Paris

timeout.com/paris

Published by Time Out Guides Ltd, a wholly owned subsidiary of Time Out Group Ltd.
Time Out and the Time Out logo are trademarks of Time Out Group Ltd.

© Time Out Group Ltd 2007
Previous editions 1989, 1990, 1992, 1995, 1997, 1998, 1999, 2000, 2001, 2002, 2003, 2004, 2005, 2006.

10 9 8 7 6 5 4 3 2 1

This edition first published in Great Britain in 2007 by Ebury Publishing
Ebury Publishing is a division of The Random House Group Ltd,
20 Vauxhall Bridge Road, London SW1V 2SA

Random House Australia Pty Limited 20 Alfred Street, Milsons Point, Sydney, New South Wales 2061, Australia
Random House New Zealand Limited 18 Poland Road, Glenfield, Auckland 10, New Zealand
Random House South Africa (Pty) Limited Isle of Houghton, Corner Boundary
Road & Carse O'Gowrie, Houghton 2198, South Africa

Random House UK Limited Reg. No. 954009

Distributed in USA by Publishers Group West
1700 Fourth Street, Berkeley, California 94710

Distributed in Canada by Publishers Group Canada
250A Carlton Street, Toronto, Ontario M5A 2L1

For further distribution details, see www.timeout.com

ISBN 10: 1-84670-006-X
ISBN 13: 978184670 0064

A CIP catalogue record for this book is available from the British Library

Colour reprographics by Wyndeham Icon, 3 & 4 Maverton Road, London E3 2JE

Printed and bound in Germany by Appl

Papers used by Ebury Publishing are natural, recyclable products made from wood grown in sustainable forests

Time Out Guides Limited
Universal House
251 Tottenham Court Road
London W1T 7AB
Tel + 44 (0)20 7813 3000
Fax + 44 (0)20 7813 6001
Email guides@timeout.com
www.timeout.com

Editorial

Editor Peterjon Cresswell
Deputy Editor Elizabeth Winding
Listings Editors Sabine Peris, Ted Milton, Alexia Loundras
Proofreader Sylvia Tombesi-Walton
Indexer Anna Norman

Editorial/Managing Director Peter Fiennes
Series Editor Ruth Jarvis
Deputy Series Editor Lesley McCave
Financial Director Gareth Garner
Guides Co-ordinator Holly Pick
Accountant Kemi Olufuwa

Design

Art Director Scott Moore
Art Editor Pinelope Kourmouzoglou
Senior Designer Josephine Spencer
Graphic Designer Henry Elphick
Digital Imaging Simon Foster
Ad Make-up Jenni Prichard

Picture Desk

Picture Editor Jael Marschner
Deputy Picture Editors Tracey Kerrigan, Monica Roche
Picture Researcher Helen McFarland

Advertising

Sales Director Mark Phillips
International Sales Consultant Ross Canadé
International Sales Executive Simon Davies
International Sales Manager Fred Durman
Advertising Sales (Paris) Matt Tembe

Marketing

Group Marketing Director John Luck
Marketing Manager Yvonne Poon
Marketing & Publicity Manager, US Rosella Albanese

Production

Group Production Director Mark Lamond
Production Manager Brendan McKeown
Production Coordinator Caroline Bradford

Time Out Group

Chairman Tony Elliott
Financial Director Richard Waterlow
TO Magazine Ltd MD David Pepper
Group General Manager/Director Nichola Coulthard
MD, Time Out International Cathy Runciman
TO Communications Ltd MD David Pepper
Group Art Director John Oakey
Group IT Director Simon Chappell

Contributors

Introduction Peterjon Cresswell. **History** Peterjon Cresswell, Simon Cropper, Andrew Hussey. **Paris Today** Rich Woodruff. **Architecture** Natalie Whittle, Natasha Edwards. **Where to Stay** Tina Isaac, Heather Stimmler-Hall, Peterjon Cresswell, Alison Culliford. **Sightseeing** Natasha Edwards, Alison Culliford, Andrew Humphreys, Natalie Whittle, Peterjon Cresswell, Rich Woodruff, Roland Lloyd Parry, Elizabeth Winding, Simon Cropper, Karen Albrecht. **Restaurants** Rosa Jackson. **Cafés & Bars** Peterjon Cresswell. **Shops & Services** Tina Isaac, Elizabeth Winding, Peterjon Cresswell, Kate van den Boogert. **Festivals & Events** Peterjon Cresswell, Simon Cropper, Elizabeth Winding. **Cabaret, Circus & Comedy** Anna Brooke. **Children** Sally Parr, Ricardo Bloch, Peterjon Cresswell. **Dance** Alison Culliford. **Film** Rich Woodruff, Simon Cropper. **Galleries** Natasha Edwards, Rich Woodruff. **Gay & Lesbian** Toby Rose, Elizabeth Winding, Nigel Guérin-Garnett. **Music: Classical & Opera** Stephen Mudge. **Music: Rock, Roots & Jazz** David McKenna, Peterjon Cresswell, David Nowell-Smith. **Nightlife** Ben Osborne. **Sport & Fitness** Peterjon Cresswell, Heather Stimmler-Hall. **Theatre** Alison Culliford, Peterjon Cresswell. **Trips Out of Town** Natasha Edwards, Peterjon Cresswell, Roland Lloyd Parry, Heather Stimmler-Hall, Anna Brooke. **Directory** Alexia Loundras, Rich Woodruff, Simon Cropper.

Maps john@jsgraphics.co.uk, except pages 415, 416.

Photography Jean-Christophe Godet, except: pages 12, 20, 23 akg-images; page19 Bridgeman Art Library; page 27 Tallandier RA/Lebrecht; page 33 Mairie de Paris; page 35 Henri Garat/Mairie de Paris; pages 64, 85, 89, 90, 217, 231, 271, 275, 277, 289, 291, 292, 293, 294, 316, 331 Heloise Bergman; page 120 David P Henry; pages 185, 200, 202, 203, 205, 207, 208, 214, 234, 235, 239, 263, 322, 323, 328, 349 Karl Blackwell; page 206 Oliver Knight; page 288 Agathe Poupeney – PhotoScene.fr; page 314 Banu Cennetoglu; page 318 R.A./Gamma; page 339 Jean-Guy Lecat.

The following images were provided by the featured establishment/artist: pages 38, 58, 281, 307, 309.

The Editor would like to thank all contributors to previous editions of *Time Out Paris*, whose work forms the basis for parts of this book.

Contents

Introduction

Paris has a new bridge. To be more accurate, it has a new *passerelle*, prosaically referred to in English as a 'footbridge'. 'Footbridge' doesn't do justice to a graceful twin-deck creation whose outline conjures a slender, elegant, female form. Naturally, the bridge – it's not some grim, graffiti-splattered walkway over a trunk road – is named after a woman. Not just any woman, mind, but that icon of feminism, Simone de Beauvoir.

The 37th in the city to span the Seine, set in its south-east corner, our humble footbridge links the developing 13th district with Bercy, Bastille and the Right Bank. Pedestrians, perhaps after pausing on the upper tier to catch a glimpse of Notre-Dame or the Eiffel Tower, can now reach this new urban hub with ease. What ten years ago was a forlorn wasteland of warehouses and railtracks today boasts a multiplex arthouse cinema, a swimming pool bobbing in the Seine and, also opened in 2006, a kilometre-long stretch of city beach. The celebrated Paris-Plage of high summer has spread from the Right to the Left Bank. By 2007, the 13th arrondissement will accommodate Docks-en-Seine, a stylish complex and new home to the French Fashion Institute. By 2010, the 13th will also house 30,000 students at four universities.

Bordering the Latin Quarter of lore, this new academic hub connects 21st-century urban development with the intellectual dynamism intrinsic to the Left Bank since medieval times. Which brings us back to Simone de Beauvoir, and the post-war Paris of Sartre and smoky jazz cafés, the Paris of Miles Davis and Juliette Gréco, of star-crossed affairs and artists starving in garrets, a Paris of the Beats, begat by the Montparnasse of the Lost Generation, begat by the Montmartre of art and absinthe. A Paris you can smell, touch, observe in scores of unsurpassable galleries and museums. A Paris, then, that is no longer with us, but that attracts us still, makes us act on impulse: lovers, intellectuals, wastrels, thinkers, talent from four corners of the globe. De Beauvoir's contemporary Gertrude Stein summed it up best when she said: 'It's not what Paris gives you, as what it doesn't take away'.

After Waterloo, Brits flocked here for war souvenirs and found the place to their liking. Two centuries on, this fashion hub has hotels of all styles, restaurants of every category and cuisine, late-night lounge bars and riverboat clubs. Gay-friendly, child-friendly and sassy with it, the city is still an easy sell: an easy-going capital that's now easier to get around.

ABOUT TIME OUT CITY GUIDES
This is the 15th edition of *Time Out Paris*, one of an expanding series of Time Out guides produced by the people behind the successful listings magazines in London, New York and Chicago. Our guides are all written by resident experts who have striven to provide you with all the most up-to-date information you'll need to explore the city or read up on its background, whether you're a local or a first-time visitor.

THE LIE OF THE LAND
To make both book and city easier to navigate, we've divided Paris into areas. They are: the Islands; Right Bank (The Louvre, Palais-Royal and Les Halles; Opéra & Grands Boulevards; the Champs-Elysées & western Paris; Montmartre & Pigalle; Beaubourg & the Marais; Bastille & eastern Paris; North-east Paris) and Left Bank (The Latin Quarter & the 13th; St-Germain-des-Prés & Odéon; Montparnasse & beyond; The 7th & the 15th). These are our own breakdowns, and not the

official arrondissements you will see signposted around town – although every address listed here gives its arrondissement number. We've also included map references that point to our street maps at the back of the guide. For further information on getting around, *see p360*.

ESSENTIAL INFORMATION
For all the practical information you might need for visiting the city, including customs information, advice on disabled facilities and access, emergency telephone numbers, a list of useful websites and the lowdown on the local transport network, turn to the Directory at the back of this guide. It starts on p360.

THE LOWDOWN ON THE LISTINGS
We've tried to make this book as easy to use as possible. Addresses, phone numbers, bus information, opening times and admission prices are all included in the listings. However, businesses can change their arrangements at any time. Before you go out of your way, we'd

strongly advise you to phone ahead to check opening times and other particulars. While every effort and care has been made to ensure the accuracy of the information contained in this guide, the publishers cannot accept responsibility for any errors it may contain.

PRICES AND PAYMENT

Prices are given in euros, and have been verified with each venue or business listed. We've noted whether shops, hotels, restaurants and other establishments accept credit cards or not, but have only listed the major cards – namely American Express (AmEx), Diners Club (DC), MasterCard (MC) and Visa (V). Many businesses will also accept other cards, however. Note that the Visa card is referred to locally as *la Carte Bleue*.

The prices we've listed in this guide should be treated as guidelines, not gospel. If prices vary wildly from those we've quoted, ask whether there's a good reason. If not, go elsewhere – then please let us know. We aim to give the best and

most up-to-date advice, so we want to know if you've been badly treated or overcharged.

TELEPHONE NUMBERS

The international country code for France is 33. All Paris and Ile-de-France telephone numbers begin with 01. If dialling Paris from abroad, drop the initial 0. If you're calling within France, dial all ten digits. A handful of numbers listed begin with 08; these can be free, at low rate or high rate – but they can only be dialled from within France. For details, check www.agence.francetelecom.com. For further information on telephones and codes, *see p378*.

MAPS

We've included a series of indexed colour street maps to the city at the back of this guide – they start on p400 – and, where possible, a grid reference for each address given in the guide. The maps now also pinpoint specific locations of hotels (❶), restaurants (❶) and cafés and bars (❶). There's an overview map on p396 and a métro map on p416.

LET US KNOW WHAT YOU THINK

We welcome tips for places that you consider we should include in future editions and take notice of your criticism of our choices. You can email us at guides@timeout.com.

There is an online version of this book, along with guides to more than 100 international cities, at **www.timeout.com**.

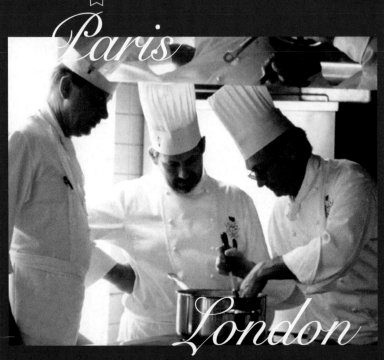

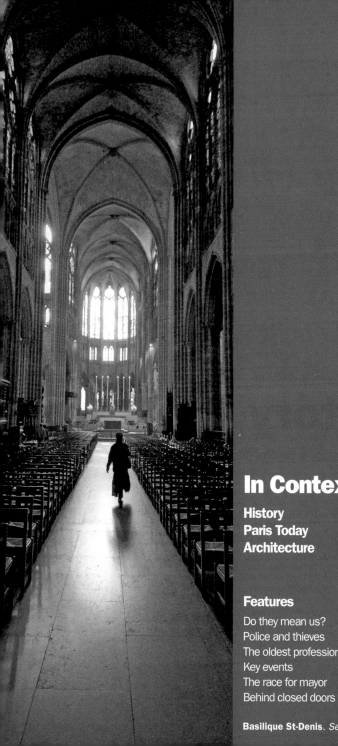

In Context

Basilique St-Denis. *See p173*.

Clovis. *See p13*.

History

Gauls, guillotines and *grands projets*.

The earliest settlers seem to have arrived in Paris around 120,000 years ago. One of them lost a flint spear-tip on the hill we now call Montmartre, and the still dangerous-looking weapon is to be seen today in the Stone Age collection at the **Musée des Antiquités Nationales** (*see p176*). There was a Stone Age weapons factory under present-day Châtelet, and the redevelopment of Bercy in the 1990s managed to unearth ten Neolithic canoes, five of which are now high and dry in the **Musée Carnavalet** (*see p112*). The fluctuating level of the river probably forced people to dwell on one of the area's many hills.

By 250 BC, a Celtic tribe known as the Parisii had put the place on the map and given the modern capital its name. The Parisii were river traders, wealthy enough to mint gold coins. The **Musée de la Monnaie de Paris** (*see p150*) has an extensive collection of their

small change. Their most important *oppidum*, a primitive fortified town, was located on an island in the Seine, which is generally thought to have been what is today's Ile de la Cité.

ROMAN PARIS

A superb strategic location and the capacity to generate hard cash were guaranteed to attract the attention of the Romans. Julius Caesar arrived in southern Gaul as proconsul in 58 BC and soon used the pretext of dealing with invading barbarians to stick his Roman nose into the affairs of northern Gaul. The Gauls didn't appreciate the attention, and in 54 BC the Eburones from the Meuse valley rebelled against the Romans. Other tribes joined in: in 52 BC the Parisii rose up with the rest of Gaul.

Caesar had his hands full dealing with the great Gaul marauder Vercingetorix, so he sent his general Labienus with four legions and part of the cavalry to secure the passage of the Seine at Lutetia, as they called Paris. The Gauls were massacred, although a contingent of Parisii escaped to be defeated later with Vercingetorix at the Battle of Alesia. The subsequent surrender of Vercingetorix left the Paris region and the rest of Gaul in Roman hands.

Roman Lutetia was a prosperous town of around 8,000 inhabitants. Apart from centrally heated villas and a temple to Jupiter on the main island (the remains of both are visible in the **Crypte Archéologique**; *see p83*), there were the sumptuous baths (now the **Musée National du Moyen Age**; *see p141*) and the 15,000-seater **Arènes de Lutèce** (*see p146*).

CHRISTIANITY

Christianity arrived in around 250 AD in the shape of Denis of Athens, who went on to become the first bishop of Paris. Legend has it that when he was decapitated by Valerian on Mons Martis, the mount of the martyrs (today better known as Montmartre), Denis picked up his head and walked with it to what is now St-Denis, to be buried there. The event is depicted in Henri Bellechose's *Retable de Saint-Denis*, now exhibited in the **Louvre** (*see pp85-91*).

> ### 'The population was decimated and the buildings on the Montagne Ste-Geneviève were pillaged and burned.'

Gaul was still a tempting prize. Waves of barbarian invaders – Alamans, Francs and others – began crossing the Rhine from 275 onwards. They sacked more than 60 cities in Gaul, including Lutetia, where the population was decimated and the buildings on the Montagne Ste-Geneviève were pillaged and burned. The bedraggled survivors used the rubble to build a rampart around the Ile de la Cité and to fortify the forum, although few citizens remained in the shadow of its walls.

It was at this time that the city was renamed Paris. Protected by the Seine and the new fortifications, its main role now was as a rear base for the Roman armies defending Gaul, and it was here in 360 that Julian was proclaimed emperor by his troops. In the same year, the first Catholic council of Paris was held, condemning the Arian branch of Christianity as heresy. The city's inhabitants, however, had concerns more pressing than theology.

Around 450, with the arrival of the Huns in the region, the people of Paris prepared once again to flee. They were dissuaded by a feisty woman named Geneviève, famed for her piety. Seeing the walls of the city defended against him, no less a pillager than Attila the Hun turned back and was defeated soon afterwards.

CLOVIS

In 464 Paris managed to resist another siege, this time by the Francs under Childeric. However, by 486, after a further blockade lasting ten years, Geneviève had no option but to surrender the city to Childeric's successor, Clovis, who went on to conquer most of Gaul and founded the Merovingian dynasty. He chose Paris as capital of his new kingdom, and it stayed that way until the seventh century, in spite of various conflicts among his successors.

Under the influence of his wife, Clotilde, Clovis converted to Christianity. He founded, and was buried in, the basilica of the Saints Apôtres, later rededicated to Ste Geneviève when the saviour and future patron saint of Paris was interred there in 512. All that remains of the basilica today is a single pillar in the grounds of the modern Lycée Henri IV; but there's a shrine dedicated to Ste Geneviève and some relics in the fine Gothic church of **St-Etienne-du-Mont** (*see p143*) next door. Geneviève and Clovis had set a trend. The Ile de la Cité was still the heart of the city, but, under the Merovingians, the Left Bank was the up-and-coming area for fashion-conscious Christians, with 11 churches built here in the period (against only four on the Right Bank and one on the Ile de la Cité). Not everyone was sold on the joys of city living, though. From 614 onwards, the Merovingian kings preferred the *banlieue* at Clichy, or wandered the kingdom trying to keep rebellious nobles in check. By the time one of the rebels, Pippin 'the Short', decided to do away with the last Merovingian in 751, Paris was starting to look passé.

Pippin's son, Charlemagne, built his capital at Aix-la-Chapelle, while his successors, known as the Carolingian dynasty, moved from palace to palace, consuming the local production. Paris, meanwhile, was doing nicely for itself as a centre for Christian learning, and had grown to house a population of 20,000 by the beginning of the ninth century. This was the high point in the popularity and political power of the great abbeys like St-Germain-des-Prés, where transcription of the Latin classics was helping to preserve much of Europe's Roman cultural heritage. Power in the Paris region was exercised by the counts of Paris.

THE VIKINGS

In 845 the Vikings appeared before the walls. Unopposed, the Norsemen sacked the city, and King Charles II, 'the Bald', had to cough up 7,000 pounds of silver to get them to leave. Recognising a soft touch when they saw one, the Vikings returned to sack the city repeatedly between 856 and 869, burning churches with heathen abandon. Better late than never, Charles organised the defence of the city and fortified bridges were built – the Grand Pont over the northern branch of the Seine and the Petit Pont over the southern, blocking the passage of the Viking ships further upstream.

In 885, Gozlin, Bishop of Paris, had just finished repairing the Roman walls when the Vikings showed up once again; this time they found the city defended against them. After a siege lasting a year, King Charles III, 'the Fat', arrived at the head of an army but, deciding that discretion is indeed the better part of valour, handed over 700 pounds of silver and politely invited the Norsemen to pillage some other part of his kingdom. The Count of Paris, Eudes, having performed valiantly in the siege of 885-6, was offered the royal crown when Charles was deposed in 888. Although the Carolingians recovered the throne after Eudes' death in 898, his great-nephew, Hugues Capet, was elected King of France in 987, adding what remained of the Carolingian dominions to his territories around Paris.

PARIS FINDS ITS FEET

Under the Capetian dynasty, although Paris was now at the heart of the royal domains, the city did not yet dominate the kingdom. Robert 'the Pious', king from 996 to 1031, stayed more often in Paris than his father, restoring the royal palace on the Ile de la Cité, while Henri I (1031-60) issued more of his charters in Paris than in Orléans. In 1112 the abbey of **St-Denis** (*see p173*) replaced St-Benoît-sur-Loire as principal monastery, so confirming the pre-eminence of Paris over Orléans.

Paris itself still consisted of little more than the Ile de la Cité and small settlements under the protection of the abbeys on each bank. On the Left Bank, royal largesse helped to rebuild the abbeys of St-Germain-des-Prés, St-Marcel and Ste-Geneviève, although it took more than 150 years for the destruction wrought there by the Vikings to be fully repaired. The Right Bank, where mooring was easier, prospered from river commerce, and three boroughs grew up around the abbeys of St-Germain-l'Auxerrois, St-Martin-des-Champs and St-Gervais. Bishop Sully of Paris began building the cathedral of Notre-Dame in 1163.

The growing complexity of government during the 12th century, and the departure of kings on crusades, meant that the administration tended to stay in the Palais de la Cité and the royal treasure in the fortress of the Temple

(built by the newly founded order of the Templars). The wisdom of this approach was confirmed by the disaster of Fréteval in 1194, where King Philippe-Auguste was defeated by Richard the Lionheart, losing much of his treasure and his archives in the process.

This minor hiccup aside, the reign of Philippe-Auguste (1180-1223) was a turning point in the history of Paris. Before, the city was a confused patchwork of royal, ecclesiastical and feudal authorities, exercising various powers, rights and privileges. Keen to raise revenues, Philippe favoured the growth of the guilds, especially the butchers, drapers, furriers, haberdashers and merchants: so began the rise of the bourgeoisie.

He also ordered the building of the first permanent market buildings at Les Halles, and a new city wall, first on the Right Bank to protect the commercial heart of Paris, and later on the Left Bank. At the western end, Philippe built a castle, the Louvre, to defend the road from the ever-menacing Normandy, whose duke was also King of England.

A GOLDEN AGE

Paris was now the principal residence of the king and the uncontested capital of France. No longer threatened by foreign invasion, the city found itself overrun by a new and altogether deadlier menace that exists to this day: lawyers. And barristers, bailiffs, prosecutors, sergeants, accountants, judges, clerks and all the bureaucratic trappings of royal government.

To accommodate the rapidly growing royal administration, the Palais de la Cité, site and symbol of power for the previous thousand years, was remodelled and enlarged. Work was begun by Louis IX (later St Louis) in the 1240s, and later continued under Philippe IV ('le Bel'). This architectural complex, of which the **Ste-Chapelle** (*see p83*) and the nearby **Conciergerie** (*see p84*) can still be seen today, was inaugurated with great pomp at Pentecost 1313. Philippe invited Edward II of England and his queen, Isabelle of France. The English were impressed: they soon came back for a long stay.

The palace was quickly filled with functionaries, so the king spent as much of his time as he could outside Paris at the royal castles of **Fontainebleau** (*see p348*) and, especially, **Vincennes** (*see p174*). The needs of the plenipotentiaries left behind to run the kingdom were met by a rapidly growing city population, piled into rather less chic buildings.

Paris was also reinforcing its identity as a major religious centre: as well as the local clergy and dozens of religious orders, the city was home to the masters and students of the university of the **Sorbonne** (established in

Where lions and gladiators did battle – the **Arènes de Lutèce**. *See p13.*

1253; *see p144*), who were already gaining a reputation for rowdiness. An influx of scholars from all over Europe gave the city a cultural and intellectual cachet it was never to lose.

By 1328 Paris was home to approximately 200,000 inhabitants, making it the most populous city in Europe. However, that year was also notable for being the last of the medieval golden age: the dynasty of Capetian kings spluttered to an inglorious halt when Charles IV died without an heir. The English quickly claimed the throne for the young Edward III, the son of Philippe IV's daughter. Refusing to recognise his descent through the female line, the late king's cousin, Philippe de Valois, claimed the French crown as Philippe VI. So began the Hundred Years War between France and England – a war that in fact would go on for 116 years.

TROUBLES AND STRIFE

To make matters worse, the Black Death (bubonic plague) ravaged Europe from the 1340s. Those not finished by the plague had to contend with food shortages, ever-increasing taxes, riots, repression, currency devaluations and marauding mercenaries. Meanwhile, in Paris, the honeymoon period for the king and the bourgeoisie was coming to an end. Rich and populous, Paris was expected to bear the brunt of the war burden; and as defeat followed defeat (notably the disaster at Crécy in August 1346), the bourgeoisie and people of the city were

increasingly exasperated by the futility of the sacrifices they were making for the hideously expensive war. To fund the conflict, King Jean II tried to introduce new tax laws – without success. When the king was captured by the English at Poitiers in 1356, his problems passed to his 18-year-old son, Charles.

The Etats Généraux, consultant body to the throne, was summoned to the royal palace on the Ile de la Cité to discuss the country's woes. The teenage king was besieged with angry demands for reform from the bourgeoisie, particularly from Etienne Marcel, then provost of the local merchants. Marcel seized control of Paris and began a bitter power struggle with the crown; in 1357, fearing widespread revolt, Charles fled to Compiègne. But as he ran, he had Paris blockaded.

Marcel called on the peasants, who were also raging against taxes, but they were quickly crushed. He then called on Charles 'the Bad' of Navarre, ally to the English, but his arrival in Paris made many of Marcel's supporters nervous. On 31 July 1358, Marcel was murdered, and the revolution was over. As a safeguard, the returning Charles built a new stronghold to protect Paris: the Bastille.

By 1420, following the French defeat at Agincourt, Paris was in English hands; in 1431 Henry VI of England was crowned King of France in Notre-Dame. He didn't last. Five years later, Henry and his army were driven back to Calais by the Valois king, Charles VII. Charles owed his grasp on power to Jeanne d'Arc, who led the victorious French in the Battle of Orléans, only to be betrayed by her compatriots, who decided she was getting too big for her boots. She was captured and sold to the English, who had her burned as a witch.

By 1436 Paris was once again the capital of France. But the nation had been nearly bled dry by war and was still divided politically, with powerful regional rulers across France continuing to threaten the monarchy. Outside of the French borders, the ambitions of the Austrian Habsburg dynasty represented a serious threat. In this general atmosphere of instability, disputes over trade, religion and taxation were all simmering dangerously in the political background.

RENAISSANCE AND REFORMATION

In the closing decades of the 15th century, the restored Valois monarchs sought to reassert their position. A wave of building projects was the public sign of this effort, giving us such masterpieces as St-Etienne-du-Mont, **St-Eustache** (*see p106*) and private homes like the Hôtel de Cluny (which today houses the Musée National du Moyen Age) and the **Hôtel de Sens**, which now accommodates the **Bibliothèque de Forney** (for both, *see p114*). The Renaissance in France had its peak under François I. As well as being involved in the construction of the magnificent châteaux at Fontainebleau, Blois and Chambord, François was equally responsible for transforming the Louvre from a fortress into a royal palace.

Do they mean us?

It is no accident that the word 'Parisian' has long been synonymous with the word 'agitator'. This tendency can be traced as far back as the Middle Ages, when Parisians were commonly described as *trublions* (disturbers of the peace) or *maillotins* (war-hammers). These terms always had a meaning that was specific and political. The word '*maillotin*', for example, was taken from the heavy lead mallets that angry rebels used in the 14th century to smash statues and heads (usually of money-lenders and tax officials, who were generally Jews and Lombards). Other agitators, *trublions*, led the disorderly and often spontaneous insurrections, or *jacqueries*, against government and king in the name of hunger and justice. The most famous and successful of such *jacqueries* was led in 1357 by Etienne Marcel, who launched a workmen's strike and killed a prince, spattering himself with blood. Marcel's statue still presides over the Seine from the front edge of the Hôtel de Ville.

Outside Paris, the rebellious Parisians were laughed at as well as feared. In the mid 16th century, Rabelais uncharitably described the Parisian as a *gros maroufle*, an unscrupulous, vulgar and dishonest alley cat. He confidently expected his description to raise a laugh of recognition throughout France as well as in Paris. Over time, the word 'Parisian' has also been used in French to describe fashionable cigarettes, numerous sexual positions (generally variants on sodomy, depending on which part of France you are in), trousers of blue material, a useless sailor, biscuits, a type of cooking

and typographical plates. For provincials, *à la parisienne* meant a job not finished, or badly done. Provincial contempt for Parisians is caught in the children's rhyme '*Parisien, tête de chien, parigot, tête de veau*' ('Parisian with a dog's head, Parisian with a calf's head').

There was (and is) a tendency to roll the 'r'. Parisian accent common to the streets. This was originally a confluence of sounds from Picardy, Flanders, Normandy and Brittany. It was most probably first heard in the early 1100s, as the low Latin of the rue de Fouarre – the ecclesiastical quarter of the fledgling city – disintegrated into French. Modified in the 16th and 17th centuries by an influx of workers, mainly boatmen and traders, from the Berry, it has otherwise remained relatively untouched by outside influence. The common feature was (and is) a tendency to roll the 'r'. The sounds 'er' or 'el' are often elongated or opened into 'ar' or 'arl'. It is a tendency that can be traced back to the 15th century and the poet François Villon, who constantly mashed rhymes such as '*merle*' (blackbird) into '*marle*'. A comic play dating from the time of Louis XIV has a character named Piarot (rather than 'Pierrot') after this same slurring tendency, and in the 19th century this sound was noted as the characteristic feature of the accent of Belleville and Ménilmontant, where a concierge was a '*conciarge*'. This is the traditional sound of the '*parigot*' – the Parisian equivalent of the Cockney – and a sound that can still be heard in the songs of Fréhel and Edith Piaf.

Andrew Hussey is the author of Paris: A Secret History *(see p384).*

He held open house for such luminaries as Leonardo da Vinci and Benvenuto Cellini. He also established the Collège de France to encourage humanist learning outside the control of the clergy-dominated universities.

Despite burning heretics by the dozen, François was unable to stop the spread of Protestantism, launched in Germany by Martin Luther in 1517. Resolutely Catholic, Paris was the scene of some horrific violence against the Huguenots, as supporters of the new faith were called. The picture was complicated by the political conflict between the Huguenot Prince de Condé and the Catholic Duc de Guise.

By the 1560s the situation had degenerated into open warfare. Catherine de Médicis, the scheming Italian widow of Henri II, was the real force in court politics. It was she who connived to murder prominent Protestants gathered in Paris for the marriage of the king's sister on St Bartholomew's Day (23 August 1572). Catherine's main aim was to dispose of her powerful rival, Gaspard de Coligny, but the situation got out of hand, and as many as 3,000 people were butchered. Henri III attempted to reconcile the religious factions and eradicate the powerful families directing the conflict, but the people of Paris turned against him and he was forced to flee. His assassination in 1589 brought the Valois line to an end.

THE BOURBONS

The throne of France being up for grabs, Henri of Navarre declared himself King Henri IV, launching the Bourbon dynasty. Paris was not impressed. The city closed its gates against the Huguenot king, and the inhabitants endured a four-year siege by supporters of the new ruler. Henri managed to break the impasse by having himself converted to Catholicism (and was later heard to quip, *'Paris vaut bien une messe'* – Paris is well worth a mass).

Henri set about rebuilding his ravaged capital. He completed the **Pont Neuf** (*see p79*), the first bridge to span the whole of the Seine. He commissioned place Dauphine and the city's first enclosed residential square – the place Royale – now **place des Vosges** (*see p113*). The square was the merry scene of jousting competitions and countless duels.

Henri also tried to reconcile his Catholic and Protestant subjects, issuing the Edict of Nantes in 1598, effectively giving each religion equal status. The Catholics hated the deal, and the Huguenots were suspicious. Henri was the subject of at least 23 attempted assassinations by fanatics of both persuasions. Finally, in 1610, a Catholic by the name of François Ravaillac fatally stabbed the king while he was stuck in traffic on rue de la Ferronerie.

TWO CARDINALS

Since Henri's son, Louis XIII, was only eight at the time of his father's death, the widow, Marie de Médicis, took up the reins of power. We can thank her for the **Palais du Luxembourg** (*see p152*) and the 24 paintings she commissioned from Rubens, now part of the Louvre collection.

Louis took up his royal duties in 1617, but Cardinal Richelieu, chief minister from 1624, was the man who ran France. Something of a schemer, he outwitted the king's mother, his wife (Anne of Austria) and a host of princes and place-seekers. Richelieu helped to strengthen the power of the monarch, and he did much to limit the independence of the aristocracy. The cardinal was also a great architectural patron. He commissioned Jacques Lemercier to build what is now the **Palais-Royal** (*see p98*), and ordered the rebuilding of the Sorbonne.

The Counter-Reformation was at its height, and lavish churches such as the baroque **Val-de-Grâce** (*see p144*) were an important reassertion of Catholic supremacy. The 17th century was 'Le Grand Siècle', a time of patronage of art and artists, even if censorship forced the brilliant mathematician and philosopher René Descartes into exile.

The first national newspaper, *La Gazette*, hit the streets in 1631; Richelieu used it as a propaganda tool. The cardinal founded the **Académie Française** (*see p150*), a sort of literary think-tank, which is still working, slowly, on the dictionary of the French language that Richelieu commissioned from them in 1634. Richelieu died in 1642; Louis XIII followed suit a few months later. The new king, Louis XIV, was five years old. Anne of Austria became regent, with the Italian Cardinal Mazarin, a Richelieu protégé, as chief minister. Rumour has it that Anne and Mazarin may have been married. Mazarin's townhouse is now home to the **Bibliothèque Nationale de France – Richelieu** (*see p99*).

Endless wars against Austria and Spain had depleted the royal coffers and left the nation drained by exorbitant taxation. In 1648 the royal family was chased out of Paris by a popular uprising, 'la Fronde', named after the catapults used by some of the rioters. Parisians soon tired of the anarchy that followed. When Mazarin's army retook the city in 1653, the boy-king was warmly welcomed. Mazarin died in 1661 and Louis XIV, now 24 years old, decided he would rule France without the assistance of any chief minister.

SHINE ON, SUN KING

The 'Roi Soleil', or Sun King, was an absolute monarch. 'L'état, c'est moi' (I am the State) was his vision of power. To prove his grandeur, the king embarked on wars against England, Holland and Austria. He also refurbished and extended the Louvre, commissioned **place Vendôme** (*see p98*) and **place des Victoires** (*see p100*), constructed the **Observatory** (*see p166*) and laid out the *grands boulevards* along the lines of the old city walls. The triumphal arches at **Porte St-Denis** and **Porte St-Martin** (for both, *see p103*) date from this time too. His major project was the palace at **Versailles** (*see p352*), a massive complex that drew on the age's finest architectural, artistic and landscape-design talents. Louis moved his court there in 1682.

Louis XIV owed much of his brilliant success to the work of Jean-Baptiste Colbert, nominally in charge of state finances, but eventually taking control of all the important levers of the state machine. Colbert was the force behind the Sun King's redevelopment of Paris. The **Hôtel des Invalides** (*see p156*) was built to accommodate the crippled survivors of Louis' wars, the **Salpêtrière** (*see p169*) to shelter fallen women. In 1702 Paris was divided into 20 *quartiers* (not until the Revolution was it re-mapped into arrondissements). **Le Procope** (*see p149*), the city's first café, opened in 1686. Although its original proprietor, Francesco Procopio dei Coltelli, would no longer recognise it since a 1989 facelift, the place is still in business. Colbert died in 1683, and Louis' luck on the battlefield ran out. Hopelessly embroiled in the War of the Spanish Succession, the country was devastated by famine in 1692.

Police and thieves

Paris was without any form of policing until the 12th century and, as such, had a Europe-wide reputation as a city where murder and banditry were the staples of daily life.

One of the first attempts to impose law and order was King Philippe-Auguste's idea of appointing bailiffs to control the city while the King and his nobles were away at the Third Crusade. The bailiffs were often referred to as *ribauds* or *ribauz*, a word related to the English 'ribaldry', and one that was used to describe the lawless troops that followed a military campaign for the pleasures of rape and pillage.

A slightly greater level of order was brought to the city with the establishment in 1160 of the office of *grand prévôt* (provost marshal), who was normally a non-Parisian and therefore independent of the city's criminal gangs. The *prévôt* was not above murder, as demonstrated by Thomas, a *grand prévôt* who was said to be involved in the killing in 1200 of five blameless German students. Other *prévôts* were excommunicated or hanged for blasphemous crimes.

Most grotesque and melancholy of all was the fate of the *prévôt* Guillaume de Tignonville who, in October 1408, ordered two students guilty of murder to be hanged at Montfaucon. The University and its famously litigious lawyers fought back, and finally won an appeal in May the following year. The unfortunate Guillaume was ordered to take down the corpses of the students, which had been rotting in the open air through the winter, and convey them to the convent of Les Mathurins, where they were to be laid to rest.

The punishment demanded by the university lawyer was that Guillaume should kiss both students on the lips to show his contrition, as the stinking bodies were taken down. The order was carried out.

Punishments were harsh throughout the Middle Ages, satisfying less a need for justice than a bloodthirsty taste for cruel entertainment. Thieves, murderers and counterfeiters were usually hanged. Other criminals had their eyes gouged out, or were whipped or branded with irons (not only on the shoulder but on the cheek or forehead). At night, the streets were to be avoided; ordinary Parisians disobeyed orders to keep lamps lit in front windows at night (an early rudimentary attempt at street lighting). Instead, they barricaded their doors and always kept weapons to hand.

There were citizen guards who also patrolled at night, but their duties were confined mainly to keeping the peace and preventing crime. This close association, even deliberate confusion, of police and judicial authority was to play a defining role in the nature of Parisian policing for decades to come: unlike British policing, which is mainly concerned with prohibiting, the Paris police system has been, and continues to be, concerned with prescriptive measures, intervention and surveillance. As one Parisian wag put it, in a remark made in the shadow of the massacres of the 1871 Commune, 'the Parisian can do what he likes, as long as it's under police supervision'.

Andrew Hussey is the author of Paris: A Secret History *(see p384).*

Pious, feisty and tasty when up against Attila the Hun – **Sainte Geneviève**. *See p13*.

The Sun King died in 1715, leaving no direct heir. His five-year-old great-grandson, Louis XV, was named king, with Philippe d'Orléans as regent. The court moved back to Paris. Installed in the Palais-Royal, the regent set about enjoying his few years of power, hosting lavish dinners that degenerated into orgies. The state, meanwhile, remained chronically in debt.

THE ENLIGHTENMENT

Some of the city's more sober residents were making Paris the intellectual capital of Europe. Enlightenment thinkers such as Diderot, Montesquieu, Voltaire and Rousseau were all active during the reign of Louis XV. Literacy rates were increasing – 50 per cent of French men could read, 25 per cent of women – and the publishing industry was booming.

The king's mistress, Madame de Pompadour, encouraged him to finance the building of the Ecole Militaire (*see p159* and the laying out of place Louis XV, known to us as **place de la Concorde** (*see p98*). The massive church of **St-Sulpice** (*see p152*) was completed in 1776. Many of the great houses in the area bounded by rue de Lille, rue de Varenne and rue de Grenelle date from the first half of the 18th century. The private homes of aristocrats and wealthy bourgeois, these would become the venues for numerous salons, the informal discussion sessions often devoted to topics raised by Enlightenment questioning.

The Enlightenment spirit of rational humanism finally took the venom out of the Catholic–Protestant power struggle, and the increase in public debate helped to change views about the nature of the state and the place and authority of the monarchy. As Jacques Necker, Louis XVI's finance minister on the eve of the Revolution, put it, popular

Come the Revolution – the execution of Louis XVI. *See p21.*

opinion was 'an invisible power that, without treasury, guard or army, gives its laws to the city, the court and even the palaces of kings'. Thanks to the Enlightenment, and an ever-growing burden of taxation on the poorest strata of society to prop up the wealthiest, that power would overturn the status quo for good.

THE FRENCH REVOLUTION

Louis XVI had poor control of his country's swelling problems, and French intervention in the Seven Years War and the American War of Independence had left the country practically bankrupt. Subsequent attempts to introduce new taxes met with strong opposition from the bourgeoisie. After a ruined harvest and a harsh winter, bread prices soared, as did discontent. Springtime in 1789 brought riots on the rue du Faubourg-St-Antoine, where factory workers' wages had been cut. The *parlements*, or high courts, urged Louis to call a meeting of the Etats Généraux – the representative body for the First Estate (the clergy), the Second Estate (the nobility) and the Third Estate (the bourgeoisie and commoners).

On 5 May 1789, the king reluctantly faced the Etats at Versailles. The Third Estate, which had as many members as the other two combined, demanded that the three merge into a single assembly, with one vote per member. Louis refused. On 20 June the Third Estate reconvened on the playing courts at the Jeu de Paumes at Versailles and swore to establish a national constitution. The embattled Louis eventually conceded and allowed the Etats to form the Assemblée Nationale. But behind the scenes, the king was gathering troops to disband the assembly; and on 12 July he publicly, and foolishly, dismissed the commoner's ally, finance minister Jacques Necker, prompting

a violent counter-coup. On 13 July Camille Desmoulins, a young unemployed lawyer, empassioned an angry crowd gathered in the Palais-Royal garden to take action. The next day, the crowd pillaged Les Invalides for arms, marched on the Bastille prison and proceeded to tear it down. Only seven prisoners were imprisoned there, but the symbolic victory was immense (and enduring, as the annual *quatorze juillet* celebrations show; *see p273*). A chastened Louis came to Paris on 17 July to acknowledge the crowds at the Hôtel de Ville.

The establishment of the constitution forged ahead, and sparked furious debate. Tax breaks for the nobility and clergy were abolished, the country was divided into local governments and Roman Catholic Church property was seized. Two Parisian convents hosted two newly formed political clubs. On the Left Bank, at a 13th-century Franciscan convent (some parts of which are still standing at 15 rue de l'Ecole de Médicine), the Cordeliers club charged its members, mostly the poor *sans-culottes* (so called because they couldn't afford breeches), a few cents to hear monarchy-bashing speeches by its leading lights. These included the figures of Desmoulins and Marat. On the Right Bank, the more radical Jacobins, who included the likes of Mirabeau, Danton and Robespierre, took up residency in a Dominican convent on rue St-Honoré, later knocked down by Napoleon.

One of Louis' original problems, the price of bread, had not budged. In October a mob of starving women marched the 12 miles (19km) to Versailles and demanded that the king come to Paris. He promised to send the women grain, an offer they rejected by decapitating some of his guards. Louis wisely transferred to the Tuileries. In the months that followed, the Jacobins roused powerful Republican feeling. Fearing greater danger at home and hoping to gain support abroad, the king and his family attempted to flee Paris on 20 June 1791. With Louis disguised as a valet, they got as far as Varennes, where a commoner recognised Louis' face from his portrait on a coin. Louis, Marie-Antoinette and family were brought back to Paris in disgrace, crowds throwing things at their coach, and poking their heads through the window and spitting.

On 14 September Louis accepted the new constitution, and the Revolution appeared to be over. But other monarchies were plotting to reinstate the king. In 1792 Austrian and Prussian troops invaded France, gaining rapidly on Paris with easy victories against a weak French army. The Republicans, rightly, suspected Louis of conspiring with the enemy, and scrabbled together their own army to capture him, ringing out the cannons on Pont Neuf to enrol the public. On the morning of 10 August, the Tuileries palace rang with gunfire. Swiss guards enlisted to defend the king put up a staunch fight, but were hacked to death along with all the palace staff. Two bloody days later, the royal family was incarcerated in the Temple prison by the radical Commune de Paris, headed by Danton, Marat and Robespierre.

> **'The guillotine stood at the place de la Révolution and took thousands of heads, including that of Louis' widow, Marie-Antoinette.'**

Rampant suspicion about possible traitors led the Revolutionaries to the gates of the city's prisons. They invaded, and murdered 2,000 so-called traitors, including the Princess of Lamballe, whose head was stuck on a spike and paraded past the royal family at the Temple. The monarchy was abolished on 22 September; the king was executed on 21 January. A trial, Robespierre claimed, was out of the question, since it would put 'the Revolution itself in the dock'. The guillotine, a symbol of the Revolution's brutality (in fact, invented by Dr Guillotin as a humane method of execution) stood at the place de la Révolution and took thousands of heads, including that of Louis' widow, Marie-Antoinette, almost a year later. She awaited her fate in a wallpapered prison cell at the Conciergerie.

There was precious little dignity to this particular period of the Revolution. Within the Revolutionary Convention, which had replaced the Assemblée Nationale, the Jacobins had expelled the monarchist Girondins (a young Girondist, Charlotte Corday, retaliated by stabbing Marat to death at his home) and were gathering dictatorial momentum. Headed by 'l'incorruptible' Robespierre, the Jacobins in September 1793 vowed to wage terror against all rebels, Girondins and dissidents. In the Great Terror of 1794, the guillotine was transferred to place du Trône Renversé ('Overturned Throne', now place de la Nation), and sliced through 1,300 necks in six weeks. The bodies were dumped in the Picpus garden (now the **Cimetière de Picpus**; *see p117*). The tumbrils, or two-wheeled carts, that carried the dead away were painted green to disguise their bloody load.

Almost everybody wanted the Terror to end. The French army had successfully beaten off foreign forces, and the incessant killing began to look unnecessary. Robespierre and his cohorts attempted some democratic reform, but most people wanted them gone. On 28 July 1794 he was executed, and the reign of terror collapsed. The biggest and bloodiest revolution was over.

NAPOLEON

Amid the post-Revolutionary chaos, power was divided between a two-housed Assembly and a Directory of five men. The French public reacted badly to hearing of England's unsuccessful attempts to promote more popular rebellion; when a royalist rising in Paris needed to be put down, a young officer from Corsica was the man to do it: Napoleon Bonaparte.

Napoleon quickly became the Directory's right-hand man. When they needed someone to lead an Italian campaign against Austria, he was the man. Victory saw France – and Napoleon – glorified. After a further, aborted, campaign to Egypt in 1799, Napoleon returned home to put down another royalist plot, made himself the chief of the newly governing three-man Consul – and by 1804 was emperor.

After failing to squeeze out the English by setting up the Continental System to block trade across the Channel, Napoleon waged massive wars against Britain, Russia and Austria. On his way to the disaster of Moscow, Napoleon gave France the *lycée* educational system, the Napoleonic Code of civil law, the Legion of Honour, the Banque de France, the **Pont des Arts** (*see p79*), the **Arc de Triomphe** (*see p121*), the **Madeleine** church (he re-established Catholicism as the state religion; *see p101*), **La Bourse** (*see p100*) and **rue de Rivoli**. He was also responsible for the centralised bureaucracy that still manages to drive the French mad.

As Russian troops – who had chased Napoleon's once-mighty army all the way from Moscow and Leipzig – invaded France, Paris itself came under threat. Montmartre, then named Montnapoléon, had a telegraph machine at its summit, one that had given so many of the emperor's orders and transmitted news of so many victories. The hill fell to Russian troops. Napoleon gave the order to blow up the city's main powder stores, and thus Paris itself. His officer refused. Paris accommodated carousing Russian, Prussian and English soldiers while Napoleon was sent to exile in Elba.

A hundred days later, he was back, leading an army against Wellington and Blücher's troops in the midsummer mud of Waterloo, near Brussels. A further defeat saw the end of him. Paris survived further foreign occupation. The diminutive Corsican died on the South Atlantic prison island of St Helena in 1821.

ANOTHER ROUND OF BOURBONS

Having sampled revolution and military dictatorship, the French were now ready to give monarchy a second chance. The Bourbons got back in business, briefly, in 1815 in the person of Louis XVIII, Louis XVI's elderly brother. Several efforts were made to adapt the monarchy to the new political realities, though the new king's Charter of Liberties was not a wholly sincere expression of how he meant to rule. Liberal intellectual activity flourished nevertheless, with figures such as the caricaturist Daumier regularly poking satirical fun at the bourgeoisie.

When another brother of Louis XVI, Charles X, became king in 1824, he decided that enough royal energy had been wasted trying to reconcile the nation's myriad factions. It was time for a spot of old-fashioned absolutism. But the forces unleashed during the Revolution, and the social divisions that had opened as a result, were not to be ignored – the people were happy to respond with some old-fashioned rebellion.

In the 1830 elections, the liberals won a hefty majority in the Chamber of Deputies, the legislative body. Charles's unpopular minister Prince Polignac, a returned émigré, promptly dissolved the Chamber, announced a date for new elections and curtailed the number of voters. Polishing off this collection of bad decisions was the 26 July decree abolishing the freedom of the press. The day after its issue, 5,000 print workers and journalists filled the streets and three newspapers went to press. When police tried to confiscate copies, they sparked a three-day riot, 'les Trois Glorieuses', with members of the disbanded National Guard manning the barricades. On 30 July Charles dismissed Polignac, but it was too late. He had little choice but to abdicate, and fled to England. As French revolutions go, it was a neat, brief affair.

Another leftover from the *ancien régime* was now winched on to the throne – Louis-Philippe, Duc d'Orléans, who had some Bourbon blood in his veins. A father of eight who never went out without his umbrella, he was eminently acceptable to the newly powerful bourgeoisie. But the poor, who had risked their lives in two attempts to change French society, were unimpressed by the new king's promise to embrace a moderate and liberal version of the Revolutionary heritage.

THE NINETEENTH CENTURY

Philosopher Walter Benjamin declared Paris 'the capital of the 19th century', and he had a point. While it was smaller in dimension than its global rival of London, in intellectual and cultural spheres it reigned supreme. On the demographic front, its population doubled to one million between 1800 and 1850. Most of the new arrivals were rural labourers, who had come to find work on the city's ever-expanding building sites. Meanwhile, the middle classes were doing well, thanks to the relatively late arrival of the industrial revolution in France, and the solid administrative structures inherited from Napoleon. The poor were as badly off as ever, only now there were more of them.

> **'Students derided the government, while workers' pamphlets gave voice to the starving poor. A wave of ill feeling slowly built up.'**

The back-breaking hours worked in the factories would not be curbed by legislation: 'Whatever the lot of the workers is, it is not the manufacturer's responsibility to improve it,' said one trade minister. In Left Bank cafés, a new bohemian tribe of students derided the materialistic government. Workers' pamphlets and newspapers, such as *La Ruche Populaire*, gave voice to the starving, crippled poor. A wave of ill feeling was gradually building up against Louis-Philippe.

On 23 February 1848, hundreds of Parisians – men, women and students – moved along the boulevards towards a public banquet at La Madeleine. The king's minister, François Guizot, had forbidden direct campaigning by opposition parties in the forthcoming election, so the parties held banquets instead of meetings. One diarist of the time noted that some of the crowd had stuffed swords and daggers underneath their shirts, but the demonstration was largely peaceful – until the troops on the boulevard des Capucines opened fire, igniting a riot.

Nice digs for the Nazis – the Gestapo had its Paris HQ at the Hôtel Meurice. *See p26.*

When it came to rebuilding the country, the uncomfortable compromises multiplied – even to the point of injustice. Companies that had worked with the Germans were the best equipped, and thus the most useful; and while a handful of collaborating industrialists, including the motor-vehicle baron Louis Renault, were imprisoned, many got off scot-free. In any case, recovery was slow to come. There were shortages of everything. Food was as hard to come by as it had been during the war; indeed, many complained they had been better off under the Germans. Medical supplies were inadequate, as were basic necessities. Even in the ministries, paper was so scarce that correspondence had to be sent out on Vichy letterhead with the sender crossing out 'Etat Français' at the top and writing 'République Française' instead. It was a poor state of affairs.

THE FOURTH REPUBLIC

On 8 May 1945, de Gaulle made a broadcast to the nation to announce Germany's surrender. Paris went wild. Cars hooted their horns, church bells rang, sirens wailed, artillery boomed and low-flying aircraft zoomed overhead. Crowds packed out the Champs-Elysées, and the city's fountains were switched back on. It was the party to end all parties.

The euphoria didn't last. There were strikes. And more strikes. Liberation had proved to be a restoration, not the revolution the Communists, now the most powerful political force in the land, had hoped for. The Communist Party was, in at least one respect, as pragmatic as everyone else: it did its utmost to turn parliamentary democracy to its advantage, to wit, getting as

many of the top jobs as it could. (It even lobbied to get members into the Académie Française.) The pragmatism stopped, however, at its tendency to see Fascists and fifth columnists in every shadow; the French Communist leader, Maurice Thorez, would travel around town only in an armoured limousine with bodyguards in tow, for fear of assassination attempts.

A general election was held on 21 October 1945. The Communists secured 159 seats, the Socialists got 146 and the Catholic Mouvement Républicain Populaire got 152. A fortnight later, at the Assemblée Nationale's first session, a unanimous vote was passed maintaining de Gaulle in his position as head of state – but he remained an antagonistic leader. His reluctance to take a firm grip on the disastrous economic situation alienated many intellectuals and industrialists who had once been loyal to him, and his characteristic aloofness only made the misgivings of the general populace worse. He, on the other hand, was disgusted by all the political chicanery – what he called its *pourriture*, or rot. On 20 January 1946, de Gaulle abruptly resigned.

France, meanwhile, looked to swift industrial modernisation under an ambitious plan put forward by internationalist politician Jean Monnet. While the economy and daily life remained grim, brash new fashion designer Christian Dior put together a stunning collection of strikingly simple clothes: the New Look. Such extravagance horrified many locals, but the fashion industry boomed. Meanwhile, the divisions in Paris between its fashionable and its run-down working-class areas became more pronounced. The northern and eastern edges – areas revived only in the late 20th century by a taste for retro, industrial decor and cheap rent – were forgotten about.

Félix Gouin, the new Socialist premier, quickly nationalised the bigger banks and the coal industry. But the right wing was growing, and there was even a rise of royalist hopes. A referendum was held in May 1946 to determine the crucial tenet of the Fourth Republic's constitution: should the Assemblée Nationale have absolute or restricted power? The results were a narrow victory for those who, like de Gaulle, had insisted the Assemblée's power should be qualified. De Gaulle's prestige increased, but it was to be another 12 years, and a whole new constitution – the Fifth Republic – before he got his hands back on the levers of power. He spent much of his *passage du désert* writing his memoirs.

THE ALGERIAN WAR AND MAY 1968

The post-war years were marked by the rapid disintegration of France's overseas interests – and her rapprochement with Germany to create what would become the European Community.

When revolt broke out in Algeria in 1956, almost 500,000 troops were sent in to protect national interests. A protest by Algerians in Paris on 17 October 1961 led to the deaths of hundreds of people at the hands of the city's police. The extent of the violence was officially concealed for decades, as was the use of torture against Algerians by French troops. Algeria became independent in 1962.

Meanwhile, the slow, painful discoveries of collaboration in World War II, often overlooked in the rush to put the country back on its feet, were also being faced. The younger generation began to question the motives of the older one. De Gaulle's Fifth Republic was felt by many to be grimly authoritarian. Some, certainly, believe that he designed it to be an elected monarchy, which is interesting when you consider that it's the constitution still in use to this day.

In the spring of 1968, students unhappy with overcrowded university conditions took to the streets of Paris at the same time as striking Renault workers. These *soixante-huitards* sprang the greatest public revolt in French living memory. For that, and for the left, at least, the revolutionaries of 1968 are still revered as heroes. At the time, they were students crammed into universities that had been somewhat cheaply expanded in order to accommodate them. The talk of politics grew across the campuses, turning against the government's stranglehold on the media and President de Gaulle's poor grasp of the economy. Ministers did indeed at the time have a sinister habit of leaning on the leading newspaper editors of the day, and television was dubbed to be 'the government in your dining room'. Inflation was high, and the gap between the working classes and the bourgeoisie was becoming a chasm.

But still, de Gaulle echoed many when he said the events of May 1968 were simply *'incompréhensible'*. The touchpaper was lit at overcrowded Nanterre university, on the outskirts of Paris, where students had been protesting against the war in Vietnam and the tatty state of the campus.

> **'Called upon to intervene, police charged into the crowd with truncheons, tear gas and a comprehensive lack of judgement.'**

On 2 May, exhausted by the protests, the authorities closed the university down and threatened to expel some of the students. The next day, a sit-in was held in sympathy at the Sorbonne. Police were called to intervene, but made things worse, charging into the crowd with truncheons, tear gas and a comprehensive lack of judgement. The city's streets were soon flooded with thousands of incensed student demonstrators, now officially on strike. The trade unions followed, as did the *lycées*. By mid May nine million people were on strike, and not just in Paris: factories all over the country were occupied by workers.

On 24 May, de Gaulle intervened – naturally, via the nation's television sets. His speech warned of civil war and pleaded for people's support. It didn't go down well: riots broke out, with students storming the Bourse, only to be thwarted by more police tear gas. Barricades sprang up all over the Latin Quarter, which had become something of a battleground, with the Odéon theatre and the Sorbonne's amphitheatre packed every night with activists and students.

Five days later, as the street violence reached its peak, de Gaulle fled briefly to Germany and Prime Minister Pompidou sent tanks to the edges of Paris. But the crisis didn't quite reach such extremes. Pompidou conceded pay rises of between seven and ten per cent and increased the minimum wage; the country went back to work. A general election was called for 23 June, by which time the right had gathered enough red-fearing momentum to gain a safe majority.

MITTERRAND

Following the largely anonymous presidencies of Georges Pompidou and Valéry Giscard d'Estaing, the Socialist François Mitterrand

The new **T3 tramway**. *See p34.*

Paris Today

Post-riot elections point the way to an uneasy future.

Whatever their outcome, the presidential elections of May 2007 will be clouded by the shocking events of 2005 and 2006 – and their aftermath. Paris saw the worst rioting and largest demonstrations since 1968, first by disaffected youths in the suburbs, then by students. While Jacques Chirac's faltering government was much criticised for its post-riot performance, dynamic interior minister Nicolas Sarkozy's hard-line stance saw his popularity leap – he's now favourite for the presidency.

A further scandal, Clearstream – branded the French Watergate – plunged the government into hot water once again. The affair centred on Chirac, Prime Minister Dominique de Villepin and their investigation of Sarkozy's fiscal dealings. It was not the first time Chirac had been embroiled in scandal: his term as Paris mayor gave rise to allegations of embezzlement and illegal party funding. However, the French constitution gives Chirac virtual immunity from the justice system as long as he is president.

The charismatic Sarkozy, meanwhile, created his own brand of controversy. Just before the riots kicked off, he made some inflammatory comments about the '*racaille*' living in the crime-ridden suburbs – which loosely translates as 'scum'. Ignited by the accidental deaths of two North African teenagers in the north-east district of Clichy-sous-Bois, the riots articulated a long-subdued anger among *banlieue* youth. In estates around Paris and other cities, warehouses, restaurants and thousands of cars were set ablaze. The government responded by calling a state of emergency, imposing curfews and banning public meetings at weekends – three weeks went by before the worst was over.

Two months later, Sarkozy entered the fray with an uncompromising immigration bill. It laid down stricter terms for immigrants: illegal aliens were no longer automatically granted papers after living in France for ten years. The bill also established a system of selective immigration, prioritising those with special skills. Sarkozy then spearheaded a widely reported eviction of an infamous immigrant squat in the southern Paris suburb of Cachan.

The leader of the ruling centre-right UMP party remains in pole position for the presidentials. His autobiography *Témoignage* topped the bestseller lists, a second instalment strategically planned for 2007. Polls suggest his closest rival is Socialist mother-of-four Ségolène Royal, whose own autobiography, *Désirs d'Avenir*, was published in September 2006. With the media billing the elections as Sarko versus Ségo, Senegal-born Royal is hoping to defy France's chauvinistic political world to become the first Madame la Présidente. Royal first came into the public eye when François Mitterand made her environment minister in 1992; in 2004 she became France's first female regional president. The 54-year-old Royal has long been in the shadow of her male left-wing colleagues, not least her romantic partner of 26 years, Socialist party leader François Hollande. Many believe her toughest battle will be winning the support of her own party.

In many ways, the riots reflected the long-standing divide between Paris and its suburbs. Unlike most major cities, Paris has rigidly defined limits: it has been composed of the same 20 districts over the same 105 square kilometres (41 square miles) since 1860. If just over two million live in Paris, the inhabitants of Greater Paris number almost ten million. Parisians regard the suburbs with a certain disdain, with the physical presence of the Périphérique ring road around the city only serving to highlight the cultural, geographic and administrative divide between Paris and its expanding suburbs.

Closing this gap is one of the main objectives of Paris mayor Bertrand Delanoë, whose public transport policies centre around improving links with the suburbs. Inaugurated in December 2006, the city's first tramway in almost a century connects with several métro lines that run to the nearby *banlieue*. The T3 line stretches over the southern edge of the city, destined to cover the whole perimeter. Another initiative is to cover sections of the congested Périphérique with landscaped gardens and sports fields, improving the quality of life of the 100,000 Parisians who live alongside it. The first area to gain relief from the eight lanes of traffic has been the north-eastern area around Porte des Lilas.

Such resourceful policy-making has been a hallmark of Delanoë's time in charge of City Hall. The mayor's next challenge is a facelift of the much-maligned Les Halles shopping centre (*see p105* **Overhauling the Halls**). Elsewhere, the Batignolles area that was to accommodate the Olympic village – Paris having lost out on the 2012 Games – will be redeveloped into a park fringed by offices, shops and housing. Delanoë remains a strong candidate for re-election when his term ends in March 2008 (*see p35* **The race for mayor**).

The major architectural event of 2006 was a pet project of Jacques Chirac. Commissioned in 1996, the Musée Quai Branly (*see p158* **A museum with a mission**) opened its vast collection of African, Asian and Oceanic art to the public ten years later. The Jean Nouvel building housing it was designed to resemble the elongated shadow of the nearby Eiffel Tower. Other major projects took place around Trocadéro, where a controversially expensive aquarium-cum-cinema complex opened beneath the gardens. (*see p119* **Trocadéro revival**). In the nearby Palais de Chaillot, the long-awaited Cité de l'Architecture et du Patrimoine will be inaugurated in early 2007.

While Paris is justly celebrated for its museums, it's undeniable that new cultural projects are often subject to a long gestation period. Billionaire businessman François Pinault got so fed up with bureaucratic

hold-ups, he abandoned his chosen site in Paris and took his new contemporary art museum to Venice instead. The city's lack of dynamism, or *muséfication*, is a criticism often levelled at mayor Delanoë. His Plan Local d'Urbanisme (PLU), adopted in 2005, has preservation at its heart. An additional 4,000 buildings and 1,500 green spaces (parks, gardens and cemeteries) will fall under state protection, while all new constructions are limited to 37m (121ft) in height.

The mayor has also been looking to the future with his Paris Ville Numérique (PARVi) project, which includes a plan to equip parks, libraries and squares with some 400 free Wi-Fi access points in 2007. Delanoë also intends to offer tax reductions to companies that lay down fibre-optic cables: the aim is to equip 80 per cent of Parisian buildings with an ultra-high speed connection by 2010. Some 60 per cent of French households already have a high speed ADSL or cable connection, making it the second most connected nation in Europe.

'With film crews allowed unprecedented access to key locations across the city, Paris is attracting big-name movie shoots.'

Despite the profusion of internet and TV channels, cinema-going remains popular in Paris (27.5 million admissions in 2005), although the trend is towards multiplexes. The city continues to attract Hollywood movie shoots (*Marie-Antoinette*, *The Da Vinci Code*), following a policy by Culture Minister Renaud Donnedieu de Vabres to promote tourism via the big screen and allow film crews greater access to key locations within the city.

Although tourist numbers are up – there's a 20 per cent rise in visitors from China alone – locals have been deserting the capital since the 1970s. One reason is escalating housing prices. Even if the rate of increase is slowing down, the annual price rise for flats in Paris stood at 12.7 per cent in the first quarter of 2006. The search for cheaper homes has sent families flocking to the suburbs, with certain neighbourhoods registering influxes of up to 45 per cent.

The trend for Parisians to move out of the city centre is another indication that the historic Paris/*banlieue* divide may eventually dissolve, and it's worth noting that some of the *banlieue* that enjoyed the most significant property booms were those that had been at the heart of the riots less than a year before. Historical divides, it seems, can quickly be forgotten in the name of profit and progress.

The race for mayor

In 2007 Bertrand Delanoë will serve the final year of his first term as Paris mayor. Given his popularity and the widespread success of his many initiatives, the 55-year-old is looking like a strong candidate for his own succession in the next municipal elections, scheduled for March 2008.

When he came to power in early 2001, at the head of a left-wing coalition, Delanoë (*pictured*) was relatively unknown to the general public. The electoral process requires Parisians to vote for representatives in their arrondissement – who in turn elect the mayor. He was the city's first Socialist mayor in over a century – and the first openly gay mayor. During his six years in one of the country's most powerful positions, Delanoë has won popular acclaim with his crowd-pleasing cultural innovations (Paris-Plage, Nuit Blanche), and political credibility with his aggressive traffic and environmental policies.

With a focus on public transport, the Tunisian-born mayor has inaugurated a new tramway, introduced multiple bus and cycle lanes, and set in motion a plan to ban cars from the central four arrondissements by 2012. As a result, traffic has been reduced by 13 per cent and pollution levels have dropped significantly. Urban regeneration has also been high on the agenda, with priority given to green spaces and social housing.

Above all, Delanoë has brought a refreshing dynamism to the position of Paris mayor, so often viewed as a springboard for ambitious politicians more interested in their own careers than in the welfare of Parisians. Corruption and scandals tainted the reign of Delanoë's predecessor Jean Tiberi, while the 18 years Jacques Chirac served as mayor have come back to haunt him in the form of embezzlement and illegal party funding accusations. In contrast, Delanoë famously chose to convert the lavish mayoral apartment into a day-care centre. He has also tried to involve Parisians in the city's politics by sending out questionnaires – local

cynics would say he is looking to win approval in time for a possible shot at the presidentials in 2012.

In the meantime, Delanoë will face stiff competition in 2008, notably from UMP candidate Françoise de Panafieu, who served as deputy to both Chirac and Tiberi during their mayoral reigns. Panafieu, a close ally of Interior Minister Nicolas Sarkozy, is currently mayor of the 17th arrondissement. She has persistently argued that Delanoë's fun-loving initiatives and green-minded policies are to the detriment of the city's economic vitality. To prove her point, she founded the Club Lutèce, an organisation that brings together economic experts and high-profile Parisians in order to plot out the city's return to prosperity.

To some surprise, the Greens announced that they will be fielding a candidate – Denis Baupin. In 2001 *les Verts* formed an alliance with the plural left, resulting in victory for Delanoë and a key position in charge of transport for Baupin. The latter is concerned that the Socialist agenda is likely to stray from that of the Greens in the future, and has decided to stand against Delanoë. Both men will face competition from the centre-right UDF's Marielle de Sarnez. A founding member of her party in 1978, she is currently a member of the European Parliament.

With two women running for the 2008 elections, there's a chance that Paris could have its first-ever mayoress – though opinion polls still show Delanoë as favourite.

Basilique St-Denis.

Architecture

A thousand years of development, destruction and development again.

Looking at the long, elegant boulevards of contemporary Paris, it's hard to imagine the city in a parlous state of ruin. But through revolution, war and tooth-and-nail sieges, the capital has often ended up in need of repair. Although it was spared bombs in World War II, Paris has been rebuilt from the rubble many times. And while Georges-Eugène Haussmann's utilitarian urban vision of straight boulevards and clean lines has stuck in the popular imagination, the Paris prior to his plans was a city of ramshackle, confusing warrens of streets and medieval houses. Paris has not always been perfect. Baron Haussmann was not the only authority to make his mark on the city's architecture, of course – Napoleon splurged on grand arches and statues, while President Giscard d'Estaing gave skyscrapers a firm no.

Today, the precious *patrimoine* of the city is closely guarded by monitors such as Bâtiments de France, and the Ville de Paris authorities are keen to develop areas with untapped potential, such as the 13th arrondissement, rather than pour money into inverted pyramids, as was the

case under Jacques Chirac's *grands travaux*. Paris still has iconic archictectural problems, however, with the ugly, maddening Les Halles mall chief among them. See *p105* **Overhauling the Halls**. Redevelopment will begin by 2008.

MEDIEVAL PARIS: ROMANESQUE TO GOTHIC

Medieval Paris congregated on the Ile de la Cité and the Latin Quarter. Sadly, the clusters of medieval housing built around Notre-Dame were razed by Haussmann in the 19th century (*see p23*). A few churches survive as examples of simple Romanesque architecture, among them **St-Germain-des-Prés** (*see p150*), with its rounded arches and decorated nave. The **Eglise St-Julien-le-Pauvre** (*see p139*), built as a pilgrim pit stop in the late 12th century, is well preserved inside.

GOTHIC

The Gothic trademarks of pointed arches, ogival vaulting and flying buttresses had their beginning at the **Basilique St-Denis** (*see p173*), completed in the 13th century by master mason Pierre de Montreuil. **Notre-Dame** (*see p80*) continued the style with its rich, delicate rose windows and fine, tendon-like buttresses (not to mention its characterful menagerie of gargoyles). Montreuil's **Sainte-Chapelle** (*see p82*), built 1246-48, represents the peak of Gothic design. The Flamboyant-Gothic style to follow saw a host of decoration. **Eglise St-Séverin** (*see p140*), with its twisting spiral column, is particularly original. The **Tour Jean-Sans-Peur** (*see p108*) is a rare fragment of an early 15th-century mansion, while the city's two finest medieval mansions are the Hôtel de Cluny (now the **Musée National du Moyen-Age**; *see p141*) and the **Hôtel de Sens** (*see p114*) in the Marais.

RENAISSANCE

Italianate town planning, with its ordered avenues, neat squares and public spaces, came late to Paris. It was instigated by François I towards the end of his reign, when he realised the beneficial effects that a well organised urban landscape could have on trade. He installed Leonardo da Vinci at Amboise and brought over Primaticcio and Rosso to work on his palace at **Fontainebleau** (*see p348*). Aristocratic quarters were established in the Faubourg St-Germain and the Marais – the latter holds the **Hôtel Carnavalet** (*see p112*) and the **Hôtel de Lamoignon** (24 rue Pavée, 4th), the finest examples of Renaissance mansions to be found in Paris.

THE ANCIEN REGIME

Henri IV, France's first Bourbon king, took control of Paris after a long siege. He found the city knee-deep in bodies and broken buildings, a chaotic mess punctuated by dilapidated churches and mansions. Public building projects were promptly organised to restore order; timber was banned, to be replaced by brick and stone, while bridges over the Seine were cleared of the houses and shops that dangerously cluttered their paths. The Pont Neuf's construction was speeded up with a new levy on wine imports.

Place Dauphine (1st) and **place des Vosges** (*see p113*) reflected Henri's taste for Italian classicism – the latter irresistibly elegant to the rich classes with its symmetrical design, red brick vaulted galleries and pitched roofs. Built on the site of an old horse market, it was intended as an affordable housing project.

The 17th century was a high point in French power and the monarchy desired buildings that reflected its grandeur, a need satisfied by the baroque style. Great architects emerged under court patronage: Salomon de Brosse, François Mansart and landscape architect André le

Nôtre. But even at **Versailles** (*see p352*), baroque never reached the excesses of Italy or Austria, as French architects followed Cartesian principles of harmony and balance.

The **Palais du Luxembourg** (*see p152*), built by de Brosse in Italianate style for Marie de Médicis, combines classic French chateau design with elements of the Pitti palace in Marie's native Florence. The **Eglise du Val-de-Grâce** (*see p143*), designed by Mansart, and later Jacques Lemercier, is one of the city's grandest examples of baroque architecture.

Nouveaux riches flocked to build mansions in the Marais and the Ile St-Louis. Those in the Marais follow a symmetrical U-shaped plan, with a secluded courtyard: look through the archways to the *cour d'honneur* of the **Hôtel de Sully** (*see p111*) or the **Hôtel Salé** (*see p112*), where façades are richly decorated, in contrast with their street faces.

Under Colbert, Louis XIV's chief minister, the creation of stage sets to magnify the Sun King's power proceeded apace. **The Louvre** (*see pp85-91*) grew as Claude Perrault created the sweeping west wing, while Hardouin-Mansart's

Boulevard Haussmann. *See p39*.

circular **place des Victoires** (*see p99*) and **place Vendôme** (*see p98*), an elegant octagon, were both designed to show off equestrian statues of the king.

ROCOCO AND NEO-CLASSICISM

In the early 18th century, the Faubourg St-Germain overtook the Marais as the city's most fashionable quarter. Most of the mansions there are now ministries or embassies, but you can still see some original carved panelling at the Hôtel Bouchardon (now home to the **Musée Maillol**; *see p157*).

Under Louis XV, a spread of sumptuous buildings was commissioned, among them **La Monnaie** (now the **Musée de la Monnaie de Paris**; *see p150*), the **Panthéon** (*see p144*), the **Ecole de Droit** (place du Panthéon, 5th) and

many new theatres. Soufflot's Panthéon, like Jacques-Ange Gabriel's neo-classical **place de la Concorde** (*see p98*), was inspired by the majestic monuments of ancient Rome.

Interior decoration took on a similarly grandiose character with the frivolous French rococo style. The best example is the **Hôtel de Soubise** (60 rue des Francs-Bourgeois, 3rd), with panelling, plasterwork and paintings by celebrated decorators of the day, including Boucher, Restout and van Loo.

THE 19TH CENTURY

The street fighting of the revolution left Paris in a desultory state, with royal statues pulled down and churches converted into 'temples of reason' or grain stores. Napoleon redressed this situation with a suitably pompous vision to

Behind closed doors

When a Parisian finally invites you into their home, it can be seen as an honour. When a Parisian architect does the same, it's an excellent opportunity to see how some of the city's creative inhabitants have broken free of the typical Haussmannian formula.

Launched in 2000, the annual **Journées de la Maison Contemporaine** (*photo above*) sees a select group of Paris-based architects open up their homes and apartments to the public – some built from scratch, but most clever reworkings of existing space.

The glossy, sumptuously shot *Architectures à Vivre* magazine (www.avivre.net) was launched at the same time. From the end of

May you can pick up a special edition of the magazine (about €10) and start plotting which houses you want to nose about first. Alternatively, you can check the event's website (www.maisons-contemporaines.com) for more information. Early booking is essential, as places are squeezed tight for each visit, and there is a minimal fee. If you're prepared to hop on a train, the event flings open doors all around France, including some interesting designs in the suburbs.

Odile Veillon, an architect who throws open her doors for the event every summer, lives in a quiet street in the 11th arrondissement in a former *atelier d'ébenisterie* (cabinet-maker's studio). When she bought the apartment it was in a fairly run-down state, with scuffed parquet floorboards and a cramped layout. But by knocking several rooms together, she created a large, light-flooded main living area, overlooking a cool, shaded courtyard.

The huddle of visitors stand politely as Veillon explains her designs, but cut straight to the chase when she's finished her speech. How much did the apartment cost? How much was the renovation? But while visitors can pick up plenty of practical information and tips, at heart this event is all about *maisons de rêve* – the loft conversion in the 1st arrondissement that you would never set foot inside otherwise, never mind afford; the stylishly bohemian family home carved out of a disused warehouse in the 20th. And with a line-up that changes each year, there are always fresh sources of envy and inspiration.

make Paris the most beautiful city in the world. He confiscated land from the aristocracy and the Church for development, and went on a massive building spree. As well as five new bridges, including the **Pont d'Austerlitz** (5th/12th) and **Pont d'Iéna** (7th/16th) and 56 ornamental fountains (such as the Fontaine de Mars), he built a rash of self-aggrandising statues and arches, most notably the **Arc de Triomphe** (*see p121*) and the shamelessly gaudy **Arc du Carrousel** (*see p94*). One of his more practical commissions was the **Canal d'Ourcq** (*see p134*) – an addition that would help improve the city's appalling water supply.

Later in the century, engineering innovations made iron-framed buildings increasingly common. Henri Labrouste's lovely reading room at the **Bibliothèque Ste-Geneviève** (1844-50; 10 place du Panthéon, 5th) was one of the first to use iron for the entire structure. Stations such as Hittorf's **Gare du Nord** (1861-65; *see p104*) and Laloux's Gare d'Orsay (now **Musée d'Orsay**; *see p157*) are simply shells around an iron frame, allowing spacious light-filled interiors. The most daring iron construction of them all was, of course, the **Eiffel Tower** (*see p159*). When it was built in 1889, it was the tallest structure in the world.

BARON HAUSSMANN

Louis Napoleon, looking enviously to the energy of London and nostalgically to the glory of Rome, decided that Paris once again needed a makeover. In 1853 he appointed Baron Haussmann as the *préfet* of Paris. A fearsome administrator rather than a professional architect, Haussmann faced problems of sanitation, sewage and traffic-clogged streets, to which he squared up with ruthless efficiency. He gave himself the rather arrogant title of 'demolition artist' (others preferred the less flattering 'Alsatian Attila'), and set about his plans for the destruction of the disorded Paris streets, cutting broad, long boulevards across the city landscape. An estimated 27,000 houses were razed to the ground in the process, including the patrician Left Bank *grands hôtels*, which made way for the boulevard St-Germain. The Haussmannian apartment block, however, has endured, its iconic utilitarian lines held in place by rows of wrought-iron balconies.

His vision also introduced English-style public parks, such as the **Buttes-Chaumont** (*see p138*), along with prisons (the **Prison de la Santé**; 14th), asylums (the **Hôpital Ste-Anne**, rue de la Santé, 14th), hospitals and sewers. Amid the upheaval, one building epitomised the grand style of the Second Empire: Charles Garnier's sumptuous **Palais Garnier** opera house (1862-75; *see p310*).

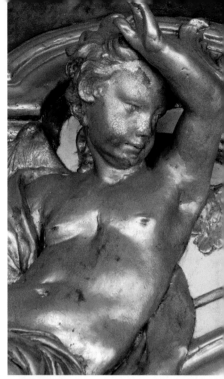

Hôtel de Soubise. *See p38.*

THE 20TH CENTURY

An outburst of extravagance for the 1900 *Exposition Universelle* marked the beginning of the 20th century. The **Train Bleu** brasserie in the Gare de Lyon (12th) is an ornate example of the heavy Beaux Arts floral style of this period. Art nouveau at its most fluid and flamboyant can be seen in Hector Guimard's métro stations and his 1901 **Castel Béranger** (*see p126*).

All this was a long way from the roughly contemporary work of Henri Sauvage, an innovative and eclectic architect. After designing several Parisian apartment blocks, he went on to create a large social housing project in **rue des Amiraux** (18th), tiled artists' studios-cum-flats in **rue La Fontaine** (16th), and the more overtly art deco 1920s extension of **La Samaritaine** (19 rue de la Monnaie, 1st). Funded by philanthropists, social housing began to be put up citywide, such as the Rothschilds' estate in **rue de Prague** (12th).

THE MODERN MOVEMENT

After World War I, two names stand out by virtue of both their innovation and influence: Auguste Perret and Le Corbusier. A third architect, Robert Mallet-Stevens, stands unrivalled for his elegance. Paris is one of the best cities in the world for Modern Movement houses and studios (often in the 16th and western suburbs like Boulogne and Garches), but also in a more diluted form for town halls and schools built in the socially minded 1930s.

Perret stayed largely within a classical aesthetic, but experimented with reinforced concrete facades. Le Corbusier tried out his ideas in private houses, such as the **Villa Savoy** in Poissy and **Villa La Roche** in the 16th, (now **Fondation le Corbusier**; *see p126*). His **Pavillon Suisse** at the **Cité Universitaire** (*see p168*) and **Armée du Salut** hostel (12 rue Cantagrel) in the 13th can be seen as an intermediary point between these villas and his Villes Radieuses mass housing schemes, which became so influential and so debased in projects across Europe after 1945.

Other notable Modern Movement buildings include Adolphe Loos' house for Dadaist poet Tristan Tzara in avenue Junot, supposedly the epitome of his maxim 'ornament is crime'. Meanwhile the new love of chrome, steel and glass found its way into art deco cafés and brasseries such as **La Coupole** (*see p210*), as well as **Le Grand Rex** cinema (*see p290*).

POST-WAR PARIS

The aerodynamic aesthetic of the post-war era saw the 1958 **UNESCO building** (*see p160*), by Bernard Zehrfuss, Pier Luigi Nervi and Marcel Breuer, and the beginnings of **La Défense** (*see p177*). The *bidonvilles*, or shanty towns, that had emerged outside town, many housing immigrants, cried out for a solution. In the 1960s and '70s, tower blocks sprouted in the suburbs and new towns: Sarcelles, Mantes la Jolie, Cergy-Pontoise, Evry, Melun-Sénart and Créteil. Redevelopment inside the city was limited, although new regulations allowed taller buildings, noticeably in Montparnasse and in the 13th and 19th. Valéry Giscard d'Estaing found the skyscraping style of projects such as place des Fêtes distasteful, however, and prevented the Paris horizon from rising any further. Piano and Rogers' high-tech **Centre Pompidou** (*see p109*), opened in 1977, was the first of the daring prestige projects that have become a trademark of modern Paris.

THE 1980S AND BEYOND

President François Mitterrand's *grands projets* dominated the 1980s and '90s as he sought to leave his stamp on the city with Nouvel's **Institut du Monde Arabe** (*see p146*) and Sprecklesen's **Grande Arche de la Défense** (*see p177*), as well as Ott's more dubious **Opéra Bastille** (*see p311*), Perrault's **Bibliothèque Nationale** (*see p171*) and Chemetov's **Bercy** (*see p116*) finance ministry. Urban renewal has transformed old industrial areas to return the balance of Paris eastwards. Stylistically, the buzzword has been 'transparency': from IM Pei's Louvre Pyramid to Jean Nouvel's **Fondation Cartier** (*see p163*) with its clever slices of glass. Christian de Portzamparc pursued a more offbeat style with his **Cité de la Musique** (*see p309*) – a series of geometrical blocks set around a colourful internal street.

The city also invested in public housing; of note are the human-scale housing round **Parc de la Villette** (*see p136*) and **Parc André-Citroën** (*see p162*), Piano's red tile and glass ensemble in **rue de Meaux** (19th) and La Poste's apartments for postal workers designed by young architects such as Frédérick Borel.

THE 21ST CENTURY

The age of the *grands projets* is over, although Jacques Chirac managed to squeeze one last legacy project into his reign with the completion of Jean Nouvel's **Musée du Quai Branly** (*see p158* **A museum with a mission**), which opened in 2006.

The city's biggest architectural challenge is now the Forum des Halles shopping centre, a drastically ugly piece of 1970s planning that is utterly discontinous with its surroundings. The Ville de Paris is launching an international architectural competition in 2007 to find a more elegant solution to managing this busy throughfare of Parisian commerce and transport.

Where to Stay

Hôtel Daniel. *See p51.*

Where to Stay

From buzzing boutique hotels to old-fashioned opulence – plus budget beds.

Hôtel du Jeu de Paume. *See p43.*

Much like restaurants and cafés, hotels here are opened, renovated and/or reinvented and reopened at a dizzying rate. Neighbourhoods fall in and out of fashion, their cachet increased by the siting of some funky boutique hotel or other – for evidence, look no further than the cultish **Hôtel du Petit Moulin**.

Among the big openings in 2006 are the **Hôtel Fouquet's-Barrière**, a luxury four-star spa job on avenue George-V scheduled for November, and the **Hôtel Daniel**, also located by the Champs-Elysées, only the second Relais & Châteaux hotel to set up in Paris. The wacky **Hôtel Amour** (*see p47* **All you need is love**) is the current talk of the town.

Whatever your needs, there's a Paris hotel to fit the bill. We've found the best in each category, from marble-clad palaces to cosy hotels with bare-stone breakfast rooms – plus no-frills budget venues (*see p68* **Low-cost lodgings**).

CLASSIFICATION AND FACILITIES

Hotels are graded according to an official star rating system designed to sort palace from pit stop – but we haven't followed it in this guide. Said star ratings usually reflect room size and the mere presence of a lift (rather than decor, staff or atmosphere), and we don't think the system is of much practical value when making your choice. Instead, we've divided the hotels into four categories, according to the price for one night in a double room with shower/bath facilities: Deluxe €300+; Expensive €200-€300; Moderate €100-€200; Budget up to €100.

Deluxe means air-conditioning, double-glazed windows, a bar and restaurant (except in the smaller boutique hotels), with babysitting and airport shuttle services; in-room facilities often include Wi-Fi internet and room service, plus other extras depending on the hotel. Expensive ones offer similar amenities and services. Moderate means an in-room phone, modem connection and breakfast service; at the budget hotels you can normally be assured of a TV and in-room phone. We provide a list of the key services below the description of each hotel. For gay hotels, *see p306*.

NEED TO KNOW

Note that all hotels in France charge an additional room tax (*taxe de séjour*) of around €1 per person per night, sometimes included in the posted rate. Hotels are often booked solid during the major trade fairs (January, May,

September), and it's hard to find a quality pillow on which to lay your head during Fashion Weeks (January, March, July and October). At quieter times, including July and August, hotels often offer reasonable special deals at short notice; phone ahead or check their websites to find out. Same-day reservations can be arranged in person for a nominal commission fee at the Office de Tourisme de Paris (*see chapter* **Resources A-Z: Tourist information**).

Several websites offer discount booking: www.parishotels.com guarantees the lowest prices online, which can be up to 70 per cent off the rack rate; and www.ratestogo.com offers big discounts on last-minute reservations.

The Islands

Expensive

Hôtel du Jeu de Paume

54 rue St-Louis-en-l'Île, 4th (01.43.26.14.18/fax 01.40.46.02.76/www.jeudepaumehotel.com). M° Pont Marie. **Rates** €180-€255 single; €225-€445 double; €545 suite; €18 breakfast. **Credit** AmEx, DC, MC, V. **Map** p409 K7 ❶

With an oh-so-discreet courtyard entrance, original 17th-century beams, private garden and a unique timbered breakfast room that was once a real tennis court built under Louis XIII, this is a charming and romantic hotel. These days it is filled with a nicely slung-together array of modern and classical art. A dramatic glass lift and catwalks lead to the rooms, which are simple and tasteful, and have Pierre Frey fabric walls. The bathrooms and lighting have recently been updated. **Photo** *p42*.

Bar. Gym. Internet (Wi-Fi). Room service.

Moderate

Hospitel Hôtel Dieu

1 pl du Parvis-Notre-Dame, 4th (01.44.32.01.00/fax 01.44.32.01.16/www.hotel-hospitel.com). M° Cité or Hôtel de Ville. **Rates** €150 single; €195 double; €215 triple; €12 breakfast. **Credit** MC, V. **Map** p408 J7 ❷

Hospitel has 14 recently renovated spotless rooms with colourful contemporary decor and a limited view of the spires of Notre-Dame. It's used by families of the Hôtel Dieu hospital's in-patients and visitors; they usually take up about half the hotel's capacity. A medical smell is present but not strong, bathrooms are quite large, and you couldn't ask for a better sightseeing base in all of Paris. Prices have gone up in the last year, but it's still good value for money. *No smoking. Room service.*

Hôtel des Deux-Îles

59 rue St-Louis-en-l'Île, 4th (01.43.26.13.35/fax 01.43.29.60.25/www.deuxiles-paris-hotel.com). M° Pont Marie. **Rates** €157 single; €178 double; €12 breakfast. **Credit** AmEx, MC, V. **Map** p409 K7 ❸

This peaceful 17th-century townhouse offers 17 soundproofed, air-conditioned rooms done out in faintly colonial style. Attractive features include a tiny courtyard off the lobby, and a vaulted stone breakfast room. All rooms are scheduled to be freshened up in January 2007. The equally pleasant Hôtel Lutèce, found at nearby No.65 (01.43.26.23.52), is run by the same management.

Concierge. Internet (Wi-Fi). TV.

The Louvre, Palais-Royal & Les Halles

Deluxe

Hôtel Costes

239 rue St-Honoré, 1st (01.42.44.50.00/fax 01.42.44.50.01/www.hotelcostes.com). M° Tuileries. **Rates** €500-€700 single or double; €1,400 suite; €30 breakfast. **Credit** AmEx, DC, MC, V. **Map** p401 G5 ❹

If attitude is more important than service, then this temple of stylish notoriety is for you. And don't even think of whipping out your autograph book, no matter how many A-listers you might find at the low-lit bar (*see p232* **'The usual, Sir?'**). The Costes boasts one of the best pools in Paris, a sybaritic Eastern-inspired affair with its own underwater music system. The same management is also responsible for the sleek Hôtel Costes K in the 16th, complete with a fabulous spa.

Bar. Concierge. Gym. Parking (€30). Pool (indoor). Restaurant. Room service. Spa. TV.

Other locations: Hôtel Costes K, 81 av Kléber, 16th (01.44.05.75.75).

Hôtel de Crillon

10 pl de la Concorde, 8th (01.44.71.15.00/fax 01.44.71.15.02/www.crillon.com). M° Concorde. **Rates** €615 single; €695 double; €8,200 suite; €47 American breakfast, €32 continental breakfast. **Credit** AmEx, DC, MC, V. **Map** p401 F4 ❺

The height of neo-classical European magnificence, the Crillon lives up to its *palais* reputation with decor strong on marble, mirrors and gold leaf. The Michelin-starred Les Ambassadeurs (*see p187*) has an acclaimed chef, Jean-François Piège, and a brand new kitchen with a glassed-in private dining area for groups of no more than six who wish to dine amid the bustle of the 80-strong kitchen staff. The Winter Garden tearoom has a gorgeous terrace and live harp music or jazz, while classes by the city's top floral designers teach guests how to recreate the chic flower arrangements seen throughout the hotel.

Bar. Business centre. Concierge. Gym. Internet. No-smoking room(s). Parking (free). Restaurants (2). Room service. TV.

▶ Green '❶' digits give the site of each hotel, shown on the maps. *See pp400-409.*

Hôtel Ritz

15 pl Vendôme, 1st (01.43.16.30.30/fax 01.43.
16.31.78/www.ritzparis.com). M° Concorde or Opéra.
Rates €710 single or double; €1,320-€9,120 suite;
€44 American breakfast, €34 continental breakfast.
Credit AmEx, DC, MC, V. **Map** p401 G4 **6**
This, the grande dame of Paris hotels, has proffered
hospitality to Coco Chanel, the Duke of Windsor,
Proust, and Dodi and Di. Today's guests have the
choice of 162 bedrooms, of which 56 are suites, from
the romantic Frédéric Chopin to the glitzy Impérial.
There are plenty of corners in which to strike poses
or quench a thirst, from Hemingway's elegant cigar
bar (*see p232* '**The usual, Sir?**') and the plush
Victorian champagne bar to the poolside hangout
inspired by Ancient Greece. **Photo** *p46.*
Bars (2). Business centre. Concierge. Gym. Hairdryer.
Internet. Parking (€44). Pool (indoor). Restaurant.
Room service. Spa. TV.

Hôtel Sofitel le Faubourg

15 rue Boissy-d'Anglas, 8th (01.44.94.14.00/fax
01.44.94.14.28/www.sofitel.com). M° Concorde.
Rates €395 single; €465-€530 double; €995 suite;
€2,000 apartment; €23-€28 breakfast.
Credit AmEx, DC, MC, V. **Map** p401 F4 **7**
This hotel is close to the major couture boutiques –
unsurprisingly, as it used to be the *Marie Claire*
offices. The rooms have Louis XVI armchairs, large
balconies, walk-in wardrobes and Roger & Gallet
smellies in the bathrooms; for shopping widowers,
there's a small gym and a hammam. It's quiet too:
the street has been closed to traffic since 2001
because the American embassy is on the corner.
Bar. Business centre. Concierge. Gym. Internet.
No-smoking room(s). Parking (€29). Restaurant.
Room service. TV.
Other locations: Sofitel Arc de Triomphe, 14 rue
Beaujon, 17th (01.53.89.50.50); Sofitel Champs
Elysées, 8 rue Jean Goujon, 8th (01.40.74.64.64); Hôtel
Scribe, 1 rue Scribe, 9th (01.44.71.24.24).

Le Meurice

228 rue de Rivoli, 1st (01.44.58.10.10/fax
01.44.58.10.19/www.lemeurice.com). M° Tuileries.
Rates €520-€610 single; €650-€760 double; €1,050-
€10,000 suite; €35-€45 breakfast. **Credit** AmEx, DC,
MC, V. **Map** p401 G5 **8**
Having spruced up its extravagant Louis XVI decor
and intricate mosaic tiled floors in a lengthy facelift,
Le Meurice is looking absolutely splendid. All of its
160 rooms are done out in distinct historical styles;
among the 36 suites (25 full and 11 junior), the Belle
Etoile on the seventh floor provides 360-degree
panoramic views of Paris from its terrace. You can
relax in the Winter Garden to the strains of regular
live jazz performances; for more intensive intervention, head over to the lavishly appointed spa with
its *vinothérapie* treatments – or get grape products
directly into your bloodstream at the gorgeous, high-
ceilinged Bar Fontainebleau.
Bar. Business centre. Concierge. Gym. Hairdryer.
Internet (Wi-Fi). No-smoking room(s). Restaurants
(2). Room service. Spa. TV.

Moderate

Hôtel Brighton

218 rue de Rivoli, 1st (01.47.03.61.61/fax
01.42.60.41.78/www.esprit-de-france.com).
M° Tuileries. **Rates** €168-€175 single or double;
€175-€255 suite; €9-€15 breakfast. **Credit** AmEx,
DC, MC, V. **Map** p401 G5 **9**
With several rooms overlooking the Tuileries garden,
the Brighton is great value (book well ahead for a
good view). All faux-marble and mosaic decor, the
recently-restored hotel was opened at the start of the
20th century as the Entente Cordiale got under way.
Concierge. Internet. TV.

Hôtel Mansart

5 rue des Capucines, 1st (01.42.61.50.28/fax
01.49.27.97.44/www.esprit-de-france.com).
M° Opéra. **Rates** €170-€310 double; €17 extra
bed; €11 breakfast. **Credit** AmEx, DC, MC, V.
Map p401 G4 **10**

The best Hotels

For contemporary chic
Hôtel le A (*p51*); Le Général (*p59*); Murano
Urban Resort (*p57*); Le Sezz (*p53*).

For gilded grandeur
Four Seasons George V (*p51*); Hôtel
de Crillon (*p43*); Le Meurice (*above*);
Hôtel Ritz (*above*).

For a peaceful hideaway
Hôtel de l'Abbaye (*p63*); Hôtel Daniel
(*p51*); Regents Hôtel (*p65*).

For seductive surroundings
Hôtel Bourg Tibourg (*p57*); Hôtel Duc
de Saint-Simon (*p66*); Hôtel du Petit
Moulin (*p57*).

For seeing and being seen
Hôtel Amour (*p49*); Hôtel Costes
(*p43*); Hôtel Plaza Athénée (*p51*); Le
Montalembert (*p66*); Murano
Urban Resort (*p57*).

For shoestring budgets
Familia Hôtel (*p62*); Grand Hôtel
Lévêque (*p67*); Hôtel Chopin (*p68*);
Hôtel Eiffel Rive Gauche (*p67*); Hôtel
Esmeralda (*p62*).

For spa aficionados
Four Seasons George V (*p51*); Hôtel
Fouquet's-Barrière (*p51*); Hôtel Ritz
(*above*); Hôtel Royal Monceau (*p51*);
InterContinental Paris Le Grand (*p49*).

Hôtel Ritz. *See p45.*

Stay near the ritzy place Vendôme without the ritzy prices. This spacious hotel has real style, with a light, roomy lobby decorated in murals inspired by formal gardens. The 57 bedrooms feature pleasant fabrics, antiques and paintings; five rooms, including the lovely Vendôme duplex, have an excellent view of the square – ideal for planning a jewel heist. *Bar. Concierge. Internet. Room service. TV.*

Hôtel des Tuileries

10 rue St-Hyacinthe, 1st (01.42.61.04.17/fax 01.49.27.91.56/www.hotel-des-tuileries.com). M° Tuileries. **Rates** €125-€140 single; €140-€195 double; €220-€250 triple; €13 breakfast. **Credit** AmEx, DC, MC, V. **Map** p401 G5 ⓫
The fashion pack adores this 18th-century hotel, located in prime shopping territory. There's a comfy *Ab Fab* feel, with ethnic rugs and a smattering of animal prints and bright art, combined with antique furniture, exposed beams and a listed staircase. *Concierge. Internet. Room service (mornings only). TV.*

Le Relais Saint-Honoré

308 rue St-Honoré, 1st (01.42.96.06.06/fax 01.42.96.17.50/www.relaissainthonore.com). M° Tuileries. **Rates** €196 double; €290-€330 suite; €12 breakfast. **Credit** AmEx, DC, MC, V. **Map** p401 G5 ⓬
There are 13 rooms and two suites with elegant, traditional decor in this 17th-century hotel. The attention to detail is immaculate – although lack of customer care sometimes lets the side down. *Concierge. Internet. No-smoking room(s). Room service. TV.*

Budget

Hôtel du Cygne

3 rue du Cygne, 1st (01.42.60.14.16/fax 01.42.21.37.02/www.hotelducygne.fr). M° Châtelet or Etienne Marcel/RER Châtelet Les Halles. **Rates** €60-€90 single; €95 double; €120 twin; €155 triple; €8 breakfast. **Credit** MC, V. **Map** p402 J5 ⓭
This traditional hotel in a 17th-century building offers 20 compact, cosy and simple rooms embellished with thoughtful, distinctive touches such as antiques and home-made furnishings. It's set on a pedestrian street in the bustling Les Halles district, so light sleepers might prefer one of the rooms that look over the courtyard; No.35 is the most spacious. *Internet. TV.*

Opéra & Grands Boulevards

Deluxe

Hôtel Ambassador

16 bd Haussmann, 9th (01.44.83.40.40/ fax 01.53.24.66.96/www.hotelambassador-paris. com). M° Richelieu Drouot or Chaussée d'Antin. **Rates** €360-€450 double; €545-€990 suite; €60 extra bed (free under-12s); €22 breakfast. **Credit** AmEx, DC, MC, V. **Map** p401 H4 ⓮
If you're looking for vintage style but can't face another gilded hotel à la Louis XIV, check into this historic, Haussmann-era hotel, which mixes tradi-

tional furniture with contemporary decor. The low-lit Lindbergh Bar is named after the pilot who dropped in for a celebratory drink and cigar after his solo transatlantic flight in 1927. The hotel is ideally situated for shopping at the *grands magasins*, and its summer rates are excellent value.
Bar. Business centre. Concierge. Gym. Internet (2nd floor). No-smoking room(s). Restaurant. Room service. TV.

Hôtel Concorde St-Lazare
108 rue St-Lazare, 8th (01.40.08.44.44/fax 01.42.93.01.20/www.concordestlazare-paris.com). M° St-Lazare. **Rates** €360-€450 double; €685-€1,580 suite; €24 breakfast. **Credit** AmEx, DC, MC, V. **Map** p401 G3 ⓯

Guests here are cocooned in soundproofed luxury – a boon after the bustling crowds of the nearby *grands magasins* department stores and St-Lazare railway station. The 19th-century Eiffel-inspired

lobby is a historic landmark: the high ceilings, marble pillars and sculptures look much as they have done for over a century. Rooms are spacious, with double entrance doors and exclusive Annick Goutal toiletries; the belle époque brasserie, Café Terminus, and sexy Golden Black Bar were styled by Sonia Rykiel. Guests also have access to a fitness centre a short distance away.
Bar. Business centre. Concierge. Internet (Wi-Fi). No-smoking room(s). Restaurant. Room service. TV.

Hôtel Edouard VII
39 av de l'Opéra, 2nd (01.42.61.56.90/fax 01.42.61.47.73/www.edouard7hotel.com). M° Opéra. **Rates** €390 single; €485 double; €525-€1,100 suite; €23 breakfast. **Credit** AmEx, DC, MC, V. **Map** p401 G4 ⓰

Owned by the same family for five generations, this refined hotel includes artful touches such as Murano glass lights, smooth wooden features and modern

All you need is love

First the wildly successful and exclusive nightclub **Le Baron**, then the slightly more accessible **Paris Paris** (for both, *see p325*) – now graffiti artist André and his fellow creative genius Lionel have hit the jackpot with the most talked-about place of 2006: the **Hôtel Amour** (*see p49*).

As ever, its success revolves around a scene. The hotel/brasserie/bar is loosely based on the English dining club model (in other words, as with Andrés nightclubs, it helps to know someone to get in).

'It's a hotel that artist friends of ours have decorated,' said André. 'A kind of club like in England, but more Bohemian. If you've gone to bed late, you're not going to get kicked out at 11.30 the next morning.' As if to prove the point, you'll find their arty set hanging out in the hotel brasserie, with live music and DJs, till the wee hours. 'We want guests to be plunged into Parisian life immediately,' enthuses André.

André is one of those entities who has become so famous that one name suffices. First known for his street art (a leggy graffiti mascot called Monsieur A), he's now a fixture on the nightlife scene in Paris, Tokyo and New York.

Each of his hotel's 20 rooms is unique, decorated around the theme of love by a coterie of contemporary artists and

designers such as Marc Newson, M&M, Stak, Pierre Le Tan and Sophie Calle – an in-house installation artist who began her career as a real chambermaid in Venice, taking note of guests' belongings to create her work *L'Hôtel*. There she got the sack. Here she's paid to peer through the bizarre keyholes and come up with something creative.

Seven of the rooms contain artists' installations, while two others have a private bar and a large terrace on which to hold your own party. Design details are quirky, colourful and risqué – Walt would blanche at the cheeky pink plastic Mickey at the check-in. This once tranquil neighbourhood is now a heaven for night owls: the late-night brasserie has an outdoor garden, and the crowd is young, beautiful and loves to party.

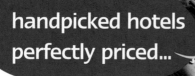

sculptures in the entrance hall. The stylish bar and restaurant Angl'Opéra (with resident star chef Gilles Choukroun) is decked out in dark mahogany and comfortable stripes (*see also p185*). Some of the individually decorated bedrooms offer wonderful balcony views of the Garnier opera house.
Bar. Concierge. Internet. No-smoking room(s). Restaurant. Room service. TV.

Hôtel Westminster

13 rue de la Paix, 2nd (01.42.61.57.46/fax 01.42.60.30.66/www.hotelwestminister.com). M° Opéra. **Rates** €750-€1,350 suite; €2,500 suite *presidentielle*; €23-€28 breakfast. **Credit** AmEx, DC, MC, V. **Map** p401 G4 🔞

This luxury hotel near place Vendôme has more than a touch of British warmth about it, no doubt owing to the influence of its favourite 19th-century guest, the Duke of Westminster (after whom the hotel was named; the current Duke reportedly still stays here). The hotel fitness centre has a top-floor location, with a beautiful tiled steam room and views over the city, while the cosy bar features deep leather chairs, a fireplace and live jazz at weekends.
Bar. Concierge. Gym. Internet (Wi-Fi). No-smoking room(s). Parking (€25). Restaurant. Room service. TV.

InterContinental Paris Le Grand

2 rue Scribe, 9th (01.40.07.32.32/fax 01.42.66.12.51/ www.paris-le-grand.intercontinental.com). M° Opéra. **Rates** €335-€1,000 double; €1,200-€4,000 suite; €35 breakfast. **Credit** AmEx, DC, MC, V. **Map** p401 G4🔞

This 1862 landmark hotel is the chain's European flagship – but, given its sheer size, perhaps 'mother ship' would be more appropriate: this landmark establishment occupies the entire block (three wings, almost 500 rooms) next to the opera house. Some 80 of the honey-coloured rooms overlook the Palais Garnier. In addition to a stylish allure bestowed by a recent multimillion-euro refit – the work of illustrious decorator Pierre-Yves Rochon, who also did up the George V (*see p51*) – the space under the vast *verrière* is one of the best oases in town. The hotel's restaurant and elegant coffeehouse, the Café de la Paix (*see p219*), has a new chef, Laurent Delarbre, recently poached from the Ritz. You can have lunch here during the week or, for a relaxing daytime break, head to the I-Spa and its seawater treatments.
Bar. Business centre. Concierge. Gym. Internet. No-smoking room(s). Parking (€40). Restaurants (2). Room service. Spa. TV.

Park Hyatt Paris-Vendôme

5 rue de la Paix, 2nd (01.58.71.12.34/fax 01.58.71.12.35/www.paris.vendome.hyatt.com). M° Opéra. **Rates** €600-€710 single or double; €810-€4,090 suite; €34-€44 breakfast. **Credit** AmEx, DC, JCB, MC, V. **Map** p401 G4 🔞

A luxurious mix of mahogany, pale limestone, matt gold and neutral fabrics under high ceilings, with rough bronze sculptures serving as light sconces and doorknobs, makes this hotel a favourite among

fashion editors. Rooms have plush Bang & Olufsen TVs and spa-like bathrooms, split into a huge dressing area and artful shower/ bath zone. There's a circular gourmet restaurant, Le Grill, where guests can watch chefs at work in the open kitchen, and a courtyard for dining in summer.
Bar. Business centre. Concierge. Gym. Internet (Wi-Fi). No-smoking room(s). Parking (free). Restaurants (2). Room service. Spa. TV.

Moderate

Hôtel Amour

8 rue Navarin, 9th (01.48.78.31.80/fax 01.48.74. 14.09/www.hotelamour.com). M° St-Georges. **Rates** €110 single; €120-€150 double; €10 breakfast. **Credit** AmEx, DC, MC, V. **Map** p402 H2 🔞

Opened in 2006, this boutique hotel is a hit with the in crowd. *See p47* **All you need is love**.
Bar. Internet (downstairs only). No-smoking rooms only. Restaurant. TV.

Hôtel Langlois

63 rue St-Lazare, 9th (01.48.74.78.24/fax 01.49.95.04.43/www.hotel-langlois.com). M° Trinité. **Rates** €99-€114 single; €114-€130 double; €130 twin; €170 suite; €20 extra bed; €10 breakfast. **Credit** AmEx, DC, MC, V. **Map** p401 H3 🔞

Built as a bank in 1870, this belle époque building became the Hôtel des Croisés in 1896. In 2001, after featuring in the Jonathan Demme film *Charade*, it changed its name to Langlois in honour of the founder of the Cinémathèque Française. Its 27 spacious, air-conditioned bedrooms are decorated in art nouveau style; larger ones have delightful hidden bathrooms.
Internet. Room service. TV.

Résidence Hôtel des Trois Poussins

15 rue Clauzel, 9th (01.53.32.81.81/fax 01.53. 32.81.82/www.les3poussins.com). M° St-Georges. **Rates** €137 single; €152 double; €187 triple; €222 quad; €152-€235 studios with kitchenette; €10 breakfast. **Credit** AmEx, DC, MC, V. **Map** p401 H2 🔞

Just off the beaten track in a pleasant *quartier*, and within uphill walking distance of Montmartre, the Résidence offers hotel accommodation in the traditional manner, but also rare self-catering studios for people who'd rather cook than eat out. Decor is traditional, with a preference for yellow. Mention *Time Out Paris* on reservation for a 15% discount.
Concierge. Internet (Wi-Fi). Room service (daytime only). TV.

Budget

Hôtel Madeleine Opéra

12 rue Greffulhe, 8th (01.47.42.26.26/fax 01.47.42.89.76/www.hotel-madeleine-opera.com). M° Madeleine. **Rates** €81-€88 single; €82-€89 double; €105 triple; €7 breakfast. **Credit** AmEx, DC, MC, V. **Map** p401 G4 🔞

Four Seasons George V. *See p51.*

This bargain hotel is just north of the Eglise Madeleine, in the heart of the city's theatre and *grands magasins* districts. Its sunny lobby sits behind a 200-year-old façade that was once a shopfront. The 24 rooms are perhaps a touch basic but still nice enough, and breakfast is brought to your room every morning.
Internet (Wi-Fi). Room service (morning). TV.

Champs-Elysées & western Paris

Deluxe

Four Seasons George V
31 av George-V, 8th (01.49.52.70.00/fax 01.49.52. 70.10/www.fourseasons.com/paris/index.html).
M° George V or Alma Marceau. **Rates** €710-€910 double/twin; €1,290-€9,500 suite; €35-€46 breakfast.
Credit AmEx, DC, MC, V. **Map** p400 D4 ②
There's no denying that the George V is serious about luxury: chandeliers, marble and tapestries; almost over-attentive staff; glorious flower arrangements; divine bathrooms; and ludicrously comfortable beds in some of the largest rooms in all of Paris. The Versailles-inspired spa includes whirlpools, saunas and a menu of treatments for an unabashedly metrosexual clientele; non-guests can now reserve appointments. It's worth every euro. **Photos** *p50*.
Bar. Business centre. Concierge. Gym. Internet (high-speed). No-smoking room(s). Pool (indoor). Restaurants (2). Room service. Spa. TV.

Hôtel le A
4 rue d'Artois, 8th (01.42.56.99.99/fax 01.42.56. 99.90/www.paris-hotel-a.com). M° St-Philippe du-Roule or Franklin D. Roosevelt. **Rates** €339-€411 double; €463 suite; €620 apartment; €23 breakfast.
Credit AmEx, DC, MC, V. **Map** p401 E4 ②
The black-and-white decor of this designer boutique hotel provides a fine backdrop for the models, artists and media types hanging out in the lounge bar area; the only splashes of colour come from the graffiti-like artworks by conceptual artist Fabrice Hybert. The 26 rooms all have granite bathrooms, and the starched white furniture slip covers, changed after each guest, make the smallish spaces seem larger than they are. The dimmer switches are a nice touch – as are the lift lights changing colour at each floor.
Bar. Concierge. Internet (Wi-Fi). No-smoking room(s). Room service. TV.

Hôtel Daniel
8 rue Frédéric-Bastiat, 8th (01.42.56.17.00/fax 01.42.56.17.01/www.hoteldanielparis.com). M° St-Philippe du-Roule or Franklin D. Roosevelt. **Rates** €320 single; €380 double; €490-€740 suite; €20 continental breakfast. **Credit** AmEx, DC, MC, V. **Map** p401 E4 ②
Paris' new Relais & Châteaux may be only a five-minute walk from the Champs-Elysées, but it feels like a world apart. A romantic gem amid the mono-

liths, it's decorated in chinoiserie and a palette of rich colours, with 26 rooms cosily appointed in toile de Jouy (the top floors have private balconies and enviable views) and an intricately hand-painted restaurant that feels like a courtyard. At about €50 per head, the gastronomic restaurant Le Lounge, run by chef Denis Fetisson, is a good deal for this neighbourhood; the bar menu is served at all hours. **Photo** *p53*.
Bar. Concierge. Internet (Wi-Fi). No-smoking room(s). Parking (€25). Restaurant. Room service. TV.

Hôtel Fouquet's-Barrière
46 av George-V, 8th (01.40.70.05.05/fax 01.40.70.57.00/www.lucienbarriere.com). M° St-Philippe du-Roule or Franklin D. Roosevelt. **Rates** €690-€910 double; €960-€8,500 suite; €46 American breakfast, €35 continental breakfast.
Credit AmEx, DC, MC, V. **Map** p400 D4 ②
Opening in November 2006, this long-awaited, grandiose five-star is built around the famous fin-de-siècle brasserie Le Fouquet's. Five buildings form the hotel complex, housing 107 rooms (including 40 suites), upscale restaurant Le Diane, a spa, indoor pool and a rooftop terrace for hire. Jacques Garcia of Hôtel Costes fame has been responsible for the interior design, retaining the Empire style of the exterior while incorporating luxurious modern touches inside – flat-screen TVs and mist-free mirrors in the marble bathrooms, for example. And, of course, it's unbeatable for location – right at the junction of avenue George-V and the Champs-Elysées.
Bar. Business centre. Concierge. Gym. Internet (Wi-Fi). No-smoking room(s). Parking (€45). Pool (indoor). Restaurants (3). Room service. Spa.

Hôtel Plaza Athénée
25 av Montaigne, 8th (01.53.67.66.67/fax 01.53.67.66.66/www.plaza-athenee-paris.com). M° Alma Marceau. **Rates** €575 single; €705-€790 double; €970-€15,000 royal suite; €36-€48 breakfast.
Credit AmEx, DC, MC, V. **Map** p400 D5 ②
This palace is ideally placed for power shopping at Chanel, Vuitton, Dior and other avenue Montaigne boutiques. Material girls and boys will enjoy the high-tech room amenities such as remote-controlled air-con, internet and video-game access on the TV via infrared keyboard, and mini hi-fi. The stylish bar full of rock stars and hotshots has modern decor, matched by a cool cocktail list and staff who know what service is (*see p232* '**The usual, Sir?**').
Bar. Business centre. Concierge. Gym. Internet (high-speed). No-smoking room(s). Restaurants (2; 4 in summer). Room service. TV.

Hôtel Royal Monceau
37 av Hoche, 8th (01.42.99.88.00/fax 01.42.99.89.90/ www.royalmonceau.com). M° Charles de Gaulle Etoile. **Rates** €560-€750 double; €1,650-€7,000 suite; €32-€45 breakfast. **Credit** AmEx, DC, MC, V.
Map p400 D3 ②
As if the acres of opulent marble and tapestries, a romantic, Michelin-starred garden restaurant and sumptuous health spa with mosaic-tiled pool weren't luxury enough, the historic Royal Monceau palace

then upped the ante with a complete renovation by Costes' darling Jacques Garcia in early 2006. The peaceful rooms have plush, tastefully muted decor.
Bar. Business centre. Concierge. Gym. Internet (high-speed). No-smoking room(s). Parking (€30). Pool (indoor). Restaurants (2). Room service. Spa. TV.

Hôtel de Sers

41 av Pierre-1er-de-Serbie, 8th (01.53.23.75.75/fax 01.53.23.75.76/www.hoteldesers.com). M° George V or Alma Marceau. **Rates** €480-€650 double; €800-€2,300 suite; additional bed €100; €29-€35 breakfast. **Credit** AmEx, DC, MC, V. **Map** p400 C5 ㉚
Behind its stately 19th-century façade, the Hôtel de Sers is an ambitious mix of minimalist contemporary furnishings (often in deep reds and mauves; nothing too austere), with a few pop art touches. Original architectural details such as the grand staircase and reception complete the picture.
Bar. Concierge. Gym. Internet. No-smoking room(s). Restaurant. Parking (€50). Room service. TV.

Hôtel de Vigny

9-11 rue Balzac, 8th (01.42.99.80.80/fax 01.42. 99.80.40/www.hoteldevigny.com). M° George V. **Rates** €395 single; €415-€495 double; €560-€725 suite; €21-€28 breakfast. **Credit** AmEx, DC, MC, V. **Map** p400 D3 ㉛
One of only two Relais & Châteaux in the city, this hotel has the feel of a private, plush townhouse. Although it's just off the Champs-Elysées, the Vigny pulls in a discerning, low-key clientele. Its 37 rooms and suites are decorated in tasteful stripes or florals, with marble bathrooms. Enjoy dinner in the art deco Baretto restaurant, or a quiet cup of tea in the library.
Bar. Concierge. Internet (Wi-Fi). No-smoking room(s). Parking (€23). Restaurant. Room service. TV.

Pershing Hall

49 rue Pierre-Charron, 8th (01.58.36.58.00/ fax 01.58.36.58.01/www.pershinghall.com). M° George V. **Rates** €351-€500 double; €720-€1,000 suite; €26 breakfast. **Credit** AmEx, DC, MC, V. **Map** p400 D4 ㉜
The refreshing mix of 19th-century grandeur and contemporary comfort makes Pershing Hall feel quite large, but this luxury establishment is really a cleverly disguised boutique hotel with just 26 rooms. Fashionable locals frequent the stylish bar and restaurant terrace, nicely set off by a dramatic vertical garden. Designed by Andrée Putman, the neat white-on-white bedrooms emphasise natural materials, with stained grey oak floors and particularly fine mosaic-tiled bathrooms with geometric styling and copious towels.
Bar. Concierge. Gym. Internet (Wi-Fi). No-smoking room(s). Restaurant. Room service. Spa. TV.

Le Sezz

6 av Frémiet, 16th (01.56.75.26.26/fax 01.56.75.26.16/www.hotelsezz.com). M° Passy. **Rates** €270-€325 single; €320-€450 double; €430-€700 suite; €25 breakfast. **Credit** AmEx, DC, MC, V. **Map** p404 B6 ㉝
Le Sezz opened its doors in 2005 with 27 sleek, luxurious rooms and suites – the work of acclaimed French furniture designer Christophe Pillet. The understated decor represents a refreshingly modern take on luxury, with black parquet flooring, rough-hewn stone walls and bathrooms partitioned off with sweeping glass façades. The bar and public areas are equally sleek and chic.
Bar. Concierge. Internet (Wi-Fi). No-smoking room(s). Room service. Sauna. TV.

Hôtel Daniel. *See p51.*

Hôtel Bourg Tibourg. *See p57*.

Expensive

Hôtel Pergolèse

3 rue Pergolèse, 16th (01.53.64.04.04/fax 01.53.64.04.40/www.hotelpergolese.com).
M° Argentine. **Rates** €195-€350 single; €220-€380 double; €18 breakfast. **Credit** AmEx, DC, MC, V. **Map** p400 B3 ㉞
The Pergolèse was one of the first designer boutique hotels in town, but still looks contemporary a decade or so after being decorated by Rena Dumas-Hermès with Philippe Starck furniture and rugs by Hilton McConnico. Rooms feature pale wood furniture, Bang & Olufsen TVs and cool, white-tiled bathrooms. *Bar. Concierge. Internet (Wi-Fi). No-smoking room(s). Room service. TV.*

Hôtel Square

3 rue de Boulainvilliers, 16th (01.44.14.91.90/fax 01.44.14.91.99/www.hotelsquare.com). M° Passy/ RER Avenue du Pdt Kennedy. **Rates** €260-€340 single or double; €420-€520 suite; €8-€20 breakfast. **Credit** AmEx, DC, MC, V. **Map** p404 A7 ㉟
Located in the upmarket 16th, this courageously modern hotel has a dramatic yet welcoming interior, and attentive service that comes from having to look after only 22 rooms. These are decorated in amber, brick or slate colours, with exotic woods, quality fabrics and bathrooms seemingly cut from one huge chunk of Carrara marble. View the exhibitions in the atrium gallery or mingle with the media types at the hip Zebra Square restaurant and DJ lounge bar. *Bar. Business centre. Concierge. Internet (Wi-Fi). No-smoking room(s). Parking (€20). Restaurant. Room service. TV.*

Moderate

Hôtel Elysées Ceramic

34 av de Wagram, 8th (01.42.27.20.30/fax 01.46. 22.95.83/www.elysees-ceramic.com). M° Charles de Gaulle Etoile. **Rates** €175 single; €200 double; €223 triple; €10 breakfast. **Credit** AmEx, DC, MC, V. **Map** p400 D3 ㊱
Situated between the Arc de Triomphe and place des Ternes, this comfortable hotel has a listed art nouveau ceramic façade dating from 1904; inside, the theme continues with a ceramic cornice around the reception. Of the 57 rooms, 29 have been renovated in sophisticated chocolate or pewter tones with art nouveau-inspired wallpaper and light fixtures; at the time of writing, the remaining rooms were scheduled to follow by early 2007. Outside is a terrace garden for taking afternoon tea or evening cocktails. *Bar. Concierge. Internet (Wi-Fi). Room service (breakfast only). TV.*

Hôtel Regent's Garden

6 rue Pierre-Demours, 17th (01.45.74.07.30/fax 01.40.55.01.42/www.hotel-regents-garden.com). M° Charles de Gaulle Etoile or Ternes. **Rates** €170 single; €180-€276 double; €12 breakfast. **Credit** AmEx, DC, MC, V. **Map** p400 C2 ㊲

This elegant hotel – built for Napoleon III's physician – features appropriately Second Empire high ceilings and plush upholstery, and a lounge looking over a lovely walled garden. There are 39 large bedrooms, some with gilt mirrors and fireplaces. An oasis of calm ten minutes from the Champs-Elysées. *Concierge. Internet (Wi-Fi). No-smoking room(s). Parking (€13). Room service (daytime only). TV.*

Montmartre & Pigalle

Expensive

Kube Rooms & Bar

1-5 impasse Ruelle, 18th (01.42.05.20.00/fax 01.42.05.21.01/www.kubehotel.com). M° La Chapelle. **Rates** €250 single; €300 double; €750 suite; €15-€25 breakfast. **Credit** AmEx, DC, V. **Map** p402 K1 ㊳
The younger sister of the Murano Urban Resort (*see p57*), Kube is an edgier and more affordable design hotel. Like the Murano, it sits behind an unremarkable façade in an unlikely neighbourhood – in this case, the ethnically diverse part of the 18th known as La Goutte d'Or. At the hotel's heart is a dimly lit bar and lounge, decorated with plasma screens and faux fur-covered sofas; upstairs, the Ice Kube bar serves up vodka in glasses that, like the bar, are carved from ice. Drinkers pay €38 to down all the vodka they like in 30 minutes. Also on the menu: 'Apérifood' and 'snackubes' by culinary designer Pierre Auge. Access to the 41 rooms – with underlit beds – is gained by fingerprint technology. *Bar. Concierge. Gym. Internet. No-smoking room(s). Parking (€30). Room service. TV.*

Terrass Hôtel

12-14 rue Joseph-de-Maistre, 18th (01.46.06.72.85/ fax 01.42.52.29.11/www.terrass-hotel.com). M° Place de Clichy. **Rates** €248 double; €340 suite; €18 breakfast. **Credit** AmEx, DC, MC, V. **Map** p401 H1 ㊴
There's nothing particularly spectacular about this classic hotel, but for those willing to pay top euro for the best views in town, Terrass fits the bill. Ask for room 704 and you can lie in the bath and look out at the Eiffel Tower (and people on the Eiffel Tower can – in theory – see you in the bath). A chef trained by Ducasse is at the helm of the gastronomic restaurant Diapason; in fine weather, opt for a table outside on the lovely seventh-floor terrace, open from June to September. *Bar. Concierge. Internet (Wi-Fi). No-smoking room(s). Restaurant. Room service. TV.*

Moderate

Hôtel Roma Sacré-Coeur

101 rue Caulaincourt, 18th (01.42.62.02.02/fax 01.42.54.34.92/www.hotelroma.fr). M° Lamarck Caulaincourt. **Rates** €75-€130 single; €75-€150 double; €7.50 breakfast. **Credit** AmEx, DC, MC, V. **Map** p401 H1 ㊵

This hotel is located on the trendier, north side of Montmartre, far from the postcard shops and coach parties, but still within walking distance (uphill) of Sacré-Coeur. From the tiny lobby, a whimsical, AstroTurf-covered staircase leads to the 57 rooms, simply decorated in pastels; the priciest enjoy views of the basilica. Air-conditioned rooms are available on floors five to seven for an extra €10 per day. *Concierge. Internet (Wi-Fi). TV.*

Timhotel Montmartre

11 rue Ravignan, 18th (01.42.55.74.79/fax 01.42.55.71.01/www.timhotel.fr). M° Abbesses. **Rates** €130 single; €145-€200 double; €150-€200 triple; €8.50 breakfast. **Credit** AmEx, DC, MC, V. **Map** p401 H1 ㊶
The location by picturesque place Emile-Goudeau makes this one of the most popular hotels in the Timhotel chain. It has 59 nice rooms, comfortable without being plush; try to bag one on the fourth or fifth floor for stunning views over Montmartre. Special offers are often available at quieter times of year; ring for details.
Concierge. Internet (high-speed). No-smoking room(s). TV.

Budget

Blanche Hôtel

69 rue Blanche, 9th (01.48.74.16.94/fax 01.49.95. 95.98). M° Blanche. **Rates** €34-€67 single; €37-€87 double; €65-€83 triple; €70-€90 quad; €6 breakfast. **Credit** AmEx, MC, V. **Map** p401 G2 ㊷
If you're prepared to forgo frills and don't mind the rather racy aspect of the neighbourhood, this is a good-value bet. The interior is far from palatial and features less-than-luxurious 1970s furniture, but the rooms are a good size and there's a bar in the lobby.
Bar. Concierge. Room service (morning only). TV.

Hôtel Ermitage

24 rue Lamarck, 18th (01.42.64.79.22/fax 01.42.64.10.33/www.ermitagesacrecoeur.fr). M° Lamarck Caulaincourt. **Rates** (incl breakfast) €79 single; €90 double; €116 triple; €136 quad. **No credit cards. Map** p402 J1 ㊸
This 12-room townhouse hotel stands on the calm, non-touristy north side of Montmartre, only five minutes from Sacré-Coeur. Rooms are large and endearingly over-decorated, with bold floral wallpaper; some higher ones have fine views over Montmartre's jumble of rooftops.
Internet (Wi-Fi). No-smoking room(s). Room service (morning only).

Royal Fromentin

11 rue Fromentin, 9th (01.48.74.85.93/fax 01.42.81. 02.33/www.hotelroyalfromentin.com). M° Pigalle. **Rates** (incl breakfast) €69-€137 single; €79-€165 double; €124-€219 triple; €144-€251 quad. **Credit** AmEx, DC, MC, V. **Map** p401 H2 ㊹
Wood panelling, art deco windows and a vintage glass lift echo the hotel's origins as a 1930s cabaret hall; its theatrical feel attracted Blondie and Nirvana.

It's just down the road from the Moulin Rouge, and many of its 47 rooms overlook the Sacré-Coeur. Rooms have been renovated in French style, with bright fabrics and an old-fashioned feel.
Bar. Concierge. Internet. Room service (breakfast only). TV.

Beaubourg & the Marais

Deluxe

Murano Urban Resort

13 bd du Temple, 3rd (01.42.71.20.00/fax 01.42.71.21.01/www.muranoresort.com). M° Filles du Calvaire or Oberkampf. **Rates** €350 single; €400-€650 double; €750-€2,500 suite; €20-€28 breakfast; €38 brunch (Sun). **Credit** AmEx, DC, MC, V. **Map** p409 L5 ㊺
Behind this unremarkable façade is a super-cool and luxurious hotel, popular with the fashion set for its slick lounge-style design and high-tech flourishes – which include Bang & Olufsen sound systems and clever coloured-light co-ordinators that enable you to change the mood of your room at the press of a button. The bar (*see p232* '**The usual, Sir?'**) has 140 varieties of vodka, which can bring the op art fabrics in the lift to life and make the fingerprint access to the hotel's 43 rooms and nine suites (two with private pools) a godsend.
Bar. Concierge. Gym. Internet (high-speed). No-smoking room(s). Parking (€30). Pool (opens Dec 2006). Restaurant. Room service. Spa (opens Dec 2006). TV.

Expensive

Hôtel Bourg Tibourg

19 rue du Bourg-Tibourg, 4th (01.42.78.47.39/ fax 01.40.29.07.00/www.hotelbourgtibourg.com). M° Hôtel de Ville. **Rates** €160 single; €220-€250 double; €350 suite; €14 breakfast. **Credit** AmEx, DC, MC, V. **Map** p409 K6 ㊻
Same owners as Hôtel Costes (*see p43*) and the same interior decorator – but don't expect this jewel box of a boutique hotel to look like a miniature replica. Aside from its enviable location in the heart of the Marais and its fashion-pack fans, this hotel is all about Jacques Garcia's neo-Gothic-cum-Byzantine decor, impressive and imaginative. Exotic, scented candles, mosaic-tiled bathrooms, luxurious fabrics in rich colours and the cool contrast of crisp white linens create the perfect escape from the outside world. There's no restaurant or bar – posing is done in the neighbourhood bars. **Photos** *p54*.
Concierge. Internet (Wi-Fi). Room service. TV.

Hôtel du Petit Moulin

29 rue de Poitou, 3rd (01.42.74.10.10/fax 01.42.74.10.97/www.hoteldupetitmoulin.com). M° St-Sébastien Froissart. **Rates** €180-€250 double; €280-€350 suite; €15 breakfast. **Credit** AmEx, MC, V. **Map** p409 L5 ㊼

Cut-price chic

Boutique hotels are all very well, but unless you're happy spending at least €300 a night, all you are going to see of them is their designer bar. Where can the city-break urbanite find a cool spot to cop some zees without having to pay a fortune in hotel rates – or taxi fares? Where they can enjoy a late, hangover-friendly breakfast, a sauna, gym and a cocktail bar? Look no further than **Le Général** (*see p59; pictured*).

Opened in 2003, two steps from place de la République and within walking distance of nightlife hub Oberkampf and café-lined Canal St-Martin, Le Général is both practical and chic. Little touches welcome the weary traveller – the shiny Granny Smith apple on the pillow, the rubber duckie on the side of

the bathtub – as well as smoked fish carpaccio or duck breast to your room at mealtimes (even drinks 24/7). Public areas, such as the trendy bar open until 2am, bear the low-key, minimalist hallmarks of designer Jean-Philippe Nuël, responsible for the Sofitel at La Défense and in Budapest.

Nuël also oversaw the look of the other two branches added to this mini-chain, as well located and well priced as the original. Le Quartier République, Le Marais, whose rooms are getting a design makeover in the winter of 2006/07, is in the heart of Oberkampf (though away from the noisiest strip of bars); and Le Quartier Bastille, Le Faubourg, opened in 2005, is near the opera and nightspots of the 12th. See www.lghhotels.com for details.

Within striking distance of the Musée Picasso and the hip shops on and around rue Charlot, this listed, turn-of-the-century façade masks what was once the oldest *boulangerie* in Paris, lovingly restored as a boutique hotel by Nadia Murano and Denis Nourry. The couple recruited fashion designer Christian Lacroix for the decor, and the result is a riot of colour, trompe l'oeil effects and a savvy mix of old and new. Each of its 17 exquisitely appointed rooms is unique, and the walls in rooms 202, 204 and 205 feature swirling, extravagent drawings and scribbles from Lacroix's sketchbook.

Bar. Internet (Wi-Fi). Parking (free).

Moderate

Hôtel de la Bretonnerie

22 rue Ste-Croix-de-la-Bretonnerie, 4th (01.48.87.77.63/fax 01.42.77.26.78/www. bretonnerie.com). M° Hôtel de Ville. **Rates** €116-€149 single or double; €180 suite; €9.50 breakfast. **Credit** MC, V. **Map** p409 K6 ⓺

With its combination of wrought ironwork, exposed stone and wooden beams, the labyrinth of corridors and passages in this 17th-century *hôtel particulier* is full of historic atmosphere. Tapestries, rich colours and the occasional four-poster bed give a sense of

individuality to the 29 suites and bedrooms. The location is convenient too, with the bars, shops and museums of the Marais just a short stroll away.
Concierge. Internet (shared terminal). TV.

Hôtel Duo
11 rue du Temple, 4th (01.42.72.72.22/fax 01.42.72. 03.53/www.duoparis.com). M° Hôtel de Ville. **Rates** €115-€155 single; €170-€300 double; €320-480 suite; €14 breakfast. **Credit** AmEx, DC, MC, V. **Map** p406 K6 ④⑨
Formerly the Axial Beauborg, this stylish boutique hotel, decorated with white marble floors, mud-coloured walls, crushed-velvet sofas and exposed beams, is close to the Centre Pompidou. Rooms are not large, but exude refinement and comfort.
Bar. Concierge. Gym. Internet. Room service. Sauna. TV.

Hôtel St-Louis Marais
1 rue Charles-V, 4th (01.48.87.87.04/fax 01.48.87.33.26/www.saintlouismarais.com). M° Sully Morland or Bastille. **Rates** €79-€99 single; €115-€140 double, twin or triple; €160 suite (quad); €10 breakfast. **Credit** AmEx, DC, JCB, MC, V. **Map** p409 L7 ⑤⓪
Built as part of a 17th-century Célestin convent, this peaceful hotel had its bathrooms redone and Wi-Fi internet access installed in 2005. Rooms are compact and cosy, with wooden beams, tiled floors and simple, traditional decor; book a more expensive one if you're claustrophobic.
Concierge. Internet (Wi-Fi). No-smoking room(s). Parking (€18). Room service (breakfast only). TV.
Other locations: Hôtel St-Louis Bastille, 114 bd Richard Lenoir, 11th (01.43.38.29.29); Hôtel St-Louis Opéra, 51 rue de la Victoire, 9th (01.48.74.71.13).

Hôtel St-Merry
78 rue de la Verrerie, 4th (01.42.78.14.15/ fax 01.40.29.06.82/www.hotelmarais.com). M° Hôtel de Ville. **Rates** €160-€230 double; €205-€275 triple; €335 suite; €11 breakfast. **Credit** AmEx, MC, V. **Map** p406 K6 ⑤①
The Gothic decor of this former presbytery attached to the Eglise St-Merry is ideal for a Dracula set, with wooden beams, stone walls and plenty of iron – behind the door of room No.9 an imposing flying buttress even straddles the carved antique bed. On the downside, the historic building has no lift and only the suite has a TV.
Concierge. No-smoking room(s). Room service (daytime only). TV (suite only).
Other locations: Hôtel Saintonge Marais, 16 rue de Saintonge, 3rd (01.42.77.91.13).

Budget

Grand Hôtel Jeanne d'Arc
3 rue de Jarente, 4th (01.48.87.62.11/fax 01.48.87.37.31/www.hoteljeannedarc.com). M° St-Paul or Chemin Vert. **Rates** €60-€72 single; €84 double; €97 twin; €116 triple; €146 quad; €6 breakfast. **Credit** MC, V. **Map** p409 L6 ⑤②

This hotel's strong point is its location on a quiet road close to pretty place du Marché-Ste-Catherine. Recent refurbishment has made the reception area striking, with a huge mirror adding the illusion of extra space. Rooms are colourful and, for the price, well sized, comfortable and clean.
Concierge. Internet (Wi-Fi). Room service (morning only). TV.

Hôtel de Roubaix
6 rue Greneta, 3rd (01.42.72.89.91/fax 01.42.72.58.79/www.hotel-de-roubaix.com). M° Réaumur Sébastopol or Arts et Métiers. **Rates** (incl breakfast) €57-€64 single; €70-€73 double; €88 triple; €92 quad. **Credit** MC, V. **Map** p402 K5 ⑤③
You're two blocks from the Centre Pompidou, the Marais and the trendy shops of rue Etienne-Marcel, with an immaculately clean bathroom, TV, telephone and even a lift. So why are the rates so low? Could be the granny-friendly decor or the squishy mattresses; but since the hotel's 53 rooms are invariably booked solid, it seems that no one is too discouraged.
Concierge. Internet. TV.

Bastille & eastern Paris

Moderate

Le Pavillon Bastille
65 rue de Lyon, 12th (01.43.43.65.65/fax 01.43.43.96.52/www.paris-hotel-pavillonbastille.com). M° Bastille. **Rates** €130-€150 single or double; €213 suite; €15 breakfast. **Credit** AmEx, DC, MC, V. **Map** p407 M7 ⑤④
The best thing about this hotel is its location between the Bastille opera house and the Gare de Lyon, but renovations in early 2007 could well up the ante. The 25 rooms may be small, but you're a stone's throw from the Viaduc des Arts, where an elevated garden has replaced the railroad's tracks and arty boutiques now occupy the arches.
Bar. Concierge. Internet (Wi-Fi). No-smoking room(s). Room service. TV.

North-eastern Paris

Moderate

Le Général
5-7 rue Rampon, 11th (01.47.00.41.57/fax 01.47.00.21.56/www.legeneralhotel.com). M° République. **Rates** €135-€155 single; €165-€225 double; €235-€265 suite; €12 breakfast. **Credit** AmEx, DC, MC, V. **Map** p402 L5 ⑤⑤
A fashionable find near the nightlife action, Le Général is notable for its remarkably moderate rates. *See p58* **Cut-price chic.**
Bar. Concierge. Gym. Internet (Wi-Fi). No-smoking room(s). Room service. Sauna. TV.
Other locations: Le Quartier Bastille, Le Faubourg, 9 rue de Reuilly, 12th (01.43.70.96.53); Le Quartier République, Le Marais, 39 rue Jean-Pierre-Timbaud, 11th (01.48.06.64.97).

Hôtel Beaumarchais

3 rue Oberkampf, 11th (01.53.36.86.86/fax 01.43.38.32.86/www.hotelbeaumarchais.com). M° Filles du Calvaire or Oberkampf. **Rates** €75-€90 single; €110-€150 double; €170 triple; €10 breakfast. **Credit** AmEx, MC, V. **Map** p409 L5 ⑤⑤
This contemporary hotel is in the Oberkampf area, not far from the Marais and Bastille. Its 31 rooms are brightly decorated with colourful walls, bathroom mosaics and wavy headboards; breakfast is served on the tiny garden patio or to your room. *Concierge. Internet (Wi-Fi). Room service. TV.*

Mercure Terminus Est

5 rue du Huit-Mai 1945, 10th (01.55.26.05.05/fax 01.55.26.05.00/www.mercure.com). M° Gare de l'Est. **Rates** €120-€200 single; €130-€215 double; €260-€350 suite; €31 extra bed; €14 breakfast. **Credit** AmEx, DC, MC, V. **Map** p402 K3 ⑤⑦
Conveniently located opposite the Gare de l'Est, this great railway hotel combines modern interior design with elements that evoke the classic age of steam: leather luggage handles on the wardrobes, retro bathroom fittings and a library in the lobby. The 200 rooms and public areas all offer Wi-Fi internet access. *Bar. Concierge. Gym. Internet (Wi-Fi). No-smoking room(s). Room service. TV.*

The Latin Quarter & the 13th

Moderate

Les Degrés de Notre-Dame

10 rue des Grands-Degrés, 5th (01.55.42.88.88/fax 01.40.46.95.34/www.lesdegreshotel.com). M° St-Michel. **Rates** (incl breakfast) €110-€160 double; €125-€190 triple; €190-€220 quad. **Credit** MC, V. **Map** p406 J7 ⑤⑧
On a vintage street across the river from Notre-Dame, this vintage hotel is a gem. Its ten rooms are full of character, with original paintings, antique furniture and exposed wooden beams (Nos.47 and 501 have views of the cathedral). It has an adorable restaurant and, a few streets away, two studio apartments that the owner rents to preferred customers only. *Bar. Restaurant. TV.*

Hôtel la Demeure

51 bd St-Marcel, 13th (01.43.37.81.25/fax 01.45.87.05.03/www.hotel-paris-lademeure.com). M° Les Gobelins. **Rates** €155-€190 double; €260 suite; €13 breakfast. **Credit** AmEx, DC, MC, V. **Map** p406 K9 ⑤⑨
This comfortable, modern hotel on the edge of the Latin Quarter is run by a friendly father and son. It has 43 air-conditioned rooms with internet access, plus suites with sliding doors to separate sleeping and living space. The wrap-around balustrades of the corner rooms offer lovely views of the city, and bathrooms feature either luxurious tubs or shower heads with elaborate massage possibilities. *Bar. Concierge. Internet (Wi-Fi). No smoking room(s). Parking (€17). Room service (breakfast only). TV.*

Hôtel des Grandes Ecoles

75 rue du Cardinal-Lemoine, 5th (01.43.26.79.23/fax 01.43.25.28.15/www.hotel-grandes-ecoles.com). M° Cardinal Lemoine. **Rates** €110-€130 single or double; €20 extra bed; €8 breakfast. **Credit** MC, V. **Map** p406 K8 ⑥⓪
A breath of fresh air in the heart of the Latin Quarter, this country-style hotel has 51 old-fashioned rooms set around a leafy garden where breakfast is served in summer. The largest of the three buildings houses the reception area and a stylish breakfast room with a gilt mirror and piano. *Concierge. Parking (€30). Room service (breakfast only).*

Hôtel du Panthéon

19 pl du Panthéon, 5th (01.43.54.32.95/fax 01.43.26.64.65/www.hoteldupantheon.com). M° Cluny La Sorbonne/RER Luxembourg. **Rates** €168-€255 single or double; €285 triple; €12 breakfast. **Credit** AmEx, DC, JCB, MC, V. **Map** p408 J8 ⑥①
The 36 rooms of this elegant hotel are beautifully decorated with classic French toile de Jouy fabrics, antique furniture and painted woodwork. Some enjoy impressive views of the Panthéon; others squint out on to a hardly less romantic courtyard, complete with chestnut tree. *Concierge. Internet (Wi-Fi). TV.*

Hôtel Résidence Henri IV

50 rue des Bernardins, 5th (01.44.41.31.81/fax 01.46.33.93.22/www.residencehenri4.com). M° Maubert Mutualité. **Rates** €107-€215 single or double; €230-€340 apartment; €6-€10 breakfast. **Credit** AmEx, DC, MC, V. **Map** p406 K8 ⑥②
This belle époque style hotel has a mere eight rooms and five apartments, so guests are assured of the staff's full attention. Peacefully situated next to leafy square Paul-Langevin, it's minutes away from Notre-Dame. The four-person apartment rooms come with a handy mini-kitchen featuring a hob, fridge and microwave – although you may be reduced to eating on the beds in the smaller ones. *Concierge. Internet (Wi-Fi). No smoking room(s). TV.*

Hôtel de la Sorbonne

6 rue Victor-Cousin, 5th (01.43.54.58.08/fax 01.40.51.05.18/www.hotelsorbonne.com). M° Cluny La Sorbonne/RER Luxembourg. **Rates** €110-€130 single or double; €8 breakfast. **Credit** AmEx, DC, MC, V. **Map** p408 J8 ⑥③
This cosy hotel between the Luxembourg gardens and the Panthéon features wooden floors, beams and a fireplace in the salon. The 39 rooms are pale green or lavender, with cheerful geranium-filled window boxes. Bathrooms are tiny but new; choose one with a shower rather than one with a gnome-sized tub. *Concierge. Internet (Wi-Fi). TV.*

Select Hôtel

1 pl de la Sorbonne, 5th (01.46.34.14.80/fax 01.46.34.51.79/www.selecthotel.fr). M° Cluny La Sorbonne. **Rates** (incl breakfast) €159-€189 double; €219 triple. **Credit** AmEx, DC, MC, V. **Map** p408 J8 ⑥④

Located at the foot of the Sorbonne, this 68-room hotel contains an appealing blend of modern art deco features and traditional stone walls and wooden beams. The winter garden and airy common areas have recently been redone in a contemporary style. *Bar. Concierge. Internet (Wi-Fi). Room service (until 10pm). TV.*

Budget

Familia Hôtel

11 rue des Ecoles, 5th (01.43.54.55.27/fax 01.43. 29.61.77/www.hotel-paris-familia.com). M° Maubert Mutualité or Jussieu. **Rates** (incl breakfast) €90 single; €97-€127 double; €128-€154 triple; €176 quad. **Credit** AmEx, DC, MC, V. **Map** p406 J8 ⑤

This old-fashioned Latin Quarter hotel has balconies hung with tumbling plants and walls draped with French tapestry replicas. Owner Eric Gaucheron offers a warm welcome, and the 30 rooms have personalised touches such as sepia murals, cherry-wood furniture and stone walls. The Gaucherons also own the Minerve next door – book in advance for both. *Concierge. Internet (Wi-Fi). Parking (€20). Room service (daytime only). TV.*
Other locations: Hôtel Minerve, 13 rue des Ecoles, 5th (01.43.26.81.89).

Hôtel Esmeralda

4 rue St-Julien-le-Pauvre, 5th (01.43.54.19.20/ fax 01.40.51.00.68). M° Maubert Mutualité or St-Michel.. **Rates** €40 single; €70-€100 double; €115 triple; €125 quad; €6 breakfast. **Credit** DC, MC, V. **Map** p408 J7 ⑤

An offbeat piece of historic Paris, the Esmeralda has 19 floral rooms with antique furnishings and aged wallpaper, as well as the uneven floors and wonky staircase you'd expect in a building that was built in 1640. Book ahead: the eight rooms overlooking Notre-Dame are popular with honeymooners. *Concierge. Room service.*

St-Germain-des-Prés & Odéon

Deluxe

L'Hôtel

13 rue des Beaux-Arts, 6th (01.44.41.99.00/fax 01.43.25.64.81/www.l-hotel.com). M° St-Germain-des-Prés or Mabillon. **Rates** €280-€640 double; €740 suite; €18 breakfast. **Credit** AmEx, DC, MC, V. **Map** p408 H6 ⑤

Guests at the luxuriously decorated L'Hôtel are more likely to be models and film stars than the starving writers who frequented it during Oscar Wilde's final days. Under Jacques Garcia's careful restoration, each room has its own special theme: Mistinguett's *chambre* retains its art deco mirror bed, and Oscar's deathbed room has, appropriately, been decorated with green peacock murals. Don't miss the cellar swimming pool or *fumoir*. *Bar. Concierge. Internet (Wi-Fi). Pool (indoor). Restaurant. Room service (daytime only). TV.*

Hôtel Lutetia

45 bd Raspail, 6th (01.49.54.46.46/fax 01.49. 54.46.00/www.lutetia-paris.com). M° Sèvres Babylone. **Rates** €400-€550 double; €750-€2,500 suite; €10-€25 breakfast. **Credit** AmEx, DC, MC, V. **Map** p405 G7 ⑥

This historic Left Bank hotel is a masterpiece of art nouveau and early art deco architecture that dates from 1910. It has a plush jazz bar and lively brasserie with views of the chic Bon Marché store across the street. Its 250 rooms, revamped in purple, gold and pearl grey, maintain a 1930s feel – slip out of those damp clothes and into a dry Martini. Big-name guests in years gone by have included Pablo Picasso, Josephine Baker and General Charles de Gaulle – the latter spent his honeymoon here. *Bar. Business centre. Concierge. Gym. Internet (high-speed; Wi-Fi). No-smoking room(s). Restaurants (2). Room service. TV.*

Villa d'Estrées

17 rue Gît-le-Coeur, 6th (01.55.42.71.11/fax 01.55.42.71.00/www.villadestrees.com). M° St-Michel. **Rates** €315 double; €355 suite; €640 apartment; €10 continental breakfast. **Credit** AmEx, DC, MC, V. **Map** p408 J6 ⑥

Jewel colours, sumptuous fabrics, stripes and patterns are the hallmarks of this polished boutique hotel – there's nothing at all minimalist about Villa d'Estrées, which was designed by Jacques Garcia. Each of the ten rooms and suites is individually decorated, all with a nod to Empire style and a crisp, slightly masculine feel. Bathrooms share striking black Moroccan tiling. **Photos** *p66.*
Bar. Concierge. Internet. Room service. TV.

L'Hôtel.

Expensive

Hôtel de l'Abbaye

*10 rue Cassette, 6th (01.45.44.38.11/fax 01.45.
48.07.86/www.hotelabbayeparis.com). M° St-Sulpice
or Rennes.* **Rates** (incl breakfast) €205-€305 single
or double; €380-€458 suite. **Credit** AmEx, MC, V.
Map p405 G7

A monumental entrance leads the way through a
courtyard into this tranquil hotel, originally part of
a convent. Wood panelling, well-stuffed sofas and
an open fireplace in the drawing room make for a
relaxed atmosphere, but, best of all, there's a surprisingly large garden where breakfast is served in
the warmer months. The 44 rooms are tasteful and
luxurious, and the suites have rooftop terraces.
Bar. Concierge. Internet (Wi-Fi). Room service. TV.

Relais Saint-Germain

*7 carrefour de l'Odéon, 6th (01.43.29.12.05/fax
01.46.33.45.30/www.hotel-paris-relais-saint-
germain.com). M° Odéon.* **Rates** (incl breakfast)
€275-€360 double; €380-€420 suite. **Credit** AmEx,
MC, V. **Map** p408 H7

The rustic wood-beamed ceilings remain intact at
the Hotel Relais Saint-Germain, a 17th-century hotel
bought and renovated by much-acclaimed chef Yves
Camdeborde (originator of the *bistronomique* dining
trend) and his wife Claudine. Each of the 22 rooms
offers a different take on eclectic-provençal charm,
and the marble bathrooms are huge by Parisian standards. Guests get first dibs on a highly sought-after
seat in the 15-table Le Comptoir next door (*see p205*).
Bar. Concierge. Internet (Wi-Fi). Room service. TV.

La Villa

*29 rue Jacob, 6th (01.43.26.60.00/fax 01.46.34.
63.63/www.villa-saintgermain.com). M° St-Germain-
des-Prés.* **Rates** €265-€335 double; €445 suite; €40
extra bed; €15 breakfast. **Credit** AmEx, DC, MC, V.
Map p408 H6

Refreshingly modern and stylish, the charismatic La
Villa has cool faux crocodile skin on the bedheads
and crinkly taffeta over the taupe-coloured walls.
Wonderfully, your room number is projected on to
the floor outside your door; useful for drunken home-
comings. Keep a look out for excellent offers on last-
minute bookings.
*Bar. Concierge. Internet (Wi-Fi). Room service
(until midnight). TV.*

Moderate

Le Clos Médicis

*56 rue Monsieur-le-Prince, 6th (01.43.29.10.80/
fax 01.43.54.26.90/www.closmedicis.com). M°
Odéon/RER Luxembourg.* **Rates** €155 single; €195-
€215 double; €280 triple or duplex; €480 suite; €13
breakfast. **Credit** AmEx, DC, MC, V. **Map** p408 H7

Designed more like a stylish, private townhouse
than a hotel, Le Clos Médicis is located by the
Luxembourg gardens: perfect if you fancy starting
every morning with a stroll among the trees. The
hotel's decor is refreshingly modern and eminently
chic, with rooms done out in taffeta curtains and che-
nille bedcovers, and antique floor tiles in the bathrooms. The cosy lounge has a working fireplace.
*Bar. Concierge. Internet (Wi-Fi). No-smoking
room(s). TV.*

Hôtel Aviatic. *See p65.*

Grand Hôtel de l'Univers

6 rue Grégoire-de-Tours, 6th (01.43.29.37.00/
fax 01.40.51.06.45/www.hotel-paris-univers.com).
M° Odéon. **Rates** €130-€170 single; €150-€215
double; €10 breakfast. **Credit** AmEx, DC, MC, V.
Map p408 H7 ⓩ
Making the most of its 15th-century origins, this
hotel features exposed wooden beams, high ceilings,
antique furnishings and toile-covered walls. Manuel
Canovas fabrics lend a posh touch, but there are also
practical features such as a laptop for rent. The same
helpful team runs the Hôtel St-Germain-des-Prés
nearby, which has a medieval-themed room and the
sweetest attic in Paris.
Bar. Concierge. Internet (Wi-Fi). No-smoking room(s).
Room service (breakfast only). TV.
Other locations: Hôtel St-Germain-des-Prés, 36 rue
Bonaparte, 6th (01.43.26.00.19).

Hôtel des Saints-Pères

65 rue des Sts-Pères, 6th (01.45.44.50.00/fax
01.45.44.90.83/www.esprit-de-france.com). M° St-
Germain-des-Prés. **Rates** €125 single; €160-€195
double; €295 suite; €13 breakfast. **Credit** AmEx,
MC, V. **Map** p405 G7 ⓩ
Built in 1658 by one of the architects of Louis XIV,
this discreet hotel now occupies an enviable place
near St-Germain-des-Prés' designer boutiques. It
boasts a charming garden and a sophisticated, if
small, bar. The most coveted room is No.100 (€325),
with its fine 17th-century ceiling by painters from
the Versailles School; it also has an open bathroom,
so you can gaze at scenes from the myth of Leda and
the Swan while you scrub.
Bar. Concierge. Internet (Wi-Fi). Room service (until
8pm). TV.

Budget

Hôtel du Globe

15 rue des Quatre-Vents, 6th (01.43.26.35.50/fax
01.46.33.62.69/www.hotel-du-globe.fr). M° Odéon.
Rates €120 single; €95-€130 double; €160 family
room; €10 breakfast. **Credit** MC, V. **Map** p408 H7 ⓩ
The Hôtel du Globe has managed to retain much of
its 17th-century character – and very pleasant it is
too. Gothic wrought-iron doors take you through
into the florid corridors, while an unexplained suit
of armour supervises guests from the tiny salon. The
rooms with baths are somewhat larger than those
with showers – all 14 underwent complete renovation in 2004. There is even a four-poster bed to be
had if you specify upon reservation.
Internet (Wi-Fi). TV.

Regents Hôtel

44 rue Madame, 6th (01.45.48.02.81/fax 01.45.44.
85.73). M° St-Sulpice. **Rates** €80 single; €80-€110
double; €110 triple; €125 quad; €7 breakfast. **Credit**
AmEx, MC, V. **Map** p410 G8 ⓩ
In Paris, it's rare to find a budget option with style,
but this discreet hotel located in a quiet street is a
lovely surprise, its courtyard garden used for break-

fast in the warmer months. The reception rooms are
a sunny provençal blue and yellow, and the bedrooms are comfortable, with new bathrooms. Some
have small balconies.
Concierge. Internet (dataport). Room service
(breakfast only). TV.

Montparnasse

Moderate

Hôtel Aviatic

105 rue de Vaugirard, 6th (01.53.63.25.50/fax
01.53.63.25.55/www.aviatic.fr). M° Montparnasse
Bienvenüe, St-Placide or Duroc. **Rates** €144-€199
double; €166-€199 twin; €295 suite; €13 breakfast.
Credit AmEx, DC, MC, V. **Map** p405 F8 ⓩ
This historic hotel has tons of character, from the
Empire-style lounge and garden atrium to the bistro-
style breakfast room. The polished floor in the lobby
(watch your feet) and the hints of marble and brass
lend impressive touches of glamour. The pricier
Supérieure rooms have such extras as bathrobes and
a modem connection.
Concierge. Internet (pay terminal). Parking (€23).
Room service (breakfast only). TV.

Budget

Hôtel Delambre

35 rue Delambre, 14th (01.43.20.66.31/fax
01.45.38.91.76/www.hoteldelambre.com). M° Edgar
Quinet or Vavin. **Rates** €85-€115 single or double;
€150-€160 suite; €9 breakfast. **Credit** AmEx, MC, V.
Map p405 G9 ⓩ
Occupying a narrow slot in a small street between
Montparnasse and St-Germain, this hotel was home
to surrealist André Breton in the 1920s. Today it's
modern and friendly, with cast-iron details in the 13
rooms and newly installed air-conditioning. The
mini suite in the attic, comprising two separate
rooms, is particularly pleasing – if not really suitable for the more generously framed.
Concierge. Internet (Wi-Fi). Room service (breakfast
only). TV.

Hôtel Istria Saint-Germain

29 rue Campagne-Première, 14th (01.43.20.91.82/
fax 01.43.22.48.45/www.istria-paris-hotel.com).
M° Raspail. **Rates** €96-€170 single; €90-€180
double; €220-€290 triple; €10 breakfast. **Credit**
AmEx, DC, MC, V. **Map** p405 G9 ⓩ
Behind this unassuming façade is the place where
the artistic royalty of Montparnasse's heyday – Man
Ray, Marcel Duchamp, Louis Aragon – once lived.
The Istria has been modernised since then, but it still
has plenty of charm, with 26 bright, simply fur-
nished rooms, a cosy cellar breakfast room and a
comfortable living area. Film fans take note: the tiled
artists' studios next door featured in Godard's
A Bout de Souffle.
Concierge. Internet (Wi-Fi). No-smoking room(s).
Room service (breakfast only). TV.

The 7th & the 15th

Deluxe

Le Montalembert

*3 rue de Montalembert, 7th (01.45.49.68.68/fax
01.45.49.69.49/www.montalembert.com). M° Rue du
Bac or Solférino.* **Rates** €370-€480 double; €600-
€830 suite; €20 breakfast. **Credit** AmEx, DC, MC, V.
Map p405 G6 ⑤

Grace Leo-Andrieu's impeccable boutique hotel
opened in 1990 and is a benchmark of quality and
service. It has everything *mode* maniacs (who flock
here for Fashion Week) could want: bathrooms
stuffed with Contemporel toiletries, a set of digital
scales and 360° mirrors to check that all-important
silhouette. Decorated in pale lilac, cinnamon and
olive tones, the entire hotel has Wi-Fi access and each
room is equipped with a flat-screen TV. Clattery
two-person staircase lifts are a nice nod to old fashioned ways in a hotel that is otherwise *tout moderne.*
*Bar. Concierge. Internet (Wi-Fi). Restaurant. Room
service. TV.*

Expensive

Hôtel Duc de Saint-Simon

*14 rue de St-Simon, 7th (01.44.39.20.20/fax
01.45.48.68.25/www.hotelducdesaintsimon.com).
M° Rue du Bac.* **Rates** €245-€275 double; €350-€375
suite; €15 breakfast. **Credit** AmEx, DC, MC, V.
Map p405 F6 ⑤

A lovely courtyard leads the way into this popular
hotel situated on the edge of St-Germain-des-Prés.
Of the 34 romantic bedrooms, four have terraces
over a closed-off leafy garden. It's perfect for lovers,
though if you can do without a four-poster bed, there
are more spacious rooms than the Honeymoon Suite.
Concierge. Internet. Room service. TV.

Le Walt

*37 av de La Motte-Picquet, 7th (01.45.51.55.83/fax
01.47.05.77.59/www.inwoodhotel.com). M° Ecole
Militaire.* **Rates** €260-€310 single; €280-€330
double; €13 breakfast. **Credit** AmEx, DC, MC, V.
Map p403 E7 ⑤

Feel like a star as you walk the spotlit red carpet to
your room at this well-appointed boutique hotel. Each
of the 25 rooms is decorated in warm milk-chocolate
tones, with wooden floors, modern walnut furniture
and, above the bed, a giant painting. Many on the sixth
floor have views of the Eiffel Tower. The hotel restaurant, decorated in burgundy velour and caramel,
with purple gossamer curtains, spills out into the chic
little courtyard on warmer days.
*Bar. Concierge. Internet (high-speed). No-smoking
room(s). Room service. TV.*

Moderate

Hôtel de La Bourdonnais

*111 av de La Bourdonnais, 7th (01.47.05.45.42/
fax 01.45.55.75.54/www.hotellabourdonnais.com).
M° Ecole Militaire.* **Rates** €125 single; €165
double or twin; €185 triple; €200 quad; €220
suite; €10 breakfast. **Credit** AmEx, DC, MC, V.
Map p404 D7 ⑤

The family-owned La Bourdonnais feels more like a
traditional French bourgeois townhouse than a
hotel, with 56 bedrooms decorated in rich colours,
antiques and Persian rugs. The main lobby opens

Villa d'Estrées. *See p62.*

on to a jungle-like winter garden and patio, where guests take breakfast, and an intimate lounge that is ideal for reading the papers over coffee.
Concierge. Internet (pay terminal). Parking (€15). Room service. TV.

Hôtel Lenox

9 rue de l'Université, 7th (01.42.96.10.95/fax 01.42.61.52.83/www.lenoxsaintgermain.com). M° St-Germain-des-Prés. **Rates** €130-€170 double; €280 duplex; €310 triple; €15 breakfast. **Credit** AmEx, DC, MC, V. **Map** p405 G6
The location may be the 7th, but this venerable literary and artistic haunt is unmistakeably part of St-Germain-des-Prés. The art deco-style Lenox Club Bar, open to the public, features comfortable leather club chairs and jazz instruments on the walls. Bedrooms, reached by an astonishing glass lift, have more traditional decor and city views.
Bar. Concierge. Internet (Wi-Fi). No-smoking room(s). Room service (until 1am). TV.

Budget

Grand Hôtel Lévêque

29 rue Cler, 7th (01.47.05.49.15/fax 01.45.50.49.36/www.hotel-leveque.com). M° Ecole Militaire. **Rates** €60 single; €90-€95 double; €90-€115 twin; €130 triple; €8 breakfast. **Credit** AmEx, MC, V. **Map** p405 E6
Recently renovated with new air-conditioning, the Lévêque is great value for its location on the market street of rue Cler. A charming tiled entrance leads to 50 well-equipped rooms, with sparkling bathrooms in all except the basin-only singles.
Concierge. Internet (dataport). TV.

Hôtel Eiffel Rive Gauche

6 rue du Gros-Caillou, 7th (01.45.51.24.56/fax 01.45.51.11.77/www.hotel-eiffel.com). M° Ecole Militaire. **Rates** €55-€95 single; €65-€105 double; €95-€125 triple; €125-€155 quad; €9 breakfast. **Credit** MC, V. **Map** p404 D6
The provençal decor and warm welcome make this a nice retreat. For the quintessential Paris view at a bargain price, ask to stay on one of the upper floors: you can see the Eiffel Tower from nine of the 29 rooms. All feature Empire-style bedheads and modern bathrooms. Outside, there's a tiny, tiled courtyard with a bridge. A nearby sister hotel in the 15th, the Hôtel Eiffel Villa Garibaldi (01.56.58.56.58), charges equally modest rates.
Concierge. Internet (pay terminal). TV.

Youth accommodation

Auberge Internationale des Jeunes

10 rue Trousseau, 11th (01.47.00.62.00/fax 01.47.00.33.16/www.aijparis.com). M° Ledru-Rollin. **Rates** (incl breakfast, per person) *Mar-June, Sept-Oct* €15. *July-Aug* €17. *Nov-Feb* €13. **Credit** AmEx, MC, V. **Map** p407 N7
Cleanliness is a high priority at this large (120 beds) hostel close to Bastille and within easy distance of the Marais. Rooms accommodate between two and four people, and the larger ones have their own shower and toilet. With the lowest hostel rates in central Paris, the place does tend to fill up fast in summer, but advance reservations can be made. Although the hostel is open all hours without any late-night curfew, the rooms are closed for cleaning every day between 10am and 3pm. **Photo** *p69.*
Internet. Microwave.

Low-cost lodgings

In addition to the great budget deals listed in this chapter, we've chosen the following hotels for their superb value and quirky style. Every one of the addresses below can supply a good night's sleep for under €90.

Hôtel Chopin

46 passage Jouffroy or 10 bd Montmartre, 9th (01.47.70.58.10/fax 01.42.47.00.70). Mº Grands Boulevards. **Rates** €68-€76 single; €81-€91 double; €109 triple; €7 breakfast. **Credit** MC, V. **Map** p402 J4
Set in a historic, glass-roofed arcade, the Chopin's original 1846 façade adds to its old-fashioned appeal. The 36 rooms are quiet and functional, with salmon-coloured walls and green carpet.

Hôtel Eldorado

18 rue des Dames, 17th (01.45.22.35.21/ fax 01.43.87.25.97/www.eldoradohotel.fr). Mº Place de Clichy. **Rates** €25-€55 single; €65-€75 double; €80-€90 triple; €7 breakfast. **Credit** MC, V. **Map** p401 G1
This eccentric hotel (*pictured*) is decorated with funky flea market finds. The Hôtel Eldorado's winning features include a wine bar, one of the best garden patios in town and a loyal local fashionista following.

Hôtel de Lille

8 rue du Pélican, 1st (01.42.33.33.42). Mº Palais Royal Musée du Louvre. **Rates** €38-€46 single; €55-€60 double; no breakfast. **No credit cards. Map** p402 H5
Tiny hotel with 14 clean, spacious rooms in belle époque style. The affiliated Hôtel du Petit Trianon (01.43.54.94.64) is in the 6th.

Hôtel de Nesle

7 rue de Nesle, 6th (01.43.54.62.41). Mº Odéon. **Rates** €55-€70 single; €75-€100 double; no breakfast. **Credit** MC, V. **Map** p408 H6
Only nine of the 20 rooms are en suite, but all are decorated with colourful murals, and many overlook a charming garden courtyard.

Hôtel Paris France

72 rue de Turbigo, 3rd (01.42.78.00.04/ fax 01.42.71.99.43/www.paris-france-hotel.com). Mº Temple. **Rates** €62-€72 single; €76-€112 double; €109-€137 triple. **Credit** AmEx, MC, V. **Map** p402 L5
A great central location, sweet lift, spruce staff and clean, pleasant rooms are on offer here. The attic has a view of Montmartre and (if you lean out far enough) the Eiffel Tower.

Hôtel Résidence Gobelins

9 rue des Gobelins, 13th (01.47.07.26.90/ fax 01.43.31.44.05/www.hotelgobelins. com). Mº Les Gobelins. **Rates** €59-€69 single; €79-€89 double; €93 triple; €103 quad; €7 breakfast. **Credit** AmEx, MC, V. **Map** p406 K10
A tiny lift leads to colourful rooms, equipped with satellite TV and telephone. The breakfast room overlooks a private garden, and there's free internet at reception. Friendly service.

Auberge Jules-Ferry

8 bd Jules-Ferry, 11th (01.43.57.55.60/fax 01.43. 14.82.09/www.fuaj.fr). M° République or Goncourt. **Rates** (incl breakfast & linens, per person) €20.50. **Credit** MC, V. **Map** p403 M4

This friendly IYHF hostel has 100 beds in rooms for two to six. There's no need – indeed, no way – to make advance bookings. No curfew, though rooms are closed between 10am and 2pm.
Internet.

BVJ Paris/Quartier Latin

44 rue des Bernardins, 5th (01.43.29.34.80/fax 01.53.00.90.91/www.bvjhotel.com). M° Maubert Mutualité. **Rates** (incl breakfast, per person) €27 dorm; €40 single; €29 double. **No credit cards**. **Map** p406 K7 ⑨

The BVJ hostel has 121 beds with homely tartan quilts in clean but bare modern dorms (for up to ten) and rooms with showers. There's also a TV lounge and a work room in which to write up your journal.
Internet.
Other locations: BVJ Paris/Louvre, 20 rue Jean-Jacques-Rousseau, 1st (01.53.00.90.90).

MIJE

6 rue de Fourcy, 4th (01.42.74.23.45/fax 01.40.27.81.64/www.mije.com). M° St-Paul. **Rates** (incl breakfast, per person; €2.50 obligatory membership) €28 dorm (18-30s); €45 single; €33 double; €29 triple. **No credit cards. Map** p409 L6 ⑨

MIJE runs three 17th-century Marais residences – one is a former convent – that provide the most attractive hostel sleeps in Paris. Its plain, clean rooms have snow-white sheets and sleep up to eight; all have a shower and basin. The Fourcy address has its own restaurant (evenings only). Curfew is 1am unless you arrange otherwise with reception.
Internet.
Other locations: (same phone) 11 rue du Fauconnier, 4th; 12 rue des Barres, 4th.

Bed & breakfast

Alcove & Agapes

Le Bed & Breakfast à Paris, 8bis rue Coysevox, 18th (01.44.85.06.05/fax 01.44.85.06.14/www.bed-and-breakfast-in-paris.com).

This B&B service offers over 100 *chambres d'hôte* (€55-€175 for a double, €95-€170 for a triple, including breakfast) with hosts who range from artists to grannies. Extras can include anything from dinner to cooking classes or tours of Paris. The multilingual website provides good descriptions and photos of each property.

Good Morning Paris

43 rue Lacépède, 5th (01.47.07.28.29/fax 01.47.07. 44.45/www.goodmorningparis.fr).

This company has 100 rooms in the city. Prices range from €54-€64 for one person, €76-€94 for doubles and €96-€106 for larger rooms for two or three. It also has apartments for two to four people, priced from €86-€122. Minimum stay is two nights.

Auberge Internationale des Jeunes.
See p67.

Apart-hotels & flat rental

A deposit is usually payable on arrival. Small ads for private short-term lets run in the fortnightly anglophone *FUSAC* (www.fusac.fr).

Citadines Apart'hotel

Central reservations 01.41.05.79.79/fax 01.41.05. 78.87/www.citadines.com. **Rates** €110-€615. **Credit** AmEx, DC, MC, V.

The 17 modern Citadines complexes across Paris (including around the Louvre and Opéra) tend to attract a mainly business clientele. Room sizes vary from slightly cramped studios to quite spacious two-bedroom apartments, all with a kitchenette and dining table suitable for those with children. Rates depend on neighbourhood, size of apartment and length of stay; although you can book for as little as one night, there are discounts for longer stays.

Paris Appartements Services

20 rue Bachaumont, 2nd (01.40.28.01.28/fax 01.40.28.92.01/www.paris-apts.com). M° Sentier. **Open** 9am-6pm Mon-Fri. **Key pick-up** 24hrs. **Rates** (5-night minimum stay) €83-€150 studio; €135-€214 2-room apartment. Monthly prices on request. **Credit** AmEx, MC, V.

This organisation specialises in short term rentals, offering furnished studios and one-bedroom flats in the 1st to 4th districts, with a weekly maid service and a 24-hour helpline manned by bilingual staff. A daily breakfast service and cleaning can also be arranged on request.

Sightseeing

Features

Jardin du Luxembourg. *See p152.*

Introduction

Sightseeing nirvana.

Real life and postcard views – Paris at its finest.

Paris is a compact capital, perfectly contained by the Périphérique and neatly divided by the Seine into Left and Right Banks, with Ile de la Cité and Ile St-Louis to add interest. Dead central, almost self-contained, is the world's most famous art museum, the Louvre. For this reason we have divided **Sightseeing** into five chapters: **The Seine & Islands** (*pp78-84*); **The Louvre** (*pp85-91*); **The Right Bank** (*pp93-138*); **The Left Bank** (*pp139-171*) and **Beyond the Périphérique** (*pp172-177*). The main sections are also sub-divided by areas that, roughly, follow district guidelines, starting from the centre and working out. To cut to the chase, follow our recipe for a potted Paris break (*see p76* **Saturday night, Sunday morning**).

You can get a good feel for Paris even on a day's sightseeing trip, something you can't say of many capital cities; and while its famed beauty certainly doesn't extend to every last nook and cranny, there are few streets here that are not worth walking along.

Walking: that's the key. The Paris métro is a world champion among public transport networks and merits a ride in its own right;

the local buses are clean, frequent and cheap; and there are plenty of **guided tours** (*see p76*) to take you around the sights. By all means, time permitting, try them all. But your best chance of hearing this city's heartbeat lies in putting one foot in front of the other, above ground, among the people who live and work here; only then will you be able to see the 'museum city' clichés for what they are. Paris is alive, thriving: joyous proof that a city can love the trappings of the contemporary world without forgetting – or fossilising – its past.

Its 20 districts spiral out, clockwise and in ascending order, from the Louvre. These are the arrondissements, the pieces that together make a jigsaw puzzle compared by novelist Julien Green to medical models of the human brain. Each piece has its connotations. 5th: intellectual. 6th: chic. 16th: affluent and stuffy. 10th, 11th: post-industrial bar hubs. 18th, 19th, 20th: lively and multicultural. Rightly or wrongly, residents are often assessed, at least at first encounter, by their postcodes – and many will tell you that Paris is not a city but, in fact, a coagulation of distinct villages.

Museums

The Louvre (see pp85-91 **The Louvre**) is so vast that it tends to overshadow the city's hundred-plus museums. The **Centre Pompidou**, **Musée d'Orsay** and **Musée Marmottan** are almost as famous, and you shouldn't miss the world-class ethnic art on show at the **Guimet** and **Dapper** museums and the **Institut du Monde Arabe**. The city's science museums are equally impressive, from the **Musée des Arts et Métiers** to the high-tech, child-friendly **Cité des Sciences et de l'Industrie** at La Villette. For lovers of the avant-garde, there's the innovative **Palais de Tokyo Site de Création Contemporain**, which houses the **Musée d'Art Moderne de la Ville de Paris**.

The reason for the rich trove is tied up with French history. After the Revolution, the huge royal collections became the property of the state; then came the 19th-century zeal for *grand tourisme* – although the ownership of foreign plunder is a matter of current debate. Both the French state and the city put large sums into the upkeep and expansion of collections, while tiny, unique private museums, like the **Musée Edith Piaf** or **Musée de l'Eventail**, struggle.

The **Musée du Quai Branly**, the new, no-expense-spared museum of tribal art beside the Eiffel Tower, was the big opening of 2006 (see p158 **A museum with a mission**). For 2007, look out for the **Cité de l'Architecture et du Patrimoine** at the **Palais de Trocadéro** (see p119 **Trocadéro revival**) and the **Pinacothèque de Paris** (see p103).

MUSEUM TICKETS AND PASSES

The most economical way to visit a large number of museums is the **Paris Museum Pass** (www.parismuseumpass.fr), formerly known as the Carte Musées et Monuments. The one-day version has been discontinued, but the pass is available in two-day (€30), four-day (€45) and six-day (€60) formats. It allows you admission into more than 60 museums and monuments in Paris, including the Louvre, Musée National Picasso and Cité des Sciences et de l'Industrie (though you will have to pay extra for special exhibitions), and also allows you to jump queues. The card is sold at participating museums and monuments, as well as tourist offices. In our listings, **PMP** indicates venues where the card is accepted.

The Galeries Nationales du Grand Palais also now operate an annual pass, the aptly named **Sésame** (www.rmn.fr), which grants handy queue-jumping rights, unlimited entry and various other discounts (€74 couples; €42 solo; €22 13-25s).

Museums often offer reduced admission for students, children and the over-60s; bring identification to prove your status. In any case, all permanent collections at municipal-run museums are free, and a reduced rate is usually applicable on Sundays. All national museums are completely free of charge on the first Sunday of the month, and most museums also throw open their doors on one Sunday in April for the **Printemps des Musées** (01.40.15.36.00, www.culture.gouv.fr; see p270).

MUSEUM OPENING HOURS

Most national museums close on Tuesdays; most municipal museums close on Mondays.

To avoid the crowds, visit on weekdays, or take advantage of the late-night opening that most of the big museums offer. Pre-booking is essential before 1pm at the Grand Palais, and it's also possible to pre-book the Louvre, the Luxembourg and major exhibitions. Most ticket counters will close 30 to 45 minutes before the official closing time.

Thousands turn out for the annual **Journées du Patrimoine** (see p273) in September to see behind the normally closed doors of some of the capital's oldest and most beautiful buildings.

TEMPORARY EXHIBITION VENUES

Non-museum exhibition centres include the **Grand Palais** and **Palais du Luxembourg**, and a host of smaller foundations, libraries and buildings of architectural interest that offer well-priced or free exhibitions. Most open only for exhibitions, so check *L'Officiel des spectacles* for details. Cultural centres include: **Centre Culturel Calouste Gulbenkian** (Portugal; 51 av d'Iéna, 16th, 01.53.23.93.93); **Centre Culturel Irlandais** (Ireland; 5 rue des Irlandais, 5th, 01.58.52.10.30); **Centre Culturel Suisse** (Switzerland; 32-38 rue des Francs-Bourgeois, 3rd, 01.42.71.38.38); **Centre Wallonie-Bruxelles** (Belgium; 127 rue St-Martin, 4th, 01.53.01.96.96); **Goethe Institut** (Germany; Galerie Condé, 31 rue de Condé, 6th, 01.40.46.69.60; 8 av Raymond-Poincaré, 16th, 01.44.43.92.30); **Institut Finlandais** (Finland; 60 rue des Ecoles, 5th, 01.40.51.89.09); **Institut Néerlandais** (Holland; 121 rue de Lille, 7th, 01.53.59.12.40) and **Maison de l'Amérique Latine** (Latin America; 217 bd St-Germain, 7th, 01.49.54.75.00).

> ▶ **Passeport Paris** is a 48-page directory of museums, shops, restaurants and tour companies, with a money-off coupon for use at each. Valid for a year, it costs €5 and is sold across the city: for more information, see www.parisinfo.com.

Sightseeing

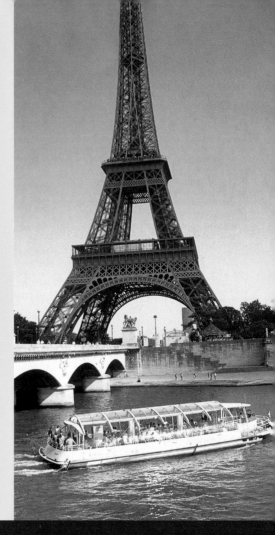

Welcome to the neighbourhood

Bastille

No so much revolutionary, these days, as creative; the area around iconic place de la Bastille is stocked with record shops, music venues (such as the Opera House) and a handful of decent bars.

Belleville

One of the city's most multicultural areas: Chinese shops rub up against halal and kosher grocers, and there's a busy street market on Tuesday and Friday mornings.

Bercy

Entertainment is a strong point, especially cinema: Bercy is the new home for Frank Gehry's Cinémathèque Française.

Grands Boulevards

Less a distinct quarter than a curving east-west stripe across several others. At the western end it's all large-scale consumerism in the *grands magasins*; to the east are seediness, buzz and exotic food shops.

Les Halles

Once the city's wholesale food market, now home to one of its unloveliest architectural landmarks, the subterranean Forum des Halles shopping mall.

Ile de la Cité

The bullseye of the capital, where its history begins – home to the law courts, Notre-Dame and a dinky flower market.

Ile St-Louis

You'd need a pile of euros to buy property on this island of calm, but it costs nothing to explore its charming streets and small, characterful shops.

Madeleine

Moneyed but lacking in character, this is where you'll find fab food shops and any number of hotels.

The Marais

With ancient buildings and a street plan largely unmolested by Haussmann, this is great pedestrian territory. The Marais is the heartland of Jewish and gay Paris, full of boutiques, art galleries and bars.

Ménilmontant

A thriving centre of alternative Paris, awash with artists' studios and trendy cafés.

Montmartre

The highest point in the city also has one of its densest concentrations of tourists. The views and Sacré-Coeur should be seen, of course – but then strike out from the crowds and explore the unabashedly romantic side streets and stairways.

Montparnasse

There's just enough of a good-time feel here after dark to recall the area's artistic heyday in the 1920s and '30s. Bars, restaurants and cinemas are abundant.

Pigalle

Sex shops and neon: that's the popular image of Pigalle. There's a lot of both, indeed – but the area has been cleaning up its act in recent years, with the relandscaping of bd de Clichy and bd de Rochechouart.

St-Germain-des-Prés

Intellectual heritage and some of the most expensive cups of coffee in the city are to be found here. The district is now best known for fashion houses and luxury brands, though a few publishers remain.

Sightseeing

Guided tours

For boat tours, *see p81*.

Coach tours

Les Cars Rouges

01.53.95.39.53/www.carsrouges.com. **Departs** *from Trocadéro. Summer* every 8-15mins 9.30am-8.50pm daily. *Winter* every 10-20mins 9.30am-7.30pm daily. **Tickets** €22; €11 4-12s. **No credit cards**.
Red buses follow a set tour of the major monuments. Hop on at any of nine stops. Recorded commentary.

Cityrama

4 pl des Pyramides, 1st (01.44.55.61.00/www. graylineparis.com). M° Palais Royal Musée du Louvre. **Departs** *Summer* 10am, 11.30am, 1.30pm, 3.30pm daily. *Winter* 10am, 11.30am, 2pm daily. **Tickets** €17; €8.50 4-11s. **Credit** AmEx, DC, MC, V.

Another double-decker outfit with multilingual recorded commentary. Also organises walking tours.

Paris L'OpenTour

13 rue Auber, 9th (01.42.66.56.56/www.paris-opentour.com). M° Havre-Caumartin/RER Auber. **Departs** *Apr-Oct* every 10-30mins 9.30am-6pm daily. *Nov-Mar* every 25-30mins 9.30am-4pm daily. **Tickets** *1 day* €25. *2 days* €28; €12 4-11s. **Credit** AmEx, DC, MC, V.
Green, open-top buses with recorded commentary in English and French. Hop on at any of 50 stops.

Paris Vision

214 rue de Rivoli, 1st (01.42.60.30.01/www. parisvision.fr). M° Tuileries. **Departs** times vary. **Tickets** €19-€163; €13.30-€114.10 under-12s. **Credit** AmEx, DC, MC, V.
Large air-conditioned coaches tour the sights – make sure you get a top-deck seat. Commentary is basic, and trips last between two hours and a full day.

Saturday night, Sunday morning

You've got a mere 48 hours to spend in the city of light. As well as the must-see list of iconic sights – the Eiffel Tower, Notre-Dame, Arc de Triomphe, the Louvre, the Musée d'Orsay, the Sacré-Coeur – there are some other delights worth squeezing into a swift *séjour*. Here are a few ideas.

Day one

Start the day with mouthfuls of crispy, buttery flakes and soft, squishy dough – in other words, a croissant from **Au Levain du Marais** (32 rue de Turenne, 3rd), an easy stroll from beautiful 17th-century place des Vosges. Sip an espresso at one of several cafés that sit facing the square.

Now for a look at a bit more of the Marais. Traditionally the Jewish quarter, it's abuzz with culture, retail and bars. Many of its imposing *hôtels particuliers* – old aristocratic mansions – now house important cultural institutions like the **Musée Carnavalet** (*see p112*), **Musée National Picasso** (*see p112*) and **Maison Européenne de la Photographie** (*see p114*). Boutique safarists, meanwhile, will find rich pickings in the streets leading off the main shopping thoroughfare of rue des Francs-Bourgeois. The area is also an enclave of contemporary art galleries and, around rue Vieille-du-Temple, a thriving bar scene, both straight and gay.

There are several unsung panoramas in Paris. The **Institut du Monde Arabe** (*see p146*), a behemoth glass building designed

by French superstar architect Jean Nouvel, has a fine collection of Middle Eastern art and a rooftop café with fabulous views looking down the Seine. Clambering up to the small temple that marks the summit of the **Parc des Buttes-Chaumont** (*see p138*) reveals beautifully landscaped swathes of green below, and miles of city beyond. Save **Sacré-Coeur** (*see p131*) for dusk, when the tourists have largely departed and the night lights have begun to smoulder.

Meander along the stone quays that border the Seine and leaf through old *revues* and tatty paperbacks at the riverside *bouquiniste* stalls (*see p242*), which are folded away into their green boxes at night. From the quays you can either hop on a sightseeing boat, or pause to explore the islands. The **Mémorial des Martyrs de la Déportation** (*see p82*) on the Ile de la Cité is an undervisited tribute to the people deported to concentration camps in World War II. On the Ile St-Louis, the deliciousness of the ice-cream from **Berthillon** (31 rue St-Louis-en-l'Ile, 4th, 01.43.54.31.61) is no secret; if the weather's warm, you'll have to queue.

Evenings start with aperitifs. Join the sociable crowd on the terrace seats at **Le Bar du Marché** (*see p233*) and watch the Left Bank people-traffic pass by over a kir, served by one of the eccentric, dungaree-wearing waiters. By now, you're almost certainly in the mood for a little nocturnal revelry. Cross the river for the **Rex** nightclub (*see p325*)

Two-wheeled tours

City-bird
08.26.10.01.00/www.city-bird.com. **Tickets** €70-
€100. **Credit** AmEx, DC, MC, V.
For the money-rich and time-poor, a new sightseeing tool: the motorbike. A friendly, knowledgeable
driver weaves you through the traffic, supplying
banter and history, while the sights whirl around you.

Fat Tire Bike Tours
01.56.58.10.54/www.fattirebiketoursparis.com. Meet
at Pilier Sud, Tour Eiffel, Champs de Mars, 7th. M°
Bir-Hakeim. **Departs** *Bike day tour* mid Feb-May &
mid Sept-mid Dec 11am daily; June-mid Sept 11am,
3pm daily. *Bike night tour* Mar & 1st 2wks Nov 7pm
Tue, Thur, Sat, Sun; Apr-15 Nov 7pm daily. *Segway
day tour* mid Feb-30 Nov 10.30am daily. *Segway
night tour* Apr-Oct 6.30pm daily. **Tickets** *Day* €24;
€22 students. *Night* €28; €26 students. *Both* €48; €44
students. *Segway* €70. **No credit cards.**

Paris, Versailles and Giverny by chunky bike or
Segway scooter. Walking tours and bike hire too.

Paris à vélo, c'est sympa!
*22 rue Baudin, 11th (01.48.87.60.01/www.paris
velosympa.com). M° Richard Lenoir.* **Departs** times
vary. **Tickets** €34; €28 13-26s; €18 under-12s.
Credit MC, V.
Multilingual themed cycle tours include nocturnal
Paris and Paris at dawn. Reservations only. Bike
hire available, from €10 for a half day or €13 for a day.

Walking tours

See above for **Cityrama** and **Fat Bike Tours.**

Paris Walking Tours
01.48.09.21.40/www.paris-walks.com. **Departs**
10.30am, 2.30pm daily. **Tickets** €10. **Credit** MC, V.
Led by long-term resident expatriates, daily walks
explore areas like the Marais and the old Left Bank.

for an electronica blowout. Post-dancefloor
hunger pangs can be satiated at welcoming
Les Halles bistro **La Poule au Pot** (10 rue
de Vauvilliers, 1st, 01.42.36.32.96), which
thoughtfully stays open until 6am. Near the
Champs Elysées, meanwhile, you'll find **La
Maison de l'Aubrac** (37 rue Marbeuf, 8th,
01.43.59.05.14), a bonhomie-filled outpost
of the Auvergne, grilling *côte du boeuf* to
perfection until 7am, every day of the week.
    Finish your *nuit blanche* in style with a coffee
at gorgeous art deco brasserie **Le Vaudeville**
(29 rue Vivienne, 2nd, 01.40.20.04.62),
which opens its doors from 7am.

Day two
Cross the Pont des Arts and head south
through the narrow Left Bank streets to
St-Sulpice church, then stroll to the **Jardin
du Luxembourg** (*see p152*), pull up two green
chairs (this is the accepted protocol – you
need the extra one as a footrest) and size up
the park life: children sailing toy boats past
the ducks on the central pond, t'ai chi groups
doing bizarre stretches and old-timers playing
unhurried chess. The adjacent museum, the
Musée National du Luxembourg (*see p152*),
hosts world-class art exhibitions – Botticelli,
Modigliani and so on.
    Amble along the tree-lined **Canal St-Martin**,
crossing from side to side over its romantic
green bridges, to explore little shops and
waterside cafés. On Sundays, traffic is
outlawed from the quai de Valmy and the

bar-lined quai de Jemmapes, to be replaced
by streams of in-line skaters, cyclists and
baby buggies. Boutiques such as princessy
outfitter **Stella Cadente** (93 quai Valmy,
10th, 01.42.09.27.00) and kitsch merchants
Antoine et Lili (*see p253*) are both open on
Sundays. For coffee and a slice of chocolate
cake, drop by wood-floored, chandeliered
café **Le Sporting** (3 rue des Récollets, 10th,
01.46.07.02.00); if you'd prefer a swift *demi*
near the water, go for friendly **L'Atmosphère**
(*see p228*) across the road.
    Modern art lovers should make a point
of visiting the wonderful collection at the
Musée de l'Art Moderne de la Ville de Paris
(*see p122*), which is neighbour to dynamic
contemporary art space the **Palais de Tokyo**
(*see p123*). From here you can walk to the
Champs-Elysées and take a nighttime hike
up the Arc de Triomphe to see the lights of
the avenue stretching into the city.
    As a parting gesture, sink into a comfy
Chesterfield and relax with an expertly shaken
cocktail at the classy neo-colonial **China Club**
(*see p224*). Cigar and cigarette smokers can
wallow in the fug of the *fumoir* upstairs.

WEEKEND TRAVEL TIPS
Buy a *carnet* of ten tickets (€10.90) if you're
staying in the city for less than two days;
for long weekends it's worth investing in a
coupon hebdomadaire, or weekly pass, for
€15.90. You can use either on the métro,
RER and buses.

The Seine & Islands

Beaches, boats and bridges – all overlooking 2,000 years of history.

The Seine

The Seine is a divide, a transport route and a tourist attraction. The division is as much psychological as physical, between a Left Bank still perceived as chic and intellectual and a Right Bank seen as mercantile. The Seine is still used to transport building materials; and, as all the boat tours attest (see p81 **Sightseeing from the Seine**), it's a must-see feature.

It hasn't always been so. For much of the 19th and 20th centuries, the Seine was barely given a second thought by anyone who didn't work on it or roar along its quay roads. Then, in the 1980s, the banks along the stretch now known as quai François-Mitterrand became a popular gay cruising area (dubbed Tata Beach), and in 1990 UNESCO added 12 kilometres (7.5 miles) of Paris riverbank to its World Heritage register. Parc Tino-Rossi was created on the Left Bank, where riverside tango became a regular event. Then the floating venues – **Batofar** (see p323) and its ilk – became super-trendy; and in the last ten years, it's been one Seine-side cultural attraction after another. Stretches of riverside roads are closed on Sundays to give free rein to cyclists and rollerskaters, port de Javel becomes an open-air dancehall in the summer and there's the summer riverside jamboree of **Paris-Plage** (see p272 **Take me to the river**), Mayor Delanoë's inspired idea to bring a bit of the south of France to the city – sand, palm trees, loungers, beach huts and all.

The bridges

From the honey-coloured arches of the ancient Pont Neuf to the swooping lines of the Passerelle Simone-de-Beauvoir (See p82 **There's a new bridge in town**), Paris' 37 bridges afford some of the most seductive reasons to visit the city – and some of the best views. The date of the very first construction traversing the Seine is lost in the fog, but there was already a bridge at the position of today's Petit Pont in the first century BC, when the Parisii Celts (see p12) ran their river trade and toll-bridge operations. The Romans put up a cross-island thoroughfare in the guise of a reinforced bridge to the south of Ile St-Louis, and another one north of it (where Pont de Notre-Dame now stands), thus creating a straight route from Orléans to Belgium.

The city's *ponts* have been bombed, bashed to bits by buses, boats and barges, weather-beaten to destruction and even trampled to the toppling point: in 1634 Pont St-Louis collapsed under the weight of a religious procession. During the Middle Ages, the handful of bridges linking the islands to the riverbanks were lined with shops and houses, but the flimsy wooden constructs regularly caught fire or got washed away. Petit Pont, for example, sank 11 times before councillors decided it would be a good idea to ban building on top of bridges.

Pont Neuf was inaugurated in 1607 and has been standing sturdy, gargoyles a-goggle, ever since. This was the first bridge to be built with no houses to obstruct the view of the river. It had a raised stretch of road at the edge to keep walkers separate from traffic and horse dung (the new-fangled 'pavement' soon caught on); the semicircular alcoves that now make handy smooching pit stops were once filled with teeth-pullers, peddlers and *bouquinistes* (*see p242*).

The 19th century saw a bridge boom – 21 of them in all, including the city's first steel, iron and suspension bridges. Pont de la Concorde used up what was left of the Bastille after the storming of 1789; the romantic Pont des Arts was the capital's first solely pedestrian crossing (built in 1803, rebuilt in the 1980s). The most glitteringly exuberant bridge is Pont Alexandre III, with its finely wrought lamps, garlanding and gilded embellishments. More practical is Pont de l'Alma, with its Zouave statue. This has long been a popular flood-level measure: when the statue's toes get wet, the state raises the flood alert and starts to close the quayside roads; when he's up to his ankles in Seine, it's no longer possible to navigate the river by boat. This offers some indication of how devastating the great 1910 flood must have been, when the plucky Zouave disappeared up to his neck – as did large areas of central Paris.

The 20th century also produced some fab additions to the line-up. Pont Charles-de-Gaulle, for example, stretches resplendent like a huge aeroplane's wing, and iron Viaduc d'Austerlitz (1905) is striking yet elegant as it cradles métro line 5. The city's newest crossing, the Passerelle Simone-de-Beauvoir, is a walkway linking the Bibliothèque Nationale to the Parc de Bercy. S*ee p82* **There's a new bridge in town**.

Ile de la Cité

In the 1st & 4th arrondissements.
The Ile de la Cité is where Paris began around 250 BC, when the Parisii, a tribe of Celtic Gauls, decided to found a settlement on this convenient bridging point of the Seine (*see p12*). Romans, Merovingians and Capetians followed, in what

became a centre of political and religious power right into the Middle Ages: royal authority concentrated at one end, around the Capetian palace; the Church at the other, by Notre-Dame.

When Victor Hugo wrote his *Notre-Dame de Paris* in 1831, the Ile de la Cité was still a bustling quarter of narrow medieval streets and tall houses: 'the head, heart and very marrow of Paris'. Assuming the metaphor was apt, Baron Haussmann performed a marrow extraction when he supervised the expulsion of 25,000 people from the island, razed tenements and some 20 churches and left behind large, official buildings – the law courts, the **Conciergerie**, Hôtel-Dieu hospital, the police headquarters and the cathedral. The lines of the old streets are traced into the parvis in front of **Notre-Dame**.

Perhaps the most charming spot on the island is the western tip, where Pont Neuf spans the Seine. Despite its name, it is in fact the oldest remaining bridge in Paris, begun under the reign of Henri III and Catherine de Médicis in 1578 and taking 30 years in all to complete. Its arches are lined with grimacing faces, said to be modelled on some of the courtiers of Henri III.

Down the steps is a leafy triangular garden, square du Vert-Galant, an ideal spot for picnics. You can also take to the water on the **Vedettes du Pont Neuf** moored on the quay (*see p81* **Sightseeing from the Seine**). In the centre of the bridge is an equestrian statue of Henri IV; the original went up in 1635, was melted down to make cannons during the Revolution, and replaced in 1818. On the bridge's eastern side, triangular place Dauphine, home to restaurants, wine bars and the ramshackle Hôtel Henri IV, was built in 1607, on what was then a sandy bar that flooded every winter. It was commissioned by Henri IV, who named it in honour of his son, the future King Louis XIII. The red-brick and stone houses, similar to those in place des Vosges (though subsequently much altered in the interest of sun terraces), look out over the quays and square. The third, eastern side was demolished in the 1860s, when the new Préfecture de Police was built. Known by its address, quai des Orfèvres, it was immortalised on screen by Clouzot's film and Simenon's Maigret novels. It's a tranquil, secluded spot.

The towers of the Conciergerie dominate the island's north bank. Along with the Palais de Justice, it was originally part of the Palais de la Cité, residential and administration complex of the Capetian kings. It occupies the site of an earlier Merovingian fortress and, before that, the Roman governor's house. Etienne Marcel's uprising prompted Charles V to move the royal retinue to the Louvre in 1358, and the Conciergerie was assigned a more sinister role as a prison for those awaiting execution. The

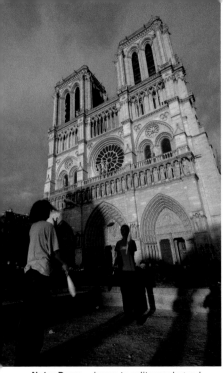

Notre-Dame – home to a literary legend.

interior is worth a visit for its prison cells and the vaulted Gothic halls. On the corner of boulevard du Palais, the Tour de l'Horloge, built in 1370, was the first public clock in Paris.

Sainte-Chapelle, Pierre de Montreuil's masterpiece of stained glass and slender Gothic columns, nestles amid the nearby law courts. Enveloping the chapel, the Palais de Justice was built alongside the Conciergerie. Behind elaborate wrought-iron railings, most of the present buildings around the fine neo-classical entrance courtyard date from the 1780s reconstruction by Desmaisons and Antoine. After passing through security, you can visit the Salle des Pas Perdus, busy with plaintiffs and barristers, and sit in on cases in the civil and criminal courts. The Palais is still the centre of the French legal system, though it's rumoured that the law courts will one day be moved to the 13th or 15th arrondissement.

Across boulevard du Palais, behind the Tribunal du Commerce, place Louis-Lépine is occupied by the green pavilions of the Marché aux Fleurs, where horticultural suppliers sell flowers, cacti and exotic trees. On Sundays, they are joined by twittering caged birds and small animals in the Marché aux Oiseaux. The Hôtel-Dieu, east of the marketplace, was founded in the seventh century. During the

Middle Ages your chances of survival here were, at best, slim; today the odds are much improved. The hospital originally stood on the other side of the island facing the Latin Quarter, but after a series of fires in the 18th century it was rebuilt here in the 1860s.

Notre-Dame cathedral dominates the eastern half of the island. On the parvis in front of the cathedral, the bronze 'Kilomètre Zéro' marker is the point from which distances to Paris from the rest of France are measured. The **Crypte Archéologique** hidden under the parvis gives a sense of the island's multi-layered past, when it was a tangle of alleys, houses, churches and cabarets. Despite all the tourists, Notre-Dame is still a place of worship, and holds its **Assumption Day procession** (*see p273*), **Christmas Mass** (*see p274*) and Nativity scene on the parvis.

Walk through the garden by the cathedral to appreciate its flying buttresses. To the north-east, a medieval feel persists in the few streets untouched by Haussmann, such as rue Chanoinesse, rue de la Colombe and rue des Ursins, though the crenellated medieval remnant on the corner of rue des Ursins and rue des Chantres was redone in the 1950s for the Aga Khan. The capital's oldest love story unfolded in the 12th century at 9 quai aux Fleurs, where Héloïse lived with her uncle Canon Fulbert, who had her tutor and lover, the scholar Abélard, castrated. Héloïse was sent to a nunnery. Behind the cathedral, in a garden at the eastern end of the island, is the **Mémorial des Martyrs de la Déportation**, remembering those sent to concentration camps.

Cathédrale Notre-Dame de Paris

Pl du Parvis-Notre-Dame, 4th (01.42.34.56.10/ www.cathedraledeparis.com). M° Cité/RER St-Michel. **Open** 7.45am-6.45pm daily. *Towers Apr-Sept* 9am-6.45pm daily. *Oct-Mar* 10am-4.45pm daily. **Admission** free. *Towers* €7.10; €5.10 18-25s; free under-18s. PMP. **Credit** MC, V. **Map** p406 J7.
One of the masterpieces of Gothic architecture, Notre-Dame was commissioned in 1160 by Bishop Maurice de Sully, who wanted to rival the smart new abbey that had just gone up in St-Denis. It replaced the earlier St-Etienne basilica, built in the sixth century by Childebert I on the site of a Gallo-Roman temple to Jupiter. Notre-Dame was constructed between 1163 and 1334, and the amount of time and money spent on it reflected the city's growing prestige. Pope Alexander III may have laid the foundation stone; the choir was completed in 1182, the nave in 1208; the west front and twin towers went up between 1225 and 1250. Chapels were added to the nave between 1235 and 1250, and to the apse between 1296 and 1330. The cathedral was plundered during the French Revolution, and then rededicated to the cult of Reason. The original statues of the Kings of

Sightseeing from the Seine

Most boats depart from the quays in the 7th and 8th arrondissements, at the foot of the Eiffel Tower, and go on a circuit around the islands, first along the Left Bank and past the Latin Quarter and Notre-Dame, then along the Right Bank, past the Marais and the Louvre.

Bateaux-Mouches

Pont de l'Alma, 8th (01.42.25.96.10/ 01.40.76.99.99/www.bateaux-mouches.fr). Mº Alma-Marceau. **Departs** *Apr-Sept* every 30mins 10am-11pm daily. *Oct-Mar* every 45 mins 11am-9pm daily. **Admission** €8; €4 under-12s, over-65s; free under-4s. **Credit** AmEx, MC, V.

If you're after a whirlwind tour of all the essential sights and don't mind crowds of tourists and schoolchildren, this, the oldest cruise operation on the Seine, is the one to choose. Still, the four languages that are crammed into the canned commentary and the high speed of the boat mean you get only the basic facts.

Bateaux Parisiens

Tour Eiffel, port de la Bourdonnais, 7th (01.44.11.33.55/www.bateauxparisiens. com). RER Champ de Mars. **Departs** *Apr-Sept* every 30mins 10am-10.30pm daily. *Oct-Mar* every hr 10am-10pm daily. **Admission** €10; €5 under-12s; free under-3s. **Credit** AmEx, MC, V.

BP's trimarans are smarter boats than most, and jaunty Parisian music flavours your cruise. Competent staff provide a live commentary in French, and good English and Spanish. The glass-topped boats should be avoided on hot days, however, as they rapidly turn into floating greenhouses.

Batobus Tour Eiffel

08.25.05.01.01/www.batobus.com. Boats stop at Tour Eiffel (Port de la Bourdonnais), Musée d'Orsay, St-Germain-des-Prés (quai Malaquais), Notre-Dame, Jardin des Plantes, Hôtel de Ville, Louvre and Champs-Elysées (Pont Alexandre III). **Departs** every 15-30mins. *Feb-mid Mar, Nov-early Jan* 10.30am-4.30pm daily. *Mid Mar-May, Sept-Oct* 10am-7pm daily. *June-Aug* 10am-9.30pm daily. *Closed 3 wks Jan.* **Admission** *Day pass* €11; €7 concessions; €5 under-16s. *2-day pass* €13; €8 concessions; €6 under-16s. *5-day pass* €16; €10 concessions; €7 under-16s. *Annual pass* €50; €30 under-16s.

A public transport and sightseeing hybrid, this is a pleasurable way to cruise through the city, with eight hop-on, hop-off stops between the Eiffel Tower and the Jardin des Plantes. The polite staff, who give tourist information on request, and the presence of some Parisians make this a classier choice. It can be combined with L'Open Tour (*see p76*) on a two-day ticket that gives you unlimited access to the 50 bus stops and eight boat stops.

Canauxrama

13 quai de la Loire, 19th (01.42.39.15.00/ www.canauxrama.fr). **Departs** *All year* Port de l'Arsenal (50 bd de la Bastille, 12th, Mº Bastille) 9.45am, 2.30pm daily. *Apr-Sept* Bassin de la Villette (13 quai de la Loire, 19th, Mº Jaurès) 9.45am, 2.45pm daily. **Admission** *Mon-Fri* €14; €8 6-12s; €11 students and concessions; free under-6s *Mon-Fri. Sat, Sun* all tickets €14 after noon. If the Seine palls, take a trip up the city's second waterway, the Canal St-Martin (*see p134*). The tree-lined canal is a pretty and characterful sight, and the 150-minute trip even goes underground for a stretch, where the tunnel walls are enlivened by a coloured light show. Reservations must be made in advance; also call for cruises between the Musée d'Orsay and La Villette.

Vedettes de Paris

Port de Suffren, 7th (01.47.05.71.29/ www.vedettesdeparis.com). Mº Bir-Hakeim. **Departs** *Easter-Oct* every 30mins 10am-11pm daily. *Nov-Easter* every hr 11am-6pm daily. **Admission** €9; €4 5-12s; free under-4s. Open boats give the most unobstructed views, and the recorded commentary can be avoided by choosing the children's cruise: the French-only tour guide on board soon tires of the bridge-naming game.

Vedettes du Pont-Neuf

Sq du Vert Galant, 1st (01.46.33.98.38/ www.vedettesdupontneuf.com). Mº Pont Neuf. **Departs** *Mar-Oct* every 30-45mins 10am-10.30pm daily. *Nov-Feb* every 45mins 10.30am-10pm Mon-Thur; 10.30am-10.30pm Fri-Sun. **Admission** €10; €5 under-12s; free under-4s.

You can sit inside just a foot or two above water level or outside on the top deck – where you may get drenched by pranksters throwing water from bridges as you pass underneath.

There's a new bridge in town

The inauguration of a new footbridge over the Seine in 2006 marks the coming of age for the area known as ZAC Rive Gauche (*see p170* **Riverside revival**). This formerly run-down, neglected stretch of land between the Gare d'Austerlitz and boulevard Masséna in the south-eastern 13th district has been extensively renovated, attracting world-renowned architects, multinational businesses and smart residents. Dominating the landscape are the four L-shaped towers of François Mitterrand's National Library, the first major development here. Ten years later, in July 2006, the 13th landed a bridge to link it to Parc de Bercy on the Right Bank: the Passerelle Simone-de-Beauvoir.

Accessible to pedestrians and cyclists, the curved footbridge was conceived by Austrian architect Dietmar Feichtinger as a 'new public space on the water', a site for temporary exhibitions, kiosks and *bouquinistes*. Feichtinger, responsible for a congress centre in Salzburg, an exhibition hall in Nice and chic motorway toll stations across France, sees the naming of the bridge after the complex,

bisexual feminist writer de Beauvoir as 'appropriate'. 'The bridge is very feminine,' says Feichtinger, 'slender and elegant.'

A cabled construction without any ground supports between the banks, it spans one of the widest stretches of the Seine, its two strands swooping in the middle. Stand on the oak planks of the higher deck, halfway along the 300-metre (984-foot) extent, and you can see the two-level Pont de Bercy of métro trains and cars, and the Josephine Baker floating pool (*see p338*), with gym, solarium, sauna, hammam and jacuzzi. In the distance, glimpses of Notre-Dame and the Eiffel Tower. On the lower deck, close to the water, you can almost touch tourist boats and coal barges.

Not only does the city's 37th bridge link to the Bibliothèque François-Mitterrand, but also to the area beyond, into which departments of Paris University are set to move in 2007. This intellectual hub, expected to house some 30,000 students, is already being referred to as a new Latin Quarter – 60 years after de Beauvoir, Sartre and associates defined the cultural direction of the old one.

Judah from the west front were torn down by the mob (who believed them to represent the kings of France) and rediscovered only during the construction of a car park in 1977 (they're now in the Musée National du Moyen-Age; *see p141*). By the 19th century, the cathedral was looking pretty shabby.

Victor Hugo, whose novel *Notre-Dame de Paris* had been a great success, led the campaign for its restoration. Gothic revivalist Viollet-le-Duc restored Notre-Dame to her former glory in the mid 19th century, although work has been going on ever since, with the replacement and cleaning of damaged and eroded finials and sculptures. Although Reims (*see p355*) was the coronation church of the French kings, that didn't deter others with monarchical pretensions: in 1430 Henry VI of England was crowned here; Napoleon made himself Emperor here in 1804; and in 1909 it hosted the beatification of Joan of Arc.

Despite its heavy restoration, the west front remains a high point of Gothic art for the balanced proportions of its twin towers and rose window, and the three doorways with rows of saints and sculpted tympanums: the *Last Judgement* (centre), *Life of the Virgin* (left) and *Life of St Anne* (right). Inside, stop a moment to admire the long nave with its solid foliate capitals and high altar with a marble *Pietà* by Coustou; the choir was rebuilt in the 18th century by Robert le Cotte but is surrounded by medieval painted stone reliefs depicting the Resurrection (south) and Nativity (north). Religious paintings, known as 'the Mays' because they were donated by the guilds on 1 May every year, hang in many of the side chapels, while the Treasury contains ornate bishops' copes, church plate and reliquaries designed to hold the Crown of Thorns (which long sat in Sainte-Chapelle; *see p84*). To truly appreciate the masonry, climb up the towers (only a limited number can ascend at one time). The route begins up the north tower and descends down the south. Between the two towers you get a close-up view of the gallery of chimeras – the fantastic birds and leering hybrid beasts designed by Viollet-le-Duc along the balustrade, including the pensive Stryga, who looks down on the capital from the first corner. After a detour to see the Bourdon, the big bell, a spiral staircase leads to the top of the south tower, from where you can look down on the spire – and see pretty much every monument in Paris. **Photo** *p80*.

La Conciergerie

2 bd du Palais, 1st (01.53.40.60.97). M° Cité/RER St-Michel Notre-Dame. **Open** *Mar-Oct* 9.30am-6pm daily. *Nov-Feb* 9am-4.30pm daily. **Admission** €6.50; €4.50 18-25s, students; free under-18s (accompanied by an adult). *With Sainte-Chapelle* €9.50; €7.50 concessions. PMP. **Credit** MC, V. **Map** p408 J6.
Marie-Antoinette was imprisoned here during the Revolution, as were Danton and Robespierre before their executions. The Conciergerie looks every inch the forbidding medieval fortress, yet much of the pseudo-medieval façade was added in the 1850s. The 13th-century Bonbec tower, built during the

reign of St Louis, the 14th-century twin towers, César and Argent, and the Tour de l'Horloge all survive from the Capetian palace. The visit takes you through the Salle des Gardes, the medieval kitchens with their four huge chimneys and the Salle des Gens d'Armes, an impressive vaulted Gothic hall built between 1301 and 1315 for Philippe 'le Bel'. After the royals moved to the Louvre, the fortress became a prison under the watch of the Concierge. The wealthy had private cells with their own furniture, which they paid for; others crowded on beds of straw. A list of Revolutionary prisoners, including a hairdresser, shows that not all victims were nobles. In Marie-Antoinette's cell, the Chapelle des Girondins, are her crucifix, some portraits and a guillotine blade.

La Crypte Archéologique

Pl Jean-Paul II, 4th (01.55.42.50.10). M° Cité/RER St-Michel Notre-Dame. **Open** 10am-6pm Tue-Sun. **Admission** €3.30; €2.20 over-60s; €1.60 13-26s; free under-14s. PMP. **Credit** (€15 minimum) MC, V. **Map** p406 J7.
Hidden under the forecourt in front of the cathedral is a large void that reveals bits and pieces of Roman quaysides, ramparts and hypocausts, medieval cellars, shops and pavements, the foundations of the Eglise Ste-Geneviève-des-Ardens (the church where Geneviève's remains were stored during the Norman invasions), an 18th-century foundling hospital and a 19th-century sewer, all excavated since the 1960s. It's not always easy to work out exactly which wall,

Where lovers meet: **Pont des Arts**. *See p79*.

column or staircase is which – but you do get a vivid sense of the sheer layers of history piled one atop another during 16 centuries. There are plans to extend the crypt to uncover part of the foundations of the Merovingian cathedral, west of the present one.

Mémorial des Martyrs de la Déportation

Sq de l'Ile de France, 4th (01.46.33.87.56). M° Cité/RER St-Michel Notre-Dame or Châtelet. **Open** *Winter* 10am-noon, 2-5pm daily. *Summer* 10am-noon, 2-7pm daily. **Admission** free. **Map** p406 J7.

This sober tribute to the 200,000 Jews, Communists, homosexuals and *Résistants* deported to concentration camps from France in World War II stands on the eastern tip of the island. A blind staircase descends to river level, where simple chambers are lined with tiny lights and the walls are inscribed with verse. A barred window looks on to the Seine.

Sainte-Chapelle

4 bd du Palais, 1st (01.53.40.60.80). M° Cité/RER St-Michel Notre-Dame. **Open** *Mar-Oct* 9.30am-5.30pm daily. *Nov-Feb* 9am-4.30pm daily. **Admission** €6.10; €4.10 18-25s, students; free under-18s (accompanied by an adult). PMP. *With Conciergerie* €9.50; €7.50 concessions. **Credit** MC, V. **Map** p408 J6.

Devout King Louis IX (St Louis, 1226-70) had a hobby of accumulating holy relics (and children: he fathered 11). In the 1240s he bought what was advertised as the Crown of Thorns, and ordered Pierre de Montreuil to design a suitable shrine. The result was the exquisite Flamboyant Gothic Sainte-Chapelle. With 15m (49ft) windows, the upper level, intended for the royal family and the canons, appears to consist almost entirely of stained glass. The windows depict hundreds of scenes from the Old and New Testaments, culminating with the Apocalypse in the rose window; on sunny days, coloured light dapples the stone. The lower chapel, with its star-painted vaulting, was for the use of palace servants.

Ile St-Louis

In the 4th arrondissement.

The Ile St-Louis is one of the most exclusive residential addresses in the city. Delightfully unspoiled, it offers fine architecture, narrow streets and pretty views from the tree-lined quays, and still retains the air of a tranquil backwater, curiously removed from city life.

For hundreds of years, the island was a swampy pasture belonging to Notre-Dame. A retreat for fishermen, swimmers and courting couples, it was then known as Ile Notre-Dame. In the 14th century Charles V built a fortified canal through the middle, thus creating the Ile aux Vaches ('Island of Cows'). Its real-estate potential wasn't realised until 1614, though, when speculator Christophe Marie persuaded Louis XIII to fill in the canal (present-day rue Poulletier) and plan streets, bridges and houses.

The island was renamed in honour of the king's pious predecessor, and the venture proved a huge success, thanks to society architect Louis Le Vau, who from the 1630s built fashionable new residences along the quai d'Anjou, quai de Bourbon and quai de Béthune, as well as the **Eglise St-Louis-en-l'Ile**. By the 1660s the island was full up; its smart reception rooms were set at the front of courtyards to give their residents riverside views (unlike the Marais, where reception rooms were at the rear).

Rue St-Louis-en-l'Ile – lined with fine historic buildings that now contain quirky gift shops and gourmet food stores (many of them open on Sunday), quaint tearooms, stone-walled bars, restaurants and hotels – runs the length of the island. The grandiose Hôtel Lambert at No.2 was built by Le Vau in 1641 for Louis XIII's secretary, and has sumptuous interiors by Le Sueur, Perrier and Le Brun. At No.51, Hôtel Chenizot, look out for the bearded faun adorning the rocaille doorway, which is flanked by stern dragons supporting the balcony. There's more sculpture on the courtyard façade, while a second courtyard hides craft workshops and an art gallery. Across the street, the Hôtel du Jeu de Paume at No.54 was once a tennis court; at No.31, famous ice-cream maker Berthillon still draws a crowd. There are great views of the flying buttresses of Notre-Dame at the western end from the terraces of the Brasserie de l'Ile St-Louis and the Flore en l'Ile café. A footbridge crosses from here to the Ile de la Cité.

Baudelaire wrote part of *Les Fleurs du Mal* while living at the Hôtel de Lauzun at No.17 quai d'Anjou; he and fellow poet Théophile Gautier also organised meetings of their dope-smokers' club here. A couple of centuries earlier, Racine, Molière and La Fontaine resided as guests of La Grande Mademoiselle, cousin of Louis XIV – and mistress of the Comte de Lauzan. The *hôtel*, built in 1657, stands out for its scaly sea-serpent drainpipes and trompe-l'oeil interiors. At 6 quai d'Orléans, meanwhile, the Adam Mickiewicz library-museum (01.43.54.35.61, open 2-6pm Thur) is dedicated to the Romantic poet, journalist and campaigner for Polish freedom, who had set off for Poland to catch the failed 1831 uprising, only to find himself unable to cross the border. He came to Paris to write poems and political pamphlets, all kept here.

Eglise St-Louis-en-l'Ile

19bis rue St-Louis-en-l'Ile, 4th (01.46.34.11.60). M° Pont Marie. **Open** 9am-noon, 3-7pm Tue-Sun. **Map** p409 L7.

The island's church was built between 1664 and 1765, following plans by Louis Le Vau and later completed by Gabriel Le Duc. The baroque interior boasts Corinthian columns and a sunburst over the altar, and sometimes hosts classical music concerts.

Napoleon III's former stables were reopened in 2004 to house princely collections of statuary acquired by Richelieu and the Borghese and Albani families during the 17th and 18th centuries. The statues, either copies of classical works or heavily restored originals, demonstrate the relationship between antique and modern sculpture. The height of the room also allows oversized works such as *Jupiter* and *Albani Alexander* to be displayed. Northern sculpture, on the lower ground floor, ranges from Erhart's Gothic *Mary Magdalene* to the neo-classical work of Thorvaldsen, while pre-Renaissance Italian pieces include Donatello's clay relief *Virgin and Child*.

Northern schools
Richelieu: 2nd floor; Sully: 1st floor. Red on Louvre maps.
Northern Renaissance works include Flemish altarpieces by Memling and van der Weyden, Bosch's fantastical, proto-surrealist *Ship of Fools*, Metsys' *The Moneylender and his Wife*, and the northern mannerism of Cornelius van Haarlem. The Galerie Médicis houses Rubens' Médicis cycle; Marie de Médicis, the widow of Henri IV, commissioned the 24 canvases for the Palais de Luxembourg in the 1620s. They blend historic events and classical mythology for the glorification of the queen, never afraid to put her best features on public display. Look out for Rubens' more personal portrait of his second wife, *Hélène Fourment and her Children*, plus van Dyck's *Charles I and his Groom* and David Teniers the Younger's peasant-filled townscapes.

Dutch paintings in this wing include early and late self-portraits by Rembrandt, his *Flayed Ox* and the warmly glowing nude *Bathsheba at her Bath*. There are Vermeer's *Astronomer* and *Lacemaker* amid interiors by De Hooch and Metsu, and the meticulously finished portraits and framing devices of Dou, plus works from the Haarlem school. German paintings in side galleries include portraits by Cranach, Dürer's *Self-Portrait* and Holbein's *Anne of Cleves*.

The rooms of Northern European and Scandinavian paintings include Caspar David Friedrich's *Trees with Crows*, the sober, classical portraits of Christian Købke, and pared-back views by Peder Balke. A fairly modest but high-quality British collection located on the first floor of the Sully includes landscapes by Wright of Derby, Constable and Turner, and portraits by Gainsborough, Reynolds and Lawrence.

Decorative arts
Richelieu: 1st floor; Sully: 1st floor. Magenta on Louvre maps.
The decorative arts collection runs from the Middle Ages to the mid-19th century, often with royal connections, and includes entire rooms

decorated in the fashion of the day. Many of the finest medieval items came from the treasury of St-Denis, amassed by the powerful Abbot Suger, counsellor to Louis VI and VII, among them Suger's 'Eagle' (a porphyry vase), a serpentine plate surrounded by precious stones, and the sacred sword of the kings of France, dubbed 'Charlemagne's Sword' by the Capetian monarchs as they sought to legitimise their line.

The Renaissance galleries take in ornate carved chests, German silver tankards and the *Hunts of Maximilien*, twelve 16th-century tapestries depicting the months, zodiac and hunting scenes. Seventeenth- and 18th-century French decorative arts are displayed in superb panelled rooms, and include characteristic brass and tortoiseshell pieces by Boulle. Displays then move on to French porcelain, silverware, watches and scientific instruments. Napoleon III's opulent apartments, used until the 1980s by the Ministry of Finance, have been preserved, with chandeliers and upholstery intact. Next to the Denon wing, the Galerie d'Apollon reopened in 2004 after four years of restoration. A precursor to the Hall of Mirrors at Versailles, it was built for Louis XIV and is a showcase of talents from this golden age: architecture by Louis Le Vau, painted ceilings by Charles Le Brun and sculpture by François Girardon, the Marsy brothers and Thomas Regnaudin. Napoleon III then commissioned Delacroix to paint the central medallion, *Apollo Vanquishing the Python*, and now it houses the crown jewels and Louis XIV vases. Merry-Joseph Blondel's *Chute d'Icare* graces the ceiling of an anteroom of the adjacent Rotonde d'Apollon.

African, Asian, Oceanic and American arts
Denon: ground floor. White on Louvre maps.
A new approach to '*arts premiers*' is seen in these eight rooms in the Pavillon des Sessions, prefiguring the Musée du Quai Branly. The spare, modern design of Jean-Michel Wilmotte allows each of the 100 key works to stand alone in something midway between an art gallery and a museum. The pure aesthetics of such objects as a svelte Zulu spoon with the breasts and buttocks of a woman, a sixth-century BC Sokoto terracotta head, a recycled iron sculpture of the god Gou that prefigures Picasso, and a pot-bellied, terracotta Chupicaro from Mexico can be appreciated in their own right. Computer terminals with mahogany benches offer visitors multimedia resources.

Temporary exhibitions
Major new exhibitions are shown in the Salle Napoleon. The 2007 programme is to include an exhibition of the work of the ancient Greek sculptor Praxiteles (23 Mar-18 June).

Bateaux Parisiens

The most Parisian journey

Yacht or glassed-in boat, dinner for two or lunch with friends, to the sounds of jazz or an Edith Piaf song. Magical Paris by night or majestic Paris by day... Paris in another way, Paris from the river, but Paris as ever. The journey begins at the foot of the Eiffel Tower, come and see Paris differently.

Sightseeing Cruises
Enchanted Cruise
Lunch Cruise
Dinner Cruise
Private Charters

At the foot of the Eiffel Tower
"Rendez-vous" at the Port de la Bourdonnais • 75007 Paris
Discover all the trips you can take on our web site: www.bateauxparisiens.com
Or book on: +33 1 46 99 43 13

The Right Bank

Rich in museums and monuments, the north bank combines commerce, culture and canalside recreation.

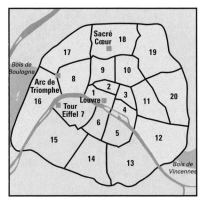

Sightseeing

The Louvre to Concorde

In the 1st arrondissement.

After the monarchs moved from the Ile de la Cité to spacious new quarters on the Right Bank, the Louvre and, later, the secondary palaces of the **Tuileries** and **Palais-Royal** became the centres of royal power.

The Louvre (*see pp85-91*) still exerts influence today: first as a grandiose architectural ensemble, a palace within the city; and, second, as a symbol of cultural Paris. What had been simply a fortress along Philippe-Auguste's city wall in 1190 was transformed into a royal residence with all the latest Gothic comforts by Charles V; François I turned it into a sumptuous Renaissance palace. For centuries it was a work in progress: everyone wanted to make their mark – including the most monarchical of presidents, François Mitterrand, who added IM Pei's glass pyramid, doubled the exhibition space and added the Carrousel du Louvre shopping mall, auditorium and food halls.

The palace has always attracted crowds: first courtiers and ministers; then artists; and, since 1793, when it was first turned into a museum, art lovers – though the last department of the Finance Ministry moved out as late as 1991. Around the Louvre, other subsidiary palaces grew up: Catherine de Médicis commissioned Philibert Delorme to begin work on one in the Tuileries; Richelieu built the Palais Cardinal, which later became the Palais-Royal.

On place du Louvre, opposite Claude Perrault's grandiose western façade of the Louvre, is **Eglise St-Germain-l'Auxerrois**, once the French kings' parish church and home to the only original Flamboyant Gothic porch in Paris, built in 1435. Mirroring it to the left of the belfry is the 19th-century neo-Gothic 1st district town hall, with its fanciful rose window and classical porch. Next door is the stylish **Le Fumoir** (*see p216*), with a Mona Lisa of its own: Amaretto, orange juice and champagne. You can walk through to the Louvre from here, through the ornate Cour Carrée, although the main museum entrance is now the pyramid or from métro Palais Royal Musée du Louvre.

Across rue de Rivoli from the Louvre, past the **Louvre des Antiquaires** antiques emporium (*see p266*) and nightspot **Le Cab** (*see p327*), stands the understatedly elegant **Palais-Royal**, once Cardinal Richelieu's private mansion and now the Conseil d'Etat and Ministry of Culture. After a stroll in its quiet gardens, it's hard to believe that this was once the most debauched corner of the capital and the starting point of the French Revolution.

In the 1780s the Palais was a boisterous centre of Paris life, where aristocrats and the financially challenged inhabitants of the *faubourgs* rubbed shoulders. The coffee-houses in its arcades generated radical debate: here Camille Desmoulins called the city to arms on the eve of Bastille Day (*see p273*); and after the Napoleonic Wars, Wellington and Field Marshal von Blücher lost so much money in the gambling dens that Parisians claimed they had won back their entire dues for war reparations. Only haute cuisine restaurant **Le Grand Véfour** (*see p183*), founded as Café de Chartres in the 1780s, survives from this era, albeit with decoration from a little later. The **Comédie Française** theatre ('La Maison de Molière'; *see p340*) stands on the south-west corner. The company, created by Louis XIV in 1680, moved here in 1799. Molière himself is honoured with a fountain on the corner of rue Molière and rue de Richelieu. Brass-fronted Café Nemours on place Colette – Colette herself used to buy cigars from old-fashioned A la Civette nearby (157 rue St-Honoré, 1st, 01.42.96.04.99) – is another thespian favourite; standing in front of it, the métro entrance by artist Jean-Michel Othoniel, all glass baubles and wonky aluminium struts, is a kitsch take on Guimard's celebrated art nouveau métro entrances.

Today, the stately arcades of the Palais-Royal house an eclectic succession of antiques dealers, philatelists, specialists in tin soldiers and musical boxes – and fashion showcases (*see p252* **Storming the palace**). Here you'll find the recently opened European flagship of renowned New York designer **Marc Jacobs** (*see p247*); chic vintage clothes specialist **Didier Ludot** (*see p255*) and the elegant perfumery **Salons du Palais-Royal Shiseido** (*see p238*). Passing through the arcades to rue de Montpensier, the neo-rococo Théâtre du Palais-Royal and the centuries-old café **Entr'acte** (*see p216*), you'll find narrow, stepped passages that run between here and rue de Richelieu. This small area, along with parallel rue Ste-Anne, is the focus of the city's Japanese community, and is full of sushi restaurants and noodle bars.

On the other side of the palace towards Les Halles, off rue Jean-Jacques-Rousseau, is galerie Véro-Dodat. Built by rich *charcutiers* during the Restoration, it has wonderfully preserved neo-classical wooden shopfronts. Browse the collections of antique dolls, the luxury leather goods and make-up boutiques. Right where rue St-Honoré meets rue Croix-des-Petits-Champs, look out for the controversial new steel lattice by architect Francis Solers across the façade of a Haussmann-era Ministry of Culture annexe.

At the western end of the Louvre, by rue de Rivoli, are the **Musée des Arts décoratifs**, the **Musée de la Mode et du Textile** and the **Musée de la Publicité**. All of these are administered independently of the Musée du Louvre, but were refreshed as part of the Grand Louvre scheme. The Decorative Arts Museum reopened in September 2006 after a ten-year, €35-million restoration. Across place du Carrousel from the Louvre pyramid, the Arc du Carrousel, a mini-Arc de Triomphe, was built in polychrome marble for Napoleon in 1806-9. The chariot on the top was originally drawn by the antique horses from San Marco in Venice, snapped up by Napoleon but returned in 1815. From the arch, the extraordinary axis along the **Jardin des Tuileries**, the **Champs-Elysées** (*see p118*) up to the **Arc de Triomphe** (*see p121*) and on to the **Grande Arche de la Défense** (*see p177*) is plain to see. **Photo** *p96*.

The Jardin des Tuileries stretched as far as the Tuileries palace, until that was destroyed in the 1871 Paris Commune. The garden was laid out in the 17th century by André Le Nôtre and remains a pleasure area, with a **funfair** (*see p285*) in summer; it also serves as an open-air gallery for modern art sculptures. Overlooking focal **place de la Concorde** is the **Musée de l'Orangerie**, reopened in May 2006 after a complete renovation; and the **Jeu de Paume**, built as a court for real tennis, now a centre for photographic exhibitions.

The best Right Bank sights

For 19th-century ingenuity
Canal St-Martin (*p134*); Gare du Nord (*p104*); Musée des Arts et Métiers (*p112*); Pavillon de l'Arsenal (*p115*).

For architecture and design
Fondation Le Corbusier (*p126*); Fondation Pierre Bergé Yves Saint Laurent (*p121*); Galerie-Musée Baccarat (*p121*); Musée des Arts décoratifs (*p97*); Musée Galliera (*p122*); Palais de Tokyo (*p123*).

For breathtaking opulence
Alexander Nevsky Cathedral (*p123*); Le Grand Rex (*p102*); Musée Jacquemart-André (*p124*); Palais Garnier (*p101*); Sacré-Coeur (*p131*).

For children's attractions
Bois de Boulogne (*p126*); Bois de Vincennes (*p116*); Cinéaqua (*p121*); La Cité des Sciences et de l'Industrie (*p134*); Jardin des

Tuileries (*p97*); Musée de la Magie (*p114*); Palais de la Découverte (*p122*); Parc des Buttes-Chaumont (*p138*); Parc Monceau (*p124*); Parc de La Villette (*p136*).

For intriguing oddities
Musée des Arts Forains (*p118*); Musée de la Contrefaçon (*p122*); Musée de l'Erotisme (*p132*); Musée de l'Eventail (*p104*); Musée du Fumeur (*p138*); Musée Gustave Moreau (*p132*); Musée National de la Marine (*p123*); Musée de Radio-France (*p127*).

For views of Paris
Arc de Triomphe (*p121*); rue de l'Ermitage (*p137*); Sacré-Coeur (*p131*); Trocadéro (*p119*); Parc des Buttes-Chaumont (p138).

For world-class art
Centre Pompidou (*p109*); Musée Marmottan – Claude Monet (*p126*); Musée National Picasso (*p112*); Musée de l'Orangerie (*p98*).

Sightseeing

Palais-Royal. *See p98.*

The stretch of rue de Rivoli running beside the Louvre towards Concorde was laid out by Napoleon's architects Percier and Fontaine in 1802-11, and is notable for its arcaded façades. It runs in a straight line between place de la Concorde and rue St-Antoine, in the **Marais** (*see p108*); at the western end it's filled with tacky souvenir shops – though old-fashioned hotels remain, and there are also gentlemen's outfitters, bookshop **WHSmith** (*see p243*) and tearoom Angelina (226 rue de Rivoli, 1st, 01.42.60.82.00). The area was inhabited by English aristocrats, writers and artists in the 1830s and '40s after the Napoleonic Wars, sleeping at the **Le Meurice** (*see p45*), buying the daily English newspaper published by bookseller **Galignani** (*see p242*), and dining in the fancy restaurants of the Palais-Royal.

Place des Pyramides, at the junction of rue de Rivoli and rue des Pyramides, contains a gleaming gilt equestrian statue of Joan of Arc. One of four statues of her in the city, it's fêted as a proud symbol of French nationalism every May Day by supporters of the Front National. Ancient rue St-Honoré, running parallel to rue de Rivoli, is one of those streets that changes style as it goes along: smart shops line it near place Vendôme, small cafés and inexpensive bistros predominate towards Les Halles. The baroque **Eglise St-Roch** is still pitted with bullet holes made by Napoleon's troops when they crushed a royalist revolt in 1795. With its old houses, adjoining rue St-Roch still feels

wonderfully authentic; a couple of shops are built into the side of the church. Further up stands Chapelle Notre-Dame de l'Assomption (1670-6), now used by the city's Polish community, its dome so disproportionately large that locals dubbed it *sot dôme* ('stupid dome'), a pun on 'Sodom'. Concept store **Colette** (*see p250*) brought some glamour to what was once a staid shopping area, drawing a swarm of similar stores in its wake. All are ideally placed for the fashionistas and film stars who touch down at **Hôtel Costes** (*see p43*) and its chic bar (*see p232* **'The usual, Sir?'**).

Opposite Colette is rue du Marché-St-Honoré, which once led to the covered Marché St-Honoré, since replaced by offices, in a square lined with trendy restaurants; to the north, rue Danielle-Casanova boasts 18th-century houses.

Further west along rue St-Honoré lies the wonderful, eight-sided **place Vendôme** and a perspective stretching from rue de Rivoli up to **Opéra** (*see p100*). At the end of the Tuileries, place de la Concorde, originally laid out for the glorification of Louis XV, is a masterclass in the use of open space, and spectacular when lit up at night. The winged Marly horses, only copies as the originals are in the Louvre, frame the entrance to the Champs-Elysées.

Smart rue Royale, leading to the **Madeleine** (*see p100*), boasts tearoom **Ladurée** (*see p221*) and the famed restaurant Maxim's (3 rue Royale, 1st, 01.42.65.27.94), with its fabulous art nouveau interior. Rue Boissy d'Anglas

The view from the **Arc du Carrousel**. *See p94*.

proffers stylish shops and the trendy Buddha Bar (No.8, 1st, 01.53.05.90.00); while sporting luxuries at **Hermès** (see p245) on rue du Fbg-St-Honoré (a westward extension of rue St-Honoré), and high-end designs at **Yves Saint Laurent** (see p249), Gucci (No.2, 1st, 01.42.96.83.27), Chloé (No.54, 1st, 01.44.94.33.00) and others set the plush tone. More tearooms and fine porcelain are displayed in the galerie and passage Royale.

Eglise St-Germain-l'Auxerrois

2 pl du Louvre, 1st (01.42.60.13.96). Mº Pont Neuf or Louvre Rivoli. **Open** 9am-7pm Mon-Sat; 9am-8.30pm Sun. **Map** p406 H6.

The architecture of this former royal church spans several eras: most striking, though, is the elaborate Flamboyant Gothic porch. Inside, there's the 13th-century Lady Chapel and a splendid canopied, carved bench by Le Brun made for the royal family in 1682. The church achieved notoriety on 24 August 1572, when its bell rang to signal the massacre of St Bartholomew's Day (see p17).

Eglise St-Roch

296 rue St-Honoré, 1st (01.42.44.13.20). Mº Pyramides or Tuileries. **Open** 8am-7pm daily. **Map** p401 G5.

Begun in the 1650s in what was then the heart of Paris, this long church was designed chiefly by Jacques Lemercier; work took so long, the church was consecrated only in 1740. Famed parishioners and patrons are remembered in funerary monuments: Le Nôtre, Mignard, Corneille and Diderot are all here, as are busts by Coysevox and Coustou, Falconet's statue *Christ on the Mount of Olives* and Anguier's superb *Nativity*. There's also a baroque pulpit and a cherub-adorned retable behind the rear altar. Bullet marks from a 1795 shoot-out between royalists and conventionists still pit the façade, recently scrubbed to honeyed cleanliness thanks to an ongoing programme of restoration.

Jardin des Tuileries

Rue de Rivoli, 1st. Mº Tuileries or Concorde. **Open** 7.30am-7pm daily. **Map** p401 G5.

Between the Louvre and place de la Concorde, the gravelled alleyways of these gardens, named after the tile factories that stood here in the Middle Ages, have been a chic promenade ever since they opened to the public in the 16th century; and the popular mood persists with the funfair that sets up along the rue de Rivoli side in summer. Renowned André Le Nôtre, who began his career as royal gardener here in 1664 before going on to Versailles, created the prototypical French garden with terraces and central vista running down the *Grand Axe* through circular and hexagonal ponds. When the Tuileries palace was burned down during the Paris Commune in 1871 (see p25), the park was expanded. As part of Mitterrand's Grand Louvre project, fragile sculptures such as Coysevox's winged horses were transferred to the Louvre and replaced by copies, and the

Maillol sculptures were returned to the Jardins du Carrousel; a handful of modern sculptures has been added, including bronzes by Laurens, Moore, Ernst, Giacometti and Dubuffet's *Le Bel Costume*. Replanting has restored parts of Le Nôtre's design and replaced damaged trees, and there's a specialist gardeners' bookshop by place de la Concorde.

Jeu de Paume

1 pl de la Concorde, 8th (01.47.03.12.50/www.jeu depaume.org). Mº Concorde. **Open** noon-9pm Tue; noon-7pm Wed-Fri; 10am-7pm Sat, Sun (last admission 30mins before closing). **Admission** €6; €3 concessions. **Credit** MC, V. **Map** p401 F5.

The Centre National de la Photographie moved into this site in 2005. The building, which once served as a tennis court, has been divided into two galleries, both stark white and with almost hangar-like proportions. It is not an intimate space, but it works well for showcase retrospectives such as Cindy Sherman and Lee Friedlander. A video-art and cinema suite in the basement offers new digital installation work, plus feature-length films made by artists. There is also a sleek café and a decent bookshop. The Jeu de Paume's smaller site is the former Patrimoine Photographique at the Hôtel de Sully (see p111).

Musée des Arts décoratifs

107 rue de Rivoli, 1st (01.44.55.57.50/ www.lesartsdecoratifs.fr). Mº Palais Royal Musée du Louvre or Pyramides. **Open** 11am-6pm Tue-Fri; 10am-6pm Sat, Sun. Closed some hols. **Admission** (with Musée de la Mode & Musée de la Publicité) €8; €6.50 18-25s; free under-18s; PMP. **Credit** MC, V. **Map** p402 H5.

Taken as a whole along with the Musée de la Mode et du Textile and Musée de la Publicité (for both, see p98), this is one of the world's major collections of design and the decorative arts. Located in the west wing of the Louvre since its opening a century ago, the venue reopened in 2006 after a decade-long, €35-million restoration, both of the building and of 6,000 of the 150,000 items collated mainly from private collectors. The major focus here is French furniture and tableware, illustrating what director Béatrice Salmon has referred to as 'the history of French taste'. From extravagant carpets to delicate crystal and porcelain, there is much to admire. Clever spotlighting and black settings show the exquisite treasures – including *châtelaines* made for medieval royalty and Maison Falize enamel work – to their best advantage. Other galleries are categorised by theme: glass, wallpaper, drawings and toys. There are cases devoted to Chinese head jewellery and the Japanese art of seduction with combs. Of most immediate attraction to the layman are the reconstructed period rooms, ten in all, showing how the other (French) half lived from the late 1400s to the early 20th century. The museum is privately run – hence the high-end contemporary design shop 107Rivoli (01.42.60.64.94; open 11am-6pm Mon, 10am-6pm Tue-Sun) attached to it, a world away from tacky caps and key rings.

Musée de la Mode et du Textile

107 rue de Rivoli, 1st (01.44.55.57.50/www.lesarts decoratifs.fr). Mº Palais Royal. **Open** for exhibitions 11am-6pm Tue-Fri; 10am-6pm Sat, Sun. **Admission** €8; €6.50 18-25s; free under-18s. PMP. **Credit** MC, V. **Map** p402 H5.

This municipal fashion museum holds Elsa Schiaparelli's entire archive and hosts exciting themed exhibitions. Dramatic black-walled rooms make a fine background to the clothes, while video screens and a small cinema space show you how the clothes move, as well as interviews with the creators.

Musée de l'Orangerie

Jardin des Tuileries, 1st (01.40.20.67.71/www. rmn.fr). Mº Concorde. **Open** 12.30-7pm Mon, Wed, Thur, Sat, Sun; 12.30-9pm Fri. **Admission** €6.50; €4.50 18-25s; free under-18s. PMP. **Credit** MC, V. **Map** p401 F5.

The long-delayed reopening of this Monet showcase finally took place in 2006, and the Orangerie is now firmly back on the tourist radar – beware long queues. Stylistically, the new look is utilitarian and fuss-free, with the museum's eight, tapestry-sized *Nymphéas* (water lilies) paintings housed in two plain oval rooms. They provide a simple backdrop for the astonishing, ethereal romanticism of Monet's works, painted late in his life and donated to the nation as a 'spiritual testimony'. Depicting Monet's 'jardin d'eau' at his house in Giverny, the *tableaux* have an intense, dreamy quality – partly reflecting the artist's absorption in the private world of his garden. Downstairs, the Jean Walter and Paul Guillaume collection of Impressionism and the Ecole de Paris is a mixed bag of sweet-toothed Cézanne and Renoir portraits, as well as works by Modigliani, Rousseau, Matisse, Picasso and Derain. **Photo** *p99.*

Musée de la Publicité

107 rue de Rivoli, 1st (01.44.55.57.50/www.lesarts decoratifs.fr). Mº Palais Royal Musée du Louvre. **Open** 11am-6pm Tue-Fri; 10am-6pm Sat, Sun. **Admission** (with Musée des Arts décoratifs & Musée de la Mode) €8; €6.50 18-25s; free under-18s. PMP. **Credit** MC, V. **Map** p402 H5.

The upstairs element of the trio of museums in the Louvre west wing, the advertising museum occupies a distressed interior by Jean Nouvel. Only a fraction of the vast collection of posters, promotional objects and packaging can be seen at one time; vintage posters are accessed through the multimedia space.

Palais-Royal

Pl du Palais-Royal, 1st, Mº Palais Royal Musée du Louvre. **Open** *Gardens* 7.30am-8.30pm daily. **Admission** free. **Map** p402 H5.

Built for Cardinal Richelieu by Jacques Lemercier, the building was once known as the Palais Cardinal. Richelieu left it to Louis XIII, whose widow Anne d'Autriche preferred it to the chilly Louvre and rechristened it when she moved in with her son, the young Louis XIV. In the 1780s the Duc d'Orléans, Louis XVI's fun-loving brother, enclosed the gardens in a three-storey peristyle and filled it with cafés, shops, theatres, sideshows and accommodation to raise money for rebuilding the burned-down opera. In complete contrast to Versailles, the Palais-Royal was a place for people of all classes to mingle in, and its arcades were a trysting venue. Daniel Buren's modern installation of black-and-white striped columns graces the main courtyard, while the stately buildings around it house the Conseil d'Etat and Ministry of Culture. **Photo** *p95.*

Place de la Concorde

1st/8th. Mº Concorde. **Map** p401 F5.

This is the city's largest square, its grand east-west perspectives stretching from the Louvre to the Arc de Triomphe, and north-south from the Madeleine to the Assemblée Nationale across the Seine. Royal architect Gabriel designed it in the 1750s, along with the two colonnaded mansions astride rue Royale; the west one houses the chic Hôtel de Crillon (*see p43*) and the Automobile Club de France, the other is the Naval Ministry. In 1792 the centre statue of Louis XV was replaced with the guillotine for Louis XVI, Marie-Antoinette and many more. The square was embellished in the 19th century with sturdy lampposts, the Luxor obelisk (from the Viceroy of Egypt), and ornate tiered fountains that represent navigation by water. The best view is by night, from the terrace by the Jeu de Paume.

Place Vendôme

1st. Mº Tuileries or Opéra. **Map** p401 G4.

Elegant place Vendôme got its name from a *hôtel particulier* built by the Duc de Vendôme that stood on the site. Opened in 1699, the eight-sided square was conceived by Hardouin-Mansart to show off an equestrian statue of the Sun King, torn down in 1792 and replaced in 1806 by the Colonne de la Grande Armée. Modelled on Trajan's Column in Rome and featuring a spiral comic strip illustrating Napoleon's military exploits, it was made from 1,250 Russian and Austrian cannons captured at the Battle of Austerlitz. During the 1871 Commune this symbol of 'brute force and false glory' was pulled down; the present column is a replica. Hardouin-Mansart only designed the façades, with their ground-floor arcade and giant Corinthian pilasters; the buildings behind were put up by nobles and speculators. Today the square houses sparkling jewellers and top fashion houses, as well as the Justice Ministry and the Hôtel Ritz (*see p45*), from where Diana and Dodi Al-Fayed set off on their last journey. At No.12, you can visit the Grand Salon where Chopin died in 1849; its fabulous allegorical decoration dates from 1777 and has been restored as part of the new museum above the venerable jewellers Chaumet (01.44.77.26.26).

The Bourse

In the 1st and 2nd arrondissements.

Far less frenzied than Wall Street, the city's traditional business district is squeezed between the elegant calm of the Palais-Royal and shopping hub the **Grands Boulevards** (*see p102*). Along rue du Quatre-Septembre and around, **La Bourse** (the stock exchange) is where financiers and stockbrokers beaver away in grandiose buildings. The Banque de France, France's national central bank, has occupied the 17th-century Hôtel de Toulouse since 1811, its long gallery still hung with Old Masters. Nearby, fashion and finance meet at stylish **place des Victoires**, designed by Hardouin-Mansart, forming an intimate circle of buildings today dedicated to fashion. West of the square, gander at shop-lined galerie Vivienne, the smartest of all the covered passages in Paris, adjoining galerie Colbert. Also look out for temporary exhibitions at the **Bibliothèque Nationale de France – Richelieu**. You can linger at the luxury food and wine merchant **Legrand** (*see p265*), or head along passage des Petits-Pères to admire the 17th- to 18th-century Eglise Notre-Dame-des-Victoires, the remains of an Augustine convent, featuring a cycle of paintings around the choir by Carle van Loo.

Rue de la Banque leads to La Bourse, behind a commanding neo-classical colonnade. The area has a relaxed feel – it's dead at weekends – but animated pockets exist at places like Le Vaudeville (29 rue Vivienne, 2nd, 01.40.20.04.62) and Gallopin (40 rue Notre-Dame-des-Victoires, 2nd, 01.42.36.45.38), busy brasseries where stockbrokers and journalists converge for lunch and post-work drinks. Rue des Colonnes is a quiet street lined with graceful porticos and acanthus motifs dating from the 1790s, while its design nemesis, the 1970s concrete-and-glass HQ of Agence France-Presse, the nation's biggest news agency, stands across busy rue du Quatre-Septembre. Although most newspaper offices have moved elsewhere, *Le Figaro* is still based in rue du Louvre. From the corner of rue Montmartre and rue du Croissant, take a look at the Café du Croissant, where Jean Jaurès, Socialist politician and founder of newspaper *L'Humanité*, was assassinated in 1914.

Bibliothèque Nationale de France – Richelieu & Musée du Cabinet des Médailles

58 rue de Richelieu, 2nd (01.53.79.53.79/www.bnf.fr). Mº Bourse. **Open** *Galeries Mansart/Mazarine, exhibitions only* 10am-7pm Tue-Sat; 1-7pm Sun. *Cabinet des Médailles* 1-5.45pm Mon-Fri; 1-4.45pm Sat; noon-6pm Sun. **Admission** *Galeries* prices vary. *Cabinet des Médailles* free. **Credit** AmEx, MC, V. **Map** p402 H4.

The history of the French National Library begins in the 1660s, when Louis XIV moved manuscripts that couldn't be housed in the Louvre to this lavish Louis XIII townhouse, formerly the private residence of Cardinal Mazarin. The library was first opened to the public in 1692, and by 1724 it had

Worth the wait: see Monet's masterpieces at the **Musée de l'Orangerie**. *See p98.*

received so many new acquisitions that the adjoining Hôtel de Nevers had to be added. Some of the original painted decoration by Romanelli and Grimaldi can still be seen in Galeries Mansart and Mazarine, now used for temporary exhibitions (and closed otherwise). The highlights, however, are the two circular reading rooms: the Salle Ovale, which is full of researchers, note-takers and readers, and the magnificent Salle de Travail, a temple to learning, with its arrangement of nine domes supported on slender columns clearly influenced by the Ottoman architecture of the Levant. The latter is now hauntingly empty, as most of its books have since been relocated to the Bibliothèque Nationale – François Mitterrand (see p171).

On the first floor is the Musée du Cabinet des Médailles, a modest two-room collection of coins and medals, including Greek, Roman and medieval examples. There is also a miscellany of other items, including Merovingian king Dagobert's throne, Charlemagne's chess set and small artefacts from the Classical world and ancient Egypt.

La Bourse

Palais Brongniart, pl de la Bourse, 2nd (01.49.27. 55.55/www.bourse-de-paris.fr). Mº Bourse. **Open** *Guided tours* call 1 wk in advance. **Admission** €8.50; €5.50 concessions. **No credit cards.** **Map** p402 H4.

After a century at the Louvre, the Palais-Royal and rue Vivienne, in 1826 the Stock Exchange was transferred to La Bourse, a dignified testament to First Empire classicism designed at Napoleon's behest by Alexandre Brongniart. It was enlarged in 1906 to create a cruciform interior, where brokers buzzed around a central enclosure, known as the *corbeille* ('basket' or 'trading floor'). Computers have made the design obsolete, but the pace remains frenetic.

Place des Victoires

1st, 2nd. Mº Bourse. **Map** p402 H5.

This circular square, the first of its kind, was designed by Hardouin-Mansart in 1685 to show off a statue of Louis XIV that marked victories against Holland. The original statue was destroyed after the Revolution (although the massive slaves from its base are now in the Louvre), and replaced in 1822 with an equestrian statue by Bosio. Among the occupants of the grand, sweeping buildings that encircle the 'square' are fashion boutiques Kenzo and Victoire.

Opéra & Grands Boulevards

In the 2nd, 8th, 9th and 10th arrondissements.

Opéra and Madeleine

Charles Garnier's wedding-cake **Palais Garnier** is all gilt and grandeur, as an opera house should be. Garnier was also responsible for the ritzy **Café de la Paix** (see p219) and the **InterContinental Paris Le Grand** (see p49) overlooking place de l'Opéra. Behind, in the Jockey Club (now the Hôtel Scribe, the centre for Allied war correspondents after the Liberation), the Lumière brothers held the world's first public cinema screening in 1895. Old England (No.12, 9th, 01.47.42.81.99), just opposite on the boulevard des Capucines, with its wooden counters, Jacobean-style ceilings and old-style goods and service, could have served as their costume consultants. The **Olympia** concert hall (see p317), the legendary venue of the Beatles, Piaf and anyone in *chanson*, was knocked down, but rose again nearby. Over the road at No.35, pioneering portrait photographer Nadar opened a studio in the 1860s, frequented by names such as Dumas père, Offenbach and Doré. In 1874 it hosted the first Impressionists' exhibition. Pedestrianised rue Edouard-VII, laid out in 1911, leads to the octagonal square of the same name with Landowski's equestrian statue of the monarch. Through an arch, another square contains the belle époque **Théâtre de l'Athénée-Louis Jouvet** (see p342).

The **Madeleine**, a monument to Napoleon, guards the end of the boulevard. At the head of rue Royale, its classical portico mirrors the **Assemblée Nationale** (see p156) on the other side of place de la Concorde over the river, while the interior is a riot of marble and altars. Well worth a browse are extravagant delicatessens **Fauchon** (see p264), **Maison de la Truffe** (see p265) and other luxury foodstores; here, too, is innovative haute cuisine restaurant **Senderens** (see p191).

Landmark department stores **Printemps** and the **Galeries Lafayette** (for both, see p237), which opened just behind the Palais Garnier in the late 19th century, also deserve investigation. Behind the latter stands the Lycée Caumartin, designed as a convent in the 1780s by La Bourse architect Brongniart, later one of Napoleon's most prestigious *lycées*. West along Haussmann's boulevard is a small square containing the **Chapelle Expiatoire** dedicated to Louis XVI and Marie-Antoinette.

Chapelle Expiatoire

29 rue Pasquier, 8th (01.42.65.35.80). Mº St-Augustin. **Open** 1-5pm Thur-Sat. **Admission** €2.50; free under-18s. PMP. **Map** p401 F3.

The chapel was commissioned by Louis XVIII in memory of his executed predecessors, his brother Louis XVI and Marie-Antoinette. Their remains, along with those of 3,000 victims of the Revolution, including Camille Desmoulins, Danton, Malesherbes and Lavoisier, were found in 1814 on the exact spot where the altar stands. The year after, the bodies of Louis XVI and Marie-Antoinette were transferred to the Basilique St-Denis (see p173); the pair are now represented by marble statues, kneeling at the feet of Religion. Every January ardent (if currently unfulfilled) royalists gather here for a memorial service.

Overhauling the Halls

In Zola's novel *Le Ventre de Paris*, Les Halles is an area groaning with food, swarming and seething with the Parisian populace. For centuries, Les Halles was the city's wholesale food market. After the market was relocated, Les Halles remained a social hub, with the opening of the RER train station of Châtelet Les Halles in 1977, a gateway for hundreds of thousands of visitors from the suburbs. Something special was needed to crown the new face of the city for the arrivals from out of town. The planners' solution? The Forum des Halles: three cavernous storeys of underground shopping beneath a concrete and glass exterior, sheltering a cinema, car park and, in its very darkest corner, a chlorine-scented public swimming pool.

Since its creation, which broke the flow of the neighbourhood with its oppressive reflective façade and the labyrinthine Jardin des Halles under which the mall stretches, the centre has come to be regarded as a blot on central Paris – unsafe at night and unlovely by day. In 2001, incoming mayor Bertrand Delanoë stepped up to civilise the soulless expanse.

Locals rushed to have a say in the redevelopment of the mall and gardens, and in 2004 the city awarded the task of redesigning them to Parisian architect David Mangin and his team from the firm Seura. Mangin presented a vision of a tree-lined open space, providing a gentle north-to-south transition from the Eglise St-Eustache towards rue de Rivoli. Seura's vast recreational garden – replacing many of the cobbles to provide four times as much open grass as there is now – will lead from the Bourse de Commerce at one end to a redesigned shopping mall topped by a tasteful glass roof. Mangin – whose other high profile public works include the capital's Denfert-Rochereau RER station – has also recruited the landscaper Philippe Raguin, the man who created the look of Parc de Bercy, for the job. And to make the whole area safer and more welcoming at night, a lighting designer has been drafted in: the aptly named Louis Clair, who has lit up such urban beacons as Notre-Dame and the Grande Arche de la Défense.

Still in the consultation stages in 2006, the revamp plans take a step forward in mid 2007, when another architect will be chosen to rebuild the shopping centre itself. Work is due to begin in earnest on the gardens in 2008, and the project is due to finish in 2012 – if all goes according to plan.

Tour Jean Sans Peur. *See p108.*

route along rue St-Denis. It was moved and reconstructed here when the nearby Cimetière des Innocents, the city's main burial ground, was demolished in 1786 after flesh-eating rats started gnawing into people's living rooms, and the bones were transferred to the catacombs.

Pedestrianised rue des Lombards is a beacon for live jazz, with **Sunset/Sunside**, **Baiser Salé** and **Au Duc des Lombards** (for all, *see pp319-320*) to choose from. In 1610, King Henri IV was assassinated by Catholic fanatic François Ravaillac on nearby rue de la Ferronnerie. Today, the street has become an extension of the Marais gay circuit.

The ancient easternmost stretch of rue St-Honoré runs into the southern edge of Les Halles. The Fontaine du Trahoir stands at the corner with rue de l'Arbre-Sec. Opposite, the Hôtel de Truden (52 rue de l'Arbre-Sec) was built in 1717 for a rich wine merchant; in the courtyard, on rue des Prouvaires, the market-traders' haunt **La Tour de Montlhéry** (*see p184*) serves up meaty fare all night. Fashion chains line the commercial stretch of the rue de Rivoli south of Les Halles. Running towards the Seine, ancient little streets such as rue des Lavandiers-Ste-Opportune and rue Jean-Lantier show a human side of Les Halles that has yet to be swept away. Between rue de Rivoli and the Pont Neuf is department store La Samaritaine, currently closed for safety reasons. Next door, a former section contains the chic Kenzo flagship, spa and the Philippe Starck-designed **Kong** restaurant and bar (*see p218*), offering more great views. From here quai de la Mégisserie, lined with horticultural suppliers and pet shops, leads towards **Châtelet** (*see p108*).

Looming over the northern edge of the Jardin des Halles is the massive **Eglise St-Eustache**, with Renaissance motifs inside and chunky flying buttresses outside. At the western end of the gardens is the circular, domed **Bourse de Commerce**. In front of it, an astrological column is all that remains from a grand palace belonging to Marie de Médicis that stood here. Nearby, the delightfully dusty **E Dehillerin** (*see p267*) supplies saucepans, knives and implements to restaurants and regular clients.

The empire of French designer **Agnès b** (*see p251*) stretches along most of rue du Jour, with streetwise outlets such as **Kiliwatch** (*see p254*) on the buzzing rue Tiquetonne becoming progressively more upscale towards the place des Victoires. On rue Etienne-Marcel, the restored **Tour Jean Sans Peur** is a weird Gothic relic of the fortified medieval townhouse of Jean Sans Peur, Duc de Bourgogne.

Busy, pedestrianised rue Montorgueil is lined with grocers, delicatessens and pavement cafés. Historic façades remain from when this was an area where the well-heeled and the working class mingled: Pâtisserie Stohrer (No.51, 2nd, 01.42.33.38.20), founded in 1730 and credited with the invention of the sugary *puits d'amour*; Le Rocher de Cancale (No.78, 01.42.33.50.29) and, back towards Les Halles, the golden snail sign hanging out in front of L'Escargot Montorgueil (No.38, 01.42.36.83.51), a restaurant that first opened in 1832. The restored glass-roofed passage du Grand-Cerf is home to several design consultancies.

Stretching north, bordered by boulevard de Bonne-Nouvelle to the north and boulevard Sébastopol to the east, lies Sentier, the historic garment district, while cocky rue St-Denis has long relied on strumpets and strip joints. The tackiness is unremitting into its northern continuation of rue du Fbg-St-Denis, which snakes north from the Forum des Halles.

Rue Réaumur houses striking art nouveau buildings with metal structures constructed as industrial premises in the early 1900s. Between rue des Petits-Carreaux and rue St-Denis is the site of the medieval Cour des Miracles – a refuge where, after a day's begging, paupers would 'miraculously' regain use of their eyes or limbs. An abandoned aristocratic estate, it was a sanctuary for the underworld until it was cleared out in 1667.

Sentier's maze of streets and passages throngs with porters shouldering linen bundles, while sweatshops churn out copies of catwalk creations. Streets such as rue du Caire, rue d'Aboukir and rue du Nil reflect the Egyptian craze following Napoleon's Egyptian campaign in 1798-99 – look out for the sphinx heads and mock hieroglyphics at No.2 place du Caire.

Bourse de Commerce

2 rue de Viarmes, 1st (01.55.65.55.65). Mº Louvre Rivoli. **Open** *for tour groups* 9am-6pm Mon-Fri. **Admission** free. **Map** p402 J5.

Housing the Paris Chamber of Commerce offices, this trade centre for coffee and sugar was built as a grain market in 1767. The circular building was then covered by a wooden dome, replaced by an avant-garde iron structure in 1809. Sadly underused, it has been mooted as a hotel, restaurant or museum.

Eglise St-Eustache

Rue du Jour, 1st (01.40.26.47.99/www.st-eustache. org). Mº Les Halles. **Open** 9am-7.30pm daily. **Map** p402 J5.

This massive barn-like church, built 1532-1640, has a Gothic structure but Renaissance decoration in its façade and Corinthian capitals. Among the paintings in the side chapels are a *Descent from the Cross* by Luca Giordano; contemporary pieces by John Armleder were added in 2000. Murals by Thomas Couture adorn the 19th-century Lady chapel. There is a magnificent 8,000-pipe organ and free recitals are held at 5.30pm on Sundays.

Forum des Halles

1st. M° Les Halles/RER Châtelet Les Halles.
Map p402 J5.
The labyrinthine mall and transport interchange
extends three levels underground and includes the
Ciné Cité multiplex cinema (*see p290*), the Forum
des Images (*see p291*) and a swimming pool (*see
p338*), as well as clothing chains, a branch of Fnac
(*see p243*) and the Forum des Créateurs, a section
for young designers. Despite an open central courtyard, a sense of gloom prevails. All should change
by 2012, with a new landscaping of the whole area.
See p105 **Overhauling the Halls**.

Pavillon des Arts

*Les Halles, 101 rue Rambuteau, 1st (01.42.33.82.50/
www.pavillon-arts.paris.fr). M° Châtelet Les Halles.*
Open 11.30am-6.30pm Tue-Sun. **Admission** €5.50;
€4 students; €2.50 14-26s; free under-14s. **No credit
cards. Map** p402 K5.
This gallery in Les Halles hosts exhibitions on anything from photography to local history.

Tour Jean Sans Peur

*20 rue Etienne-Marcel, 2nd (01.40.26.20.28/www.
tourjeansanspeur.com). M° Etienne Marcel.* **Open**
Termtime 1.30-6pm Wed, Sat, Sun. *School hols* 1.30-
6pm Tue-Sun. *Tour* 3pm. **Admission** €5; €3 7-18s,
students; free under-7s. *Tour* €8. **No credit cards.**
Map p402 K5.
This Gothic turret (1409-11) is the remnant of the
townhouse of Jean Sans Peur, Duc de Bourgogne. He
was responsible for the assassination of his rival
Louis d'Orléans, which sparked the Hundred Years'
War and saw Burgundy allied to the English crown.
Jean had this show-off tower added to his mansion
to protect him from vengeance by the aggrieved
widow. In 1419 he was assassinated by a partisan
of the dauphin, the future Charles VII. You can climb
the tower, which has rooms leading off the stairway.
Carved vaulting halfway up depicts naturalistic
branches of oak, hawthorn and hops, symbols of
Jean Sans Peur and Burgundian power. The huge
mansion originally spanned Philippe-Auguste's city
wall. **Photo** *p106*.

Beaubourg & the Marais

In the 3rd and 4th arrondissements.
Between boulevard Sébastopol and the Bastille
are Beaubourg – site of the **Centre Pompidou**
since 1977 – and the Marais, largely built
between the 16th and 18th centuries and now
jam-packed with boutiques, museums and bars.

Beaubourg & Hôtel de Ville

Contemporary Parisian architecture began
with the Centre Pompidou, designed by Richard
Rogers and Renzo Piano. This international
benchmark of inside-out high-tech is as much
of an attraction as its contents, which include
the **Musée National de l'Art Moderne**.

The piazza outside attracts street performers
and pavement artists, while the reconstructed
Atelier Brancusi, the sculptor's studio, which
he left to the state, was moved here from the
15th district. On the other side of the piazza, rue
Quincampoix houses galleries, bars and cobbled
passage Molière, with its old shopfronts and
the Théâtre Molière (01.44.54.53.00). Beside
the Centre Pompidou is place Igor-Stravinsky
and the Fontaine Stravinsky – full of spraying
kinetic fountains, and a colourful snake by the
late artists Nikki de St-Phalle and Jean Tinguély
– and the red-brick **IRCAM** music institute (*see
p309*), designed by Renzo Piano.

The church of St-Merri (78 rue St-Martin, 4th,
01.42.71.93.93), which has a Flamboyant Gothic
façade complete with an androgynous demon
leering over the doorway, sits on the south side
of the square. Inside are a carved wooden organ
loft, the joint contender (along with **Eglise
St-Séverin**; *see p140*) for the oldest bell in
Paris (1331), and 16th-century stained glass.

South of here stands the spiky Gothic **Tour
St-Jacques**. Towards the river, on the site of
the Grand Châtelet, a fortress put up in the 12th
century to defend Pont au Change, place du
Châtelet features an Egyptian-themed fountain
framed by twin theatres designed by Davioud
as part of Haussmann's urban improvements in
the 1860s. They are now two of the city's leading
arts venues: the **Théâtre de la Ville** (*see p312
and p342*) and **Théâtre du Châtelet** (*see
p288 and p309*), an opera and concert hall.

Beyond Châtelet, the **Hôtel de Ville**, the
City Hall, has been the symbol of municipal
power since 1260. The equestrian statue in
front of the building is of 14th-century merchant
leader and rebel Etienne Marcel. Revolutionaries
made City Hall their base in the 1871 Commune,
but it was set on fire by the Communards
themselves and wrecked during savage fighting.
It was rebuilt according to the original model,
on a larger scale, in fanciful neo-Renaissance
style, with knights in armour along the roof and
statues of French luminaries dotted all over the
walls. The square outside was formerly called
place de Grève, after the nearby riverside wharf
on which goods were unloaded for market. *Grève*
has come to be the French word for 'strike',
thanks to the number of demonstrations and
protests that gathered here. During the 16th-
century Wars of Religion, Protestant heretics
were burned in the square, and the dreadful
guillotine stood here during the Terror, when
Danton, Marat and Robespierre made the Hôtel
de Ville their own seat of government. Today
the square hosts an ice rink in December (*see
p274*) and screenings of major sports events.
Across the road stands the Bazar de l'Hôtel de
Ville department store, or **BHV** (*see p237*).

Atelier Brancusi

Piazza Beaubourg, 4th (01.44.78.12.33/www
.centrepompidou.fr). M° Hôtel de Ville or Rambuteau.
Open 2-6pm Mon, Wed-Sun. **Admission** free.
Credit AmEx, V. **Map** p406 K6.
When Constantin Brancusi died in 1957 he left his
studio and its contents to the state, later rebuilt by
the Centre Pompidou. His fragile works in wood and
plaster, the endless columns and streamlined bird
forms, show how Brancusi revolutionised sculpture.

Centre Pompidou
(Musée National d'Art Moderne)

Rue St-Martin, 4th (01.44.78.12.33/www.centre
pompidou.fr). M° Hôtel de Ville or Rambuteau.
Open 11am-9pm (last entry 8pm) Mon, Wed, Fri-Sun
(until 11pm some exhibitions); 11am-11pm Thur.
Admission *Museum & exhibitions* €10; €8 18-25s;
free under-18s, 1st Sun of mth (museum only). PMP.
Credit AmEx, DC, MC, V. **Map** p406 K6.
The primary colours, exposed pipes and air ducts
make this one of the best-known sights in Paris. The
then-unknown Italo-British architectural duo of
Renzo Piano and Richard Rogers won the competition with their 'inside-out' boilerhouse approach,
which put air-conditioning, pipes, lifts and the escalators on the outside, leaving an adaptable space
within. The multi-disciplinary concept of modern art
museum (the most important in Europe), library,
exhibition and performance spaces and repertory
cinema was also revolutionary. When the centre
opened in 1977, its success exceeded all expectations. After a two-year revamp, the centre reopened
in 2000 with an enlarged museum, renewed performance spaces, vista-rich Georges restaurant and a
mission to get back to the stimulating interdisciplinary mix of old. Entrance to the forum is free (as is
the library, which has a separate entrance), but you
now have to pay to go up the escalators.

The Centre Pompidou (or 'Beaubourg') holds the
largest collection of modern art in Europe, rivalled
only in its breadth and quality by MOMA in New
York. Sample the contents of its vaults (50,000
works of art by 5,000 artists) on the website, as only
a fraction – about 600 works – can be seen for real
at any one time. There is a partial rehang each year.
For the main collection, buy tickets on the ground
floor and take the escalators to level four for post-
1960s art. Level five spans 1905 to 1960. There are
four temporary exhibition spaces on each of these
two levels (included in the ticket). Main temporary
exhibitions take place on the ground floor, in gallery
two on level six, in the south gallery, level one and
in the new Espace 315, devoted to the under-40s.

On level five, the historic section takes a chronological sweep through the history of modern art,
via Primitivism, Fauvism, Cubism, Dada and
Surrealism up to American Color-Field painting and
Abstract Expressionism. Masterful ensembles let
you see the span of Matisse's career on canvas and
in bronze, the variety of Picasso's invention, and the
development of cubic orphism by Sonia and Robert
Delaunay. Others on the hit list include Derain,

Braque, Duchamp, Picabia, Mondrian, Malevich,
Kandinsky, Dix, Ernst, Miró, Klee, Magritte, Rothko
and Bacon. Don't miss the reconstruction of a wall
of André Breton's studio, combining the tribal art,
folk art, flea-market finds and drawings by fellow
artists that the Surrealist artist and theorist had
amassed. The photography collection also has an
impressive roll call, including Brassaï, Kertész, Man
Ray, Cartier-Bresson and Doisneau.

Level four, post-'60s art, has been entirely rehung.
Thematic rooms concentrate on the career of one
artist; others focus on movements such as Anti-form
or *arte povera*. Recent acquisitions line the central
corridor, while at the far end you can find architecture and design. Video art and installations by the
likes of Mathieu Mercier and Dominique Gonzalez-
Foerster are in a frequently changing room devoted
to *nouvelle création*.

Shows for 2007 include 'Airs de Paris' (2 April-20
August), celebrating Beaubourg's 30th birthday and
revealing how design and architecture reflect modern urban life. The Galerie des Enfants hosts 'BD
Reporters' (until 23 April), a follow-up to an exhibition of works by Tintin creator Hergé, showing how
cartoonists present the world. *See also chapters*
Architecture, **Right Bank**, **Children** and **Film**.

Hôtel de Ville

29 rue de Rivoli, 4th (01.42.76.43.43/www.paris.fr).
M° Hôtel de Ville. **Open** 10am-7pm Mon-Sat. **Map**
p406 K6.
Rebuilt by Ballu after the Commune, the palatial,
multi-purpose Hôtel de Ville is both the heart of the
city administration and a place to entertain visiting
dignitaries. Free exhibitions are held in the Salon
d'Accueil (open 10am-6pm Mon-Fri); the rest of the
building, accessible only by weekly guided tours
(book in advance), features parquet floors, marble
statues, crystal chandeliers and painted ceilings.

Tour St-Jacques

Square de La-Tour-St-Jacques, 4th. M° Châtelet.
Map p406 J6.
Loved by the Surrealists, this solitary Flamboyant
Gothic belltower with its leering gargoyles is all that
remains of the St-Jacques-La-Boucherie church, built
for the powerful Butchers' Guild in 1508-22. The
statue of Blaise Pascal at the base commemorates
his experiments on atmospheric pressure, carried
out here in the 17th century. A weather station now
crowns the 52m (171ft) tower, not open to the public.

The Marais

The narrow streets of the Marais contain
aristocratic *hôtels particuliers*, art galleries,
boutiques and stylish cafés, with beautiful
carved doorways and early street signs carved
into the stone. The Marais, or 'marsh', started
life as a piece of swampy ground inhabited by
a few monasteries, sheep and market gardens.
This was one of the last parts of central Paris to

be built up. In the 16th century the elegant Hôtel Carnavalet and Hôtel Lamoignon saw the area's phenomenal rise as an aristocratic residential district; Henri IV began building **place des Vosges** in 1605. Nobles and royal officials followed, building smart townhouses where literary ladies such as Mme de Sévigné held court. The area fell from fashion a century later; many of the narrow streets remained unchanged as mansions were transformed into workshops, crafts studios, schools, tenements, and even the fire station on rue de Sévigné. Several can be visited as museums, others can be seen only on walking tours or on the **Journées du Patrimoine** (*see p273*). The Marais is a favourite spot for a Sunday stroll, as many of the shops are open – though if you come during the week you have more chance of wandering into some of the elegant courtyards.

Rue des Francs-Bourgeois, crammed with impressive mansions and original boutiques, runs like a backbone right through the Marais, becoming more aristocratic as it leaves the food shops of rue Rambuteau behind. Two of the most refined early 18th-century residences are Hôtel d'Albret (No.31), a venue for jazz concerts at the **Paris Quartier d'été** festival (*see p273*), and the palatial Hôtel de Soubise (No.60), the national archives. Begun in 1704 for the Prince and Princesse de Soubise, it boasts interiors by Boucher and Lemoine and currently hosts the **Musée de l'Histoire de France**, along with the neighbouring Hôtel de Rohan. There's also a surprising series of rose gardens. On one side

of its colonnaded Cour d'Honneur, architect Delamair incorporated the turreted, medieval gateway of the Hôtel de Clisson, visible on rue des Archives. Facing the Archives Nationaux, the Crédit Municipal (No.55) still acts as a sort of municipal pawnshop: people bring in goods for cash; items never reclaimed are sold off at auction. On the corner of rue Pavée is the austere Renaissance Hôtel Lamoignon, with a magisterial courtyard adorned with Corinthian pilasters. Built in 1585, it now contains the Bibliothèque Historique de la Ville de Paris (No.24, 01.44.59.29.40). Further up, the **Musée Carnavalet** runs across the Hôtel Carnavalet and the Hôtel le Peletier de St-Fargeau. The Hôtel Carnavalet set the pattern for many of the *hôtels* to follow, with its U-shaped plan behind an entrance courtyard; the façade reliefs of the four seasons are possibly by Jean Goujon.

At its eastern end, rue des Francs-Bourgeois leads into the beautiful brick-and-stone place des Vosges. At one corner is the **Maison de Victor Hugo**, where the writer lived from 1833 to 1848. An archway in the south-west corner leads to the **Hôtel de Sully**, accommodating the Patrimoine Photographique. Designed in 1624, the building belonged to Henri IV's minister, the Duc de Sully. Its two beautifully proportioned courtyards contain reliefs of the four seasons and a rare, surviving orangery.

Several other important museums are also found in sumptuous *hôtels*. The Hôtel Salé on rue de Thorigny, built in 1656, was nicknamed ('salty') after its owner, Fontenay, who collected

Le Marais. *See p108*.

the salt tax. Beautifully restored and extended to house the **Musée National Picasso**, it has an elegant courtyard adorned with sphinxes and a grand baroque stairwell carved with garlands, imperial busts and gambolling cupids. Nearby, the pretty Hôtel Donon, built in 1598, contains the **Musée Cognacq-Jay** and has remarkable 18th-century panelled interiors, while the Hôtel Guénégaud contains the **Musée de la Chasse et de la Nature** hunting museum.

The Marais has also long been a focus for the Jewish community. Jews were expelled from France in the Middle Ages, but when they were granted citizenship after the Revolution, the Marais became their point of arrival. Today's community is centred on rue des Rosiers, rue des Ecouffes and rue Pavée (where there's a synagogue designed by Guimard). Originally made up mainly of Ashkenazi Jews, who arrived after the pogroms in Eastern Europe at the end of the 19th century (many were later deported during World War II), the community expanded in the 1950s and '60s with a wave of Sephardic Jewish immigration after French withdrawal from North Africa. As a result, there are now many falafel shops alongside Central European Jewish bakers and delis, such as **Finkelsztajn** (*see p264*) and late-opening Jo Goldenberg (7 rue des Rosiers, 4th, 01.48.87.20.16).

The lower ends of rue des Archives and rue Vieille-du-Temple are the centre of café life – including **Petit Fer à Cheval** (*see p223*) and **La Chaise au Plafond** in neighbouring rue du Trésor (*see p222*) – and the hub of the gay scene. Bars such as the **Open Café** (*see p303*) draw gay crowds for the early-evening happy hour. In their midst, at 22-26 rue des Archives, the 15th-century Cloître des Billettes is the only surviving Gothic cloister in Paris.

Workaday rue du Temple is full of surprises. Near rue de Rivoli, **Le Latina** (*see p293*) specialises in Latin American films and holds tango balls in the room above. At No.41, an archway leads into the former Aigle d'Or coaching inn, now the **Café de la Gare** café-théâtre (*see p276*). Further north, at No.71, the grandiose Hôtel de St-Aignan, built in 1650, contains the **Musée d'Art et d'Histoire du Judaïsme**. The majestic courtyard with giant Corinthian pilasters, oval galleried staircase and traces of fresco in the café hint at just how splendid this must have been before it was converted into a town hall, workshops and a warren of apartments, prior to being rescued in the 1990s. The top end of rue du Temple and adjoining streets such as rue des Gravilliers are packed with costume jewellery, handbag and rag-trade wholesalers in what is the city's oldest Chinatown. The Quartier du Temple was once a fortified, semi-independent entity under

the Knights Templar, until the order grew so powerful it rivalled the monarchy and was suppressed in 1313. Their Tour du Temple, a monastery under the Knights Hospitalier de St-Jean, became a prison in the Revolution, and held the royal family in 1792. The church and keep have been replaced by square du Temple and the Carreau du Temple clothes market.

The north-west corner of the Marais hinges on the **Musée des Arts et Métiers**, a science museum with early flying machines displayed in the 12th-century chapel of the former priory of St-Martin-des-Champs, and the adjoining Conservatoire des Arts et Métiers. Across rue St-Martin on square Emile-Chautemps, the Théâtre de la Gaîté Lyrique is to be renovated as a cultural centre. Among the ancient buildings here, No.3 rue Volta, once considered the oldest house in Paris, is now thought to date from the early 17th century, in defiance of the then laws against half-timbered structures. A much older house is at 51 rue de Montmorency, built in 1407 by notorious alchemist Nicolas Flamel.

Despite the Marais' rise to fashion, the less gentrified streets around the northern stretch of rue Vieille-du-Temple towards place de la République are awash with designers on the rise and old craft workshops. Rue Charlot, housing an occasional contemporary art gallery at the passage de Retz at No.9 (01.48.04.37.99), is typical of the prevailing trend. At the top, the Marché des Enfants-Rouges (once an orphanage whose inhabitants were attired in red uniforms) is one of Paris' oldest markets, founded in 1615.

Hôtel de Sully

62 rue St-Antoine, 4th (01.42.74.47.75). M° St-Paul. **Open** noon-7pm Tue-Fri; 10am-7pm Sat, Sun. **Admission** €8; €4 concessions. **Credit** MC, V. **Map** p409 L7.
Along with the Jeu de Paume (*see p97*), the former Patrimoine Photographique forms part of the two-site home for the Centre National de la Photographie.

Maison de Victor Hugo

Hôtel de Rohan-Guéménée, 6 pl des Vosges, 4th (01.42.72.10.16/www.paris.fr/musees). M° Bastille or St-Paul. **Open** 10am-6pm Tue-Sun. **Admission** free. *Exhibitions* prices vary. **Credit** MC, V. **Map** p409 L6.
Victor Hugo lived here from 1833-48, and today the house is a museum devoted to the life and work of France's favourite son. On display are his first editions, nearly 500 drawings and, more bizarrely, the great man's home-made furniture.

Musée d'Art et d'Histoire du Judaïsme

Hôtel de St-Aignan, 71 rue du Temple, 3rd (01.53.01.86.60/www.mahj.org). M° Rambuteau. **Open** 11am-6pm Mon-Fri; 10am-6pm Sun. Closed Jewish hols. **Admission** €6.80; €4.50 18-26s; free under-18s. **Credit** *Shop* MC, V. **Map** p409 K6.

It is fitting that a museum of Judaism should be lodged in one of the grandest mansions of the Marais, the epicentre of local Jewish life. It sprung from the collection of a private association formed in 1948 to safeguard Jewish heritage after the Holocaust. Pick up a free audioguide in English to help you navigate through displays illustrating ceremonies, rites and learning, and showing how styles were adapted across the globe through examples of Jewish decorative arts. Photographic portraits of modern French Jews, each of whom tells his or her own story on the audio soundtrack, brings a contemporary edge. There are documents and paintings relating to the emancipation of French Jewry after the Revolution and the Dreyfus case, from Zola's *J'Accuse!* to anti-Semitic cartoons. Paintings by the early 20th-century avant-garde include works by El Lissitsky and Chagall. The Holocaust is marked by Boris Taslitzky's stark sketches from Buchenwald and Christian Boltanski's courtyard memorial to the Jews who lived in the building in 1939, 13 of whom died in the camps. **Photos** *p113*.

Musée des Arts et Métiers

60 rue Réaumur, 3rd (01.53.01.82.00/www.arts-et-metiers.net). M° Arts et Métiers. **Open** 10am-6pm Tue, Wed, Fri-Sun; 10am-9.30pm Thur. **Admission** €6.50; €4.50 students; free under-18s. PMP. **Credit** V. **Map** p402 K5.

After the monks of St-Martin-des-Champs lost their heads in the Revolution, Abbé Henri Grégoire kept his by thinking up a new use for the building – as a repository of technological marvels that could act as a 3D encyclopedia for investors and industrialists in the new republic. The collection has since expanded to fill three floors of a neighbouring modern building with glass cases of beautifully crafted scientific instruments, from astrolabes to steam engines, plus reconstructions of famous inventors' workshops. It's pretty dry and static, though, and not child-friendly. The exception is the restored church, the earliest example of Parisian Gothic, which removes invention from the realm of science and presents it as some sort of divinely inspired alchemy. Here, in soaring ecclesiastical surrounds, you'll find an original Foucault's Pendulum, set in motion at noon and 5pm daily, Blériot's biplane, a model of Bartholdi's Statue of Liberty and Alain Prost's Formula 1 Renault.

Musée Carnavalet

23 rue de Sévigné, 3rd (01.44.59.58.58/www.paris.fr/musees). M° St-Paul. **Open** 10am-6pm Tue-Sun. **Admission** free. *Exhibitions* €7; €5.50 over-60s; €3.50 14-26s; free under-13s. **Credit** *Shop* AmEx, MC, V. **Map** p409 L6.

Here, 140 chronological rooms depict the history of Paris, from pre-Roman Gaul to the 20th century. Built in 1548 and transformed by Mansart in 1660, this fine house became a museum in 1866, when Haussmann persuaded the city to preserve its beautiful interiors. Original 16th-century rooms house Renaissance collections, with portraits by Clouet and furniture and pictures relating to the Wars of

Religion. The first floor covers the period up to 1789, with furniture and paintings displayed in restored, period interiors; neighbouring Hôtel Le Peletier de St-Fargeau covers from 1789 onwards. Displays relating to 1789 detail its convoluted politics and bloodshed, with prints and memorabilia, including a chunk of the Bastille prison. There are items belonging to Napoleon, a cradle given by the city to Napoleon III – and Proust's cork-lined bedroom.

Musée de la Chasse et de la Nature

Hôtel Guénégaud, 60 rue des Archives, 3rd (01.53.01.92.40/www.chassenature.org). M° Rambuteau. **Open** hours and prices vary; call for details. **Map** p409 K5.

Currently closed, the museum is due to re-open in 2007. Housed on three floors of a 17th-century mansion, it's a store of ornate hunting weapons and studies by Alexandre-François Desportes, including his portrait of Louis XIV's hunting dogs.

Musée Cognacq-Jay

Hôtel Donon, 8 rue Elzévir, 3rd (01.40.27.07.21/www.paris.fr/musees). M° St-Paul. **Open** 10am-5.40pm Tue-Sun. **Admission** free. **Map** p409 L6.

This cosy museum houses the collection put together in the early 1900s by La Samaritaine founder Ernest Cognacq and his wife Marie-Louise Jay. They stuck mainly to 18th-century French works, focusing on rococo artists such as Watteau, Fragonard, Boucher, Greuze and pastellist Quentin de la Tour, though some English artists (Reynolds, Romney, Lawrence) and Dutch and Flemish names (an early Rembrandt, Ruysdael, Rubens), plus Canalettos and Guardis, have managed to slip in. Pictures are displayed in panelled rooms with furniture, porcelain, tapestries and sculpture of the same period.

Musée de l'Histoire de France

Hôtel de Soubise, 60 rue des Francs-Bourgeois, 3rd (01.40.27.60.96/www.archivesnationales.culture.gouv.fr/chan). M° Hôtel de Ville or Rambuteau. **Open** 10am-12.30pm, 2-5.30pm Mon, Wed-Fri; 2-5.30pm Sat, Sun. **Admission** €3; €2.30 18-25s; free under-18s. **Credit** V. **Map** p409 K6.

Generally housed in one of the grandest Marais mansions, the Hôtel de Rohan, this museum is currently undergoing renovation. In the meantime, documents and artefacts covering everything from the founding of the Sorbonne to an ordinance about umbrellas are displayed in the neighbouring Hôtel de Soubise. Its rococo interiors, decorated for the Prince and Princesse de Soubise in the 1730s, feature paintings by Boucher and van Loo.

Musée National Picasso

Hôtel Salé, 5 rue de Thorigny, 3rd (01.42.71.25.21/www.musee-picasso.fr). M° Chemin Vert or St-Paul. **Open** *Oct-Mar* 9.30am-5.30pm Mon, Wed-Sun. *Apr-Sept* 9.30am-6pm Mon, Wed-Sun. **Admission** *Mon-Sat* €6.50, *Sun* €4.50; free under-18s, 1st Sun of mth. PMP. *With exhibitions* prices vary. **Credit** *Shop* AmEx, MC, V. **Map** p409 L6.

Picasso's paintings, sculptures, collages, drawings and ceramics are shown off in style in this stately Marais mansion, complete with sweeping staircase. The collection, donated to the state by Picasso's family in lieu of inheritance tax, gives a panorama of his career from precocious early sketches to later stylistic whimsies, via delightful oddities such as a papier-mâché goat. Many of the 'greatest hits' hang in other state-owned Paris museums, but to get a feeling for Picasso's artistic development this is the best resource in the city. (Photography, one of his late conquests, is the only under-represented medium.) From a haunting, blue-period self-portrait and rough studies for the *Demoiselles d'Avignon,* the collection moves to Picasso's Cubist and classical phases, the surreal *Nude in an Armchair* and assorted portraits of his abundant lovers, in particular Marie-Thérèse and Dora Maar. A small covered sculpture garden displays pieces that sat around Picasso's studio until his death, and there is a pleasant summer café.

Place des Vosges

4th. M° St-Paul. **Map** p409 L6.

Paris' first planned square was commissioned in 1605 by Henri IV and inaugurated by his son Louis XIII in 1612. With harmonious red-brick-and-stone arcaded façades and steeply pitched slate roofs, it differs from the later pomp of the Bourbons. Laid out symmetrically with carriageways through the taller Pavillon de la Reine on the north side and Pavillon du Roi on the south, the other lots were sold off as concessions to royal officials and nobles (some façades are imitation brick). Originally called place Royale, its name dates from the Napoleonic Wars, when the Vosges was the first region of France to pay its war taxes. Mme de Sévigné, salon hostess and letter-writer, was born at No.1bis in 1626. At that time the garden hosted duels and trysts; now it attracts children from the nearby nursery school.

The St-Paul district

In 1559 Henri II was fatally wounded jousting on today's rue St-Antoine, marked by Pilon's marble *La Vierge de Douleur* in the **Eglise St-Paul-St-Louis**. South of rue St-Antoine is the sedate residential area of St-Paul, lined with dignified 17th- and 18th-century façades. The linked courtyards of Village St-Paul house antiques sellers (*see p266*). On rue des Jardins-St-Paul is the largest surviving section of the **fortified wall of Philippe-Auguste**. The infamous poisoner Marquise de Brinvilliers, who killed her father and brothers to inherit the family fortune, lived at Hôtel de Brinvilliers (12 rue Charles-V) in the 1630s.

By St-Paul métro station on the corner of rue François-Miron and rue de Fourcy is the Hôtel Hénault de Cantorbe, renovated and given a minimalist modern extension as the **Maison Européenne de la Photographie**. Down rue

Musée d'Art et d'Histoire du Judaïsme. *See p111.*

de Fourcy towards the river, across a medieval formal garden, you can see the rear façade of the Hôtel de Sens, a rare medieval mansion built as the Paris residence of the Archbishops of Sens in the 15th century, with a lovely array of turrets. It houses the **Bibliothèque Forney**, specialising in graphic design.

Near Pont Sully are square Henri-Galli, with a rebuilt piece of Bastille prison, and the **Pavillon de l'Arsenal**, built by a rich timber merchant to put on art shows, and home to displays about Parisian architecture.

Winding rue François-Miron leads you back towards the Hôtel de Ville. At 17 rue Geoffroy l'Asnier, the Mémorial du Martyr Juif Inconnu is being extended as part of the **Mémorial de la Shoah**, a museum, memorial and study centre devoted to the Holocaust that opened in 2005. As you pass No.26, note the Cité des Arts complex of artists' studios, and the ornate lion's head and giant shell motif on the doorway of the 17th-century Hôtel de Châlon-Luxembourg. At 11 and 13 rue François-Miron, two half-timbered houses probably date from the 14th century, although they were heavily rebuilt in the 1960s. Rue du Pont-Louis-Philippe contains jewellers, designer furniture and gift shops, while stepped rue des Barres boasts tearooms overlooking the spiky chevet of the **Eglise St-Gervais-St-Protais**.

Bibliothèque Forney
Hôtel de Sens, 1 rue du Figuier, 4th (01.42.78. 14.60). Mº Pont Marie. **Open** times vary. **Admission** free. **No credit cards**. **Map** p409 L7.
The Forney library specialises in exhibitions of applied and graphic arts. Although closed at the time of writing, it was due to re-open in April 2007.

Eglise St-Gervais-St-Protais
Place St-Gervais, 4th (01.48.87.32.02). Mº Hôtel de Ville. **Open** times vary. **Map** p409 K6.
Gothic at the rear and classical at the front, this church also has an impressive Flamboyant Gothic interior, most of which dates from the 16th century. The nave gives an impression of enormous height, with tall columns that soar up to the vault. There are plenty of fine funerary monuments, especially the baroque statue of Chancellor Le Tellier.

Eglise St-Paul-St-Louis
99 rue St-Antoine, 4th (01.42.72.30.32). Mº St-Paul. **Open** 9am-8pm daily. **Map** p409 L6.
This domed baroque Counter-Reformation church is modelled, like all Jesuit churches, on the Chiesa del Gesù in Rome. Completed in 1641, it features a single nave, side chapels and a three-storey hierarchical façade featuring statues of Saints Louis, Anne and Catherine – all replacements. The provider of confessors to the kings of France, the Eglise St-Paul-St-Louis was richly endowed until Revolutionary iconoclasts pinched its treasures, including the

hearts of Louis XIII and XIV. Afterwards, in 1802, it was converted back into a church, and today it houses Delacroix's *Christ in the Garden of Olives*.

Fortified wall of Philippe-Auguste
Rue des Jardins-St-Paul, 4th (www.philippe-auguste. com). Mº Pont Marie or St-Paul. **Map** p409 L7.
King Philippe-Auguste (1165-1223), the first great Parisian builder since the Romans, enclosed his city within a great wall. The largest surviving section, complete with towers, extends along rue des Jardins-St-Paul. Another chunk is at 3 rue Clovis (5th), and odd remnants of towers are dotted around the Marais, rue du Louvre and St-Germain-des-Prés.

Maison Européenne de la Photographie
5-7 rue de Fourcy, 4th (01.44.78.75.00/www.mep-fr.org). Mº St-Paul. **Open** 11am-7.30pm Wed-Sun. **Admission** €6; €3 students, 8-26s; free under-8s, all 5-7.30pm Wed. **Credit** MC, V. **Map** p409 L6.
Probably Paris' best photographic centre, housing retrospectives by Martin Parr and Don McCullin, along with work by emerging photographers. The building, an airy mansion with a modern extension, contains a huge permanent collection. The venue organises the biennial Mois de la Photo and the Art Outsiders festival of new media web art in September.

Le Mémorial de la Shoah
17 rue Geoffroy-l'Asnier, 4th (01.42.77.44.72/ www.memorialdelashoah.org). Mº St-Paul or Pont Marie. **Open** 10am-6pm Mon-Wed, Fri-Sun; 10am-10pm Thur. *Research centre* 10am-5.30pm Mon-Wed, Fri, Sun; 10am-7.30pm Thur. **Admission** free. **Map** p409 K6.
Airport-style security checks mean queues, but don't let that put you off. The Mémorial du Martyr Juif Inconnu is an impressively presented and moving memorial to the Holocaust. Enter via the Wall of Names, where limestone slabs are engraved with the first and last names of each of the 76,000 Jews deported from France from 1942 to 1944 with, as an inscription reminds the visitor, the say-so of the Vichy government. The excoriation continues in the basement-level permanent exhibition, which documents the plight of French and European Jews through photographs, texts, films and individual stories: 'The French,' reads one label (captioning is also given in English), 'were not particularly interested in the fate of French Jews at this point.' Expect to spend the remainder of your day in deep contemplation.

Musée de la Magie
11 rue St-Paul, 4th (01.42.72.13.26/www.museedela magie.com). Mº St-Paul. **Open** 2-7pm Wed, Sat, Sun (longer during school hols). **Admission** €7; €5 under-12s. **No credit cards**. **Map** p409 L7.
This interactive museum of magic is run in the spirit of Robert-Houdin, the 19th-century conjurer whose name was taken by Harry Houdini. The sleight of hand starts outside in the queue and gets craftier as you go through the exhibition. Conjuring tools are put into practice before your very eyes.

Pavillon de l'Arsenal

21 bd Morland, 4th (01.42.76.33.97/www.pavillon-arsenal.com). M° Sully Morland. **Open** 10.30am-6.30pm Tue-Sat; 11am-7pm Sun. **Admission** free. **Credit** *Shop* MC, V. **Map** p409 L7.

The setting is a fantastic 1880s gallery with an iron frame and glass roof; the subject is the built history of Paris; the result is disappointing. The ground floor houses a permanent exhibition on the city's development, but space and funds are lacking to the extent that exhibits are limited to a few story boards, maps and photos, and three city models inset in the floor (done far more impressively at the Musée d'Orsay). Upstairs you'll find temporary displays on local building projects, a library and a *vidéothèque*.

Bastille & eastern Paris

Mainly in the 11th and 12th arrondissements.

Place de la Bastille has been a potent symbol of popular revolt ever since the prison-storming that inaugurated the Revolution. While still a gathering point for demonstrations, and the setting for the Bastille Day ball every July (*see p273*), the area was transformed in the 1980s with the arrival of the **Opéra Bastille** (*see p311*), trendy cafés, restaurants and bars. The site of the prison itself is now a bank, while the gap left by the castle ramparts forms the present-day square, dominated by the massive, curved façade of the Opéra. Opened in 1989 on the bicentennial of Bastille Day, the venue remains controversial, criticised for its poor acoustics and construction. South of the square is the Port de l'Arsenal marina, while north of the square the canal continues underground, beneath the broad boulevard Richard-Lenoir, site of an outdoor market on Sunday mornings.

Rue du Fbg-St-Antoine has been the heart of the furniture-makers' district for centuries. Gaudy furniture showrooms still line the street, slowly being colonised by clothes shops and bars. Cobbled rue de Lappe typifies the shift, as the last remaining furniture workshops hold out against theme bars that teem with teens at weekends. Pockets of arty resistance remain on rue de Charonne with the hip Pause Café (No.41, 11th, 01.48.06.80.33) and its busy terrace, bistro Chez Paul (No.13, 11th, 01.47.00.34.57) and dealers in colourful 1960s furniture. Rues des Taillandiers and Keller are a focus for record stores, streetwear shops and fashion designers.

Narrow street frontages hide cobbled alleys, lined with craftsmen's workshops or quirky bistros dating from the 18th century. Note the cours de l'Ours, du Cheval Blanc, du Bel Air (and hidden garden) and de la Maison Brûlée, the passage du Chantier on Fbg-St-Antoine, the rustic-looking passage de l'Etoile d'Or and the passage de l'Homme, with wooden shopfronts on rue de Charonne. This area was originally located outside the city walls on the lands of the Convent of St-Antoine (parts of which survive as the Hôpital St-Antoine). In the Middle Ages skilled furnituremakers not belonging to the city's restrictive guilds began a tradition of free thinking, a development that made this an incendiary area during the 1789 Revolution.

Further down rue du Fbg-St-Antoine is place d'Aligre, home to a rowdy, cheap produce market, a more sedate covered market and the only flea market within the city walls, where a handful of *brocanteurs* sell junk and old books. The road ends in the major intersection of place de la Nation, another grand square. Originally it was called place du Trône, after a throne that was placed here when Louis XIV and his bride Marie-Thérèse entered the city in 1660. After the Revolution, between 13 June and 28 July 1799, thousands were guillotined here, their bodies carted to the nearby **Picpus Cemetery**. The square still has two of Ledoux's toll houses and tall Doric columns from the 1787 Mur des Fermiers-Généraux. In the centre stands Jules Dalou's sculpture *Le Triomphe de la République*, erected for the centenary of the Revolution in 1889. East of place de la Nation, broad cours de Vincennes has a market on Wednesday and Saturday mornings and kerb-crawlers by night.

North of place de la Bastille, boulevard Beaumarchais divides Bastille from the Marais. East of place Voltaire, on rue de la Roquette, which heads east towards the **Ménilmontant** area (*see p136*) and **Père-Lachaise** cemetary (*see p137*), a small park and playground marks the site of the prison de la Roquette, where a plaque remembers the 4,000 Resistance members imprisoned here in World War II.

La Maison Rouge – Fondation Antoine de Galbert

10 bd de la Bastille, 12th (01.40.01.08.81/ www.lamaisonrouge.org). M° Quai de la Rapée. **Open** 11am-7pm Wed-Sun. **Admission** €6.50; €4.50 students, 13-25s; free under-13s. **Credit** MC, V. **Map** p406 M7.

Founded by collector Antoine de Galberg, and set in a former printworks, the Red House is an independently run space that alternates monographic shows of contemporary artists with exhibitions giving an insight into different private art collections (such as Arnulf Rainer's collection of Art Brut). There are also occasional projects commissioned for the patio. *See also p295.*

Place de la Bastille

4th/11th/12th. M° Bastille. Map p407 M7.

Nothing remains of the prison that, on 14 July 1789, was stormed by revolutionary forces. Though only seven prisoners remained, the event provided the rebels with arms and gave the insurrection momentum. The prison was quickly torn down, its stones

Sightseeing

used to build Pont de la Concorde. Parts of the foundations can be seen in the métro; some of the reconstructed tower stands at sq Henri-Galli, near Pont de Sully (4th). The Colonne de Juillet, topped by a gilded *génie* of Liberty, is a monument to Parisians who fell in the revolutions of July 1830 and 1848.

Bercy & Daumesnil

The **Viaduc des Arts** is a former railway viaduct along av Daumesnil; its glass-fronted arches showcase a row of craft boutiques and workshops. Above sprout the blooms and bamboo of the **Promenade Plantée**, which continues through the Jardin de Reuilly and east to the **Bois de Vincennes**.

Eglise du St-Esprit is a copy of Istanbul's Hagia Sofia, while the nearby **Cimetière de Picpus** contains the graves of many of the Terror's victims, as well as American War of Independence hero General La Fayette. Just before the Périphérique, the **Palais de la Porte Dorée** (*see p283*) was built in 1931 for the Exposition Coloniale. It features striking, if politically incorrect, reliefs on the façade and two beautiful art deco offices designed by Ruhlmann. Originally the Musée des Colonies, then the Musée des Arts d'Afrique et d'Océanie (its collections now absorbed by the Musée du Quai Branly, *see p158*), it is currently used for design exhibitions – but still has an aquarium complete with crocodiles in the basement.

As recently as the 1980s, wine was unloaded off barges at Bercy, but this stretch of the Seine has now been redeveloped with the vast Ministère de l'Economie et du Budget and, to the west, the events venue **Palais Omnisports de Paris-Bercy** (*see p313* and *p330*). To the east is the Bercy Expo exhibition and trade centre. In between lie the modern **Parc de Bercy** and the former American Center, built in the 1990s by Frank Gehry, before his Bilbao Guggenheim. It has since reopened as the **Cinémathèque Française** (*see p291*). At the eastern edge of the park is **Bercy Village**, where stone wine warehouses have been restored and opened as shops and cafés along a cobbled street. The result is lively, if somewhat antiseptic; typical is mainstream **Club Med World** (*see p328*). Another conversion is the Pavillons de Bercy, with the **Musée des Arts Forains**, a collection of fairground rides and carnival salons.

Bois de Vincennes

12th. M° Porte Dorée or Château de Vincennes.
This is Paris' biggest park, created, like the Bois de Boulogne in the west, when former royal hunting forest was landscaped by Alphand for Baron Haussmann. There are boating lakes, a Buddhist temple, a racetrack, restaurants, a baseball field (*see p332*) and a small farm. The park also contains the city's main zoo (*see p283*), now largely closed because of lack of maintenance, though the rugged fake mountains look impressive against the skyline,

Palais de la Porte Dorée. *See p117.*

concrete. The **Musée du Vin** is of interest if
only for its setting in the vaulted cellars of the
wine-producing Abbaye de Minimes, destroyed
in the Revolution. Rue de Passy, formerly the
village high street, and parallel rue de
l'Assomption are the focus of local life, with
fashion shops and *traiteurs*, the revamped
department store Franck et Fils (80 rue de
Passy, 16th, 01.42.15.00.37) and an upmarket
covered market. The former Passy station is
now La Gare restaurant (19 chaussée de la
Muette, 16th, 01.42.15.15.31). Ladies who shop
stop by the lovely art deco La Rotonde café
(12 chaussée de la Muette, 16th, 01.45.24.45.45)
or stock up on cakes at Japanese *pâtisserie*
Yamakasi (6 chaussée de la Muette), while a
curiosity are three wooden dachas on Villa
Beauséjour, built by Russian craftsmen for the
1867 Exposition Universelle and rebuilt here.

West of the former high-society pleasure
gardens of the Jardin du Ranelagh you'll find
the **Musée Marmottan**, with its superb
collection of Monet's late water-lily canvases,
other Impressionists and Empire furniture.

Next to the Pont de Grenelle stands the
circular **Maison de Radio-France**, the giant
home of state broadcasting. You can attend
concerts (*see p310*) or take a tour around its
endless corridors; employees nickname the
place 'Alphaville', after the Jean-Luc Godard
film. From here, in more upmarket Auteuil, you
can head up rue Fontaine, the best place to find
art nouveau architecture by Hector Guimard, of
métro entrance fame. Despite extravagant iron

balconies, **Castel Béranger** at No.14 was
originally low-rent lodgings; Guimard designed
outside and in, right down to the wallpaper and
stoves. He also designed the less ambitious
Nos.19 and 21, and tiny Café Antoine at No.17.
The long neglected Hôtel Mezzara at No.60 is
sometimes open for exhibitions. Pay homage at
No.96, where Marcel Proust was born. Guimard
lived in the house he built at 122 avenue Mozart.

Nearby, around the métro station Jasmin,
is Le Corbusier territory. The **Fondation Le
Corbusier** occupies two of his avant-garde
houses in square du Dr-Blanche. A little further
up rue du Dr-Blanche, rue Mallet-Stevens is
almost entirely made up of refined houses by
Robert Mallet-Stevens, while sculptor Henri
Bouchard himself commissioned the studio and
house that is now the dusty **Atelier-Musée
Henri Bouchard**. Much of the rest of Auteuil
is private territory, with exclusive streets of
residences off rue Chardon-Lagache, although
you can still find villagey parts around the
Eglise d'Auteuil; the studio of 19th-century
sculptor Jean-Baptiste Carpeaux also remains,
looking rather lost, at 39 boulevard Exelmans.
The top storey was later added by Guimard.

West of the 16th, across the Périphérique,
sprawls the **Bois de Boulogne**, a royal
hunting-reserve-turned-park that includes a
boating lake and cycle paths. At porte d'Auteuil
are the romantic **Serres d'Auteuil** and sports
venues the **Parc des Princes**, home of
flagship football club **Paris St-Germain**
(for both, *see p330*), and **Roland Garros**

(see p330), host of the French Tennis Open. Another attraction will open in 2009: the Fondation Louis-Vuitton, to be housed in a Frank Gehry-designed glass building.

Atelier-Musée Henri Bouchard
25 rue de l'Yvette, 16th (01.46.47.63.46/ www.musee-bouchard.com). M° Jasmin. **Open** 2-7pm Wed, Sat. Closed last 2wks Mar, June, Sept & Dec. **Admission** €4; €2.50 students under-26; free under-6s. **No credit cards.**
Sculptor Henri Bouchard had this house and studio built in 1924. Tended by his son, his dusty workroom, crammed with sculptures, sketchbooks and tools, gives an idea of the official art of his day. He began with Realist-style peasants and maidens, but around 1907 adopted a pared-down, linear style, as seen in his reliefs for the Eglise St-Jean-de-Chaillot and the monumental *Apollo* at the Palais de Chaillot.

Bois de Boulogne
16th. M° Porte Dauphine or Les Sablons.
Covering 865 hectares, the Bois was once the Forêt de Rouvray hunting grounds. It was landscaped in the 1860s, when romantic artificial grottoes and waterfalls were created around the Lac Inférieur. The Jardin de Bagatelle (route de Sèvres à Neuilly, 16th, 01.40.67.97.00) is famous for its roses, daffodils and water lilies and contains an orangery that rings to the sound of tinkling Chopin in summer. The Jardin d'Acclimatation (*see p283*) is a children's amusement park, complete with a miniature train, farm, rollercoaster and boat rides. The Bois also boasts two racecourses (Longchamp and Auteuil; *see pp330-332*), sports clubs and stables, and restaurants, including Le Pré Catelan (route de Suresnes, 16th, 01.44.14.41.14).
Today there are plans to reduce the traffic and replant some of the scrubby woodland. The opening of the Fondation Louis-Vuitton in 2009 should also change the character of the area. For the time being, it attracts picnickers and dog walkers, with boats rented on the lake and cycle hire nearby. By night the Bois is transformed into a parade ground for transsexuals and swingers of every stripe.

Castel Béranger
14 rue La Fontaine, 16th. M° Jasmin. Closed to the general public.
Guimard's masterpiece of 1895-8 epitomises art nouveau in Paris. From outside you can see his love of brick and wrought iron, asymmetry and renunciation of harsh angles not found in nature. Green seahorses climb the façade, and the faces on the balconies are thought to be self-portraits, inspired by Japanese figures, to ward off evil spirits.

Fondation Le Corbusier
Villa La Roche, 8-10 square du Dr-Blanche, 16th (01.42.88.41.53/www.fondationlecorbusier.fr). M° Jasmin. **Open** 1.30-6pm Mon; 10am-12.30pm, 1.30-6pm Tue-Thur; 10am-12.30pm, 1.30-5pm Fri; 10am-5pm Sat. Closed Aug. **Admission** €3-€4; free under-12s. **No credit cards.**
This house, designed by Le Corbusier in 1923 for a Swiss art collector, shows the visionary architect's ideas in practice, with its stilts, strip windows, roof terraces and balconies, built-in furniture and an unsuspected use of colour inside: sludge green, blue and pinky beige. A sculptural cylindrical staircase and split volumes create a variety of geometrical vistas; inside is decked out with Le Corbusier's own neo-Cubist paintings and furniture, along with pieces by Perriand. Adjoining Villa Jeanneret houses the foundation's library. **Photos** *p124 & p125.*

Le Jardin des Serres d'Auteuil
3 av de la Porte d'Auteuil, 16th (01.40.71.75.23). M° Porte d'Auteuil. **Open** *Winter* 10am-5pm daily. *Summer* 10am-6pm daily. **Admission** free.
These romantic glasshouses were opened in 1895 to cultivate plants for Parisian parks and public spaces. Today there are seasonal displays of orchids and begonias. Look out for the steamy tropical pavilion with palms, birds and Japanese ornamental carp.

Maison de Balzac
47 rue Raynouard, 16th (01.55.74.41.80/www. paris.fr/musees). M° Passy. **Open** 10am-6pm Tue-Sun. **Admission** free. **Credit** MC, V. **Map** p404 B6.
Honoré de Balzac rented this apartment in 1840 to escape his creditors, and quickly established a password to sift friends from bailiffs. Converted into a museum, the collection of mementos is spread over several floors. Although the displays are rather dry, the garden gives an idea of how chic the villas here were when Passy was a stylish 19th-century spa. Memorabilia includes first editions and letters, plus portraits of friends and the novelist's mistress Mme Hanska, with whom he corresponded for years before they married. Along with a 'family tree' of his characters that extends across several walls, you can see Balzac's desk and the monogrammed coffee pot that fuelled all-night work on his epic *Comédie Humaine.* From late 2007, Paul Jouve's illustrations for *Une Passion dans le Desért* will be on display.

Musée Marmottan – Claude Monet
2 rue Louis-Boilly, 16th (01.44.96.50.33/www. marmottan.com). M° La Muette. **Open** 10am-6pm Tue-Sun (last entry 5.30pm). **Admission** €8; €4.50 8-25s; free under-8s. **Credit** MC, V.
Originally a museum of the Empire period left to the state by collector Paul Marmottan, this old hunting pavilion has become a famed holder of Impressionist art thanks to two bequests: the first by the daughter of the doctor of Manet, Monet, Pissarro, Sisley and Renoir; the second by Monet's son Michel. Its Monet collection, the largest in the world, numbers 165 works – including the seminal *Impression Soleil Levant* – plus sketchbooks, palette and photos. A special circular room was created for the breathtaking late water lily canvases; upstairs are works by Renoir, Manet, Gauguin, Caillebotte and Berthe Morisot, 15th-century primitives, the Wildenstein collection of medieval manuscripts, a Sèvres clock and a collection of First Empire furniture.

Sacré-Coeur. See p131.

Musée de Radio-France

Maison de Radio France, 116 av du Président-Kennedy, 16th (01.56.40.15.16/01.56.40.21.80/ www.tourisme.fr/radio-france). M° Ranelagh or Passy/RER Kennedy Radio France. **Open** *Guided tours 10.30-11am, 2.30pm, 4pm Mon-Fri.* **Admission** €5; €3 concessions. **No credit cards. Map** p404 A7.
Audio-visual history is presented with an emphasis on French pioneers such as Edouard Branly and Charles Cros, including documentary evidence of the first radio message transmitted between the Eiffel Tower and the Panthéon. Look out also for the London broadcast of the Free French, carried out in delightfully obscure coded messages.

Musée du Vin

Rue des Eaux, 16th (01.45.25.63.26/www.musee duvinparis.com). M° Passy. **Open** *10am-6pm Tue-Sun.* **Admission** (with guidebook and glass of wine) €8.50; €7 over-60s; €5.70 students; free under-14s, diners in the restaurant. **Credit** *Shop, restaurant* AmEx, DC, MC, V. **Map** p404 B6.
Here the Confrères Bacchiques defend French wines from imports and advertising laws. In the cellars of an old wine-producing monastery are displays on the history of viticulture, with waxwork peasants, old tools, bottles and corkscrews. Visits finish with a wine tasting and, a paid extra, a meal.

Montmartre & Pigalle

In the 9th and 18th arrondissements.
The highest point in Paris, Montmartre resembles some perched southern hill village, with its tight-packed houses spiralling round the mound below the sugary-white oversized dome of **Sacré-Coeur**. Despite the onslaught of tourists, it is surprisingly easy to leave them all behind and to fall under the spell of the most unabashedly romantic district of Paris. Climb and descend quiet stairways, peer into little alleys, ivy-covered houses and deserted squares, and explore streets like rue des Abbesses, rue des Trois-Frères and rue des Martyrs, with their cafés, quirky boutiques and young, arty community.

For centuries, Montmartre was a tranquil, windmill-packed village. When Haussmann sliced through the city centre, working-class families started to move out and peasant migrants poured into an industrialising Paris from across France. Montmartre swelled. The hill was absorbed into the city of Paris in 1860, but remained proudly independent. Its key role in the Commune in 1871, fending off government troops, is marked by a plaque on rue du Chevalier-de-la-Barre.

Artists moved into the area from the 1880s. Renoir found subject matter in the cafés and *guinguettes*. Toulouse-Lautrec enthusiastically patronised the local bars and immortalised its cabarets in his famous posters; later it was

Musée de Montmartre. See p131.

Sightseeing

frequented by Picasso and artists of the Ecole de Paris, Utrillo and Modigliani. *See p128* **Artists' Paris 1 Montmartre**.

You can start a wander from Abbesses métro station, one of only two in Paris (along with porte Dauphine) to retain its original art nouveau metal-and-glass awning designed by Hector Guimard. Across place des Abbesses is art nouveau St-Jean-de-Montmartre church, a pioneering reinforced concrete structure studded with turquoise mosaics around the door. Along rue des Abbesses and adjoining rue Lepic, which winds its way up the hill, are food shops, wine merchants and cafés, including the ever-popular **Le Sancerre** (*see p222*), and offbeat boutiques. The famous **Studio 28** cinema (*see p293*), opened in 1928 and still going strong, is where Luis Buñuel's controversial Surrealist classic *L'Age d'Or* had its riotous première in 1930.

In the other direction from Abbesses, at 11 rue Yvonne-Le-Tac, is the Chapelle du Martyr where, according to legend, St Denis picked up his head after his execution in the third century (hence the name Montmartre – martyr's mount). Rue Orsel, with a typical local cluster of retro design, ethnic and second-hand clothes shops, leads to place Charles-Dullin, where a cluster of cafés overlook the respected Théâtre de l'Atelier (1 pl Charles-Dullin, 18th, 01.46.06.49.24).

Up the hill, the cafés of rue des Trois-Frères are a popular spot for an evening drink. The street leads into sloping place Emile-Goudeau, whose staircases, wrought-iron streetlights and

Artists' Paris 1 Montmartre

Follow in the footsteps of the artistic greats with a short but strenuous walk on the Butte Montmartre. Be prepared for a steep climb, with numerous cobbles and stairs, and don't tackle the walk with a pushchair or in heels.

Start at Mº Pigalle (❶). Though it competes with the neon of the Folies Pigalle and the Sexodrome, the square's elegant fountain recalls the era when **place Pigalle** hosted a market of artists' models. Monet began his love affair with the model who would become his wife at No.1 (now a restaurant, Léon de Bruxelles, housed in a newer building), and the Café de la Nouvelle Athènes, the scene of Degas' *L'Absinthe*, was between rue Frochet and rue Pigalle. Place Pigalle was effectively the crossroads between Impressionism, based down in the 9th, and the radical art movements that would follow, up on the Butte.

Head north up cobbled rue André-Antoine, just to the left of place Pigalle, noting the recently-added anti-Sarkozy mosaic on the right wall. Follow the road as it kinks to the left then right, and take the steps up to place des Abbesses. Go straight up through the archway of passage des Abbesses, which has a window on to the little square that features the graffiti-esque 'Mur des je t'aime' – the 'Wall of I Love Yous'. More steps take you to rue des Trois-Frères, and the grocers featured in the film *Amélie*. It's upwards, ever upwards along rue Androïet, with its vertiginous layer upon layer of former artists' studios.

Heading left up rue Berthe you'll reach the lovely **place Emile-Godeau** (❷), shaded by 16 chestnut trees and with a working Wallace fountain for refreshment. A shop window next to the Timhotel has a display on the Bâteau Lavoir, the piano-factory-turned-artist's-studios where Picasso, Juan Gris, Modigliani and the poet Apollinaire worked in acute squalor. 'None of us were truly happy except there,' said Picasso after he moved into more bourgeois lodgings. The building burned down in 1970 and only the façade remains, though turning left into rue d'Orchampt reveals that artists' studios have been recreated here. Curving right and ever upwards you emerge on rue Lepic, opposite the **Moulin de la Galette** (❸). This is the site of the *guinguette* painted by Renoir; its delightful garden with the wooden windmill now houses a restaurant.

Continue up rue Girardon to place Marcel-Aymé, where a modern scupture evokes the writer's 'man who walked through walls'. Turning right, rue Norvins takes you past what looks like a country lane (where the truly rich own houses with car ports), before you reach the edge of the tourist madness that centres on place du Tertre. Avoid this by going left, up then down rue des Saules, where you can turn right at the Maison Rose for the **Musée de Montmartre** (*see p131*), or drop down the hill to the **Lapin Agile** cabaret (❹ *see p131*) made famous by Picasso. Turn right to walk past the lovely Montmartre vineyard and a secret wild garden. Continue on rue St-Vincent till you reach Parc de la Turlure, which you can cut through before skirting round the Sacré-Coeur to reach its forecourt – and the welcome relief of the funicular and the cluster of cafés around Abbesses métro below.

old houses are particularly evocative of days gone by. The Bâteau Lavoir, a piano factory that stood at No.13, witnessed the birth of Cubism. Divided into a warren of studios in the 1890s for impoverished artists of the day, it was here that Picasso painted *Les Demoiselles d'Avignon* in 1906-7, when he, Braque and Juan Gris all happened to be residents. The building burned down in 1970, but has since been reconstructed. On rue Lepic, which winds up the hill from rue des Abbesses, are the village's two remaining windmills: the Moulin du Radet, which was moved here in the 17th century from its hillock in rue des Moulins near the Palais-Royal; and the Moulin de la Galette, site of the celebrated dancehall famously depicted by Renoir (now in the Musée d'Orsay; *see p157*) and today a smart restaurant. Vincent van Gogh and his beloved brother Theo resided at No.54 from 1886 to 1888.

On tourist-swamped place du Tertre at the top of the hill, portrait painters compete to sketch you or flog lurid sunset views of Paris; nearby Espace Dali (11 rue Poulbot, 18th, 01.42.64.40.10) offers a slightly more illustrious alternative. Round here, or so legend has it, the word 'bistro' was born in the early 1800s, when Russian soldiers shouted '*Bistro*!' ('Quickly!') to be served. Just off the square is the oldest church in the district, St-Pierre-de-Montmartre, whose columns have grown bent with age. Founded by Louis VI in 1133, it is an example of early Gothic, in contrast to its extravagant neighbour, the basilica of Sacré-Coeur.

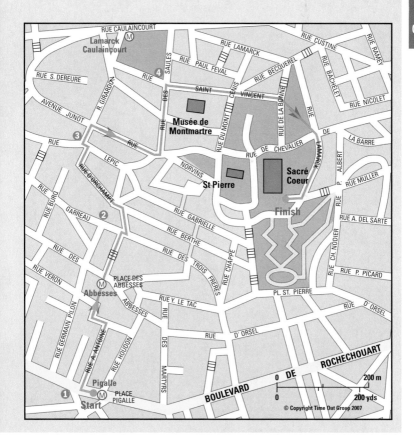

La Goutte d'Or. *See p133.*

For all its kitsch and swarms of tourists, though, Sacré-Coeur is well worth the visit for its sheer 19th-century excess. Rather than the main steps, take the staircase down rue Maurice-Utrillo to pause on a café terrace on the small square at the top of rue Muller, or wander down through the adjoining park to the Halle St-Pierre. The old covered market is now used for shows of naïve art, but the surrounding square and streets, known as the Marché St-Pierre, are packed with fabric shops and are a great source of discounted bin ends.

On the north side of place du Tertre in rue Cortot is the quiet 17th-century manor that houses the **Musée de Montmartre**, dedicated to the neighbourhood and its former famous inhabitants. Dufy, Renoir and Utrillo all used to have studios in the entrance pavilion. Nearby in rue des Saules is the Montmartre vineyard, planted by local artist Poulbot in 1933 in commemoration of the vines that once covered the area. The grape-picking here every autumn is a local ritual, celebrated with great pomp.

Further down the hill, amid rustic, shuttered houses, is the **Au Lapin Agile** cabaret (*see p276*). This old meeting point for local artists got its name from André Gill, who painted the inn sign of a rabbit (lapin A. Gill). Singers still churn out nostalgia here today.

A series of pretty squares leads to rue Caulaincourt, crossing the ravine of the oddly romantic **Cimetière de Montmartre** (enter on avenue Rachel, reached by staircase from rue Caulaincourt or place de Clichy). Winding down the back of the hill, avenue Junot is lined with exclusive residences, such as the avant-garde house built by Adolf Loos for Dadaist poet Tristan Tzara at No.15, exemplifying his Modernist maxim: 'Ornament is crime.'

Cimetière de Montmartre

20 av Rachel, access by stairs from rue Caulaincourt, 18th (01.53.42.36.30). M° Blanche or Place de Clichy. **Open** *6 Nov-15 Mar* 8am-5.30pm Mon-Fri; 8.30am-5.30pm Sat; 9am-5.30pm Sun & public hols. *16 Mar-5 Nov* 8am-6pm Mon-Fri; 8.30am-6pm Sat; 9am-6pm Sun & public hols. **Map** p403 G1.
Truffaut, Nijinsky, Berlioz, Degas, Offenbach, German poet Heine and Surrealist painter Victor Brauner are all buried here. So too are La Goulue, the first great cancan star and model for Toulouse-Lautrec, celebrated local beauty Mme Récamier, and the consumptive heroine Alphonsine Plessis, inspiration for Dumas' *La Dame aux Camélias* and Verdi's *La Traviata*. Flowers are still left for pop diva and gay icon Dalida, who lived on nearby rue d'Orchampt.

Musée d'Art Halle St-Pierre

2 rue Ronsard, 18th (01.42.58.72.89/www.halle saintpierre.org). M° Anvers. **Open** 10am-6pm daily. Closed Aug. **Admission** €7; €5.50 students, 4-26s; free under-4s. **Credit** *Shop* MC, V. **Map** p402 J2.

The former covered market in the shadow of Sacré-Coeur specialises in *art brut, art outsider* and *art singulier* from its own and other collections. Shows for 2007 include a retrospective on local artist and writer Unica Zürn, who died in 1974 when she threw herself off her balcony.

Musée de Montmartre

12 rue Cortot, 18th (01.46.06.61.11/www.musee demontmartre.fr). M° Lamarck Caulaincourt or Abbesses. **Open** 11am-6pm Wed-Sun. **Admission** €7; €5.50 students, over-60s; free under-10s. **Credit** *Shop* MC, V. **Map** p402 H1.
At the back of a garden, this 17th-century manor shows the history of the historic hilltop, with rooms devoted to composer Gustave Charpentier and a tribute to the Lapin Agile cabaret, with original Toulouse-Lautrec posters. There are paintings by Suzanne Valadon, who had a studio above the entrance pavilion, as did Renoir, Raoul Dufy and Valadon's son Maurice Utrillo. **Photo** *p127*.

Sacré-Coeur

35 rue du Chevalier-de-la-Barre, 18th (01.53.41. 89.00/www.sacre-coeur-montmartre.com). M° Abbesses or Anvers. **Open** *Basilica* 6am-10.30pm daily. *Crypt & dome Winter* 10am-5.45pm daily. *Summer* 9am-6.45pm daily. **Admission** free. *Crypt & dome* €5. **Credit** MC, V. **Map** p402 J1.
Work on this enormous mock Romano-Byzantine edifice began in 1877. It was commissioned after the nation's defeat by Prussia in 1870, voted for by the Assemblée Nationale and built from public subscription. Finally completed in 1914, it was consecrated in 1919 – by which time a jumble of architects had succeeded Paul Abadie, winner of the original competition. The interior boasts lavish mosaics, and there's a fine view from the dome. **Photo** *p127*.

Pigalle

Pigalle is the sleaze centre of Paris. Despite a recent police blitz to counteract tourist rip-offs and rough-ups, passers-by may still be hassled by barkers and hawkers trying to muscle them in to some peep show or other.

In the 1890s Toulouse-Lautrec's posters of Jane Avril at the Divan Japonais, Le Chat Noir, the Moulin Rouge, and of *chansonnier* Aristide Bruant immortalised the area's cabarets, and were a landmark in both art and the art of advertising. At the end of the 19th century, of the 58 buildings on rue des Martyrs, 25 were cabarets (a few, such as the drag shows Michou and Madame Arthur, remain today); others were *maisons closes*. But it's still a happening street: Le Divan Japonais is now **Le Divan du Monde** (*see p315*), a club and music venue; a hip crowd packs into **La Fourmi** (*see p222*) opposite, and up the hill there's a cluster of *atelier*-boutiques where designers have set up their sewing machines at the back of the shop.

Along the boulevard, behind its bright red windmill, the **Moulin Rouge** (*see p276*), once the image of naughty 1890s Paris, is now a cheesy tourist draw. Its befeathered dancers still cancan and cavort across the stage, but are no substitute for La Goulue and Joseph Pujol – *le pétomane* who could pass wind melodically. In stark contrast is the Cité Véron next door, a cobbled alley with curlicue iron entrance sign, a small theatre and cottagey buildings, among them 6bis where writer and jazz musician Boris Vian lived between 1953 and 1958. The famous **Elysée Montmartre** belle époque music hall today programmes an array of concerts (*see p315*) and club nights, but the **Folies Pigalle** (*see p324*) nightspot retains undeniable Pigalle flavour with its after-parties and drag queens.

Musée de l'Erotisme

72 bd de Clichy, 18th (01.42.58.28.73/www.musee-erotisme.com). M° Blanche. **Open** 10am-2am daily. **Admission** €8; €6 students. **Credit** MC, V. **Map** p401 H2.

Seven floors of erotic art and artefacts amassed by collectors Alain Plumey and Joseph Khalif. The first three run from first-century Peruvian phallic pottery through Etruscan fertility symbols to Yoni sculptures from Nepal; the fourth gives a history of Paris brothels; and the recently refurbished top floors host exhibitions of modern erotic art. In the basement you'll find titillations such as a vagina dinner plate.

La Nouvelle Athènes

Just south of Pigalle and east of rue Blanche lies this mysterious and often overlooked quarter, dubbed the New Athens when it was colonised by a wave of artists, writers and composers in the early 19th century. Long-forgotten actresses and *demi-mondaines* had mansions built here; some are set in tiny rue de la Tour-des-Dames, which refers to one of the many windmills owned by Couvent des Abbesses. To glimpse more of these miniature palaces, wander through the adjoining streets and passageways, such as rue St-Lazare (the painter Paul Delaroche lived at No.58) and rue de La Rochefoucauld.

Just off rue Taitbout stands square d'Orléans, a remarkable housing estate built in 1829 by the English architect Edward Cresy. These flats and studios attracted the glitterati of the day, including George Sand and her lover Chopin. In the house built for Dutch painter Ary Scheffer in nearby rue Chaptal, the **Musée de la Vie Romantique** displays the writer's mementos.

The **Musée Gustave Moreau** on rue de La Rochefoucauld is reason alone to visit, featuring the artist's cramped apartment and magnificent studio. Fragments of bohemia can still be gleaned in the area, although the Café La Roche,

where Moreau would meet Degas for drinks and rows, has been downsized to La Joconde (57 rue Notre-Dame-de-Lorette, 9th, 01.48.74.10.38). The area is steeped in history: Degas painted most of his memorable ballet scenes in rue Frochot, while Renoir hired his first proper studio at 35 rue St-Georges. A few streets away in Cité Pigalle, a collection of studios, is van Gogh's last Paris house (No.5), from where he moved to Auvers-sur-Oise. There is a plaque here, but nothing marks the building in rue Pigalle where Toulouse-Lautrec sat and slowly drank himself to an early grave.

The area around the neo-classical Eglise Notre-Dame-de-Lorette, built in the form of a Greek temple, was built up in Louis-Philippe's reign and was famous for its courtesans or *lorettes*, elegant ladies named after their haunt of rue Notre-Dame-de-Lorette. In 1848, Gauguin was born at No.56; from 1844 to 1857, Delacroix had a studio at No.58. The latter then moved to place de Furstemberg in the 6th (now **Musée Delacroix**). Rue St-Lazare still contains some delightfully old-fashioned shops and bistros, including perfumier **Détaille 1905** (*see p238*), and bistro **Chez Jean** (No.8, 01.48.78.62.73). The lower stretch of rue des Martyrs is packed with tempting food shops, while a little further up the hill you should look out for the prosperous residences of the Cité Malesherbes and avenue Trudaine. The circular place St-Georges was home to the true Empress of Napoleon III's Paris: the Russian-born Madame Païva. She lived in the neo-Renaissance No.28, thought to be outrageous at the time of its construction. 'La Païva' shot herself in the head after a passionate affair with the millionaire cousin of Chancellor Otto von Bismarck.

Musée Gustave Moreau

14 rue de La Rochefoucauld, 9th (01.48.74.38.50/ www.musee-moreau.fr). M° Trinité. **Open** 10am-12.45pm, 2-5.15pm Mon, Wed-Sun. **Admission** €5; €3 18-25s, Sun; free under-18s. PMP. **Credit** MC, V. **Map** p401 G3.

A wonderful private museum, this combines the small private apartment of Symbolist painter Gustave Moreau (1825-98) with the vast two-floor gallery he built to display his work – set out as a museum by the painter himself, and opened in 1903. Downstairs shows his obsessive collector's nature with family portraits, Grand Tour souvenirs and a boudoir devoted to the object of his unrequited love, Alexandrine Durem. Upstairs is Moreau's fantasy realm, which plunders Greek mythology and biblical scenes for canvases filled with writhing maidens, trance-like visages, mystical beasts and strange plants. Printed on boards that you can carry around are the artist's lengthy, rhetorical and mad commentaries. Don't miss the trippy masterpiece *Jupiter et Sémélé* on the second floor.

Musée de la Vie Romantique

16 rue Chaptal, 9th (01.55.31.95.67/www.paris.fr/ musees). M° Blanche or St-Georges. **Open** 10am-6pm Tue-Sun. *Tearoom May-Oct* 11.30am-5.30pm Tue-Sun. **Admission** free. *Exhibitions* €7; €3.50 18-26s; free under-14s. **Credit** AmEx, DC, MC, V. **Map** p401 G2.

When Dutch artist Ary Scheffer lived in this small villa, this area thronged with composers, writers and artists. Aurore Dupin, Baronne Dudevant (George Sand) was a guest at Scheffer's soirées, and many other great names crossed the threshold, including Chopin, Delacroix and Liszt. The museum is devoted to Sand, although the watercolours, lockets, jewels and plastercast of her right arm that she left behind reveal little of her ideas or affairs. But the house itself is quite lovely, decorated with restraint and good taste. A couple of ancillary buildings are used for temporary exhibitions, and there's a pretty rose garden and a conservatory that serves as a café.

La Goutte d'Or

The area north of Barbès Rochechouart métro station was used by Zola as a backdrop for *L'Assommoir*, his novel set among the district's laundries and absinthe cafés. Today, heroin has replaced absinthe as the means of escape.

La Goutte d'Or is primarily an African and Arab neighbourhood, and can seem like a colourful slice of Africa or a state under perpetual siege due to the frequent police raids. Down rue Doudeauville you'll find lively African music shops, while rue Polonceau contains African grocers and Senegalese restaurants. Mayor Delanöe has tried to attract young designers to the area by designating rue des Gardes 'rue de la mode', while square Léon is the focus for **La Goutte d'Or en Fête** (*see p273*) in June, which brings together local musicians. Some of them, such as Africando and the Orchestre National de Barbès, have become well known across Paris. A market sets up under the métro tracks on Monday, Wednesday and Saturday mornings along boulevard de la Chapelle, with stalls of exotic vegetables and rolls of African fabrics.

Further north, at porte de Clignancourt, is the city's largest flea market, the **Marché aux Puces de Clignancourt** (*see p266*).

North-east Paris

In the 10th, 11th, 19th and 20th arrondissements.
Gigantic place de la République stands like a frontier between the old aristocratic Marais and the more proletarian north-east, an area in transition. Charming areas stand abreast grotty ones, and modern housing developments beside relics from the old villages of Belleville, La Villette, Ménilmontant and Charonne.

Column cull

As iconic as Guimard's art nouveau métro entrances, the 150-year-old Morris columns, advertising everything from local election candidates to obscure theatre productions, are due for the chop.

Invented by printer Gabriel Morris in 1850, and built by a company named after him, the columns were replaced by illuminated versions in the 1980s.

Nearly 800 of these cylindrical billboards were dotted around the capital in 2005. Following a directive by Bertrand Delanoë's Mairie, a third of them are due to be pulled down with immediate effect, to rid the city of clutter in public spaces.

Those with most to lose from the decision are the smaller theatre and music venues, much of whose publicity – and, as a result, income – depends on having their posters glued up all over Paris. After much protest, the City Hall agreed to limit the cull to 550. It also plans to introduce a new, five-sided column, replacing the three-sided models installed 25 years ago.

Canal St-Martin to La Villette

Canal St-Martin, built 1805-25, begins at the Seine at Pont Morland (where there's a small marina at Port de l'Arsenal), disappears underground at Bastille, hides under boulevard Richard-Lenoir, then re-emerges after crossing rue du Faubourg-du-Temple, east of place de la République. Faubourg-du-Temple itself, once the country lane that led to Belleville, is scruffy and cosmopolitan, lined with cheap grocers and discount stores, hidden courtyards and colourful stalwarts of Paris nightlife: **Le Gibus** (see p324), Brazilian bar-restaurant **Favela Chic** (see p329) and the vintage dancehall **La Java** (see p329), as well as the Palais des Glaces (No.37, 10th, 01.42.02.27.17), which programmes seasons of French comics.

The first stretch of the canal, lined with shady trees and crossed by iron footbridges and locks, has the most appeal. The quays are traffic-free on Sundays. Many canalside warehouses have been snapped up by artists and designers or turned into loft apartments. You can take a boat up the canal as far as La Villette.

East of here, the Hôpital St-Louis (entrance rue Bichat) was commissioned in 1607 by Henri IV to house plague victims, and was built as a series of isolated pavilions in the same brick-and-stone style as **place des Vosges** (see p113), far enough from the town to prevent risk of infection. Behind the hospital, the rue de la Grange-aux-Belles housed the Montfaucon gibbet, put up in 1233, where victims were hanged and left to the elements. Today the street contains music cafés **Chez Adel** (see p317) and L'Apostrophe (No.23, 10th, 01.42.08.26.07). East of the hospital, the lovely cobbled rue Ste-Marthe and place Ste-Marthe have a provincial air, busy at night with multi-ethnic eateries like Le Panier (32 pl Ste-Marthe, 10th, 01.42.01.38.18) and the Sainte-Marthe (32 pl Ste-Marthe, 10th, 01.44.84.36.96).

North is the Parti Communiste Français, on place du Colonel-Fabien, a surrealist, curved glass curtain wall raised off the ground on a concrete wing, built in 1968-71 by Brazilian architect Oscar Niemeyer with Paul Chemetov and Jean Deroche. The canal disappears briefly again under place de Stalingrad, a dodgy locale at night. The square was landscaped in 1989 to showcase the Rotonde de La Villette, one of Ledoux's grandiose 1780s toll houses that once marked the boundary of Paris; it now displays exhibitions and archaeological finds.

Here the canal widens into the Bassin de La Villette, and the new developments along the quai de Loire and further quai de la Marne, as well as some of the worst of 1960s and '70s housing in the colossal blocks that stretch along

rue de Flandres. At 104 rue d'Aubervilliers, the old Pompes Funèbres – former municipal undertaker – is being turned into a multimedia art space, scheduled to open in 2007.

At the eastern end of the basin is an unusual 1885 hydraulic lifting bridge, Pont de Crimée. Thursday and Sunday mornings add vitality with a canalside market at place de Joinville. East of here, the Canal de l'Ourcq (created in 1813 to provide drinking water, as well as for freight haulage) divides: Canal St-Denis runs north towards the Seine, while Canal de l'Ourcq continues east through La Villette and the suburbs. Long the city's main abattoir district, still reflected in the Grande Halle de La Villette and in some of the old meaty brasseries along boulevard de La Villette, the neighbourhood has been revitalised since the late 1980s by the postmodern **Parc de La Villette** leisure and education complex, with the **Cité des Sciences et de l'Industrie** science museum (which also incorporates the **Cité des Enfants**; see p281), and the **Cité de la Musique** concert hall (see p309 and p319), with its rich and varied line-up.

La Cité des Sciences et de l'Industrie

La Villette, 30 av Corentin-Cariou, 19th (01.40.05.70.00/www.cite-sciences.fr). M° Porte de la Villette. **Open** 10am-6pm Tue-Sat; 10am-7pm Sun. **Admission** €7.50; €5.50 7-16s, students under 25, over-60s; free under-7s. PMP. **Credit** MC, V. **Map** p403 (inset).

The ultra-modern science museum at La Villette pulls in five million visitors every year. Explora, the permanent show, occupies the upper two floors, whisking visitors through 30,000sq m (320,000sq ft) of space, life, matter and communication: scale models of satellites including the Ariane space shuttle, planes and robots make for an exciting journey. Experience weightlessness in the space section. In the Espace Images, try the delayed camera and other optical illusions, draw 3D images on a computer or lend your voice to the *Mona Lisa*. The hothouse garden investigates futuristic developments in agriculture and bio-technology. The lower floors host exhibitions; the Cité des Enfants runs workshops for children. *See chapter* **Children**. **Photos** p135.

Musée de la Musique

Cité de la Musique, 221 av Jean-Jaurès, 19th (01.44.84.44.84/www.cite-musique.fr). M° Porte de Pantin. **Open** noon-6pm Tue-Sat; 10am-6pm Sun. **Admission** €7; €5.60 6-25s; free under-6s, over-60s. PMP. **Credit** AmEx, MC, V. **Map** p403 (inset).

Alongside the concert hall, this innovative music museum houses a gleamingly restored collection of instruments from the old Conservatoire, interactive computers and scale models of opera houses and concert halls. Visitors are supplied with an audio guide in a choice of languages, and the musical commentary is a joy, playing the appropriate instrument

La Cité des Sciences et de l'Industrie. *See p134.*

as you approach each exhibit. Alongside the trumpeting brass, curly woodwind instruments and precious strings are more unusual items, such as the Indonesian gamelan orchestra, whose sounds influenced the work of Debussy and Ravel. Concerts in the amphitheatre use historic instruments from the collection. Exhibitions for 2007 include the videos of US musician and visual artist Christian Marclay.

Parc de La Villette

Av Corentin-Cariou, 19th (01.40.03.75.03/ www.villette.com). M° Porte de La Villette. Av Jean-Jaurès, 19th. M° Porte de Pantin. **Map** p403 inset.
La Villette's programmes range from avant-garde music to avant-garde circus. Once the city's main cattle market and abattoir, it was to be replaced by a high-tech slaughterhouse but instead was transformed into the Cité des Sciences et de l'Industrie, a futuristic, interactive science museum. Outside you'll find the shining, spherical La Géode IMAX cinema (*see p290*) and the Argonaute submarine. Dotted with red pavilions, or *folies*, the park was designed by Swiss architect Bernard Tschumi and is a postmodern feast (guided tours 08.03.30.63.06, 3pm Sun in summer). The *folies* serve as glorious giant climbing frames, as well as a first-aid post, burger bar and children's art centre. Kids shoot down a Chinese dragon slide, and an undulating suspended path follows the Canal de l'Ourcq. As well as the lawns, which are used for an open-air film festival in summer, there are ten themed gardens bearing evocative names such as the Garden of Mirrors, of Mists, of Acrobatics and of Childhood Horrors (all of this can be terribly spooky if you lose your way en route to the Cabaret Sauvage circus or nightclub venue; *see p277 and p329*). South of the canal are the Zénith (*see p314*), used for rock concerts, and the Grande Halle de La Villette – a remnant of the former cattle market that's now used for trade fairs, exhibitions and September's jazz festival (*see p273*). It is flanked by the Conservatoire de la Musique and the Cité de la Musique, designed by Christian de Portzamparc, with rehearsal rooms, concert halls and the Musée de la Musique (*see above*).

Belleville, Ménilmontant & Charonne

When the city boundaries were expanded in 1860, Ménilmontant, Belleville and Charonne, once villages that provided Paris with fruit, wine and weekend escapes, were all absorbed. They were built up with housing for migrants, first from rural France and later from former colonies in North Africa and South-east Asia. The main tourist attraction is **Père-Lachaise** cemetery, but the area also encompasses one of the city's most beautiful parks, the romantic **Buttes-Chaumont**. Despite attempts to dissipate workers' agitation by splitting the village between the 11th, 19th and 20th

administrative districts, Belleville became the centre of opposition to the Second Empire. Cabarets, artisans and workers typified 1890s Belleville; colonised by artists in the 1990s, today Belleville is a trendy hangout.

On bd de Belleville, Chinese and Vietnamese shops rub shoulders with Muslim and kosher groceries, couscous and falafel eateries, and a street market takes place on Tuesday and Friday mornings. Legend has it that Edith Piaf was born on the pavement outside No.72 rue de Belleville, as marked on the plaque: 'On the steps of this house was born on the 19 December 1915, in the greatest poverty, Edith Piaf, whose voice would later move the world.' Devotees run the nearby appointment-only **Musée Edith Piaf**, a modest two-room museum.

North of here, along avenue Simon-Bolivar, is the Parc des Buttes-Chaumont. This is the most des-res part of north-east Paris, with Haussmannian apartments overlooking the

Rue de Belleville.

set pieces: looking on to it are the elegant 5th arrondissement town hall and, opposite, the law faculty. On the north side, the Ste-Geneviève university library (No.10, 5th, 01.44.41.97.97), built by Labrouste with an iron-framed reading room, contains medieval manuscripts. On the other side you'll find the historic Hôtel des Grands Hommes (No.17, 5th, 01.46.34.19.60, www.hoteldesgrandshommes.com), where Surrealist mandarin André Breton invented 'automatic writing' in the 1920s.

Pascal, Racine and the remains of Sainte Geneviève are all interred within **Eglise St-Etienne-du-Mont**, on the north-east corner of the square. Just behind it, within the illustrious and elitist Lycée Henri IV, is the Gothic-Romanesque Tour de Clovis, part of the former Abbaye Ste-Geneviève. Take a look through the entrance (open during termtime) and you'll also catch glimpses of the cloister and other sundry monastic structures. Further from place de Panthéon, along rue Clovis, is a chunk of Philippe-Auguste's 12th-century city wall (other chunks can be spotted at 62 rue du Cardinal-Lemoine and at the rear of buildings on rue Descartes; *see also p114*). The exiled monarch James II once resided at 65 rue du Cardinal-Lemoine, in the severe buildings of the former Collège des Ecossais (now a school), founded in 1372 to house Scottish students; King James' brain was preserved here until carried off and lost during the French Revolution. Other well known ex-residents include Hemingway, who lived at both 79 rue du Cardinal-Lemoine (note the plaque) and 39 rue Descartes in the 1920s, and James Joyce. The latter completed *Ulysses* while staying at 71 rue du Cardinal-Lemoine (*see also p239* **Turning over a new leaf**). Rimbaud lived in rue Descartes, while Descartes himself lived on nearby rue Rollin.

This area is still a mix of tourist picturesque and gentle village, where some of the buildings hide surprising courtyards and gardens. Pretty place de la Contrescarpe has been a famous rendezvous since the 1530s, when writers Rabelais, Ronsard and Du Bellay frequented the Cabaret de la Pomme de Pin at No.1; it still has some lively cafés. When George Orwell stayed at 6 rue du Pot-de-Fer in 1928 and 1929 (he described his time here and his work as a dishwasher in *Down and Out in Paris and London*), it was a place of astounding poverty; today the street is lined with bargain bars and restaurants, while the restored houses along rue Tournefort bear little relation to the garrets of Balzac's *Le Père Goriot*. Rue Mouffetard, originally the road to Rome and one of the oldest streets in the city, winds southwards as a suite of cheap bistros, Greek and Lebanese

tavernas and knick-knack shops thronged with tourists; the vibe described by Hemingway – 'that wonderful narrow crowded market street, beloved of bohemians' – has somewhat faded. The busy street market (Tue-Sat, Sun morning) on the lower half seethes on weekends, when it spills on to the square and around the cafés in front of the **Eglise St-Médard**. There's another busy market, more frequented by locals, at **place Monge** (Wed, Fri, Sun morning). *See also p263* **Super marchés**.

Back to the west of the Panthéon, head south beyond rue Soufflot and you'll notice rue St-Jacques becomes prettier. Here you'll find several ancient buildings, including the elegant *hôtel* at No.151, good food shops, vintage bistro Perraudin (No.157, 5th, 01.46.33.15.75) and the Institut Océanographique (No.195, 5th, 01.44.32.10.70, www.oceano.org/io), which has plentiful aquariums much loved by schoolkids. Rue d'Ulm contains the blue-chip Ecole Normale Supérieure (No.45, 5th, 01.44.32.30.00, www.ens.fr), once occupied in protest by the unemployed in January 1998; in an echo of 1968, students also joined in.

Turn off up hilly rue des Fossés-St-Jacques to discover place de l'Estrapade; in the 17th century the *estrapade* was a tall wooden tower from which deserters were dropped repeatedly until they died. Nearby, in rue des Irlandais, the **Centre Culturel Irlandais** (*see p73*) hosts concerts, exhibitions, films, plays and spoken-word events promoting Irish culture. Back to the west of rue St-Jacques, rue Soufflot and broad rue Gay-Lussac (a hotspot of the May 1968 revolt), with their Haussmannian apartment buildings, lead to boulevard St-Michel and the **Jardin du Luxembourg** (*see p152*). Further south along rue St-Jacques, in the potters' quarter of Roman Lutetia, is the least altered and most ornate of the city's baroque churches, the landmark **Eglise du Val-de-Grâce**. Round the corner, at 6 rue du Val-de-Grâce, is the former home of Alfons Maria Mucha, the influential Moravian art nouveau painter, known for his posters of Sarah Bernhardt.

Collège de France

11 pl Marcelin-Berthelot, 5th (01.44.27.12.11/ 01.44.27.11.47/www.college-de-france.fr). M° Cluny La Sorbonne or Maubert Mutualité/RER Luxembourg. **Open** 9am-5pm Mon-Fri. **Map** p408 J7. Founded in 1530 with the patronage of François I, the college is both a place of learning and a research institute. The present building dates from the 16th and 17th centuries; there's also a later annexe. All lectures are free and open to the public; some have been given by such eminent figures as anthropologist Claude Lévi-Strauss, philosopher Maurice Merleau-Ponty and mathematician Jacques Tits.

Sightseeing

Eglise St-Etienne-du-Mont

Pl Ste-Geneviève, 5th (01.43.54.11.79). M° Cardinal Lemoine/RER Luxembourg. **Open** 10am-7pm Tue-Sun. **Map** p408 J8.

Geneviève, patron saint of Paris, is credited with having miraculously saved the city from the ravages of Attila the Hun in 451 (*see p13*), and her shrine has been a popular site of pilgrimage ever since. The present church was built in an amalgam of Gothic and Renaissance styles between 1492 and 1626, and once adjoined the abbey church of Ste-Geneviève. The façade mixes Gothic rose windows with rusticated classical columns and reliefs of classically draped figures. The interior is wonderfully tall and light, with soaring columns and a classical balustrade. The stunning Renaissance rood screen, with its double spiral staircase and ornate stone strapwork, is the only surviving one in Paris, and was possibly designed by Philibert Delorme. Also worth a look is the ornate canopied wooden pulpit by Germaine Pillon dating from 1651, adorned with figures of the Graces and supported by a muscular Samson sitting on the defeated lion. Sainte Geneviève's elaborate neo-Gothic brass-and-glass shrine (shielding the ancient tombstone) is located to the right of the choir, surrounded by an assorted collection of reliquaries and dozens of marble plaques bearing messages of thanks. At the back of the church (reached through the sacristy), the catechism chapel constructed by Baltard in the 1860s has a cycle of paintings relating the saint's life story.

Eglise St-Médard

141 rue Mouffetard, 5th (01.44.08.87.00). M° Censier Daubenton. **Open** 8am-noon, 2.30-7.30pm daily. **Map** p406 J9.

The original chapel here was a dependency of the Abbaye Ste-Geneviève. The rebuilding towards the end of the 15th century created a somewhat larger, late Gothic structure best known for its elaborate vaulted ambulatory.

Eglise du Val-de-Grâce

Pl Alphonse-Laveran, 5th (01.40.51.47.28). RER Luxembourg or Port-Royal. **Open** noon-6pm Tue, Wed, Sat, Sun. **Admission** €5; €2.50 children, 6-12s; free under-6s. **No credit cards. Map** p406 H9.

Anne of Austria, the wife of Louis XIII, vowed to erect 'a magnificent temple' if God blessed her with a son. She got two. The resulting church and surrounding Benedictine monastery – these days a military hospital and the Musée du Service de Santé des Armées – were built by François Mansart and Jacques Lemercier. This is the most luxuriously baroque of the city's 17th-century domed churches, its ornate altar decorated with twisted barley-sugar columns. The swirling colours of the dome frescoes painted by Pierre Mignard in 1669 (which Molière himself once eulogised) are designed to give a foretaste of heaven. In contrast, the surrounding monastery offers the perfect example of François Mansart's classical restraint. Phone in advance if you're after a guided visit.

Musée du Service de Santé des Armées

Val de Grâce, pl Alphonse-Laveran, 5th (01.40.51.51.94). RER Luxembourg or Port Royal. **Open** noon-6pm Tue, Wed, Sat, Sun. **Admission** €5; €2.50 6-12s; free under-6s. **No credit cards. Map** p406 J9.

Housed in the royal convent designed by Mansart, next door to a military hospital, this museum traces the history of military medicine via replicas of field hospitals and ambulance trains, and antique medical instruments. The chilling section on World War I demonstrates how speedily the conflict propelled progress in medical science.

Le Panthéon

Pl du Panthéon, 5th (01.44.32.18.00). M° Cardinal Lemoine/RER Luxembourg. **Open** 10am-5.15pm (until 5.45pm summer) daily. **Admission** €7.50; €4.50 18-25s; free under-18s (if accompanied by an adult). PMP. **Credit** MC, V. **Map** p408 J8.

Soufflot's neo-classical megastructure, with its huge dome, was the architectural *grand projet* of its day, commissioned by a grateful Louis XV as an appropriately grandiose way to thank Sainte Geneviève for his recovery from illness. But by the time it was ready in 1790, a lot had changed; during the Revolution, the Panthéon was rededicated as a 'temple of reason' and the resting place of the nation's great men. The austere barrel-vaulted crypt now houses Voltaire, Rousseau, Hugo and Zola; new heroes are installed but rarely: Pierre and Marie Curie's remains were transferred here in 1995. André Malraux, writer, Résistance hero and de Gaulle's culture minister, arrived in 1996; Alexandre Dumas in 2002. Inside are Greek columns and domes, and 19th-century murals of Geneviève's life by Symbolist painter Puvis de Chavannes, a formative influence on Picasso during the latter's blue period.

Mount the steep spiral stairs to the colonnade encircling the dome for superb views across the city. A replica of Foucault's Pendulum hangs here; the original proved that the earth does indeed spin on its axis, via a universal joint that lets the direction of the pendulum's swing rotate as the earth revolves.

La Sorbonne

17 rue de la Sorbonne, 5th (01.40.46.22.11/www.sorbonne.fr). M° Cluny La Sorbonne. **Open** *Tours* by appointment. Closed July & Aug. **Map** p408 J7.

Founded in 1253 by Robert de Sorbon, the University of the Sorbonne was at the centre of the Latin Quarter's intellectual activity from the Middle Ages until 1968, when it was occupied by students and stormed by the riot police. The authorities then split the University of Paris into safer outposts, but the Sorbonne still houses the Faculté des Lettres. Rebuilt by Richelieu and reorganised by Napoleon, the present buildings date from the late 1800s, and have a labyrinth of classrooms and lecture theatres, as well as an observatory tower. The elegant dome of the 17th-century chapel dominates place de la Sorbonne; Cardinal Richelieu is buried inside. It's only open to the public for exhibitions or concerts.

Institut du Monde Arabe. *See p146.*

The Jardin des Plantes district

The quiet, easternmost part of the 5th district is home to more academic institutions, the Paris mosque and another Roman relic. Old-fashioned bistros on rue des Fossés-St-Bernard contrast with the slab-sided 1960s architecture of the massive university campus of Paris VI and VII, the science faculty (known as Jussieu) built on what had been the site of the important Abbaye St-Victor. Between the Seine and Jussieu is the strikingly modern, glass-faced **Institut du Monde Arabe**, which has a programme of concerts and exhibitions and a restaurant with a great view. The **Jardin Tino Rossi**, by the river, contains the slightly dilapidated **Musée de la Sculpture en Plein Air**. In summer this is a spot for dancing and picnicking.

Hidden among the many hotels of rue Monge is the entrance to the **Arènes de Lutèce**, a Roman amphitheatre. The circular arena and its tiers of stone seating were rediscovered in 1869, when the street was being built. Their excavation started in 1883, thanks to lobbying by Victor Hugo. Nearby rise the white minaret and green pan-tiled roof of the **Mosquée de Paris**, built in 1922. This is the official focus for the city's Muslim community, as opposed to more makeshift or clandestine mosques that have since sprung up around the city. Its beautiful Moorish tearoom is a student haunt.

The mosque looks over the **Jardin des Plantes** botanical garden. Opened in 1626 as a garden for medicinal plants, it features an 18th-century maze and a winter garden bristling with rare species. It also houses the Museum National d'Histoire Naturelle, with its brilliantly renovated **Grande Galerie de l'Evolution**, and a zoo, La Ménagerie, an unlikely by-product of the Revolution, when royal and noble collections of wild animals were impounded. Street names and the lovely animal-themed fountain on the corner of rue Cuvier pay homage to the many naturalists and other scientists who worked here. A short way away, at 11-13bis rue Geoffroy-St-Hilaire, the words 'Chevaux', 'Poneys' and 'Anes' are still visible on the façade of the old horse market.

Arènes de Lutèce

Rue Monge, rue de Navarre or rue des Arènes, 5th. Mº Cardinal Lemoine or Place Monge. **Open** *Summer* 8am-10pm daily. *Winter* 8am-5.30pm daily. **Admission** free. **Map** p406 K8.

This Roman arena, where wild beasts and gladiators fought, could seat 10,000 people. It was still visible during the reign of Philippe-Auguste in the 12th century, then disappeared under rubble. The site was rediscovered in 1869 and now incorporates a romantically planted garden. These days, it attracts skateboarders, footballers and boules players.

Grande Galerie de l'Évolution

36 rue Geoffroy-St-Hilaire, 2 rue Bouffon or pl Valhubert, 5th (01.40.79.54.79/56.01/www.mnhn.fr). Mº Gare d'Austerlitz or Jussieu. **Open** *Grande Galerie* 10am-6pm Mon, Wed-Fri, Sun; 10am-8pm Sat. *Other galleries* 10am-5pm Mon, Wed-Fri; 10am-6pm Sat, Sun. **Admission** *Grande Galerie* €8; €7 4-18s; free under-4s. *Other galeries* (each) €6; €4 4-18s; free under-4s. **No credit cards. Map** p406 K9.

One of the city's most child-friendly attractions is guaranteed to bowl adults over too. Located within the Jardin des Plantes (*see p147*), this beauty of a 19th-century iron-framed, glass-roofed structure has been modernised with lifts, galleries and false floors, and filled with life-size models of tentacle-waving squids, open-mawed sharks, tigers hanging off elephants and monkeys swarming down from the ceiling. The centrepiece is a procession of African wildlife across the first floor that resembles the procession into Noah's Ark. Glass-sided lifts take you up through suspended birds to the second floor, which deals with man's impact on nature and rewiring of evolution (crocodile into handbag, lama into alpaca overcoat). The third floor traces endangered and extinct species. The separate Galerie d'Anatomie Comparée et de Paléontologie contains over a million skeletons and a fossil collection of world importance. *See also p282.*

Institut du Monde Arabe

1 rue des Fossés-St-Bernard, 5th (01.40.51.38.38/ www.imarabe.org). Mº Jussieu. **Open** *Museum* 10am-6pm Tue-Sun. *Library* 1-8pm Tue-Sat. *Café* noon-6pm Tue-Sun. *Tours* 3pm Tue-Fri; 3pm & 4.30pm Sat, Sun. **Admission** *Roof terrace, library* free. *Museum* €5; €4 concessions; free under-12s. PMP. *Exhibitions* varies. *Tours* €8. **Credit** MC, V. **Map** p406 K7.

A clever blend of high-tech steel-and-glass architecture and Arab influences, this Seine-side *Grand Projet* was constructed between 1980 and 1987 to a design by Jean Nouvel (whose latest triumph is the Musée du Quai Branly; *see p158* **A museum with a mission**). Shuttered windows, inspired by the screens of Moorish palaces, act as camera apertures, contracting or expanding according to the amount of sunlight available. A museum covering the history and archaeology of the Islamic Arab world occupies the upper floors: start at the 7th with Classical-era finds and work your way down via early Islamic dynasties to the present day. Unfortunately, the presentation and layout are somewhat uninspired – objects in glass cases with little in the way of context – and there is little to engage the non-specialist. However, the Institut hosts several major crowd-pleasing exhibitions throughout the year, there's an excellent Middle East bookshop on the ground floor and the views from the roof terrace (to which access is free) are fabulous. The Institut also organises a varied programme of dance and classical Arab music, and every Saturday at 4pm you can take a tour of 'Paris arabe historique' (€15 per person). **Photos** *p145.*

Jardin des Plantes

36 rue Geoffroy-St-Hilaire, 2 rue Bouffon,
pl Valhubert or 57 rue Cuvier, 5th. M° Gare
d'Austerlitz, Place Monge or Jussieu. **Open** *Main*
garden winter 8am-dusk daily; summer 7.30am-8pm
daily. *Alpine garden* Apr-Sept 8am-4.30pm Mon-Fri;
1-5pm Sat, Sun. Closed Oct-Mar. *Greenhouses*
Closed 2007. *Ménagerie* Apr-Sept 9am-5pm daily.
Admission *Alpine Garden* free Mon-Fri; €1 Sat,
Sun. *Jardin des Plantes* free. *Ménagerie* €7; €5 4-18s;
free under-4s. **Credit** AmEx, MC, V. **Map** p406 L8.
Although small and slightly dishevelled, the Paris
botanical garden – which contains more than 10,000
species and includes tropical greenhouses and rose,
winter and Alpine gardens – is an enchanting place.
Begun by Louis XIII's doctor as the royal medicinal
plant garden in 1626, it opened to the public in 1640.
The formal garden, which runs between two dead-
straight avenues of trees parallel to rue Buffon, is
like something out of *Alice in Wonderland*. There's
also the Ménagerie (a small zoo) and the terrific
Grande Galerie de l'Évolution (*see p146*). Ancient
trees on view include a false acacia planted in 1636
and a cedar that dates from 1734; climbing up a little hill is an 18th-century spiral yew. A plaque on
the old laboratory declares that this is where Henri
Becquerel discovered radioactivity in 1896.

Jardin Tino Rossi (Musée de la Sculpture en Plein Air)

Quai St-Bernard, 5th. M° Gare d'Austerlitz. **Open**
8am-dusk Mon-Fri; 9am-dusk Sat, Sun. **Admission**
free. **Map** p406 K8.
Despite recent replanting, this open-air sculpture
museum by the Seine fights a constant battle against
graffiti. Still, it's a pleasant enough, if traffic-loud,
place for a stroll. Most of the works are second-rate,
aside from Etienne Martin's bronze *Demeure I* and
the Carrara marble *Fenêtre* by Cuban artist Careras.

La Mosquée de Paris

2 pl du Puits-de-l'Ermite, 5th (01.45.35.97.33/
tearoom 01.43.31.38.20/baths 01.43.31.18.14/
www.mosquee-de-paris.net). M° Monge. **Open** *Tours*
9am-noon, 2-6pm Mon-Thur, Sat, Sun (closed Muslim
hols). *Tearoom* 10am-11.30pm daily. *Restaurant*
noon-2.30pm, 7.30-10.30pm daily. *Baths* (women)
10am-9pm Mon, Wed, Sat; 2-9pm Fri; (men) 2-9pm
Tue, Sun. **Admission** €3; €2 7-25s, over-60s; free
under-7s. *Tearoom* free. *Baths* €15-€35. **Credit** MC,
V. **Map** p406 K9.
Some distance removed from the Arabic-speaking
inner-city enclaves of Barbès Rochechouart and
Belleville, this vast Hispano-Moorish construct is
nevertheless the spiritual heart of France's Algerian-
dominated Muslim population. Built from 1922 to
1926 with elements inspired by the Alhambra and
the Bou Inania Medersa in Fès, the Paris mosque is
dominated by a stunning green-and-white tiled
square minaret. In plan and function it divides into
three sections: religious (grand patio, prayer room
and minaret, all for worshippers and not curious
tourists); scholarly (Islamic school and library); and,
via rue Geoffroy-St-Hilaire, commercial (café and

domed hammam, *see p241*). La Mosquée café (open
9am-midnight daily) is delightful – a modest courtyard of whitewashed walls and blue-and-white
mosaic-topped tables shaded beneath green foliage
and scented with the sweet smell of sheesha (€6)
smoke. Charming waiters distribute glasses of *thé à
la menthe* (€2), along with syrupy, nutty North African
pastries, sorbets and fruit salads. **Photo** *p148*.

St-Germain-des-Prés & Odéon

In the 6th arrondissement.
The Left Bank once symbolised scholarship;
now it has some of the most expensive
property in Paris. It's also serious fashion
territory, but still home to publishers.

The lore of Paris café society and intellectual
life has been amply fed by the tales that leaked
out of St-Germain-des-Prés. Verlaine and
Rimbaud drank here; later, Sartre, Camus and
de Beauvoir scribbled and squabbled, and
musicians congregated around Boris Vian in
the post-war jazz boom. Today earnest types
still pose with weighty tomes, and the literati
and glitterati assemble on café terraces – to
give interviews: with all the local price hikes,
the only writers living here these days are the
well-established ones.

In 1990s a band of intellectuals founded
'SOS St-Germain' to battle against the tide of
commercialism. The association's honorary
president was bohemian singer Juliette Gréco,
who performed in the local clubs in the 1950s,
when she was living in a poky hotel room on
the rue de Seine. Fashion designer **Sonia
Rykiel** (*see p248*), long in the camp of the
germanopratins (as residents are called), also
joined the campaign. The campaigners' efforts
have been largely in vain: St-Germain almost
rivals avenue Montaigne (*see p246* **Montaigne
makeover**) for designer boutiques. Armani,
Louis Vuitton, Dior, Cartier and Céline have all
set up shop here, and **Karl Lagerfeld** (*see
p246*) opened his photography gallery on rue de
Seine – but the jazz clubs and musicians have
largely moved away.

From the boulevard to the Seine

Hit by shortages of coal during World War II,
Sartre shunned his cold flat on rue Bonaparte.
'The principal interest of the Café de Flore,' he
noted at the time, 'was that it had a stove, a
nearby métro and no Germans.' Although you
can spend more on a few coffees here than on a
week's heating these days, the **Café de Flore**
(*see p233*) remains an arty favourite and hosts
café-philo evenings in English. Its rival, **Les
Deux Magots** (*see p233*), facing historic

La Mosquée de Paris. *See p147.*

Eglise St-Germain-des-Prés, is frequented largely by tourists. Nearby is the celebrity favourite Brasserie Lipp (151 bd St-Germain, 6th, 01.45.48.53.91); art nouveau fans prefer Brasserie Vagenende (142 bd St-Germain, 6th, 01.43.26.68.18). The swish late-night bookshop **La Hune** (*see p243*) provides sustenance of a more intellectual kind.

St-Germain-des-Prés grew up around the medieval abbey, the oldest church in Paris and site of an annual fair that drew merchants from across Europe. There are traces of its cloister and part of the abbot's palace behind the church on rue de l'Abbaye. Constructed in 1586 in red brick with stone facing, the palace prefigured the architecture of **place des Vosges** (*see p113*). Charming place de Furstemberg (once the palace stables) is home to upmarket furnishing fabric stores and the house and studio where the elderly Delacroix lived when painting the murals in St-Sulpice; today it houses the **Musée National Delacroix**. Wagner, Ingres and Colette all lived on nearby rue Jacob; its elegant 17th-century *hôtels particuliers* now contain specialist book, design and antiques shops, a handful of pleasant hotels and the odd bohemian establishment.

Further east, rue de Buci hosts a street market and upmarket food shops, and is home to cafés Les Etages (No.5, 6th, 01.46.34.26.26) and Bar du Marché (No.16, 6th, 01.43.26.55.15). Hôtel La Louisiane (60 rue de Seine, 6th, 01.44.32.17.17, www.hotellalouisiane.com) has housed jazz stars Chet Baker and Miles Davis, and Existentialist powerhouses Sartre and de Beauvoir. Rue de Seine, rue des Beaux-Arts and rue Bonaparte (Manet was born in the latter, at No.5, in 1832) are still packed with small art galleries, mostly specialising in 20th-century abstraction, tribal art and art deco furniture. It was in rue des Beaux-Arts, at the Hôtel d'Alsace, that Oscar Wilde complained about the wallpaper and then checked out for good. Now renovated and fashionably over the top, it has rechristened itself **L'Hôtel** (*see p62*). La Palette (43 rue de Seine, 6th, 01.43.26.68.15) and Bistro Mazarin (42 rue Mazarine, 6th, 01.43.29.99.01) are good stopping-off points with enviable terraces; rue Mazarine, with boutiques selling lighting, vintage toys and jewellery, also has Terence Conran's brasserie **L'Alcazar** at No.62 (*see p231 and p322*) and hipster club **Wagg** (*see p324*) located in a former cabaret.

On quai de Conti stands the neo-classical Hôtel des Monnaies, built at the demand of Louis XV by architect Jacques-Denis Antoine; formerly the mint (1777-1973), it's now the **Musée de la Monnaie**, a coin museum. Behind the colonnaded façade is a curious

combination of elegant salons and industrial premises; commemorative medals are still engraved and struck here today. Next door stands the domed **Institut de France**, cleaned to within an inch of its crisp, classical life. Opposite, the iron Pont des Arts footbridge leads directly to the **Louvre** (*see pp85-91*). Further along, the city's main fine-arts school, the **Ecole Nationale Supérieure des Beaux-Arts**, occupies an old monastery.

Coffee was first drunk in Paris in 1686 at Café Procope (13 rue de l'Ancienne-Comédie, 6th, 01.40.46.79.00), whose customers have included Voltaire, Rousseau, Benjamin Franklin, Danton, Verlaine – and, today, tourists. Look out for Voltaire's desk and a postcard from Marie-Antoinette. The back opens on to the twee, cobbled passage du Commerce-St-André, home to toy shops, jewellers, chintzy tearooms and tapas trove Bistrot La Catalogne (No.4, 6th, 01.55.42.16.19). In the 18th century Dr Joseph-Ignace Guillotin first tested out his notorious device – designed, believe it or not, to make executions more humane – in the cellars of what is today the Pub St-Germain (17 rue de l'Ancienne-Comédie, 6th, 01.56.81.13.13); the first victim was, reputedly, a sheep. Jacobin regicide Billaud-Varenne was among those who felt the steel of Guillotin's gadget; his former home at 45 rue St-André-des-Arts was the site of the first girls' *lycée* in Paris, the Lycée Fénelon, founded in 1883. Today rue St-André-des-Arts, which winds towards boulevard St-Michel, features gift shops, crêperies and an arts cinema. Veer off it into quiet side streets such as rue des Grands-Augustins, rue de Savoie and rue Séguier, and you find printers, bookshops and dignified 17th-century *hôtels particuliers*. On the corner of rue and quai des Grands-Augustins, **Lapérouse** restaurant (*see p207*) has a row of intimate private dining rooms, where gentlemen entertained their mistresses; Les Bouquinistes (53 quai des Grands-Augustins, 6th, 01.43.25.45.94) is easier to peek into. Begun in 1292, the Hôtel de Fécamp, at 5 rue de Hautefeuille, was the townhouse of the abbots of Fécamp; nearby No.13, is the birthplace of poet Baudelaire. Legend has it that rue Gît-le-Coeur ('here lies the heart') is so called because a mistress of Henri IV lived here; at No.9 is the Hôtel du Vieux Paris (6th, 01.44.32.15.90), the 'Beat Hotel' where William Burroughs revised *Naked Lunch*.

Ecole Nationale Supérieure des Beaux-Arts (Ensb-a)

14 rue Bonaparte, 6th (01.47.03.52.15/www.ensba.fr). M° St-Germain-des-Prés. **Open** *Courtyard* 9am-5pm Mon-Fri. *Exhibitions* 1-7pm Tue-Sun. **Admission** €4; €2 concessions. *Exhibitions* prices vary. **Credit** V. **Map** p408 H6.

The city's most prestigious fine-arts school resides in what remains of the 17th-century Couvent des Petits-Augustins, the 18th-century Hôtel de Chimay, some 19th-century additions and some chunks of assorted French châteaux moved here after the Revolution (when the buildings briefly served as a museum of French monuments, before becoming the art school in 1816). Exhibitions are often held here; the entrance is on quai Malaquais.

Eglise St-Germain-des-Prés

3 pl St-Germain-des-Prés, 6th (01.55.42.81.33/ www.eglise-sgp.org). M° St-Germain-des-Prés. **Open** 8am-7.45pm Mon-Sat; 9am-8pm Sun. **Map** p408 H7.
The oldest church in Paris. On the advice of Germain (later Bishop of Paris), Childebert, son of Clovis, had a basilica and monastery built here around 543. It was first dedicated to St Vincent, and came to be known as St-Germain-le-Doré ('the gilded') because of its copper roof, then later as St-Germain-des-Prés ('of the fields'). During the Revolution the abbey was burned and a saltpetre refinery installed; the spire was added in a clumsy 19th-century restoration. Still, most of the present structure is 12th century, and ornate carved capitals and the tower remain from the 11th. Tombs include those of Jean-Casimir, the deposed King of Poland who became Abbot of St-Germain in 1669, and of Scots nobleman William Douglas. Under the window in the second chapel is the funeral stone of philosopher-mathematician René Descartes; his ashes have been here since 1819.

Institut de France

23 quai de Conti, 6th (01.44.54.19.30/www.institut-de-france.fr). M° Louvre Rivoli or Pont Neuf. **Open** Guided tours Sat, Sun (01.44.54.19.30/www. monum.fr; call for times). **Admission** €3.10. **No credit cards. Map** p408 H6.
This elegant domed building with two sweeping curved wings was designed as a school (founded by Cardinal Mazarin for provincial children) by Louis Le Vau and opened in 1684. The five academies of the Institut (Académie Française, Académie des Inscriptions et Belles-Lettres, Académie des Beaux-Arts, Académie des Sciences, Académie des Sciences Morales et Politiques) moved here in 1805. Inside is Mazarin's ornate tomb by Hardouin-Mansart, and the Bibliothèque Mazarine (open to over-18s with ID and two photos; €15/year). The Académie Française, zealous guardian of the French language, was founded by Cardinal Richelieu in 1635 with the aim of preserving the purity of French from corrupting outside influences (such as English). Les Immortels, Academy members are still modestly known, have never stopped trying to impose rules on a language and population that embrace multicultural input.

Musée de la Monnaie de Paris

11 quai de Conti, 6th (01.40.46.55.35/www.monnaie deparis.fr). M° Odéon or Pont Neuf. **Open** 11am-5.30pm Tue-Fri; noon-5.30pm Sat, Sun. Closed Aug. **Admission** (includes audio guide) €8; free under-16s. **Credit** *Shop* AmEx, MC, V. **Map** p408 H6.

Housed in the handsome neo-classical mint built in the 1770s, this high-tech museum tells the tale of global and local coinage from its pre-Roman origins, using sophisticated displays and audio-visual presentations. The history and development of the franc, from its war-time debut in 1360, is outlined in precise detail.

Musée National Delacroix

6 pl de Furstemberg, 6th (01.44.41.86.50/ www.musee-delacroix.fr). M° St-Germain-des-Prés. **Open** 9.30am-4.30pm Mon, Wed-Sun. **Admission** €5; free under-18s, all on 1st Sun of mth. PMP. **Credit** MC, V. **Map** p408 H6.
Romantic painter Eugène Delacroix moved to this apartment and studio in 1857 in order to be near the Eglise St-Sulpice, where he was painting murals. The Louvre and the Musée d'Orsay house his major canvas works, but this collection includes small oil paintings – among them an early self-portrait in the stance of a Walter Scott hero and *Madeleine au Désert* – free pastel studies of skies, sketches and lithographs, as well as his palette and some Moroccan memorabilia. Exhibits include correspondence between Baudelaire and George Sand.

St-Sulpice & the Luxembourg

Crammed with historic buildings and interesting shops, the quarter south of boulevard St-Germain between Odéon and Luxembourg epitomises civilised Paris. Just off the boulevard lies the covered market of St-Germain, once the site of the medieval St-Germain fair. It's now the site of a shopping arcade, auditorium, food hall and underground swimming pool. There are bars and bistros along rue Guisarde, nicknamed rue de la Soif ('thirst street') thanks to its carousers; it contains the late-night Birdland bar (No.8, 6th, 01.43.26.97.59) and a couple of notable bistros: Mâchon d'Henri (No.8, 6th, 01.43.29.08.70) and Brasserie Fernand (No.13, 6th, 01.43.54.61.47). Rue Princesse and rue des Canettes are a beguiling mix of budget eateries, pizzerias and nocturnal haunts known to a determined few: the Bedford Arms pub (17 rue Princesse, 6th, 01.46.33.43.54) and nightspot Castel (15 rue Princesse, 6th, 01.40.51.52.80).

Pass the fashion boutiques, high-class pâtisseries and antiquarian book and print shops and you come to **Eglise St-Sulpice**, a surprising 18th-century exercise in classical form with two unmatching turrets and a colonnaded façade. The square in front was designed in the 19th century by Visconti; it contains his imposing, lion-flanked Fontaine des Quatre Points Cardinaux (a pun on cardinal points and the statues of Bishops Bossuet, Fénelon, Massilon and Flechier, none of whom was actually a cardinal) and is the centrepiece

Parks and palaces – **Jardin & Palais du Luxembourg**. *See p152*.

for today's **Foire St-Germain** (*see p273*), a summer fair for antiques, books and poetry. The Café de la Mairie (8 pl St-Sulpice, 6th, 01.43.26.67.82) is a favourite with Left Bank intellectuals and students.

Amid shops of religious artefacts, the chic boutiques on place and rue St-Sulpice include **Yves Saint Laurent** (*see p249*), Christian Lacroix (2-4 pl St-Sulpice, 6th, 01.46.33.48.95, www.christian-lacroix.com), **Agnès b** (*see p251*), **Vanessa Bruno** (*see p248*), Catherine Memmi (11 rue St-Sulpice, 6th, 01.44.07.02.02), popular perfumier Annick Goutal (12 pl St-Sulpice, 6th, 01.46.33.03.15) and milliner **Marie Mercié** (*see p259*). Prime shopping continues further west: clothes on rue Bonaparte and rue du Four, and accessory and fashion shops on rue du Dragon, rue de Grenelle and rue du Cherche-Midi. If you spot a queue in the latter street, it's most likely for the famous bread at **Poilâne** (*see p261*). Across the street, at the junction of rue de Sèvres and rue du Cherche-Midi, César's spiky bronze *Centaur* is a tribute by the French sculptor to Picasso.

The early 17th-century chapel of St-Joseph-des-Carmes – once a Carmelite convent, now hidden within the Institut Catholique (21 rue d'Assas, 6th, 01.44.39.52.00, www.icp.fr) – was the scene of the murder of 115 priests during the Terror in 1792. To the east lies wide rue de Tournon, lined by such grand 18th-century residences as the elegant Hôtel de Brancas (No.6), with figures of Justice and Prudence over the door. This street opens up to the **Palais du Luxembourg**, which now serves as the Senate, and the adjoining **Jardin du Luxembourg**, the quintessential Paris park.

Towards boulevard St-Germain is the neo-classical **Odéon, Théâtre de l'Europe** (*see p342*), built in 1779 and recently renovated. Beaumarchais' *Le Mariage de Figaro* was first performed here in 1784. A house in the square in front was home to Revolutionary hero Camille Desmoulins, who incited the mob to attack the Bastille in 1789. Now it's occupied by La Méditerranée (2 pl de l'Odéon, 6th, 01.43.26.02.30); an arty rendezvous in the 1940s, the restaurant's menus and plates were designed by Jean Cocteau. Joyce's *Ulysses* was first published in 1922 by Sylvia Beach at the iconic Shakespeare & Co at 12 rue de l'Odéon (no relation to the current Latin Quarter bookshop, whose first owner was given permission to use the name; *see p239* **Turning over a new leaf**). Next door is the venerable jukebox-blessed café **Le Bar Dix** (*see p233*).

Further along the street, located at 12 rue de l'Ecole-de-Médecine, is the colonnaded neo-classical Université René Descartes (Paris V) medical school, and the **Musée d'Histoire de la Médecine**. The Club des Cordeliers, set up by Danton in 1790, devised revolutionary plots across the street at the Couvent des Cordeliers (No.15); the 14th-century refectory, all that remains of the monastery founded by St Louis, houses contemporary art exhibitions. Marat, one of the club's leading lights, was stabbed to death in the bathtub at his home in the same street; David depicted the moment after the crime in his iconic painting, the *Death of Marat*. This was the surgeons' district: observe the sculpted doorway of the neighbouring *hôtel* and the domed building at No.5, once the barbers' and surgeons' guild (the two were nearly the same thing in early medicine), now university premises. Climb rue André-Dubois to rue Monsieur-le-Prince to reach budget restaurant Polidor (No.41, 6th, 01.43.26.95.34), in business since 1845; further along is the arts cinema Les 3 Luxembourg (No.67, 6th, 01.46.33.97.77).

Eglise St-Sulpice

Pl St-Sulpice, 6th (01.46.33.21.78). M° St-Sulpice. **Open** 7.30am-7.30pm daily. **Map** p408 H7.

It took 120 years (starting in 1646) and six architects to finish the church of St-Sulpice. The grandiose Italianate façade, with its two-tier colonnade, was designed by Jean-Baptiste Servandoni. He died in 1766 before the second tower was finished, leaving one tower a good five metres shorter than the other. The trio of murals by Delacroix you see in the first chapel – *Jacob's Fight with the Angel, Heliodorus Chased from the Temple* and *St Michael Killing the Dragon* – create a suitably sombre atmosphere.

Jardin & Palais du Luxembourg

Pl Auguste-Comte, pl Edmond-Rostand or rue de Vaugirard, 6th (01.42.34.23.89/www.senat.fr/visite). M° Odéon/RER Luxembourg. **Open** *Jardin* summer 7.30am-dusk daily; winter 8am-dusk daily. **Map** p408 H8.

The palace was built in the 1620s for Marie de Médicis, widow of Henri IV, by Salomon de Brosse on the site of the former mansion of the Duke of Luxembourg. Its Italianate style, with Mannerist rusticated columns, was intended to remind her of the Pitti Palace in her native Florence. In 1621 she commissioned Rubens to produce the 24 huge paintings, now in the Louvre, celebrating her life. Reworked by Chalgrin in the 18th century, the palace now houses the French parliament's upper house, the Sénat (open only by guided visits or on the Journées du Patrimoine; *see p273*).

The mansion next door (Le Petit Luxembourg) is the residence of the Sénat's president. The gardens, though, are the real draw: part formal (terraces and gravel paths), part 'English garden' (lawns and mature trees), they are the quintessential Paris park. The garden is almost crowded with sculptures: a looming Cyclops (on the 1624 Fontaine de Médicis), queens of France, a miniature Statue of Liberty, wild animals, busts of literary giants Flaubert and Baudelaire, and a monument to Delacroix. There are orchards (300 varieties of apples and pears) and an apiary where you can take beekeeping courses. The Musée du Luxembourg (*see below*) hosts prestigious art exhibitions, with lesser art shows held in the former Orangerie. Most interesting, though, are the people: an international mixture of *flâneurs* and *dragueurs*, chess players and martial-arts practitioners; as well as children on ponies, in sandpits, up climbing frames, on roundabouts and playing with the old-fashioned sailing boats on the pond (*see p283*). Then there are the tennis courts (*see p338*), *pétanque* pitches (*see p334* **Too cool for boules**), a bandstand showcasing concerts on summer afternoons – and hundreds of park chairs. **Photos** *p151*.

Musée d'Histoire de la Médecine

Université René Descartes, 12 rue de l'Ecole-de-Médecine, 6th (01.40.46.16.93). Mº Odéon or St-Michel. **Open** *Mid July-Sept* 2-5.30pm Mon-Fri. *Oct-mid July* 2-5.30pm Mon-Wed, Fri, Sat. **Admission** €3.50; €2.50 students; free under-8s. **No credit cards. Map** p408 H7.
The history of medicine is the subject of the medical faculty collection. There are ancient Egyptian embalming tools, a 1960s electrocardiograph and a gruesome array of saws used for amputations. You'll also find the instruments of Dr Antommarchi, who performed the autopsy on Napoleon, and the scalpel of Dr Félix, who operated on Louis XIV.

Musée des Lettres et Manuscrits

8 rue de Nesle, 6th (01.40.51.02.25/www.museedeslettres.fr). Mº Odéon. **Open** 1-9pm Wed; 10am-6pm Thur-Sun. **Admission** €6; €4.50 under-25s. **Credit** (€16 minimum) MC, V. **Map** p408 H7.
This intimate space in the heart of the Latin Quarter presents modern history as recorded on paper. More than 2,000 documents and letters give an insight into the lives of the great and the good, from Magritte to Mozart and Freud to François Mitterrand. Einstein arrives at the theory of relativity on notes scattered in authentic disorder, Baudelaire complains about his money problems in a letter to his mother and HMS *Northumberland*'s log-book records the day Napoleon boarded the ship to be taken to St Helena.

Musée National du Luxembourg

19 rue de Vaugirard, 6th (01.42.34.25.95/www.museeduluxembourg.fr). Mº Cluny La Sorbonne or Odéon/RER Luxembourg. **Open** 11am-10pm Mon, Fri, Sat; 11am-7pm Tue-Thur; 9am-7pm Sun. **Admission** €10; €8 students, 8-25s; free under-8s. **Credit** MC, V. **Map** p408 H7.
When it opened in 1750, this small but imposing museum was the first public gallery in France. Its current stewardship by the national museums and the French Senate has brought imaginative touches and some impressive coups. For 2007, look out for a rare chance to see 150 pieces by the influential fin-de-siècle jewel-maker René Lalique and his contemporaries. The exhibition runs from 7 March to 29 July. Book ahead to avoid queues.

The 7th & western Paris

Mainly 7th arrondissement, parts of 15th.
Townhouses spread west from St-Germain into the profoundly establishment 7th district, as the streetlife and café culture give way to tranquil residential blocks and government offices. The 7th divides into the intimate Faubourg St-Germain, with historic mansions and fine shops, and **Les Invalides**, wide windswept avenues and the **Eiffel Tower**.

The Faubourg St-Germain

In the early 18th century, when the Marais went out of fashion, aristocrats built palatial new residences on the Faubourg St-Germain, the district developing around the site of the former city wall. It is still a well-bred part of the city, government ministries and foreign embassies colouring the area with flags and diplomatic number plates. Many fine *hôtels particuliers* survive; glimpse their stone gateways and elegant entrance courtyards on rues de Grenelle, St-Dominique, de l'Université and de Varenne.

Just west of St-Germain, the 'Carré Rive Gauche' or 'Carré des Antiquaires' – the quadrangle of streets enclosed by quai Voltaire, rue des Sts-Pères, rue du Bac and rue de l'Université – is filled with antiques shops. On rue des Sts-Pères, *chocolatier* Debauve & Gallais (No.30, 7th, 01.45.48.54.67), with its period interior, has been making chocolates since 1800, originally for medicinal purposes. Rue du Pré-aux-Clercs, named after a field where students used to sort out their differences by duelling, is today a favourite with fashion insiders. There are still students to be found on adjoining rue St-Guillaume, home of the prestigious Fondation Nationale des Sciences-Politiques (No.27, 7th, 01.45.49.50.50), more commonly known as 'Sciences-Po'.

Rue de Montalembert is home to two of the Left Bank's most fashionable hotels: the **Hôtel Montalembert** (*see p66*) and the Hôtel du Pont-Royal, a gastronomic magnet ever since the addition of the trendy **Atelier de Joël Robuchon** (*see p211*). By the river, a Beaux-Arts train station – the towns once served still listed on the façade – houses the unmissable art collections of the **Musée d'Orsay**; outside on the esplanade are 19th-century bronze *animalier* sculptures. Next door is the lovely 1780s Hôtel de Salm, a mansion built for a German count, once the Swedish embassy, and now the Musée National de la Légion d'Honneur et des Ordres de Chevalerie (2 rue de Bellechasse, 7th, 01.40.62.84.25), devoted to France's honours system since Louis XI. The Legion of Honour was formed by Napoleon in 1802. Across the street,

The muse in the museum

Few of the visitors enjoying a sedate Sunday walk around the house and gardens comprising the **Musée National Rodin** (*see p157*) will have heard of a sculptress called Camille Claudel – although an entire room in the museum is devoted to her work and influence on the world-famous sculptor.

Born in 1864, Camille moved to Montparnasse in 1881, determined to become an artist. Two years later she became Rodin's assistant, working on the *Burghers of Calais*. Rodin, then 43, was smitten by his 19-year-old pupil's beauty: her brother, the poet Paul Claudel, later remembered 'a superb brow above magnificent eyes of that rare blue so seldom encountered outside the covers of a novel'.

A *grand amour* began, with the couple working alongside each other in Rodin's studio. Camille posed for a number of Rodin's pieces, and their sculptures show a mutual influence: in fact, after Rodin's death, several of her pieces were mistakenly attributed to him and cast in bronze.

But to Camille's increasing torment, Rodin refused to leave Rose Beuret, his lifetime partner and the mother of his son. His artistic success compounded her resentment. As his

a modern footbridge, the Passerelle Solférino, crosses the Seine to the Tuileries. The fancy Hôtel Bouchardon today houses the **Musée Maillol**. Right beside its curved entrance, the Fontaine des Quatre-Saisons by Edmé Bouchardon features statues of the seasons surounding allegorical figures of Paris above the rivers Seine and Marne.

You'll have to wait for the open-house Journées du Patrimoine (*see p273*) to see the decorative interiors and private gardens of other *hôtels*, such as the Hôtel de Villeroy (Ministry of Agriculture; 78 rue de Varenne, 7th), Hôtel Boisgelin (Italian Embassy; 47 rue de Varenne, 7th), Hôtel d'Avaray

(Dutch ambassador's residence; 85 rue de Grenelle, 7th), Hôtel d'Estrées (Russian ambassador's residence; 79 rue de Grenelle, 7th) or Hôtel de Monaco (Polish Embassy; 57 rue St-Dominique, 7th). Among the most beautiful is the Hôtel Matignon (57 rue de Varenne, 7th), residence of the prime minister. Once used by French statesman Talleyrand for lavish receptions, it contains the biggest private garden in Paris. The Cité Varenne at No.51 is a lane of exclusive houses with private gardens.

Rue du Bac is home to the city's oldest and most elegant department store, **Le Bon Marché** ('the good bargain'; *see p237*), and to an unlikely pilgrimage spot, the **Chapelle de**

popular acclaim grew and commissions poured in, she struggled to escape from his shadow, despite the success of pieces such as *Sakuntala* and *La Valse*, both exhibited in Paris in 1888. By the 1890s their relationship was deteriorating; by 1893, it was over.

Camille was devasted. *L'Age Mûr* (1899) vividly captured her predicament: in it, a young woman on her knees beseechingly holds out her arms to a man being torn away by an older woman. In turn, Camille haunted Rodin's work, as he returned to unfinished portraits of her that became works such as *La France*, *La Pensée* and *L'Aurore*.

After the break, Camille fought to find her own artistic voice, producing art nouveau-influenced works like *La Vague* and *Les Causeuses* and finding an agent of her own, Eugène Blot. But by 1905 – the year that the Rodin Pavilion at place de l'Alma was triumphantly opened – she had become paranoid and delusional. A virtual recluse in her studio, she raged that Rodin had stolen her ideas and wanted to destroy her. On 10 March 1913, her family committed her to a mental asylum. In 1914 she was transferred to another asylum at Montfavet, where she remained alone until her death 29 years later.

la **Médaille Miraculeuse**. On nearby rue de Babylone, handy budget bistro Au Babylone (No.13, 7th, 01.45.48.72.13) has been serving up lunches for decades, but the Théâtre de Babylone, where Beckett's *Waiting for Godot* was premièred in 1953, is long since gone.

At the foot of boulevard St-Germain, facing place de la Concorde across the Seine, is the **Assemblée Nationale**, the lower house of the French parliament. Behind, elegant place du Palais-Bourbon leads into rue de Bourgogne, a rare commercial thoroughfare amid the official buildings, with some delectable pâtisseries and designer-furniture showrooms. Nearby, the mid 19th-century Eglise Ste-Clothilde (12 rue

Martignac, 7th, 01.44.18.62.60), with its skeletal twin spires, is an early example of Gothic Revival. Beside the Assemblée is the Foreign Ministry, often referred to by its address, 'quai d'Orsay'. Beyond it, a long, grassy esplanade leads up to golden-domed Les Invalides. The vast military hospital complex, with its Eglise du Dôme and St-Louis-des-Invalides churches, all built by Louis XIV, epitomises the official grandeur of the Sun King as expression of royal and military power. It now houses the **Musée de l'Armée**, as well as Napoleon's tomb inside the Eglise du Dôme. Stand with your back to the dome to survey the cherubim-laden Pont Alexandre III and the **Grand** and **Petit Palais** (*see p119*) over the river, all three put up for the 1900 Exposition Universelle. Just beside Les Invalides is the **Musée National Rodin**, occupying the charming 18th-century Hôtel Biron and its romantic gardens. Rodin was invited here in 1908, on the understanding that he would give his work to the state. Many of his great sculptures, including the *Thinker*, the *Burghers of Calais* and the swarming *Gates of Hell*, are displayed in the building and around the gardens – as are those of his lesser known mistress, Camille Claudel. *See p154* **The muse in the museum**.

Assemblée Nationale

33 quai d'Orsay, 7th (01.40.63.60.00/www. assemblee-nat.fr). M° Assemblée Nationale. **Map** p405 F5.
Like the Sénat, the Assemblée Nationale (also known as the Palais Bourbon) is another royal building adapted for republicanism. It was built in 1722-8 for the Duchesse de Bourbon, daughter of Louis XIV and Madame de Montespan, who also put up the neighbouring Hôtel de Lassay (now the official residence of the Assembly's president) for her lover, the Marquis de Lassay. the *palais* was modelled on the Grand Trianon at Versailles, with a colonnaded *cour d'honneur* opening on to rue de l'Université and gardens running down to the Seine. The Prince de Condé extended the palace, linked the two *hôtels* and laid out place du Palais-Bourbon. The Greek temple-style façade facing Pont de la Concorde (actually the rear of the building) was added only in 1806 to mirror the Madeleine. Flanking this riverside façade are statues of four great statesmen: L'Hôpital, Sully, Colbert and Aguesseau. The Napoleonic frieze on the pediment was replaced by a monarchist one after the restoration: between 1838 and 1841, Cortot sculpted the figures of France, Power and Justice. After the Revolution, the palace became the meeting place for the Conseil des Cinq-Cents, the new legislative body. It was the forerunner of the parliament's lower house, which set up here for good in 1827, radically altering the interior with the building of the Hémicycle debating chamber. Visits are possible only by arrangement through a serving *député* (if you're French) – or, after long queuing, during the Journées du Patrimoine (*see p273*).

Chapelle de la Médaille Miraculeuse

Couvent des Soeurs de St-Vincent-de-Paul, 140 rue du Bac, 7th (01.49.54.78.88). M° Sèvres Babylone. **Open** 7.45am-1pm, 2.30-7pm daily. **Map** p405 F7.
In 1830 saintly Catherine Labouré was said to have been visited by the Virgin, who gave her a medal that performed miracles. This kitsch chapel – murals, mosaics, statues and the embalmed bodies of Catherine and her mother superior – is one of France's most visited sites, attracting two million pilgrims every year. Reliefs in the courtyard tell the nun's story – and slot machines sell medals.

Espace EDF Electra

6 rue Récamier, 7th (01.53.63.23.45/www.edf.fr). M° Sèvres Babylone. **Open** noon-7pm Tue-Sun. **Admission** free. **Map** p405 G7.
This former electricity substation, converted by Electricité de France for PR purposes, is now used for varied, well-presented exhibitions examining the likes of garden designer Gilles Clément and pioneer filmmaker Georges Méliès.

Les Invalides & Musée de l'Armée

Esplanade des Invalides, 7th (01.44.42.40.69/www. invalides.org). M° La Tour Maubourg or Les Invalides. **Open** Apr-Sept 10am-6pm daily. Oct-Mar 10am-5pm daily. Closed 1st Mon of mth. **Admission** *Courtyard* free. *Musée de l'Armée & Eglise du Dôme* €7.50; €5.50 students under 26; free under-18s. PMP. **Credit** MC, V. **Map** p405 E6.
Its imposing gilded dome is misleading: the Hôtel des Invalides was (and in part still is) a hospital. Commissioned by Louis XIV for wounded soldiers, it once housed as many as 6,000 invalids. Designed by Libéral Bruand (the foundations were laid in 1671) and completed by Jules Hardouin-Mansart, it's a magnificent monument to Louis XIV and Napoleon. Behind lines of topiaried yews and cannons, the main (northern) façade has a relief of Louis XIV (Ludovicus Magnus) and the Sun King's sunburst. Wander through the main courtyard and you'll see grandiose two-storey arcades, sundials on three sides and a statue of Napoleon glaring out from the end; the dormer windows around the courtyards are sculpted in the form of suits of armour.
The complex contains two churches – or, rather, a sort of double church: the Eglise St-Louis was for the soldiers, the Eglise du Dôme for the king, and each had its own separate entrance. You'll find an opening behind the altar that connects the two. The long, barrel-vaulted nave of the church of St-Louis is hung with flags captured from enemy troops. Since 1840 the baroque Eglise du Dôme has been solely dedicated to the worship of Napoleon, whose body was supposedly brought here from St Helena (although this is now in doubt).
On the ground floor, under a dome painted by De la Fosse, Jouvenet and Coypel, are chapels featuring monuments to such generals as Vauban, Foch and Joseph Napoleon (Napoleon's older brother and King of Italy and Spain). Napoleon II (King of Rome) is buried in the crypt with his father the emperor. Two dramatic black figures holding up the entrance to the crypt, the red porphyry tomb, the ring of giant figures, and the friezes and texts eulogising the emperor's heroic deeds give the measure of the cult of Napoleon, cherished in France for ruling large swaths of Europe and for creating an administrative and educational system that endures to this day.
The Invalides also houses the Musée de l'Ordre de la Libération and the Musée des Plans-Reliefs, the collection of scale models of cities begun by Vauban, and once used as an aid to military strategy. Also included in the entry price is the impressive Musée de l'Armée. For the military historian, the museum

is a must, but even if sumptuous uniforms and hefty cannons are not your thing, the building is itself a splendour. Besides military memorabilia, the rooms are filled with fine portraiture, such as Ingres' *Emperor Napoleon on his Throne*. The World War I rooms are moving, with the conflict brought into vivid focus by documents and photos. The Général de Gaulle wing deals with World War II, taking in not only the Résistance but also the Battle of Britain and the war in the Pacific, alternating artefacts with contemporary film footage.

Musée Maillol

59-61 rue de Grenelle, 7th (01.42.22.59.58/www. museemaillol.com). M° Rue du Bac. **Open** 11am-6pm (last admission 5.15pm) Mon, Wed-Sun. **Admission** €8; €6 students; free under-16s. **Credit** Shop AmEx, MC, V. **Map** p405 G7.

Dina Vierny was 15 when she met Aristide Maillol (1861-1944) and became his principal model for the next decade, idealised in such sculptures as *Spring*, *Air* and *Harmony*. In 1995 she opened this delightful museum above the renovated 18th-century Hôtel Bouchardon, exhibiting Maillol's drawings, engravings, pastels, tapestry panels, ceramics and early Nabis-related paintings, as well as the sculptures and terracottas that epitomise his calm, modern classicism. Vierny also set up a Maillol Museum in his Pyrenean village of Banyuls-sur-Mer. This Paris venue also has works by Picasso, Rodin, Gauguin, Degas and Cézanne, a whole room of Matisse drawings, rare Surrealist documents and works by naïve artists. Vierny has also championed Kandinsky and Ilya Kabakov, whose *Communal Kitchen* installation recreates the atmosphere of Soviet domesticity. Monographic exhibitions are devoted to modern and contemporary artists. The highlight for 2007 is a retrospective show of works by Pascin (14 February-4 June), the Bulgarian-American member of the Montparnasse set of the 1920s.

Musée National Rodin

Hôtel Biron, 77 rue de Varenne, 7th (01.44.18. 61.10/www.musee-rodin.fr). M° Varenne. **Open** Apr-Sept 9.30am-5.15pm Tue-Sun (gardens until 6.45pm). Oct-Mar 9.30am-4.15pm (gardens until 5pm) Tue-Sun. **Admission** €6; €4 18-25s, all on Sun; free under-18s, all on 1st Sun of mth. PMP. *Exhibitions* €7; €5 18-25s. *Gardens* €1. **Credit** MC, V. **Map** p405 F6.

The Rodin museum occupies the *hôtel particulier* where the sculptor lived in the final years of his life. *The Kiss*, the *Cathedral*, the *Walking Man*, portrait busts and early terracottas are exhibited indoors, as are many of the individual figures or small groups that also appear on the *Gates of Hell*. Rodin's works are accompanied by several pieces by his mistress and pupil, Camille Claudel (*see p154* **The muse in the museum**). The walls are hung with paintings by Van Gogh, Monet, Renoir, Carrière and Rodin himself. Most visitors have greatest affection for the gardens, spotted with trees and treasures: look out for the *Burghers of Calais*, the elaborate *Gates of Hell* (inspired by Dante's *Inferno*), the *Thinker*, *Orpheus*

under shade, and unfinished nymphs emerging from their marble matrix. From March to April 2007 'Rodin et le Rêve Japonais', will display the artist's personal collection of Japanese work, as well as his drawings of the Japanese dancer Hanako. Fans can also visit the Villa des Brillants at Meudon (19 av Rodin, Meudon, 01.41.14.35.00, closed Mon-Thur and Oct-Apr), where Rodin worked from 1895.

Musée d'Orsay

1 rue de la Légion-d'Honneur, 7th (01.40.49.48.14/ recorded information 01.45.49.11.11/www.musee- orsay.fr). M° Solférino/RER Musée d'Orsay. **Open** July-May 9.30am-6pm Tue-Sun. June 9.30am-9.45pm Tue-Sun. **Admission** €7.50; €5.50 concessions, all on Sun; free under-18s, all on 1st Sun of mth. PMP. **Credit** Shop MC, V. **Map** p405 G6.

The building was originally a train station, designed by Victor Laloux to coincide with the Exposition Universelle in 1900. The platforms proved too short for modern trains and by the 1950s the station was threatened with demolition; it then became home to a theatre (the Renaud-Barrault), and scenes in Orson Welles' *The Trial* were filmed here. It was saved in the late 1970s when President Giscard d'Estaing decided to turn it into a museum spanning the fertile art period between 1848 and 1914. (The painter Edouard Détaille had said it looked like a palace of fine art when it was built.) Italian architect Gae Aulenti remodelled the interior, keeping the iron-framed coffered roof and creating galleries either side of a light-filled canyon. The arrangement has its drawbacks – upstairs, the Impressionists and post-Impressionists are knee-deep in tourists, while too much space is given downstairs to Couture's languid nudes and Meissonier's history paintings – but it somehow manages to keep its open-plan feel.

The museum follows a chronological route, from the ground floor to the upper level and then to the mezzanine, showing links between Impressionist painters and their forerunners. Running down the centre of the tracks, a central sculpture aisle takes in monuments and maidens by Rude, Barrye and Carrier-Belleuse, but the outstanding pieces are by Carpeaux, including his controversial *La Danse* for the façade of the Palais Garnier. The Lille side, on the right of the central aisle, is dedicated to the Romantics and history painters: Ingres and Amaury-Duval contrast with the Romantic passion of Delacroix's North African period, Couture's vast *Les Romains de la Décadence* and the cupids of Cabanel's *Birth of Venus*. Further on are early Degas canvases and works by Symbolists Moreau and Puvis de Chavannes; another gallery shows selections from the vast holdings of early photography.

The first rooms to the Seine side of the main aisle are given over to the Barbizon landscape painters: Corot, Daubigny and Millet. One room is dedicated to Courbet, with the *Artist and his Studio*, the monumental *Burial at Ornans* and the show-stopping *L'Origine du Monde*. This floor also covers pre-1870 works by the Impressionists, including Manet's provocative *Olympia*, and their precursor Boudin.

A museum with a mission

Paris' newest museum is the last pet project of outgoing French president Jacques Chirac. Pompidou had his Centre, Mitterrand his Bibliothèque and, since the summer of 2006, Chirac has his **Musée du Quai Branly** (*see p161*). Surrounded by trees on the banks of the Seine, Branly is a vast showcase for non-European cultures. Dedicated to the ethnic art of Africa, Oceania, Asia and the Americas, it joins together the collections of the Musée des Arts d'Afrique et d'Océanie and the Laboratoire d'Ethnologie du Musée de l'Homme, as well as contemporary indigenous art. Intended to 'recognise the rightful place of these civilisations, together with the heritage of peoples who are sometimes forgotten, in the present culture of the world', this is a museum with a mission.

Factor in an extraordinary building by Jean Nouvel (whose last foray in the Paris museums circuit was the stunning Fondation Cartier; *see p163*) on a prime riverside site within spitting distance of the Eiffel Tower and covering 40,000sq m (430,556 sq ft), and Paris has a new big hitter in its powerful museum line-up. With its angular forms and protruding, coloured metal boxes, Nouvel's creation is a surprisingly baroque construction, a hotchpotch of visual metaphors: a bridge museum between

Upstairs are the Impressionists, Pissarro, Renoir and Caillebotte, Manet's *Déjeuner sur l'Herbe*, Monet's paintings of Rouen cathedral and works by Degas. Among the Van Goghs are *Church at Auvers* and *Wheat Field with Crows*. You'll also find the primitivist jungle of Le Douanier Rousseau, the gaudy lowlife of Toulouse-Lautrec, the colourful exoticism of Gauguin's Breton and Tahitian periods, and Cézanne's still lifes, landscapes and the *Card Players*, as well as works by Seurat and Signac, and the mystical pastel drawings of Odilon Redon.

On the mezzanine are works by the Nabis painters – Vallotton, Denis, Roussel, Bonnard and Vuillard.

Several rooms are given over to art nouveau decorative arts, including furniture by Majorelle, and Gallé and Lalique ceramics. Paintings by Klimt and Burne-Jones reside here, and there are sections on architectural drawings and early photography. The sculpture terraces include busts by Rodin, heads by Rosso and bronzes by Bourdelle and Maillol.

The exhibitions scheduled for 2007 continue a series in which contemporary artists present an example of their own works as well as that currently hanging in the museum. Programmed for the spring is Charles Sandison introducing Van Gogh's *La Chambre de l'Artiste*.

Europe (the one continent not represented here) and the four other continents; a river; a snake; a tropical jungle within an urban one. It also looks to be a pleasing addition to the *quartier*: the landscaped gardens that take up half the site incorporate an open-air amphitheatre and extend to the building itself, with a 'vertical garden' of 15,000 plants scaling the façade.

Inside, dimly lit to create a shadowy, mysterious aura, the permanent collection is reached via a curving white ramp, a huge space divided into four zones for the four featured continents that also lets you wander from one to another along a central path or 'river'. Treasures include a tenth-century anthropomorphic Dogon statue from Mali, Vietnamese costumes, Gabonese masks, Aztec statues, Peruvian feather tunics, rare frescoes from Ethiopia, animal hide and bark cloth garments from the Americas, and the Harter bequest of masks and sculptures from Cameroon. A mezzanine gallery is used for pan-continental exhibitions.

Yet the museum's remit goes beyond merely presenting relics from the 300,000-strong collection. Music is a key feature of the interdisciplinary approach, with musical exhibits, a 500-seat auditorium for a full programme of theatre, music and dance performances, plus the opportunity to relay the oral tradition inherent to so many global cultures. A striking circular glass drum, or 'silo', rises up through the building to allow intriguing glimpses of the instruments in reserve.

All in all, Quai Branly promises to be an extraordinary, and much needed, addition to the traditionally stuffy museum scene.

West of Les Invalides

South-west of the Invalides is the massive Ecole Militaire (av de La Motte-Picquet, 7th), the military academy built by Louis XV to educate the children of penniless officers; it would later train Napoleon. The severe neo-classical building was designed by Jacques Ange Gabriel. It's still used by the army and closed to the public. From the north-western side of the Ecole Militaire begins the vast Champ de Mars, a market garden converted into a military drilling ground in the 18th

century. It has long been home to the most celebrated Paris monument of all, the **Eiffel Tower**. At the south-eastern end of the Champ de Mars stands the Mur pour la Paix ('wall for peace'), erected in 2000 to articulate hopes for peace. South-east of the Ecole are the Y-shaped **UNESCO** building, built in 1958, and the modernist Ministry of Labour. Fashionable apartments line broad avenues Bosquet and Suffren, though there's much architectural eclecticism in the area: look at the pseudo-Gothic and pseudo-Renaissance houses on avenue de Villars, Lavirotte's fabulous art nouveau doorway at 27 avenue Rapp and the striking, box-shaped Notre-Dame de l'Arche de l'Alliance church (81 rue d'Alleray, 15th, 01.56.56.62.56), which was completed in 1998. For signs of life, visit the Saxe-Breteuil street market (*see p263* **Super marchés**), and the old-fashioned bistros Thoumieux (79 rue St-Dominique, 7th, 01.47.05.49.75) and, on an arcaded square next to a pretty fountain, Fontaine de Mars (129 rue St-Dominique, 7th, 01.47.05.46.44). The upper reaches of rue Cler contain classy food shops.

Les Egouts de Paris

Entrance opposite 93 quai d'Orsay, by Pont de l'Alma, 7th (01.53.68.27.81). M° Alma Marceau/ RER Pont de l'Alma. **Open** 11am-4pm (until 5pm May-Sept) Wed-Sat. Closed 3wks Jan. **Admission** €3.80; €3.05 5-12s; free under-5s. **No credit cards.** **Map** p400 D5.
For centuries the main source of drinking water in Paris was the Seine, which was also the main sewer. Construction of an underground sewerage system began at the time of Napoleon. Today the Egouts de Paris constitutes a smelly museum; each sewer in the 2,100km (1305-mile) system is marked with a replica of the street sign above. The Egouts can be closed after periods of heavy rain.

Eiffel Tower

Champ de Mars, 7th (01.44.11.23.45/recorded information 01.44.11.23.23/www.tour-eiffel.fr). M° Bir-Hakeim/RER Champ de Mars Tour Eiffel. **Open** *16 June-Aug* 9am-12.45am daily. *Sept-15 June* 9.30am-11.45pm daily. **Admission** *By stairs* (1st & 2nd levels, 9am-12.30am) €3.80; €3 under-25s. *By lift* (1st level) €4.20; €2.30 3-12s; (2nd level) €7.70; €4.20 3-12s; (3rd level) €11; €6 3-12s; free under-3s. **Credit** AmEx, MC, V. **Map** p404 C6.
No building better symbolises Paris than the Tour Eiffel. Maupassant claimed he left Paris because of it, William Morris visited daily to avoid having to see it from afar – and it was originally meant to be a temporary structure. The radical cast-iron tower was built for the 1889 World Fair and the centenary of the 1789 Revolution by engineer Gustave Eiffel (whose construction company still exists today). Eiffel made use of new technology that already popular in iron-framed buildings. Construction took

Maison de la Culture du Japon. *See p161.*

more than two years and used some 18,000 pieces of metal and 2,500,000 rivets. The 300m (984ft) tower stands on four massive concrete piles; it was the tallest structure in the world until overtaken by New York's Empire State Building in the 1930s. Vintage double-decker lifts ply their way up and down, or you can walk as far as the second level. There are souvenir shops, an exhibition space, café and even a post office on the first and second levels. Also on the first, an ice rink is set up every Christmas (*see p274*). The smart Jules Verne restaurant, on the second level, has its own lift in the north tower. At the top (third level), there's Eiffel's cosy salon and a viewing platform with panels pointing out what to see in every direction. Views can reach over 65km (40 miles) on a good day, although the most fascinating perspectives are of the ironwork itself, whether gazing up from underneath or enjoying the changing vision as the lift rises. At night, for ten minutes on the hour, 20,000 flashbulbs attached to the tower provide a beautiful shimmering effect. The tower has some six million visitors a year; to avoid the queues, come late at night.

UNESCO

7 pl de Fontenoy, 7th (01.45.68.10.00/tours 01.45. 68.16.42/www.unesco.org). M° Ecole Militaire. **Open** 9.30am-5.30pm Mon-Fri. *Tours* 3pm Mon-Fri (in English on Tue). **Admission** free. **Map** p405 D7.

The Y-shaped UNESCO headquarters, built in 1958, is home to a swarm of international diplomats. It's worth visiting for the sculptures and paintings – by Picasso, Arp, Giacometti, Moore, Calder and Miró – and for the Japanese garden, with its contemplation cylinder by minimalist architect Tadao Ando.

Village Suisse

38-78 av de Suffren or 54 av de La Motte-Picquet, 15th (www.levillagesuisse.com). M° La Motte Picquet Grenelle. **Open** 10.30am-7pm Mon, Thur-Sun. **Map** p404 D7.

The mountains and waterfalls created for the Swiss Village at the 1900 Exposition Universelle are long gone, but the village lives on. Rebuilt as blocks of flats, the street level has been colonised by some 150 boutiques offering various high-quality, if pricy, antiques and collectibles.

Along the Seine

Downstream from the Eiffel Tower is the recently opened **Musée du Quai Branly** (*see p158* **A museum with a mission**), the Chirac-sponsored museum of primitive arts. A short way further on, the high-tech **Maison de la Culture du Japon** stands near Pont Bir-Hakeim on quai Branly. Beyond, the 15th arrondissement Fronts de Seine riverfront, with its tower-block developments, was the scene of some of the worst architecture of the 1970s. This would-be brave new world of walkways, suspended gardens and tower blocks has no easily discoverable means of access. The adjacent Beaugrenelle shopping centre is more straightforward to get into, but remains woefully dingy – although there are plans for an extensive redevelopment in the next few years. Further west, things look up: the sophisticated former headquarters of the Canal+ TV channel (2 rue des Cévennes, 15th), designed by American architect Richard Meier, is surrounded by fine modern housing; and the pleasant **Parc André Citroën**, created in the 1990s on the site of the former Citroën car works, runs all the way down to the Seine quayside, where you'll find the occasional cruise ship and summer party-goers.

Maison de la Culture du Japon

101bis quai Branly, 15th (01.44.37.95.00/www. mcjp.asso.fr). Mᵒ Bir-Hakeim/RER Champ de Mars Tour Eiffel. **Open** noon-7pm Tue, Wed, Fri, Sat; noon-8pm Thur. Closed Aug. **Admission** free. **Map** p404 C6.

Constructed in 1996 by the Anglo-Japanese architectural partnership of Kenneth Armstrong and Masayuki Yamanaka, this opalescent glass-fronted cultural centre screens films and puts on exhibitions and plays. It also contains a library, an authentic Japanese tea pavilion on the roof, where you can watch the tea ceremony, and a well-stocked book and gift shop. **Photo** *p160.*

Musée du Quai Branly

29-55 quai Branly, 7th (01.56.61.70.00/www. quaibranly.fr). RER Pont de l'Alma. **Open** 10am-6.30pm Tue-Wed, Fri-Sun; 10am-9.30pm Thur. **Admission** €10; free under-18s, concessions. **Credit** AmEx, DC, MC, V. **Map** p404 C6.

The great opening of 2006 is this four-building collection of art and artefacts relating to non-European cultures. An auditorium stages regular concerts – programmed for 14-17 June 2007 is Desert Blues, musicians and video projections from Mali. *See p158* **A museum with a mission.**

Parc André Citroën

Rue Balard, rue St-Charles or quai Citroën, 15th. Mᵒ Javel or Balard. **Open** 8am-dusk Mon-Fri; 9am-dusk Sat, Sun, public hols. **Map** p404 A9.

This park is a fun, postmodern version of a French formal garden by Gilles Clément and Alain Prévost. It comprises glasshouses, computerised fountains, waterfalls, a wilderness and themed gardens featuring different coloured plants and even sounds. Stepping stones and water jets make it a garden for pleasure as well as philosophy. The tethered Eutelsat helium balloon takes visitors up for marvellous panoramic views over the city. If the weather looks unreliable, call 01.44.26.20.00 to check the day's programme. *See also p283.* **Photos** *p162.*

Montparnasse & beyond

Mainly 14th & 15th arrondissements, parts of 6th.

Artists such as Picasso, Léger and Soutine fled to 'Mount Parnassus' in the early 1900s to escape the rising rents of Montmartre. They were soon joined by Chagall, Zadkine and other escapees from the Russian Revolution, and by Americans such as Man Ray, Henry Miller, Ezra Pound and Gertrude Stein. Between the wars the neighbourhood symbolised modernity: studio buildings with large north-facing windows were built by avant-garde architects all over this part of Paris; artists, writers and intellectuals drank and debated in the quarter's showy bars; and naughty pastimes – such as the tango – flourished. *See p164* **Artists' Paris 2 Montparnasse.**

Today Montparnasse has lost much of its soul. The high-rise **Tour Montparnasse**, the first skyscraper in central Paris, is the most visible of several redevelopment projects of the 1970s; horror at its construction prompted a change in building regulations for central Paris. At least there are fabulous views from the panoramic café on the 56th floor, and the tower is an inescapable landmark. At its foot are a shopping centre, the **Red Light** and **Club Mix** nightclubs (*see p325 and p329*) and, in winter, an open-air **ice rink** (*see p337*). The old Montparnasse railway station witnessed two events of historic significance: in 1898 a runaway train burst through its façade (you've almost certainly seen the photograph), and on 25 August 1944 the German forces surrendered Paris here. The train station was rebuilt in the 1970s, a grey affair that contains the surprising **Jardin Atlantique**, the **Mémorial du Maréchal Leclerc** and the **Musée Jean Moulin** above its tracks.

Rue du Montparnasse, appropriately enough for a street near the station that sends trains to Brittany, is clustered with crêperies. Nearby, strip joints have replaced most of the theatres on the ever-saucy rue de la Gaîté, but boulevard Edgar-Quinet has pleasant cafés and a street market (Wed, Sat), and the entrance to the **Cimetière du Montparnasse**. Nearby boulevard du Montparnasse still buzzes at night, thanks to its many cinemas and eating and drinking spots: giant art deco brasserie **La Coupole** (*see p210*); opposite, classic café **Le Select** (*see p234*); Le Dôme (No.108, 14th, 01.43.35.25.81), now a top-notch fish restaurant and bar; and restaurant La Rotonde (No.105, 6th, 01.43.26.48.26). All were popularised by the heavyweight literary and arty set between the wars, and all now use this heritage to their advantage. Of the bunch, Le Select seems the least forced – but only just. Nearby, on bd

Sightseeing

Parc André Citroën. *See p161.*

Raspail, stands Rodin's statue of Balzac, whose rugged rather than flattering appearance caused such a scandal that it was put in place only after the sculptor's death.

For a whiff of Montparnasse's artistic past, wander down rue de la Grande-Chaumière. Bourdelle and Friesz taught at the venerable Académie de la Grande-Chaumière (No.14), frequented by Calder, Giacometti and Pompon among others (it still offers drawing lessons today); Modigliani died at No.8 in 1920, ruined by tuberculosis, drugs and alcohol; nearby **Musée Zadkine** occupies the sculptor's old house and studio. Rue Vavin and rue Bréa, leading to the **Jardin du Luxembourg** (*see p152*), have become an enclave of children's shops. Make sure you look out for the sleek, white-tiled apartment building where art nouveau architect Henri Sauvage lived at 6 rue Vavin, built in 1912.

Further east on boulevard du Montparnasse, literary café La Closerie des Lilas (No.171, 6th, 01.40.51.34.50) was a pre-war favourite with everyone from Lenin and Trotsky to Picasso and Hemingway; brass plaques on the tables illustrate which historic figure used to sit where. Next to it is the lovely Fontaine de l'Observatoire, featuring bronze turtles and thrashing sea horses by Frémiet and figures of the four continents by Carpeaux. From here, the Jardins de l'Observatoire form part of the green axis 1900 between the **Palais du Luxembourg** (*see p152*) and the original royal observatory, the **Observatoire de Paris**. A curiosity next door is the Maison des Fontainiers, built over an expansive (now dry-ish) underground reservoir originally commissioned by Marie de Médicis to supply water to fountains around the city.

A recent addition to boulevard Raspail is the glass-and-steel **Fondation Cartier**; designed by Jean Nouvel, it contains the jewellery company's headquarters and an exhibition centre for contemporary art.

West of the train station, the redevelopment of Montparnasse is also evident in the circular place de Catalogne, a piece of 1980s postmodern classicism by Mitterrand's favourite architect, Ricardo Bofill, and the housing estates of rue Vercingétorix. Traces of old, arty Montparnasse remain too: in impasse Lebouis, an avant-garde studio building has recently been converted into the **Fondation Henri Cartier-Bresson**; at 21 avenue du Maine, an ivy-clad alleyway of old studios contains the artist-run exhibition space Immanence, as well as the **Musée du Montparnasse**, housed in the former academy and canteen of Russian painter Marie Vassilieff; on rue Antoine-Bourdelle, the **Musée Bourdelle** includes another old cluster of

studios, where sculptor Bourdelle, Symbolist painter Eugène Carrière and, briefly, Marc Chagall worked. Towards Les Invalides, on rue Mayet, craft and restoration workshops still hide in old courtyards.

Cimetière du Montparnasse

3 bd Edgar-Quinet, 14th (01.44.10.86.50). M° Edgar Quinet or Raspail. **Open** *16 Mar-5 Nov* 8am-6pm Mon-Fri; 8.30am-6pm Sat; 9am-6pm Sun. *6 Nov-15 Mar* 8am-5.30pm Mon-Fri; 8.30am-5.30pm Sat; 9.30am-5.30pm Sun. **Admission** free. **Map** p405 G9.
This 1,800-acre cemetery was formed by commandeering three farms (you can still see the ruins of a rural windmill by rue Froidevaux) in 1824. As with much of the Left Bank, the Montparnasse cemetery scores highly for literary credibility: Beckett, Baudelaire, Sartre, de Beauvoir, Maupassant, Ionesco and Tristan Tzara all reside here; the artists include Brancusi, Henri Laurens, Frédéric Bartholdi (sculptor of the Statue of Liberty) and Man Ray. The celebrity roll-call continues with Serge Gainsbourg, André Citroën (of automobile fame), comic Coluche and actress Jean Seberg.

Fondation Cartier pour l'Art Contemporain

261 bd Raspail, 14th (01.42.18.56.72/recorded info 01.42.18.56.51/www.fondation.cartier.fr). M° Raspail or Denfert-Rochereau. **Open** noon-8pm Tue-Sun. **Admission** €6.50; €4.50 concessions; free under-10s. **Credit** AmEx, MC, V. **Map** p405 G9.
Jean Nouvel's glass-and-steel building, an exhibition centre with Cartier's offices above, is as much a work of art as the installations inside. Shows by contemporary artists and photographers often have wide-ranging themes, such as 'Birds' or 'Desert'. Live events around the shows are called Nuits Nomades.

Fondation Dubuffet

137 rue de Sèvres, 6th (01.47.34.12.63/www. dubuffetfondation.com). M° Duroc. **Open** 2-6pm Mon-Fri. Closed Aug. **Admission** €4; free under-10s. **No credit cards. Map** p405 E8.
You have to walk up a winding garden path to get to this museum housed in an old three-storey mansion. Set up by Jean Dubuffet, wine merchant and master of *art brut*, a decade before his death in 1985, the foundation ensures that a fair body of his works is accessible to the public. There's a changing display of Dubuffet's lively drawings, paintings and sculptures, plus models of the architectural sculptures from the *Hourloupe* cycle. The foundation looks after the *Closerie Falballa*, the 3D masterpiece of the cycle, housed at Périgny-sur-Yerres, east of Paris (viewings by appointment only, €8).

Fondation Henri Cartier-Bresson

2 impasse Lebouis, 14th (01.56.80.27.00/www.henri cartierbresson.org). M° Gaîté. **Open** 1-6.30pm Tue-Fri, Sun; 1-8.30pm Wed; 11am-6.45pm Sat. Closed Aug & between exhibitions. **Admission** €4; €3 students, under-26s; over-60s, all 6.30-8.30pm Wed. **No credit cards. Map** p405 F10.

Artists' Paris 2 Montparnasse

With its sleazy dance halls and cheap rents, Montparnasse was a natural choice when the Montmartre artists' colony decamped in search of cheaper lodgings in the 1910s. Founder members such as Picasso and Modigliani were joined by Russian and South American refugees, who scrounged drinks at its cafés and filled up at Marie Vassilieff's artists' soup kitchen. With American writers and jazzers such as Josephine Baker adding spice to the mix, the area soon became a hedonistic playground that epitomised *les années folles*. The 1970s saw the ghastly Tour Montparnasse plonked bang in the middle, but walking around you can still spot the artists' ateliers, and stop for a *verre* in its famous watering holes, which retain the decorative allure of their glory days.

Start at Mº Falguière and take rue Falguière, which goes off to the left. At No.11 the gates of the Villa Gabriel are sometimes left open; wander in to get a taste of the tiled, glass-fronted studios. Turn left into **rue Antoine Bourdelle**, where at No.16 you can pop in to this monumental sculptor's museum (❶ *see p165*), or peer through the railings to see the outsized mythological works in its garden. The road comes out on avenue du Maine just opposite Marie Vassilieff's old soup kitchen, now the **Musée du Montparnasse** (❷ *see p166*). Green light softly filters in through wisteria-clad windows in the old studios, where changing exhibitions explore different aspects of Montparnasse artistic life.

Turn left out of the museum and take the steps at the end of the avenue to cross the plaza in front of the bustling Gare Montparnasse. Continue up avenue du Maine on the other side and take the first left on to peaceful rue du Maine, which joins rue de la Gaîté at the trendy Café Tournesol. To the right down this theatre-filled street you can see the neon sign for Bobino. Although most famous for hosting iconic singer-songwriter Georges Brassens and actress-turned-singer Juliette Gréco in the '60s, the dance hall was also the place where Man Ray's lover Kiki and other saucy cabaret performers bared their bits before a rapt and penniless audience.

Continue left to the sycamore-shaded place Edgar-Quinet, which offers a choice of café terraces. To gawp at some truly dreadful artistic efforts, stroll by the art market on boulevard Edgar-Quinet.

Nearby rue Delambre was a favourite with those artists who did not live in **La Ruche** (*see p168*), the artists' colony in passage Dantzig in the 15th. Man Ray had his studio at No.15 (now the Hôtel Lenox) and at No.10 the Auberge de Venise was once the Dingo Bar, where Hemingway first met F Scott Fitzgerald. Just along the road at No.5, a plaque commemorates the Japanese artist Foujita – by all accounts one of the craziest of a crazy bunch (❸).

At the end of the road is place Pablo-Picasso, with four of the original five cafés that made this, according to an exhibition in

Opened in 2003, this two-floor gallery is dedicated to the photographer Henri Cartier-Bresson. It consists of a tall, narrow *atelier* in a 1913 building, with a minutely catalogued archive, open to researchers, and a lounge on the fourth floor screening films. In the spirit of Cartier-Bresson, who assisted on three Jean Renoir films and drew and painted all his life (some drawings are also found on the fourth floor), the Fondation opens its doors to other disciplines with three annual shows. The convivial feel of the Fondation – and its Le Corbusier armchairs – foster relaxed discussion with staff and other visitors.

Jardin Atlantique

Gare Montparnasse or pl des Cinq-Martyrs-du-Lycée-Buffon, 15th. Mº Montparnasse Bienvenüe or Gaîté. **Open** 8am-dusk Mon-Fri; 9am-dusk Sat, Sun. **Map** p405 F9.

Perhaps the hardest of all the gardens in Paris to find, the Jardin Atlantique was opened in 1995. It's an engineering feat in itself: a modest oasis of gran-

ite paths, trees and bamboo is spread over the roof 18m (59ft) above the tracks of Montparnasse train station. Small openings allow you to peer down on the trains below; children seem to love the randomly triggered fountain jets.

Mémorial du Maréchal Leclerc de Hauteclocque et de la Libération de Paris & Musée Jean Moulin

Jardin Atlantique, 23 allée de la 2e DB (above Gare Montparnasse), 15th (01.40.64.39.44/www.paris.fr). *Mº Montparnasse Bienvenüe.* **Open** 10am-6pm Tue-Sun. **Admission** free. *Exhibitions* €4; €3 students, over-60s; €2 under-26s; free under-13s. **Credit** *Shop* MC, V. **Map** p405 F9.

This double museum retraces World War II and the Résistance through the Free French commander General Leclerc and left-wing hero Jean Moulin. Documentary material and film archives complement an impressive 270º slide show, complete with sound effects retelling the Liberation of Paris.

the now-defunct Café Parnasse in 1921, 'the centre of the world'. Chose from the sedate **Dôme**, the showbiz **Select** and the **Rotonde**, where Picasso and Man Ray once held court. Or, most splendid of all, **La Coupole** (❹, *see p210*). Opened in 1927, its splendid pillars

feature paintings by eight artists of the day, including Marie Vassilieff. Artists and writers flocked in, among them André Derain, Man Ray and Henry Miller. If you're interested in its illustrious past, a souvenir booklet reveals more than the waiters are prepared to tell you.

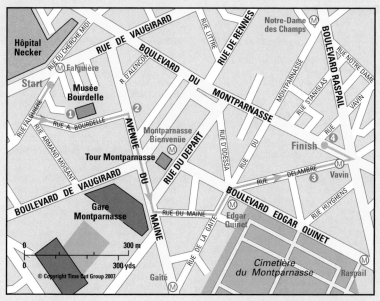

Musée-Atelier Adzak

3 rue Jonquoy, 14th (01.45.43.06.98). M° Plaisance. **Open** usually 3-7pm Sat, Sun, call in advance. **Admission** free.
The eccentric house, studio and garden built by the late Roy Adzak harbour traces of the conceptual artist's plaster body columns and dehydrations. Now a registered British-run charity, it gives artists (generally foreign) a chance to exhibit in Paris.

Musée Bourdelle

16-18 rue Antoine-Bourdelle, 15th (01.49.54.73.73/ www.paris.fr/musees/bourdelle). M° Montparnasse Bienvenüe or Falguière. **Open** 10am-6pm Tue-Sun. **Admission** free. *Exhibitions* prices vary (approx €4.50/€3 concessions). **Credit** MC, V. **Map** p405 F8.
The sculptor Antoine Bourdelle (1861-1929), pupil of Rodin, produced monumental works like the Modernist relief friezes at the Théâtre des Champs-Elysées, inspired by Isadora Duncan and Nijinsky. Set around a small garden, the museum includes the

artist's apartment, and studios used by him, as well as by Eugène Carrière, Dalou and Chagall. A 1950s extension tracks the evolution of Bourdelle's equestrian monument to General Alvear in Buenos Aires, and his masterful *Hercules the Archer*. A new wing by Christian de Portzamparc houses bronzes such as studies of Beethoven in various guises.

Musée du Montparnasse

21 av du Maine, 15th (01.42.22.91.96/www.musee dumontparnasse.net). M° Montparnasse Bienvenüe. **Open** 12.30-7pm Tue-Sun. **Admission** €5; €4 students, 12-18s; free under-12s. **No credit cards**. **Map** p403 F8.
Set in one of the last surviving alleys of studios, this was home to Marie Vassilieff, whose own academy and cheap canteen welcomed poor artists Picasso, Cocteau and Matisse. Trotsky and Lenin were also guests. Shows focus on the area's creative past and present-day artists. Until April 2007, a temporary exhibition celebrates Modigliani's Paris, 1906-20.

Musée Pasteur

*Institut Pasteur, 25 rue du Dr-Roux, 15th
(01.45.68.82.83/www.pasteur.fr). M° Pasteur.* **Open**
2-5.30pm Mon-Fri. Closed Aug. **Admission** €3;
€1.50 students. **Credit** MC, V. **Map** p405 E9.
The flat where the famous chemist and his wife lived
at the end of his life (1888-95) has not been touched;
you can see their furniture and possessions, photos
and instruments. An extravagant mausoleum on the
ground floor houses Pasteur's tomb, decorated with
mosaics depicting his scientific achievements.

Musée de la Poste

*34 bd de Vaugirard, 15th (01.42.79.23.45/www.
museedelaposte.fr). M° Montparnasse Bienvenüe.*
Open 10am-6pm Mon-Sat. **Admission** €5; €3.50
students under 26; free under-13s. PMP. *Permanent
& temporary exhibitions* €6.50; free under-18s. **No
credit cards**. **Map** p405 E9.
Among uniforms, pistols, carriages, official decrees
and fumigation tongs emerge snippets of history:
during the 1871 Siege of Paris, hot-air balloons and
carrier pigeons were used to get post out of the city,
and *boules de Moulins*, balls crammed with hundreds of letters, were floated down the Seine in
return, mostly never to arrive. The second section
covers French and international philately.

Musée Zadkine

*100bis rue d'Assas, 6th (01.55.42.77.20/www.paris.
fr/musees/zadkine). M° Notre-Dame-des-Champs/
RER Port-Royal.* **Open** 10am-6pm Tue-Sun.
Admission free. *Exhibitions* €4; €3 students, over-
60s; €2 under-26s; free under-13s. **Credit** (€15
minimum) MC, V. **Map** p408 G8.
Works by the Russian-born Cubist sculptor Ossip
Zadkine are displayed around this tiny house and
garden near the Jardin du Luxembourg, where he
lived from 1928 until his death in 1967. Zadkine's
works cover musical, mythological and religious
subjects, and his style varies with his materials: his
bronzes tend to be geometrical, his wooden sculptures more sensuous. Works are displayed at eye
level, with drawings and poems by Zadkine and
paintings by his wife, Valentine Prax. Changing
exhibitions of contemporary artists are held in the
former studio.

Observatoire de Paris

*61 av de l'Observatoire, 14th (www.obspm.fr).
M° St-Jacques/RER Port-Royal.* **Open** *Tours* 1st Sat
of mth (except Aug) by written reservation only to:
Service de la Communication (service des visites),
Observatoire de Paris, 61 av de l'Observatoire, 75014
Paris. **Map** p405 H10.
The Paris observatory was founded by Louis XIV's
finance minister, Colbert, in 1667; it was designed
by Claude Perrault (who also worked on the Louvre),
with labs and an observation tower. The French
meridian line drawn by François Arago in 1806
(which was in use before the Greenwich meridian
was adopted as an international standard) runs
north-south through the centre of the building; the
dome on the observation tower was added in the

1840s, but what with urban light pollution, most
stargazing is now carried out in Meudon and
Provence. A visit entails a prior written appointment, but check the website for openings linked to
astronomical happenings – or visit on the Journées
du Patrimoine (*see p273*).

Tour Montparnasse

*33 av du Maine, 15th (01.45.38.52.56/www.tour
montparnasse56.com). M° Montparnasse Bienvenüe.*
Open *Winter* 9.30am-10.30pm daily. *Summer*
9.30am-11.30pm daily. **Admission** €9; €6.50
students; €4 7-15s; free under-7s. **Credit** MC, V.
Map p405 F9.
Built in 1974 on the site of the old station, this 209m
(686ft) steel-and-glass monolith is shorter than the
Eiffel Tower, but better placed to get a fabulous
view of the city – including, of course, the Eiffel
Tower itself. A lift whisks you up in 38 seconds to
the 56th floor, where you'll find a display of aerial
scenes of Paris, an upgraded café-lounge, a souvenir
shop – and sky. On a clear day you can see up to
40km (25 miles). Another, shorter, lift gets you up to
the roof. Classical concerts are held on the terrace.

Denfert-Rochereau & Montsouris

In the run-up to the 1789 Revolution, the bones
of six million Parisians were taken from the
handful of overcrowded city cemeteries and
wheelbarrowed to the **Catacombs**, a network
of tunnels that spreads under much of the 13th
and 14th arrondissements. The gloomy Denfert-
Rochereau public entrance to one section is next
to one of the toll gates of the Mur des Fermiers-
Généraux built by Ledoux in the 1780s.
    The bronze *Lion de Belfort* dominates the
traffic-laden place Denfert-Rochereau, a
favourite starting point for the city's countless
political demonstrations. The regal beast was
sculpted by Bartholdi, of Statue of Liberty fame,
and is a scaled-down replica of one in Belfort
that commemorates the brave defence by
Colonel Denfert-Rochereau of the town in 1870.
Nearby, the southern half of rue Daguerre is a
sociable, pedestrianised market street
(Tue-Sat, Sunday mornings) brimming with
cafés and food shops.
    One of the big draws here is the **Parc
Montsouris**, containing lovely lakes, dramatic
cascades and an unusual history. Surrounding
the western edge of the park are a number of
modest, quiet streets – including rue du Parc
Montsouris and rue Georges-Braque – that
used to be lined in the 1920s and '30s with
charming villas and artists' studios by avant-
garde architects such as Le Corbusier and
André Lurçat. On the southern edge of the park
sprawls the **Cité Universitaire** complex,
containing three dozen internationally themed
halls of residence and 6,000 students.

Montparnasse.

Les Catacombes

*1 av Colonel Henri-Rol-Tanguy, 14th (01.43.22.
47.63/www.catacombes.info). M°/RER Denfert
Rochereau.* **Open** 9.30am-4pm Tue-Sun. **Admission**
€5; €3.30 over-60s; €2.50 students, 14-26s; free
under-14s. **Credit** (€15 minimum) MC, V.
Map p407 H10.

Official entrance for the extensive network of subterranean passages that runs under much of the city,
particularly the 13th and 14th arrondissements. The
3,000km (1864 miles) tunnel network originated as
quarries, providing limestone for huge building projects such as Notre-Dame. By the late 18th century,
when the city had extended this far south, many
streets began to collapse. The authorities set about
building tunnels and supports to prop up the earth.
At the same time, with public burial pits rising in
the era of the Revolutionary Terror, the bones of six
million people were transferred to the *catacombes*.
The bones of Marat, Robespierre and their cronies
are tightly packed in with wall upon wall of their fellow citizens. It's an extraordinary sight, and one not
for the claustrophobic: visitors descend an 85-step
spiral staircase that takes them some 20m (66ft)
below ground, to a mass of bones and carvings.
Make sure you carry a torch – and don't try to take
away one of the bones as a souvenir: your bags will
be checked at the end.

Cité Universitaire

*Bd Jourdan, 14th (01.44.16.64.00/www.ciup.fr).
RER Cité Universitaire.*

The Cité Internationale Universitaire de Paris is an
odd mix. Created between the wars in a mood of
internationalism and inspired by the model of
Oxbridge colleges, the 37 halls of residence spread
across landscaped gardens were designed in a variety of supposedly appropriate national styles, some
by appropriate national architects (Dutchman
Willem Dudok drew the De Stijl-style Collège
Néerlandais); others, like the Asie du Sud-Est building, with its Khmer sculptures and bird-beak roof,
are exotic pastiches. The Brits get what looks like a
minor public school; the Maison Internationale is
based on Fontainebleau; the Swiss and Brazilians
get Le Corbusier. You can visit the sculptural white
Pavillon Suisse (01.44.16.10.10, www.fondation
suisse.fr), which has a Le Corbusier mural on the
ground floor. The Cité's spacious landscaped gardens are open to the public, and the newly renovated theatre stages a mix of drama and modern dance.
To apply to rent a room here, *see p379*.

Parc Montsouris

Bd Jourdan, 14th. RER Cité Universitaire. **Open**
8am-dusk Mon-Fri; 9am-dusk Sat, Sun.

The most colourful of the capital's many parks,
Montsouris was laid out for Baron Haussmann by
Jean-Charles Adolphe Alphand. It includes sweeping, gently sloping lawns, an artificial lake and artificial cascades. On its opening day in 1878 the lake
inexplicably emptied, and the engineer responsible
committed suicide.

The 15th arrondissement

Centred on the shopping streets of rue du
Commerce and rue Lecourbe, the expansive
15th has little to offer tourists, though as a
largely residential district it has plenty of good
restaurants and street markets. It's worth
making a detour to visit **La Ruche** ('beehive'),
designed by Eiffel as a wine pavilion for the
1900 Exposition Universelle and moved here
to serve as artists' studios. Nearby is **Parc
Georges Brassens**, opened in 1983, while at
the porte de Versailles, the sprawling **Paris-
Expo** exhibition centre was created in 1923.

Parc Georges Brassens

*Rue des Morillons, 15th. M° Porte de Vanves or
Porte de Versailles.* **Open** 8am-dusk Mon-Fri; 9am-
dusk Sat, Sun. **Map** p404 D10.

Built on the site of the old Abattoirs de Vaugirard,
Parc Georges Brassens prefigured the industrial
regeneration of Parc André Citroën and La Villette.
The gateways, crowned by bronze bulls, have been
kept, as have a series of iron meat-market pavilions,
which house a second-hand book market at weekends. The Jardin des Senteurs is planted with aromatic species, and a small vineyard yields 200
bottles of Clos des Morillons every year.

Paris-Expo

*Porte de Versailles, 15th (01.72.72.17.00/www.
paris-expo.fr). M° Porte de Versailles.* **Map** p404 B10.
The vast exhibition centre, spread over different
halls, hosts all kinds of trade and art fairs. Many,
such as the Foire de Paris (*see p270*) and art fair
FIAC (*see p274*), are open to the public.

La Ruche

*Passage de Dantzig, 15th. M° Convention or Porte de
Versailles.* **Map** p404 D10.
Take a peek through the fence or sneak in behind an
unsuspecting resident to see the iron-framed former
wine pavilion built by Eiffel for the 1900 Exposition
Universelle, and rebuilt by philanthropic sculptor
Alfred Boucher to be let as studios for struggling
artists. Chagall, Soutine, Brancusi, Modigliani,
Lipchitz and Archipenko spent periods here, and the
140 studios are still sought after by artists today.

The 13th arrondissement

The contrasts are immediate in the 13th, where
villagey clusters of little houses alternate with
1960s tower blocks and the new ZAC Rive
Gauche development zone. Here is where you'll
find the newest bridge in Paris, the Passerelle
Simone-de-Beauvoir; next to it, a new floating
swimming pool and sundeck, both inaugurated
in the summer of 2006. Soon to come will be a
university complex to house 30,000 students
and staff. It's all happening in the 13th. *See
p170* **Riverside revival**.

Les Gobelins & La Salpêtrière

Its defining features may be tower blocks, but the 13th arrondissement is also historic, especially in the area bordering the 5th. The **Manufacture Nationale des Gobelins**, home to the state weaving companies, continues a tradition founded in the 15th century, when tanneries, dyers and weaving workshops lined the River Bièvre. The waterway became notorious for its pollution, and the slums that grew up around it were depicted in Hugo's *Les Misérables*. The area was tidied up in the 1930s, when square René-Le-Gall, a small park, was laid out on the allotments used by tapestry workers. The river was built over, but local enthusiasts have opened up a small stretch in the park. Nearby, through a gateway at 17 rue des Gobelins, you can spot the turret and first floor of a medieval house, recently renovated as apartments. The so-called Château de la Reine Blanche on rue Gustave-Geffroy is named after Queen Blanche of Provence, who had a château here; it was probably rebuilt in the 1520s for the Gobelin family. Blanche was also associated with a nearby Franciscan monastery, of which a fragmentary couple of arches survive on the corner of rue Pascal and rue de Julienne.

In the northern corner of the 13th, next to Gare d'Austerlitz (the station that serves most of central France), sprawls the huge Hôpital de la Pitié-Salpêtrière founded in 1656, with its striking **Chapelle St-Louis**.

The busy intersection of place d'Italie has seen further recent developments. Opposite the 19th-century town hall stands the Centre Commercial Italie 2, a bizarre high-tech confection designed by Kenzo Tange. It houses a shopping centre but, sadly, no longer the Gaumont Grand Ecran Italie cinema, closed in 2006 due to competition from multiplexes. You'll also find a thrice-weekly food market on boulevard Auguste-Blanqui (Tue, Fri, Sun).

Chapelle St-Louis-de-la-Salpêtrière
47 bd de l'Hôpital, 13th (01.42.16.04.24). M° Gare d'Austerlitz. **Open** 8.30am-6pm Mon-Fri, Sun; 11am-6pm Sat. **Admission** free. **Map** p406 L9.
This austerely beautiful chapel, designed by Libéral Bruand and completed in 1677, features an octagonal dome in the centre and eight naves in which they used to separate the sick from the insane, the destitute from the debauched. Around the chapel sprawls the vast Hôpital de la Pitié-Salpêtrière, founded on the site of a gunpowder factory (hence the name, derived from saltpetre) by Louis XIV to house rounded-up vagrant women. It became a centre for research into insanity in the 1790s, when renowned doctor Philippe Pinel began to treat some of the inmates as sick rather than criminal; Charcot later pioneered neuropsychology here, receiving a famous visit from Freud. Salpêtrière is today one of the city's main teaching hospitals, but the chapel is also used for contemporary art installations, notably for the Festival d'Automne (*see p273*), when its striking architecture provides a backdrop for artists such as Bill Viola, Anish Kapoor and Nan Goldin.

Manufacture Nationale des Gobelins
42 av des Gobelins, 13th (tours 01.44.54.19.33). M° Les Gobelins. **Open** *Tours* 2pm, 2.45pm Tue-Thur. **Admission** €8; €6 7-24s; free under-7s. **No credit cards. Map** p406 K10.
The royal tapestry factory was founded by Colbert when he set up the Manufacture Royale des Meubles de la Couronne in 1662; it's named after Jean Gobelin, a dyer who owned the site. It reached the summit of its renown during the *ancien régime*, when Gobelins tapestries were produced for royal residences under artists such as Le Brun and Oudry. Tapestries are still made here (mainly for French embassies around the world), and visitors can watch weavers at work. The tour (in French) through the 1912 factory takes in the 18th-century chapel and the Beauvais workshops. Arrive 30 minutes before the tour starts.

Chinatown & La Butte-aux-Cailles

South of rue de Tolbiac, the shop signs suddenly turn Chinese or Vietnamese, and even McDonald's is decked out *à la chinoise*. The city's main Chinatown runs along avenue d'Ivry, avenue de Choisy and into the 1960s tower blocks between. While many of the tower blocks in the Paris suburbs are bleak, here they have a distinctly eastern vibe, with restaurants, Vietnamese *pho* noodle bars and Chinese pâtisseries, hairdressers and purveyors of exotic groceries, not to mention the expansive Tang Frères supermarket (48 avenue d'Ivry, 13th, 01.45.70.80.00), the main supplier for Chinatown. There's even a Buddhist temple hidden in a car park beneath the tallest tower (avenue d'Ivry, opposite rue Frères d'Astier-de-la-Vigerie, 13th). Lion and dragon dances, and martial arts demonstrations, take place on the streets at Chinese New Year (*see p274*).

In contrast to Chinatown, the villagey Butte-aux-Cailles, occupying the wedge between boulevard Auguste-Blanqui and rue Bobillot, is a neighbourhood of old houses, winding cobblestone streets, funky bars and restaurants. This workers' neighbourhood, home in the 19th century to many small factories, was one of the first to fight during the 1848 Revolution and the Paris Commune. The Butte has preserved its rebellious character: residents wear Fidel Castro T-shirts and resist the aggressive forces of city planning and construction companies. The cobbled rue de la Butte-aux-Cailles and rue des Cinq-Diamants are the hub of the bohemian

Riverside revival

With the inauguration of an elegant footbridge (*see p82* **There's a new bridge in town**) and an ultra-modern floating swimming pool (*see p337*) on the Seine, 2006 in many ways marked the coming of age for the area officially known as the ZAC Rive Gauche. The Zone d'Aménagement Concerté ('Multi-partner Development Zone'), more simply referred to by its district number on the Left Bank, the 13th, extends between the Gare d'Austerlitz and boulevard Masséna. At the same time as the bridge and pool were opened, Paris-Plage, a popular summer feature previously reserved for the Right Bank, expanded for the first time across the river to set up along a one-kilometre (0.6 mile) stretch of the 13th (*see p272* **Take me to the river**).

Since 1996, and the inauguration of the **Bibliothèque Nationale François Mitterrand** (*see p171*) here, there have been major changes in this once industrial wasteland – the arrival of the high-tech driverless métro line 14, a new RER station at the library, the opening of the 14-screen **MK2** arthouse cinema (*see p289*) – but all this is only part of equally ambitious development plans to be realised in the next 12 months.

Now that the new footbridge – with its capacity to host temporary exhibitions and rows of book stalls – provides a link with the four L-shaped towers of the Bibliothèque Nationale, there is a tangible sense of what is to come. Combine this with the proximity of the city's tramway (*see p362* **Green machine**) launching in December 2006, plus the recent

opening of shops such as a vast Decathlon sports store, and you have the infrastructure in place for a new hub of arts and education, within easy reach of both sides of the city.

The advent of the city's biggest university site is already upon us. The Paris VII Denis-Diderot University has moved into several of the renovated industrial buildings near the Seine, including the landmark Grands Moulins de Paris and the Halles aux Farines (Flour Hall). Like Les Frigos, an old refrigerated warehouse converted into a ramshackle complex of artists' studios and rehearsal rooms, the university premises stand as a reminder of the area's heritage, and form a stark contrast to the surrounding glass-fronted offices and glitzy modern flats. With more university departments set to migrate to the area in 2007, ZAC Rive Gauche is already being billed as the new Latin Quarter, an intellectual stronghold that will eventually house some 30,000 students and staff at four separate universities.

The university developments are only part of the ongoing plans. From 2007, métro line 14 will call at a new station at Olympiades, to the west of Bibliothèque. Just south of the Gare d'Austerlitz, a strip of run-down warehouses is to be reincarnated as the Docks-en-Seine. With a completion date pencilled in for November 2007, the project will see the existing concrete buildings covered with a stylish wooden framework and topped by a panoramic garden. Offering riverside views, the complex will house the

soixante-huitard forces, where you'll find relaxed, inexpensive bistros like the eccentric Le Temps des Cérises (18 rue Butte-aux-Cailles, 13th, 01.45.89.69.48), run as a co-operative, Chez Gladines (30 rue des Cinq-Diamants, 13th, 01.45.80.70.10) and the more upmarket **Chez Paul** (*see p203*). The cottages built in 1912 in a mock-Alsatian style around a central green at 10 rue Daviel were among the earliest public-housing schemes in Paris. Just across rue Bobillot, the **Piscine de la Butte-aux-Cailles** (*see p338*) is a charming Arts and Crafts-style swimming pool, fed by artesian wells. Further south, you can explore passage Vandrezanne, the little houses and gardens of square des Peupliers, rue des Peupliers and rue Dieulafoy, and the flower-named streets of the Cité Florale. By the Périphérique, the Stade

Charléty (17 av Pierre-de-Coubertin, 13th, 01.44.16.60.60), designed by father and son Henri and Bruno Gaudin, is a superb piece of stadium architecture headed by swooping, bird-like floodlights.

The developing east

The construction of the **Bibliothèque Nationale de France** breathed life into the desolate area between Gare d'Austerlitz and the Périphérique, formerly an expanse of lonesome railway yards, and now known as the ZAC Rive Gauche (*see p170* **Riverside revival**). The ambitious, long-term ZAC project calls for a new university quarter, an eastwards extension of the Latin Quarter, aided by the recent introduction of a footbridge capable of hosting

Institut Français de la Mode (the French Fashion Institute), being uprooted from the prestigious Champs-Elysées area, as well as shops, restaurants and a nightclub. The club will be in good company – the presence of landmark DJ spot the **Batofar** (*see p323*) and the more eclectic floating entertainment venue alongside it, the **Guinguette Pirate**

(*see p319*), has already established the 13th as a suitable destination for a summer night out on the tiles.

A bridge, swimming pool, multiplex cinema, summer beach, city university and national institute of fashion – not bad for a site that was a sprawling mess of old railway tracks and abandoned buildings only a decade ago.

exhibitions (*see p82* **There's a new bridge in town**) and a tramway linking to the suburbs (*see p362* **Green machine**).

Further east, towards Porte d'Ivry, curious rue Watt is the lowest street in Paris (it runs below river level). At 12 rue Cantagrel you can see Le Corbusier's Cité de Réfuge de l'Armée de Salut hostel, a long, reinforced-concrete structure built from 1929 to 1933 to accommodate 1,500 homeless men, and a precursor of the architect's Unités d'Habitation.

Bibliothèque Nationale de France François Mitterrand

10 quai François-Mauriac, 13th (01.53.79.59.59/ www.bnf.fr). M° Bibliothèque François Mitterrand. **Open** 2-7pm Mon; 9am-7pm Tue-Sat; 1-7pm Sun. **Admission** *1 day* €3.30. *2 weeks* €20. *1 year* €35; €18 students, 16s-25s. **Credit** MC, V. **Map** p407 M10.

Opened in 1996, the new national library was the last and costliest of Mitterrand's *Grands Projets*, the first stage in the redevelopment of the 13th district. Its architect, Dominique Perrault, was criticised for his curiously dated design, which hides readers underground and stores the books in four L-shaped glass towers. He also forgot to specify blinds to protect books from sunlight; they had to be added afterwards. In the central void is a garden (filled with 140 trees, transported from Fontainebleau at enormous expense). The library houses over ten million volumes and can accommodate 3,000 readers. The research section, just below the public reading rooms, opened in 1998. Much of the library is open to the public: books, newspapers and periodicals are accessible to anyone over 18, and you can browse through photographic, film and sound archives in the audiovisual section. There are regular classical music concerts and exhibitions too.

Beyond the Périphérique

The sound of the suburbs.

Magnificent men's flying machines: the **Musée de l'Air et de l'Espace**. *See p173.*

Closing the divide – social, cultural, economic – between Paris and its suburbs is one of the avowed policies of city mayor Bertrand Delanoë. Improved transport links is the most tangible evidence of this, such as the recently inaugurated T3 tramway (*see p370* **High-tech travel**) running along the southern edge of the Périphérique, the ring road separating city from suburb. Another initiative is to landscape sections of it to give those living alongside a better quality of life. One by one, district councils of the outer boroughs are signing co-operation agreements with the City Hall for closer links. The latest, signed in September 2006 and involving Ivry-sur-Seine, puts forward an ambitious plan for a local history museum to be built on a bridge across the river.

For many Parisians, though, the suburbs evoke images of the terrible riots of 2005, an expression of long-subdued anger of *banlieue* youth. An expedition to the *banlieue* (especially the undesirable northern and eastern suburbs) takes on the aura of a journey to a foreign land, a land ventured into only for cheap supermarket petrol and DIY stores. For them, the *banlieue*

(a term rarely used to include the sought-after districts such as Neuilly, St-Cloud or Boulogne, but with much the same implied tag of 'inner city' when applied to UK towns) is as much a mindset as a physical reality, with its image of housing estates, large immigrant populations, unemployment, drugs and urban gangs, even its own accent, argot and style of dress. Part of the negative rep is accurate: there are dangerous estates, where the fire brigade is attacked as it puts out blazes, and where attempts to reopen local shops are answered by vandalism. But there are also swaths of respectable residential districts, with their own self-contained provincial atmosphere quite different from the city itself.

There are signs of change too. A major new gallery, the MAC/VAL, is the first permanent collection of contemporary art to open in the Paris suburbs (*see p298* **A breath of fresh art**). A handful of destination restaurants have been enjoying significant custom from residents travelling out to dine (*see p210* **Supper in the suburbs**). The rising property prices within Paris mean that many families are now being forced out into the inner ring of suburbs. High

Sculptor Paul Landowski (1875-1961) won the Prix de Rome in 1900, and never lacked for state commissions, his work treating classical and modern themes on a monumental scale. One of his most intriguing creations is *Temple* – four sculpted walls depicting the history of humanity. Some 100 sculptures are on show in this garden and studio.

Musée National de la Céramique

Pl de la Manufacture, 92310 Sèvres (01.41.14.04.20). Mº Pont de Sèvres. **Open** 10am-5pm Mon, Wed-Sun. Closed most public hols. **Admission** €4.60; €2.60 18-25s; free under-18s, all on 1st Sun of mth. *Exhibitions* €5.20; €3.80 CM. **Credit** MC, V.
Founded in 1738 as a private concern, the famous porcelain factory moved to Sèvres from Vincennes under the state in 1756. Finely painted, delicately modelled pieces that epitomise French rococo style, together with later Sèvres, adorned with copies of Raphaels and Titians, demonstrate a technical virtuosity. The collection also includes Delftware, Meissen and wonderful Ottoman plates.

La Défense

The skyscrapers and walkways of La Défense – named after a stand against the Prussians in 1870 – create a whole new world. The area has been a showcase for French business since the mid 1950s, when the CNIT hall was built to host trade shows, but it was the arrival of the **Grande Arche** that gave the district its most dramatic monument. Today, more than 100,000 people work here, and another 35,000 live in the blocks of flats on the southern edge, served by the inevitable mall, an IMAX cinema, a huge multiplex and a leisure complex. For summer

2007, Jean-Christophe Choblet, the creator of **Paris-Plage** (*see p272*), is to create a series of outdoor cultural events to encourage workers to socialise in the neighbourhood rather than take the usual commuter train home. On the central esplanade are fountains and sculptures by Miró and Serra. No particular skyscraper displays architectural distinction, although together they make an impressive sight.

La Grande Arche de La Défense

92044 Paris La Défense (01.49.07.27.57/www.grande arche.com). Mº La Défense. **Open** *Apr-Sept* 10am-8pm daily. *Oct-Mar* 10am-7pm daily. **Admission** €7.50; €6 students, 6-18s; free under-6s. **Credit** MC, V.
Completed for the bicentenary of the Revolution, in 1989, the Grande Arche was designed by Danish architect Johan Otto von Spreckelsen. Though it lines up neatly on the Grand Axe – from the Louvre, up the Champs-Elysées to the Arc de Triomphe – the building itself is skewed. A vertigo-inducing glass lift soars up through the 'clouds' to the roof, and a fantastic view over Paris.

Musée Mémorial Ivan Tourguéniev

16 rue Ivan-Tourguéniev, 78380 Bougival (01.45.77.87.12). Mº La Défense then bus 258. **Open** *Apr-Oct* 10am-6pm Sun. Also by appointment for groups (weekdays). **Admission** €5.50; €4.60 students, 12-25s; free under-12s. **No credit cards.**
The dacha where novelist Ivan Turgenev lived until his death in 1883 was a gathering spot for composers Saint-Saëns and Fauré, divas Pauline Viardot and Maria Malibran, and writers Henry James, Flaubert, Zola and Maupassant. Letters and editions are on the ground floor; above are the music room where Viardot held court and the writer's deathbed.

NEW TIME OUT
SHORTLIST GUIDES 2007

Barcelona
2007
WHAT'S NEW | WHAT'S ON | WHAT'S NEXT

London
2007
WHAT'S NEW | WHAT'S ON | WHAT'S NEXT

New York
2007
WHAT'S NEW | WHAT'S ON | WHAT'S NEXT

Paris
2007
WHAT'S NEW | WHAT'S ON | WHAT'S NEXT

Prague
2007
WHAT'S NEW | WHAT'S ON | WHAT'S NEXT

Rome
2007
WHAT'S NEW | WHAT'S ON | WHAT'S NEXT

The MOST up-to-date guides to the world's greatest cities

UPDATED ANNUALLY

WRITTEN BY LOCAL EXPERTS

Available at all major bookshops at only
£6.99 and from timeout.com/shop

Eat, Drink, Shop

Features

Restaurants

The dining spots *du choix*.

Un Jour à Peyrassol. *See p184.*

Gone are the days when Paris offered culinary wonders on every corner. Sadly, despite the quality of the products available, the overall standard seems to be on a downhill slide that could put the city's reputation as a gastronomic capital in real peril – especially when compared to the much more adventurous food scenes in cities such as London, New York and Sydney.

Thankfully, an increasing number of young chefs are valiantly battling this general trend – many of them working alone in tiny kitchens. Cyril Lalanne at **La Cerisaie**, Sylvain Endra at **Le Temps au Temps**, Nadège Varigny and Guy Bommefront at **Ribouldingue**, Philippe Tredgeu at **L'Entredgeu** and Chris Wright at **Le Timbre** are a few of the idealists whose diminutive restaurants prove that Paris dining has a future. Christian Constant, mentor to many a Paris chef, also shows what bistro cooking can and should be at **Le Café Constant**, where you can taste the lack of shortcuts in classic dishes such as lentils braised with pork and pike-perch *quenelles*.

The chef's bistro has come to be known as the neo-bistro, setting it apart from old-time stalwarts such as **Josephine 'Chez Dumonet'** and **Chez La Vieille**, which continue to soldier on in diminishing numbers.

If bistros are still the major genre in Paris, there is a growing number of more ambitious restaurants where the price you pay for contemporary cooking still looks reasonable compared to haute cuisine. Some of these are run by haute cuisine chefs such as Pierre Gagnaire (**Gaya Rive Gauche**), Guy Savoy (**Atelier Maître Albert**) and Joël Robuchon (**L'Atelier de Joël Robuchon**) in a bid to make their cooking more accessible, while others showcase the styles of former bistro chefs such as William Ledeuil (Ze Kitchen Galerie, 4 rue des Grands Augustins, 6th, 01.44.32.00.32) and Gilles Choukroun (**Angl'Opéra**). Most offer reasonable value for money, though it is easy to spend €100 or more per person at haute cuisine annexes.

Brasseries have sunk particularly low, with most now run by chains – go for the historic settings, buzzy atmospheres, seafood platters and occasional surprisingly good dish (the desserts at least are usually reliable).

Like any world capital, Paris has a dizzying number of international restaurants to choose from. Best among these are the North African restaurants, though you'll also find good Japanese, Chinese, Korean, Middle Eastern and Italian food if you're extremely selective.

Except for the very simplest restaurants, it's wise to book ahead. This can usually be done on the same day as your intended visit, although really top-notch establishments require bookings weeks in advance and confirmation the day before (remember that lunch can be much more affordable than dinner). If you've failed to get a reservation, try putting yourself on a waiting list a couple of days ahead, as last-minute cancellations are common.

All listings have been checked at time of press but are often liable to change. Many venues close for their annual break in August,

Purple '❶' numbers given in this chapter correspond to the location of each restaurant as marked on the street maps. See pp400-409.

Eat, Drink, Shop

Price codes

With our reviews, we give the average price for a standard main course chosen from the à la carte menu. If 'Main courses' is not listed, only prix fixe options are available. 'Prix fixe' indicates the price of the venue's set menu at lunch and/or dinner. All bills include a service charge, but an additional tip of a few euros (for the whole table) is polite unless you're unhappy with the service.

some at Christmas. Restaurants in this chapter are presented by area, then by type: French or international. For more reviews, refer to *Time Out Paris Eating & Drinking*, available at www.timeout.com/shop.

The Islands

French

Brasserie de l'Ile St-Louis
55 quai de Bourbon, 4th (01.43.54.02.59). Mº Pont Marie. **Open** noon-midnight Mon, Tue, Fri-Sun; 6pm-midnight Thur. Closed Aug. **Main courses** €20. **Credit** MC, V. **Map** p409 K7 ❶
Happily, this old-fashioned brasserie soldiers on while exotic juice bars and fancy tea shops on the Ile St-Louis come and go. The terrace has one of the best summer views in Paris and is invariably packed; the dining room exudes shabby chic. Nicotined walls make for an agreeably authentic Paris mood, as does the slightly gruff waiter, though nothing here is gastronomically gripping: a well-dressed *frisée aux lardons*, a slab of fairly ordinary terrine, a greasy slice of *foie de veau* prepared *à l'anglaise* with a rasher of bacon, and a more successful pan of warming tripes. A dash more sophistication in the kitchen would transform this delightful place into something more exceptional.

Mon Vieil Ami
69 rue St-Louis-en-l'Ile, 4th (01.40.46.01.35). Mº Pont Marie. **Open** noon-2.30pm, 7-10.30pm Wed-Sun. Closed 1st 3wks Aug. **Main courses** €21. **Prix fixe** €39. **Credit** AmEx, DC, MC, V. **Map** p409 K7 ❷
Antoine Westermann from the Buerehiesel in Strasbourg has created a true foodie destination here. He may be one of Alsace's greatest chefs, but the modernised bistro cooking draws from all the regions of France – more unusually, he pays as much attention to vegetables as to meat and fish. Starters such as a tartare of finely diced raw vegetables with sautéed baby squid on top impress with their deft seasoning and accuracy of preparation. Typical of

the mains is a cast-iron casserole of roast duck with caramelised turnips and couscous, or gleamingly fresh, chunky flakes of hake on a generous *barigoule* of stewed artichoke hearts and fennel. Desserts revisit bistro favourites – rum baba, chocolate tart or a light variation on the *café liègeois* in a cocktail glass. Even the classic high-ceilinged Ile St-Louis dining room has been successfully refreshed with black beams, white perspex panels between wall timbers, and a long black *table d'hôte* down one side.

The Louvre, Palais-Royal & Les Halles

French

L'Ardoise
28 rue du Mont-Thabor, 1st (01.42.96.28.18). Mº Concorde or Tuileries. **Open** noon-2.30pm, 6.30-11pm Tue-Sat; 6.30-11pm Sun. Closed 1st 3wks Aug. **Main courses** €19. **Prix fixe** €32. **Credit** MC, V. **Map** p401 G5 3 ❸
One of the city's outstanding modern bistros, L'Ardoise is also one of the few to open on Sundays. The rather anonymous room is soon packed with gourmets eager to sample Pierre Jay's reliably delicious cooking. A wise choice might be six oysters with warm chipolatas and a pungent shallot dressing, an unusual combination from Bordeaux; equally attractive are a gamey hare pie with an escalope of foie gras nestling in its centre, or firm, shelled langoustines placed around a mousseline of celery and coated in a luscious chervil sauce. A lightly chilled, raspberry-scented Chinon, from a wine list sensibly arranged by price, provides a perfect complement.

La Bourse ou la Vie
12 rue Vivienne, 2nd (01.42.60.08.83). Mº Bourse. **Open** noon-3pm, 7-10pm daily. **Main courses** €20. **Credit** MC, V. **Map** p402 H4 ❹
After a career as an architect, the round-spectacled owner of La Bourse ou la Vie has a new mission in life – to revive the dying art of the perfect *steak-frites*. His vivid yellow and red dining room is an unlikely setting for the meat fest that takes place here daily. The only decision you'll need to make is which cut of beef to order with your chips, unless you inexplicably pick the cod from the perfunctory laminated menu. Choose between ultra-tender *coeur de filet* or a huge, surprisingly un-chewy *bavette*. Rich, creamy pepper sauce is the speciality here, but the real surprise is the frites, which gain a distinctly animal flavour and inimitably crunchy texture from the suet in which they are cooked. Own-made desserts are temptingly displayed at the entrance.

Chez La Vieille
37 rue de l'Arbre-Sec, 1st (01.42.60.15.78). Mº Louvre Rivoli. **Open** noon-2pm Mon-Wed, Fri; noon-2pm, 7.30-9.30pm Thur. **Main courses** €26. **Prix fixe** Lunch €27. **Credit** AmEx, MC, V. **Map** p406 J6 ❺

Eat, Drink, Shop

The rustic ground floor of this bistro bursts with well-rounded regulars, while upstairs is plain and bright. A wondrous ad-lib selection of starters might include hot *chou farci* and home-made *terrine de foie gras*, both delivered by a smiling waitress. Equally impressive is *foie de veau*, coated in a pungent reduction of shallots and vinegar and served with potato purée. Puddings follow the same cornucopian principle as the starters, and the wine list includes a fine selection of wines from Corsica (birthplace of the eponymous *vieille* who now runs the dining room). Opening hours are limited and booking is essential, but the lunchtime prix fixe is a bargain for the quantity and quality of the fare.

Drouant

18 rue Gaillon, 2nd (01.42.65.15.16/www.drouant .com). M° Quatre Septembre or Pyramides. **Open** noon-2.30pm, 7pm-midnight daily. **Main courses** €67. **Prix fixe** *Lunch* €45. **Credit** AmEx, DC, MC, V. **Map** p401 H4. ⑥

Star Alsatian chef Antoine Westermann, who runs the successful Ile St-Louis bistro Mon Vieil Ami (*see p182*), has whisked this landmark 1880 brasserie into the 21st century with bronze-upholstered banquettes and armchairs, a pale parquet floor and rather incongruous butter-yellow paint and fabrics. Black suits are de rigueur in a dining room heavy with testosterone (at least at lunch). Westermann has dedicated this restaurant to the art of the hors d'oeuvre, served in themed sets of four ranging from the global (a surprisingly successful Thai beef salad with brightly coloured vegetables, coriander, and a sweet and spicy sauce) to the nostalgic (silky leeks in vinaigrette). The bite-sized surprises continue with the main course accompaniments – four of them for each dish, to be shared among the diners – and the multiple mini-desserts.

Le Grand Véfour

17 rue de Beaujolais, 1st (01.42.96.56.27/www. relaischateaux.com). M° Palais Royal Musée du Louvre. **Open** 12.30-2pm, 8-10pm Mon-Thur; 12.30-2pm Fri. Closed Aug. **Main courses** €74. **Prix fixe** *Lunch* €78. **Credit** AmEx, DC, MC, V. **Map** p402 H5 ⑦

Opened in 1784 (as the Café de Chartres), this is one of the oldest and most historical restaurants in Paris. Many of the greats of this world once feasted on this very spot, from Napoleon and his Josephine to the literary elite – André Malraux, Colette, Sartre, Simone de Beauvoir and Victor Hugo, who was a regular. Each member of staff is perfectly charming, particularly the knowledgeable sommeliers and the dashing maître d'hôtel, Christian David. An à la carte meal begins with a fantasia suite of delicacies: tiny frogs' legs, for example, artistically arranged within a circle of sage sauce; a first course of creamed Breton sea urchins served in their spiny shells with a quail's egg and topped with caviar; flash-fried langoustines with tangy mango sauce nestling inside a curled shell, with tiny girolles and a swirl of coriander juice. Fish dishes may be a touch

overcooked, and the adventurous desserts are not always entirely successful – but you'll forgive all after a glass of vintage Armagnac.

Le Meurice

Hôtel Meurice, 228 rue de Rivoli, 1st (01.44.58. 10.10/www.meuricehotel.com). M° Tuileries. **Open** noon-2pm, 7.30-10pm Tue-Fri; 7.30-10pm Sat. Closed Aug. **Main courses** €70. **Prix fixe** *Lunch* €75. *Dinner* €170. **Credit** AmEx, DC, MC, V. **Map** p401 G5 ⑧

Yannick Alléno, chef here since 2003, has hit his stride and is doing some glorious, if understated, contemporary French luxury cooking. Few chefs working in Paris today exercise such restraint when it comes to letting superb produce star at the table, but Alléno has a light touch, teasing the flavour out of every leaf, frond, fin or fillet that passes through his hands. Turbot is sealed in clay before cooking and then sauced with celery cream and a coulis of

The best Restaurants

For confirmed carnivores

Boucherie Roullière (*p206*); La Bourse ou la Vie (*p182*); Chez Paul (*p203*); Ribouldingue (*p206*); La Tour de Montlhéry (Chez Denise) (*p184*).

For dinner à deux

Lapérouse (*p209*); La Madonnina (*p202*); Mon Vieil Ami (*p182*).

For hearty appetites

L'Ambassade d'Auvergne (*p195*); Le Bistrot Napolitain (*p193*); Chez Omar (*p196*); Le Souk (*p201*).

For lunch on a budget

A la Bière (*p201*); L'Encrier (*p199*); Le Reminet (*p206*).

For oysters by the dozen

Ballon & Coquillages (*p187*); La Coupole (*p210*); Huîtrerie Régis (*p207*).

For star chefs at work

L'Arpège (*p212*); L'Atelier de Joël Robuchon (*p212*); Le Bistrot d'à Côté Flaubert (*p188*); Le Meurice (*p183*); Pierre Gagnaire (*p190*); Senderens (*p191*).

For terroir cuisine

L'Ambassade d'Auvergne (*p195*); L'Ami Jean (*p211*); Chez Michel (*p201*); Granterroirs (*p189*); Mon Vieil Ami (*p182*).

For vegetarians

Chez Omar (*p196*); Le Petit Marché (*p196*); Crêperie Bretonne Fleurie (*p197*).

Eat, Drink, Shop

flat parsley, while Bresse chicken stuffed with foie gras and served with truffled *sarladais* potatoes (cooked in the fat of the bird) is breathtakingly good. A fine cheese tray, with a stunning extra-aged comté, comes from Quatrehomme (*see p262*), and the pastry chef amazes with his signature millefeuille. The bemused complicity of the courtly but friendly waiters and sommeliers makes for a memorable meal.

Scoop

154 rue St-Honoré, 1st (01.42.60.31.84/www. scoopcafe.com). M° Palais Royal Musée du Louvre. **Open** 11am-7pm Mon-Sat; noon-7pm Sun. **Main courses** €15. **Prix fixe** €10-€14. **Credit** MC, V. **Map** p402 H5 ❾

What started out as an American-style ice-cream parlour has taken on a Parisian personality well suited to its fashionable surroundings just behind the Louvre. For lunch, choose from healthy wraps, soups such as the delectable pumpkin concoction, savoury tarts and hot dishes. But be sure to save room for the main event – ice-creams in flavours such as chocolate espresso, toasted pecan or Vermont maple syrup. For even more indulgence, order the turtle sundae (vanilla ice-cream with chocolate and caramel sauce and pecans). Service isn't ultra-speedy during peak times, so arrive early if you're rushed (later on, they run out of wraps and tarts). Delicious pancakes are served for Sunday brunch (noon-4.30pm), as well as hot dishes such as salmon and ratatouille for the more conventional French eater.

Table d'Hôte du Palais Royal

8 rue de Beaujolais, 1st (01.42.61.25.30/www. carollsinclair.com). M° Bourse or Pyramides. **Open** 11.30am-2.30pm, 6pm-midnight daily. **Main courses** €40. **Prix fixe** €28. **Credit** AmEx, MC, DC, V. **Map** p401 H5 ❿

Caroll Sinclair's new restaurant, in a gorgeous setting just outside the Palais-Royal garden, has a more informal atmosphere than her previous establishment Le Safran, and is all the better for it. The idea of *table d'hôte* is that diners should feel like guests in a private home. Though the excellent prix fixe pulls a younger crowd, it's rewarding to go à la carte with a wonderful crayfish bisque, smoked salmon served with dill-sprinkled potato salad, an exceptional, spicy *boeuf tartare* with ginger as part of its secret recipe, and an interesting hybrid meat and fish dish of tuna steak served with warm foie gras and wild mushrooms. A perfectly quaffable carafe wine, served in beautiful antique decanters, provides an alternative to the pricy but well-chosen wine list. Delicious ice-creams are made on the premises.

La Tour de Montlhéry (Chez Denise)

5 rue des Prouvaires, 1st (01.42.36.21.82). M° Les Halles/RER Châtelet Les Halles. **Open** noon-3.30pm, 7.30pm-6am Mon-Fri. Closed 14 July-15 Aug. **Main courses** €22. **Credit** MC, V. **Map** p402 J5 9 ⓫

At the stroke of midnight, the place is packed, jovial and hungry. The busy red-checked dining room is intimate – you end up tasting a portion of your neighbour's roasted lamb or chatting by the barrels of wine stacked atop the bar. Savoury traditional dishes, washed down by litres of the house Brouilly, are the order of the day. Les Halles was the city's wholesale meat market, and game, beef and offal still rule here. Diners devour towering rib steaks served with marrow and a heaped platter of fries, home-made and among the best in town. Brave souls can try *tripes au calvados*, grilled *andouillette* or lamb's brain, or go for a stewed venison, served with succulent celery root and home-made jam.

Un Jour à Peyrassol

13 rue Vivienne, 2nd (01.42.60.12.92/www. peyrassol.com). M° Bourse. **Open** noon-2pm, 8-10pm daily. **Main courses** €25. **Credit** MC, V. **Map** p402 H4. ⓬

As anyone who has travelled around Provence will know, come winter the restaurants there go truffle-crazy, putting the black tuber into everything from soups to ice-cream. This casually chic little offshoot of the Commanderie de Peyrassol, a picturesque wine-producing castle in the Var, keeps up the game with its blackboard menu, full of truffle treats. They can be eaten on toast, atop a baked potato, in scrambled eggs or in a rich, creamy sauce enveloping fluffy gnocchi. The natural complement is the Commanderie's wine – white, red and rosé AOC Côtes de Provence, which is also available at the shop two doors away. **Photo** *p181.*

International

Chez Vong

10 rue de la Grande-Truanderie, 1st (01.40.26.09.36). M° Etienne Marcel or Les Halles. **Open** noon-2.30pm, 7pm-midnight Mon-Sat. **Main courses** €50. **Prix fixe** *Lunch* €23.50. **Credit** AmEx, DC, MC, V. **Map** p402 J5 ⓭

The staff at this intimate Chinese restaurant take pride in its excellent cooking, which covers the great dishes of Canton, Shanghai, Beijing and Sichuan. From the greeting at the door to the knowledgeable and trilingual service (Cantonese, Mandarin and French), each part of the experience is thoughtfully orchestrated to showcase China's diverse and delicious cuisines. Tables, draped in pink cloth, are widely spaced; low lighting and green ceramic bamboo partitions heighten the sense of intimacy. Any doubts about authenticity are extinguished with the first arrival of the beautifully presented dishes, which are placed on heated stands at the table. Expertly cooked spicy shrimp glistens in a smooth, characterful sauce of onions and ginger, while Ma Po tofu melts in the mouth, its spicy and peppery flavours melding with those of the fine pork mince.

Kai

18 rue du Louvre, 1st (01.40.15.01.99). M° Louvre-Rivoli. **Open** noon-2pm, 7-10.30pm Tue-Sat; 7-10.30pm Sun. Closed Aug. **Main courses** €60. **Prix fixe** *Lunch* €27-€38. *Dinner* €58-€90. **Credit** MC, V. **Map** p402 H5 ⓮

occur seamlessly, yet Vrinat is not afraid to hire young chefs with character. A recent decision was to put Alain Solivérès in charge of the kitchen, which is turning out flawless food. Past the spacious and rather subdued front room is a livelier, brasserie-like second room. Prices here are not as shocking as in some restaurants at this level; there's a €70 lunch menu, though you might have to make a point of asking for it. *Rémoulade de coquilles St-Jacques* is a technical feat, with slices of raw, marinated scallop wrapped in a tube shape around a finely diced apple filling, encircled by a mayonnaise-like *rémoulade* sauce. An earthier and lip-smacking dish is the trademark *épeautre* – known in English as spelt – cooked 'like a risotto' with bone marrow, black truffle, whipped cream and parmesan, and topped with sautéed frogs' legs. *Ravioli au chocolat araguani* is a surprising and wonderful dessert: pillowy pockets of soft chocolate pasta explode in the mouth, releasing liquid bitter chocolate.

International

Le Bistrot Napolitain

18 av Franklin-D.-Roosevelt, 8th (01.45.62.08.37). Mº St-Philippe du-Roule. **Open** noon-2.30pm, 7-10.30pm Mon-Fri; noon-3pm Sat. Closed Aug. **Main courses** €25. **Credit** MC, V. **Map** p401 E4 **②**
This chic Italian bistro off the Champs-Elysées is as far from a tourist joint as it is possible to be. On weekday lunchtimes (it doesn't open on Saturday night or on Sunday) it is full of suave Italianate businessmen in modish pinstripes. The decor is plain, the tablecloths starched white, and the kitchen open, with the *pizzaiolo* shoving fluffy pizzas in and out of the oven while orders are shouted over the heads of diners. Generosity defines the food – not just big plates, but lashings of the ingredients that others skimp on, such as the slices of tangy parmesan piled high over rocket on the fresh and tender beef carpaccio. The pizzas are as good as they say they are: the Enzo comes with milky, almost raw *mozzarella di bufala* and tasty tomatoes, which prove how good the crust is as it doesn't become a soggy mush. For pasta you can choose between dried and fresh, with variations such as fresh saffron tagliatelle.

Man Ray

34 rue Marbeuf, 8th (01.56.88.36.36/www.manray.fr). Mº Franklin D. Roosevelt. **Open** *Sept-July* 7pm-midnight daily. *Aug* 7pm-midnight Tue-Sat. **Main courses** €25. **Prix fixe** €27, €35. **Credit** AmEx, MC, V. **Map** p401 D4 **③**
At the perenially hip Man Ray, conversation tends to involve whispering, 'Don't look now, but that's Mick Jagger', punctuated by lengthy gawping at the extravagant pan-Asian decor – the cavernous space has the feel of a 21st-century opium den. The food is an afterthought and comically bland, though you might have more luck with the sushi or sashimi platters. Normally safe-bet fried spring rolls, labelled *'comme je les aime'*, are greasy, and the insipid foie gras with chutney is like a butter and fig-jam breakfast. Dry tuna steak is beached on spinach leaves drowned in tangy ginger sauce, turning blacker by the minute as you wait for your partner's course to arrive. Tiramisu comes in a sundae glass, with coffee jelly lurking beneath. Be warned. Better to taste the buzz from the mezzanine bar for the 'After Work' drink and free massage in the week – a far more appetising way to mingle with the beautiful people.

Eat, Drink, Shop

Taillevent. *See p191.*

Montmartre & Pigalle

French

Chez Toinette

20 rue Germain-Pilon, 18th (01.42.54.44.36).
M° Abbesses or Pigalle. **Open** 7.30-11.30pm Mon-Sat.
Closed last 3wks Aug. **Main courses** €16. **Credit**
MC, V. **Map** p401 H2 **34**

This stalwart purveyor of bistro fare behind the
Théâtre de Montmartre has steadily upped its prices
in line with its burgeoning success. However, the
blackboard menu is still good value in an area
known for rip-offs. As you squeeze into the seats,
the amiable waiter describes each dish with pride,
then presents an appetiser of olives, ripe cherry
tomatoes and crisp radishes. Of the starters, try the
red-blooded wild boar terrine, the gloriously creamy
chèvre chaud or the soufflé-like asparagus quiche.
Carnivorous mains include *mignon de porc*, spring
lamb and assorted steaks – the lamb seared in rosemary is a deliciously lean morsel. The desserts cover
standard ground, but you can round off on a high
note with Armagnac-steeped prunes.

Georgette

*29 rue St-Georges, 9th (01.42.80.39.13). M° Notre-
Dame-de-Lorette.* **Open** noon-2.45pm, 7.30-11pm
Tue-Fri. Closed Aug. **Main courses** €15. **Credit**
AmEx, MC, V. **Map** p402 H3 **35**

A mix of 1950s formica tables (with matching bar)
and ancient wooden beams provides the external
charm, but what has won Georgette a loyal following since it opened three years ago is the chef's lov-
ing use of seasonal ingredients. Forget pallid
supermarket tomatoes; here, in late summer, they're
orange, yellow and green, layered in a salad or
blended up in a flavour-packed gazpacho. Hearty
meat dishes satisfy the local business crowd, while
lighter options might include slightly bony sea
bream with provençal vegetables, or a charlotte of
juicy lamb chunks and aubergine. For calorie counters there's an unsweetened prune and pear compote
– though the creamy, cloud-like fontainebleau cheese
with raspberry coulis is worth abandoning a diet for.

Pétrelle

34 rue Pétrelle, 9th (01.42.82 11.02). M° Anvers.
Open 8-10pm Tue-Sat. Closed 4wks July/Aug & 1wk
Dec. **Main courses** €23. **Prix fixe** €27. **Credit**
MC, V. **Map** p402 J2 **36**

Jean-Luc André is as inspired a decorator as he is a
cook, and the quirky charm of his dining room has
made it popular with fashion designers and film
stars alike. A faded series of early 20th-century
tableaux is one recent flea market find, but behind
the style is some serious substance. André seeks out
the very best ingredients from local producers, and
the quality shines through. The €27 no-choice menu
is huge value for money (on our last visit, marinated sardines with tomato relish, rosemary-scented

Le Petit Marché. *See p196.*

rabbit with roasted vegetables, deep purple poached figs), or you can splash out with luxurious à la carte dishes such as tournedos Rossini. If you're looking for a quick and delicious lunch near Montmartre, visit André's annexe, Les Vivres, next door.

International

Kastoori
4 pl Gustave-Toudouze, 9th (01.44.53.06.10).
M° St-Georges. **Open** 6.30-11.30pm Mon; 11.30am-2.30pm, 6.30-11.30pm Tue-Sun. **Main courses** €16. **Prix fixe** *Lunch* (Mon-Fri) €8, €10. *Dinner* €15. **Credit** MC, V. **Map** p401 H2 ④

It's no surprise that Kastoori's terrace, on a delightful 19th-century square, is often full: this friendly, family-run Indian restaurant is one of the few good-value eateries in the area. We're not talking ubiquitous mass-produced buffets: each dish on the lunch and dinner set menus is prepared with care and home-mixed spices, and you can taste the difference. Amid dangling lanterns, Indian fabrics and (perhaps too much) incense inside, or under hot lamps outside, order some popadoms to taste the home-made chutneys served in an ornate metal boat, and choose from tangy raita and *kaleji* (coriander-sprinkled, curried lamb liver) as starters, followed by a choice of tandoori chicken, chicken curry, *saag paneer* or the dish of the day, selected from the à la carte menu. You can bring your own wine for no corkage fee, and don't miss the delicious lassis or kulfis for afters.

Rose Bakery
46 rue des Martyrs, 9th (01.42.82.12.80). M°
Notre-Dame-de-Lorette. **Open** 9am-7pm Tue-Sat; 10am-5pm Sun. Closed 2wks Aug. **Main courses** €20. **Credit** MC, V. **Map** p402 H2 ③

This English-themed café run by a Franco-British couple stands out for the quality of its ingredients – organic or from small producers – as well as the too-good-to-be-true puddings, carrot cake, sticky toffee pudding and, in winter, a chocolate-chestnut tart. The DIY salad plate is crunchily satisfying, but the thin-crusted *pizzettes*, daily soups and occasional risottos are equally good choices. Don't expect much beyond scones in the morning except at weekends, when brunch is served to a packed-out house. Popular with health-conscious locals who love the smoke-free atmosphere and expats who can't believe their luck, the dining room – which looks as if it might have once been a garage – is minimalist but welcoming. The service is friendly, if overwhelmed.

Beaubourg & the Marais

French

L'Ambassade d'Auvergne
22 rue du Grenier-St-Lazare, 3rd (01.42.72.31.22/
www.ambassade-auvergne.com). M° Arts et Métiers.
Open *Sept-July* noon-2pm, 7.30-10.30pm daily.
Aug noon-2pm, 7.30-10.30pm Mon-Fri, Sun. **Main courses** €15. **Prix fixe** €32. **Credit** AmEx, MC, V. **Map** p402 K5 ③

This rustic auberge is a fitting embassy for the hearty, filling fare of central France. Go easy on the complimentary pâté and thick-sliced country bread while you look at the menu – you're going to need your appetite later. An order of cured ham comes as two hefty, plate-filling slices, while the salad bowl is chock-full of green lentils cooked in goose fat, studded with bacon and shallots. The *rôti d'agneau* arrives as a pot of melting chunks of lamb in a rich meaty sauce with a helping of tender white beans. Dishes arrive with the flagship *aligot*, served with great pomp as the waiter lifts great strands of the creamy, elastic mash-and-cheese concoction into the air and lets it plop on to the plates with a dramatic flourish. Of the regional wines (Chanturgue, Boudes, Madargues), the rather fruity AOC Marcillac makes a worthy partner for a successful meal.

Le Dôme du Marais
53bis rue des Francs-Bourgeois, 4th (01.42.74.
54.17). M° Rambuteau. **Open** noon-2.30pm, 7.15-11pm Tue-Sat. Closed 2wks Jan & 3wks Aug. **Main courses** €18. **Prix fixe** *Lunch* €17, €23. *Dinner* €32, €45. **Credit** AmEx, MC, V. **Map** p409 K6 ④

Lying somewhere between casual and formal, bistro and haute cuisine, Le Dôme du Marais seems to have got it just about right. The staff won't turn a hair if you show up in jeans, but should you feel the urge to mark the occasion with finery, the octagonal, domed dining room would provide a fine backdrop.

The building pre-dates the French Revolution and once served as the auction room for state-owned pawnbrokers; today it has been done up (but, thankfully, not overdone) in burgundy and gilt, with tables dressed in sparkling white linen. Owner-chef Pierre Lecoutre loves to work with seasonal produce, serving, say, *filet de courbine*, a white fish available for three weeks a year, in a chorizo cream sauce next to fresh little broad beans that also have a brief season. *Monceau de chocolat* and strawberry *dacquoise* live up to their stunning good looks.

Le Hangar

12 impasse Berthaud, 3rd (01.42.74.55.44).
M° Rambuteau. **Open** noon-2.30pm, 7-11.30pm
Tue-Sat. Closed Aug. **Main courses** €16. **No credit cards. Map** p402 K5 ④

It's worth making the effort to check out this bistro by the Centre Pompidou, with its terrace and excellent cooking. The exposed stone walls and smartly set tables are immediately welcoming, and the long, airy room fills with locals and slightly baffled tourists. A bowl of tapenade and toast is supplied to keep you going while choosing from the comprehensive *carte*. It yields, for starters, tasty and grease-free *rillettes de lapereau* (rabbit) alongside perfectly balanced pumpkin and chestnut soup. Main courses include a well-seasoned steak tartare, served with a crisp salad and *pommes dauphines*, and a superb *ris de veau* on a bed of melting chicory. Puddings such as chocolate soufflé and warm white-wine tart with cinnamon are also tempting – but if you're going to splurge, remember that payment is on cash only.

Le Petit Marché

9 rue de Béarn, 3rd (01.42.72.06.67). M° Chemin Vert. **Open** noon-3pm, 8pm-midnight Mon-Fri; noon-4pm, 8-10pm Sat, Sun. **Main courses** €16. **Prix fixe** *Dinner* €40. **Credit** MC, V. **Map** 406 L6 ④

Just a step away from place des Vosges, Petit Marché attracts a fashion-conscious crowd. The woody interior is warm and welcoming, while the heated terrace offers a view of the *gendarmerie*. The menu is short and modern with Asian touches. Raw tuna is flash-fried in sesame seeds and served with a Thai sauce, making for an original and refreshing starter; crispy-coated deep-fried king prawns have a similar oriental lightness. The main vegetarian risotto is rich in basil, coriander, cream and al-dente green beans, contrasting winningly with the unctuous rice. Pan-fried scallops with lime are precision-cooked to avoid any hint of rubberiness, and accompanied by a good purée and more beans. There's a short wine list; the carafe of house red is unusually good. **Photo** *p194.*

Le Petit Pamphlet

15 rue St-Gilles, 3rd (01.42.71.22.21) M° Chemin Vert. **Open** 7.30-11pm Mon, Sat; noon-2.30pm, 7.30-11pm Tue-Fri. Closed 2wks Jan & 2wks Aug. **Main courses** €30. **Credit** MC, V. **Map** p409 L6 ④

His solid success at the chic Marais bistro Le Pamphlet inspired chef Alain Carrère to open this casual annexe just to the north of place des Vosges.

Jacquard table runners and framed sketches liven up a dining room that otherwise feels a tiny bit bland, but the flavours are as bold as ever in starters such as tomato stuffed with confit lamb, followed by black cod in a tomato and caper dressing served with crushed potatoes, or parmesan risotto topped with prawns cooked *a la plancha*. Typical of the seasonal desserts are roasted figs with caramel ice-cream and mirabelle plums with a crumble topping. The very professional staff are anxious to please, and prices are more than fair for the neighbourhood.
Other locations: Le Pamphlet, 38 rue Debelleyme, 3rd (01.42.72.39.24).

International

Anahi

49 rue Volta, 3rd (01.48.87.88.24). M° Arts et Métiers, Temple or République. **Open** 8pm-midnight daily. **Main courses** €20. **Credit** MC, V. **Map** p409 L5 ④

A rickety old building in a narrow and ill-lit street deep in the Marais houses this trendy Argentinian restaurant. Slabs of grilled beef fresh (well, vacuum-packed) from the pampas pull in the crowds, cheerily welcomed by Carmina and Pilat, the sisters who started up in this old charcuterie some 20 years ago. The original white-tiled walls feature black-and-white photos of the pair, and the art deco ceiling was painted by Albert Camus' brother. Tuck into *torta pascualina*, a sweetish spinach tart with onions, or try the standout ceviche made with sea bass. Mains of skewered chicken breast marinated in lemon and served with apple and pineapple salsa and sweet potato purée, and *cururú de camarao* (grilled *gambas* with peanuts and okra) are satisfying, but the *bif angosto* – a juicy fillet served with a green salad – is the star. Match it with a choice Chilean red.

Chez Omar

47 rue de Bretagne, 3rd (01.42.72.36.26).
M° Temple or Arts et Métiers. **Open** noon-2.30pm, 7-11.30pm Mon-Sat; 7-11.30pm Sun. **Main courses** €16. **No credit cards. Map** p402 L5 ④

The once-fashionable Omar doesn't take reservations, and the queue can stretch the length of the zinc bar and through the door. Everyone is waiting for the same thing: couscous. Prices range from €11 (vegetarian) to €24 (*royale*); there are no tagines or other traditional Maghreb mains, only a handful of French classics (duck, fish, steak). Overstretched waiters slip through the crowds with mounds of semolina, steaming vats of vegetable-laden broth and steel platters heaving with meat and more meat, including the stellar *merguez*. Even on packed nights there's an offer of seconds – gratis, of course – to encourage you to stay; big appetites might find room for the giant platter of Algerian pastries the waiter leaves at your table. Non-smokers beware: the proximity of your neighbours means you'll share more than just their conversation.
Other locations: Café Moderne, 19 rue Keller, 11th (01.47.00.53.62).

Bastille & eastern Paris

French

Le Bistrot Paul Bert

18 rue Paul Bert, 11th (01.43.72.24.01).
M° Charonne. **Open** noon-2pm, 7.30-11pm Tue-Thur;
noon-2pm, 7.30-11.30pm Fri, Sat. Closed Aug. **Main
courses** €30. **Prix fixe** *Lunch* €16. *Dinner* €30.
Credit MC, V. **Map** p407 N7
This heart-warming bistro gets it right almost down
to the last crumb, and is a popular haunt of local
businessmen and artisans. No-nonsense, pared-
down cooking is its forte: expect high-quality seasonal produce, very simply prepared. A starter salad
of *ris de veau* illustrates the point, with lightly
browned veal sweetbreads perched on a bed of green
beans and baby carrots and lightly nipped with a
sauce of sherry vinegar and deglazed cooking juices.
Though this approach is appealing, there are times
when it can be too plain. Cod steak with a fan of
roasted carrots and white asparagus is perfectly
cooked, but could do with a sprinkling of grey sea
salt and a squirt of lemon juice. Carnivores seem to
fare better under the minimalist regimen; a roasted
shoulder of suckling pig and a thick steak with a raft
of golden, clearly homemade thick-cut frites look
inviting indeed. This is one of the rare bistros that
still offer a help-yourself cheese tray, and it's unfail-
ingly a pleasant selection of nicely aged, seasonal
cheeses. Desserts are superb too, including what
may be the best floating island in Paris and a truly
top-notch *Paris Brest* (choux pastry filled with
mocha-hazelnut cream). If you're in the area at
lunchtime, the prix fixe menu is remarkable value.

Bofinger

*5-7 rue de la Bastille, 4th (01.42.72.87.82/www.
bofingerparis.com). M° Bastille.* **Open** noon-3pm,
6.30pm-1am Mon-Fri; noon-1am Sat, Sun. **Main
courses** €28. **Prix fixe** €30. **Credit** AmEx, DC,
MC, V. **Map** p409 L7
Opposite the Bastille opera house, Bofinger is a post-
show haunt that draws big crowds at other times for
its authentic art nouveau setting and brasserie
atmosphere. Downstairs is the prettiest place to eat,
but upstairs is air-conditioned. As at many Flo
group restaurants, the food is always adequate but
rarely aspires to great culinary heights. An à la carte
choice might start with plump, garlicky escargots
or a well-made langoustine terrine, followed by an
intensely seasoned salmon tartare, a generous (if
uneventful) cod steak, or calf's liver accompanied by
cooked melon. Alternatively, you could go for the
foolproof brasserie meal of oysters and fillet steak,
followed by a rabidly pungent plate of munster
cheese and accompanying bowl of cumin, washed
down by the fine Gigondas at €35.50 a bottle.

Crêperie Bretonne Fleurie

*67 rue de Charonne, 11th (01.43.55.62.29).
M° Ledru-Rollin or Charonne.* **Open** noon-2.30pm,
7pm-midnight Mon-Fri; 7-11pm Sat. Closed Aug.
Main courses €5. **Credit** MC, V. **Map** p407 N7
Everything about this place is authentic, including
the crêpe chef's own pointy chin thatch, wiggly pipe
and striped sailor shirt. The menu is straightforward: to fill your savoury, freshly cooked buckwheat
galette, choose a ham/cheese/egg combination (all
three is a *complète*, presented in a square topped
with a gleaming egg yolk), *andouille* (tripe sausage)
or the more unusual camembert with walnuts. Old-

Crêperie Bretonne Fleurie.

Eat, Drink, Shop

DISCOVER MORE CITIES

Tell us what you think and you could win £100-worth of City Guides

Your opinions are important to us and we'd like to know what you like and what you don't like about the Time Out City Guides

For your chance to win, simply fill in our short survey at **timeout.com/guidesfeedback**

Every month a reader will win £100 to spend on the Time Out City Guides of their choice – a great start to discovering new cities and you'll have extra cash to enjoy your trip!

fashioned manners prevail: the sashaying waitresses serve ladies first as gents politely contemplate the Celtic flags, Breton Tintin book and puzzling tribal mask. Dessert crêpes feature pear 'n chocolate and banana 'n chocolate fillings. Dry cider would be the logical accompaniment, but a Breton Breizh cola in its nifty glass bottle is hard to resist. **Photo** *p197*.

L'Encrier

55 rue Traversière, 12th (01.44.68.08.16).
Mº Ledru-Rollin or Gare de Lyon. **Open** noon-2.15pm, 7.30-11pm Mon-Fri; 7.30-11pm Sat. Closed Aug. **Main courses** €14. **Prix fixe** *Lunch* €13. *Dinner* €17, €21. **Credit** MC, V. **Map** p407 M7 **49**
Through the door and past the velvet curtain, you find yourself face to face with the kitchen – and a crowd of locals, many of whom seem to know the charming boss personally. Value is tremendous here, with a €13 lunch menu and a choice of €17 or €21 menus in the evening, as well as a few à la carte choices. Start with fried rabbit kidneys on a bed of salad dressed with raspberry vinegar, an original and wholly successful combination, and follow with goose *magret* with honey – a welcome change from the usual duck version and served with crunchy, thinly sliced sautéed potatoes. To end, share a chocolate cake, or try the popular profiteroles. The fruity Chinon is a classy red at a rather steep €24, but worth every cent.

Le Temps au Temps

13 rue Paul-Bert, 11th (01.43.79.63.40).
Mº Faidherbe Chaligny. **Open** noon-2pm, 8-10.30pm Tue-Sat. **Main courses** €19-€26. **Prix fixe** *Lunch* €11, €13, €16. *Dinner* €27. **Credit** MC, V. **Map** p407 N7 **50**

This bistro's friendly new owners have retained the name, but replaced the bric-a-brac of inaccurate timepieces with just two or three clocks, opening up the room with a clear glass frontage. Chef Sylvain Sendra is a bright talent. The €27 menu might begin with a home-made *fromage de tête*, well worth the three days it took in the making, or a cleverly balanced dish of warm *ratte* potatoes and sundried tomatoes topped with anchovies. The quality of the main courses doesn't flag, with, for instance, a delicate fillet of verbena-steamed John Dory on a bed of cauliflower 'couscous'. Ice-creams are home-made, and include an exquisite violet sorbet.

Le Train Bleu

Gare de Lyon, cour Louis-Armand, 12th (01.43.43.09.06/www.le-train-bleu.com). Mº Gare de Lyon. **Open** 11.30am-3pm, 7-11pm daily. **Main courses** €26. **Prix fixe** €43. **Credit** AmEx, DC, MC, V. **Map** p407 M8 **51**
This listed dining room – with vintage frescoes of the alluring destinations of the Paris-Lyon-Marseille railway and big oak benches with shiny brass coat racks – exudes a pleasant air of expectation. Don't expect cutting-edge cooking, but rather fine renderings of French classics using first-rate produce. Lobster served on walnut oil-dressed salad leaves is a generous, beautifully prepared starter, as is the pistachio-studded *saucisson de Lyon* with a warm salad of small *ratte* potatoes. Mains of veal chop topped with a cap of cheese, and *sandre* (pike-perch) with a 'risotto' of *crozettes* are also pleasant, although given the size of the starters and the superb cheese tray, you could have a satisfying meal here even if you forgo a main course. A few reasonably priced wines would be a welcome addition.

Le Temps au Temps.

No guts, no glory

Andouillette. Tête de veau. Rognons. For the offal-shy, these are words to be wary of on French menus. Yet, ever since France lifted the two-year ban on organ meats that followed the mad cow crisis in the 1990s, offcuts have been regaining their cult status thanks to young bistro chefs who proudly serve up humble ingredients in a bid to keep their prices reasonable. Many haute cuisine chefs share this penchant for the unusual textures and flavours of organ meats: veal sweetbreads appear on the menus of both **Alain Ducasse au Plaza Athénée** (see p187) and **Pierre Gagnaire** (who pan-fries them with rhubarb, ginger and maple syrup; see p190).

Even if most Parisians take their offal in stride – andouillette (tripe sausage) is a frequent plat du jour on café menus and rognon de veau (veal kidney) with potato gratin has long been a bistro classic – only a handful of restaurants have made obscure animal parts their speciality. Historic Les Halles brasserie **Au Pied de Cochon** (6 rue Coquillière, 1st, 01.40.13.77.00) serves up pig's trotters and tails round the clock (though many diners come here for the onion soup), while long-established Bastille bistro **Le Passage des Carmagnoles** (18 passage de la Bonne Graine, 11th, 01.47.00.73.30) celebrates the andouillette in all its pungent glory. At the time-worn budget joint **La Ravigotte** (41 rue de Montreuil, 11th, 01.43.72.96.22), consenting adults can eat a big plate of fat (in the form of tête de veau, or veal head) unchallenged, and **Boucherie Roulière** (see p206; pictured) is the place to go for once-forbidden marrowbones. Newest and perhaps the most original on the sparsely populated offal scene is **Ribouldingue** (see p206), an elegant yet homely little bistro that opened next to St-Julien-le-Pauvre church in May 2006.

Owner Nadège Varigny worked as a waitress for 12 years at La Régalade – where former chef Yves Camdeborde made his name serving such rustic fare as sheep's testicles – before opening this restaurant on his advice. Though Varigny isn't in the kitchen (the chef is Guy Bommefront, who previously worked at Le Troquet and Ledoyen), she designed the menu based on the Lyonnais fare she ate as a child.

One of the most surprising dishes is the tétine de vache, which translates as 'cow's teat' but in fact consists of thin slices of udder, breaded and pan-fried. Varigny promises a milky taste and, indeed, you would think the mild, inoffensive meat has been coated in cheese. Just as intriguing is the groin de cochon – actually the tip of the muzzle, again breaded and fried (which seems to be a good way of disguising the more challenging parts of a beast).

More recognisable main courses run from daube de joue de boeuf (beef cheek stew) with macaroni and veal kidney with potato gratin to seared tuna atop aubergine confit; desserts include a rather unusual ice-cream made with ewe's milk. So far, Varigny says, her customers have been most enthusiastic. 'We haven't had many tourists yet, but recently we did have a table of Americans who all seemed delighted to sample the offal dishes. Most foreigners, however, do look very surprised.'

Whether or not you're an offal person, a little vocabulary will always come in useful: **andouille** cold tripe sausage **andouillette** hot tripe sausage **coeur** heart **foie** liver **gras double** the lining of the cow's stomach **langue** tongue **moelle** bone marrow **museau** muzzle **oreille** ear **pied** trotter **queue** tail **ris** sweetbreads **rognon** kidney **tête** head.

Au Vieux Chêne

7 rue du Dahomey, 11th (01.43.71.67.69).
M° Faidherbe Chaligny. **Open** noon-2pm, 8-10.30pm
Mon-Fri; 8-10.30pm Sat. Closed 1wk July & 2wks
Aug. **Main courses** €35. **Prix fixe** *Dinner* €29.
Credit MC, V. **Map** p407 N7 ⑤②
While everyone loves the fly-in-amber atmosphere
of old enamelled advertisements, the zinc-capped
bar by the door when you come in, and the tile floor,
what makes this bistro so special is the earnestness
of their desire to please – everyone here wants you
to eat and drink to your heart's content. And you
will indeed, as chef Stéphane Chevassus just gets
better and better. A starter of langoustines encased
in fine crunchy angel hair and garnished with slices
of fresh mango is delicious and refreshing, while
chilled tomato soup is garnished with mint, a ball of
tomato sorbet and a drizzle of olive oil. Chevassus
is a gifted game cook too, as proved by the tender
roast pigeon sautéed with Chinese cabbage and its
accompaniment of mushrooms cooked with galan-
gal root, which brings out the sweetness of the bird.
Puddings sustained the high standard with a mor-
eish *moelleux d'abricots*, and a chocolate ganache
layered between buttery shortbread with a silky praline ice-cream. The Faugères goes down a treat with
a plate of perfectly ripened cheeses from Alléosse.

International

Le Souk

1 rue Keller, 11th (01.49.29.05.08). M° Ledru-Rollin
or Bastille. **Open** 7.30-11.30pm Tue-Fri; 12.15-7.30pm
Sat, Sun. **Main courses** €15. **Prix fixe** (for 8 or
more) €31, €35. **Credit** DC, MC, V. **Map** p407 N7 ⑤③
Potted olive trees mark the entrance to this lively
den of Moroccan cuisine. Start with savoury *b'stilla*,
a pasty stuffed with duck, raisins and nuts,
flavoured with orange-blossom water and sprinkled
with cinnamon and powdered sugar, or creamy
aubergine dip scooped up with fluffy Moroccan
bread, made on the premises. Don't fill up, though,
as the first-rate tagines and couscous are enormous.
The *tagine canette*, duckling stewed with honey,
onions, apricots, figs and cinnamon then showered
with toasted almonds, is terrific; *couscous bidaoui*
arrives in handsome earthenware, a hefty shank of
lamb on the side. Cold beer goes down well, but you
might prefer a bottle of Algerian or Moroccan red
wine. For dessert try the excellent millefeuille with
fresh figs, while sweet mint tea is poured in a long
stream by a djellaba-clad waiter.

North-eastern Paris

French

A la Bière

104 av Simon-Bolivar, 19th (01.42.39.83.25).
M° Colonel Fabien. **Open** noon-3pm, 7pm-1.30am
daily. **Main courses** €8.60. **Prix fixe** €12.30.
Credit AmEx, MC, V. **Map** p403 M3 ⑤④

A la Bière looks like one of those nondescript corner
brasseries with noisy pop music and lots of smoke,
but what makes it stand out is an amazingly good-
value €12.30 prix fixe full of fine bistro favourites,
all served with a smile. White tablecloths and finely balanced kirs set the tone; starters of thinly sliced
pig's cheek with a nice French dressing on the salad,
and a home-made rabbit terrine exceed expectations.
The mains live up to what's served before: charcoal-
grilled entrecôte with hand-cut chips, and juicy
Lyonnais sausages with potatoes drenched in olive
oil, garlic and parsley. The staff know their wine and
never hurry the diners; there's usually jolly banter
going on at the bar. This is one of the few bargains
left in Paris – let's hope it stays that way.

Le Chateaubriand

129 av Parmentier, 11th (01.43.57.45.95).
M° Goncourt. **Open** noon-2pm, 8-11pm Tue-Fri;
8-11pm Sat. Closed 3wks Aug. **Prix fixe** *Dinner*
€30-€36. **Credit** MC, V. **Map** p403 M4 ⑤⑤
After a hit debut at La Famille in Montmartre, self-
taught Basque chef Iñaki Aizpitarte has taken over
this very stylish bistro. His menu displays the same
set of gastronomic balls that made La Famille a hit
– come at dinner to try the cooking at its most adventurous, as a much simpler (albeit cheaper) menu is
served at lunch. Dishes have been deconstructed
down to their very essence and then put back together again. You'll understand immediately if you try
starters such as chunky steak tartare garnished with
a quail's egg, Vietnamese-style dipping sauce with
whole peanuts, or asparagus with a sublime tahini
foam and little splinters of sesame-seed brittle. The
chef doesn't always need to be cerebral to make you
wildly happy either – his Spanish goat's cheese with
stewed apple jam is brilliant, as is his chocolate cus-
tard with Espelette pepper. A fantastic list of easy
drinking wines, a sassy bunch of waiters and one of
the coolest crowds to be found anywhere in Paris –
book a few days ahead if you want to join the party.

Chez Michel

10 rue de Belzunce, 10th (01.44.53.06.20). M° Gare
du Nord. **Open** 7pm-midnight Mon; noon-2pm, 7pm-
midnight Tue-Fri. Closed 3wks Aug. **Prix fixe** €30.
Credit MC, V. **Map** p402 K2 ⑤⑥
Chez Michel is just behind the imposing St-Vincent-
de-Paul church and a few minutes' walk from Gare
du Nord – and while the area isn't particularly
classy, the food is. Thierry Breton is from Brittany,
and so proud of his origins that he sports the Breton
flag on his chef's whites. His menu is stacked with
hearty offerings from said hearty region. Marinated
salmon with purple potatoes served in a preserving
jar, pickled herring-style, is succulently tender; so,
too, is the fresh abalone. As for the rabbit, braised
with rosemary and Swiss chard, it might just be the
best bunny in town. Blackboard specials, which
carry a €5-€25 supplement, follow the seasons:
game-lovers are spoilt in the cooler months with
wood pigeon, wild boar and venison, and there are
usually some juicy, fat, fresh scallops on offer too.

Kazaphani.

International

Bharath Café

67 rue Louis-Blanc, 10th (01.58.20.06.20). M° La Chapelle. **Open** 9am-midnight daily. **Main courses** €7. **Prix fixe** €7.50, €13.50. **Credit** AmEx, DC, MC, V. **Map** p402 L2 ⑤⑦

For the most authentic South Indian/Sri Lankan food in town, venture to La Chapelle. Don't be deterred by the basic decor, brusque service or the throngs of men loitering round about. These Tamil immigrants are fussy about their food. Start with tempting meat rolls, compact deep-fried pancakes stuffed with mutton, potatoes and spices – though don't take more than two, or you'll have no room for the more tantalising main dishes, such as lamb *kotta roti* (shredded thick chapattis mixed with tender meat, eggs, green chillies and onions), big enough for two. Another house speciality is the *masala dosai* (crêpes filled with yellow curry, potatoes and mustard seed), originally a filling breakfast dish but equally suitable at dinner. Braver souls should try the stronger dishes, including the spicy chicken curry with rice and a small helping of lentil curry. You'll be mopping your brow while begging for more.

Dong Huong

14 rue Louis-Bonnet, 11th (01.43.57.18.88). M° Belleville. **Open** noon-11pm Mon, Wed-Sun. Closed 3wks Aug. **Main courses** €7. **Credit** (€15 minimum) MC, V. **Map** p403 N4 ⑤⑧

The excellent food attracts a buzzy crowd, but this is also, significantly, one of the few Paris restaurants to banish smokers to a separate room (on the lower floor). Dishes arrive promptly and in most generous portions. The delicious *bành cuôn*, steamed Vietnamese ravioli stuffed with minced meat, mushrooms, bean sprouts, spring onions and deep-fried onion, are served piping hot. *Com ga lui*, chicken kebabs with tasty lemongrass, though not as delicate, come with tasty rice. *Bô bùn chà giò* (noodles with beef and small *nem* topped with onion strips, spring onion and crushed peanuts) makes a meal in itself. For dessert, the mandarin, lychee and mango sorbets are tasty and authentic – and don't miss out on the dark, sickly sweet iced lotus-flower tea, with lotus seeds, lychees and seaweed jelly.

Ile de Gorée

70 rue Jean-Pierre-Timbaud, 11th (01.43.38.97.69). M° Parmentier. **Open** 7pm-1am daily. **Main courses** €14. **Credit** MC, V. **Map** p403 M4 ⑤⑨

Gorée Island is a 15-minute ferry ride off the Senegal coast. At for its namesake in the most happening bar quarter of Paris, mango and peach punch and live kora music set the mood. Simple but well-prepared *boudin créole* (black pudding with cinnamon) and *aloco* (sautéed plantains) with sweet tomato relish can be followed with a hearty *dem farci* (stuffed mullet) in brown sauce or *thiou poisson* (whole fish) with tomatoes, bell peppers, carrots, potatoes and basmati rice, richly marinated with a sauce that tingles with flavour. Muomuo, the friendly house cat, will happily lap up the rest of your rum-raisin ice-cream from the bowl, but disdains the exotic selection of coconut, mango and pistachio sorbets. The cooks wave goodbye – an enchanted isle indeed.

Kazaphani

122 av Parmentier, 11th (01.48.07.20.19). M° Parmentier or Goncourt. **Open** noon-3pm, 7.30pm-midnight Tue-Fri, Sun; 7.30pm-midnight Sat. Closed last 2wks Aug. **Main courses** €30. **Prix fixe** *Lunch* €18. *Dinner* €27, €32. **Credit** AmEx, MC, V. **Map** p403 M5 ⑥⓪

The atmosphere at this family-run Cypriot restaurant is so relaxed that you might feel you've walked into someone's home. The room is pleasantly decorated with rhododendron boughs and paintings of Cyprus. The €32 meze menu brings dish after dish of food; highlights include the octopus in olive oil, lemon and garlic; wonderfully lemony mushrooms; a tasty paste of broad beans; and a taramasalata so pale and creamy it's a world away from the usual lurid pink concoction that dares to bear the same name. Next arrive plates of calamares, deep-fried whitebait and huge, aniseed-flavoured *gambas*. Meat dishes are of excellent quality too, particularly the crisp meatballs and stuffed pork. You can match the food with any of the good red wines on offer – Hatzimichalis, say, or Nemea.

La Madonnina

10 rue Marie-et-Louise, 10th (01.42.01.25.26). M° Goncourt or Jacques Bonsergent. **Open** noon-2.30pm, 8-11pm Mon-Thur; noon-2.30pm, 8-11.30pm Fri, Sat. Closed 2wks Aug. **Main courses** €13. **Prix fixe** *Lunch* €11. **Credit** MC, V. **Map** p402 L4 ⑥①

Yves Camdeborde was one of the first chefs to introduce the accessibly priced, market-inspired menu at La Régalade in the early 1990s. He now runs the bijou 17th-century Hôtel Le Relais Saint-Germain, whose art deco dining room, modestly dubbed Le Comptoir, serves brasserie fare from noon to 6pm and on weekend nights – salads and a hot *plat du jour*, such as duck confit with smooth mashed potatoes – and a five-course *prix fixe* feast on weekday evenings. The single dinner sitting lets the chef take real pleasure in his work. On the daily menu, you might find dishes like an iced cream of chicken soup spiked with *vin jaune du Jura* and dotted with chanterelle mushrooms, or rolled saddle of lamb with vegetable-stuffed 'Basque ravioli' – Camdeborde is from South-west France. In summer, the handful of pavement tables makes for fine people-watching. It's very popular, so book well in advance. **Photo** *p206.*

La Ferrandaise

8 rue de Vaugirard, 6th (01.43.26.36.36). M° Odéon or RER Luxembourg. **Open** noon-2.30pm, 7-10.30pm Tue-Thur; noon-2.30pm, 7pm-midnight Fri; 7pm-midnight Sat. **Main courses** €30. **Prix fixe** €30, €38. **Credit** AmEx, MC, V. **Map** p405 E9 ⑦⓪
This newly opened bistro with stone walls, a giant chandelier and portraits of cows on the walls has quickly established a faithful clientele, seemingly dominated by local business people. In the modern bistro tradition, the young, northern French chef serves solid, classic food with a twist. A platter of excellent ham, sausage and terrine arrives as you study the blackboard menu, while the bread is crisp-crusted, thickly sliced sourdough. Almost every dish is a variation on standards: two specialities are the potato stuffed with escargots in a camembert sauce,

and a wonderfully flavoured, slightly rosé slice of veal. Desserts might include intense chocolate with rum-soaked bananas and a layered glass of mango and meringue. Wines start at €14.

Huîtrerie Régis

3 rue de Montfaucon, 6th (01.44.41.10.07). M° Mabillon. **Open** 11am-midnight Tue-Sun. Closed mid-July-Sept. **Main courses** €35. **Prix fixe** €21.50, €30. **Credit** MC, V. **Map** p408 H7 ⑦①
Parisian oyster fans are often obliged to use one of the city's big brasseries to get their fix of shellfish, but what if you just want to eat a reasonably priced platter of oysters? Enter Régis and his 14-seat oyster bar in the heart of St-Germain. The tiny white room feels pristine, the tables are properly laid, and it's non-smoking. Here you can enjoy the freshest oysters from the Marenne for around €25 a dozen. The bread and butter is fresh and wines are well-chosen. Régis attracts an enviable crowed of fans who have discovered that oysters make a sexy prelude or postlude to an evening at the cinema. Hungry souls can supplement their feast with a rather ordinary scallop terrine or more happily enjoy a slice of rustic home-made apple tart or the cheese of the day. Régis waxes lyrical about his oysters and the welcome could not be warmer. **Photo** *p208.*

Josephine 'Chez Dumonet'

117 rue du Cherche-Midi, 6th (01.45.48.52.40). M° Duroc. **Open** 12.30-2.30pm, 7.30-10.30pm Mon-Fri. **Main courses** €22. **Credit** AmEx, MC, V. **Map** p405 F8 ⑦②
At this bastion of bistro cooking, luxury ingredients bring a touch of glamour and attract a well-heeled, loyal clientele. The dining room is comfortingly

La Ferrandaise.

Huîtrerie Régis. *See p207.*

old-fashioned, and formal staff give the impression of serious eating. Dishes can come as half-portions, letting you try some classy numbers without breaking the bank. In truffle season, the salad of lamb's lettuce, warm potatoes and truffle shavings is €31 in its half-portion version. Delicious sautéed potatoes, rich in goose fat and garlic, accompany both the tournedos and a quality *andouillette*. Puddings are sumptuous too.

Lapérouse
51 quai des Grands-Augustins, 6th (01.43.26.68.04).
M° St-Michel. **Open** noon-2.30pm, 7.30-10.30pm Mon-Fri; 7.30-10.30pm Sat. Closed Aug. **Main courses** €32. **Prix fixe** *Lunch* €30. *Dinner* €90. **Credit** AmEx, DC, MC, V. **Map** p408 J6 🕖
One of the most romantic spots in Paris, Lapérouse was formerly a clandestine rendezvous for French politicians and their mistresses; the tiny private dining rooms upstairs used to lock from the inside. Chef Alain Hacquard does a modern take on classic French cooking: his beef fillet is smoked for a more complex flavour; a tender saddle of rabbit is cooked in a clay crust, flavoured with lavender and rosemary and served with ravioli of onions. The only snag is the cost, especially of the wine – a half-bottle of Pouilly-Fuissé is nearly €35. The lunch menu is limited, but frankly, the seductive Seine-side dining room has always been best savoured at night.

Le Timbre
3 rue Ste-Beuve, 6th (01.45.49.10.40). M° Vavin.
Open 7.30-11pm Mon; noon-2pm, 7.30-11pm Tue-Sat. Closed 3wks Aug. **Main courses** €17. **Prix fixe** *Lunch* €22. **Credit** MC, V. **Map** p405 G8 🕖
Chris Wright's restaurant, open kitchen included, might be the size of the average student garret, but this Mancunian aims high. His menu of three to four starters, main courses and desserts changes every week, and he uses the same suppliers as the city's top chefs. Typical of his cooking is a spring-like plate of fresh green asparagus elegantly cut in half lengthwise and served with dabs of anise-spiked sauce and balsamic vinegar, and a little crumbled parmesan. Main courses are also pure in presentation and flavour – a thick slab of pork, pan-fried but not the least bit dry, comes with petals of red onion that retain a light crunch, while juicy guinea fowl is served on a bed of tomato and pineapple chutney. Should you opt for cheese, you'll have a choice between '*le vrai*' (British cheddar) and '*le faux*' (a goat's cheese from the Ardèche).

International

Bread & Roses
7 rue de Fleurus, 6th (01.42.22.06.06).
M° St-Placide. **Open** 8am-8pm Mon-Sat. **Main courses** €20. **Credit** MC, V. **Map** p405 G8 🕖
Come for a morning croissant and you might find yourself staying for lunch, so tempting are the wares at this Anglo-influenced *boulangerie/épicerie/*café. Giant wedges of cheesecake nestle next to French

pastries, while immense savoury puff-pastry tarts are perched on the counter. Attention to detail shows even in the authentically pale tarama, which is matched with buckwheat-and-seaweed bread. Prices reflect the quality of the often-organic ingredients, but that doesn't seem to deter the moneyed locals, who order towering birthday cakes here for their snappily dressed offspring. Given the cheerful setting – pale wood with plenty of natural light inside and a few pavement tables – it's a mystery why the staff can't crack a smile.

Il Gattopardo
29 rue Dauphine, 6th (01.46.33.75.92). M° Odéon.
Open noon-2.30pm, 7.30-11.30pm Mon-Sat; 8-11.30pm Sun. **Main courses** €14. **Prix fixe** *Lunch* €14. **Credit** AmEx, MC, V. **Map** p408 H7 🕖
This cosy restaurant is up a steep flight of stairs in an old Left Bank house. The cheerful, slightly corny service sets a laid-back mood for some good eating – and Angelo Procopio knows what locals want from Italian food. One of the best pasta cooks in town, he offers a short but tempting menu, tantalising with tagliolini under white truffle shavings (costly but worth it), fettucine with a superb home-made tomato sauce, ravioli and tortellini. Another of his signature dishes, *tagliata*, is a delicious, thinly sliced steak in a herby, garlicky green sauce. A changing line-up of fish is also available. Desserts aren't very interesting, but the wine list has some good buys, especially in the Sardinian and Sicilian categories. A great little hole in the wall for dinner with friends.

Montparnasse & beyond

French

Apollo
3 pl Denfert-Rochereau, 14th (01.45.38.76.77/
01.43.22.02.15). M° Denfert Rochereau/RER Denfert Rochereau. **Open** noon-3pm, 8pm-midnight daily. **Main courses** €20. **Prix fixe** *Lunch* €18. **Credit** AmEx, DC, MC, V. **Map** p405 H10 🕖
From the same team that conceived Quai Ouest, this high-design restaurant in the former RER offices of Denfert Rochereau brings a breath of novelty into a staid part of Paris. The decor fits nicely with the original design, but the menu is firmly in the 21st century. Modern takes on comfort food include herring caviar and potatoes, *blanquette de coquilles St-Jacques* and braised beef with carrots. The food is generally good and generously served, as are desserts such as pineapple and bananas sautéed in vanilla-flavoured cream.

La Cerisaie
70 bd Edgar Quinet, 14th (01.43.20.98.98).
M° Edgar Quinet or Montparnasse. **Open** noon-2pm, 7-10pm Mon-Fri. Closed Aug & 1wk Dec. **Main courses** €30. **Credit** MC, V. **Map** p405 G9 🕖
Nothing about La Cerisaie's unprepossessing red façade in the shadow of the Montparnasse Tower hints at the talent that lurks inside. The chef's wife

Eat, Drink, Shop

quickly makes you feel welcome in the minuscule ochre-and-red room. With a simple starter of white asparagus served with preserved lemon and drizzled with bright green parsley oil, chef Cyril Lalanne proves his ability to choose and prepare the finest produce. On the daily changing blackboard menu you might find *bourride de maquereau*, a thrifty take on the garlicky southern French fish stew, or *cochon noir de Bigorre*, an ancient breed of pig that puts ordinary pork to shame. *Baba à l'Armagnac*, a variation on the usual rum cake, comes with stunningly good chantilly. There is a good selection of wines from small producers, many of them at affordable prices – look for Armagnacs and other alcohols from the South-west too.

La Coupole

102 bd du Montparnasse, 14th (01.43.20.14.20). M° Vavin. **Open** 8.30am-1am Mon-Thur, Sun; 8.30am-1.30am Fri, Sat. **Main courses** €40. **Prix fixe** €34.50. **Credit** AmEx, DC, MC, V. **Map** p405 G9 ⑲

Though Montparnasse today is a far cry from its avant-garde heyday when this restaurant opened in 1927 – as a *bar américain* with cocktails and basement dancing, where you could savour the indecency of the tango – La Coupole still glows with some of the old glamour. The people-watching remains superb, inside and out, while the long ranks of linen-covered tables, highly professional waiters, 32 art deco columns painted by different artists of the epoch, mosaic floor and the sheer scale of the operation still make coming here an event. What's more, it continues to be a favourite with Parisians of all ages, as well as out-of-towners and tourists. The set menu offers unremarkable steaks, foie gras, fish and autumn game stews, but the real treat is the shellfish, displayed along a massive counter. Take your pick from the *claires*, *spéciales* and *belons*, or go for a platter brimming with crabs, oysters, prawns, periwinkles and clams.

Wadja

10 rue de la Grande-Chaumière, 6th (01.46.33. 02.02). M° Vavin. **Open** noon-2pm, 7.30-11pm Mon-Sat. **Main courses** €23. **Prix fixe** *Lunch* €11, €14. *Dinner* (2 courses) €15. **Credit** MC, V. **Map** p405 G9 ⑳

Striking the right balance between simplicity and sophistication, this creamy-yellow bistro has become a favourite destination for families, foreign visitors and artists from the adjacent studios. À la carte, you might find foie gras sautéed with prunes, monkfish with bacon, seasonal game or a classic

Supper in the suburbs

Parisians are at last overcoming their reluctance to step outside the *Périphérique*, thanks to a new breed of restaurants that is giving the *banlieue* a much-needed boost. Within metres of the city limits, prices go down dramatically and the surroundings can become surprisingly countrified. Whether you're seeking cutting-edge cuisine, gleaming fresh shellfish or a country-style buffet, you'll find it in the 'burbs. While a couple of these restaurants require a short traipse on the RER or SNCF train line, most are on the métro.

Boulogne Sur Mer

11bis av Jean-Baptiste Clement, 92100 Boulogne-Billancourt (01.46.04.12.87). M° Boulogne Jean Jaurès. **Open** noon-2.30pm Tue-Thur; noon-2.30pm, 8-10pm Fri, Sat. **Main courses** €40. **Credit** AmEx, MC, V.

This seven-table spot is the place to go if you're staying in Boulogne-Billancourt and want bargain seafood – or if you're looking for suburban local colour among your fellow diners. Shrimp served as an appetiser are ultra-fresh, the shellfish platters are enormous and fish comes straight from the restaurant's own glistening fish shop. Wine is reasonably priced, starting at €14. **Photos** *p211* & *p213*.

La Cave est Restaurant

45 rue de Paris, 93100 Montreuil (01.42.87.09.48). M° Croix-de-Chavaux. **Open** noon-2.30pm, 7-10.30pm Mon-Fri; 7-10:30pm Sat. **Main courses** €28. *Lunch menu* €14.50. **Credit** MC, V.

Wine bar? Restaurant? Who cares? Inside what appears to be a converted wine warehouse, with spigots coming out of the walls, you'll find tables, place settings and an extremely appealing menu. In keeping with current fashions, you can choose from plenty of 'natural' unfiltered wines, largely priced around the €14-€20 mark, but the food is every bit as impressive – try the langoustines in a spicy crustacean sauce and a towering main course of green beans, smashed potatoes, a crunchy potato *galette* and crisp-skinned *confit de canard*.

L'Escarbille

8 rue de Vélizy, 92190 Meudon (01.45.34.12.03). SNCF train from Gare Montparnasse to Bellevue on the Rambouillet/Mantes line (12mins). **Open** noon-2pm, 7.30-10pm Tue-Fri; 7.30-10pm Sat. **Main courses** €50. **Prix fixe** €36. **Credit** MC, V.

agneau de sept heures, but you can opt for the daily changing *menu du jour*. With a choice of two main courses (one meat, one fish) and either a starter or dessert for only €14, this is one of the best bargains in town. Wadja is also a place for some interesting wine discoveries – say, a little-known white Burgundy, or an unfiltered organic red Bergerac.

The 7th & the 15th

French

Le 144 Petrossian
18 bd de La Tour-Maubourg, 7th (01.44.11.32.32/ www.petrossian.fr). M° La Tour Maubourg. **Open** noon-2.30pm, 7.30-10.30pm Tue-Sat. **Main courses** €80. **Prix fixe** €45. **Credit** AmEx, DC, MC, V. **Map** p401 E5 ③
Young Senegalese-French chef Rougui Dia now directs the kitchen in which she worked for several years, with intriguing results. As before, you'll find Russian specialities such as blinis, salmon and caviar (at €39 an ounce) from the Petrossian boutique downstairs, but Dia has thrown in preparations and spices from all over the world. You might start with the Tsar's cup of three different slices of

marinated salmon on a bed of artichoke hearts with cumin, or a divine risotto made with carnaroli rice, codfish caviar and crisp parmesan. In a similar vein, Med-meets-Russia are main courses of lamb 'cooked for eleven hours' on a raisin-filled blini, and roast sea bream with a terrific lemon-vodka sauce, accompanied by tasty *kasha*. A cool runny-centred chocolate cake with ice-cream and jellied quince finishes things off in modern French style. A caution: while at lunch glasses of wine are offered for €5, at dinner bottles start at €40.

L'Ami Jean
27 rue Malar, 7th (01.47.05.86.89). M° Invalides. **Open** noon-2pm, 7pm-midnight Tue-Sat. Closed Aug. **Main courses** €22. **Prix fixe** €28. **Credit** MC, V. **Map** p405 D6 ③
This long-running Basque address has become a hit since the arrival of chef Stéphane Jégo. Excellent bread from Poujauran is a perfect nibble when slathered with a tangy, herby *fromage blanc* – as are starters of sautéed baby squid on a bed of ratatouille, and little rolls of aubergine stuffed with perfectly seasoned braised lamb. Tender veal shank comes de-boned with a lovely side of baby onions and broad beans with tiny cubes of ham, while house-salted cod is soaked, sautéed and doused with an

Régis Douysset, former sous-chef at the stately La Grande Cascade in the Bois de Boulogne, took over this restaurant adjacent to the Meudon train station in 2005. From the tapenade that kicks off the meal to the concluding *cannelés* (custardy, vanilla-infused little cakes from Bordeaux), the food is a bargain for the price. The foie gras '*croque monsieur*' is a must, but from the langoustine bisque to the extra-bitter chocolate dessert, it's hard to go wrong. All in all, well worth the trip out of town.

elegant vinaigrette. There's a great wine list, and some lovely Brana *eau de vie* should you decide to linger; a party spirit sets in as the night grows long.

L'Arpège

84 rue de Varenne, 7th (01.45.51.47.33/www.alain-passard.com). M° Varenne. **Open** noon-2.30pm, 8-10.30pm Mon-Fri. **Main courses** €100. **Prix fixe** €320. **Credit** AmEx, DC, MC, V. **Map** p405 F6 🕙
Assuming you can swallow a brazenly high bill – we're talking €42 for a potato starter – and forsake the normal full-dress drill of a haute cuisine meal, the chances are you'll have a spectacular time at chef Alain Passard's Left Bank establishment. His attempt to plane down and simplify the haute experience – the chrome-armed chairs in the already minimalist dining room look like something from old East Germany – seems a bit of a misstep; but then something edible comes to the table, such as tiny smoked potatoes served with a horseradish mousseline. Delicate vegetable-stuffed ravioli in lobster bouillon are elegant and quietly sexy, but nowhere near as satisfying, especially at €58. A main course of sautéed free-range chicken garnished with a roasted shallot, an onion, potato mousseline and pan juices is the apotheosis of comfort food. Desserts are elegant and edgy, and service is impeccable. The one terrible drawback to eating out here is the sky-high pricing of the wine list.

L'Atelier de Joël Robuchon

5 rue de Montalembert, 7th (01.42.22.56.56/ www.robuchon.com). M° Rue du Bac. **Open** 11.30am-3.30pm, 6.30pm-midnight daily. **Main courses** €30. **Prix fixe** €98. **Credit** MC, V. **Map** p405 G6 🕙
This is star chef Joël Robuchon's Paris take on a New York coffee-shop-cum-sushi-and-tapas-bar. The lacquer interior and two U-shaped bars – you sit on stools at a wenge-wood counter by Pierre-Yves Rochon – are the epitome of sassy Left Bank chic, and the food is fine, with inspiration from Astrance (*see p187*) and Spain's El Bulli. The menu is split into three different *formules*: start with caviar, Spanish ham, a large seasonal salad or maybe an assortment of little tasting plates, perhaps bearing veal sweetbreads skewered with a bay leaf twig and served with Swiss chard in cream. Then go classic (a steak), fanciful (*vitello tonnato*, veal in tuna and anchovy sauce) or lush (sublime cannelloni of roasted Bresse chicken, stuffed with foie gras and served with wild mushrooms). Desserts are less inspired, the fluffy, melting passionfruit soufflé with pistachio ice-cream being the best.

Le Café Constant

139 rue St-Dominique, 7th (01.47.53.73.34). M° Ecole Militaire/RER Pont de l'Alma. **Open** noon-2.30pm, 7-10.30pm Tue-Sat. **Main courses** €12. **Credit** MC, V. **Map** p404 D6 🕙

▶ ## Suburban dining (continued)

L'Instant Gourmand

113 rue Louis Rouquier, 92300 Levallois Perret (01.47.37.13.43). M° Louise Michel, then 15min walk/bus 53, 94, 165 or 174. **Open** noon-2pm, 7.30-10pm Mon-Fri; 7.30-10pm Sat. **Prix fixe** €34. **Credit** AmEx, MC, V. This restaurant, located just 400m from the city limits, serves a combination of old and new French cuisine. Levallois Perret is awash with flowers, flowering trees and plants and, while the surrounding high-rises are a bit disconcerting, it's almost like being in the country. Expect satisfying, great-value fare such as chicken morsels on a bed of forcemeat with fresh spring herbs in the centre, and a main dish of quail cooked two ways with wild grains – all accompanied by wine from a wonderful, informed list, decent coffee and fine *mignardises*.

Jarrasse l'Ecailler de Paris

4 av Madrid, 92200 Neuilly-sur-Seine (01.46.24.07.56). M° Argentine. **Open** noon-2pm, 7.15-10.30pm daily. **Prix fixe** €38. **Credit** MC, V.

Star chef Michel Rostang and his daughter Caroline have successfully revived this fish bistro in Neuilly, which now serves seafood to rival the best in Paris. The restaurant has a classy new look, right down to the plates from Jersey featuring bold paintings of squid, mussels and the like. The prix fixe might include *fines de claire* oysters, crisp-skinned sea bream and a gold-standard *moelleux au chocolat*. However, most business diners opt for the bistro's signature dish of a whole fish for two, which is ample and delicious. There's an impressive selection of white wines at around €20.

Les Magnolias

48 av de Bry, 94170 Le Perreux-sur-Marne (01.48.72.47.43/www.lesmagnolias.com). RER Nogent Le Perreux on the 'E' line from St-Lazare or the Gare du Nord (20mins). **Open** noon-1.30pm, 7.30-9.30pm Tue-Fri; 7.30-9.30pm Sat. Closed 1st wk Jan, Aug. **Prix fixe** €48. **Credit** MC, V.
In six years, Breton chef Jean Chauvel has put the suburb of Le Perreux-sur-Marne on the map. This is a destination restaurant, where

This simple and brightly lit neighbourhood café is a fitting showcase for the brilliance of chef Christian Constant, formerly of the kitchens at Hôtel de Crillon (*see p187*). Café Constant purrs with good times, good food and good value, as an appealingly diverse crowd of locals and Constant fans have quickly sussed out. The blackboard menu changes constantly; if you're hungry, start with the peppery *pâté de campagne* or even the salmon-wrapped poached eggs in gelatin with salad, and follow with the steak, grilled steak tartare or calf's liver, all served with generous side dishes. For a lighter feed, begin with the green bean salad then opt for *pasta au pistou* or salmon tartare. All of the food served here is fresh and flavourful, portions are more than fair, and the wine list is a blessing. No booking.

Chez les Anges

54 bd La Tour-Maubourg, 7th (01.47.05.89.86/ www.chezlesanges.com). M° La Tour Maubourg. **Open** noon-3pm, 7.30-11pm Mon-Sat. **Main courses** €25. **Prix fixe** €40. **Map** p401 E6 ❸❺
Jacques Lacipière of the bistro Au Bon Accueil is behind the revival of this restaurant, which was known for its superb Burgundian cooking in the 1960s and '70s (hence the decor). You can order à la carte, with main dishes priced at around €20 to €30, or opt for the good-value 'Menu Surprise'. This takes a tapas-style approach, with each course arriving in

sets of two or three tiny portions. These change from day to day, but might include creations such as cauliflower bavarois and little frogs' leg fritters. Though the cooking isn't on the level of, say, Joël Robuchon, the chef is clearly making an effort and the waiters are full of goodwill. **Photo** *p214*.

Gaya Rive Gauche

44 rue du Bac, 7th (01.45.44.73.73). M° Rue du Bac. **Open** 12.15-2.30pm, 7.15-10.45pm Mon-Fri; 7.15-10.45pm Sat. **Main courses** €30. **Credit** AmEx, MC, V. **Map** p405 G6 ❸❼
Pierre Gagnaire, a chef known for his individuality, runs this Left Bank seafood restaurant, redecorating with a fish-scale wall and cloth-less white tables. The line is blurred between starters and main courses, with menu titles such as '*insolites*' (unexpected) and '*essentiel*'. What a relief, though, to see starters at less than €20 and main courses at less than €30, even if the great man himself is not in the kitchen. Typical of his style is a seafood jelly with neatly arranged *coco de Paimpol* white beans and Spanish ham, followed by strips of wild sea bass simply sautéed and deglazed with manzanilla sherry. As so often happens with Gagnaire, not everything works; nonetheless, it's exciting to experience his unique take on French cuisine. Gaya is particularly refreshing in a city where most seafood restaurants have fallen into a minimalist rut.

Eat, Drink, Shop

Parisians and foreigners come to be delighted, baffled and surprised. Why? Because of Chauvel's skillful, unexpected layering of tastes and textures – roast pigeon in a verbena infusion with roasted pine nuts and vegetables sautéed with fennel seeds, for instance. Try not to be intimidated by the menu's literary style – staff will be more than happy to help decipher the more complex dishes.

Les Symples de l'Os à Moelle

18 av de la République, 92130 Issy-Les-Moulineaux (01.41.08.02.52). M° Mairie d'Issy. **Open** noon-2.30pm, 7.30-9.30pm Mon-Fri; 7.30-9.30pm Sat. **Prix fixe** €22. **Credit** MC, V.
Though Les Symples advertises itself as a 'wine bar-buffet', it's more like a country inn from another era. Food is simple but excellent, and every available space is occupied by crocks of pâté, lentils, cucumbers, shredded

beetroot, carrot and fennel. They serve two set specials each day, such as creamy mushroom soup and leg of lamb with ratatouille. Then in come the piles of pudding: rice pudding, prunes soaked in orange-scented wine, apple crumble, prune *clafoutis* and fruit salad – plus a huge selection of cheeses. Marvellous!

Restaurant Thierry Burlot

8 rue Nicolas-Charlet, 15th (01.42.19.08.59).
M° Pasteur. **Open** noon-2.30pm, 7.30-10.30pm
Mon-Fri; 7.30-11.30pm Sat. Closed 10 days Aug.
Main courses €32. **Credit** AmEx, MC, V.
Map p405 E9 ⑱

Thierry Burlot's modern bistro continues to draw
crowds with an enticing menu of artistically prepared food served in stylish and upbeat surroundings. Produced with fresh ingredients, the offerings
vary from earthy truffle-laden dishes to lighter fish
and seafood numbers, including the quite exquisite
langoustines grilled with vanilla, served as a starter
or main course. A meal might start with excellent
lightly poached egg topped with shards of truffles
and framed by fresh leeks, followed by oven-cooked
sea bass in a delightful herb and mushroom sauce.
Original desserts include intricate chocolate creations and home-made caramel ice-cream. Service is
undertaken by an efficient, if rather charmless,
coterie of black-clad Parisian twentysomethings.

Le Troquet

21 rue François-Bonvin, 15th (01.45.66.89.00).
M° Sèvres Lecourbe. **Open** noon-2.30pm, 7.30-11pm
Tue-Sat. Closed 1wk May, Aug & 1wk Dec. **Prix
fixe** *Lunch* €24, €28. *Dinner* €30, €40. **Credit** MC,
V. **Map** p405 D8 ⑲

After polishing his technique in Christian Constant's
kitchens, chef Christian Etchebest took over this
bistro from his uncle. Decorated with 1930s light fixtures and a proud Crillon certificate, the restaurant
feels deceptively old-fashioned but is one of the most

Chez les Anges. See p213.

reliable bets in the city. Etchebest's Basque-inspired
cooking may have rustic touches, but his style is
modern. From a brief but tempting lunch menu, start
with fresh goat's cheese on crisp pastry, sprinkled
with Espelette pepper and served with just-cooked
red cabbage. Vegetable soup turns out to be a
creamy, cardamom-scented blend, which you ladle
yourself on to foie gras and a spoonful of crème
fraîche. The mains are stunning: a thick tuna steak
wrapped in cured ham and served with a rich
squash purée or plump farm chicken breast stuffed
with tapenade, and cabbage cooked with juniper,
pork and olive oil. Desserts are less remarkable.

International

Odori

*18 rue Letellier, 15th (01.45.77.88.12). M° La Motte
Picquet Grenelle or Avenue Emile Zola.* **Open** noon-
3pm, 7-10.30pm Tue-Sun. Closed 2wks Dec. **Main
courses** €17. **Credit** AmEx, MC, V. **Map** p404 C8 ㉚

It may be out of the way, hidden down an obscure
street, yet Odori is perpetually packed with Korean
diners – an encouraging sign of delicious, authentic
food, confirmed at the first piquant bite. A sublime
starter of steak tartare is worth the trek alone: the
ice-cold meat, scented with sesame oil and textured
with slivers of Fuji apple, raw garlic and a raw egg,
is fresh and cleanly prepared. Follow this mild dish
with a comforting beef and leek soup, a Korean staple that's just hot and spicy enough to be warming
rather than blazing. The classic Korean barbecue
comes with the usual side dishes of *kimchi* and various root vegetables, marinated in vinegar or tossed
in a lively chilli paste; Korean beef arrives sizzling
on a hot plate surrounded by a moat of sweet but
mild stock (wear machine-washable clothes). The
service is friendly but harried.

Restaurant Al Wady

153-155 rue de Lourmel, 15th (01.45.58.57.18).
M° Lourmel. **Open** noon-3pm, 7pm-midnight daily.
Main courses €16. **Prix fixe** *Lunch* €11, €14.
Dinner €19. **Credit** AmEx, MC, V. **Map** p404 B9 ㉛

Al Wady is not the type of place to which you'd take
someone keen for a postcard Paris dining experience. But if said acquaintance has a hankering for a
Lebanese feast to rival the best they might find in
the Middle East, you're on to a winner. The long
menu makes for an agony of indecision, so it's wise
to settle for the meze platter – at €38 for two, a great
way to sample house specialities like garlicky hou-
mous, moist tabouleh and smoky *baba ganoush*.
And that's just for starters. Golden-brown pastries
hold the perfect bite of delicately spiced lamb, while
succulent chicken pieces in a caramelised orange
glaze will appeal to those with a sweet palate. The
yardstick for true greatness in Lebanese kitchens is
measured by the falafel; neither too grainy nor too
moist, Al Wady's are orbs of herbed wonder. The
coffee is suitably strong, and the delicious honeyed
pastries can be bought to take away.

Cafés & Bars

What was wrong with zinc?

Le Baron Rouge: nobly resisting change. *See p224.*

Pink '❶' numbers in this chapter mark the location of each café as shown on the street maps. *See pp400-409.*

Take any bar in central Paris – the Taverne on place de la République, for example, or the Relais round the corner. Popping in for a *verre* in 2004 would have been a similar experience to doing the same in 1974: shiny Bordeaux red banquettes, much neon, an older male clientele seeking solace in each other's company. No longer. The Taverne – sorry, la taverne – has added arty decorative touches to its new lower-case moniker and extended its opening hours and beer range to attract younger, professional customers from both sexes. The Relais: dark wood and proper breakfasts. And this is happening all over Paris. Lampshades or window blinds of thin paper, upmarket snacks, neutral colours, understated murals. The price for the punter is often €3 for a small glass of beer – the humble *demi* – and little to choose between any venue. Counter service is more common, particularly during the ubiquitous happy hour, plus there'll be some electronic aural backdrop and regular appearances by hawkers from the Indian sub-continent trying to flog roses or strings of jasmin.

The traditional café is a dying breed. A few years ago there was one on almost every street corner, 10,000 in all. Today only 1,500 remain, providing locals with strong coffee, cheap plonk and lively conversation around the zinc bar counter from early morning to long past dusk.

In some cases, modernisation has been a boon – at **Bar Ourcq**, **L'Alimentation Général** and **L'Ile Enchantée**, for instance. More established venues of cosmopolitan character are clustered in the city's nightlife hub in the 11th arrondissement between Parmentier and Ménilmontant métro stops, an area named after its main bar-lined street: Oberkampf. Parallel to rue Oberkampf runs rue Jean-Pierre-Timbaud, which delivers a more offbeat and varied selection of bars, as does the street connecting them, rue St-Maur. Other destinations include the Canal St-Martin in the 10th, the Marais (and its north-western overspill between

The best Bars

For beer types

Le Baron Rouge (*p224*); Le Brébant
(*p218*); Le Sancerre (*p222*); La Taverne de
Nesle (*p233*); Le Truskel (*p221*).

For drinking past bedtime

Le Bar (*p231*); Le Brébant (*p218*); La
Maizon (*p229*); Le N'Importe Quoi (*p218*);
L'Objectif Lune (*p225*); Le Tambour
(*p219*); Le Truskel (*p221*).

For friendly prices

L'Antenne Bastille (*p224*); Le Baromètre
(*p222*); Le Cinquante (*p229*); Le Fanfaron
(*p224*); Le Phénix (*p230*).

For sounds

L'Alimentation Générale (*p225*); Bar Ourcq
(*p228*); Café Chéri(e) (*p228*); Le Detone
(*p230*); Le Fanfaron (*p224*); La Fourmi
(*p222*); La Jungle (*p219*); La Liberté
(*p225*); La Maizon (*p229*); Le Mange
Disque (*p229*); Le N'Importe Quoi (*p218*);
L'Opa (*p225*); Au P'tit Garage (*p230*).

For stuffy waiters

Café de Flore (*p233*); Café Marly (*right*);
Au Petit Suisse (*p233*).

For weird cocktails

L'Alimentation Générale (*p225*); Café
Chéri(e) (*p228*); Le Crocodile (*p230*);
Impala Lounge (*p221*); La Jungle (*p219*);
Pop Corner (*p231*).

For wine buffs

Le Baromètre (*p222*); Le Baron Rouge
(*p224*); Le Cinquante (*p229*).

Etienne Marcel and Arts et Métiers métro
stations) and the area around Abbesses in
Montmartre. The Left Bank and Montparnasse
boast a proud if overplayed literary heritage,
while the west still has its swank and glitz.

It's cheaper to drink at the counter than be
served at a table, cheaper inside than on the
terrace, and cheaper before 10pm, when a *tarif
de nuit* might be imposed. Wine in three colours
is ubiquitous, and coffee comes as a strong
espresso unless otherwise requested. The sturdy
brasserie and noble bistro provide food with
formality akin to a restaurant, so if you're just
there for a drink, you'll pay more for the social
nicety of aproned-and-waistcoated service. You
can usually run a tab, and tipping is optional;
just a few small coins left in the silver dish.

The Louvre, Palais-Royal & Les Halles

Le Café des Initiés

*3 pl des Deux-Ecus, 1st (01.42.33.78.29). Mº Louvre
Rivoli or Les Halles.* **Open** 7.30am-1am Mon-Sat.
Credit AmEx, MC, V. **Map** p402 H5 ❶
Once a crumbling corner café, now a designer hangout, the Café des Initiés is a top spot for a trendy
tipple. The main room is lined with ergonomic red
banquettes, a long zinc bar provides character, and
sleek black articulated lamps peer down from the
ceiling. Dotted across the windowsills are tall, slender vases filled with fresh, scented lilies. The friendly
staff and central location have helped put this place
firmly on the aperitif map.

Café Marly

*93 rue de Rivoli, cour Napoléon du Louvre, 1st
(01.49.26.06.60). Mº Palais Royal Musée du Louvre.*
Open 8am-2am daily. **Credit** AmEx, DC, MC, V.
Map p401 H5 ❷
A class act, this, as you might expect of a Costes café
whose lofty arcaded terrace overlooks the Louvre's
glass pyramid. Accessed through the passage
Richelieu (the entrance for advance Louvre ticket-
holders), Marly offers a sophisticated and pricy break
from the world's most famous collection of art. It's €6
for a Heineken, so you might as well splash out €12
on a Chocolate Martini or a Shark of vodka, lemon-
ade and grenadine. Most of the well-chosen wines are
under €10 a glass and everything is impeccably
served by razor-sharp smart staff. Brasserie fare and
sandwiches are on offer too. **Photo** *p217*.

Entr'acte

*47 rue de Montpensier, 1st (01.42.97.57.76).
Mº Pyramides or Palais Royal.* **Open** noon-midnight
daily. **Credit** MC, V. **Map** p402 H5 ❸
There's something happening around the Palais-
Royal – and it's not just Marc Jacobs and the fashion crowd moving in. A little detour off avenue de
l'Opéra, down a staircase, and you find an unexpected congregation of imbibers and diners spread
over a corner of pavement, half here for this little bar
near the Comédie Française, half for the adjoining
Sicilian pizza restaurant. There's food to be had at
Entr'acte too – €10 plates of cheese and charcuterie,
standard pastas and so on – but most customers are
here to enjoy an early evening glass of house
Bourgueil somewhat sharper than they'd find at the
place du Palais-Royal itself. If it's raining, though,
the interior is tiny (with toilet and kitchen close
together – watch as you come out), with an equally
poky basement. Free Wi-Fi access and even
laptop lending are on offer.

Le Fumoir

*6 rue de l'Amiral-de-Coligny, 1st (01.42.92.00.24/
www.lefumoir.fr). Mº Louvre Rivoli.* **Open** 11am-
2am daily. Closed 2wks Aug. **Credit** AmEx, MC, V.
Map p402 H6 ❹

Eat, Drink, Shop

who give the 24-hour clock their best shot. Neither tatty nor threatening, Le Tambour comprises a small counter area where staff and souses banter, a busy conservatory, and a long dining room memorable for its retro métro map from Stalingrad station and iconic image of Neil Armstrong.

Le Truskel
10 rue Feydeau, 2nd (01.40.26.59.97/www.truskel. com). M° Bourse. **Open** 8pm-2am Tue, Wed; 8pm-5am Thur-Sat. Closed Aug. **Credit** MC, V. **Map** p402 H4 ⑯
The formula is quite simple at this pub-cum-disco: an excellent selection of beers, fruity Belgian and quality Czech included, attends to your throat while an extensive repertoire of Britpop assaults your ears. The back area is for dancing, just like a school disco. Malcontent expats love it, but not as much as French boys who can't hold their Murphy's. To add to the mystique, a bar bell rings for no reason whatsoever, causing first-time UK visitors to down their drinks in one and dive for the bar.

Champs-Elysées & western Paris

Le Dada
12 av des Ternes, 17th (01.43.80.60.12). M° Ternes. **Open** 6am-2am Mon-Sat; 6am-10pm Sun. **Credit** AmEx, MC, V. **Map** p400 C3 ⑰
Perhaps the hippest café on this classy avenue in a stuffy part of town, Le Dada is best known for its well-placed, sunny terrace, though the kookily Dada-influenced two-floor interior is ideal for a cheeky afternoon tipple. The wood-block carved tables and red walls provide a warm atmosphere for a crowd that tends towards the well heeled, well spoken and, well, loaded. That said, the atmosphere is friendly and relaxed and, if terracing is your thing, you could happily spend a summer's day here.

Impala Lounge
2 rue de Berri, 8th (01.43.59.12.66). M° George V. **Open** noon-2am Mon-Thur, Sun; noon-4am Fri, Sat. **Credit** AmEx, MC, V. **Map** p400 D4 ⑱
Dubbed the 'African Bar' by regulars, this wannabe hip spot hams up the colonial with zebra skins, tribal masks and a throne hewn from a tree trunk. Beer, wine, tea and standard favourites can all be had, but best are the cocktails, one of which claims to boost a waning libido with its mystery mix of herbs and spices. DJs rock Sunday afternoon away, and the snack-and-mains menu includes ostrich.

Ladurée
75 av des Champs-Elysées, 8th (01.40.75.08.75/ www.laduree.fr). M° George V or Franklin D. Roosevelt. **Open** 7.30am-midnight daily. **Credit** AmEx, DC, MC, V. **Map** p400 D4 ⑲
Everything in this elegant tearoom suggests decadence, from the 19th-century-style interior and service to the labyrinthine corridors that lead to the

toilets. But you came here not merely to wallow in the warm glow of bygone wealth: you came for the teas, pastries and, above all, the hot chocolate. It's thick, bitter and creamier than heaven; on a first tasting, you'll say to yourself, 'This is tar.' And so it is; a rich, velvety tar that will leave you in the kind of stupor requisite for any lazy afternoon. The original branch at 16 rue Royale (8th, 01.42.60.21.79) is better known for its macaroons.

Petit Défi de Passy
18 av du Président-Kennedy, 16th (01.42.15.06.76/ www.defidepassy.com). M° Passy/RER Avenue du Pdt Kennedy. **Open** 10am-midnight daily. **Credit** AmEx, DC, MC, V. **Map** p404 B6 ⑳
In permanent rebellion against its posh postcode, this refreshingly no-fuss bar-restaurant challenges the local chi-chi rule, jollying along friendly students and English teachers through happy hour in a distinct whiff of late adolescence. It's positively bursting with toff totty (albeit rather on the young side), and the best bit is, it's cheap. Chaps can impress the fillies by buying a bottle of Absolut for €60 and keeping it behind the bar with their name on.

Le Rival
20 av George V, 8th (01.47.23.40.99). M° George V. **Open** 7am-2am daily. **Credit** MC, V. **Map** p400 D4 ㉑
Stylish but low-key, this four-star contemporary bar makes a mean Martini: fresh fruit, Polish or Detroit, with a wellyful of Zubrowka or Krupnik chucked in and served with pzazz. Other highlights of the €12 cocktail range are a Saigon Russian Mule with Poire Williams, lemon and ginger beer, and a Spiced Swizzle of rum and amaretto. A decent glass of Brouilly or Chablis sets you back €7, par for the course – but God knows how they can charge €18 for a cheeseburger and hash browns or €10 for a *croque-monsieur*. Still, the shopaholic and business clientele seem happy to pay up.

Sir Winston
5 rue de Presbourg, 16th (01.40.67.17.37). M° Charles de Gaulle Etoile. **Open** 9am-3am Mon-Wed, Sun; 9am-4am Thur-Sat. **Credit** AmEx,V. **Map** p400 C4 ㉒
A bit of an anomaly, this. Grand and imperial, in a location on the corner of avenue d'Iéna within sight of very high-end glitz, Sir Winston does a nice line in jazz and gospel brunches on a Sunday; chicken tandoori and Scottish salmon feature among the main courses (€15-€20). Colonial knick-knacks, chesterfields and chandeliers make up the decor, while Winnie himself is framed behind a sturdy bar counter equipped with a well-worn armrest groove. A battalion of whiskies stands guard beside him, and the wine list is equally *recherché*; nothing wrong with the €10 cocktails, either. Where this place falters is in veering from the established standards, especially in its girly cocktail menu. A Sir Winston Breezer of Bacardi, melon liqueur, pineapple and banana juice? Harrumph!

Montmartre & Pigalle

La Divette de Montmartre

136 rue Marcadet, 18th (01.46.06.19.64). M°
Lamarck Caulaincourt. **Open** 5pm-1am Mon-Sat;
5-11pm Sun. **Credit** MC, V.

This cavern of colourful nostalgia is run by Serge,
its barrel-bellied barman. Tucked away among
Montmartre's hilly backstreets but worth the trek,
this is Serge's *Recherche du temps perdu* in album-
cover, poster and table-football form. Beatles albums
line up over the bar, Rolling Stones ones under it and
an Elvis clock ticks in between; this decorative trin-
ity is interrupted by *yé-yé* pop tack, the occasional
green of St-Etienne football iconography and an old
red telephone box. On tap are Wieckse Witte,
Afflighem, Pelforth and gossip about the days when
Manu Chao were regulars.

La Fourmi

74 rue des Martyrs, 18th (01.42.64.70.35).
M° Pigalle. **Open** 8.30am-2am Mon-Thur; 8.30am-
4am Fri, Sat; 10am-2am Sun. **Credit** MC, V.
Map p402 H2 ㉓

Set on the cusp of the 9th and 18th, La Fourmi is
retro-industrial at its best. It's an old bistro that has
been converted for today's tastes, with picture windows giving natural light and visual bustle to the
spacious, roughshod, sand-coloured main interior,
whose prime seats are on the podiums at the back.
The classic zinc bar counter is crowned by industrial lights, the ornately carved back bar featuring
the odd titular ant. An excellent music policy and
cool clientele – although they'd have to go some to
beat the bar staff – ensure a pile of flyers. As good
a place as any to find out what's happening in town.

Le Sancerre

35 rue des Abbesses, 18th (01.42.58.08.20). M°
Abbesses. **Open** 7am-2am Mon-Thur; 7am-4am Fri,
Sat; 9am-2am Sun. **Credit** MC, V. **Map** p402 H1 ㉔
Of the many choices on rue des Abbesses, this is the
most popular, its terrace full, its large, dark-wood
interior an attractive mix of cool and cosy. Taps of
Paulaner, Grimbergen and Record accompany bot-
tled Belgian beauties Kriek and Mort Subite; standard cocktails, €5.50 on Mondays, are presented
with the same care as the couple of *plats du jour* and
a good range of mains and salads. Sadly, the service
can be teeth-grindingly slow, truly galling when a
duo is murdering your favourite Roy O number.

Beaubourg & the Marais

Andy Whaloo

69 rue des Gravilliers, 3rd (01.42.71.20.38). M° Arts
et Métiers. **Open** 4pm-2am Mon-Sat. **Credit** AmEx,
MC, V. **Map** p409 K5 ㉕
Andy Whaloo – created by the people behind its
neighbour 404 and London's Momo and Sketch – is
Arabic for 'I have nothing'. Bijou? The place brings
new meaning to the word. A formidably fashionable

Le Petit Fer à Cheval.
See p223.

set crowds in here and fights for a coveted place on an
upturned paint can (who needs a divan when you've
got Dulux?). From head to toe, it's a beautifully
designed venue, crammed with Moroccan artefacts
and enough colours to fill a Picasso. It's quiet early on,
but there's a surge around 9pm, and the atmosphere
heats up as the night gets longer.

Le Baromètre

17 rue Charlot, 3rd (01.48.87.04.54). M° Arts et
Métiers. **Open** 8am-11pm Mon-Sat. **Credit** MC, V.
Map p409 L5 ㉖
Unpretentious but serious wine bar and eaterie,
favoured by the craftsmen and artisans originally
native to this now sought-after street before the fashionistas and designers moved in. Lunchtimes tend
to be heaving, so unless you're after a €12 sit-down
menu du jour in the intimate area of green banquettes at the back, you're better off passing through
on a lazy afternoon, ordering up a *tartine* thickly
spread with pâté, or a plate of cheese, and choosing
from a 20-strong selection of wines by the glass,
most at under €2.

La Chaise au Plafond

10 rue du Trésor, 4th (01.42.76.03.22/
www.cafeine.com). M° St Paul. **Open** 9am-2am daily.
Credit MC, V. **Map** p409 K6 ㉗
This is one of a modest coterie of venues in the
Vieille-du-Temple locality owned and designed by
Xavier Denamur. Set just off the main drag, its terrace facing neat squares of shrubbery on a pedestrianised side street, it adjoins Les Philosophes, with
whom it shares the same menu. You can nab a plate
of scrambled eggs (perhaps with smoked salmon) or
a house salad with smoked duck breast and a glass

Terrace oases downtown are hard to come by. One gem, not five minutes from the Gare de l'Est, enclosed in its own secluded, walled garden, is the **Café A** (148 rue du Fbg-St-Martin, 10th, no phone). Open until 10pm every day except Monday, the Café A is part of the Maison des Architectes set in the Couvent des Récollets – there's something meticulously planned about the setting sun falling over the tree-lined terrace.

Verdant surroundings can also be found at the **Péniche El Alamein** (opposite 11 quai François-Mauriac, 13th, 01.46.86.41.60), a floating garden and bar aboard a moored barge, near two landmark waterside venues – the **Batofar** (*see p323*) and the **Guinguette Pirate** (*see p319*). Here, in the shadow of the new Passerelle Simone-de-Beauvoir bridge, the Seine embankment is broader, and the tables spread out around the Guinguette Pirate form an alfresco bar hub.

Diagonally opposite the 13th, past quai de la Rapée, the nearby marina also allows for waterside relaxation. **Le Grand Bleu**

(Port de l'Arsenal, bd de la Bastille, 12th, 01.43.45.19.99) is half-fish restaurant, half-café, facing the water and set in greenery. Further north, the waterside scene along the Canal St-Martin is well documented – half the clientele of **Le Jemmapes** (No.82, 10th, 01.40.40.02.35) congregate on the adjacent quay of the same name.

Continuing past Jaurès métro station, the water broadens into the Bassin de la Villette, providing the ideal backdrop for the facing **MK2** arthouse cinemas and their terrace cafés at 7 quai de la Loire and 14 quai de la Seine. Up quai de la Loire, past joggers, snoggers, *pétanque* players and children scrambling over climbing frames, stands the **Bar Ourcq** (*see p228; pictured below*). A world and three métro stops away from the grimy Gare du Nord, the Bar Ourcq offers the best of bar relaxation: a switched-on crowd, funky furniture, decently priced drinks, DJ sounds and even deckchair hire. All you need do is drag it the 50 metres to the embankment. You could even be on holiday.

Le Phénix. See p230.

L'Atmosphère

49 rue Lucien-Sampaix, 10th (01.40.38.09.21).
M° Gare de l'Est or Jacques Bonsergent. **Open**
9.30am-1.45am Mon-Sat; 9.30am-midnight Sun.
No credit cards. Map p402 L3 ㊸

L'Atmosphère remains at the centre of the Canal St-Martin renaissance and sums up the spirit of the area. Parisians of all kinds chat, read and gaze from the waterside terrace; within, the simple, tasteful interior, animated conversation and cheapish drinks provide entertainment enough. It's always packed, but brave the crowds on Sundays for the early evening world and experimental music slots.

Bar Ourcq

68 quai de la Loire, 19th (01.42.40.12.26/www.
barourcq.com). M° Laumière. **Open** *Winter* 5pm-midnight Wed-Thur, Sun; 3pm-2am Fri, Sat. *Summer*
5-9.30pm Wed-Fri, Sun; 3pm-2am Sat. **No credit**
cards. Map p403 N1 ㊹

A little turquoise-framed corner bar, the Ourcq is set back from a canal embankment broad enough to accommodate *pétanque* games (ask at the bar), a cluster of deckchairs and a kids' playground nearby. It's a completely different scene from the crowded bustle along Canal St-Martin; more discerning and less self-satisfied. Inside, Ourcq is a vivacious, recently declared smoke-free cabin, with an intimate raised area at the back. Drinks are listed in a hit parade of prices, starting with €2 for a *demi* or glass of red wine, €3 for a Pelforth or Kir, and €4 for a lively Mojito. Pastas at €7, exhibitions and a regular DJ agenda keep the cool clientele sated and entertained. The bar closes on rainy weekdays in summer. *See*
p226 **A** *rouge* **with a view. Photo** *p225.*

Café Charbon

109 rue Oberkampf, 11th (01.43.57.55.13/www.
nouveaucasino.net). M° Parmentier or Ménilmontant.
Open 9am-2am Mon-Thur, Sun; 9am-4am Fri, Sat.
Credit MC, V. **Map** p403 N5 ㊾

This beautifully restored belle époque building sparked the Oberkampf nightlife boom, its booths, mirrors, chandeliers and adventurous music policy putting trendy locals at their ease, capturing the essence of café culture spanning each end of the 20th century. It was cool, it was *fine dining*, sound DJing, retro chic and high ceilings. After 15 years or more, the formula still works, inspiring scores of bars nearby. The management opened the equally popular Nouveau Casino nightclub next door (*see*
p324) and has continued the empire-building with the groovified De la Ville Café (*see p219*) in the 10th.

Café Chéri(e)

44 bd de la Villette, 19th (01.42.02.02.05). M°
Belleville. **Open** 8am-2am daily. **Credit** MC, V.
Map p403 M3 ㊻

This splendid DJ bar (*see p322*) has expanded its brief and its opening hours to become an all-day café – without watering down any of the funky chic that keeps it well ahead of the pack after dark. Set in a gloomy corner of Belleville, the Chéri(e) sparkles with wit and invention. Large sealed jars on the bar pack all kinds of punches, such as the €5 Chéri(e) of dark rum; fruit vodkas also a speciality. DJ nights are conceived with equal craft, and the atmosphere is one of sass and seduction – note the marvellous mural alluding to the personal sacrifices made to squeeze into a life of coupledom. There's a front terrace if you need a little conversational respite from the BPM.

L'Ile Enchantée

*65 bd de la Villette, 10th (01.42.01.67.99). M°
Colonel Fabien.* **Open** 8am-2am Mon-Fri; 5pm-2am
Sat. **Credit** MC, V. **Map** p403 M3
The latest DJ bar on the burgeoning scene north-
west of Belleville, the Enchanted Island has just the
right understated touches of chic and retro and
equally minimal house/electro sounds to keep the
focus firmly fixed on conversation. The tall, tall ceilings and French windows let in acres of Belleville
skyline, and there's space aplenty amid the studded
banquettes and tables. The wine list is formidable,
there's Kriek by the bottle and sturdy cocktails come
in at €6.50 a hit. An up-for-it and slightly older
crowd keeps a steady buzz without any pressing
need to be the next best thing in town. On busier DJ
nights (*see p322*), a cool lounge operates upstairs.

La Maizon

*123 rue Oberkampf, 11th (01.58.30.62.12). M°
Ménilmontant.* **Open** 4pm-2am Mon-Thur, Sun; 4pm-
6am Fri, Sat. **Credit** AmEx, MC, V. **Map** p403 N5
The best DJ bar on the Oberkampf strip – although
inexplicably less frequented than the cod salsa and
pseudo Brazilian bars you have to pass to get here.
This means you're guaranteed a cosy spot, if not by
the bar, then certainly at a table in the back of the
narrow room, fringed with Arabic touches. Its location opposite madly popular late-night music venue
Cithéa helps, but stick around here for Maes on
draught, Gin Fizz and other long drinks at €7 and
thumping but imaginative sounds. Actually, that
might be a drawback, as conversation gets tricky
once the DJ hits his groove approaching dawn of a
Saturday – but hey, who needs talk at that time?

Le Mange Disque

*58 rue de la Fontaine, 11th (01.58.30.87.07/
www.mangedisque.fr). M° Goncourt.* **Open** 5pm-
2am Tue-Sat. Closed Aug. **No credit cards.**
Map p403 M4
This remarkably cool bar shows just what you can
do with a little art, a fine taste in music, the most
mundane of furniture and the right connections. If
you want to launch a CD, introduce a DJ or throw
any kind of bash where word of mouth counts, do it
here. There are other factors, of course. Savvy owner
Hubert has brought in choice wines from little-
known producers in south-west France but only
charges €2-€3 a glass for them. Likewise, the smallish snacks at under €10. Stacks of vinyl are left out
for browsing – is there anything more satisfying
than browsing through vinyl? – and with the constant traffic of events and launches, no two evenings
are the same. A good name to drop.

La Marquise

*74 rue Jean-Pierre-Timbaud, 11th (01.43.55.86.96).
M° Couronnes, Parmentier or St-Maur.* **Open** 8am-
2am daily. **Credit** AmEx, MC, V. **Map** p403 M4
Overdone things on Oberkampf? Jaded with Jean-
Pierre-Timbaud? Then venture up the street con-
necting them, rue St-Maur, for a less celebrated,

Le Cinquante

*50 rue de Lancry, 10th (01.42.02.36.83). M° Jacques
Bonsergent.* **Open** *Sept-July* 5.30pm-2am daily.
Aug 5.30pm-2am Tues-Sun. **No credit cards**.
Map p402 L4
Spunky little place, this, just down from the Canal
St-Martin. Bare brick, formica and framed ads from
the immediate post-war period form the decor,
although the ambience comes with the inner circle of
regulars: boho types in on the scene. These days it's
established enough to produce its own T-shirts and
customised bar stools. Reasonable prices – 50cl
pitchers of sauvignon, Brouilly and Chablis in the
€10 range, all available by the glass – attract a
mixed bag of tastes and generations in the cabin-
sized space. The two rooms in the main bar are
for dining (affordable classics) and performances
(minimal and generally acoustic). Last orders are at
1.20am – no arguments there, then.

La Gouttière

*96 av Parmentier, 11th (01.43.55.46.42).
M° Parmentier.* **Open** 8am-2am Mon-Fri; 3pm-2am
Sat. **Credit** V. **Map** p403 M4
Far enough (five minutes) from rue Oberkampf to
feel off the beaten track, the Gutter is not quite out
and out libertine, but you're on the right lines.
Certainly, a come-what-may approach to music,
drinking and eye contact abounds, in a crowded,
smoky room thankfully aired by French windows
of stripped wood. Inside, assuming you can see it,
decor consists of a few LP covers and the kind of
colour scheme often put to good use in adventure
playgrounds. Cheap lunches and animated seducing
techniques complete the picture.

more haphazard strip of bars. Dark, North African hookah haunts, late-night billiard bars, the slightly trendier Nun's Café and, facing each other at the JPT end of things, Le Chat Noir and this mauve gem, whose official address belies its St-Maur location. Whereas the former is frequented by Parisiennes beyond dating age but up for a good time, the latter attracts younger drinkers, who banter away on high-backed chairs while the barman plays cards with the regulars. Apart from the eponymous Marquess in a gilt-edged frame, the Manneken-Pis and Miles Davis portrait provide visual accompaniment. Finding a table is never usually a problem.

La Mercerie

98 rue Oberkampf, 11th (01.43.38.81.30). Mº Parmentier. **Open** 7pm-2am daily. **Credit** MC, V. **Map** p403 N5 ⓺

Opposite the landmark Charbon (*see p228*) and infinitely more grungy, the spacious Mercerie does indeed look like a haberdasher's – one that's been stripped out and then scuffed by the collective feet of boho Paris. Bare walls – bare everything, in fact – allow room for the usual Oberkampf shenanigans of death-wish drinking against a loud, eclectic musical backdrop. A DJ programme is lipsticked on to the back-bar mirror. Happy hour stretches to 9pm, so you can cane the house vodkas (apricot, mango, honey) and still have enough euros to finish the job after dusk. The back area, with its tea lights, provides intimacy if that's where the evening takes you.

Mon Chien Stupide

1 rue Boyer, 20th (01.46.36.25.49). Mº Gambetta. **Open** 6pm-2am Tue-Sun. **Credit** MC, V. **Map** p403 P4 ⓸

As the action moves relentlessly eastwards from Oberkampf, the once-distant outposts of Gambetta and Bagnolet appear on the radar of the discerning bar-hopper. Mon Chien Stupide, set at a quiet, hilly Gambetta crossroads, can be considered a port of call rather than a blip. Colourful and humorous, a bar for grown-ups rather than the kids' hangouts the other side of rue Sorbier, My Stupid Dog calls itself with some justification a 'Bar Expo'; the portraits of black musicians are striking, the swirling lightshades unusual and the strings of pretty lights a talking point. An undercurrent of jazzy sounds drifts along nicely. Commendably unsympathetic to canines – note the 'Dog Paste' sign by the bar.

Au Passage

1bis passage St-Sébastien, 11th (01.43.55.07.52). Mº St Sébastien Froissart. **Open** 9am-11pm daily. **Credit** MC, V. **Map** p409 M5 ⓺

A strange find, this, tucked down a long, narrow alleyway off rue Amelot, opposite the back entrance of Pop In. Look out for the green Stella sign if you're lost. Inside is red and black and Bohemian all over. Artists and artisans cluster around the corner bar, passing over the €2 bottles of Tsingtao beer for dark glasses of teeth-staining *vin rouge*, perhaps dipping into their neighbour's plate of meat or cheese

nibbles (€5/€8). There's a little art on the far wall, some retro cookbooks and a feeling that entire decades could pass and no one would really notice.

Au P'tit Garage

63 rue Jean-Pierre-Timbaud, 11th (01.48.07.08.12). Mº Parmentier. **Open** 6pm-2am daily. **Credit** AmEx, MC, V. **Map** p403 M4 ⓺

As sweetly tuned as Chuck Berry's cherry-red '53, this quite marvellous rock 'n' roll bar is the pick of the bunch on rue J-P-T. Not that the owners have fitted it with Americana or waitresses on rollerskates; the L'il Garage is as basic as the real car-fit business a few doors down the road. The stuffing bursts out of the bar stools and skip-salvage chairs accompany wobbly tables of ill-matched colours. Regulars cluster around the twin decks at the bar, while music-savvy Frenchettes giggle and gossip at the back. Dancing and death-wish drinking are interrupted by Lily the cackling Korean, hawking her carrier bag of tacky souvenirs. **Photo** *p231.*

Le Phénix

18 rue des Panoyaux, 20th (no phone). Mº Ménilmontant. **Open** noon-1am daily. **No credit cards. Map** p403 P5 ⓺

Of the cluster of bars near the junction of Panoyaux and Ménilmontant, this is the brightest and wittiest, with a neat little back garden to boot. The main front bar area, beneath a ceiling of erotic tiles, is dominated by a table football over which a scarf exclaims: 'FC Ferraille – Death To The Referee.' Here is where the action is, and where a regular may bring out the house ukulele for a tuneful strum. Belgian Maes runs at an affordable €2 a *demi*, while McEwan's is a baffling €3. Shouldn't someone tell them? **Photo** *p228.*

The Latin Quarter & 13th

Le Crocodile

6 rue Royer-Collard, 5th (01.43.54.32.37). RER Luxembourg. **Open** 10pm-late Mon-Sat. Closed Aug. **Credit** MC, V. **Map** p408 J8 ⓼

Ignore the apparently boarded-up windows for a cocktail at Le Crocodile – if you're here late, it's open. Young, friendly regulars line the sides of this small, narrow bar and try to decide on a drink: not easy, given the length and complexity of the cocktail list. It trots out 311 choices (the number increases on a yearly basis), each one more potent than the last. Pen and paper are provided to note your decision; the pen comes in handy for point-and-choose decisions when it all gets hazy. Given the €6-per-cocktail happy hour (Mon-Thur before midnight; €9 other times), this can be rather soon. We think we can recommend an *accroche-coeur*, a supremely 1970s mix of champagne and Goldschläger, served with extra gold leaf; after that, we had to start pointing.

Le Detone

10 rue Laplace, 5th (01.40.46.99.32). Mº Maubert-Mutualité. **Open** 7pm-2am Tue-Sat. **No credit cards. Map** p408 J8 ⓼

Au P'tit Garage. *See p230.*

In a different time zone to the neighbouring Piano Vache – this a savvy DJ bar, the other a student-indie throwback – Le Detone is nonetheless tardis-like in its size and appearance. It's all very earnest, with open decks early evening, followed by regular rumblings of jungle or drum 'n' bass. Drinks range to shorts, slings and longs, though most nod their heads over a *demi*, dancing kept to a minimum by space restrictions. This is a good place to pick up flyers to see what's going on in town.

Le Pantalon
7 rue Royer-Collard, 5th (no phone). RER Luxembourg. **Open** 5.30pm-2am Mon-Sat. **No credit cards. Map** p408 J8 ⑥⓪
Le Pantalon is a local café that seems familiar yet is utterly surreal. It has the standard fixtures and fittings, including the old soaks at the bar – plus a strange vacuum-cleaner sculpture, disco-light toilets and the world's most prosaic proposal of marriage. Offbeat decor aside, the regulars and staff are enough to tip the balance firmly into eccentricity. Friendly and very funny French grown-ups and foreign students chat in a mishmash of languages; happy hours are generous, but drinks are always cheap enough to make you tipsy without the worry of a cash-crisis hangover.

Pop Corner
16 rue des Bernadins, 5th (01.44.07.12.47). M° Maubert-Mutualité. **Open** 6pm-2am Tue-Thur; 6pm-4am Fri, Sat. **Credit** MC, V. **Map** p406 K7 ⑥①
Smoky and successful marriage of music bar and Brit pub, set between St-Germain and the river. The clientele is a mix of with-it attractive young, professional Parisiennes and anglophone expats unloos-

ening their ties – all very post-work, pre-shag stuff. There's even a bed in the corner. Abstract art on bare brick, a garlanded TV and €5 Poptions Magiques cocktails (Indi Pop: vodka and honey) add alternative touches – but both sexes are here to sink pints and peruse the possibilities.

St-Germain-des-Prés & Odéon

Alcazar
62 rue Mazarine, 6th (01.53.10.19.99/www.alcazar.fr). M° Odéon. **Open** 7pm-2am daily. **Credit** AmEx, DC, MC, V. **Map** p408 H7 ⑥②
It would be fair to assume that the Alcazar would be over by now, hip bars tending to fade once their first flush of youth is gone. But the 'AZ bar' still pulls it off somehow. The sleek velvet banquettes, polished aluminium bar and the vantage point over the oh-so-trendy restaurant and into the private dining room all help, of course, but really this place is worth paying for because it's posh without being poncey – and the drinks are great. The easy-listening sessions on Monday evenings are *un must* in local hip circles, and the weekend aperitif crowd still shows no sign of defecting.

Le Bar
27 rue de Condé, 6th (01.43.29.06.61). M° Odéon. **Open** 8pm-late Mon-Sat. **No credit cards. Map** p408 H7 ⑥③
Le Bar is one of those strange little places that you only ever visit when it's very, very late and you're very, very drunk. It'll all come back to you: how it's almost completely pitch black, has a shrine-type affair at the back of the bar and gravel on the floor; and how everyone talks in whispers – and the drinks

'The usual, Sir?'

Some exclusive, others legendary, most tucked away from the outside world, Paris hotel bars make for some of the best and most mythical drinking dens in the city.

The daddy of them all, the **Hemingway Bar at the Ritz** (15 pl Vendôme, 1st, 01.43.16.33.65; *pictured*) is a wonderfully civilised place in which to get smashed. Bartenders Colin and Ludo dispense fabulous cocktails (and compliments and flowers for the ladies) in a gloriously suave manner. **Bar Cambon** opposite (entrance at 38 rue Cambon, 1st, 01.43.16.30.90) is a good spot for posh partying, while the **Bar Vendôme** (01.43.16.33.63) at the front of the hotel has a perfect summer terrace.

If it hasn't been reserved for VIPs for the night, stunning sundowners can also be found on the seventh-floor roof terrace of the **Hôtel Raphaël** (17 av Kléber, 16th, 01.53.64.32.00). Downstairs, the Bar Anglais, while staid, is the stuff of history: Eisenhower toasted liberation here, and contemporaries Ava Gardner, Marlon Brando and Cary Grant all popped in for a *verre* at some point. Serge Gainsbourg wrote many of his songs while propping up the bar.

Champagne bar **Le Dokhan's** (Hôtel Trocadéro Dokhan's, 117 rue Lauriston, 16th, 01.53.65.66.99) is the perfect choice for amorous encounters. Think high ceilings, ornate gilt, decorative panelling and service so discreet it's practically invisible. Superb cocktails are served too.

Those looking for something just a little less subtle should head to the **V** (Four Seasons George V, 31 av George-V, 8th, 01.49.52.70.06) for a glitzy beverage or three. Champagne at €25 a glass, €28 for a club sandwich – it's sure swank at the Cinq. Higher on the see-and-be-seen scale is **Le Bar du Plaza** (Hôtel Plaza Athénée, 25 av Montaigne, 8th, 01.53.67.66.00), a cocktail bunny's most outré fantasy, with flattering lighting, high chairs offering maximum leg-crossing opportunities and ridiculous drinks. Avoid the savoury concoctions and speciality vodka jellies, and instead go for an old-fashioned but expertly mixed standard or join the PR crowd and indulge in a Fashion Ice: alcoholic ice lollies that offer maximum flirting and slurping potential.

Traditionalist trendies still make a beeline for the **Costes** (239 rue St-Honoré, 1st, 01.42.44.49.80), all champers and air kisses, or the **Murano** (13 bd du Temple, 3rd, 01.42.71.20.00) and its inventive interior, sassy staff and creative, vodka-based *boissons* – go for the Red Fruits and Love combo, vodka and summer fruits artfully served up in test tubes.

These days, hotels can make a name for themselves purely through the buzz around the bar alone. A classic example is the **Hôtel Amour** (*see p49*), brainchild of nightlife entrepreneur André, whose slightly retro brasserie (with leafy garden) has wowed the in crowd as much as the arty guest rooms.

are exceedingly strong. A couple of words of warning about this place: once you've been here, you'll find yourself strangely drawn back at inappropriate times when you really should be going home to bed, and at least one member of the party is guaranteed to fall asleep on the comfy black leather banquettes. There's a strange echo effect in the corridor leading down to the toilet, so if Le Bar is your last chance to pull before the sun comes up, don't discuss your strategy too loudly.

Le Bar Dix

10 rue de l'Odéon, 6th (01.43.26.66.83). M° Odéon. **Open** 6pm-2am daily. **No credit cards.** **Map** p408 H7 ❻❹

It's been here forever, this homely cavern of a bar, certainly longer than the brash Irish Horse's Tavern at one end of the street. Generations of students have glugged back jugs of the celebrated home-made sangria while squeezed into the cramped, twilit upper bar, tattily authentic with its Jacques Brel record sleeves, Yves Montand handbills and pre-war light fittings. The jukebox sadly no longer runs on vinyl, but the CDs weep suitably nostalgic pop nectar. Spelunkers and hopeless romantics negotiate the hazardous stone staircase to drink in the cellar bar, with its candlelight and century-old advertising murals. Someone please come and slap a preservation plaque on the place.

Le Bar du Marché

75 rue de Seine, 6th (01.43.26.55.15). M° Mabillon or Odéon. **Open** 8am-2am daily. **Credit** MC, V. **Map** p408 H7 ❻❺

The market in question is the Cours des Halles, the bar a convivial corner café opening out on to a pleasing blur of St-Germain-des-Prés bustle. It's all wonderfully simple, with easy dishes like a ham omelette or a plate of herring in the €7 range, half-decent Brouilly or muscadet at €4-€5 a glass, a few retro posters – Campari, Piaf, the Frères Jacques – and the regular passing of a beret-topped waiter. It couldn't be anywhere else in the world. Locals easily outnumber the tourists, though, the long afternoons underlining Rod Stewart's unusually astute observation that Paris gives you the impression that no one is ever working. Recommended.

Café de Flore

172 bd St-Germain, 6th (01.45.48.55.26/www.cafe-de-flore.com). M° St-Germain-des-Prés. **Open** 7.30am-1.30am daily. **Credit** AmEx, DC, MC, V. **Map** p408 H7 ❻❻

Bourgeois locals crowd the terrace tables at lunch, eating club sandwiches with knives and forks, as anxious waiters frown at couples with pushchairs or single diners occupying tables for four. This historic café, former HQ of the Lost Generation intelligentsia, attracts many tourists who eye passers-by hopefully. And, yes, celebs have been known to alight here from time to time. But a *café crème* is €4.60, a Perrier €5 and the omelettes and *croque-monsieurs* are best passed over for better dishes on

the menu (€15-€25). Upstairs, play readings are held on Mondays and philosophy discussions on the first Wednesday of the month, both at 8pm, in English.

Les Deux Magots

6 pl St-Germain-des-Prés, 6th (01.45.48.55.25/www.lesdeuxmagots.com). M° St-Germain-des-Prés. **Open** 7.30am-1am daily. Closed 1wk Jan. **Credit** AmEx, DC, MC, V. **Map** p408 H7 ❻❼

Stand outside here too long and be prepared to photograph visitors wanting proof of their encounter with French philosophy. The former haunt of Sartre, de Beauvoir et al now draws a less pensive crowd that can be all too '*m'as-tu vu*', particularly on weekends, when anglophone and Anglophile hordes pack the terrace. The hot chocolate is still good (and the only item served in generous portions) – but, like everything else, it's pricey. Visit on a weekday afternoon when the editors return, manuscripts in hand, to the inside tables, leaving enough elbow room to engage in some serious discussion. **Photo** *p234.*

Au Petit Suisse

16 rue de Vaugirard, 6th (01.43.26.03.81). M° Odéon. **Open** 7am-midnight Mon-Sat; 7am-10.30pm Sun. **Credit** DC, MC, V. **Map** p408 H7 ❻❽

Named after Marie de Médicis' Swiss Guards, the compact Au Petit Suisse has an enviable location next to the Jardin du Luxembourg and so pulls in a range of posh locals, harassed au pairs escaping from their charges and Gauloise-puffing Sorbonne students. The formal waiters excel in French snottiness, but do at least make this place all the more authentic and blissfully tourist-free. Brave the haughty stares for one of the handful of tables, order a Kir with a side of sneer and lap up a genuine 6th-arrondissement café experience.

Le Rostand

6 pl Edmond-Rostand, 6th (01.43.54.61.58). RER Luxembourg. **Open** 8am-2am daily. **Credit** MC, V. **Map** p408 H6 ❻❾

Le Rostand has a truly wonderful view of the Jardin du Luxembourg from its classy interior, decked out with oriental paintings, a long mahogany bar and wall-length mirrors. It's a terribly well-behaved place, and you should definitely consider arriving draped in furs or sporting the latest designer sunglasses if you want to fit in with the well-heeled regulars. The drinks list is lined with whiskies and cocktails, pricey but not as steep as the brasserie menu. Perfect for a sedate and civilised drink after a spin round the gardens.

La Taverne de Nesle

32 rue Dauphine, 6th (01.43.26.38.36). M° Odéon. **Open** 6pm-4am Mon-Thur, Sun; 6pm-6am Fri, Sat. **Credit** V. **Map** p408 H6 ❼❿

La Taverne, a late-night staple for people who just can't go home before daylight, has four distinct drinking areas: a zinc bar at the front, a sort of Napoleonic campaign tent in the middle, a trendily lit ambient area at the back, and a dreadful 1980s disco downstairs, where girls in pearls do their best to look sexy. The separate spaces correspond to stages of drunkenness and seem to encourage a gradual progression to the horizontal state. Among the 100 or so brews on offer you'll find the best of Belgium, but it's the excellent choice of French beers that really sets this place apart. Don't miss sampling the house special – L'Epi, brewed in three different versions: Blond (100% barley), Blanc (oats) and Noir (buckwheat) – or Corsican Pietra on tap.

Montparnasse

Le Select
99 bd de Montparnasse, 6th (01.42.22.65.27). Mº Vavin. **Open** 7am-2am Mon-Thur, Sun; 7am-4am Fri, Sat. **Credit** MC, V. **Map** p405 G9 ⓔ
For a decade between the wars, the junction of boulevards Raspail and Montparnasse was the centre of the known universe. Man Ray, Cocteau and Lost Generation Americans hung out at its vast glass-fronted cafés (Le Dôme, La Coupole), socialising, snubbing and snogging. Eight decades on, Le Select is the best of these inevitable tourist traps. Sure, its pricy menu is big on historical detail and short on authenticity (take the 'Cockney Brunch' of eggs, bacon and jam at €15, for example), but by and large Le Select manages to hold on to its heyday with dignity. *Intello* locals hang out at the bar, spreading out the highbrow culture section as Mickey the house cat strolls insouciantly across the newsprint. Happy hour from 7pm makes history affordable, the cocktail and whisky list is extensive, and pleasingly it's Mickey (not Ern Hemingway) who is honoured with a prominent framed portrait.

The 7th & the 15th

Le Café du Marché
38 rue Cler, 7th (01.47.05.51.27). Mº Ecole Militaire. **Open** 7am-midnight Mon-Sat; 7am-5pm Sun. **Credit** MC, V. **Map** p405 D6 ⓐ
This well-loved address is frequented by trendy locals, shoppers hunting down a particular type of cheese along this busy market street and tourists who've managed to make it this far from the Eiffel Tower. Le Café du Marché really is a hub of neighbourhood activity. Its *pichets* of decent house plonk go down a treat, and while it's fine just to have a drink here, mention must be made of the food – such as the huge house salad featuring lashings of foie gras and Parma ham.

Café Thoumieux
4 rue de la Comète, 7th (01.45.51.50.40/www. thoumieux.com). Mº La Tour Maubourg. **Open** noon-2am Mon-Fri; 5pm-2am Sat. Closed 3wks Aug. **Credit** AmEx, MC, V. **Map** p405 E6 ⓑ
The little brother to vintage bistro Thoumieux is a laid-back destination for cocktails, tapas or big-screen sport. Banquettes snake around the room and spiky Aztec-pattern lamps send light flickering up the walls and the faces of pretty young locals who have made this place their own. The flavoured vodkas are delicious and include vanilla, caramel and banana. Don't blame them for any difficulties you might be suffering with the treacherous, extra-high bar stools (the banquettes are definitely the safest option) or for the sight of the monstrous, pebble-dashed sink in the toilets – it's real.

Elevated conversation and lofty prices at **Les Deux Magots**. *See p233.*

Shops & Services

Fashion booms, family shops fold and flea markets flourish.

Rustic, tasty and traditional – **Saxe-Breteuil** market is known for its cheeses. *See p263.*

The world's fashion capital is booming. The Golden Triangle around the Champs-Elysées has taken a youth cure, anchored by **Louis Vuitton**'s new global concept store with a significant trickle-down along avenue Montaigne (*see p246* **Montaigne makeover**). But this is no longer a city with one golden triangle; it has several. The one on the Left Bank has **Le Bon Marché** as its apex (*see p249* **Walk this way**) while the trendiest one of all continues to blossom along rue Charlot and rue Vieille-du-Temple in the 3rd district.

Extensive renovations along rue Saint-Honoré between place Vendôme and the Palais-Royal – and especially rue du Mont-Thabor, near landmark concept store **Colette** – have made this an attractive area for new designer shops, from arrivals such as Roberto Cavalli (whose flagship opens in 2007) and Diane von Furstenberg to small fashionable boutiques such as **Jay Ahr**. Back at the Palais-Royal, the 2006 inauguration of **Marc Jacobs**' first European flagship in Paris has made the neighbourhood a magnet for fashionistas (*see p252* **Storming the palace**).

The real Paris is sourced in those specialist boutiques that have always been a vibrant part of the city's fashion culture. Likewise, family-run food shops, outlets for artisan tradition and rustic markets barely changed in over a century (*see p263* **Super *marchés***). Although recent years have seen the closure of many family-run *fromageries*, *boulangeries*, *charcuteries* and quirky little treasure troves, and the chain concept is catching on quickly, the overall variety and quality remains impressive, and almost everything, from a vintage bottle of Armagnac to a single praline chocolate, is lovingly served, wrapped and presented, whatever the store. Informative discussion is still very much part of the purchasing process; and beautiful, old-style arcades – such as the galerie Vivienne or passage Jouffroy – make shopping a sightseeing pleasure as well.

Different areas have different specialities (*see p256* **Shopping by area**). There are clusters of antiques shops in the 7th district and second-hand and rare book outlets in the 5th (a reminder of the days when there were publishing guilds there); crystal and porcelain

A shrine to shopping – the **Galeries Lafayette**. *See p237.*

manufacturers still dot rue de Paradis in the 10th; furniture craftsmen inhabit rue du Faubourg-St-Antoine; bikes and cameras are clustered on bd Beaumarchais and the world's top jewellers can be found on place Vendôme. Street-chic and lifestyle boutiques live side by side in the Marais and around rue Etienne-Marcel, while quirky newcomers settle in Abbesses or near the Canal St-Martin. Designer labels are scattered all over the 1st, 6th and 8th.

No shopping trip would be complete without a visit to a flea market, where haggling is still de rigueur and cash is the payment of choice.

SALES AND OPENING HOURS

Shops open 10am-7pm Monday to Saturday, with specialist boutiques closing for an hour at lunch. Sunday shopping is no longer frowned upon – the shopping galleries inside the Louvre and selected shops on the Champs-Elysées are open – but is not as common as in the UK. Small corner grocery stores open late for essentials. Many family-run concerns close in August. Twice a year, in January and July, boutiques sell off seasonal stock at reduced prices to make way for incoming collections. The exact national dates for the sales (*soldes*) are imposed by the state-run consumer office; call 01.40.27.16.00 for details.

One-stop shops

Department stores

The revamped *grands magasins* have brought in trendy designers and luxury spaces to lure shoppers away from independent boutiques.

BHV (Bazar de l'Hôtel de Ville)

52-64 rue de Rivoli, 4th (01.42.74.90.00/DIY hire 01.42.74.97.23/www.bhv.fr). M° Hôtel de Ville. **Open** 9.30am-7.30pm Mon, Tue, Thur-Sat; 9.30am-9pm Wed. **Credit** AmEx, MC, V. **Map** p406 J6.
Hardware heaven – there's even a Bricolage Café, with internet access. Upper floors have a good range of men's outdoor wear, upmarket bedlinen, toys, books, household appliances – and a large space devoted to every type of storage utility.

Le Bon Marché

24 rue de Sèvres, 7th (01.44.39.80.00/www.bon marche.fr). M° Sèvres Babylone. **Open** 9.30am-7pm Mon-Wed, Fri; 10am-9pm Thur; 9.30am-8pm Sat. **Credit** AmEx, DC, MC, V. **Map** p405 G7.
Paris' oldest department store, opened in 1848, is also its most swish and user-friendly, thanks to an extensive redesign by LVMH. Luxury boutiques, Dior and Chanel among them, take pride of place on the ground floor; escalators designed by Andrée Putman take you up to the fashion floor, which has

an excellent selection of global designer labels, from Lanvin to APC. Designer names also abound in Balthazar, the prestigious men's section, while VIP services include personal shopping stylists for both men and women. The adjoining Grande Epicerie food hall (01.44.39.81.00, www.lagrandeeicerie.fr, 8.30am-9pm Mon-Sat) has a café and restaurant.

Galeries Lafayette

40 bd Haussmann, 9th (01.42.82.34.56/ fashion shows 01.42.82.30.25/fashion advice 01.42.82.35.50/www.galerieslafayette.com). M° Chaussée d'Antin La Fayette/RER Auber. **Open** 9.30am-7.30pm Mon-Wed, Fri, Sat; 9.30am-9pm Thur. **Credit** AmEx, DC, MC, V. **Map** p401 H3.
The store has revamped its fashion, beauty and accessories sections, and, in hot competition with Printemps (*see below*), opened a third-floor lingerie department. More than 90 designers are spread over the first and second floors, including Cavalli, Lacroix and Givenchy. There are five fashion and beauty consultants to guide you through the sartorial maze, and the men's fashion space on the third floor, Lafayette Homme, has natty designer corners and a 'Club' area with internet access. On the first floor, Lafayette Gourmet has exotic foods galore, and a vast wine cellar. The domed ceiling is eminently photogenic, and there's a rooftop café. Over the road, Lafayette Maison (www.lafayettemaison.com) offers five floors of design for the home. **Photo** *p236.*
Other locations: Centre Commercial Montparnasse, 14 rue de Départ, 14th (01.45.38.52.87).

Printemps

64 bd Haussmann, 9th (01.42.82.50.00/www. printemps.com). M° Havre Caumartin/RER Auber. **Open** 9.35am-7pm Mon-Wed, Fri, Sat; 9.35am-10pm Thur. **Credit** AmEx, DC, MC, V. **Map** p401 G3.
Printemps is the home of superlatives – its shoe department (on the fifth floor of Printemps de la Mode) and beauty department are both the largest in the world, the latter stocking some 200 brands. The lingerie department is the stuff of fantasy too with gorgeous smalls from Erès, Gaultier, Pucci and the like. In all, there are six floors of fashion in both the men's and women's stores. On the second floor of Printemps de la Mode, French designers APC, Zadig et Voltaire sit side by side with Moschino and Dolce e Gabbana; Miss Code, on the fifth floor, targets the teen miss. Along with furnishings, Printemps de la Maison contains the more conceptual 'function floor', with saucepans and coffee machines neatly organised on steel shelving. The ninth-floor terrace restaurant sports an art nouveau cupola.

Tati

4 bd de Rochechouart, 18th (01.55.29.52.50/ www.tati.fr). M° Barbès Rochechouart. **Open** 10am-7pm Mon-Sat. **Credit** MC, V. **Map** p402 J2.
Expect to find anything from T-shirts to wedding dresses, as well as bargain children's clothes and household goods at this discount heaven. It's unbeatably cheap, but don't expect high quality.
Other locations: throughout the city.

Shopping centres

Drugstore Publicis

133 av des Champs-Elysées, 8th (01.44.43.79.00/ www.publicisdrugstore.com). M° Charles de Gaulle Etoile. **Open** 8am-2am Mon-Fri; 10am-2am Sat, Sun. **Credit** MC, V. **Map** p400 D4.

A 1960s legend, the Drugstore Publicis has been clad with neon swirls by architect Michele Saee following a long renovation in 2004; a glass-and-steel café oozes on to the pavement. On the ground floor a newsagent, pharmacy, bookshop and upmarket deli full of quality olive oils and elegant biscuits; a video screen reminds you that Publicis is an advertising agency. The basement is a macho take on Colette (*see p250*), keeping selected design items and lifestyle mags, but replacing high fashion with wines and a cigar cellar.

La Galerie du Carrousel du Louvre

99 rue de Rivoli, 1st (01.43.16.47.10/www. lecarrouseldulouvre.com). M° Palais Royal Musée du Louvre. **Open** 10am-8pm daily. **Credit** AmEx, MC, V. **Map** p406 J6.

This massive underground centre – open every day of the year – is home to more than 35 shops, mostly big-name chains vying for your attention and your cash. It's great for last-minute gifts.

Beauty

Cosmetics

L'Artisan Parfumeur

24 bd Raspail, 7th (01.42.22.23.32). M° Rue du Bac. **Open** 10.30am-7.30pm Mon-Sat. **Credit** AmEx, DC, MC, V. **Map** p405 G7.

Among scented candles, potpourri and charms, you'll find the best vanilla perfume Paris can offer – Mûres et Musc, a bestseller for two decades. **Other locations**: throughout the city.

By Terry

36 galerie Véro-Dodat, 1st (01.44.76.00.76/www. byterry.com). M° Palais Royal Musée du Louvre. **Open** 10.30am-7pm Mon-Sat. **Credit** AmEx, MC, V. **Map** p402 H5.

Terry de Gunzburg, who earned her reputation at Yves Saint Laurent, offers made-to-measure 'haute couleur' make-up by skilled chemists and colourists combining high-tech treatments and handmade precision. There's prêt-à-porter, too. **Other locations**: 1 rue Jacob, 6th (01.46.34.00.36); 10 av Victor-Hugo, 16th (01.55.73.00.73).

Conceptual Scent

48-50 rue de l'Université, 7th (01.45.44.50.14). M° Rue du Bac. **Open** 10am-7pm Mon-Sat. **Credit** AmEx, MC, V. **Map** p405 G6.

Invisible from the street, this minimal space is a temple to fragrance, selling its own delicious lines of perfumes, gels and candles. Sniff out the Eau Interdite, a curious, absinthe-scented eau de cologne.

Détaille 1905

10 rue St-Lazare, 9th (01.48.78.68.50/www.detaille. com). M° Notre-Dame de-Lorette. **Open** 3-7pm Mon; 10am-7pm Tue-Fri; 11am-4pm Sat. **Credit** MC, V. **Map** p401 H3.

Step back in time at this shop, opened, as the name suggests, in 1905 by the war artist Edouard Détaille. Six fragrances (three for men and three for women) are made from century-old recipes.

Editions de Parfums Frédéric Malle

37 rue de Grenelle, 7th (01.42.22.77.22/www. editionsdeparfums.com). M° Rue du Bac or St-Sulpice. **Open** 1-7pm Mon; 11am-7pm Tue-Sat. **Credit** AmEx, DC, MC, V. **Map** p405 F6.

Choose from eight perfumes by Frédéric Malle, former consultant to Hermès and Lacroix. Carnal Flower by Dominique Ropion is seduction in a bottle. **Other locations**: 21 rue du Mont-Thabor, 1st (01.42. 22.77.22); 140 av Victor-Hugo, 16th (01.45.05.39.02).

Galerie Noémie

92 av des Champs-Elysées, 8th (01.44.76.06.26/ www.galerienoemie.com). M° George V. **Open** 11am-7pm Mon-Thur; 11am-9pm Fri, Sat. **Credit** AmEx, DC, MC, V. **Map** p402 J5.

You can tell owner Noémie is a painter by the way all the make-up is set out in palettes. Little pots of gloss (starting from €7.50) in myriad colours triple as lip gloss, eyeshadow or blusher. Check out Noemie's blog at http://blog.galerie-noemie.com/. **Other locations**: Galeries Lafayette, 40 bd Haussmann, 9th (01.42.82.34.56).

Guerlain

68 av des Champs-Elysées, 8th (01.45.62.52.57/ www.guerlain.com). M° Franklin D. Roosevelt. **Open** 10.30am-8pm Mon-Sat; 3-7pm Sun. **Credit** AmEx, DC, MC, V. **Map** p401 E4.

Perfume's great golden oldie recently had a facelift and is looking more ravishing than ever. Head to the first floor to get the full measure of the history behind the house that created the mythic Samsara, Mitsouko and L'Heure Bleue.

L'Occitane

55 rue St-Louis-en-l'Ile, 4th (01.40.46.81.71/ www.loccitane.com). M° Pont Marie. **Open** 11am-7pm Mon; 10am-7pm Tue; 10am-7.30pm Wed-Fri; 10am-8pm Sat, Sun. **Credit** AmEx, DC, MC, V. **Map** p409 K7.

The many branches of this popular Provençal chain proffer natural beauty products in neat packaging. Soap stalls, along with essential oils and perfumes. **Other locations**: throughout the city.

Salons du Palais-Royal Shiseido

Jardins du Palais-Royal, 142 galerie de Valois, 1st (01.49.27.09.09/www.salons-shiseido.com). M° Palais Royal Musée du Louvre. **Open** 10am-7pm Mon-Sat. **Credit** AmEx, DC, MC, V. **Map** p401 H5.

Under the arcades of the Palais-Royal, Shiseido's perfumer Serge Lutens practises his aromatic arts. A former photographer at Paris *Vogue* and artistic director of make-up at Christian Dior, Lutens is a

Eat, Drink, Shop

Turning over a new leaf

Its modest yellow frontage facing the Seine in the shadow of Notre-Dame, **Shakespeare & Co** (*see p243*) is surely the most famous English-language book emporium in the world. Its story is interwoven with the leading literary personalities of the 20th century, straddling the war, three premises and two owners.

The current one, George Whitman, is now in his 93rd year, grey-haired and lucid, riven with the morals learned from his impoverished wanderings in central America. The founder, Sylvia Beach, died in Paris in 1962, and ran the original store at nearby Odéon. The present manager, responsible for introducing a telephone, a credit-card machine and, most notably, a biennial summer literary festival, is Sylvia Beach Whitman, George's daughter. 'When I took over in 2003, everyone was constantly talking about the shop's history,' says Sylvia. 'It was always Sylvia Beach and the Lost Generation, George Whitman and the Beat Generation. It was infuriating!' Without tampering with the homely feel of the shop's interior, or her father's core philosophy of offering penniless writers a dark recess of the shop in which to sleep, Sylvia has set about giving Shakespeare a modern direction. As well as the festival, set up in a marquee on a patch of riverside green alongside the store – after the travel writing theme of 2006, 'Real Lives, Memoirs and Biographies' is the theme for 2008 – Sylvia has plans for a café and cultural centre, realising the idea her father

nurtured in 1951to fashion Shakespeare into a local literary hub.

Both Whitman senior and Beach were riding a wave of post-war literary euphoria. Beach opened her first shop almost exactly a year after Armistice Day, in 1919. Paris was permissive if impoverished, and most welcoming to Americans. Her circle of clients and acquaintances included Hemingway, Fitzgerald and James Joyce. It was Beach who published the first 1,000 copies of *Ulysses*, on Joyce's 40th birthday in 1922. Two decades later, after Beach refused to sell a Nazi officer her last copy of *Finnegan's Wake*, her shop was closed. Famously and symbolically, it had to be Hemingway, amid the sound of shelling and sniper fire, who liberated it in 1944.

Beach never officially opened the shop again. Victorious GIs stayed over and studied in Paris, including Whitman and new associate Lawrence Ferlinghetti. With a modest inheritance, Whitman bought his current premises and converted them into a bookshop and library. While Ferlinghetti worked on his literary thesis (before heading to San Francisco to open the City Lights bookstore in 1953), a new generation gathered at what was then known as Le Mistral. The Beats, Burroughs, Ginsberg and the incorrigible kleptomaniac Gregory Corso gave poetry readings and drank their way through literary evenings.

After Beach's death, Whitman renamed his shop in honour of her heritage. Walk in today and you hear the clacking of old typewriters from upstairs, your eyes falling upon a few bronze coins in a symbolic dry wishing well, and mottos ('Live for Humanity') engraved in between the steps. Outside, amid the stalls and small ads, the 'Paris Wall Newspaper' is a chalked history written by Whitman on New Year's Day 2004. No bar codes, no security gates, no shrink wrap. As former regular Gertrude Stein said: 'It's not what Paris gives you, as what it doesn't take away'.

Eat, Drink, Shop

Bercy Village

a break from **Parisian life**

There is a place in Paris that is different from the rest, far from the noise and bustle ; where shopping comes down to strolling around, stopping at terraces and breathing village air. You are welcomed by shops, exhibitions, activities and restaurants nestled in the historical wine and spirit storehouses of the capital.

There is no need to look further afield to find yourself elsewhere ; come off at the Cour Saint Emilion metro station (line 14), **and take a break.**

 Une parenthèse à Paris

Shops – leisure pastimes – activities – restaurants – cinemas UGC

Ⓜ ⑭ **Cour Saint-Émilion**

www.bercyvillage.com

maestro of rare taste. Bottles of his concoctions – Tubéreuse Criminelle, Rahat Loukoum and Ambre Sultan – can be sampled by visitors. Look out for Fleurs d'Oranger, which the great man defines as the smell of happiness. Many of the perfumes are exclusive to the Salons; prices start at around €100. **Other locations**: 2 place Vendôme, 1st (01.42.60.68.61); 29 rue de Sèvres, 6th (01.42.22.46.60); 66 bd Montparnasse, 15th (01.43.20.95.40).

Sephora

70 av des Champs-Elysées, 8th (01.53.93.22.50/ www.sephora.fr). M° Franklin D. Roosevelt. **Open** *Sept-Jun* 10am-midnight daily. *July, Aug* 10am-1.30am. **Credit** AmEx, DC, MC, V. **Map** p401 E4.
The late-opening flagship of the cosmetic supermarket chain houses 12,000 French and foreign brands of scent and slap. Sephora Blanc (14 cour St-Emilion, 12th, 01.40.02.97.79) features beauty products in a blindingly minimalist interior.
Other locations: throughout the city

Salons & spas

Anne Sémonin

Le Bristol, 108 rue du Faubourg-Saint-Honoré, 8th (01.42.66.24.22/www.lebristolparis.com). M° Miromesnil or Champs Elysées Clemenceau. **Open** 10am-7pm Tue-Sat. **Credit** AmEx, DC, MC, V. **Map** p401 E3.
Facials involve delicious concoctions of basil, lavender, lemongrass, ginger and plant essences. Also on offer are reflexology and a selection of massage styles, from Thai to Ayurvedic. Body treatments cost from €70 to €210. Sémonin's renowned seaweed skincare products and essential oils are also on sale.
Other locations: 2 rue des Petits-Champs, 2nd (01.42.60.94.66).

Les Bains du Marais

31-33 rue des Blancs-Manteaux, 4th (01.44.61.02.02/ www.lesbainsdumarais.com). M° St-Paul. **Open** *Men* 11am-11pm Thur; 10am-8pm Fri. *Women* 11am-8pm Mon; 11am-11pm Tue; 10am-7pm Wed. *Mixed* 7-11pm Wed; 10am-8pm Sat; 11am-11pm Sun. Closed Aug. **Credit** AmEx, MC, V. **Map** p409 K6.
This hammam and spa mixes modern and traditional (lounging beds and mint tea). Facials, waxing and essential oil massages (€60) are also available. The hammam is €30, a standard massage €30.

La Bulle Kenzo

1 rue du Pont-Neuf, 1st (01.73.04.20.04/www.labulle kenzo.com). M° Pont Neuf. **Open** 10am-8pm Mon-Sat. **Credit** AmEx, DC, MC, V. **Map** p406 J6.
Kenzo's flagship store houses a chic beauty salon of high concept. The two massage rooms offer two different vibes: Pétillante has a disco ball, while Japanese Zen cocoon provides calmer pleasures.

L'Espace Payot

62 rue Pierre-Charon, 8th (01.45.61.42.08). M° George V. **Open** 7am-10pm Mon-Fri; 9am-7pm Sat; 10am-5pm Sun. **Credit** AmEx, MC, V. **Map** p400 D4.

Opened in 2006 by Dr Nadia Payot, one of the leading ladies in French skincare, this institute offers the entire gamut of luxurious face and body treatments. One of the largest spas in Paris, it has a gym, pool, sauna and steam bath, and health food bar. Prices range from €40 to €80, while a day pass is €150.

L'Esthétique de Demain

15 rue de la Grande-Truanderie, 1st (01.40.26.53.10). M° Châtelet or Etienne Marcel. **Open** 2-7pm Mon; 10am-8.30pm Tue-Fri; 10am-7pm Sat. **Credit** MC, V. **Map** p402 J5.
If you're looking to get the job done without a lot of hoopla, this low-key, low-cost salon specialising in hair removal is for you. Waxing for men and women starts at €9, facials from €28. Massages 'per minute' are also on offer (it's €10 for ten minutes) along with reflexology, Reiki and more.

Hammam de la Grande Mosquée

1 pl du Puits-de-l'Ermite, 5th (01.43.31.18.14). M° Censier Daubenton. **Open** *Men* 2-9pm Tue; 10am-9pm Sun. *Women* 10am-9pm Mon, Wed, Sat; 2-9pm Fri. **Credit** MC, V. **Map** p406 K9.
Be steamed, scrubbed and massaged to the sound of soft voices and Arabic music in this 1920s mosque. Follow a session with a *gommage* (exfoliation with a rough mitt), then a massage. The hammam is €15, *gommage* €10 and massage €10. Swimwear is compulsory. Towel and gown hire is also available.

Hammam Med Centre

43-45 rue Petit, 19th (01.42.02.31.05/www. hammammed.com). M° Ourcq. **Open** *Women* 11am-10pm Mon-Fri; 9am-7pm Sun. *Mixed* 10am-9pm Sat. **Credit** MC, V. **Map** p403 N5.
This hammam is hard to beat – spotless mosaic-tiled surroundings, flowered sarongs and a relaxing pool. The exotic 'Forfait florale' option (€139) will have you cloaked in rose petals and massaged with *huile d'Argan* from Morocco, while the more simple hammam and *gommage* are €39.

Institut Lancôme

29 rue du Fbg-St-Honoré, 8th (01.42.65.30.74/ www.lancome.fr). M° Madeleine or Concorde. **Open** 10am-7pm Mon-Sat. **Credit** AmEx, DC, MC, V. **Map** p401 F4.
Lancôme's flagship salon offers its affluent clientele just about every treatment going: exfoliation, massage, facials, waxing, tanning and manicure. Facials cost €45 to €90; body treatments cost from €90.

Toni & Guy

248 rue St-Honoré, 1st (01.40.20.98.20/www.toni andguy.com). M° Palais Royal Musée du Louvre or Pyramides. **Open** 10am-8pm Mon-Sat. **Credit** AmEx, DC, MC, V. **Map** p401 G5.
At prime spots in Paris, Toni & Guy's salons charge from €49 to €92, depending on the 'artist' working on your hair. Book a cut on a Friday and Saturday afternoon for DJs as well, or get a free cut at the academy (122 rue du Fbg-St-Honoré, 8th, 01.40.20.15.93).
Other locations: throughout the city.

Eat, Drink, Shop

All that jazz and more at **Crocojazz**. *See p243.*

Books, CDs, DVDs

Books

Artazart

*83 quai de Valmy, 10th (01.40.40.24.00/www.
artazart.com). M° Jacques Bonsergent.* **Open**
10.30am-7.30pm Mon-Fri; 2-8pm Sat, Sun. **Credit**
AmEx, MC, V. **Map** p402 L4.
A bright yellow beacon on trendy Canal St-Martin,
this bookshop and gallery stocks cutting-edge publications on fashion, art, architecture and design.

Bouquinistes

*Along the quais, especially quai de Montebello & quai
St-Michel, 5th. M° St-Michel.* **Open** times vary from
stall to stall, generally Tue-Sun. **No credit cards.**
Map p406 J7.
The green, open-air boxes along the *quais* are one of
the city's oldest institutions. Most sell second-hand
books – ignore the nasty postcards and rummage
through boxes packed with ancient paperbacks for
something existential. Feel free to haggle.

Brentano's

*37 av de l'Opéra, 2nd (01.42.61.52.50/www.
brentanos.fr). M° Opéra or Pyramides.* **Open** 10am-
7.30pm Mon-Sat. **Credit** (€45 minimum) AmEx, DC;
(€17 minimum) MC, V. **Map** p401 G4.
Brentano's is good for American classics, modern
fiction and bestsellers, plus business titles. The children's section is in the basement. It hosts monthly
reading groups and children's clubs.

La Flûte de Pan

*49, 53 & 59 rue de Rome, 8th (01.42.93.65.05/www.
laflutedepan.fr). M° Europe.* **Open** 10am-6.30pm Tue,
Thur-Sat; 2.30-6.30pm Wed. **Credit** V. **Map** p401 F3.
Three shops stock books on classical music and
scores for all instruments. There's learning material at No.49; brass, sax and percussion at No.53; and
piano, organ and vocal at No.59.

Galignani

224 rue de Rivoli, 1st (01.42.60.76.07). M° Tuileries.
Open 10am-7pm Mon-Sat. **Credit** MC, V.
Map p401 G5.
Opened in 1802, this was the first English-language
bookshop in Europe. Today it stocks fine arts books,
French and English literature, and magazines.

Gibert Jeune

*10 pl St-Michel, 5th (01.56.81.22.22/www.gibert
jeune.fr). M° St-Michel.* **Open** 9.30am-7.30pm Mon-
Sat. **Credit** MC, V. **Map** p408 J7.
This 'Langues et lettres' branch of the Left Bank
chain stocks books published in 320 languages.
Other locations: 15bis bd St-Denis, 2nd; 36 rue de
la Huchette, 5th; 23 & 27 quai St-Michel, 5th; 5 pl St-
Michel, 5th; 2, 4 & 6 pl St-Michel, 6th.

Gibert Joseph

*26 bd St-Michel, 6th (01.44.41.88.88/www.gibert
joseph.com). M° St-Michel.* **Open** 10am-7.30pm Mon-
Sat. **Credit** MC, V. **Map** p408 J7.
Erudite Gibert Joseph was formed separately from
Gibert Jeune in 1929. Stationery, CDs, DVDs and art
supply branches are found further up the boulevard.
Other locations: 30, 32 & 34 bd St-Michel, 6th.

La Hune

170 bd St-Germain, 6th (01.45.48.35.85). M° St-Germain-des-Prés. **Open** 10am-11.45pm Mon-Sat; 11am-7.45pm Sun. **Credit** AmEx, MC, V. **Map** p405 G7.

This Left Bank institution boasts a global selection of art and design books, and a magnificent collection of French literature and theory.

Librairie Flammarion

Centre Pompidou, 19 rue Beaubourg, 4th (01.44.78.43.22/www.flammarioncentre.com). M° Rambuteau. **Open** 11am-10pm Mon, Wed-Sun. Closed 2wks Sept. **Credit** AmEx, MC, V. **Map** p402 K5.

A pleasant place to peruse first-rate art, design, photography and cinema titles, this also stocks children's books, postcards (the post office next door is the quietest in town) and arty magazines.

Librairie 7L

7 rue de Lille, 7th (01.42.92.03.58). M° Rue du Bac or Solférino. **Open** 10.30am-7pm Tue-Sat. **Credit** AmEx, DC, MC, V. **Map** p405 G6.

Karl Lagerfeld's love of books gets street frontage in this chic shop, with fashion, art, design and poetry titles – and every magazine worth reading.

Shakespeare & Co

37 rue de la Bûcherie, 5th (01.43.26.96.50/http://shakespeareco.org). M° St-Michel. **Open** noon-midnight daily. **Credit** MC, V. **Map** p406 J7.

Opened in 1951, George Whitman's bookshop is still going strong (*see p239* **Turning over a new leaf**).

Village Voice

6 rue Princesse, 6th (01.46.33.36.47/www.village voicebookshop.com). M° Mabillon. **Open** 2-7.30pm Mon; 10am-7.30pm Tue-Sat; noon-6pm Sun. **Credit** AmEx, DC, MC, V. **Map** p405 H7.

New fiction, non-fiction and literary magazines in English, plus literary events and poetry readings.

WHSmith

248 rue de Rivoli, 1st (01.44.77.88.99/www.whsmith. fr). M° Concorde. **Open** 9am-7.30pm Mon-Sat; 1-7.30pm Sun. **Credit** AmEx, MC, V. **Map** p401 G5.

Some 70,000 English-language titles and a near impenetrable crush around the magazine section; the first floor has books, DVDs and audiobooks.

CDs & DVDs

Gibert Joseph (*see p242*) also stocks CDs and DVDs; WHSmith (*see above*) stocks British DVDs. For new and second-hand vinyl, head over to rue Keller in the 11th for electronica and rue de Navarre (5th) for jazz.

Blue Moon Music

84 rue Quincampoix, 3rd (01.40.29.45.60). M° Rambuteau. **Open** 11am-7pm Mon-Fri; noon-7pm Sat. **Credit** MC, V. **Map** p406 J6.

Specialises in reggae and ragga. Authentic Jamaican sounds imported on a weekly basis.

Crocodisc

40-42 rue des Ecoles, 5th (01.43.54.47.95). M° Maubert Mutualité. **Open** 11am-7pm Tue-Sat. Closed 2wks Aug. **Credit** MC, V. **Map** p408 J7.

The excellent, if expensive, range includes rock, funk, African, country and classical. For jazz and blues, try sister shop Crocojazz. **Photo** *p242*. **Other locations:** Crocojazz, 64 rue de la Montagne-Ste-Geneviève, 5th (01.46.34.78.38).

Fnac

74 av des Champs-Elysées, 8th (01.53.53.64.64/ticket office 08.92.68.36.22/www.fnac.com). M° George V. **Open** 10am-midnight Mon-Sat; noon-midnight Sun. **Credit** AmEx, MC, V. **Map** p400 D4.

Fnac is a supermarket of culture: books, DVDs, CDs, audio kit, computers and photographic equipment. Most branches – notably the vast Forum des Halles address – stock everything; others specialise, including kids' stuff (*see p244*). All branches operate as a concert box office. If you plan on a large purchase, you can save by signing up for Fnac membership. **Other locations:** throughout the city.

Monster Melodies

9 rue des Déchargeurs, 1st (01.40.28.09.39). M° Les Halles. **Open** noon-7pm Mon-Sat. **Credit** MC, V. **Map** p402 J5.

The owners are prepared to help you on a treasure hunt – with more than 10,000 second-hand CDs of every variety, that's just as well.

Virgin Megastore

52-60 av des Champs-Elysées, 8th (01.49.53.50.00/ www.virginmega.fr). M° Franklin D. Roosevelt. **Open** 10am-midnight Mon-Sat; noon-midnight Sun. **Credit** AmEx, DC, MC, V. **Map** p401 E4.

The luxury of perusing CDs and DVDs till midnight makes this a choice spot, and the listening posts let you sample any CD by scanning its barcode. Tickets for concerts and sports events are available here too. This main branch has the best selection of books. **Other locations:** Carrousel du Louvre, 99 rue de Rivoli, 1st (01.44.50.03.10); 5 bd Montmartre, 2nd (01.40.13.72.13); 15 bd Barbès, 18th (01.56.55.53.70).

Children

Clothes & shoes

Children's shops are clustered on rues Bréa (6th), Vavin (6th) and du Fbg-St-Antoine (12th).

Bonton

82 rue de Grenelle, 7th (01.44.39.09.20/www. bonton.fr). M° Rue du Bac. **Open** 10am-7pm Mon-Sat. Closed 2wks Aug. **Credit** AmEx, DC, MC, V. **Map** p405 F6.

At this concept store for kids and trendy parents, T-shirts and trousers come in rainbow colours, and at pretty steep prices. Furniture and accessories are also available, plus a children's hairdresser.

Eat, Drink, Shop

Jacadi

76 rue d'Assas, 6th (01.45.44.60.44/www.jacadi.fr).
M° Vavin. **Open** 10am-7pm Mon-Sat. **Credit** MC, V.
Map p405 G8.
Jacadi's well-made clothes for babies and children –
pleated skirts, smocked dresses, dungarees and Fair
Isle knits – are a hit with well-to-do parents.
Other locations: throughout the city.

Du Pareil au Même

15-17 & 23 rue des Mathurins, 9th (01.42.66.93.80/
www.dpam.com). M° Havre Caumartin/RER Auber.
Open 10am-7pm Mon-Sat. **Credit** AmEx, MC, V.
Map p401 G3.
Bright, cleverly designed basics for children aged
three months to 14 years, at low prices. The Bébé
branch, with fashionable accessories and clothing
for kids up to two years, is a good source of gifts that
look more expensive than they really are.
Other locations: throughout the city.

Petit Bateau

26 rue Vavin, 6th (01.55.42.02.53/www.petit-bateau.
com). M° Vavin. **Open** 10am-7pm Mon-Sat. **Credit**
AmEx, MC, V. **Map** p405 G8.
Renowned for comfortable, well-made cotton T-
shirts, vests and other separates, Petit Bateau carries an equally coveted teen range.
Other locations: throughout the city.

Six Pieds Trois Pouces

222 bd St-Germain, 7th (01.45.44.03.72).
M° Solférino. **Open** 10.30am-7pm Mon-Sat.
Credit AmEx, DC, MC, V. **Map** p405 F6.
The excellent array of children's and teens' shoes
runs from Start-rite and Aster to Timberland and
New Balance, plus the shop's own-label series.
Other locations: 19 rue de la Monnaie, 1st (01.40.
41.07.79); 85 rue de Longchamp, 16th (01.45.53.64.21);
78 av de Wagram, 17th (01.46.22.81.64).

Toys & books

Traditional toyshops abound. Department
stores (*see p237*) go overboard at Christmas.
For children's books in English, try **WHSmith**
(*see p242*) or **Brentano's** (*see p243*).

Arche de Noé

70 rue St-Louis-en-l'Ile, 4th (01.46.34.61.60).
M° Pont Marie. **Open** 10.30am-7pm daily. **Credit**
AmEx, MC, V. **Map** p409 L6.
'Noah's Ark' is a great place for Christmas shopping,
with traditional wooden toys from eastern Europe,
games and jigsaws, and finger puppets.

Fnac Junior

19 rue Vavin, 6th (01.56.24.03.46/www.eveiletjeux.
com). M° Vavin. **Open** 10am-7.30pm Mon-Sat.
Credit AmEx, MC, V. **Map** p405 G8.
Fnac carries books, toys, DVDs, CDs and CD-Roms
for the under-12s. Storytelling and other activities
(Wed, Sat) take place for three-year-olds and up.
Other locations: throughout the city.

Village Joué Club

3-5 bd des Italiens, 2nd (01.53.45.41.41/www.joue
club.fr). M° Richelieu Drouot. **Open** 10am-8pm Mon-
Sat. **Credit** AmEx, MC, V. **Map** p402 H4.
The largest toy store in Paris is spread out on
ground level in and around the passage des Princes.

Fashion

All big-name international designers have
their own shops in Paris. **Marc Jacobs**' recent
opening has helped make the Palais-Royal a
shopping destination (*see p252* **Storming the
palace**) away from the heavyweight names
in the Golden Triangle between the Champs-
Elysées, George-V and avenue Montaigne.
Montaigne itself is enjoying a trendy upgrade
(*see p246* **Montaigne makeover**). Elsewhere
across the city, the label-filled boutiques are a
fashionista's dream. Concept stores, where
fashion, art, music and design all collide
under one roof, are defined by the landmark
Colette, still ahead of **Surface to Air**,
Spree and **Castelbajac Concept Store**.
   In addition to pan-European brands like
Mango, H&M and Zara, the high street has its
fair share of Gallic cheapies: think **Etam**,
Jennyfer and Pimkie. The highest density is in
the Forum des Halles (1st) and on nearby rue de
Rivoli, between the métro stations of Châtelet
and Louvre Rivoli. For more on the different
shopping districts, *see p256-257* **Shopping by
area**. For children's clothes, *see p243*.

Designer

A-poc

47 rue des Francs-Bourgeois, 4th (01.44.54.07.05).
M° St-Paul or Rambuteau. **Open** 11am-7pm Mon-
Sat. Closed 3wks Aug. **Credit** AmEx, DC, MC, V.
Map p409 L6.
Its unusual name an acronym for 'A Piece of Cloth',
Issey Miyake's lab-style boutique takes a conceptual
approach to fashion. Alongside ready-to-wear cotton
Lycra clothes are rolls of seamless tubular wool jer-
sey that is cut *sur mesure*; Miyake's assistants will
be happy to advise. His original shop (3 pl des Vosges,
4th, 01.48.87.01.86) today houses the creations of
Naoki Takizawa, design protégé to the old master.

Balenciaga

10 av George V, 8th (01.47.20.21.11/www.
balenciaga.com). M° Alma Marceau or George V.
Open 10am-7pm Mon-Sat. **Credit** AmEx, DC, MC,
V. **Map** p400 D5.
With Nicolas Ghesquière at the helm, the Spanish
fashion house is ahead of Japanese and Belgian
designers in the hipness stakes. Floating fabrics contrast with dramatic cuts, producing a sophisticated
urban style that the fashion *haut monde* can't wait
to slip into. Bags and shoes are also available.

Chanel

31 rue Cambon, 1st (01.42.86.28.00/www.chanel.
com). M° Concorde or Madeleine. **Open** 10am-7pm
Mon-Sat. **Credit** AmEx, DC, MC, V. **Map** p401 G4.
Fashion legend Chanel has managed to stay relevant
– thanks to Karl Lagerfeld. Coco opened her first
boutique in this street, at No.21, in 1910, and the tradition continues in this elegant space. Lagerfeld has
been designing for Chanel since 1983 and keeps on
rehashing the classics, like the little black dress and
the Chanel suit, with great success.
Other locations: 42 avenue Montaigne, 8th
(01.47.23.74.12).

Christian Dior

30 av Montaigne, 8th (01.40.73.54.44/www.dior.
com). M° Franklin D. Roosevelt. **Open** 10am-7pm
Mon-Sat. **Credit** AmEx, DC, MC, V. **Map** p400 D5.
To judge from the gaggles in from the suburbs for
a Dior bag, Nick Knight's ad campaigns have been
successful. Outrageous, acclaimed John Galliano is
behind the label's upbeat, youthful and sexy image.
Other locations: throughout the city.

Comme des Garçons

54 rue du Fbg-St-Honoré, 8th (01.53.30.27.27/www.
doublestreetmarket.com). M° Madeleine or Concorde.
Open 11am-7pm Mon-Sat. **Credit** AmEx, DC, MC,
V. **Map** p401 F4.
Rei Kawakubo's design ideas and revolutionary mix
of materials have influenced fashions of the past two
decades, and are showcased in this fire-engine-red,
fibreglass store. Exclusive perfume lines get a futuristic setting at Comme des Garçons Parfums (23 pl
du Marché-St-Honoré, 1st, 01.47.03.15.03).

Costume National

5 rue Cambon, 1st (01.40.15.04.36/www.costume
national.com). M° Concorde. **Open** 11.30am-7pm
Mon; 10.30am-7pm Tue-Sat. **Credit** AmEx, MC, V.
Map p401 G4.
This Milan-based label produces young, sexy
clothes for men and women. Designer Ennio Capasa
used to work for Yohji Yamamoto and is as keen on
black as he is on giving women hourglass figures.

Gaspard Yurkievich

43 rue Charlot, 3rd (01.42.77.55.48/www.gaspard
yurkievich.com). M° Filles du Calvaire. **Open** 11am-
7pm Tue-Sat. **Credit** MC, V. **Map** p402 L5.
The first boutique of this native Parisian fashion
missile. Hot men's and women's designs and a dangerous line of shoes are all on display.

Hermès

24 rue du Fbg-St-Honoré, 8th (01.40.17.46.00/
www.hermes.com). M° Concorde or Madeleine. **Open**
10.30am-6.30pm Mon-Sat. **Credit** AmEx, DC, MC, V.
Map p401 F4.
Once a saddler, this fashion and accessories house
is still an independent family business. Its horse-
themed scarves were staid until avant-garde designer Martin Margiela became head of womenswear.
He handed the reins to Jean-Paul Gaultier in 2004.
The fifth generation of the Hermès clan directs
things from this venerable 1930s building.

Isabel Marant

16 rue de Charonne, 11th (01.49.29.71.55).
M° Ledru-Rollin. **Open** 10.30am-7.30pm Mon-Sat.
Credit AmEx, MC, V. **Map** p407 M7.

Eat, Drink, Shop

This year's model – star designer **Marc Jacobs** opens his first Paris store. *See p247.*

Marant's style is easily recognisable in her ethno-babe brocades, blanket-like coats and decorated sweaters. It's a favourite among young trendies and artsy *parisiennes*.
Other locations: 1 rue Jacob, 6th (01.43.26.04.12).

Jean-Paul Gaultier
*6 rue Vivienne, 2nd (01.42.86.05.05/www.
jeanpaulgaultier.fr). M° Bourse.* **Open** 10.30am-7pm Mon-Fri; 11am-7pm Sat. **Credit** AmEx, DC, MC, V. **Map** p402 H4.
King of couture Gaultier has restyled his original boutique as a boudoir with trapunto-quilted, peach taffeta walls. Men's and women's ready-to-wear and the reasonably priced JPG Jeans lines are all on sale here, with the haute couture department upstairs (01.42.97.48.12, by appointment only).
Other locations: 44 av George-V, 8th (01.44.43.00.44).

John Galliano
*384-386 rue St-Honoré, 1st (01.55.35.40.40/www.
johngalliano.com). M° Concorde or Madeleine.* **Open** 11am-7pm Mon-Sat. **Credit** AmEx, DC, MC, V. **Map** p401 G4.
At Dior since 1996, Gibraltar-born Galliano still has his own range and a reputation as one of the UK's most original designers. You can view the small but diverse collection of flamboyant and feminine delights through the showcase window, or from the Louis XVI-style leather chairs inside.

Lagerfeld Gallery
40 rue de Seine, 6th (01.55.42.75.50). M° Odéon. **Open** 11am-7pm Tue-Sat. Closed Aug. **Credit** AmEx, DC, MC, V. **Map** p408 H6.
Andrée Putman helped create this shrine to King Karl's brand of stylish minimalism: Lagerfeld's fashion creations and photography are both on display.

Montaigne makeover

Fashion's old grey lady is looking decidedly sprite these days. Long the bastion of blue-rinse bourgeois shopping, avenue Montaigne has emerged as the most interesting leg of the Golden Triangle. It still caters to the well-heeled shopper of a certain age and means, but the tone is becoming resolutely younger. Luxury's mega-watt brands – Chanel, Prada, Valentino, Harry Winston and Dior – now keep company with neighbours sporting serious fashion cred among the young and slim.

Walking north from the Seine, **Paul & Joe** (*see p248*) offers a line of pretty bohemian chic separates for women. The hot LA-based jewellery brand **Chrome Hearts** recently opened at No.18 (01.40.70.17.35; *pictured*) and on the corner of the rue François I-er there is **Zadig & Voltaire** (18 rue Francois-Ier, 01.40.70.97.89), whose oversize cashmere V-neck jumpers in dusty lilac, taupe and grey have made the company the success story in affordable luxury. This is the only Z&V De Luxe boutique in the capital (for others, *see p253*), meaning that it carries customised and limited edition pieces not found in other stores – as well as the brand's new line of semi-precious jewellery and shoes by Marc Jacobs and the Italian brand NDC.

Other newcomers include a **Chloe** boutique (No.44), a 1940s-inspired 'boudoir' for **Jimmy Choo** (No.34) and a **Bonpoint**, purveyor of storybook-precious outfits for fashion's youngest set (No.49). **Montaigne Market**, the avenue's lone multi-brand boutique, carries fashion labels that serious fashionistas would have trouble sourcing elsewhere in Paris,

including Behnaz Sarafpour, Zac Posen, Matthew Williamson, True Religion and Juicy Couture. For sustenance, there is always **L'Avenue** (No.41, 01.40.70.14.91), a Costes restaurant brimming with beautiful people and Parisian attitude. At cocktail hour, the chic destination bar at the **Plaza Athenée Hotel** (*see p232* **'The usual, Sir?'**) serves up mean Mojitos to a chic clientele.

All the fashion brands under one roof at the **Montaigne Market**. *See p246.*

You could just sneak in to browse the latest fashion, beauty and art publications, scattered over a handsome round table at the front of the gallery.

Louis Vuitton

101 av des Champs-Elysées, 8th (08.10.81.00.10/ www.vuitton.com). M° George V. **Open** 10am-8pm Mon-Sat. **Credit** AmEx, DC, MC, V. **Map** p400 D4.
The 'Promenade' flagship sets the tone for Vuitton's global image, from the 'bag bar', bookstore and new jewellery department to the women's and men's ready-to-wear. Contemporary art, videos by Tim White Sobieski and a pitch-black elevator by Olafur Eliasson complete the picture. Accessed by lift, the Espace Vuitton hosts temporary art exhibits – but the star of the show is the view over Paris.
Other locations: 6 pl St-Germain-des-Prés, 6th; 22 av Montaigne, 8th.

Marc Jacobs

34 galerie de Montpensier, 1st (01.55.35.02.60/ www.marcjacobs.com). M° Palais Royal Musée du Louvre or Pyramides. **Open** 11am-8pm Mon-Sat. **Credit** AmEx, DC, MC, V. **Map** p402 H5.
Marc Jacobs is on a roll. Not only is he fashion king of luxury's top-selling house, he is also the only designer to have captured that distinctive downtown New York vibe and make it real for grunge fans and Park Avenue princesses alike. Now, Parisians are snapping up his perfect little shifts, funky T-shirts and 'mouse' flats at his first signature boutique in Europe. With its marble floors, Christian Liaigre-designed furniture and muted grey and white walls, the new arrival blends in perfectly with its elegant surroundings. Stocking womenswear, menswear, accessories and shoes, it's already becoming a place of pilgrimage for the designer's legion of admirers. His decision to set up operations in the Palais-Royal, rather than in the traditional designer shopping enclaves, has brought new life (and an influx of fashionistas) to the area. *See p252* **Storming the palace. Photo** *p245.*

Marni

57 av Montaigne, 8th (01.56.88.08.08/www.marni. com). M° Franklin D. Roosevelt. **Open** 10am-7pm Mon-Sat. **Credit** AmEx, DC, MC, V. **Map** p400 D5.
Consuelo Castiglioni has fun mixing leather, fur, silk, cashmere and prints, creating an eccentric but cool jostle of textures and colours.

Martin Grant

10 rue Charlot, 3rd (01.42.71.39.49/www.martin grantparis.com). M° Temple. **Open** 10am-6pm Mon-Fri. Closed 3wks Aug. **Credit** MC, V. **Map** p406 K6.
Grant's shop is now tucked away on a second-floor Marais apartment, chipped tiled floor and worn velvet chairs recalling a retrofied Prada ad. This is couture, though, as interpreted by Australian designer Martin Grant. If you're a stickler for steady cuts, pure textiles and unfussy designs, pay him a visit.

Martin Margiela

23 & 25bis rue de Montpensier, 1st (01.40.15.07.55/ www.maisonmartinmargiela.com). M° Palais Royal Musée du Louvre. **Open** 11am-7pm Mon-Sat. **Credit** AmEx, DC, MC, V. **Map** p402 H5.
The first Paris outlet for the JD Salinger of fashion is a pristine, white, unlabelled space. His collection for women (Line 1) has a blank label but is recognisable by external white stitching. You'll find Line 6 (women's basics) and Line 10 (menswear), plus accessories for men and women, and shoes.
Other locations: 13 rue de Grenelle, 7th (01.45.49.06.45).

Miu Miu

16 rue de Grenelle, 7th (01.53.63.20.30/www. miumiu.com). M° Sèvres Babylone. **Open** 11am-7pm Mon; 10am-7pm Tue-Sat. **Credit** AmEx, DC, MC, V. **Map** p405 G7.
Miu Miu is Prada's colourful younger (and cheaper) sister – with a reckless style and fab shoes. This two-floor store has men's and women's fashions; the one at 219 rue St-Honoré (01.53.63.20.30) is smaller.

Paul & Joe.

Paul & Joe

64 rue des Sts-Pères, 7th (01.42.22.47.01/www.paul andjoe.com). M° Rue du Bac or St-Germain-des-Prés. **Open** 10am-7pm Mon-Sat. **Credit** AmEx, DC, MC, V. **Map** p405 G6.

Fashionistas have taken a real shine to Sophie Albou's weathered 1940s-style creations (named after her sons), so much so that she has opened a menswear branch in addition to this flagship, with its out-to-be-noticed, bubblegum-pink gramophone. **Other locations:** *Men* 62 rue des St-Pères, 7th (01.42.22.47.01). *Men & women* 46 rue Etienne-Marcel, 2nd (01.40.28.03.34); 2 av Montaigne, 8th (01.47.20.57.50); 123 rue de la Pompe, 16th (01.45.53.01.08).

Paul Smith

22-24 boulevard Raspail, 7th (01.42.84.15.30/ www.paulsmith.co.uk). M° Sèvres Babylone, Rue du Bac or Saint-Sulpice. **Open** 11am-7pm Mon; 10am-7pm Tue-Sat. **Credit** AmEx, DC, MC, V. **Map** p405 G7.

Le style anglais in a wood-panelled interior. Smith's great suits and classic shoes are on the upper floor; women and kids get a funkier space below.

Prada

10 av Montaigne, 8th (01.53.23.99.40/www.prada. com). M° Alma Marceau. **Open** 11am-7pm Mon; 10am-7pm Tue-Sat. **Credit** AmEx, DC, MC, V. **Map** p400 D5.

Fashionistas just can't seem to get enough of Miuccia Prada's elegant designs. Handbags of choice are complemented by a ready-to-wear line, amid lime-green walls uniform to Paris branches. **Other locations:** 5 rue de Grenelle, 6th (01.45.48.53.14); 6 rue du Fbg-St-Honoré, 8th (01.58.18.63.30).

Sonia Rykiel

175 bd St-Germain, 6th (01.49.54.60.60/www. soniarykiel.com). M° St-Germain-des-Prés or Sèvres Babylone. **Open** 10.30am-7pm Mon-Sat. **Credit** AmEx, DC, MC, V. **Map** p405 G6.

The queen of stripes produces skinny rib knitwear evoking the Left Bank babes of yore. Menswear is across the street, while two newer boutiques stock the younger, more affordable Sonia by Sonia Rykiel range (59 rue des Sts-Pères, 6th, 01.49.54.61.00) and kids' togs (4 rue de Grenelle, 6th, 01.49.54.61.10). Also on rue de Grenelle, on the site of Sonia's original 1966 shop, the Rykiel Woman store at No.6 (01.49.54.66.21) stocks a range of designer sex toys. **Other locations:** throughout the city.

Tsumori Chisato

20 rue Barbette, 3rd (01.42.78.18.88). M° St-Paul or Hôtel de Ville. **Open** 11am-7pm Mon-Sat. Closed 2wks Aug. **Credit** AmEx, MC, V. **Map** p409 L6.

Known for her inventive use of colour and wispy fabrics, this designer has a cult following thanks to poetic, romantic designs big on ingenious detail.

Vanessa Bruno

25 rue St-Sulpice, 6th (01.43.54.41.04/www.vanessa bruno.com). M° Odéon. **Open** 10.30am-7.30pm Mon-Sat. **Credit** AmEx, DC, MC, V. **Map** p408 H7.

Mercerised cotton tanks, flattering trousers and feminine tops have a Zen-like quality that stems from Bruno's stay in Japan, and they look good on any figure. She also makes great bags; the ample Lune was created to mark ten years in the business. **Other locations:** 12 rue de Castiglione, 1st (01.42.61.44.60); 100 rue Vieille-du-Temple, 3rd (01.42.77.19.41).

Yohji Yamamoto

25 rue du Louvre, 1st (01.42.21.42.93/www.yohji yamamoto.co.jp). M° Sentier or Les Halles. **Open** 10.30am-7pm Mon-Sat. **Credit** AmEx, DC, MC, V. **Map** p405 G7.

One of the few true pioneers working in fashion today, Yamamoto is a master of cut and finish, both strongly inspired by the kimono and traditional Tibetan costume. His dexterity with form makes for unique shapes and styles, largely black, but when he does colour, it's a blast of brilliance. This is womenswear; you can find the men's boutique over at 47 rue Etienne-Marcel (1st, 01.45.08.82.45).

Yves Saint Laurent

6 pl St-Sulpice, 6th (01.43.29.43.00/www.ysl.com). M° St-Sulpice. **Open** 11am-7pm Mon; 10.30am-7pm Tue-Sat. **Credit** AmEx, DC, MC, V. **Map** p408 H7.

Yves Saint Laurent retired in 2002 after a 40-year career that began at Dior and continued with the androgynous revolution he fomented in the 1960s under his own name, getting women into dinner and jump suits. This is the main women's store; you'll find menswear at No.12 (01.43.26.84.40).

Other locations: *Men* 32 rue du Faubourg Saint-Honoré, 8th (01.53.05.80.80). *Women* 38 rue du Faubourg-Saint-Honoré, 8th (01.42.65.74.59).

Boutiques & concept stores

AB33 and N°60

33 & 60 rue Charlot, 3rd (01.42.71.02.82/01.44. 78.91.90). M° Filles du Calvaire. **Open** 11am-8pm Tue-Sun. **Credit** AmEx, MC, V. **Map** p409 L5.

In under two years, AB33, the original boutique run by fashion addict Agathe Buchotte, has become a must in every like-minded woman's address book for its eclectic mix of pieces from smaller brands like Odd Molly and Laundry Industry. The newer N°60 revels in a more rock 'n' roll attitude, courtesy of labels like McQ, Chalayan and April 77.

Base One

47bis rue d'Orsel, 18th (01.53.28.04.52/ www.baseoneshop.com). M° Anvers. **Open** 12.30-8pm Tue-Sat; 3.30-8pm Sun. Closed 2wks Aug. **Credit** MC, V. **Map** p402 J2.

Princesse Léa and Jean-Louis Faverole, the couple behind Espace Lab 101 *(see p254)* and Project 101 *(see p322)* squeeze items from little known local and international designers (Shai Wear, Li-Lei, Drolaic, 0K47), plus small, established brands (Fenchurch, Motel, Consortium) into their sitting-room style boutique. Calling it an underground Colette would be somewhere near the mark.

Walk this way

Among the winding, tony shopping streets surrounding the Left Bank store **Le Bon Marché** *(see p237)*, rue du Cherche-Midi in the 6th has long been a shoe shopper's delight – but recently, nearby rue de Grenelle, starting in the 6th and stretching into the 7th, has stepped up the footwear stakes with a line-up of star names.

The street begins at the carrefour de la Croix-Rouge with small shops such as **Jean-Claude Monderer** (No.1, 01.42.84.36.02), who sells comfort shoes as well as killer heels of his own design, and **Laure Bassal** (No.3, 01.42.22.44.24), who specialises in classic 1920s and '30s designs. **Charles Kammer** (No.14, 01.42.22.35.13) is a Parisienne's staple for shoes that are just trendy enough for everyday at comparatively moderate prices, while tiny boutiques by footwear darlings such as Vivier revivalist **Bruno Frisoni** and **Christian Louboutin** (for both, *see p260*) are a hardy fashionista's first stops. If you can't find the red-soled shoe that fits at Louboutin, fear not: he has just launched a custom service.

Scattered among the boudoir boutiques are outposts belonging to well-established global brands such as **Patrick Cox**, **Freelance** by Jean-Baptiste Rautureau, **Ferragamo**, **Miu Miu**, **Moschino**, **Tod's** and **Yves Saint Laurent** – even **LK Bennett** decided to set up shop here.

Among this constellation of names, two multi-brand indies stand out: **Iris** *(see p260)* features the most attractive selection of Marc Jacobs shoes this side of the Palais-Royal, along with models by Viktor & Rolf, John Galliano and Proenza-Schouler; **Moss** (No.22, 01.42.22.01.43) is run by three sisters who pride themselves on sourcing cutting edge couture shoes hard to find elsewhere, such as creations by former Celine stylist Avril Gau and signature styles by Laurence Dacade, Duccio del Duca and Hartian Bourdin. You'll also find haute scarves by Octavio Pizzaro and jewellery by KarryO', the fourth sister, whose tiny shop nearby (62 rue des Saints-Pères, 01.45.48.94.67) is well worth a visit. Paris socialites come here to source vintage jewellery, as well as modern creations by owner **Karine Berrebi**. Her adjacent gallery, **Unique**, features one-of-a-kind finds from jewellery to decorative objects to Hermès bags and the occasional Schiaparelli fur – all stand-out pieces to pair with a closetful of fabulous new shoes.

Eat, Drink, Shop

Les Belles Images

74 rue Charlot, 3rd (01.42.76.93.61/www.lesbelles images.com). Mº Filles du Calvaire. **Open** 11am-7.30pm Tue-Sat. **Credit** MC, V. **Map** p402 L5.
A serious retro '60s vibe reigns at this chic boutique, where owner Sandy Bontout showcases items from current collections of obscure and big-name French and international labels, such as Ambali separates, Walk that Walk shoes and editor's picks from Veronique Leroy and Vivienne Westwood. A men's section was added in the autumn of 2006.

Castelbajac Concept Store

10 rue Vauvilliers, 1st (01.55.34.10.28/www.jc-de-castelbajac.com). Mº Les Halles or Louvre Rivoli. **Open** 11am-7pm Mon-Sat. **Credit** AmEx, DC, MC, V. **Map** p402 J5.
Jean-Charles de Castelbajac's humorous, colourful world of fashion – developed by the aristo designer during 30 years on both sides of the Atlantic – is showcased in this gleaming white store.

Colette

213 rue St-Honoré, 1st (01.55.35.33.90/www. colette.fr). Mº Tuileries or Pyramides. **Open** 11am-7pm Mon-Sat. **Credit** AmEx, DC, MC, V. **Map** p401 G4.
Renowned and much-imitated one-stop concept and lifestyle store Colette is still influential. This shrine to the limited edition displays must-have accessories inside clinical glass cases away from sticky fingers. Books, media, shiny new gadgets, and the hair and beauty brands själ, Kiehl's and uslu airlines are scattered amid the magazines and photo albums on the ground floor and mezzanine. Upstairs has a selection of 'in' clothes and accessories. Lunch, with a global selection of mineral water, can be nibbled in the chic basement Water Bar.

L'Eclaireur

3ter rue des Rosiers, 4th (01.48.87.10.22/www. leclaireur.com). Mº St-Paul. **Open** 11am-7pm Mon-Sat. **Credit** AmEx, DC, MC, V. **Map** p409 L6.
Housed in a dandified warehouse, L'Eclaireur stocks uncompromising designs by Comme des Garçons, Martin Margiela, Dries van Noten, Carpe Diem and Junya Watanabe. A new space near Concorde sells chic fashions for men and women, plus homeware items with an accent on Fornasetti. **Photo** *p251.*
Other locations: 131 galerie de Valois, 1st (01.40.20.42.52); 10 rue Hérold, 1st (01.40.41.09.89); 8 rue Boissy d'Anglas, 8th (01.53.43.03.70).

Jay Ahr

2-4 rue du 29-Juillet, 1st (01.42.96.95.23/www.jay ahr.com). Mº Tuileries. **Open** 10am-7pm Mon-Sat. **Credit** AmEx, MC, V. **Map** p401 G5.
Former jewellery designer Jonathan Riss opened this shop as a fashion stylist in 2004, and struck gold with simple, figure-flaunting '60s inspired dresses. Think plunging necklines and Bianca Jagger in her heyday, with Ali McGraw and Anita Pallenberg in the mix. There are no price tags on the dresses, so you have to ask; prices start at around €500.

Joseph

147 bd St-Germain, 6th (01.55.42.77.56). Mº St-Germain-des-Prés. **Open** 11am-7pm Mon, Sat; 10.30am-7pm Tue-Fri. **Credit** AmEx, DC, MC, V. **Map** p405 G6.
Taking a cue from its London store, Joseph has opened a multi-brand shop in place of Onward. Still here are pieces by Ann Demeulemeester, Dries van Noten and Bruno Pieters, plus accessories by Bijoux de Sophie and handbags by Jerome Dreyfus.

Kabuki Femme

25 rue Etienne-Marcel, 1st (01.42.33.55.65/www. babarabui.com). Mº Etienne Marcel. **Open** 10.30am-7.30pm Mon-Sat. Closed 29 July-22 Aug. **Credit** AmEx, DC, MC, V. **Map** p402 J5.
On the ground floor there's intrepid footwear and bags by Costume National, Miu Miu and Prada, plus Fendi's cult creations; Burberry belts and Miu Miu sunglasses are also stocked. Upstairs are outfits by Véronique Leroy, Prada and Costume National.
Other locations: Kabuki Homme, 21 rue Etienne-Marcel, 1st (01.42.33.13.44).

Kokon To Zai

48 rue Tiquetonne, 2nd (01.42.36.92.41/www. kokontozai.co.uk). Mº Etienne Marcel. **Open** 11.30am-7.30pm Mon-Sat. **Credit** AmEx, DC, MC, V. **Map** p402 J5.
Always a spot-on spotter of the latest creations, this tiny style emporium is sister to the Kokon To Zai in London. The neon and club feel of the mirrored interior match the dark glamour of the designs. Unique pieces straight off the catwalk share space with creations by Marjan Peijoski, Noki, Raf Simons, Two Tom, Ziad Ghanem and new Norwegian designers.

Maria Luisa

40 rue de Mont-Thabor, 1st (01.47.03.48.08). Mº Concorde. **Open** 10.30am-7pm Mon-Sat. **Credit** AmEx, DC, MC, V. **Map** p401 G4.
Venezuelan Maria Luisa Poumaillou was one of the city's first stockists of Galliano, McQueen and the Belgians, and has an eye for rising stars such as Bernhard Willhelm, Eley Kishimoto, Undercover and Emma Cook. Nearby branches cover up-and-coming young designers (No.38, 01.42.96.47.81), menswear (No.19bis, 01.42.60.89.83) and shoes and accessories (2 rue Cambon, 01.47.03.96.15).

Me

29 rue du Dragon, 6th (01.53.63.02.52). Mº St-Germain-des-Prés. **Open** 10am-7pm Mon-Sat. **Credit** AmEx, MC, V. **Map** p405 G7.
Oversized dolls are the mannequins at Me, the most youthful division of Issey Miyake, created by this disciples as an offshoot of Pleats Please. Washable, pleated stretch tops make up 80% of the collection.

Mona

17 rue Bonaparte, 6th (01.44.07.07.27). Mº St-Germain des-Prés. **Open** 11am-1.30pm, 2.30-7pm Mon-Fri; 11am-7pm Sat. **Credit** AmEx, MC, V. **Map** p408 H6.

This concept boutique features tightly edited selections and sales assistants who double as stylists, not to mention a red carpet (ideal for practice runs). The eponymous owner used to run a shoe boutique; designers often customise models to her wishes.

Shine
15 rue de Poitou, 3rd (01.48.05.80.10). Mº Filles du Calvaire. **Open** 11am-7.30pm Mon-Sat. **Credit** AmEx, MC, V. **Map** p407 M7.
For funkier clothes than Maria Luisa (*see p250*), Vinci d'Helia has what you need: sexy T-shirts with unusual detailing, Luella's chunky knits and Earl Jeans trousers and jackets.

Spree
16 rue de La Vieuville, 18th (01.42.23.41.40). Mº Abbesses. **Open** 2-7pm Mon; 11am-7.30pm Tue-Sat. Closed 1wk Aug. **Credit** AmEx, MC, V. **Map** p402 H1.
Artistic director Bruno Hadjadj and fashion designer Roberta Oprandi offer fashion, design and art with a Montmartre vibe – 1960s chairs draped in the latest fashions by Preen and Isabel Marant.
Other locations: 1 rue St-Simon, 7th (01.42.22.05.04).

Surface to Air
46 rue de l'Arbre-Sec, 1st (01.49.27.04.54/ www.surface2air.com). Mº Pont Neuf. **Open** 12.30-7.30pm Mon-Sat. Closed 2wks Aug. **Credit** MC, V. **Map** p406 J6.
This non-concept concept store also acts as a gallery and graphic design agency. The cult clothing selection takes in Alice McCall's sassy frocks, Fifth Avenue Shoe Repair jeans and printed dresses by Wood Wood. For men, labels include Marios, Wendy & Jim and F-Troupe.

Womenswear

Agnès b
2, 3, 6 & 19 rue du Jour, 1st (men 01.42.33.04.13/ women 01.45.08.56.56/www.agnesb.com). Mº Les Halles. **Open** *Oct-Apr* 10am-7pm Mon-Sat. *May-Sept* 10am-7.30pm Mon-Sat. **Credit** AmEx, MC, V. **Map** p402 J5.
Agnès b rarely wavers from her design vision: pure lines in fine quality cotton, merino wool and silk. Best buys are shirts, pullovers and cardigans that keep their shape for years. Her mini-empire of men's, women's, children's, travel and sportswear shops is compact; see the website for details.
Other locations: throughout the city

American Apparel
31 pl du Marché-St-Honoré, 1st (01.42.60.03.72/ www.americanapparel.net). Mº Pyramides, Opéra or Tuileries. **Open** 10.30am-7.30pm Mon-Sat. **Credit** AmEx, DC, MC, V. **Map** p401 G4.
Paris has acquired a taste for American Apparel's ethically spotless, colourful cotton basics. After setting up base here in 2005, the LA brand opened a second shop off the Canal St-Martin and another in the Marais, with the down-to-earth style that has made its slim-fit T-shirts a hit on the rock scene.
Other locations: 41 rue du Temple, 4th (01.42.74.71.03); 10 rue Beaurepaire, 10th (01.42.49.50.01).

Antoine et Lili
95 quai de Valmy, 10th (01.40.37.41.55/www. antoineetlili.com). Mº Jacques Bonsergent or Gare de l'Est. **Open** 11am-7pm Mon, Sun; 11am-8pm Tue-Fri; 10am-8pm Sat. **Credit** AmEx, DC, MC, V. **Map** p402 L3.

Eat, Drink, Shop

L'Eclaireur. *See p250.*

Storming the palace

Not long ago the Palais-Royal was a sleepy destination filled with numismatists, antiques dealers and the odd boutique, anchored at the south by the Comédie Française and at the north by the three-star gastronomic temple Le Grand Véfour, where Napoleon and Josephine once canoodled.

Today, Cardinal Richelieu's palace houses the state council, the ministry of culture and a collection of boutiques that has transformed this once quiet garden into a must-shop destination. For that, Paris has **Marc Jacobs** to thank, since where Jacobs leads, the fashion world follows. The designer's first European flagship (*see p247*) is just down the gallery from two of three boutiques belonging to fashion expert, vintage collector and renowned designer **Didier Ludot** (*see p255*). Ludot's third shop, La Petite Robe Noire, offers re-editions of fashion's greatest hits plus seasonal collections of his own little black dresses, under the eastern arcades. An elegant outpost of the fashion editor's favourite jewellery shop **Casoar** (29 galerie de Montpensier, 01.42.96.39.54) displays intricate re-editions of Napoleon III, belle

epoque and art deco jewellery such as intaglio rings and earrings in *pâte de verre*.

The **Salons du Palais-Royal Shiseido** (*see p238*) is an anomaly even in the cradle of haute perfumery, for it was entirely handpainted to the intricate specifications of the house perfumer Serge Lutens, whose heady creations, such as Ambre Sultan and Tubéreuse Criminelle, come in the bell-shaped bottle available nowhere else in the world. Fashion darling **Pierre Hardy** (*see p261*) is the talent behind the fabulous jewellery at Hermès, but he also designs shoes that become cult pieces season in, season out. The latest string to his bow is a collection of handbags that has garnered a similar reception. Designer **Jérôme Lhuiller** (138-139 galerie de Valois, 01.49.26.07.07) may not be widely known, but his colourful collection of trapeze dresses and top trousers make him a very Parisian choice. On the other end of the spectrum, the brand new Paris boutique of LA-based designer **Rick Owens** (130 galerie de Valois, 01.40.20.42.52) brings a certain rock 'n' roll glamour to these 17th-century arcades. Roll over, Richelieu.

Rue du Fbg-St-Honoré & the Champs-Elysées

When St-Honoré crosses into the 8th and becomes **rue du Fbg-St-Honoré**, it takes on an air of exclusivity. The area covers the lovely shops around **Madeleine**, the A-grade fashion strip of **avenue Montaigne** (see p246 **Montaigne makeover**) – home to **Christian Dior** (p245), **Marni** (p247) and **Prada** (p248) – and the **Champs-Elysées**. Famous names include **Balenciaga** (p244), **Hermès** (p245) and **Louis Vuitton** (p247); a less familiar fashionista fave is **Loft Design by** (p253). For failsafe gourmet goodies, try **Alléosse** (p262), **Jabugo Ibérico & Co** (p262) or **La Maison du Chocolat** (p262). Beauty salons and stores include **Anne Sémonin** (p241), **Guerlain** (p238), **Institut Lancôme** (p241) and **Sephora** (p241); while for music and books there's **La Flûte de Pan** (p242), **Fnac** (p243) and **Virgin Megastore** (p243). **Drugstore Publicis** (p238) is handy for late-night buys.

Opéra & Grands Boulevards

Department stores **Printemps** (p237) and **Galeries Lafayette** (p237) provide the commercial heartbeat to this busy quartier. Here, too, are children's shops **Du Pareil au Même** (p244) and **Village Joué Club** (p244); books at **Brentano's** (p242); plus sports and games equipment at **Citadium** (p267) and **René Pierre** (p267). The historic **Cartier** store stands on rue de la Paix (p260); wine shop **Les Caves Augé** (p265) is another old-timer.

Montmartre

Funky, independent designers cluster around the winding streets by Sacré-Coeur. **Boulevard de Rochechouart** is known for its discount shops – the populist **Tati** is at No.4 (see p237). Fashionable types gravitate towards the hip **Espace Lab 101** (p254), **Spree** (p251), **Base One** (p249) or vintage store **Wochdom** (p258). If you need a reviving cake or two, **Arnaud Delmontel** (p261) and **Arnaud Lahrer** (p264) are on hand. Just north is the biggest flea market in Paris, the **Marché aux Puces de Clignancourt** (p266).

Canal St-Martin

This mini quartier provides the perfect canalside esplanade for relaxed browsing; **Antoine et Lili** sells riotously colourful clothing (p251), while design-focused bookshop **Artazart** stocks impressive coffee table tomes (p242).

Bastille

Traditionally home to fine furniture craftsmen, **rue du Fbg-St-Antoine**, **rue de Charonne** and **rue Keller** are peppered with designer fashion and interiors shops, such as **Caravane Chambre 19** (p266), **Galerie Patrick Seguin** (p267) and **Silvera** (p267). Of particular note for clothes are **The Lazy Dog** (p255), **Isabel Marant** (p245) and **Ladies & Gentlemen** (p253). Local food and wine shops include **L'Autre Boulange** (p261) and **Moisan** (p261).

The Marais

Rue des Rosiers, **rue des Francs-Bourgeois** and offshoots house designer boutiques and interiors shops. Label-lovers should look out for **Les Belles Images** (p250) and **L'Eclaireur** (p250) – plus discount outlet **L'Habilleur** (p258). Men are well catered for, with **L'Eclaireur Homme** (p253), **Jack Henry** and **Nodus** (for both, p254). Jewish bakeries include the famous **Finkelsztajn** (p264). For everything else, there's the landmark **BHV** department store (p237).

St-Germain-des-Prés & Odéon

Stores line up on **boulevard St-Germain**, by **St-Sulpice church** and along **rue de Buci**. There's a fashionable name around every corner: **Miu Miu** (p247), **Sonia Rykiel** (p248), **Yves Saint Laurent** (p249) and more; **Le Bon Marché** department store (see p237) also stocks designer labels. Hip **APC** (p253), **Camper** (p260), **Hervé Chapelier** (p260) and **Vanessa Bruno** (p248) provide head-to-toe garb – as do seconds store **Le Mouton à Cinq Pattes** (p258) and lingerie shop **Princesse Tam Tam** (p259). Interspersed are the children's clothes shops of rue Vavin (p243) and plenty of bookshops: **Fnac Junior** (p244), **La Hune** (p243), **Librairie 7L** (p243), and **Village Voice** (p243). The area also houses seven master chocolate-makers (see p262). For more savoury edibles, head for **Da Rosa**, **Huilerie Artisanale Leblanc** (for both, p264) and the famous **Poilâne** (p261).

St-Michel & the 5th

St-Germain's bookish cousin is the hub of publishing: stock up on reading material at **Gibert Jeune**, **Gibert Joseph** (for both, p242), **Shakespeare & Co** (see p239 **Turning over a new leaf**) and the **Bouquinistes** (p242). Here, too, are the fragrant **Diptyque** (p265) and the **Hammam de la Grande Mosquée** (p241).

Bag your heart's desire at **Hervé Chapelier**. *See p260.*

Free 'P' Star
8 rue Ste-Croix-de-la-Bretonnerie, 4th (01.42.76.
03.72). M° St-Paul. **Open** noon-11pm Mon-Sat;
2-10pm Sun. **Credit** MC, V. **Map** p409 K6.
This Aladdin's cave of retro glitz, ex-army wear and
glad rags is the cheapest of the bargain basements.

L'Habilleur
44 rue de Poitou, 3rd (01.48.87.77.12). M° St-
Sébastien Froissart. **Open** noon-8pm Mon-Sat.
Credit MC, V. **Map** p402 L5.
Urbanites use this slick store for its mens- and
womenswear by Roberto Collina, Paul & Joe and
Stefano Mortari. Items are end-of-line or straight
from the catwalk, with 60% off their original prices.

Le Mouton à Cinq Pattes
138 bd St-Germain, 6th (01.43.26.49.25). M° Odéon.
Open 10am-7pm Mon-Sat. **Credit** AmEx, MC, V.
Map p408 H7.
Designer vintage and last season's collection in mint
condition: Buscat, Chanel and Lagerfeld. Labels are
cut out so make sure you know what you're buying.
Other locations: *Men & women* 18 rue St-Placide,
6th (01.42.84.25.11). *Women* 8 rue St-Placide, 6th
(01.45.48.86.26).

Rag
83-85 rue St-Martin, 4th (01.48.87.34.64).
M° Rambuteau or Châtelet/RER Châtelet Les Halles.
Open 10am-8pm Mon-Sat; noon-8pm Sun. **No**
credit cards. Map p402 K5.
One half focuses on pilots' navy jumpers and 1970s
shirts at €15, colourful puffer jackets, and '70s heels;
the other may yield a vintage Hermès scarf, a 1960s
Paco Rabanne dress or a Gucci accessory.

Son et Image
87 rue St-Denis, 1st (01.40.41.90.61). M° Châtelet.
Open 10.30am-8pm Mon-Sat. **Credit** AmEx, DC,
MC, V. **Map** p402 J6.
This popular little second-hand clothes store is filled
with vintage leather, fur coats and hip boots.

Wochdom
72 rue Condorcet, 9th (01.53.21.09.72). M° Pigalle
or Anvers. **Open** noon-8pm Mon-Sat. **Credit** AmEx,
DC, MC, V. **Map** p402 J2.
This temple to vintage stocks a mainly female collection, inclined towards the spotty and stripy 1980s.
Copies of *Interview, Elle* and *Vogue*, and old vinyl
too; there's a concession at Printemps (*see p237*).

Yesterday Never Dies
53 rue du Four, 6th (01.45.49.14.80) M° St-Sulpice
or Sèvres Babylone. **Open** 10.30am-7pm Mon-Sat.
Credit AmEx, MC, V. **Map** p405 G7.
Walking into this cosy shop feels like unearthing
treasures from granny's closet, with *armoires*
stuffed with real vintage as well as original fashions
inspired by the '60s, '70s and '80s, designed by the
shop's owners. Even the furniture is for sale.

Lingerie & swimwear

Most of the third floor of **Galeries Lafayette**
(*see p237*) is devoted to underwear; for
swimwear, *see also p267* **Sport & games**.

Alice Cadolle
4 rue Cambon, 1st (01.42.60.94.22/www.cadolle.
com). M° Concorde or Madeleine. **Open** 10am-1pm,
2-7pm Mon-Sat. Closed Aug. **Credit** AmEx, MC, V.
Map p401 G4.
Five generations of lingerie-makers are behind this
boutique, founded by Hermine Cadolle, inventor of
the bra. Great-great-granddaughter Poupie Cadolle
continues the tradition in a cosy space devoted to a
luxury ready-to-wear line. The couture division has
its own modern setting, Loft Couture (255 rue St-
Honoré, 1st, 01.42.60.94.94; by appointment only).

Erès
2 rue Tronchet, 8th (01.47.42.28.82/www.eres.fr).
M° Madeleine. **Open** 10am-7pm Mon-Sat. **Credit**
AmEx, DC, MC, V. **Map** p401 G4.

Super *marchés*

Paris markets have eternal appeal, and their products – like a farmer's pungent goat's cheese, a dozen fresh Cancale oysters, a bunch of ruby chard or a jar of sunflower-yellow honey – are seen as more 'natural' alternatives to supermarket fare.

The city council has made markets more accessible to working people by extending their opening hours. There are now more than 70 markets – including a handful of the covered variety – in Paris. The city council's website (www.paris.fr) has full details of each one; below is a selection of the best:

Marché Monge (place Monge, 5th, Mº Place Monge; 7am-2.30pm Wed, Fri; 7am-3pm Sun; *photo above*), though compact, is pretty and set on a leafy square. It has a high proportion of producers and is much less touristy than nearby rue Mouffetard. Be prepared to queue for the best quality.

Saxe-Breteuil (av de Saxe, 7th, Mº Ségur; 7am-2.30pm Thur; 7am-3pm Sat) has an unrivalled setting facing the Eiffel Tower, as well as the city's most chic produce. Look for farmer's goat's cheese, rare apple varieties, Armenian specialities, abundant oysters and a handful of dedicated small producers.

Marché Anvers (pl d'Anvers, 9th, Mº Anvers; 3-8pm Fri) is an afternoon market that adds to the village atmosphere of a peaceful *quartier*

down the hill from Montmartre. Among its highlights are untreated vegetables, hams from the Auvergne, lovingly aged cheeses and award-winning honey.

Marché Bastille (bd Richard-Lenoir, 11th, Mº Richard-Lenoir; 7am-2.30pm Thur; 7am-3pm Sun) is one of the biggest and most boisterous in Paris. A favourite of political campaigners, it's also a great source of local cheeses, farmer's chicken and excellent affordable fish.

Marché Beauvau (pl d'Aligre, 12th, Mº Ledru-Rollin; 8.30am-1pm, 4-7.30pm Tue-Sat; 8.30am-1.30pm Sun), a covered market, is proudly working class. Stallholders do their utmost to out-shout each other, while price-conscious shoppers don't compromise on quality. There's a flea market nearby.

Marché Président-Wilson (av Président-Wilson, 16th, Mº Alma-Marceau or Iéna; 7am-2.30pm Wed; 7am-3pm Sat) is a classy market attracting the city's top chefs, who snap up ancient vegetable varieties.

Marché Batignolles (bd de Batignolles, 17th, Mº Brochant; 9am-2pm Sat) is more down to earth than the better-known Raspail organic market, with a quirky selection of stallholders, many of whom produce what they sell. Prices are higher here than at ordinary markets but the goods are worth it.

Eat, Drink, Shop

Pâtisseries

Arnaud Lahrer
53 rue Caulaincourt, 18th (01.42.57.68.08).
M° Lamarck Caulaincourt. **Open** 10am-7.30pm
Tue-Sat. **Credit** MC, V. **Map** p401 H1.
Look out for the strawberry-and-lychee flavoured
bonheur and the chocolate-and-thyme *récif.*

Finkelsztajn
27 rue des Rosiers, 4th (01.42.72.78.91/www.la
boutiquejaune.com). M° St-Paul. **Open** 10am-7pm
Mon, Wed-Sun. Closed 15 July-15 Aug. **Credit**
(€20 minimum) AmEx, MC, V. **Map** p409 L6.
This motherly, yellow-fronted shop, in business
since 1946, stocks dense Jewish cakes filled with
poppy seeds, apples or cream cheese.

Gérard Mulot
76 rue de Seine, 6th (01.43.26.85.77). M° Odéon.
Open 6.45am-8pm Mon, Tue, Thur-Sun. Closed
Easter & Aug. **Credit** V. **Map** p408 H7.
Gérard Mulot rustles up stunning pastries. A popular example is the *mabillon*: caramel mousse with
apricot marmalade.
Other locations: 93 rue de la Glacière, 13th
(01.45.81.39.09).

Pierre Hermé
72 rue Bonaparte, 6th (01.43.54.47.77). M° Saint-
Germain des-Prés, Mabillon or Saint-Sulpice.
Open 10am-7pm Tue-Fri, Sun; 10am-7.30pm Sat.
Closed 1st 3wks Aug. **Credit** AmEx, DC, MC, V.
Map p405 G7.
Pastry superstar Hermé attracts connoisseurs from
St-Germain and afar with his seasonal collections.
Other locations: 185 rue de Vaugirard, 15th
(01.47.83.89.96).

Treats & *traiteurs*

Da Rosa
62 rue de Seine, 6th (01.40.51.00.09/www.darosa.fr).
M° Odéon. **Open** 10am-11pm daily. **Credit** AmEx,
MC, V. **Map** p408 H7.
José Da Rosa sourced ingredients for top restaurants
before filling his own shop with Spanish hams,
Olivier Roellinger spices and Luberon truffles.

Fauchon
26 & 30 pl de la Madeleine, 8th (01.70.39.38.00/
www.fauchon.com). M° Madeleine. **Open** *No.26* 8am-
9pm Mon-Sat. *No.30* 9am-8pm Mon-Sat. **Credit**
AmEx, MC, V. **Map** p401 F4.
The city's most famous food shop is worth a visit –
particularly for the beautifully packaged gift items.

Hédiard
21 pl de la Madeleine, 8th (01.43.12.88.88/
www.hediard.fr). M° Madeleine. **Open** 8.30am-9pm
Mon-Sat. **Credit** AmEx, DC, MC, V. **Map** p401 F4.
The first to introduce exotic foods to Paris, Hédiard
specialises in rare teas and coffees, spices, jams and
candied fruits. The original shop, dating from 1880,
has a posh tearoom upstairs, La Table d'Hédiard.
Other locations: throughout the city.

Huilerie Artisanale Leblanc
6 rue Jacob, 6th (01.46.34.61.55/www.huile-leblanc.
com). M° St-Germain-des-Prés. **Open** noon-7pm Tue-
Fri; 10am-7pm Sat. Closed 2wks Aug. **No credit**
cards. Map p405 H6.
The Leblanc family started out making walnut oil
from its family tree in Burgundy before branching
out to press pure oils from hazelnuts, almonds, pine
nuts, grilled peanuts, pistachios and olives.

Brie? boursin? There's even runny camembert at **Fromagerie Quatrehomme**. *See p262.*

La Maison de la Truffe
19 pl de la Madeleine, 8th (01.42.65.53.22/
www.maison-de-la-truffe.com). M° Madeleine.
Open 9.30am-9pm Mon-Sat. **Credit** AmEx, DC,
MC, V. **Map** p401 F4.
Truffles worth more than gold, more affordable (artificial) truffle oils, sauces and vinegars, truffle-
enhanced foie gras – Guy Monier offers them all.

Torréfacteur Verlet
256 rue St-Honoré, 1st (01.42.60.67.39). M° Palais
Royal Musée du Louvre. **Open** 9.30am-6.30pm Mon-
Sat. **Credit** MC, V. **Map** p401 G5.
Eric Duchaussoy roasts rare beans to perfection –
sip here or take home some of finest coffee in Paris.

Wine, beer & spirits

Les Caves Augé
116 bd Haussmann, 8th (01.45.22.16.97). M° St-
Augustin. **Open** 1-7.30pm Mon; 9am-7.30pm Tue-
Sat. Closed Mon in Aug. **Credit** AmEx, MC, V.
Map p401 E3.
The oldest wine shop in Paris – Marcel Proust was
a regular customer – is serious and professional.

Les Caves Taillevent
199 rue du Fbg-St-Honoré, 8th (01.45.61.14.09/
www.taillevent.com). M° Charles de Gaulle Etoile or
Ternes. **Open** 9am-7.30pm Tue-Sat. Closed 1st 3wks
Aug. **Credit** AmEx, DC, MC, V. **Map** p400 D3.
Choose from the half a million wines here for your
meal at the nearby Taillevent restaurant (*see p190*).

Julien, Caviste
50 rue Charlot, 3rd (01.42.72.00.94). M° Filles du
Calvaire. **Open** 9am-1.30pm, 3.30-7.30pm Tue-Sat;
10.30am-1.30pm Sun. Closed 3rd wk Aug. **Credit**
AmEx, MC, V. **Map** p402 L5.
Julien promotes the small producers he has discovered, and often holds wine tastings on Saturdays.

Lavinia
3 bd de la Madeleine, 1st (01.42.97.20.20/www.
lavinia.fr). M° Madeleine. **Open** 10am-8pm Mon-
Fri; 9am-8pm Sat. **Credit** AmEx, DC, MC, V.
Map p401 G4.
This emporium stocks 5,000 wines, half from outside France. There's a vast selection of spirits too.

Legrand Filles et Fils
1 rue de la Banque, 2nd (01.42.60.07.12).
M° Bourse. **Open** 11am-7pm Mon-Sat. Closed Mon in
July & Aug. **Credit** AmEx, MC, V. **Map** p402 H4.
Fine wines and brandies, teas and *bonbons,* plus a
showroom for regular wine tastings.

Ryst Dupeyron
79 rue du Bac, 7th (01.45.48.80.93/www.
dupeyron.com). M° Rue du Bac. **Open** 12.30-7.30pm
Mon; 10.30am-7.30pm Tue-Sat. Closed 2wks Aug.
Credit AmEx, MC, V. **Map** p405 F7.
The Dupeyrons have sold Armagnac for four generations, and still have bottles from 1868. Treasures
include 200 fine Bordeaux wines and vintage Port.

Gifts

Florists

Monceau Fleurs
92 bd Malesherbes, 8th (01.53.77.61.77/www.
monceaufleurs.com). M° Villiers. **Open** 8.30am-9pm
Mon-Sat; 9am-7.30pm Sun. **Credit** V. **Map** p400 B6.
The citywide branches sell an affordable range of
fresh *fleurs.* Order and pay for bouquets online too.
Other locations: throughout the city.

Au Nom de la Rose
87 rue St-Antoine, 4th (01.42.71.34.24/www.aunom
delarose.fr). M° St-Paul. **Open** Sept-Jul 10am-9pm
daily. *Aug* 10am-9pm Mon-Sat. **Credit** AmEx, DC,
MC, V. **Map** p409 L7.
Specialising in roses, Au Nom can supply a bouquet,
as well as rose-based beauty products and candles.
Other locations: throughout the city.

Souvenirs & eccentricities

Diptyque
34 bd St-Germain, 5th (01.43.26.45.27/www.
diptyqueparis.com). M° Maubert Mutualité. **Open**
10am-7pm Mon-Sat. **Credit** V. **Map** p405 G6.
Diptyque's divinely scented candles in 48 different
varieties are probably the best you'll ever find.

Pa Design
2bis rue Fléchier, 9th (01.42.85.20.85/www.pa-
design.com). M° Notre-Dame-de-Lorette. **Open** 11am-
2pm, 3-7pm Wed-Fri; 10am-1pm, 2-7pm Sat. **Credit**
MC, V. **Map** p402 H3.
Ingenious objects: vases, toys and photo frames.

Paris Accordéon
80 rue Daguerre, 14th (01.43.22.13.48/www.paris
accordeon.com). M° Gaîté or Denfert Rochereau.
Open 9am-noon, 1-7pm Tue-Fri; 9am-noon, 1-6pm
Sat. **Credit** AmEx, MC, V. **Map** p405 G10.
Accordions, from simple squeeze-boxes to beautiful
tortoiseshell models, both second-hand and new.

Paris-Musées
29bis rue des Francs-Bourgeois, 4th (01.42.74.13.02).
M° St-Paul. **Open** 2-7pm Mon; 11am-1pm, 2-7pm
Tue-Fri; 11am-7pm Sat; noon-7.30pm Sun. **Credit**
AmEx, DC, MC, V. **Map** p409 L6.
Run by the museum federation, this shop sells lamps
and ceramics from local museums. **Photo** *p266.*

Sennelier
3 quai Voltaire, 7th (01.42.60.72.15/www.magasin
sennelier.fr). M° St-Germain-des-Prés. **Open**
2-6.30pm Mon; 10am-12.45pm, 2-6.30pm Tue-Sat.
Credit AmEx, DC, MC, V. **Map** p405 G6.
Old-fashioned colour merchant Sennelier sells oil
paints, watercolours and pastels, including rare pig-
ments, plus primered boards, varnishes and paper.
Other locations: 4bis rue de la Grande-Chaumière,
6th (same phone).

Eat, Drink, Shop

Home

Antiques & flea markets

Knowing who specialises in what is essential for antiques buying in Paris. Classy traditional antiques can be found in the **Louvre des Antiquaires**, **Carré Rive Gauche** (6th), **Village Suisse** and rue du Fbg-St-Honoré (1st). You'll find art deco in St-Germain-des-Prés (7th) and retro by rue de Charonne (11th). For books, look in the **bouquinistes** (*see p242*) and at Parc Georges Brassens (15th).

As well as flea markets, don't forget auction house **Drouot** (*see p103*). There are also frequent *brocantes* and *braderies* – antiques' and collectors' markets.

Louvre des Antiquaires

2 pl du Palais-Royal, 1st (01.42.97.27.27/www.louvre-antiquaires.com). M° Palais Royal Musée du Louvre. **Open** 11am-7pm Tue-Sun. Closed Sun in July & Aug. **Credit** varies. **Map** p406 H5.
This upmarket antiques centre houses 250 antiques dealers: perfect for Louis XV furniture, tapestries, porcelain, jewellery, model ships and tin soldiers.

Marché aux Puces d'Aligre

Pl d'Aligre, rue d'Aligre, 12th. M° Ledru-Rollin. **Open** 7.30am-1.30pm Tue-Sun. **Map** p407 N7.
The only flea market in central Paris, Aligre stays true to its junk tradition with a handful of *brocanteurs* peddling books, phone cards, kitchenware and oddities at what seem to be optimistic prices.

Marché aux Puces de Clignancourt

Av de la Porte de Clignancourt, 18th. M° Porte de Clignancourt. **Open** 7am-7.30pm Mon, Sat, Sun.
The mother of all flea markets is home to some 2,500 dealers at ten main markets. For classic furniture, head to the Marché Dauphine (No.138-140) or the Marché Biron (No.85); for jewellery, try the Marché Serpette (No.110) and for vintage bric-a-brac, the Marché Paul Bert (No.104). Don't bother to arrive early for bargains – most stalls don't open till 9am.

Marché aux Puces de Vanves

Av Georges-Lafenestre & av Marc-Sangnier, 14th. M° Porte de Vanves. **Open** 7am-7.30pm Sun.
Begun in the 1920s, Vanves is the smallest and friendliest of the Parisian flea markets, perfect for a Sunday morning. If you get there early enough, there are decent second-hand clothes, dolls, 1950s costume jewellery and silverware.

Le Village St-Paul

Rue St-Paul, rue Ch arlemagne & quai des Célestins, 4th. M° St-Paul. **Open** 10am-7pm Mon-Sat. **No credit cards. Map** p409 L7.
This colony of antiques sellers, spread across small linking courtyards, is a source of retro furniture, kitchenware and wine gadgets.

Random gifts at **Paris-Musées**. *See p265*.

Design & interiors

The vast **Lafayette Maison** (*see p237*) offers a selection of current design and homewares.

Astier de Villatte

173 rue St-Honoré, 1st (01.42.60.74.13/www.astier devillatte.com). M° Palais Royal Musée du Louvre. **Open** 11am-7.30pm Mon-Sat. Closed 3wks Aug. **Credit** AmEx, MC, V. **Map** p401 G4.
Once home to Napoléon's silversmith, this ancient warren now houses ceramics inspired by 17th- and 18th-century designs, handmade by the Astier de Villatte siblings in their Bastille workshop.

Caravane Chambre 19

19 rue St-Nicolas, 12th (01.53.02.96.96/www.caravane.fr). M° Ledru-Rollin. **Open** 11am-7pm Tue-Sat. Closed 2wks Aug. **Credit** AmEx, MC, V. **Map** p407 M7.
This offshoot of Françoise Dorget's original Marais shop has goodies such as exquisite hand-sewn quilts from west Bengal, crisp cotton and organdie tunics, Berber scarves, lounging sofas and daybeds. **Other locations**: 22 rue St-Nicolas, 12th (01.53.17.18.55); 6 rue Pavée, 4th (01.44.61.04.20).

Christian Liaigre

42 rue du Bac, 7th (01.53.63.33.66/www.christian-liaigre.fr). M° Rue du Bac. **Open** 10am-7pm Mon-Sat. Closed 3wks Aug. **Credit** AmEx, MC, V. **Map** p405 G6.

This French interior decorator fitted out Marc Jacobs' boutiques. His showroom displays his elegant lighting and furniture designs, in trademark tones of cream and brown.
Other locations: 61 rue de Varenne, 7th (01.47.53.78.76).

Christophe Delcourt
39 rue Lucien Sampaix, 10th (01.42.71.34.84/ www.christophedelcourt.com). M° Jacques Bonsergent. **Open** 9am-noon, 1-6pm Mon-Fri. Closed Aug. **Credit** AmEx, DC, MC, V. **Map** p401 G4.
Delcourt's art deco-influenced, geometrical lights and furniture are given a contemporary spin by their combination of stained wood and black steel.

CSAO
9 rue Elzévir, 3rd (01.44.54.55.88/www.csao.fr). M° St-Paul. **Open** 11am-7pm Mon-Sat; 2-7pm Sun. **Credit** AmEx, DC, MC, V. **Map** p409 L6.
This boutique offers African craftwork created according to fair-trade principles. The artisans often fashion their objects out of recycled materials, such as funky furniture constructed from tins.

FR 66
25 rue de Renard, 4th (01.44.54.35.36/www.fr66. com). M° Hôtel de Ville. **Open** 10am-7pm Mon-Sat. Closed 2-3wks Aug. **Credit** AmEx, MC, V. **Map** p406 K6.
Somewhere between a gallery and a shop, this two-level experimental space accommodates contemporary artists and designers who produce exciting and original products for the home – not only furniture, but electrical fittings, and floor and wall coverings.

Galerie Patrick Seguin
5 rue des Taillandiers, 11th (01.47.00.32.35/www. patrickseguin.com). M° Ledru-Rollin or Bastille. **Open** 10am-7pm Tue-Sat. Closed 2wks Aug. **Credit** AmEx, DC, MC, V. **Map** p407 M7.
Seguin specialises in French design from the 1950s: items by Jean Prouvé and Charlotte Perriand are on display in a showroom designed by Jean Nouvel.

Sentou Galerie
24 rue du Pont-Louis-Philippe, 4th (01.42.77.44.79/ 01.42.71.00.01/www.sentou.fr). M° Pont Marie. **Open** 10am-7pm Tue-Sat. **Credit** AmEx, MC, V. **Map** p409 K7.
A trend-setting shop for colourful tableware and furniture: painted Chinese flasks, vases and so on.
Other locations: 29 rue François-Miron, 4th (01.42.78.50.60); 26 bd Raspail, 7th (01.45.49.00.05).

Silvera
41 rue du Fbg-St-Antoine, 11th (01.43.43.06.75/ www.silvera.fr). M° Bastille or Ledru-Rollin. **Open** 10am-7pm Mon-Sat. Closed 2wks Aug. **Credit** AmEx, MC, V. **Map** p407 M7.
The former Le Bihan taken over by Silvera in 2005 is a three-floor showcase for modern design. Look out for furniture and lighting from Perriand, Pesce, Pillet, Morrison, Arad and others.
Other locations: 58 av Kléber, 16th (01.53.65.78.78).

Kitchen & bathroom

Bains Plus
51 rue des Francs-Bourgeois, 4th (01.48.87.83.07). M° Hôtel de Ville. **Open** 2-7pm Mon, Sun; 11am-7.30pm Tue-Sat. **Credit** AmEx, MC, V. **Map** p409 K6.
This is the ultimate gentlemen's shaving shop: stock includes duck-shaped loofahs, seductive dressing gowns, chrome mirrors, bath oils and soaps.

E Dehillerin
18 rue Coquillière, 1st (01.42.36.53.13/www. e-dehillerin.fr). M° Les Halles. **Open** 9am-12.30pm, 2-6pm Mon; 9am-6pm Tue-Sat. **Credit** MC, V. **Map** p402 J5.
Suppliers to great chefs since 1820, this no-nonsense warehouse stocks just about every kitchen utensil ever invented. A saucepan from Dehillerin is for life.

Laguiole Galerie
1 pl Ste-Opportune, 1st (01.40.28.09.42/www.forge-de-laguiole.com). M° Châtelet. **Open** 10.30am-1pm, 2-7pm Mon-Sat. **Credit** MC, V. **Map** p406 J6.
Philippe Starck designed this chic boutique, a showcase for France's classic knife, the Laguiole.

Sport & games

Unless you need specialised equipment, you'll find what you want at **Go Sport** (www.go-sport.com) or **Décathlon** (www.decathlon.fr).

Citadium
50-56 rue de Caumartin, 9th (01.55.31.74.00/www. citadium.com). M° Havre Caumartin. **Open** 9am-8pm Mon, Tue, Fri, Sat; 10am-8pm Wed; 9am-9pm Thur. **Credit** AmEx, DC, MC, V. **Map** p401 G3.
Cultish emporium of sports goods – from hip watches to cross-country skis – on four themed floors.

Nauti Store
40 av de la Grande-Armée, 17th (01.43.80.28.28/ www.nautistore.fr). M° Argentine. **Open** 11am-7pm Mon; 10.30am-7pm Tue-Sat. **Credit** DC, MC, V. **Map** p400 C3.
This shop stocks a vast range of sailing clothes and shoes from labels such as Helly Hansen and Sebago.

René Pierre
35 rue de Maubeuge, 9th (01.44.91.91.21/www.rene-pierre.fr). M° Poissonnière. **Open** 10am-1pm, 2-6.30pm Mon-Sat. **Credit** MC, V. **Map** p402 H3.
France's finest table-football tables, ready for free delivery as far as Calais to UK buyers. Jukeboxes and billiard tables are also available.

Subchandlers – Plongespace
80 rue Balard, 15th (01.45.57.01.01/www. subchandlers.com). M° Balard. **Open** 10.30am-7.30pm Tue-Sat. **Credit** AmEx, MC, V. **Map** p404 A9.
This diving specialist stocks all apparatus, plus underwater cameras. Monthly soirées on diving too.

Eat, Drink, Shop

© Bal du Moulin Rouge 2003/2007 - Moulin Rouge

Kris Gautier

Discover the Show of the Most Famous Cabaret in the World !

Dinner & Show at 7pm from €145 • Show at 9pm : €99 & at 11pm : €89

Montmartre - 82, bd de Clichy - 75018 Paris - Reservations : 01 53 09 82 82
www.moulin-rouge.com

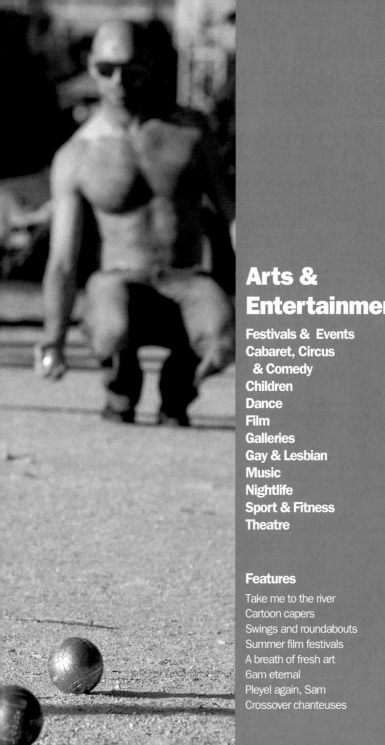

Arts & Entertainment

Festivals & Events

Many of them free, some outdoor, festivals make a big splash all year round.

Along with a panoply of cultural events throughout the year, Paris hosts any number of anniversaries and religious festivals. Indeed, the city seems to turn every commemoration into a serious, state-funded event – and the pro-active reign of Mayor Delanoë has done much to refresh the capital's diary. **Paris-Plage** (*see p272* **Take me to the river**), an urban beach set up by the Seine for the summer, and **Nuit Blanche**, an autumnal, all-night culture fest, have brought high-profile successes.

In terms of cultural seasons, Paris starts up in October, keeping busy until the beginning of summer, when companies heads south. Many summer events are free, such as Paris-Plage, the **Fête de la Musique** and **Bastille Day**. *See also p292* **Summer film festivals**.

PUBLIC HOLIDAYS

On *jours feriés*, banks, many museums, most businesses and a number of restaurants close; public transport runs a Sunday service. Bastille Day, New Year's Day, May Day and Christmas Day are the most piously observed holidays.

The bank holiday calendar runs as follows: New Year's Day (*Jour de l'An*); Easter Monday (*Pâques*); May Day (*Fête du Travail*); VE Day (*Victoire 1945*) 8 May; Ascension Day (*Jour de l'Ascension*); Whit Monday (*Pentecôte*); Bastille Day (*Quatorze Juillet*) 14 July; Feast of the Assumption (*Fête de l'Assomption*) 15 Aug; All Saints' Day (*Toussaint*) 1 Nov; Remembrance Day (*L'Armistice 1918*) 11 Nov; Christmas Day (*Noël*).

Spring

Six Nations

Stade de France, 93210 St-Denis (08.92.70.09.00/ www.stadefrance.fr). RER B La Plaine Stade de France or RER D Stade de France St-Denis. **Admission** varies. **Date** Feb-Mar.
Paris is invaded by Brits and Celts for three big rugby weekends in winter. Tickets are hard to come by – log on to www.rbs6nations.com at least three months in advance.

Fashion Week

Various venues (www.modeaparis.com). **Date** Mar & Oct.
Paris presents its haute couture and prêt-à porter collections to invited guests only. Everyone who's anyone shows here, from Valentino to Viktor & Rolf. The better hotels fill up, as do the trendier bistros.

Le Printemps des Poètes

Various venues (www.printempsdespoetes.com). **Date** Mar.
Celebrating the centenary of the poet René Char's birth, the 2007 edition of this popular national poetry festival, set up by Jack Lang in 1999, has 'Lettera amorosa' as its theme.

Printemps du Cinéma

Various venues (www.printempsducinema.com). **Date** Mar.
Film tickets all across the city are cut to a bargain €3.50 for this popular three-day film event.

Banlieues Bleues

Various venues in Seine St-Denis (01.40.03.75.01/ www.banlieuesbleues.org). **Admission** €10-€16. **Date** Mar-Apr.
Five weeks of quality French and international jazz, blues, R&B, soul, funk, flamenco and world music.

Le Chemin de la Croix

Square Willette, 18th (01.53.41.89.00). Mᵒ Anvers or Abbesses. **Date** Good Friday.
Mini-pilgrimage as crowds follow the Archbishop of Paris from the bottom of Montmartre up to Sacré-Coeur as he performs the Stations of the Cross.

Foire du Trône

Pelouse de Reuilly, 12th (www.foiredutrone.com). Mᵒ Porte Dorée. **Admission** free; rides €1.50-€4. **Date** early Apr-end May.
France's biggest funfair: stomach-churning rides, bungee jumping and *barbe à papa* (candyfloss).

Marathon de Paris

Av des Champs-Elysées, 8th, to av Foch, 16th (01.41.33.15.68/www.parismarathon.com). **Date** Apr.
From the Champs-Elysées all along the Right Bank to the Bois de Vincennes and back again to the Bois de Boulogne, 35,000 marathon runners take in the city's sights for the 31st staging of this event in 2007.

Foire de Paris

Paris-Expo, pl de la Porte de Versailles (01.49.09. 60.00/www.foiredeparis.fr). Mᵒ Porte de Versailles. **Admission** €12; €10 concessions; €7 under-7s. **Date** 27 Apr-8 May 2007.
This enormous lifestyle salon includes world crafts and foods, plus the latest health and house gizmos.

Fête du Travail

Date 1 May.
May Day is strictly observed. Key sights (the Eiffel Tower aside) close, and unions march in eastern Paris via Bastille. Vendors sell sweet-smelling posies of lily of the valley (*muguet*) on every street corner.

Jazz à la Villette. *See p273.*

Printemps des Musées

Various venues (http://printempsdesmusees.
culture.fr). **Date** May.
The Ministry of Culture's annual treat sees selected
museums across France open their doors for free.

La Nuit des Musées

All over France (www.nuitdesmusees.culture.fr).
Admission free. **Date** mid May.
For one night, landmark museums across Paris open
late and organise various special entertainments.

Festival de St-Denis

Various venues in St-Denis (01.48.13.12.10/
www.festival-saint-denis.fr). M° St-Denis Basilique.
Admission €9-€55. **Date** end May-end June.
The Gothic St-Denis basilica and other historic
buildings in the neighbourhood host four weeks of
quality classical concerts through the month of June.

Quinzaine des Réalisateurs

Forum des Images, Porte St-Eustache, Forum
des Halles, 1st (01.44.89.99.99/www.quinzaine-
realisateurs.com). M° Les Halles. **Admission** €5.50.
Date May-June.
As soon as the dust has settled at Cannes, the
Directors' Fortnight programme comes to Paris.

French Tennis Open

Stade Roland-Garros, 2 avenue Gordon-Bennett,
16th (01.47.43.52.52/www.frenchopen.org).
M° Porte d'Auteuil. **Admission** €21-€53.
Date late May-early June.

The glitzy Grand Slam tennis tournament is always
well attended by showbiz stars. The tricky clay
courts have been the downfall of many a champion.

Summer

Le Printemps des rues

01.47.97.36.06/www.leprintempsdesrues.com.
Admission free. **Date** June.
Despite financial worries, this annual street-theatre
fest is all set to continue in 2007.

Prix de Diane Hermès

Hippodrome de Chantilly, 16 av du Général-Leclerc,
90209 Chantilly (03.44.62.41.00/www.france-
galop.com). **Admission** €8; €4 concessions; free
under-18s. **Date** 10 June 2007.
The French Derby draws la crème de la crème of
high society to the races at Chantilly, sporting silly
hats and keen to take a flutter.

Fête de la Musique

All over France (01.40.03.94.70/www.fetedela
musique.fr). **Admission** free. **Date** 21 June.
Concerts are held all over the city – and indeed
nationwide – for this free music festival.

Gay Pride March

Information: Centre Gai et Lesbien (01.43.57.21.47/
www.fiertes-lgbt.org). **Date** 30 June 2007.
Outrageous floats and flamboyant costumes parade
towards Bastille, followed by an official fête and various club events.

Arts & Entertainment

Take me to the river

It just keeps getting bigger and better. Now in its sixth year, the month-long city beach of **Paris-Plage** (*see p273*) spread itself over both banks of the Seine for the first time in 2006. In addition to the original Right Bank site, from the Louvre to Sully-Morland, there's now a kilometre of riverside attractions on the Left. With the **Piscine Josephine-Baker** as its centrepiece (*see p338*), this new and relatively uncrowded stretch opposite Parc de Bercy in the 13th district also offers picnic areas, speedball and a toddlers' sandpit.

The idea for Paris-Plage, conceived by Jean-Christophe Choblet in 2002, was simple – not dissimilar to the one used in Barcelona during the Olympics a decade before. For city mayor Bertrand Delanoë, its main role was to give those who couldn't otherwise afford it (notably suburban families) an annual holiday. Everything would be free, a principle that still endures – only now Plage involves 2,000 tonnes of sand, 300 loungers, 240 parasols, 68 palm trees and two dozen sports activities, including trampolining, t'ai chi and volleyball. There are hammocks and a 1,000-volume lending library in four languages, again free of charge with a €5 refundable deposit.

Each hour of the day brings its own attractions. Sporting types pitch up in the morning for jogging;

sun-worshippers and picnickers find their spot in the hotter hours; and the evening brings a *passeggiata* where licensed buskers – tango, salsa and so on – get festive under the bright lights (powered by solar energy, of course). The Plage is open from 7am to midnight, after which an army of beach sweepers and a special Seine-cleaning boat arrive to make it pristine for the next day. Each summer sees a new theme: 2006 was the year of Polynesia.

Successfully exported to Hamburg, Berlin, Budapest, Rome, Tokyo and any number of French cities, Paris-Plage is a peach of an idea that attracts more than four million visitors to an otherwise-empty city every August. The only problem is, where can you find room for improvement?

Foire St-Germain
Pl St-Sulpice and venues in St-Germain-des-Prés, 6th (01.43.29.61.04/www.foiresaintgermain.org). M° St-Sulpice. **Admission** free. **Date** June-July.
St-Germain-des-Prés lets its hair down for a month of concerts, theatre and workshops.

Paris Jazz Festival
Parc Floral de Paris, Bois de Vincennes (39.75/www. parcfloraldeparis.com/www.paris.fr). M° Château de Vincennes. **Admission** *Park* €3. **Date** June-July.
Free jazz weekends at the lovely Parc Floral.

Festival Chopin à Paris
Orangerie de Bagatelle, Parc de Bagatelle, Bois de Boulogne, 16th (01.45.00.22.19/www.frederic-chopin. com). M° Porte Maillot, then bus 244. **Admission** €16-€31. **Date** June-July.
Candlelit evening recitals in the Bagatelle gardens.

La Goutte d'Or en Fête
Square Léon, 18th (01.46.07.61.64/www.gouttedor enfete.org). M° Barbès Rochechouart. **Admission** free. **Date** late June-early July.
Established and local artists play reggae, raï and rap in this Arab and African neighbourhood.

Paris Cinéma
Various venues (www.pariscinema.org). **Admission** varies. **Date** early July.
Premières, tributes and restored films make up the programme of Paris' summer film-going initiative.

Solidays
Longchamp Hippodrome (01.53.10.22.22/www. solidays.com). M° Porte d'Auteuil. **Admission** *Day* €20. *Weekend* €35. **Date** early July.
A three-day music festival with a mix of French, international and new talent, all for the benefit of AIDS charities. *See also p313.*

Miss Guinguette
38 quai Victor Hugo, Ile du Martin-Pêcheur, Champigny-sur-Marne (information 01.49.83.03.02/ www.guinguette.fr). RER Champigny-sur-Marne. **Admission** €7. **Date** 14 July.
A quest to find the light-footed queen of the open-air dancehall scene at this river-island venue.

Le Quatorze Juillet (Bastille Day)
All over France. **Date** 14 July.
France's national holiday commemorates the events of 1789. On the eve, Parisians dance at place de la Bastille. At 10am on the 14th, crowds line up down the Champs-Elysées as the President reviews a full military parade. By night, the Champ de Mars fills for the firework display.

Le Tour de France
Av des Champs-Elysées, 8th (01.41.33.15.00/ www.letour.fr). **Date** July.
The ultimate endurance test climaxes after some 3,500km (2,175 miles) of calf-busting action. Blink and you'll miss the winner as the event ends on the Champs-Elysées in a blur of pedals and Lycra.

Le Cinéma en Plein Air
Parc de La Villette, 19th (01.40.03.75.75/www. villette.com). M° Porte de Pantin. **Admission** free. **Date** mid July-end Aug.
Settle back on the lawn at this summer fixture – a themed season of films screened under the stars on Europe's largest inflatable screen.

Paris, Quartier d'été
Various venues (01.44.94.98.00/www.quartierdete. com). **Admission** free-€15. **Date** mid July-mid Aug.
A series of classical and jazz concerts, dance and theatre performances in outdoor venues.

Paris-Plage
Pont des Arts to Pont de Sully (08.20.00.75.75/ www.paris.fr). M° Sully Morland, Louvre Rivoli, Châtelet, Hôtel de Ville, Pont Marie. **Admission** free. **Date** mid July-mid Aug.
Over a month, for the sixth consecutive year in 2007, palm trees, huts, hammocks and 2,000 tonnes of fine sand bring a seaside atmosphere now spread over both sides of the Seine embankment. *See p272* **Take me to the river.**

Fête de l'Assomption
Cathédrale Notre-Dame de Paris, pl du Parvis Notre-Dame, 4th (01.42.34.56.10). M° Cité/RER St-Michel Notre-Dame. **Admission** free. **Date** 15 Aug.
A national holiday. Notre-Dame again becomes a place of religious pilgrimage for Assumption Day.

Rock en Seine
Domaine National de St-Cloud (08.92.68.08.92/ www.rockenseine.com). **Admission** *Day* €39. *2 days* €65. **Date** end Aug.
Two days, two stages, and one world-class line-up of rock and indie groups. *See also p313.*

Autumn

Jazz à la Villette
Parc de la Villette, 211 av Jean-Jaurès, 19th (01.40.03.75.75/01.44.84.44.84/www.villette.com/ www.jazzalavillette.com). M° Porte de Pantin. **Admission** €12-€30. **Date** early Sept.
One of the best local jazz fests. **Photo** *p271.*

Techno Parade
01.42.47.84.75/www.technopol.net. **Date** mid Sept.
This parade (finishing at Bastille) marks the start of electronic music festival Rendez-vous Electroniques.

Journées du Patrimoine
Across France (08.20.20.25.02/www.jp.culture.fr). **Date** Sept.
Embassies, ministries, scientific establishments and corporate headquarters open their doors. The festive Soirée du Patrimoine takes place on the first Journée. Get *Le Monde* or *Le Parisien* for a full programme.

Festival d'Automne
Various venues. Information: 156 rue de Rivoli, 1st (01.53.45.17.17/www.festival-automne.com). **Admission** €9-€30. **Date** mid Sept-mid Dec.

Major annual festival of challenging contemporary theatre, dance and modern opera, intent on bringing non-Western culture into the French consciousness. 'Autumn Festival' is a bit of a misnomer, as some exhibitions run over the new year into January.

Nuit Blanche
Various venues (39.75/www.paris.fr). **Admission** free. **Date** early Oct.
Culture by moonlight: galleries and museums host one-off installations, while swimming pools, bars and clubs stay open till very late.

Prix de l'Arc de Triomphe
Hippodrome de Longchamp, Bois de Boulogne, 16th (01.49.10.20.30/www.france-galop.com). M° Porte d'Auteuil, then free shuttle bus. **Admission** €8; €4 concessions; free under-18s. **Date** early Oct.
France's richest flat race attracts the elite of horse racing amid much pomp and ceremony.

Fête des Vendanges à Montmartre
Rue des Saules, 18th (01.30.21.48.62/www.fete desvendangesdemontmartre.com). M° Lamarck Caulaincourt. **Date** 2nd weekend in Oct.
Folk music, speeches, locals in costume and a parade celebrate the 800-bottle Montmartre grape harvest. *Chansons* accompany the village-fête atmosphere, with produce stands in Montmartre all weekend.

FIAC
01.41.90.47.47/www.fiacparis.com. **Admission** €20; €10 concessions. **Date** 26-30 Oct 2007.
Now held at the Louvre and the Grand Palais, this respected international art fair gives France a chance to strut its contemporary stuff. *See also p295.*

Les Puces du design
Passage du Grand-Cerf, pl Goldoni, 2nd (01.53.40. 78.77/www.pucesdudesign.com). M° Etienne Marcel. **Admission** free. **Date** Oct.
Set in the cobbled pedestrian streets of the shabby-but-chic Montorgueil district, this modern design market draws specialist retailers from all over France.

Festival Inrockuptibles
Various venues (01.42.44.16.16/www.lesinrocks.com). **Admission** varies. **Date** early Nov.
Once indie-centred, this festival curated by popular rock magazine *Les Inrockuptibles* today champions trance, techno and trip hop – but that could all change by autumn 2007. *See also p313.*

Armistice Day
Arc de Triomphe, 8th. M° Charles de Gaulle Etoile. **Date** 11 Nov.
To commemorate French combatants who served in the World Wars, the President lays wreaths at the Tomb of the Unknown Soldier under the Arc de Triomphe. The *bleuet* (a cornflower) is worn.

Fête du Beaujolais Nouveau
www.beaujolaisgourmand.com. **Date** mid Nov.
The third Thursday in November sees cafés and wine bars throng as patrons assess the new vintage.

Winter

Africolor
Various venues in the suburbs, including Montreuil, St-Denis and St-Ouen (01.47.97.69.99/www. africolor.com). **Admission** approx €13. **Date** late Nov-mid Dec.
A month-long African music festival, held at a handful of venues in the *banlieue*.

Paris sur Glace
Pl de l'Hôtel de Ville, 4th; M° Hôtel de Ville. Pl Raoul Dautry, 15th; M° Montparnasse Bienvenüe. Pl de la Bataille de Stalingrad, 19th; M° Stalingrad. Information: 39.75/www.paris.fr. **Admission** free (skate hire €6). **Date** Dec-Mar.
Totter around the edges of these outdoor rinks while fearless five-year-olds zoom past. There's also skating on the Eiffel Tower – *see below, Patinoire de Noël.*

Patinoire de Noël
Eiffel Tower, Champ de Mars, 7th (01.44.11.23.45/ recorded info 01.44.11.23.23/www.tour-eiffel.fr). M° Bir-Hakeim/RER Champ de Mars Tour Eiffel. **Admission** €2.30-€4.20. **Dates** mid Dec-late Jan.
Hire a pair of free skates (you don't have to bring your own) and experience the city's snazziest winter wonderland as the first floor of the illuminated tower gets a seasonal icy makeover.

Noël (Christmas)
Date 24-25 Dec.
Christmas is a family affair in France, with a dinner on Christmas Eve (*le réveillon*), normally after mass. Notre-Dame cathedral fills for the 11pm service. Usually the only bars and restaurants are the ones in the city's main hotels.

New Year's Eve/New Year's Day
Date 31 Dec-1 Jan.
Crowds running into the tens of thousands swarm along the Champs-Elysées and let off bangers. Nightclubs and restaurants hold expensive soirées. On New Year's Day the Grande Parade de Paris brings floats, bands and dancers.

Fête des Rois (Epiphany)
Date 6 Jan.
Pâtisseries sell *galettes des rois*, cakes with a frangipane filling in which a *fève*, or tiny charm, is hidden.

Mass for Louis XVI
Chapelle Expiatoire, 29 rue Pasquier, 8th (01.42.65. 35.80). M° St-Augustin. **Date** Jan.
On the Sunday closest to 21 January, anniversary of the beheading of Louis XVI in 1793, royalists and right-wing crackpots mourn the end of the monarchy.

Nouvel An Chinois
Around av d'Ivry & av de Choisy, 13th. M° Porte de Choisy or Porte d'Ivry. Also av des Champs Elysées, 8th (www.parisinfo.com). **Date** Jan.
Lion and dragon dances, and lively martial arts demonstrations, celebrate the Chinese New Year.

Cabaret, Circus & Comedy

On with the show.

Le Lido. *See p276.*

Glam girls dancing in a provocative way may be an age-old stereotype, but it's one that shows no sign of disappearing in Paris; it's still boobs and boas in the city's traditional cabarets. Beyond these coach-tour magnets, satire thrives in good old-fashioned *café-théâtres*, where songs and sketches come with supper and a bottle of plonk. Away from the glitz, venues range from cellars to converted cinemas.

On the comedy front, veteran Anglo venue **Laughing Matters** is still going strong at La Java, drawing acts from across the Channel, the US and Australia; for the city's other comedy venues, you'll need to speak the lingo.

Cabaret & café-théâtre

Back in 1889, the **Moulin Rouge** presented a risqué, skirt-raising dance called *Quadrille Réaliste* – later coined the cancan. The rest, as they say, is history; a century after cancan was born, busty babes are still slinking across the cabaret stages of Paris. These days, cabaret

is an all-evening, smart-dress extravaganza, complete with a pre-show gourmet meal and champers. It may be touristy and expensive (you won't get much change from €100), but it is an unrivalled spectacle. Male dancers, acrobats and magicians complement the foxy foxtrots; the dancing is perfectly synchronised, the costumes beautiful, and the whole caboodle now unreservedly respectable.

Glitzy cabaret

La Belle Epoque
36 rue des Petits-Champs, 2nd (01.42.96.33.33/ www.belleepoqueparis.com). M° Opéra or Quatre Septembre. **Dinner** 9pm daily. **Shows** 10pm daily. **Admission** *Show* (incl champagne) €52. *Dinner & show* €72-€102. **Credit** AmEx, DC, MC, V. **Map** p401 H4.
Prices are slightly cheaper at La Belle Epoque, which was reopened as a cabaret venue in 1987. There's a slightly tacky feel, though, and less of a sense of history than you'll find at the *grandes dames* of the city's cabaret scene.

Crazy Horse Saloon

12 av George-V, 8th (01.47.23.32.32/www.
crazyhorse.fr). M° Alma Marceau or George V.
Shows 8.30pm, 11pm Tue-Fri, Sun; 7.30pm, 9.45pm,
11.50pm Sat. **Admission** *Show* (incl 2 drinks) €90.
Credit AmEx, DC, MC, V. **Map** p400 D4.

A cheaper, more risqué show than the offerings at
the Lido or Moulin Rouge runs at the Horse, whose
art du nu was invented in 1951 by Alain Bernadin.
Since then, this ode to feminine beauty has entertained punters with 11 lookalike dancers whose
names (Nooka Caramel and Misty Flashback) are as
real as their wigs. Clad only in rainbow light and
strategic squares of black tape, the girls put on some
tantalising numbers, with titles such as *Va Va Voom*.

Le Lido

116bis av des Champs-Elysées, 8th (01.40.76.56.10/
www.lido.fr). M° George V or Franklin D. Roosevelt.
Dinner 7.30pm. **Shows** 9.30pm, 11.30pm daily.
Admission *Show* (incl champagne) €80-€210; €20
under-12s. *Dinner & show* €140-€210; €30 under-12s.
Credit AmEx, DC, MC, V. **Map** p400 D4.

This is the largest, priciest cabaret of the lot: high-
tech touches (descending balcony and disappearing
lamps) optimise visibility, and star chef Paul Bocuse
has revolutionised the menu. The slightly tame
show has 60 Bluebell Girls, boob-shaking, wacky
costumes and numerous oddities: courtesan cats
meeting Charlie Chaplin, for example. **Photo** *p275.*

Moulin Rouge

82 bd de Clichy, 18th (01.53.09.82.82/www.moulin-
rouge.com). M° Blanche. **Dinner** 7pm. **Shows** 9pm,
11pm daily. **Admission** *9pm show* (incl champagne)
€97. *11pm show* €87 (incl champagne). *Dinner & show*
€140-€165. **Credit** AmEx, DC, MC, V. **Map** p401 G2.

Toulouse-Lautrec posters, glittery lamp-posts and
fake trees lend tacky charm to this most traditional
of glamour revues, while 60 Doriss dancers cavort
with faultless synchronisation. Costumes are flamboyant, the *entr'acte* acts funny and the sets solid:
one daring number even takes place inside a giant
tank of underwater boa constrictors. Elbow room is
nil, with hundreds of tables packed in like sardines.
But if you can bear intimacy with international businessmen, the Moulin Rouge won't disappoint.

Café-théâtre

L'Ane Rouge

3 rue Laugier, 17th (01.47.64.45.77). M° Ternes.
Shows 8.30pm-12.30am daily. **Admission** *Show*
(incl 1 drink) €35. *Dinner & show* €55-€85. **Credit**
MC, V. **Map** p400 C2.

The 'Red Donkey' is a glittery *café-théâtre* happy to
combine comic cabaret with a great atmosphere.
The menu features some unusual regional dishes.

Au Bec Fin

6 rue Thérèse, 1st (01.42.96.29.35). M° Pyramides.
Shows 7pm, 8.15pm, 9.45pm Mon-Sat. *Matinées for
children* 2.30pm, 4.30pm Wed, Sat, Sun. *Show for*

3s-6s 11am Wed, Sat, Sun. Closed Aug. **Admission**
Show €16; €9-€12 concessions. *Dinner & show* €30-
€36. **Credit** AmEx, MC, V. **Map** p401 H5.

With a 300-year-old pedigree, this tiny *café-théâtre*
offers wholesome family entertainment. After dining
downstairs, head up the rickety staircase to see anything from Oscar Wilde to a modern-day *Cendrillon*.

Les Blancs Manteaux

15 rue des Blancs-Manteaux, 4th (01.48.87.15.84/
www.blancsmanteaux.fr). M° Hôtel de Ville. **Shows**
from 7pm daily (phone for details). **Admission**
Show €16; €13 concessions. *Double show* €26. *Dinner
& show* €27. **No credit cards. Map** p409 K6.

This Marais institution has two theatres, multiple
weekly performances and new stand-up on the first
Wednesday of the month. With a dinner-and-show
ticket, you can dine at the nearby Epices et Délices.

Chez Michou

80 rue des Martyrs, 18th (01.46.06.16.04/www.
michou.com). M° Pigalle. **Dinner** 9pm daily. **Shows**
11pm approx. **Admission** *Show* (incl 1 drink) €35.
Dinner & show €97. **Credit** MC, V. **Map** p402 H2.

Drag, sparkling costumes, good food and wine: come
to Michou's if you're looking for larger-than-life
impersonations of Brigitte Bardot and Tina Turner.

Au Lapin Agile

22 rue des Saules, 18th (01.46.06.85.87).
M° Lamarck Caulaincourt. **Shows** 9pm-2am
Tue-Sun. **Admission** *Show* (incl 1 drink) €24.
No credit cards. Map p402 H1.

The prices have gone up, but that's all that seems to
have changed since this quaint, pink bar first opened
in 1860. Tourists now outnumber the locals, but the
Lapin harbours an echo of old Montmartre.

Comedy & fringe theatre

Le Bout

6 rue Frochot, 9th (01.42.85.11.88/www.lebout.com).
M° Pigalle. **Shows** daily. **Admission** €14; €7.50
concessions. *Two shows* €15. **No credit cards.**
Map p402 H2.

In the heart of Pigalle, this ex-*café-théâtre* school has
been cramming them into its 40-seater venue since
1999. The emphasis is on newcomers but not nec-
essarily amateurs. Annual comedy festival too.

Café de la Gare

41 rue du Temple, 4th (01.42.78.52.51/www.cafe-
de-la-gare.fr.st). M° Hôtel de Ville. **Shows** 7.30pm,
9.30 pm Mon, Tue, Sun; 8pm, 10pm Wed-Sat.
Admission €10-€22. **Credit** MC, V. **Map** p406 K6.

House specialities at this atmospheric, 300-seater
venue include lively French stand-up and raucous,
irreverent comedies.

Caveau de la République

1 bd St-Martin, 3rd (01.42.78.44.45/www.caveau.fr).
M° République. **Shows** 8.30pm Wed-Sat; 3.30pm Sun.
Closed Aug. **Admission** €29.50 Tue-Thur; €37 Fri-
Sun; €10 under-26s (except Sat); €23.50 concessions
(except Sat). **Credit** MC, V. **Map** p402 L4.

Open since 1901, this is one of the last *chansonniers* on the block, where artists spurt out golden oldies before presenting their own sardonic compositions. The humour is of a political-satirical bent.

Le Point Virgule

7 rue Ste-Croix-de-la-Bretonnerie, 4th (01.42.78. 67.03/www.netkiri.fr). M° Hôtel de Ville. **Shows** 7pm, 8pm, 9.15pm, 10.30pm daily. **Admission** €17; €9-€13 concessions. **No credit cards.** **Map** p409 K6.

This small Marais theatre is an ideal launch pad for up-and-coming comedians and hosts an annual comedy festival in November, Top In Humour. On Wednesday afternoons there's a children's show.

Le Zèbre

63 bd de Belleville, 20th (01.43.55.55.55). M° Belleville. **Shows** days vary. **Admission** €12; €10 children. **Credit** MC, V. **Map** p403 N4.

After forays in all kinds of directions, the art deco Z now sticks to satirical cabaret and chirruping *chanson*, with children's shows at the weekend.

Comedy in English

Laughing Matters

La Java, 105 rue du Fbg-du-Temple, 10th (01.53.19.98.88/www.anythingmatters.com). M° Goncourt. **Shows** days vary. **Admission** €20; €17 students. **No credit cards.** **Map** p403 M4.

This anglophone comedy spot now has the monopoly in Paris, with promoter Karel Beer luring UK and US comedians across the water to perform here.

Circus

Circus – traditional big tops and avant-garde acts – is a year-round fixture. See *Cirque* in the children's section of *Pariscope* for listings and also *pp278-285* **Children.**

Cabaret Sauvage

Parc de La Villette, 19th (01.42.09.01.09/ www.cabaretsauvage.com). M° Porte de la Villette. **Shows** days vary. **Admission** €12-€20. **Credit** MC, V. **Map** p403 inset.

Housed in an old circus venue, this mixture of tent, saloon and hall of mirrors provides a platform for contemporary jugglers and acrobats.

Cirque d'Hiver Bouglione

110 rue Amelot, 11th (01.47.00.28.81/www.cirque dhiver.com). M° Filles du Calvaire. **Shows** *Late Oct-late Feb* days vary. **Admission** €10-€39. **Credit** AmEx, MC, V. **Map** p409 L5.

Inaugurated in 1852, this traditional circus has been in the same family for seven decades. **Photo** *below.*

Cirque Pinder

Pelouse de Reuilly, Bois de Vincennes, 12th (01.45.90.21.25/www.cirquepinder.com). M° Porte Dorée or Porte de Charenton. **Shows** *Mid Nov-mid Jan* days vary. **Admission** €15-€40; free under-2s. **Credit** AmEx, DC, MC, V.

With horses, lions, elephants and monkeys, Pinder is the oldest and most traditional travelling circus in France. The final leg of its annual tour is the Christmas show at the Pelouse de Reuilly.

Espace Chapiteaux

Parc de La Villette, 19th (01.42.09.01.09/www. villette.com). M° Porte de la Villette. **Shows** days vary. **Admission** varies. **Credit** MC, V. **Map** p403 inset.

This big top hosts companies such as Cirque Plume, Cirque Vent d'Autan and aerialists Les Arts Saut.

Grand Céleste Cirque

22 rue Paul Meurice, 20th (01.53.19.99.13/ www.grandceleste.com). M° Porte des Lilas. **Open** Nov-end Feb. **Shows** 8.30pm Thurs, Fri, Sat; 4pm Sun. *Matinées* Wed, Fri, Sat, Sun (times vary). **Admission** €10-€26. **No credit cards.**

Three blue tents host this circus of traditional acts. If you fancy a go, circus courses are on offer.

Cirque d'Hiver Bouglione.

Children

Enjoy one of Europe's most family-friendly capitals.

The railway children: **Parc Zoologique de Paris**. *See p283.*

The city of high fashion and smoky bistros may not seem like the most family-friendly of destinations – in fact, Paris welcomes kids of all ages, with an impressive array of entertainment options geared towards *les p'tits*. And any notion that Parisians are standoffish will soon disappear under a barrage of praise and advice.

Most of the famous sights on any child's wish list can be ticked off without undue stress – although it may be wise to head for the **Eiffel Tower** (*see p160*) early in the morning, when the queues are less daunting. For a relaxing overview of the heart of the city, a boat trip down the Seine is hard to beat. The waterborne **Batobus** links eight prime sights, including the Eiffel Tower, the Louvre and Notre-Dame. *See p81* **Sightseeing from the Seine**.

Children are made welcome at most cafés and restaurants, where set mini-menus (€5-€8) are commonplace. Failing that, simple standbys such as a *croque-monsieur* or a crêpe should pass muster even with fussy eaters.

The city excels when it comes to parks and playgrounds; generations of Parisians have grown up among the sandpits, swings, puppet shows, pony rides and boating ponds of the **Luxembourg** and **Tuileries** gardens. *See p284* **Swings and roundabouts**.

Paris has become much more cycle- and skate-friendly in recent years, so you can take a spin *en famille* along the cycle lanes by the Seine and the Canal St-Martin. The RATP rents out hard-to-steal blue and white bikes, plus junior bikes and child seats, at a number of locations across the city (www.rouelibre.fr). For a day out in beautiful surroundings, the **Bois de Vincennes** (*see p116*) in the east and the **Bois de Boulogne** (*see p126*) in the west provide woodlands, picnic areas, boating lakes and cycle rental.

Gaps in the academic schedule – Wednesday afternoons, weekends and school holidays – are filled with all kinds of organised children's activities, ranging from museum workshops to special film screenings and theatre productions. Listings weeklies such as *Pariscope, L'Officiel des Spectacles* and *Télérama*'s *Sortir* supplement have children's sections; daily paper *Libération* also publishes a bi-monthly supplement for parents, *Paris-Mômes*.

GETTING AROUND

Parisian drivers can be fast and furious, so only cross at a zebra crossing – and stay alert even then. Turning traffic should give priority to pedestrians, but often doesn't. Keep an eye out for skaters, scooter-riders and motorcyclists speeding down narrow pavements.

Turnstiles, stairs and crowded carriages make negotiating the métro tricky with a pushchair. Travel between 10.30am and 4pm to avoid the crowds, or use the easier, driverless line 14 (Gare St-Lazare to Bibliothèque François Mitterrand) – a big hit with kids, who can sit at the front and peer down the tunnel as the train advances. The mostly overground lines 6 (Nation to Charles de Gaulle Étoile) and 2 (Nation to Porte Dauphine) offer attractive city views, and a number of RER stations have lifts.

It's often better to take the bus. Some, such as Nos.24 and 63 (www.ratp.fr) pass all the sights, and dozens are accessible with a pushchair. Some have four priority seats near the front for those travelling with under-fours, who go free on public transport. Four- to ten-year-olds qualify for a half-price *carnet* (a book of ten tickets) for all transport, including the Balabus tourist bus, Montmartrobus minibus and Montmartre funicular. Taxi drivers will generally take a family of four, as under-tens count as half; they charge €1 to carry a folding pushchair. If you're stuck miles from anywhere, try G7 taxis (01.41.27.66.99), with an English-speaking booking line.

HELP AND INFORMATION

The English-speaking support group Message (01.58.60.00.53, www.messageparis.org, annual membership €47) aims to provide a social network for parents and parents-to-be, and publishes the handy *ABCs of Motherhood in Paris* (€25 for non-members, €20 for members).

Babies & toddlers

Nappy-changing facilities are few and far between, so always pack a portable changing mat. A spot worth remembering is the WC chalet in the **Jardin du Luxembourg**, where €0.40 gives you access to loos with a padded changing table; the **Galeries Lafayette** and **Printemps** (*for both, see p237*) department stores have clean, well-equipped change rooms.

Breastfeeding in public places is often frowned upon in France, so you may have to feed *en plein air*, or in a quiet corner of a museum or restaurant. Take a scarf for places where modesty is essential.

A city break with tots in tow doesn't have to mean missing out on the city's galleries and museums. Almost all of the main attractions have child-friendly activities or green spaces nearby – handy as a reward for good behaviour, or if you're prepared to split into two groups. There's a carefully tended garden by **Notre-Dame** (*see p80*), for example, and even the quiet and dignified **Musée Rodin** (*see p157*) has its outdoor distractions, with a sandpit to dig in and sculpture-filled gardens to explore. And if the heady heights of the Eiffel Tower prove too daunting, more down-to-earth amusements can be found at the adjacent Champ de Mars, with its play areas and donkey rides. Alternatively, ride the carousel opposite the tower, at the foot of the Trocadéro gardens – one of many old-style merry-go-rounds dotted around the city.

Babysitting

The American Church in Paris

65 quai d'Orsay, 7th (01.40.62.05.00/www.ac paris.org). M° Invalides or Pont de l'Alma. **Open** 9am-10.30pm Mon-Sat; 2.30-7pm Sun. **Map** p405 E5. The free noticeboard inside the main entrance has 'situations wanted' ads from recommended English-speaking babysitters and au pairs, as well as others for rooms and useful services.

Baby Sitting Services

01.46.21.33.16/www.babysittingservices.com. **Open** 24hrs daily. *Office* 7am-9pm Mon-Fri; 7am-8pm Sat. **Rates** *Mon-Sat* 8am-10pm €6.80/hr; 10pm-8am €7.50/hr. *Sun* €8/hr + €11.90 fee. *Bank hols* €15.90/hr. €1/hr/child supplement for 3 or more children. **Credit** MC, V. Babysitting can be organised at two hours' notice. School pickup, outings, children's parties and long-term babysitting can also be arranged.

Activity museums

Egyptian mummies at the **Louvre** (*see pp85-91*), dinosaur skeletons at the Galeries de Paléontologie et d'Anatomie Comparée at the **Muséum National d'Histoire Naturelle**, flying machines at the **Musée de l'Air et de l'Espace** at Le Bourget (*see p173*), model boats at the **Musée National de la Marine**, the Planetarium at the **Palais de la Découverte** (*see p122*), the Argonaut submarine at **La Cité des Sciences et de l'Industrie** (*see p134*) – there's plenty to feed a child's imagination. Under-4s get in free at most museums, while under-13s pay half price. Several museums provide activity sheets and a handful offer children's workshops (in French) on Wednesday afternoons, at weekends and in the holidays. Most museums close on Mondays or Tuesdays.

At the Louvre the programme for kids is led by artists, architects and filmmakers, with workshops, readings and performances. Next

Arts & Entertainment

Cartoon capers

The two huge theme parks outside Paris – **Disneyland Paris** (*pictured*) 32km (20 miles) south-east and **Parc Astérix** 36km (22 miles) to the north – attract millions of visitors every year. The former draws families over from the UK by the bucketload, with a special direct Eurostar service laid on from London. Astérix, meanwhile, scores heavily with the domestic and European market. Astérix is cheaper and offers more educational benefits, but Disneyland Paris also boasts the Walt Disney Studios Park and white-knuckle rides of Adventureland and Frontierland. In turn, Astérix has hit back with Le Grand Splatch and Goudurix. While Disneyland Paris turns out thousands of satisfied customers every week, all the year round, Parc Astérix closes for winter; Disneyland Paris also comes into its own at Hallowe'en and Christmas, when there are parades and performances.

Split into neat historical sections (Ancient Greece, the Roman Empire, the Middle Ages and 19th-century Paris), Parc Astérix is full of variety and easy to get around. Thrill-seekers can defy gravity on Goudurix, Europe's largest rollercoaster with seven stomach-churning loop-the-loops, while younger kiddies will squirm to get wet on Le Grand Splatch log-flume. Astérix, Obélix and company hang out in the Gaul Village (an exact replica of Albert Uderzo's comic-book creation), which adjoins the Druid's Forest adventure playground and nearby magic school, where evil Romans have been turned into real pigmy goats. A jamboree of live acts pumps up the pace, with quality shows from dancing dolphins in the Théâtre de Poséidon to acrobatics and synchronised swimming inside the Roman Circus. The food in the park is reassuringly French; among the huge choice of eateries is the Rélais Gaullois canteen, with three courses for €11.

Disneyland Paris, one-fifth the size of Paris, comprises the main Disneyland park and adjacent film studio complex. Enter the studios via the Front Lot and head into Animation Courtyard for a lesson in cartoon production at Animagique, a 'black light' show based on cult moments from Disney classics. From there, the special-effects Studio Tram Tour in Production Courtyard takes you on to an imitation film set with real fireballs and cascading torrents of water. Daredevils should try the Rock 'n' Roller Coaster in the Back Lot, which hurtles round hairpin turns and loops to the sounds of Aerosmith. In the main park, little ones can enjoy Fantasyland, with Sleeping Beauty's fairy-tale castle; white-knuckle seekers will prefer Adventureland and Frontierland, with bone-shaking rides like Indiana Jones et le Temple du Péril.

The cartoon characters cavorting around the park are continually besieged by autograph hunters, and you won't get close to the most popular ones. Look out for any special appearances at the restaurants – times will be posted up inside. If you're short of time, get to the park early for a free Fastpass so you can queue-jump on most big rides.

For both Disneyland Paris and Parc Astérix, certain rides have height restrictions.

Disneyland Paris/ Walt Disney Studios Park
Marne-la-Vallée (08.25.30.60.30/UK 0870 503 0303/www.disneylandparis.com). RER A or TGV Marne-la-Vallée-Chessy. By car A4

---

door, the **Musée des Arts Décoratifs** (*see p97*) offers hands-on art workshops for ages four to 12, as well as special tours tailored to different age groups. The **Palais de Tokyo** (*see p123*) has inventive 'Tok Tok' workshops, often led by contemporary artists, and the Musée Rodin sets up children's clay-modelling workshops in August. The **Musée National Picasso** (*see p112*) offers family visits on Sundays, with children's workshops on Wednesdays in term-time that explore animal sculptures and pictures by the great man himself. **Paris Walks** (01.48.09.21.40, www.paris-walks.com) organises a series of child-friendly city strolls in the school holidays.

Centre Pompidou – Galerie des Enfants
Rue St-Martin, 4th (01.44.78.49.13/www.centre pompidou.fr). M° Rambuteau/RER Châtelet Les Halles. **Open** *Museum* 11am-10pm Mon, Wed-Sun. *Workshops* most Wed & Sat afternoons. **Admission** *Museum* €10; free under-18s. *Workshops* €10. **Credit** MC, V. **Map** p402 K5.
Lively, child-friendly exhibitions by top artists and designers introduce children to modern art, design and architecture, as well as hands-on workshops for six- to 12-year-olds, and family workshops one Sunday afternoon a month. Outside, look for the colourful Stravinsky fountain on the south side, designed by Niki de Saint-Phalle and Jean Tinguely, and the animated clock in the Quartier de l'Horloge

Metz-Nancy exit 14. **Open** *Sept-mid July* 10am-8pm Mon-Fri; 9am-8pm Sat, Sun. *Mid July-Aug* 9am-11pm daily. **Studios Park** *Winter* 10am-6pm Mon-Fri; 9am-6pm Sat, Sun. *Summer* 9am-6pm daily. All times may vary for public hols. **Admission** *Disneyland Park or Walt Disney Studio Park* €43; €35 3-11s; free under-3s. *One-day Hopper for both parks* €53; €45 3-11s; free under-3s. *Three-day Hopper* €115; €95 3-11s; free under-3s. **Credit** AmEx, MC, V. One-day tickets are valid for the main Park *or* the Studio Park; and for both only after 6pm in summer and 5pm in winter. They are also sold at UK Disney stores, and in Paris at

Fnac, Virgin Megastore (*see p243*) and at tourist offices. All-in one-day RER-Disneyland Paris tickets are sold at major stations. Hoppers for both parks are sold at the venue.

Parc Astérix

60128 Plailly (08.26.30.10.40/www.parc asterix.fr). RER B Roissy-Charles de Gaulle 1, then shuttle bus (9.30am-1.30pm, 4.30pm-closing time). By car A1 exit Parc Astérix. **Open** *Apr-Jun* 10am-6pm daily. *July-Aug* 9.30am-7pm daily. *Sep-Oct* 10am-6pm Wed, Sat, Sun. Closed Nov-Mar. Call ahead for extra closure dates. **Admission** €34; €24 3-11s; free under-3s. **Credit** MC, V.

on the piazza's north side: every hour, its man-size automaton Le Défenseur du Temps ('Defender of Time') valiantly fights off a crab, a dragon or a cockerel (and all three at midday and 6pm). *See p109.*

Cité des Enfants

Niveau 0, Cité des Sciences et de l'Industrie, 30 av Corentin-Cariou, 19th (01.40.05.80.00/www.cite-sciences.fr). M° Porte de la Villette. **Open** (90min visits) 10.30am, 12.30pm, 2.30pm, 4.30pm Tue-Sun. **Admission** €5 per session. **Credit** AmEx, MC, V. **Map** p403 inset.

Two vast hands-on discovery zones cater for three- to five-year-olds and five- to 12-year-olds at the Cité des Enfants, part of the vast Cité des Sciences et de l'Industrie (*see p134*). Highlights include the water

cascades (switch the points and watch the wheels spin) and a building site with foam blocks, wheelbarrows, cranes and pulleys. Older kids can try out the working TV studio or explore the walk-in anthill.

Musée Grévin

10 bd Montmartre, 9th (01.47.70.85.05/www.musee-grevin.com). M° Grands Boulevards. **Open** 10am-5.30pm (last admission 4.30pm) Mon-Fri; 10am-7pm (last admission 6pm) Sat, Sun & hols. **Admission** €17.50; €15.50 6-14s; free under-6s. **Credit** AmEx, DC, MC, V. **Map** p402 H4.

Paris' waxworks museum, opened in 1882, is home to more than 300 models of entertainers, artists, writers and historical figures, from Einstein to Arnold Schwarzenegger, Gandhi to Britney Spears, and

Elvis to Spiderman. You can also see a re-creation of Louis XIV's lavish wedding, or Neil Armstrong's first step on the moon. The renovated Palais de Mirages (Hall of Mirrors) was reopened in June 2006.

Musée National de la Marine
Palais de Chaillot, 17 place du Trocadéro, 16th (01.53.65.69.69/www.musee-marine.fr). M° Trocadéro. **Open** 10am-6pm Mon, Wed-Sun. **Admission** €8; €4 6-18s; free under-6s. **Credit** *Shop* MC, V. **Map** p400 B5.
If your children dream of adventure on the high seas, this maritime museum is for them. Highlights are a 20ft-tall model of the *Océan*, a 19th-century sailing vessel equipped with an impressive 120 cannons; a gilded barge built for Napoleon; and some extravagant, larger-than-life prow figures – from serene-faced angels to leaping seahorses. There are also dozens of model boats, dating from the 18th to the 20th century, plus a window through which you can watch the in-house restoration team at work. New for 2007 is an exhibition of toy boats. *See also p123.*

Muséum National d'Histoire Naturelle
36 rue Geoffroy-St-Hilaire, 8 rue Bouffon, 57 rue Cuvier, pl Valhubert, 5th (01.40.79.54.79/ www.mnhn.fr). M° Gare d'Austerlitz or Jussieu. **Open** 10am-6pm Mon, Wed-Fri, Sun (last admission 5.15pm); 10am-8pm Sat. **Admission** *Grande Galerie de l'Evolution* €8; €6 4-13s; free under-4s. *Galeries de Paléontologie et d'Anatomie Comparée* or *Galerie de Minéralogie et de Géologie.* €6; €4 4-13s; free under-4s. **No credit cards**. **Map** p406 K9.
The Grande Galerie de l'Evolution houses stuffed creatures shown to great effect in the lofty central forum, creating a Noah's Ark-like parade that also includes Louis XV's pet rhinoceros. The Salle de Découverte has temporary exhibitions, microscopes and interactive games, while hunks of meteorites and crystals occupy the Galerie de Minéralogie et de Géologie. The bony remains of fish, birds, monkeys, dinosaurs and humans are located in the Galerie de Paléontologie et d'Anatomie Comparée. You can also visit a modest menagerie (*see p283*) at this Jardin des Plantes complex (see *p284*).

Musée de la Poupée
Impasse Berthaud, 3rd (01.42.72.73.11/ www.museedelapoupeeparis.com). M° Rambuteau. **Open** 10am-6pm Tue-Sun. **Admission** €6; €3 3-18s; free under-3s. **No credit cards. Map** p406 L7.
This small private museum displays some 400 dolls (mostly of French origin) with their accompanying accessories and pets, arranged in thematic tableaux. Temporary exhibits, covering topics such as Barbie or dolls in regional costumes, are presented in the last three rooms. A shop and doll's hospital, run by doll doctor Véronique Derez, share the premises.

Aquaria, menageries & zoos

Cinéaqua
2 av des Nations Unies, 16th (01.40.69.23.23/www. cineaqua.com). M° Trocadéro. **Open** 10am-8pm daily. **Admission** €19.50; €15 students; €12 under-12s; free under-3s. **Credit** MC, V. **Map** p400 B5.
This superb new aquarium contains 500 fish and

Jardin du Luxembourg. *See p283.*

invertebrates, sharks and coral aplenty, plus a three-screen cinema. The problem is the price – a bone of contention when it opened in 2006. There are kids' clubs (ages three to ten) from 1pm to 4pm on Wednesdays, Saturdays and Sundays, a touch pool and set feeding times – 4pm is the sharks' tea party.

Ménagerie du Jardin des Plantes
57 rue Cuvier, 5th (01.40.79.37.94). Mº Jussieu, Place Monge or Gare d'Austerlitz. **Open** 9am-6pm Mon-Sat; 9am-6.30pm Sun. **Admission** €7; €5 4-16s, students; free under-4s. **Credit** AmEx, MC, V. **Map** p406 K8.
This small zoo was founded in 1794, when the Royal Ménagerie was moved here from Versailles. Its inhabitants include vultures, monkeys, orang-utans, reptiles, a century-old turtle and a lovely red panda.

Palais de la Porte Dorée Aquarium Tropical
293 av Daumesnil, 12th (01.44.74.84.80/www.palais-portedoree.org). Mº Porte Dorée. **Open** 10am-5.15pm Mon, Wed-Sun. **Admission** €5.50; €8 for an adult with children under-12; €4.20 4-25s; free under-4s.
This art deco palace houses the city aquarium and its colonial crocodiles, brought over from Dakar in 1948; other watery residents include cuttlefish, clownfish and sharks. Though the art from Africa and Oceania have been moved to the Musée du Quai Branly (*see p161*), you can still visit several of its main rooms. *See also p117.*

Parc de Thoiry
78770 Thoiry-en-Yvelines (01.34.87.53.76/www.thoiry.tm.fr). 45km (28 miles) west of Paris; by car A13, A12, then N12 direction Dreux until Thoiry. **Open** *Summer* 10.30am-6.30pm daily. *Winter* 11am-5pm daily. **Admission** Free under-3s. *Safari park* €22; €15 3-14s. *Château* €10; €7.40 3-14s. *Park & château* €26.50; €18.80 3-14s. **Credit** AmEx, MC, V.
A well as a fine château, the Parc de Thoiry houses one of Europe's first animal reserves. Inquisitive zebras rub their noses over your windscreen, lions stretch out in the shade, and bears amble down forest tracks. Rarities include Siberian lynx and Tonkean macaques. The park is only accessible by car; the ticket is valid for the zoo, maze and gardens.

Parc Zoologique de Paris
53 av de St-Maurice, 12th (01.44.75.20.00/www.mnhn.fr). Mº Porte Dorée. **Open** *Summer* 9am-6pm Mon-Sat; 9am-6.30pm Sun & bank hols. *Winter* 9am-5pm Mon-Sat; 9am-5.30pm Sun & bank hols. **Admission** €5; free under-4s. **Credit** MC, V.
More than 200 species can be seen at this spacious zoo in the heart of the Bois de Vincennes. Gibbons leap around the trees, baboons slide on the rocks, and human over-sevens can ascend the 65m (213ft) Grand Rocher – take the lift, or be prepared to climb 352 steps. Check the notice at the entrance for information about newborn animals and feeding times (especially for seals). If the walking gets too much, a miniature train tours the zoo. **Photo** *p278.*

Parks, gardens & views

You're allowed to sit on the grass and picnic in most Paris parks. Two pretty spots for an alfresco lunch are **Parc Monceau** (*see p124*) and **Parc Montsouris** (*see p168*). Most public gardens offer playgrounds with climbing frames, sandpits and concrete ping-pong tables; the **Tuileries** (*see p97*) contains trampolines, a carousel and ducks to feed, while at **place des Vosges** (*see p113*) there are wooden slides and rocking horses. Some parks, such as the one at the **Rond Point des Champs-Elysées** (*see p118*) have puppet shows at weekends and most Wednesday afternoons. The language might be hard to follow, but the enthusiastic audience participation is contagious.

If the queue at the Eiffel Tower is too much, there's always the pushchair-friendly **Tour Montparnasse** (*see p166*) – take the lift to the 56th floor, then another to the 59th. The ninth-floor terrace at the **Musée de l'Institut du Monde Arabe** (*see p146*) also has great views, as well as sticky treats served on mosaic-topped tables. You can also climb to giddy heights at the **Arc de Triomphe** (*see p121*) and **Notre-Dame** (*see p80*). For a more dynamic, stair-free ascent, the hot-air balloon at the **Parc André Citroën** (01.44.26.20.00, www.aeroparis.com; *see p161*), rises 150m every half-hour, from 9am till dusk. It costs €12/€6/€4, free under-3s.

Jardin d'Acclimatation
Bois de Boulogne, 16th (01.40.67.90.82/www.jardindacclimatation.fr). Mº Les Sablons. **Open** *June-Sept* 10am-7pm daily. *Oct-May* 10am-6pm daily. **Admission** €2.70; €1.35 concessions; free under-3s. **Credit** (€15 minimum) MC, V.
Founded in 1860, its opening presided over by Napoleon III, this amusement park and garden has bears, a Normandy-style farm and an aviary, as well as boat rides, a Chinese dragon rollercoaster and the Enchanted House for children aged two to four. Older kids can visit the interactive Explor@dome, designed by San Francisco's Exploratorium (€5/€4), or try out the mini racetrack and minigolf. Many of the attractions cost €2.50 (€30 for 15); others are free. A miniature train (€5.20/€3.85 including entrance fee) runs from Porte Maillot through the Bois de Boulogne to the park entrance. The peaceful Chinese teahouse is open only at weekends, offering a menu of eight different blends.

Jardin du Luxembourg
Pl Edmond-Rostand, pl Auguste-Comte or rue de Vaugirard, 6th (01.42.34.23.89/www.paris.fr). Mº Odéon or St-Sulpice/RER Luxembourg. **Open** *Summer* 7.30am-dusk daily. *Winter* 8am-dusk daily. **Map** p405 H8.
The biggest and best play area on the Left Bank, with an imaginative playground (€2.50 for children, €1.50 for accompanying adults), a merry-go-round,

Swings and roundabouts

There is a playground around every corner all over Paris. Built as much for adults as for children, they provide fresh air, space and relative calm for beleaguered parents and nannies, while the kids play in the sand or swoop down the slide.

Swings are few and far between – though you will find industrial-looking metal ones at the **Jardin du Luxembourg** (*see p283*), the **Parc Monceau** (*see p124*) and square des Batignolles (17th), hired from and powered by an attendant (€1.40/5mins).

For older ones, there is a more challenging playground at the Jardin du Luxembourg (*pictured*), which includes a huge jungle gym spider web (€2.50, €1.50 for adults). At the Jardin des Enfants at the Jardin des Halles (porte St-Eustache, M° Rambuteau, free, closed Mondays), a fantastical multi-sensory playground designed by sculptor Claude Lalanne for the sevens to 11s, visits begin on the hour and adults are not allowed in. At the **Jardin des Tuileries** (*see p97*) there is a charming playground with tubular structures, a swinging carousel and various devices that are hard to climb onto or stay on, plus a set of trampolines a little further west (€2/5min). At the **Jardin d'Acclimatation** (*see p283*) in the Bois de Boulogne, attractions include a water ride, rollercoaster and mini racing circuit.

For the younger set, the most magical ride is still the carousel or *manège* – and there are plenty to choose from. At €2 per ride it isn't a cheap proposition, but it is a delight and comes in many varieties. Near the **Eiffel Tower** (*see p160*) alone there are three: one whirling enticingly near the waiting lines at the foot of the tower; a beautiful double-decker affair by the **Trocadéro**, just across the river; and, most charming of all, a hand-cranked antique carousel at the south end of the **Champ de Mars**, with hand-painted horses named Rocky and Dora and rings to be caught with a wooden baguette.

Indeed, you'll find *manèges* in all of the major parks. Some, like the one near the porte Lescot in the Jardin des Halles, seem dwarfed by their urban setting, but most of them, such as the ones at the foot of the **Sacré-Cœur** (*see p131*) or in the Jardin des Tuileries, have an enchanted feel. The Dodo *manège* at the **Jardin des Plantes** (*see p284*) is also worth a spin – it features extinct animals instead of horses. At Christmas the Mairie de Paris sets up free carousels around the city, including one at the **Hôtel de Ville** (*see p109*), with helicopters and motorcycles in place of galloping steeds.

Unlike carousels in the UK, French *manèges* rotate counter-clockwise – handy for right-handed kids to spear the dangling rings.

pony rides, marionette shows, tennis courts and, in summer, a toy boating pond – hiring a model boat costs €2 for half an hour. *See above* **Swings and roundabouts**. Photo *p282*.

Jardin des Plantes

57 rue Cuvier or pl Valhubert, 5th (01.40.79.30.00/ www.mnhn.fr). M° Gare d'Austerlitz or Jussieu. **Open** *Summer* 7.30am-8pm daily. *Winter* 7.30am-5.30pm daily. **Map** p406 K9.

France's main botanical garden is surrounded by a small zoo (*see p283*) and the three museums that make up the Musée National d'Histoire Naturelle (*see p282*). There are playgrounds, stalls and constantly changing plant life, including hundreds of varieties of flowers, grasses and alpine plants, most of them labelled with their Latin names. The garden first opened its gates to the public in 1640, and its rich history is very much in evidence: the maze dates back to 1739; the bears' dens to 1805.

Arts & Entertainment

Parc des Buttes-Chaumont
Rue Botzaris, rue Manin or rue de Crimée, 19th.
M° Buttes Chaumont. **Open** *Oct-Apr* 7am-8.15pm
daily. *May, mid Aug-Sept* 7am-9.15pm daily. *June-mid Aug* 7am-10.15pm daily. **Map** p403 N2.
Set on the site of a disused lime quarry, the park was
created in the 1860s. Views over the city are superb,
and there are man-made grottoes and waterfalls to
explore, plus a playground, puppet shows and car-riage and pony rides in summer. *See p138.*

Parc Floral
Bois de Vincennes, 12th (01.43.28.41.59).
*M° Château de Vincennes, then 10min walk or bus
112.* **Open** 9.30am-dusk daily. **Admission** *Mon-Fri*
€1; €0.50 7-25s; free under-7s. *Sat, Sun* €3; €1.50
7-25s; free under-7s. **No credit cards.**
The miniature train (€1.50) is just one outstanding
feature of this verdant park, one of the city's best
play areas for children of all ages. There's a nature
resource centre and butterfly garden, plus a huge
adventure playground with any number of slides,
swings and climbing frames. Older kids will enjoy the
Parisian-themed minigolf course and pedal-powered
carriages. Wednesday afternoons bring free theatre
shows, suitable for threes to tens. *See p116.*

Parc de La Villette
*211 av Jean-Jaurès, 19th (01.40.03.75.03/www.
villette.com). M° Porte de Pantin or Porte de la
Villette.* **Open** 6am-1am daily. **Map** p403 inset.
Part of the redeveloped Villette canal basin, this is
a series of themed gardens. Quirky attractions
include an 80m-long dragon, whose tongue forms a
huge slide, and the Jardin des Miroirs, a bizarre land-scape of trees and giant mirrors. Strangest of all is
the other-worldly Garden of Childhood Fears,
designed to recreate a fairy-tale forest – visitors
walk through rustling silver birch and blue spruce
trees, while spooky music plays. *See p136.*

Entertainment & sports

Funfairs are a perennial pleasure, the best
being **La Fête à Neu-Neu** (Bois de Boulogne,
autumn) and the **Foire du Trône** (Bois de
Vincennes, spring). In summer, **La Fête des
Tuileries** offers views from the big wheel,
along with other rides. Other family-friendly
events include the **Chinese New Year** parade
in February, the outdoor **Fête de la Musique**
on 21 June and, in July and August, **Quartier
d'Eté** (www.quartierdete.com), when the city's
parks host music, dance, cinema and theatre
events. **Bastille Day** (14 July) brings a parade,
aerial military fly-past and fireworks display;
with Christmas come cute window displays at
the city's department stores, free carousels and
outdoor skating rinks at the Eiffel Tower, the
Hôtel de Ville and Montparnasse. Traditional
circuses (*see p277*) come to town each year.
See also pp270-274 **Festivals & Events.**

Fables, fairy tales and folk stories from all
over francophone Africa are favourites at
children's shows at the city's theatres and *café-théâtres* on Wednesday afternoons, at weekends
and in the holidays. The varied programme of
theatre, dance and musical creations at the
Théâtre Dunois (7 rue Louise-Weiss, 13th,
01.45.84.72.00, www.theatredunois.org) is
specifically geared towards children and young
people. Look for listings in *Pariscope* and on the
last page of *Télérama*'s *Sortir* supplement.
Children's films are generally dubbed into
French, but you can see VO (*version originale*)
screenings of the latest Hollywood hits at
dozens of cinemas across town (*see pp289-294*
Film). Keep a lookout for children's showings
on Wednesdays and Saturday afternoons at the
Cinémathèque Française (*see p291*). The
IMAX cinema in La Villette's **Géode** (*see p290*)
will keep kids goggle-eyed and enthralled.
Paris is good for watery entertainment
too. The 35 public pools (www.paris.fr) include
the new **Piscine Josephine-Baker** (*see
p337*), moored on the Seine and filled with
purified water pumped from the river. A less
sophisticated but popular alternative is the
indoor **Aquaboulevard** (*see p337*), where
over-threes can splash down different slides
and ride the waves. In summer, **Paris-Plage**
(*see p272* **Take me to the river**) sees a
plunge pool installed by the Seine along with
2,000 tonnes of sand. For details of all sports
activities, *see pp330-338* **Sport & Fitness.**

Theme parks

Two theme parks tower over the others:
Disneyland Paris and **Parc Astérix**. *See
p280* **Cartoon capers.** Lesser-known ones
include the Wild West-themed **La Mer de
Sable** ('the Sea of Sand'; €17/€14 3-11s,
03.44.54.18.44, www.merdesable.fr), France's
first theme park. Current attractions include
water rides and a big wheel, plus a more sedate
miniature train and carousels for smaller
visitors – not to mention the bison and camel
farm. For more modern-day entertainment,
head out to **Futuroscope** (€31/€24 5-16s,
www.futuroscope.com), which provides 3D
cinemas, simulators rides and games. Located
near Poitiers, it's an 80-minute TGV ride from
Gare Montparnasse. Tickets aren't cheap, but
if you visit after 5pm the price comes down
considerably. If you hanker after more simple
(and inexpensive) pleasures, spend an afternoon
at the **Playmobil FunPark**, where children
invent their own games in the 12 themed zones
(22-24 rue des Jachères, ZA La Cerisaie, 94260
Fresnes, €1.50/free under-3s, 01.49.84.94.44,
www.playmobil.com).

Dance

Spectacular contemporary dance keeps Paris on its toes.

Centre de Danse du Marais. *See p288*.

Although the sumptuous ballet productions at the **Opéra Garnier** and international ballet companies at **Châtelet** will always delight audiences, it is in the contemporary scene that Paris currently shines. Opened in 2004, the prestigious **Centre National de la Danse** outside the city centre in Pantin has given France an impressive HQ for its 600-plus regional dance companies and welcomes international big names, with the emphasis firmly on new creation.

Older but no less daring contemporary dance venues pepper the city, the most respected being **Théâtre de la Ville**. At **Chaillot**, meanwhile, the programme is packed with global names and choreographed versions of popular dance forms such as tango or flamenco. Festivals play a large part in the roster of big-name appearances; dancers from the Alvin Ailey American Dance Theater were the guests of honour at 2006's open-air **Les Etés de la Danse** in the gardens of the National Archives. Look out too for the three-month long **Festival d'Automne**, which has long-standing links with Merce Cunningham and William Forsythe.

For would-be performers there are masses of dance classes, from ballet through oriental to hip hop. Finally, the open-air salsa and tango dancing on the Left Bank offers a chance for anyone who fancies kicking up their heels on a summer night.

INFORMATION AND RESOURCES

For listings, see *Pariscope* and *L'Officiel des Spectacles*, and the *Aden* supplement in *Le Monde*. For events coverage, look out for two monthlies: *La Terrasse* (distributed free at major dance venues) and the glossy *Danser*.

For shoes and equipment, **Repetto** (22 rue de la Paix, 2nd, 01.44.71.83.12) supplies the Opéra with pointes and slippers; **Menkes** (12 rue Rambuteau, 3rd, 01.40.27.91.81) sells serious flamenco gear as well as outsize glam-rock boots.

Festivals

Every season sees some kind of contemporary dance festival in or near Paris. The year starts with **Faits d'Hiver** (www.faitsdhiver.com) in January; May/June welcomes the **Rencontres Chorégraphiques de Seine-St-Denis** (www.rencontreschoregraphiques.com) and the **IRCAM Agora festival** (www.ircam.fr). **Onze Bouge** (www.festivalonze.org) in June is followed by the street-dance **Rencontres de la Villette** (www.rencontresvillette.com) at various surburban locations every October. You will find smaller dance festivals at the **Maison des Arts de Créteil**, as well as the **Ménagerie de Verre** in the 11th. *See also pp270-274* **Festivals & Events**.

Les Etés de la Danse

Hôtel Rohan, 60 rue des Francs-Bourgeois, 3rd (www.lesetesdeladanse.com). M° Hôtel de Ville or Rambuteau. **Dates** *July.*

Created in 2005, this festival puts the spotlight on one company or choreographer, with a month of performances in the atmospheric open-air setting of a *hôtel particulier* in the Marais.

Paris quartier d'été

01.44.94.98.00/www.quartierdete.com. **Dates** *July-Aug.*

This festival features eclectic programmes and free outdoor performances. Public rehearsals and talks give audiences the chance to meet prestigious international choreographers.

Festival d'Automne

01.53.45.17.00/www.festival-automne.com. **Dates** *Sept-Dec.*

For 35 years, the Festival d'Automne has shown the way forward in the performing arts. Performances are highbrow and experimental, with works by big-name choreographers as well as newcomers.

Major dance venues

Centre National de la Danse

1 rue Victor-Hugo, 93507 Pantin (01.41.83.27.27/ box office 01.41.83.98.98/www.cnd.fr). M° Hoche/ RER Pantin. **Open** *Box office* 10am-7pm Mon-Fri. **Admission** €6-€14. **Credit** AmEx, MC, V.

This impressive new centre aims to break down the barriers between dancers and audience. Performances are in studios rather than on a stage, and dancers and choreographers hang out in the communal areas between rehearsals. There's a phenomenal archive of films and choreographic material too. **Photo** *p288.*

Maison des Arts de Créteil

Pl Salvador-Allende, 94000 Créteil (01.45.13.19.19/ www.maccreteil.com). M° Créteil-Préfecture. **Open** *Box office* 1-7pm Tue-Sat. Closed mid July-Aug. **Admission** €8-€30. **Credit** MC, V.

Ballet Angelin Preljocaj and dancers from the Kathlehong township in South Africa are highlights for 2007 at this arts centre in the suburbs. Don't miss the Festival International Exit in the spring.

Palais Garnier

Pl de l'Opéra, 9th (08.92.89.90.90/www.opera-de-paris.fr). M° Opéra. **Open** *Box office* 11am-6pm Mon-Sat. *Telephone bookings* 9am-6pm Mon-Sat.

Closed 15 July-end Aug. **Admission** €7-€160. *Concessions* 1hr before show. **Credit** AmEx, MC, V. **Map** p401 G4.

The Ballet de l'Opéra National de Paris manages to tread successfully between tutu classics and new productions, between the Opéra Bastille (*see p311*) and lavish Palais Garnier, where the renovated grand foyer is a must-see. *Giselle, Copelia* and Nureyev's *Don Quichotte* and *Cinderella* are joined by contemporary work by Robyn Orlin in 2007.

Théâtre National de Chaillot

1 pl du Trocadéro, 16th (01.53.65.30.00/www. theatre-chaillot.fr). M° Trocadéro. **Open** *Box office* 11am-7pm Mon-Sat; 1-5pm Sun. *Telephone bookings* 11am-7pm Mon-Sat. Closed July-Aug. **Admission** €27-€33; €12-€27 concessions. **Credit** MC, V. **Map** p400 C5.

Tango fanatic Ariel Goldenberg always pulls together an exciting international dance programme at Chaillot. Hiroaki Umeda, Béatrice Masson's baroque dance and Abou Lagraa's hip-hop-influenced choreography are among the offerings in 2007.

Théâtre de la Ville – Les Abbesses

2 pl du Châtelet, 4th (01.42.74.22.77/www.theatre delaville-paris.com). M° Châtelet. **Open** *Box office* 11am-8pm Mon-Sat. *Telephone bookings* 11am-7pm Mon-Sat. Closed July & Aug. **Admission** €12-€23; €12 under-28s. **Credit** MC, V. **Map** p404 J6.

This leading contemporary dance venue has become a showcase for established choreographers; Akram Khan and Meg Stuart will visit in 2006-2007, and Pina Bausch in June. Book early: most shows sell out well before opening night. Sister venue Théâtre des Abbesses specialises in classical Indian performers. **Other locations**: Théâtre des Abbesses, 31 rue des Abbesses, 18th (01.42.74.22.77).

Other dance venues

L'Etoile du Nord

16 rue Georgette-Agutte, 18th (01.42.26.47.47). M° Guy Môquet. **Open** *Box office* 1-6pm Mon-Fri. Closed July-Aug. **Admission** €19; €10-€14 concessions. **Credit** V.

Provides a welcome platform for the contemporary multimedia dance scene.

Ménagerie de Verre

12-14 rue Léchevin, 11th (01.43.38.33.44/ www.menagerie-de-verre.org). M° Parmentier. **Open** *Box office* 1-7pm Mon-Fri. Closed July-Aug. **Admission** €13; €10 concessions. **No credit cards. Map** p403 N5.

This multidisciplinary hothouse is rooted in the avant-garde, with contemporary dance and classes. It also hosts bi-annual festival Les Inaccoutumés.

Regard du Cygne

210 rue de Belleville, 20th (01.43.58.55.93/redcygne. free.fr). M° Télégraphe. **Open** *Box office* 1hr before show. Closed Aug. **Admission** €6-€15. **No credit cards. Map** p403 Q3.

Arts & Entertainment

This picturesque, pared-down studio in Belleville is one of the capital's few alternative spaces. Pieces are original and often experimental, and its Spectacles Sauvages nights allow unknowns to show a ten-minute piece to the public.

Théâtre de la Bastille
76 rue de la Roquette, 11th (01.43.57.42.14/www. theatre-bastille.com). M° Bastille or Voltaire. **Open** *Box office* 10am-6pm Mon-Fri; 2-6pm Sat. Closed July-Aug. **Admission** €13-€20. **Credit** MC, V. **Map** p407 M6.
Small theatre showcasing innovative contemporary dance and drama pieces.

Théâtre du Châtelet
1 pl du Châtelet, 1st (01.40.28.28.00/www. chateletheatre.com). M° Châtelet. **Open** *Box office* Sept-June 11am-7pm daily. *July, Aug* 1-6pm daily. **Admission** from €10. **Credit** AmEx, MC, V. **Map** p402 J5.
A classical music institution across the square from the Théâtre de la Ville (*see p342*), Châtelet indulges dance audiences every year with international acts such as American Ballet Theatre (in February) and Les Ballets de Monte Carlo (in mid June). French regional ballets also receive regular invites.

Théâtre de la Cité Internationale
21 bd Jourdan, 14th (01.43.13.50.50/www.theatre delacite.com). RER Cité Universitaire. **Open** *Box office* 2-7pm Mon-Fri. *Telephone bookings* 2-7pm Mon-Sat. Closed July-Aug. **Admission** €21; €7.50-€12.50 concessions; €14 for all Mon. **Credit** MC, V.
A well-established contemporary dance venue at the Cité Universitaire, hosting shows, workshops and other festive events.

Dance classes & events

Centre de Danse du Marais
41 rue du Temple, 4th (01.42.72.15.42/ 08.92.68.68.70/www.parisdanse.com). M° Rambuteau or Hôtel de Ville. **Open** 9am-9pm Mon-Fri; 9am-8pm Sat; 9am-7pm Sun. **Classes** €18. **Map** p402 K5.
There's a huge choice of classes here, with big-name teachers such as belly-dance star Leila Haddad and ballet's Casati-Lazzarelli team. The five-class 'sampler' pass is a good deal at €68. **Photo** *p286.*

Centre Momboye
25 rue Boyer, 20th (01.43.58.85.01/www.momboye. com). M° Gambetta. **Open** 9am-10.30pm daily. **Classes** €14-€15. **Map** p403 P4.
This is the only centre devoted entirely to African dance, taught to live drumming. There's hip hop too.

Dance on the banks of the Seine
Jardins Tino Rossi, 5th. M° Austerlitz. Daily from 7pm May-Sept. Free.
In summer, the amphitheatres of this Seine-side park fill up with salsa, rock, tango, Irish, hip hop and just about any other dance form you can think of. Informal classes are held around 7 or 8pm, then the *bal* begins.

Studio Harmonic
5 passage des Taillandiers, 11th (01.48.07.13.39/ www.studioharmonic.fr). M° Bastille. **Open** *Office* 10am-5pm Mon-Fri. *Classes* 9.30am-10pm Mon-Fri; 9am-7.30pm Sat. Closed 3wks Aug. **Classes** €15. **Map** p407 M7.
The rising star among Paris dance schools, Studio Harmonic's claim to fame is teacher Laure Courtellemont and her trademark raggajam, a blend of hip hop and Afro-Caribbean dance.

Centre National de la Danse. See p287.

Film

A city of silver screens.

La Géode. *See p290.*

Cinema-going is a serious pastime in Paris. More tickets per capita are bought here than anywhere else in Europe and, in any given week, there's a choice of around 230 movies – not counting festivals. If the city's cinematic landscape is constantly evolving, the overall picture remains healthy. Paris now possesses more screens than ever, thanks to the opening of the **MK2 Quai de Loire**, not to mention the **UGC Ciné-Cité** at La Défense. In 2006, the UGC Convention and the Gaumont Grand Ecran Italie (once the city's biggest screen) closed due to competition from multiplexes.

In Paris, multiplexes regularly show films from Eastern Europe, Asia and South America, while countless independent cinemas continue to screen a hugely eclectic assortment of cult, classic and just plain obscure films. As well as retrospectives and cut-price promotions, there are often visits from a major director or star.

The city's enduring passion for cinema is reciprocated by the film industry, with some 662 crews shooting movies here in 2005 alone. A recent ministerial decision to boost tourism via the movies and grant unprecedented access to historical monuments has also helped to entice Hollywood filmmakers. Beneficiaries

of the new policy have so far included Sophia Coppola, who filmed *Marie-Antoinette* at Versailles, and Ron Howard, who shot scenes from *The Da Vinci Code* inside the Louvre.

Local interest is large enough to sustain a small avalanche of monthly movie magazines and there's an entire book fair, the **Salon du Livre de Cinéma et du DVD**, devoted to writing on film. Meanwhile, French DVD labels produce some of the most expertly curated discs in the world. Take a look at the extensive film sections of **Fnac** or **Virgin Megastore** (for both, *see p243*) and you're more than likely to find American and British titles otherwise unavailable in the US or UK.

INFORMATION AND TICKETS

New releases, sometimes 15 or more, hit the screens on Wednesdays. Hollywood is well represented, of course, but Paris audiences have a balanced cinematic diet that includes an insatiable appetite for international films as well as shorts and documentaries. On top of this there are the 150-plus annual releases funded or part-funded with French money (the French film industry is still the world's third largest, after the US and India).

Arts & Entertainment

For venues, times and prices, consult one of the city's two main weekly listings mags: *L'Officiel des Spectacles* and *Pariscope*. *Films nouveaux* are new releases, *Exclusivités* are the also-showing titles, and *Reprises* means rep. For non-francophone flicks, look out for two letters somewhere near the title: VO (*version originale*) means a screening in the original language with French subtitles; VF (*version française*) means that it has been dubbed into French.

Buy tickets in the usual way at the cinema – for new blockbusters, especially at multiplexes, it pays to buy tickets at least one screening in advance. You can also phone **AlloCiné** (08.92.89.28.92, www.allocine.fr). Online booking may entail a booking fee. Seats are often discounted by 20 to 30 per cent at Monday or Wednesday screenings, and the Mairie sponsors cut-price promotions throughout the year (*see p292* **Summer film festivals**).

All multiplex chains offer *cartes illimitées,* season tickets that allow unlimited access.

Cinemas

Giant screens & multiplexes

La Géode
26 av Corentin-Cariou, 19th (08.92.68.45.40/www. lageode.fr). M° Porte de la Villette. **Admission** €9; €7 under-25s. **Credit** MC, V. **Map** p403 inset.
The IMAX cinema at the Cité des Sciences occupies a shiny geodesic sphere. The huge 1,000sq m hemispheric screen lets you experience 3D plunges through natural scenery, and animated adventures where figures zoom out to grab you. **Photo** *p289.*

Le Grand Rex
1 bd Poissonnière, 2nd (08.92.68.05.96/www. legrandrex.com). M° Bonne Nouvelle. **Admission** €9; €7 students, over-60s; €5.95 under-12s. *Les Etoiles du Rex tour* €7.50; €6.50 under-12s; €5.50 for all 5-7pm. **Credit** MC, V. **Map** p402 J4.
With its wedding-cake exterior, fairy-tale interior and the largest auditorium in Europe (2,750 seats), this is one of the few cinemas to upstage whatever it screens: no wonder it's a listed historic monument. Its blockbuster programming (usually in French) is suited to its vast, roll-down screen; it also hosts concerts and rowdy all-night compilation events. There are six smaller screens too. The Etoiles du Rex tour is a 50-minute, SFX-laden taste of movie magic.

Max Linder Panorama
24 bd Poissonnière, 9th (08.92.68.00.31/www.max linder.com). M° Grands Boulevards. **Admission** €8.50; €6.50 Mon, Wed, Fri, students (except weekends), under-12s. **Credit** MC, V. **Map** p402 J3.
This state-of-the-art cinema (THX surround sound and an 18m screen) is named after the dapper French silent comedian who owned it between 1914 and

1925. The walls and 700 seats are all black to prevent even the tiniest twinkle of reflected light distracting the audience from what's happening on the screen. Look for all-nighters and one-off showings of rare vintage films or piano-accompanied silents.

MK2 Bibliothèque
128-162 av de France, 13th (08.92.69.84.84/www. mk2.com). M° Bibliothèque François Mitterrand or Quai de la Gare. **Admission** €9-€9.20; €6.70 (Mon-Fri before 6pm) students, 12s-18s; €5.50 under-12s; €5.10 before noon; €19.80 monthly pass. **Credit** MC, V. **Map** p407 M10.
The MK2 chain's flagship offers an all-in-one night out: 14 screens, three restaurants, a bar open until 5am at weekends and two-person 'love seats'. A paragon of imaginative programming, MK2 is growing all the time; it has added ten more venues in town, two along the Bassin de la Villette with waterside cafés. For €19.80 a month, its Le Pass card is excellent value, offering film buffs unlimited screenings at any MK2, Pathé or Gaumont venue, as well as some independents.

UGC Ciné Cité Bercy
2 cour St-Emilion, 12th (08.36.68.68.58/www.ugc.fr). M° Cour St-Emilion. **Admission** €9.20; €6.50 students, over-60s; €5.50 under-12s; €18 monthly pass. **Credit** MC, V. **Map** p407 N10.
This ambitious 18-screen development screens art movies and mainstream fodder, and hosts regular meet-the-director events. The 19-screen UGC Ciné Cité Les Halles original (7 pl de la Rotonde, Nouveau Forum des Halles, 1st, 08.92.70.00.00) serves the same mix. The UGC Illimitée card provides all-you-can-watch access for €18 per month; new applicants pay a non-refundable €30 handling fee. **Photo** *p291.*

Showcases

Auditorium du Louvre
Musée du Louvre, 99 rue de Rivoli, 1st (01.40.20. 55.55/www.louvre.fr). M° Palais Royal Musée du Louvre. **Admission** €8.50; €3.50 under-26s; free under-18s. **Credit** MC, V. **Map** p402 H5.
This 420-seat auditorium was designed by IM Pei. Film screenings are often related to the exhibitions; silent movies with live music are regulars.

Centre Pompidou
Rue St-Martin, 4th (01.44.78.12.33/www.centre pompidou.fr). M° Hôtel de Ville or Rambuteau. **Admission** €10; €8 students. **Credit** MC, V. **Map** p406 K6.
The varied programme here features themed series, experimental and artists' films, and a weekly documentary session. This is also the venue for the Cinéma du Réel festival; held in March, it champions documentary films (www.cinereel.org).

Le Cinéma des Cinéastes
7 av de Clichy, 17th (01.53.42.40.20). M° Place de Clichy. **Admission** €8.50; €6.80 students, under-12s, over-60s. **Credit** MC, V. **Map** p401 G2.

Done out to evoke the studios of old, this three-screen showcase of world cinema holds meet-the-director sessions and festivals of classic, foreign, gay and documentary films. Also offers a monthly pass.

La Cinémathèque Française

*51 rue de Bercy, 12th (01.71.19.33.33/www.
cinematheque.fr). M° Bercy.* **Admission** *Permanent
exhibitions* €2.50-€3. *Temporary exhibitions* €7-€9;
€6 under-12s. *Films* €6; €5 students, 13s-18s; €3
under-12s; free for members. *Membership* €10/month.
Credit MC, V. **Map** p407 N9.
Relocated to Frank Gehry's striking, spacious cubist building in 2005, the Cinémathèque Française now boasts four screens, a bookshop, a restaurant, a temporary exhibition space and the Musée du Cinéma, where it displays a fraction of its prolific collection of movie memorabilia. In the spirit of its founder Henri Langlois, the Cinémathèque hosts major retrospectives, cult movies, classics, experimental cinema and Q&A sessions with directors.

Forum des Images

*2 Grande Galerie, Porte St-Eustache, Forum des
Halles, 1st (01.44.76.62.00/www.forumdesimages.
net). M° Les Halles.* **Open** 1-9pm Tue-Sun. Closed
2wks Aug. **Admission** (per day) €5.50; €4.50
students, under-26s. Membership available.
Credit AmEx, MC, V. **Map** p402 J5.
Following a major facelift, the hyperactive Forum des Images reopens in February 2007. The new, open layout makes it easier to move between spaces: a film archive dedicated to Paris on celluloid; a photo library; and four auditoriums, screening a thought-provoking, entertaining programme of films grouped around such themes as 'Gangsters' or 'Death'. A new addition is the François Truffaut library, where users are able to consult both books and DVDs. The Forum hosts Les Rencontres, the trash treats of L'Etrange Festival, films from the critics' favourites at Cannes, and Pocket Films, a festival of films shot on mobile phones.

Arthouses

Accattone

*20 rue Cujas, 5th (01.46.33.86.86). M° Cluny La
Sorbonne/RER Luxembourg.* **Admission** €7; €6
Wed, students, under-20s (except Fri nights and
weekends). **No credit cards. Map** p408 J8.
Named after Pasolini's first film, this tiny Latin Quarter cinema has a clear preference for old Italian arthouse. That said, there's still plenty of room on the rolling weekly programme of around 30 films for the likes of Buñuel, Oshima, Roeg and Ken Russell. In the 1960s the cinema was managed by none other than François Truffaut.

Action

Action Christine *4 rue Christine, 6th
(01.43.29.11.30). M° Odéon or St-Michel.*
Admission €7.50; €6 students, under-20s.
No credit cards. Map p408 J7.

UGC Ciné Cité Bercy. *See p290.*

Action Ecoles *23 rue des Ecoles, 5th
(01.43.29.79.89). M° Maubert Mutualité.*
Admission €7.50; €6 students, under-20s.
No credit cards. Map p408 J8.
Grand Action *5 rue des Ecoles, 5th
(01.43.29.44.40/www.legrandaction.com). M°
Cardinal Lemoine.* **Admission** €8; €6.50 students,
under-20s. **No credit cards. Map** p406 K8.
A Left Bank stalwart, the Action group is renowned for screening new prints of old movies. With a programme that might range from *Annie Hall* to *Citizen Kane*, it's heaven for anyone who's nostalgic for Tinseltown classics and quality US independents.

Le Balzac

*1 rue Balzac, 8th (01.45.61.10.60/www.cinema
balzac.com). M° George V.* **Admission** €8; €6 Mon,
Wed, students, under-18s, over-60s. **No credit
cards. Map** p400 D4.
Built in 1935 and boasting a mock ocean-liner foyer, Le Balzac scores highly both for design and programming. Jean-Jacques Schpoliansky, the ever-genial manager, is often found welcoming punters in person at the start of each screening. The Balzac recently acquired a digital projector, and awards prizes according to audience votes. It now accepts the UGC Illimité card.

Le Champo

*51 rue des Ecoles, 5th (01.43.54.51.60).
M° Cluny La Sorbonne or Odéon.* **Admission**
€7.50; €6 Wed, last screening Sun, lunchtime
matinées, students, under-20s. **No credit cards.**
Map p408 J7.

Summer film festivals

range from classic Hollywood to modern arthouse, and they are all screened in the original language with French subtitles. The theme in 2006 was 'Men and Beasts', and included films as varied as *Batman Returns*, *The Birds* and Pedro Almodóvar's *Matador*.

More free outdoor movie-going is on offer during **Cinéma au Clair de Lune**, providing the chance to watch Paris-based movies, often in the areas they were filmed or are set. Organised by the Forum des Images, this festival brings its giant screen to a host of different parks and squares across the city during August. Similarly to Cinéma Plein Air, movies begin at nightfall.

The Mairie de Paris, meanwhile, offers up over 400 films at €4 and many more for free during its two week-long **Paris Cinéma**. This July festival includes short films, *avant-premières*, retrospectives and yet more free open-air projections; it also screens the odd French film with English subtitles. A splattering of stars is at hand to introduce some movies. One noteworthy innovation of the festival is CinéRando. These guided or self-guided city walks allow you to discover parts of Paris that have served as backdrops for famous movie scenes.

To ease punters into the summer festivals, the **Fête du Cinéma** in June offers film buffs a three-day-long promotion of unlimited movies at the entry price of €2 per film. Most cinemas in Paris participate, and the only catch is that you have to buy one full-priced ticket to benefit from the offer. Similarly, **3 jours 3 euros** eases punters out of the summer festival season. As the name suggests, this late August promotion lasts for three days and gives entry to most Parisian cinemas for €3.

As if cinema wasn't already popular enough in Paris, the Mairie has devised a series of special festivals and programmes to get even more bums on seats. Most of these initiatives take place in summer, taking advantage of the warm evenings to screen films under the stars. They usually cost nothing or next to nothing at all. For listings details, *see pp293-294*.

The most established is the **Cinéma Plein Air** (*pictured*) at Parc de la Villette. Celebrating its 17th edition in 2007, this highly popular festival gives *cinéphiles* the opportunity to enjoy open-air cinema on a huge inflatable screen every night (except Mondays) throughout the summer. Movies

The two-screen Champo has been in operation for nearly seven decades, a venerable past recognised in 2000 when it was conferred with historic monument status. In the 1960s it was a favourite haunt of *nouvelle vague* directors such as Claude Chabrol.

Le Cinéma du Panthéon
13 rue Victor-Cousin, 5th (01.40.46.01.21/ www.cinemapantheon.com). RER Luxembourg. **Admission** €7; €5.50 Mon, Wed, students, 13s-18s; €4 under-13s. **Credit** MC, V. **Map** p408 J8.
The city's oldest surviving movie house (founded in 1907) is one of the few to have retained its balcony. It screens new, often obscure international films and hosts meet-the-director nights and discussions.

Le Denfert
24 pl Denfert-Rochereau, 14th (01.43.21.41.01/ www.allocine.fr). Mº Denfert Rochereau/RER Denfert Rochereau. **Admission** €6.50; €5 Mon, Wed, students, over-60s; €4.60 under-15s. **No credit cards. Map** p405 H10.
This friendly little cinema offers an eclectic repertory selection that ranges from François Ozon and Hayao Miyazaki to shorts and animation, as well as new-release foreign films.

L'Entrepôt
7-9 rue Francis-de-Pressensé, 14th (01.45.40.07.50/ www.lentrepot.fr). Mº Pernety or Plaisance. **Admission** €7; €5.60 students, over-60s; €4 under-12s. **No credit cards. Map** p405 F10.

A diverse array of documentaries, shorts, gay cinema and productions from developing nations are more common here than mainstream stuff. Films are often accompanied by a debate or a chance to meet the director.

Images d'Ailleurs
21 rue de la Clef, 5th (01.45.87.18.09). M° Censier Daubenton. **Admission** €6; €5.50 concs; €4.70 under-12s, for all Mon. **No credit cards.** **Map** 406 K9.
Opened in 1990, this cinema focuses on films from Africa and other rare movie treats.

Le Latina
20 rue du Temple, 4th (01.42.78.47.86/www. lelatina.com). M° Hôtel de Ville. **Admission** €7.50; €6 Mon, Tue, students, under-20s. **No credit cards.** **Map** p406 K6.
The programming at this flag-bearer for Latin cultures runs from Argentinian to Romanian films. Latin dance features at the €17 film-dinner-dancing deals on Monday and Wednesday evenings.

Le Mac Mahon
5 av Mac-Mahon, 17th (01.43.80.24.81/www. cinemamacmahon.com). M° Charles de Gaulle Etoile. **Admission** €6.50; €4.50 students. **No credit cards.** **Map** p400 C3.
This single-screen, 1930s-era cinema has changed little since its 1960s heyday (tickets are still, delightfully, of the tear-off variety), when its all-American programming fostered the label 'mac-mahonisme' among the buffs who haunted the place. Americana of the 1930s to '60s is still the bulk of what lights up the screen. **Photo** *p294.*

La Pagode
57bis rue de Babylone, 7th (01.45.55.48.48). M° St-François-Xavier. **Admission** €8; €6.50 Mon, Wed, students, under-21s. **No credit cards.** **Map** p405 F7.
This glorious edifice is not, as local legend might have it, a block-by-block import, but a 19th-century replica of a pagoda by a French architect (although there are several authentic Japanese elements present, including the carved beams). Renovated in the late 1990s, this is certainly one of the loveliest cinemas in the world.

Studio 28
10 rue Tholozé, 18th (01.46.06.36.07/www.cinema studio28.com). M° Abbesses or Blanche. **Admission** €7.50; €6.30 students, under-18s. **No credit cards.** **Map** p401 H1.
The venue for the screening of Buñuel's scandalous *L'Age d'Or,* this historic cinema also features in the more heartwarming *Amélie.* It offers a decent repertory mixture of classics and recent movies, complete with Dolby sound and a civilised bar for a pre-or post-screening tipple.

Studio Galande
42 rue Galande, 5th (01.43.26.94.08). M° St-Michel or Cluny La Sorbonne. **Admission** €7; €5.50 Wed, students.* **No credit cards.** **Map** p408 J7.

Some 20 different films are screened in subtitled versions at this Latin Quarter venue every week: international arthouse with the occasional *Matrix.* On Fridays, fans of *The Rocky Horror Picture Show* turn up in drag, equipped with rice and water pistols.

Festivals & special events

The city plays host to a range of film festivals, some of them free, some taking place outdoors. *See also p292* **Summer film festivals** and *pp270-274* **Festivals & Events**.

Festival International de Films de Femmes
Maison des Arts, pl Salvador-Allende, 94040 Créteil (01.49.80.38.98/www.filmsdefemmes.com). M° Créteil – Préfecture. **Date** Mar.
A selection of retrospectives and new international films by female directors.

Printemps du Cinéma
Various venues (www.printempsducinema.com). **Date** Mar.
Three days of bargain €3.50-entry films at cinemas all across Paris.

Côté Court
Ciné 104, 104 av Jean-Lolive, 93500 Pantin (01.48.46.95.08/www.cotecourt.org). M° Eglise de Pantin. **Date** Mar-Apr.
A great selection of new and old short films shown at Ciné 104 and a handful of neighbouring venues.

La Pagode.

Arts & Entertainment

Paris Cinéma

Various venues (01.55.25.55.25/www.paris cinema.org). **Date** July.
Mairie-sponsored programme of shorts and documentaries. *See p292* **Summer film festivals**.

Les Rencontres

Forum des Images (see p291). **Date** July.
Map p404 J5.
A global choice of new independent features, documentaries and short films, usually screened in the presence of their directors.

Cinéma au Clair de Lune

Various venues (01.44.76.62.18/www.forum desimages.net). **Date** Aug.
Night-time films on giant open-air screens in squares and public gardens around town: party atmosphere guaranteed. *See p292* **Summer film festivals**.

3 Jours/3 Euros

All cinemas throughout Paris (www.paris.fr/fr/ culture/missioncinema). **Date** Aug.
This Mairie-sponsored promotion is timed to start getting kids into cinemas before the schools go back. For three days, every screening costs just €3.

L'Etrange Festival

Forum des Images (see p291/www.etrange festival.com). **Date** Sept. **Map** p404 J5.
Explicit sex, gore and weirdness in the screenings and 'happenings' at this annual feast of all things unconventional draw large crowds.

Salon du Livre de Cinéma et du DVD

Espace des Blancs-Manteaux, 48 rue Vieille-du-Temple, 4th (www.cinemathequefrançaise.com). M° Hôtel de Ville. **Date** Oct. **Map** p409 K6.
European publishers of cinema-related books sell their wares; there are round-table discussions and a chance to meet filmmakers. After a two-year hiatus, this (usually) annual event returns in 2007.

Bookshops

Paris is well supplied with film bookshops.
Virgin Megastore (*see p243*) also stocks a range of English-language movie books.

Cinédoc

45-53 passage Jouffroy, 9th (01.48.24.71.36/ www.cine-doc.fr). M° Grands Boulevards. **Open** 10am-7pm Mon-Sat. **Credit** V. **Map** p402 J4.
Finding what you're looking far isn't easy in this narrow, tobacco-scented bookshop. Ask the helpful staff or take pot luck among the old photos, US film mags and fanzines, disquisitions on the *nouvelle vague* and books about special effects in *Star Wars*.

Ciné Reflet

14 rue Serpente, 6th (01.40.46.02.72). M° Cluny La Sorbonne. **Open** 1-8pm Mon-Sat; 3-7pm Sun.
Credit MC, V. **Map** p408 J7.

An old projector stands in a corner of this sprawling shop, well stocked with old photos, posters, and new and second-hand books. Subjects covered range from Lithuanian formalism to Laurel and Hardy. The strong English-language selection includes the *Time Out Film Guide* and mags like *Sight & Sound*. Current and back issues of *Les Cahiers du Cinéma* and *Première* fill shelf after shelf, as do fanzines and old press dossiers. The shop is planning to move premises in 2007, so call before your visit.

Contacts

24 rue du Colisée, 8th (01.43.59.17.71/www.media librairie.com). M° St-Philippe-du-Roule or Franklin D. Roosevelt. **Open** 10am-7pm Mon-Fri; 2-7pm Sat.
Credit MC, V. **Map** p401 E4.
Truffaut's favourite *librairie* has been selling books on film for over 40 years. The stock is well organised, with a large and up-to-date selection of English-language titles. You'll also find *Film Comment* and *American Cinematographer*, plus a few videos.

Scaramouche

161 rue St-Martin, 3rd (01.48.87.78.58). M° Rambuteau. **Open** 11am-1pm, 2-8pm Mon-Sat.
Credit MC, V. **Map** p402 K5.
This large-ish shop covers cinema and *gestuelle* (mime and puppetry). The film section includes a wide range of new and second-hand titles in English, plus a huge collection of publicity photos and portraits filed in manilla envelopes under film title or actor's or director's name. Wim Wenders and Alain Renais have been known to pop in.

Le Mac Mahon. *See p293.*

Galerie G-P et N Vallois

36 rue de Seine, 6th (01.46.34.61.07/www.galerie-vallois.com). M° Mabillon or Odéon. **Open** 10.30am-1pm, 2-7pm Mon-Sat. **Map** p408 H7.
Interesting conceptual work in all media includes American provocateur Paul McCarthy, Turner Prize winner Keith Tyson and a clutch of French thirty- and fortysomethings, including Tatiana Trouvé, Alain Bublex and Gilles Barbier.

Galerie Kamel Mennour

60 & 72 rue Mazarine, 6th (01.56.24.03.63/ www.galeriemennour.com). M° Odéon. **Open** 10.30am-7.30pm Mon-Sat. **Map** p408 H7.
After bursting on to the St-Germain scene with chic, often provocative, shows by fashion photography crossovers David LaChapelle and Ellen von Unwerth and filmmaker Larry Clark, Mennour now exhibits some of France's most talked-about young talents, including Kader Attia and Adel Abdessemed.

Galerie Lara Vincy

47 rue de Seine, 6th (01.43.26.72.51/www.lara-vincy.com). M° Mabillon, St-Germain-des-Prés or Odéon. **Open** 2.30-7pm Mon; 11am-1pm, 2.30-7pm Tue-Sat. **Map** p408 H7.
Liliane Vincy, daughter of the founder, is one of the few characters to retain something of the old St-Germain spirit and a sense of 1970s Fluxus-style happenings. Interesting theme and solo shows include master of the epigram Ben, as well as artists' text-, music- and performance-related pieces.

Galerie Loevenbruck

40 rue de Seine, 6th (01.53.10.85.68/www.loevenbruck.com). M° Mabillon or Odéon. **Open** 2-7pm Tue-Sat. **Map** p408 H6.
Funky Loevenbruck injected a dose of humour into St-Germain with a bunch of young artists – Virginie Barré, Bruno Peinado and Olivier Blankaert – who treat conceptual concerns with a light touch.

13th arrondissement

&: - in situ Fabienne Leclerc

10 rue Duchefdelaville, 13th (01.53.79.06.12/ www.insituparis.fr). M° Chevaleret. **Open** 11am-7pm Tue-Sat. **Map** p407 M10.
Fabienne Leclerc works on the long term with an interesting and international range of artists that includes Andrea Blum, Bruno Perramant, Subodh Gupta, Patrick van Caeckenbergh and Gary Hill.

Air de Paris

32 rue Louise-Weiss, 13th (01.44.23.02.77/www.airdeparis.com). M° Chevaleret. **Open** 11am-7pm Tue-Sat. **Map** p407 M10.
This gallery, named after Duchamp's famous bottle of air, shows experimental, neo-conceptual and often somewhat chaotic material. A hip international stable of artists includes Liam Gillick, Carsten Höller and Philippe Parreno. Don't miss the 'Random Gallery' – displays in the shop window between Air de Paris and neighbour Praz-Delavallade.

Art:Concept

16 rue Duchefdelaville, 13th (01.53.60.90.30/www.galerieartconcept.com). M° Chevaleret or Bibliothèque François Mitterrand. **Open** 11am-7pm Tue-Sat. **Map** p407 M10.
This offers an eclectic list: installations by artists Michel Blazy and Martine Aballéa, the photoworks or happenings of Roman Signer and the intricate cartoon-style drawings of Philippe Perrot.

Galerie Kréo

22 rue Duchefdelaville, 13th (01.53.60.18.42/www.galeriekreo.com). M° Chevaleret. **Open** 2-7pm Tue-Fri; 11am-7pm Sat. **Map** p407 M10.
Occupying the ambiguous area between design as function and design as art, Kréo commissions limited-edition pieces by leading contemporary designers. Look for Marc Newson, Jasper Conran, Ron Arad, young Dutch superstar Hella Jongerius, and native talent such as the Bouroullec brothers.

gb agency

20 rue Louise-Weiss, 13th (01.53.79.07.13/www.gbagency.fr). M° Chevaleret. **Open** 11am-7pm Tue-Sat. **Map** p407 M10.
The gb agency revealed young artists Loris Gréaud and Elina Brotherus, and rediscovered the likes of Robert Breer. Shows group several artists together in an exploration of temporality and the exhibition concept itself.

Jousse Entreprise

24 & 34 rue Louise-Weiss, 13th (01.53.82.10.18/ www.jousse-entreprise.com). M° Chevaleret or Bibliothèque François Mitterrand. **Open** 11am-1pm, 2-7pm Tue-Sat. **Map** p407 M10.
Philippe Jousse shows contemporary artists – such as Matthieu Laurette, photographer Frank Perrin and challenging young video artist Clarisse Hahn – alongside 1950s avant-garde furniture by Jean Prouvé and ceramics by Georges Jouve.

Alternative spaces

La Bellevilloise

21 rue Boyer, 20th (01.53.27.35.77/www.la bellevilloise.com). M° Gambetta. **Open** hours vary. **Map** p403 P4.
This was a radical institution founded after the Paris commune. Reborn in 2005, its focus is artistic experimentation and innovation, with exhibitions, concerts, debates, recording studios and a café.

Café au Lit

16 rue de la Liberté, 19th (01.46.36.18.85/ www.cafeaulit.com). M° Place des Fêtes. **Open** selected dates or by rental.
Live with – and in – art in this apartment-cum-installation rehabilitated by Franco-Portuguese architect-artist Didier Faustino. Exhibitions, curated by 'Weiswald' (a pair of German critics and journalists), generally last around three months and are open to those who rent the flat (three nights minimum), as well as for selected events.

Gay & Lesbian

The party scene gets political.

Open Café. *See p303*.

These days, the gay scene is an integral part of local life – in 2006 more than 700,000 revellers took to the streets to celebrate the city's annual **Gay Pride March**. Leading the parade were two of France's most prominent gay politicians: Paris mayor Bertrand Delanoë and Jean-Luc Romero, national secretary of the conservative UMP party. Also in attendance was the (heterosexual) Socialist party leader François Hollande, partner of presidential candidate Ségolène Royal. With national elections coming up, the pink vote is a force to be reckoned with.

'*Pour l'égalité en 2007*!' was this year's chosen rallying cry: now the gay community has gained acceptance, the next step is to achieve equality. The hot issues are same-sex adoption and marriage. Although civil unions (PACS) are allowed, the decree annulling France's first gay marriage in 2004 still stands.

But the gay scene's integration into the mainstream does have its downside. While the Marais still has its fair share of quirky characters and kinky clubs, some say it's in danger of becoming another money-making machine. As the chains move in (Le Pain Quotidien and Starbucks, for example), the trendsetters have moved out, heading for new

spots due north: **Les Bains Douches** (*see p325*), **De la Ville Café** and **Le Réconfort** are all towards the Grands Boulevards and Arts et Métiers. Here, too, is trailblazing lesbian club **Pulp**, a key player in the city's sapphic scene.

Back in the Marais, a spate of muggings of gay men has been making headlines in city daily *Le Parisien*. Victims meet their attackers in bars and follow them out on to the street, only to get robbed. According to Flag, an association set up for gay and lesbian members of the Paris police force, the attacks are more about opportunism than homophobia. Criminals simply see the Marais scene as an easy target; these days, its wealth and voting power seem to be more of interest to the wider world than the sexual leanings of its community.

INFORMATION AND RESOURCES

Both *Têtu* (www.tetu.com) and *Préf* magazines (www.preferencesmag.com) report on goings-on in gay life and have text in English. Freebies found in gay venues include *e-illico* (www.e-llico.com), *2 Weeks-Paris* (www.2xparis.fr) and *Tribumove* (www.tribumove.com). Find current information at www.paris-gay.com, www.citegay.fr and www.gayvox.com.

Arts & Entertainment

Neat boutique: **Pierre Talamon**. *See p305.*

Centre Gai et Lesbien
3 rue Keller, 11th (01.43.57.21.47/www.cglparis.org).
Mº Ledru-Rollin or Bastille. **Open** 4-8pm Mon-Sat.
Library 2-6pm Fri, Sat. **Map** p407 M7.
This multifunctional community centre, library and
meeting space hosts support groups as well as associations for gay and lesbian parents-to-be.

Inter-LGBT
c/o Maison des Associations du l'Île, boite 8, 5 rue
Perrée, 3rd (01.72.70.39.22/www.inter-lgbt.org).
The Interassociative Lesbienne, Gaie, Bi et Trans is
an umbrella group of 50 French LGBT associations.
It organises the Printemps des Assoces in the Espace
des Blancs Manteaux (48 rue Vieille-du-Temple, 4th)
every April and the annual Pride March.

SNEG
59 rue Beaubourg, 3rd (01.44.59.81.01/www.
sneg.org). Mº Rambuteau. **Open** 1-7pm Mon-Fri.
Map p409 K5.
The Syndicat National des Entreprises Gaies is a
nationwide organisation for gay and lesbian businesses, with over 1,000 members.

SOS Homophobie
01.48.06.42.41/www.sos-homophobie.org
Victims and witnesses of homophobic crimes and
discrimination can report them to this confidential
service, which offers support and publishes an annual report on homophobia.

Gay Paris

Bars & cafés

Le Bear's Den
6 rue des Lombards, 4th (01.42.71.08.20/www.
bearsden.fr). Mº Châtelet Les Halles or Hôtel de Ville.
Open 4pm-2am Mon-Thur, Sun; 4pm-4am Fri, Sat.
Credit MC, V. **Map** p406 J6.

A friendly local for bears, muscle bears, chubbies
and those who admire their rotund brethren. Visit
the website for details on comically named theme
nights such as 'Charcuterie'.

Café Cox
15 rue des Archives, 4th (01.42.72.08.00). Mº Hôtel
de Ville. **Open** 11pm-2am daily. **No credit cards**.
Map p409 K6.
Beefy, hairy, shaven-headed folk congregate along
the pavement in front of Cox for post-work drinks,
before moving on to more intimate surroundings.
Sport jeans and sneaks, grab a beer and you're in.

Le Carré
18 rue du Temple, 4th (01.44.59.38.57). Mº Hôtel de
Ville. **Open** 10am-4am daily. **Credit** AmEx, MC, V.
Map p406 K6.
Enjoy coffee, lunch, dinner or as many highballs as
you care to consume in this stylish café-bar. After
which, you can follow your newly found target across the
street to RAIDD (*see p303*) should you so desire.

De la Ville Café
34-36 bd de Bonne-Nouvelle, 10th (01.48.24.48.09/
www.delavillecafe.com). Mº Bonne Nouvelle. **Open**
11am-2am Mon-Sat; noon-2am Sun. **Credit** AmEx,
MC, V. **Map** p402 J4.
Although not strictly gay, this place does have quite
a following. Attractions include a huge patio, imaginative design, decent fare and a stylish clientele.

Le Feeling
43 rue Ste-Croix-de-la-Bretonnerie, 4th (01.48.04.
70.03). Mº Rambuteau or Hôtel de Ville. **Open** 5pm-
2am daily. **Credit** V. **Map** p409 K6.
This Marais institution is generally peopled by a
slightly older crowd until the wee hours of the night.

Les Maronniers
18 rue des Archives, 4th (01.40.27.87.72). Mº
Hôtel de Ville. **Open** noon-2am daily. **Credit** MC, V.
Map p409 K6.

Right on the main drag, this bar is central in every sense of the word. A few hours on the crowded terrace give you real insight into the inner workings of Paris' gay milieu.

Mixer Bar

23 rue Ste-Croix-de-la-Bretonnerie, 4th (01.48. 87.55.44/www.mixerbar.com). Mº Hôtel de Ville. **Open** 5pm-2am daily. **Credit** AmEx, MC, V. **Map** p409 K6.

This used to be the hang-out *du jour*, but has fallen somewhat by the wayside with its gaudy and dated decor. There's a mixed lesbian and gay crowd, although some nights are exclusively for the girls.

Open Café

17 rue des Archives, 4th (01.42.72.26.18). Mº Hôtel de Ville or Rambuteau. **Open** 11am-2am Mon-Thur, Sun; 11am-4am Fri, Sat. **Credit** MC, V. **Map** p409 K6.

Cruise and be cruised in the café that everybody passes through at some point in the evening. Great staff and prompt service help. **Photo** *p301.*

Le Pick-Clops

16 rue Vieille-du-Temple, 4th (01.40.29.02.18). Mº Hôtel de Ville or St-Paul. **Open** 7am-2am Mon-Sat; 8am-2am Sun. **Credit** V. **Map** p406 L6.

An old tobacco shop in the heart of the Marais, Le Pick-Clops offers rock 'n' roll kitsch in a laid-back Parisian café. Fills with couples, gay and straight.

RAIDD Bar

23 rue du Temple, 4th (01.42.77.04.88/www.raidd bar.com). Mº Hôtel de Ville. **Open** 6.30pm-5am daily. **Credit** (minimum €10) MC, V. **Map** p406 K6.

Standing room only at street level, with another bar and red velvet couches down under. Herculean bartenders take turns in the wall-mounted shower for nightly shows, a DJ spins and the place gets jam-packed after other bars close between 1am and 2am.

Restaurants

B4 Le Resto

6-8 sq Ste-Croix-de-la-Bretonnerie, 4th (01.42.72. 16.19/www.b4resto.com). Mº Hôtel de Ville. **Open** noon-2pm, 8pm-midnight Mon-Sat; noon-5pm, 8-11pm Sun. **Credit** MC, V. **Map** p409 K6.

Have a drink at the little bar while you wait for your table, or just gaze at the ever-attractive clientele in sleek and stylish surroundings. The food here lies somewhere between fusion and contemporary French, and the service is attitude-free. Book for weekend evenings, when it's a popular spot.

Le Kofi du Marais

54 rue Ste-Croix-de-la-Bretonnerie, 4th (01.48.87. 48.71). Mº Hôtel de Ville. **Open** noon-11pm daily. **Credit** AmEx, MC, V. **Map** p406 K6.

Modern and simple cooking with an American twist is the speciality here. Club sandwiches, burgers and salads are menu staples, while the *frites* are more like fries. Prices are reasonable and service good.

Le Loup Blanc

42 rue Tiquetonne, 2nd (01.40.13.08.35/ www.loup-blanc.com). Mº Etienne Marcel. **Open** 7.30pm-12.30am Mon-Sat. *Sunday brunch* 11am-4pm. **Credit** MC, V. **Map** p402 J5.

This gay-run eaterie offers a different take on dinner: make your selection from the meat, seafood or vegetarian categories on the menu and pay for the number of components you have ordered. **Other locations:** 37 rue Quincampoix, 4th (01.42.77.10.03/www.ozoreso.com).

Le Réconfort

37 rue de Poitou, 3rd (01.49.96.09.60). Mº St-Sébastien Froissart. **Open** noon-2.30pm, 8-11pm Mon-Fri; 8-11.30pm Sat, Sun. **Credit** AmEx, MC, V. **Map** p409 L5.

The chef, Guillem, was once a fashion designer, and his creativity shines through in this romantic restaurant. Rotating artwork, a constantly changing decor and a simple but well-chosen menu make for an enjoyable dining experience.

Clubs

Diversity is the watchword when it comes to the city's club scene, with everything from old-fashioned disco knees-ups to offbeat electro nights. A mixed but increasingly gay crowd mingles at **Les Bains Douches** (*see p325*), **Nouveau Casino** (*see p324*) and **La Scène Bastille** (*see p325*). For details of the hippest nights and afterparties, *see p305* **6am eternal**.

Club 79

22 rue Quentin-Bauchard, 8th (01.47.23.69.17/ www.club79.fr). Mº Georges V. **Open** 10.30pm-4am daily. **Admission** €6-€15. **Credit** V. **Map** p400 D4.

Not a gay venue as such, but Under (every second Sunday morning of the month) is the gay place to be.

Follow Me

24 rue Keller, 11th (04.34.08.03.22/www.follow me-paris.com). Mº Bastille. **Open** 6am-midday Mon, Thur-Fri; 6am-4pm Sat; 6am-7pm Sun. **Admission** (incl 1 drink) €20. **Credit** V. **Map** p407 M6.

A mixed after-hours club, brimming with talent.

L'Insolite

33 rue des Petits-Champs, 1st (01.40.20.98.59). Mº Pyramides. **Open** 11pm-5am daily. **Admission** free Mon-Thur; €10 Fri, Sat. **Credit** V. **Map** p402 H5.

Everyone under the sun comes here and has a blast – just don't expect cutting edge, underground tracks.

Queen

102 av des Champs-Elysées, 8th (08.92.70.73.30/ www.queen.fr). Mº George V. **Open** midnight-7am Mon-Thur, Sun; midnight-8am Fri, Sat. **Admission** €15 Mon-Thur, Sun; €20 Fri, Sat. **Drinks** €10. **Credit** *Bar* AmEx, MC, V. **Map** p400 D4.

One of the oldest and largest clubs, Le Queen's main gay nights are Saturday@Queen and Overkitsch on Sundays. *See also p329.*

Arts & Entertainment

Le Tango

13 rue au Maire, 3rd (01.42.72.17.78). M° Arts et Métiers. **Open** 8pm-2am Thur; 10.30pm-5am Fri, Sat; 6-11pm Sun. **Admission** €7; free Thur. **Credit** V. **Map** p409 K5.

Wacky crowd, Madonna songs and accordion tunes.

Sex clubs & saunas

Le Dépot

10 rue aux Ours, 3rd (01.44.54.96.96/www.ledepot. com). M° Etienne Marcel. **Open** midnight-7am daily. **Admission** €7.50 before 11pm, €10 after Mon-Thur, Sun; €12 (incl 1 drink) Fri, Sat. **Credit** MC, V. **Map** p402 K5.

A very busy dance club with a labyrinthine maze of cubicles, glory holes and darkrooms downstairs.

IDM

4 rue du Fbg-Montmartre, 9th (01.45.23.10.03). M° Grands Boulevards. **Open** noon-1am Mon-Thur, Sun; noon-2am Fri, Sat. **Admission** €15 Mon-Fri; €17 Sat, Sun; €10 under-30s. **Credit** MC, V. **Map** p402 J4.

The city's largest gay sauna is split over three levels and has plenty of cabins and corridors to prowl.

L'Impact-Cruising Bar

18 rue Greneta, 2nd (01.42.21.94.24/www.impact-bar.com). M° Châtelet Les Halles. **Open** 8pm-3am Mon-Thur; 10pm-6am Fri, Sat; 3pm-3am Sun. **Admission** €11. **Credit** MC, V. **Map** p402 K5.

Paris' first gay sex club offers various theme nights, a plentiful supply of condoms and lube, and a 2-3am happy hour. €11 gets you a plastic bag for all your clothes save your shoes, plus a drink. Most of the action happens downstairs in the cubicles, sling, labyrinth and giant bed. Tuesdays are Horse Man Naked nights, where interested parties can be measured up. Should they surpass the 20cm (eight-inch) stipulation, they're granted free admission.

Sun City

62 bd de Sébastopol, 3rd (01.42.74.31.41). M° Etienne Marcel. **Open** midnight-6am daily. **Admission** €16 Mon-Fri; €17.50 Sat, Sun; €9 under-26s. **Credit** MC, V. **Map** p402 J5.

Bollywood-themed dry saunas, a jacuzzi, hammams, video rooms, a pool, private rooms, a gym and a bar.

Le Transfert

3 rue de La Sourdière, 1st (01.42.60.48.42). M° Tuileries or Pyramides. **Open** midnight-6am Mon-Fri; midnight-8am Sat, Sun. **Admission** free; 1 drink obligatory. **Credit** AmEx, MC, V. **Map** p401 G5.

A well-known club for men sporting leather, S&M gear and denim, so don't forget your chaps and harnesses. Nights include Trash Naturist Theme on Saturdays and Sneakers Trip on Sundays.

Univers Gym Paris-Sauna Hammam Musculation

20-22 rue des Bons-Enfants, 1st (01.42.61.24.83, 08.25.70.04.29/www.universgym.fr). M° Palais Royal or Les Halles. **Open** noon-2am Mon-Sat; 6pm-2am

Sun. **Admission** €13 before 2pm, €17.50 after; €9 after 10pm. *Under-26s*: €7 before 2pm, €9 after; €6 after 10pm; €5 Tues after 8pm. **Credit** AmEx, DC, MC, V. **Map** p402 H5.

Although more sauna than gym, complete work-out facilities are available. A towel must be worn in the bar and gym areas – do as you please everywhere else. In late 2006 the gym closed for renovation, due to reopen in 2007: check the website before visiting.

Shops & services

L'Eclaireur

Homme: 12 rue Malher, 4th (01.44.54.22.11/ www.leclaireur.com). Femme: 3ter rue des Rosiers, 4th (01.48.87.10.22). M° St-Paul. **Open** 11am-7pm Mon-Sat. **Credit** AmEx, DC, MC, V. **Map** p409 L6.

You'll find a chic array of labels at this multi-brand designer shop; highlights include the colourful creations of German milliner Reinhard Plank.

Other locations: throughout the city.

iEM

208 rue St-Maur, 10th (01.40.18.51.51/www.iem.fr). M° Goncourt. **Open** 10.30am-7.30pm Mon-Sat. **Credit** AmEx, MC, V. **Map** p403 M4.

This sex hypermarket emphasises the harder side of gay life. Videos, clothes and gadgets can all be found, with leather and rubber upstairs.

Other locations: throughout the city.

Legay Choc

45 rue Ste-Croix-de-la-Bretonnerie, 4th (01.48. 87.56.88/www.legaychoc.fr). M° Hôtel de Ville. **Open** 8am-8pm Mon, Tue, Thur-Sun. **No credit cards. Map** p409 K6.

Run by two brothers (one gay, one straight) whose surname just so happens to be Legay, this Marais *boulangerie* and pâtisserie is exceedingly popular – expect lengthy breakfast and lunchtime queues. For special occasions, a penis-shaped loaf can be made to order. There's now also a sandwich shop in the 4th.

Other locations: 17 rue des Archives, 4th (01.48.87.24.61)

Les Mots à la Bouche

6 rue Ste-Croix-de-la-Bretonnerie, 4th (01.42.78. 88.30/www.motsbouche.com). M° Hôtel de Ville or St-Paul. **Open** 11am-11pm Mon-Sat; 1-9pm Sun. **Credit** AmEx, MC, V. **Map** p409 K6.

Something of an institution in the Marais, this bookshop carries gay-interest literature from all over the world and has a good English-language section.

Nickel

48 rue des Francs-Bourgeois, 4th (01.42.77.41.10/ www.nickel.fr). M° Hôtel de Ville or Rambuteau. **Open** 11am-7.30pm Mon, Tue, Fri, Sat; 11am-9pm Wed, Thur. **Credit** AmEx, MC, V. **Map** p406 L6.

Nickel offers body and skincare treatments, strictly for menfolk. A one-hour facial is €45-€55, a manicure €13 and an hour-long relaxing massage €45. Staff are adept, but speak to manager Franck Tainier for your truly complicated epidermal needs.

6am eternal

Clubbing in gay Paree isn't on the same scale as the scenes in New York or London – but its random nature is precisely its charm.

La Scène Bastille (*see p325*) has some unmissable monthly nights. Although it's not strictly a gay venue, here 'electro-queer' night Eyes Need Sugar attracts a stylish, fashion-focused crowd and top-notch DJs with an ear for gritty beats. House and electro aficionados should also head to the ever-popular Monoculture, while the after-party Progress with DJ Nicholas Nucci is always packed. The multi-talented venue is also a restaurant and a space for live concerts. If you happen to be dining on the right night, you get to see concert for free.

The club of the moment is the recently refurbished **Les Bains Douches** (*see p325*). Housed in old Turkish bath-house, it's well promoted around the Marais. Keep your eyes peeled for flyers – you'll need them to make up for the €10 drinks. On the second Saturday of the month, the lively Yes Sir, I Can Boogie is held here, while every Saturday the club's first floor hosts the Brooklyn Sessions for R&B-loving gays. Les Bains is also a good bet at weekends, with the party continuing from 6am at A.F.T.E.R. and Boudoir. Dedicated clubbers can keep going from Saturday night through to Sunday afternoon.

Under at **Club 79** (*see p303*) is another after-hours club that is hugely popular with the gay crowd. It's just across the street from **Queen** (*see p303*), so try to get there well before it opens at 6.30am to avoid the sprawling queue.

Another club where the party kicks off in the early hours of the morning is **Follow Me** (*see p303*), which opens its doors from 6am except Tuesdays and Wednesdays. Here, too, tireless clubbers can party until 7pm on Sunday. Although it's a mixed night, a quick trawl around the dancefloor will reveal a significant gay contingent. Another club for hets and homos alike is **Le Nouveau Casino** (*see p324*) in the Oberkampf district. The monthly Disco Queer night, dubbed 'The Other Side of Disco', invariably gets them dancing.

Often the most colourful and memorable nights out are those spent at the more eccentric **Le Tango** (*see p304*) and **l'Insolite** (*see p303*). The former is an ancient dancehall; the latter some sort of converted wine cellar. Le Tango is a welcome change from the usual mainstream gay scene, and the beloved haunt of ageing but fabulous transvestites, skinny twinks, diesel dykes, muscle Marys and all other creatures of the Parisian night. The playlist is composed of accordion music until midnight and 'everything else but techno' from then on – and there will always be a Madonna track or six. The club also throws regular 100 per cent Madonna nights, with monikers like 'Confessions on a Tango Floor'. Meanwhile, L'Insolite perches its DJ astride the bar – and although the mixing is often suspect and the tunes undeniably cheesy, it doesn't dampen the mood in the slightest. It may not be not cool, but it is tremendous fun. To find it, go through the gate at No.33 to the courtyard, and the entrance to the cavern is on your left.

Pierre Talamon

15 rue du Temple, 4th (01.42.71.06.17/www.pierretalamon.com). M° Hôtel de Ville. **Open** noon-7.30pm Mon-Sat. **Credit** AmEx, MC, V. **Map** p402 K6. Understated, moderately conservative menswear for the discerning urban male. **Photo** *p302*.

Wooyoungmi

44 rue Vieille-du-Temple, 4th (01.42.77.76.84). M° Hôtel de Ville or St-Paul. **Open** 11am-8pm Tue-Sat; 2-8pm Sun. **Credit** AmEx, MC, V. **Map** p409 K6. Beautifully cut casual and formal clothes are displayed to great effect in this Korean designer's shop.

Plus Que Parfait

23 rue des Blancs-Manteaux, 4th (01.42.71.09.05). M° Hôtel de Ville or St-Paul. **Open** 3-8pm Mon; noon-8pm Tue-Sat; 3-7pm Sun. Clothes deposit Mon-Fri. **Credit** MC, V. **Map** p409 K6.

A *dépôt vente*, where pristine condition, second-hand designer clothing is sold on commission, and a veritable treasure trove of men's fashion finds.

Point Soleil

15 rue du Temple, 4th (01.48.87.81.13). M° Hôtel de Ville. **Open** 8am-8.30pm Mon-Sat; 9am-7.30pm Sun. **Credit** AmEx, MC, V. **Map** p406 K6. One of a chain of tanning salons, this branch is favoured by body-beautiful types. Bronzing is €7 for ten minutes, with a range of tanning options.

Space Hair

10 rue Rambuteau, 3rd (01.48.87.28.51). M° Rambuteau. **Open** noon-10pm Mon; 11am-11pm Tue-Fri; 9am-10pm Sat. **Credit** MC, V. **Map** p409 K6. Divided into two salons, Cosmic and Classic, the 1980s kitsch feel, late opening hours and cute stylists keep this place packed; it's best to book ahead.

Arts & Entertainment

Where to stay

Hôtel Duo

11 rue du Temple, 4th (01.42.72.72.22/fax 01.42. 72.03.53/www.duoparis.com). M° Hôtel de Ville. **Rates** €115-€155 single; €170-€300 double; €320-480 suite; €14 breakfast. **Credit** AmEx, DC, MC, V. **Map** p406 K6

Gay-friendly, but not marketed as strictly gay, the Duo is a stylish place to rest your head. What's more, it has helpful staff at the reception – a rarity in this trendy area. Unbeatable location.

Hôtel Central Marais

33 rue du Vieille-du-Temple, 4th (01.48.87.56.08/ www.hotelcentralmarais.com). M° Hôtel de Ville or St- Paul. **Rates** €87 double; €7 breakfast. **Credit** MC, V. **Map** p409 K6.

If location and affordable rates are more important to you than plush surroundings, then this aptly named hotel is a good choice. The barmen of Le Central bar (located below the hotel) act as receptionists from 5pm until 2am daily, and can keep you updated on the local nightlife.

Lesbian Paris

Despite the loss of the buzzing Bliss Kfé lounge, the girly scene continues to gain momentum. The remaining bars are thriving, while the main sapphic club, **Pulp**, now gets the best DJs in town. In-the-know gay men tag along with their girlfriends here, the cutting edge of the queer music scene, and superior to the repetitive techno trash that dominates the gay clubs. The crowd at **Le Troisième Lieu** is now also more diverse, with drag kings and queens rubbing epaulettes with fashion-forward girls and nerdy gays.

La Champmeslé

4 rue Chabanais, 2nd (01.42.96.85.20). M° Bourse or Pyramides. **Open** 3pm-early morning Mon-Sat. **Credit** MC, V. **Map** p402 H4.

This veteran girl bar remains a popular hangout for lesbian locals and visitors. Beer is the drink of choice – pull up a seat and enjoy the regular cabaret nights.

Le Day Off

10 rue de l'Isly, 8th (01.45.22.87.90). M° Gare St-Lazare. **Open** 11am-3am Mon-Fri. **Credit** MC, V. **Map** p401 G3.

Apt name for this weekday-only pub-restaurant – heavy drinking enjoyed by work-weary lesbians.

Pulp

25 bd Poisonnière, 2nd (01.40.26.01.93/www.pulp-paris.com). M° Grands Boulevards. **Open** midnight-5am Thur-Sat. **Admission** (incl 1 drink) €10. **Credit** MC, V. **Map** p402 J4.

No wonder the boys are keen to accompany their gal pals to Pulp, considering the DJs it attracts. Ramona, Olivier and DJ Yvan have all taken up residencies here, offering up the dirtiest of electro, '80s and plain ol' house tunes, while Tom le Wanker is a guaranteed fixture. *See also p325.*

Le Troisième Lieu

62 rue Quincampoix, 4th (01.48.04.85.64/www.le troisiemelieu.com). M° Rambuteau. **Open** 6pm-2am Mon-Sat. **Credit** MC, V. **Map** p406 K5.

Elaborate *tartines*, delicious desserts and strong drinks are the fare at this lesbian-run bar and restaurant. Despite its militant subtitle ('Cantine des Ginettes Armés'), the vibe is jovial. *See also p323.*

Unity Bar

176-178 rue St-Martin, 3rd (01.42.72.70.59/ http://unity.bar.free.fr). M° Rambuteau. **Open** 4pm-2am daily. **No credit cards. Map** p402 K5.

Located more in the gay 'hood than the other girly spots, Unity offers pool and beverages.

Pulp.

Music

From opera to Les Plastiscines via jazz, rap and *chanson*.

Ensemble Orchestral de Paris.
See p308.

Classical & Opera

The recent reopening of the capital's only large concert hall, the **Salle Pleyel** (*see p310* **Pleyel again, Sam**), shifted attention briefly away from Gérard Mortier, director of the Opéra National de Paris, and a season that has divided music lovers into vociferous opposing camps. Some see Mortier's strong modernist theatrical convictions as part of an exciting musical adventure, while others find the repertoire, production values and even the orchestral performances a betrayal of all they hold dear. The absence of a permanent musical director has led to unsettled musical standards; in terms of new productions there have been both notable successes, such as André Engel's elegant staging of Hindemiths's *Cardillac*, and spectacular failures – like the much-denigrated version of Verdi's *Simon Boccanegra* by Johan Simons. But perhaps this is just the sort of rollercoaster of emotions on which an opera house thrives. Over at the **Châtelet**, Jean-Luc Choplin has chosen to please the crowds, whose tastes are often condescendingly ignored. He

opened his mandate with *Le Chanteur de Mexico* by Francis Lopez – a French Ivor Novello figure. Critics howled in derision, but the public were delighted to rediscover this familiar music, part of a shared cultural heritage. The **Opéra Comique** have also flourished – having been promoted to National Theatre status, they are guaranteed serious funding for the foreseeable future.

Other public institutions have been going through more troubled waters. No sooner had Jacques Taddei been appointed as director of music at **Radio France** than news of his resignation was announced. This difficult job is now in the hands of Thierry Beauvert, whose main role must be to balance the books.

Radio France is also responsible for two of the city's main orchestras: the **Orchestre Philharmonique de Radio France**, whose musical director is Myung-Whun Chung, and the **Orchestre National de France**, led by Kurt Masur. Both are currently being challenged and outpaced in terms of publicity and tight programming by the **Orchestre de Paris**, with its new home and dynamic conductor Christoph Eschenbach.

Contemporary creation remains a strong suit in the city's musical make-up, thanks to the work of the **IRCAM**, the **Ensemble Intercontemporain** and the still active presence of Pierre Boulez. Important premières scheduled for 2007 include works by leading French composers of the new generation, such as Dusapin, Fénelon and Mantovani.

The early music scene is still led by William Christie's **Les Arts Florissants**, with French conductor Emmanuelle Haïm joining other native specialists, such as Christophe Rousset and Jean-Claude Malgoire. The thirst for rediscovering long-lost works of the distant past is unquenchable, and record companies are happy to share this enthusiasm.

There's plenty going on in churches too. The **Festival d'Art Sacré** (01.44.70.64.10, www.festivaldartsacre.new.fr) presents church music in authentic settings in the run-up to Christmas; **Les Grands Concerts Sacrés** (01.48.24.16.97) and **Musique et Patrimoine** (01.42.50.96.18) also offer concerts at various churches, while music in Notre-Dame cathedral is taken care of by **Musique Sacrée Notre-Dame** (01.44.41.49.99, tickets 01.42.34.56.10).

The main musical provider in summer is the **Paris Quartier d'Eté** festival (www.quartierdete.com), with concerts in gardens across the city. The **Festival de Saint-Denis** (www.festival-saint-denis.fr) also offers top names in a spectacular setting. *See also pp270-274* **Festivals & Events**.

INFORMATION AND TICKETS

For listings, see *L'Officiel des Spectacles* or *Pariscope*. Monthly magazines *Le Monde de la Musique* and *Diapason* also list classical concerts, while *Opéra Magazine* provides good coverage of all things vocal. Look out too for *Cadences* and *La Terrasse*, two free monthlies distributed outside concerts. Another source of information is www.concertclassic.com.

Many venues and orchestras offer cut-rate tickets to students (under 26) an hour before curtain-up. Be wary of smooth-talking ticket touts around the Opéra and at big-name concerts. For the **Fête de la Musique** (21 June), all events are free, and year-round freebies crop up at the **Maison de Radio France** and the **Conservatoire de Paris**, as well as in certain churches.

Orchestras & ensembles

Les Arts Florissants

01.43.87.98.88/www.arts-florissants.com.
William Christie's 'Arts Flo' are France's most highly regarded early music group, and have been honoured with invitations from the Opéra National and

the Comédie Française, joining forces with the ballet of the Opéra for Handel's *Allegro, il Penseroso, ed il Moderato*. The standards of the ensemble in Rameau and Lully have become benchmarks in authentic European performance. Arts Flo have also formed the 'Jardin des Voix' to promote young baroque talent, and participate in educational work to help children know their viols from their theorbos.

Ensemble Intercontemporain

01.44.84.44.50/www.ensembleinter.com.
Glamorous Finnish conductor Susanna Mälkki is the new musical director of this prestigious bastion of contemporary music, founded by Pierre Boulez (who still occasionally conducts the ensemble). The standard of the 31 soloists is beyond reproach, and the ensemble regularly commissions new work as well as participating in the thematic programming of the Cité de la Musique.

Ensemble Orchestral de Paris

08.00.42.67.57/www.ensemble-orchestral-paris.com.
John Nelson remains one of the finest conductors in France, and if his orchestra does not have the best players in the world, it nonetheless provides a stimulating addition to the city's musical life. Highlights to watch out for in 2007 include performances of Handel's *Messiah* for the Festival de Saint-Denis in June 2007, set against the suitably grandiose backdrop of the basilica. **Photos** *p307 & p309.*

Orchestre Colonne

01.42.33.72.89/www.orchestrecolonne.fr.
This venerable but underachieving orchestra now seem in better form. Led by composer Laurent Petitgirard, their musical and artistic director, the orchestra seem eager to promote the preference of new music. Each concert teams a contemporary work with more popular pieces, including a world première in 2007 from composer Michel Decoust.

Orchestre Lamoureux

01.58.39.30.30/www.orchestrelamoureux.com.
Saved from closure by the government at the eleventh hour, this worthy orchestra still suffer from insufficient funding, and their concert appearances in the capital are sparse. In 2006-07 the band celebrate their 125th birthday, and their fine musical director, Yutaka Sado, will conduct some of the core Romantic repertoire in honour of the occasion – works by Wagner and Debussy among them.

Orchestre National de France

01.56.40.15.16/www.radiofrance.fr.
The firm hands of Kurt Masur have changed the profile of this prestigious orchestra, based at the Maison de Radio France, for the better. Their performances of the German symphonic repertoire now rank with the best in the world. In 2007 the centenary of Shostakovich is to the fore, before the season ends with a spell in the pit of the Théatre des Champs-Elysées, playing Debussy's *Pelléas et Mélisande* under the legendary Bernard Haitink.

Orchestre de Paris

01.56.35.12.12/www.orchestredeparis.com.
Christoph Eschenbach and his orchestra have left
the Théâtre Mogador with no regrets to take up residence in the newly restored Salle Pleyel (*see p310*
Pleyel again, Sam). The big cycles of Mozart and
Shostakovitch reach their climax, and the 150th
anniversary of Schumann's death is the occasion to
programme his symphonies. French musicians are
not neglected, and Dutilleux's 90th birthday will be
equally celebrated. Guest conductors include Esa-
Pekka Salonen, Rostropovitch and Marek Janowski.

Orchestre Pasdeloup

01.42.78.10.00/www.concertspasdeloup.com.
The Pasdeloup are the oldest orchestra in Paris, but
the time when they premièred works by Ravel and
Bizet has long gone. Programming now concentrates
on a light repertoire of popular easy-listening classics, enlivened by the odd interesting soloist.

Orchestre Philharmonique de Radio France

www.radiofrance.fr.
The highly respected musical director Myung-
Whun Chung and his orchestra play to a high standard, and in 2007 they let their hair down by playing
in the pit of the Châtelet for the operetta *Le Chanteur
de Mexico* by Lopez – a welcome lighthearted departure for this conservative institution, whose programming lacks any strong thematic identity.

Venues

Auditorium du Louvre

*Entrance through Pyramid, Cour Napoléon, Musée
du Louvre, rue de Rivoli, 1st (01.40.20.55.55/
reservations 01.40.20.55.00/www.louvre.fr).
M° Palais Royal Musée du Louvre.* **Box office**
9am-7pm Mon, Wed-Fri. Closed July, Aug.
Admission €6-€30. **Credit** MC, V. **Map** p401 H5.
A fine series for 2007 is proposed at the Louvre, with
a full season of chamber music, lunchtime concerts
and music on film. Shostakovitch is paid homage to,
and a highlight of the chamber music series is an
appearance by gifted French countertenor Philippe
Jaroussky in cantatas by Scarlatti and Handel.

Châtelet – Théâtre Musical de Paris

*1 pl du Châtelet, 1st (01.40.28.28.40/www.chatelet-
theatre.com). M° Châtelet.* **Box office** 11am-7pm
daily. *By phone* 10am-7pm Mon-Sat. Closed July,
Aug. **Admission** €10-€125. **Credit** AmEx, DC,
MC, V. **Map** p408 J6.
New director Jean-Luc Choplin looks set to bring
more French music back to the theatre, and to create
a more popular cultural experience than that provided by the esoteric programming at the Opéra
National (*see p311*). Choplin is even bringing Bizet's
Carmen back to the capital in May 2007, which may
please the public more than the critics. Besides
opera, the theatre also holds fine series of chamber
music and symphonic concerts.

Cité de la Musique

*221 av Jean-Jaurès, 19th (01.44.84.45.00/
www.cite-musique.fr). M° Porte de Pantin.* **Box
office** noon-6pm Tue-Sun. *By phone* 11am-7pm
Mon-Sat; 10am-6pm Sun. **Admission** €5.60-€33.
Credit MC, V. **Map** p403 (inset).
The energetic programming here tends to focus on
contemporary and baroque music, but there's also a
vast non-classical repertoire that includes ethnic
music and jazz. Concerts are frequently split up into
series with a pedagogic aim, and the whole place has
an exciting atmosphere of discovery. The museum
has a smaller concert space, while the Conservatoire
(01.40.40.45.45) is host to world-class performers and
professors, and features many free concerts.

IRCAM

*1 pl Igor-Stravinsky, 4th (01.44.78.48.16/
www.ircam.fr). M° Hôtel de Ville.* **Box office**
10am-1pm, 2-6pm Mon-Fri. **Admission** €5-€14.
Credit AmEx, DC, MC, V. **Map** p406 K6.
The bunker set up in 1969 to create microtonal microtonal music for the new century is looking rather less
redundant nowadays, thanks largely to its full programme of conferences and courses, and the showcase IRCAM Festival in June 2007. Particularly
interesting is the Concerts Cursus, a series that presents new work by ten young composers from different cultural backgrounds. IRCAM's concerts are
performed here, in the main hall of the neighbouring Centre Pompidou and at the Théâtre des Bouffes
du Nord. The current director at IRCAM is Frank
Madlener, who took the reins in January 2006.

John Nelson of the **Ensemble Orchestral de Paris**. *See p308.*

Maison de Radio France

116 av du Président-Kennedy, 16th (01.56.40.15.16/ information 01.42.30.15.16/www.radiofrance.fr). M° Passy/RER Avenue du Pdt Kennedy. **Box office** 11am-6pm Mon-Sat. **Admission** €5-€55. **Credit** AmEx, DC, MC, V. **Map** p404 A7.

State-owned radio station France Musique broadcasts a superb range of classical concerts, operas and ethnic music from here. The main stage (the Salle Olivier Messiaen) may be charmless, but the quality of music-making from the Orchestre National de France and the Orchestre Philharmonique de Radio France makes up for it. The Passe Musique offers under-26s admission to four concerts for €18, or a year of concerts for €99. Occasional free events are spread over themed weekends, and the Présences contemporary music festival is held in February.

Musée National du Moyen Age

6 pl Paul-Painlevé, 5th (01.53.73.78.16/www.musee-moyenage.fr). M° Cluny La Sorbonne. **Admission** €16; €13 students, under-18s. **Credit** AmEx, MC, V. **Map** p408 J7.

The museum presents a worthy programme of medieval concerts in which troubadours and the use of polyphony reflect the museum's collection.

Musée d'Orsay

62 rue de Lille, 7th (01.40.49.47.57/www.musee-orsay.fr). M° Solférino/RER Musée d'Orsay. **Admission** €11-€30; €6-€20 under-26s. **Credit** MC, V. **Map** p405 G6.

The museum runs a full and enterprising series of lunchtime and evening concerts. The 2006/7 season spotlights the chamber music of Fauré and Brahms, together with music that influenced the painter Maurice Denis, tied into an exhibition of his work.

Opéra Comique – Théâtre National

Pl Boieldieu, 2nd (01.42.44.45.40/www.opera-comique.com). M° Richelieu Drouot. **Box office** 9am-9pm Mon-Sat. *By phone* 11am-6pm Mon-Sat. **Admission** €7-€100. **Credit** AmEx, DC, MC, V. **Map** p402 H4.

Jérôme Savary has done a fine job of promoting this bijou theatre, which saw the premières of so many great operas. However, its new status as a Théâtre

Salle Pleyel (*pictured; see p312*)

Pleyel again, Sam

Arpeggios of relief could be heard from the Orchestre de Paris when the **Salle Pleyel** (*pictured; see p312*) reopened in September 2006, finally bringing to an end its four years of exile in the Théâtre Mogador. The heavily significant work chosen to mark the occasion was Mahler's *Resurrection* symphony, making for the sort of grand celebrity opening evening that Paris does so well.

This brought to the end a long and torturous debate about major symphonic concert halls in the capital. Despite a plethora of museums and public buildings, Paris lacks major purpose-built venues for the symphonic repertoire. Prior to the renovations, the Salle Pleyel was a lacklustre auditorium, both architecturally and acoustically. Built by the famous Pleyel piano-makers, the original 3,000-seat hall opened in 1927 – only to burn down nine months later. Successive renovations were done on the cheap, and only tinkered superficially with the look and acoustics of the place.

Matters reached a head when the owners of the Pleyel, the troubled Crédit Lyonnais, sold it for a song in 1998, and the new owners initially seemed hesitant about the musical future of the dusty old venue. In 2004 the government stepped in and agreed to rent the building back, and massive works were undertaken to provide a concert hall worthy

of the city and a suitable permanent home for the Orchestre de Paris. Against this backdrop of financial manoeuvring, the orchestra's musical director, conductor Christoph Eschenbach, put his job on the line; either it was a new hall, or no more dynamic German maestro. The move to Mogador had been a near-disaster for the band: not only were the audience unfamiliar with the theatre, but the boxy and boomy acoustics were completely inadequate for performances.

Architect François Ceria was brought in to restore the Pleyel's art deco elegance, while American acoustic experts Artec Consultants were responsible for improving the acoustics. The result is a stunning new concert space, white and chic, with beechwood trimmings, a pale oak stage and plush raspberry velvet seating. More importantly, the infamous, now-you-hear-it, now-you-hear-it-again acoustics have been fixed. The improvements have produced a crystal-clear and slightly brutal acoustic that won't allow for any orchestral imprecision to pass unnoticed. This aural clarity will certainly keep orchestras and soloists on their toes, but analytical listeners will be well pleased. A 20 per cent increase in volume has also been achieved, thanks in part to the loss of nearly 500 seats; the seating capacity is now just under 2,000.

La Cigale/La Boule Noire

120 bd de Rochechouart,18th (01.49.25.89.99/
www.lacigale.fr). M° Anvers or Barbès Rochechouart.
Credit MC, V. **Map** p402 J2.
Easily one of Paris' finest venues, this beautiful,
horseshoe-shaped theatre is wonderfully atmospheric, and recently hosted Massive Attack and
Jarvis Cocker's first major solo performance.

Le Divan du Monde

75 rue des Martyrs, 18th (01.42.52.02.46/
www.divandumonde.com). M° Anvers or Pigalle.
Credit MC, V. **Map** p402 H2.
It's come a long way since the days when Toulouse-
Lautrec sipped absinthe here, but the decadent spirit of this old Montmartre joint has just about
survived. Indie, hip hop and electro are the staples.

Elysée Montmartre

72 bd de Rochechouart, 18th (08.92.69.23.92/www.
elyseemontmartre.com). M° Anvers. **Open** *Bar* 11am-
midnight daily. *Concerts* 7pm daily. **Admission**
€15-€30. **Credit** *Bar* V. **Map** p402 J2.
This reliable, if uninspiring, mid-sized venue once
staged cancan, but today you're more likely to catch
Peaches or the Brian Jonestown Massacre.

La Flèche d'Or

102bis rue de Bagnolet, 20th (01.44.64.01.02/
www.flechedor.com). M° Alexandre Dumas. **Open**
8pm-2am Mon, Sun; 8pm-5am Wed-Sat. **Credit** MC,
V. **Map** p403 Q5.
Revitalised indie and electro venue with credible
French and foreign names, and a restaurant. This is
definitely worth a look for its frequent free nights.

sustained note that runs through the length of
the album. Acclaimed by the critics and public
alike, *Le Fil* soon became a gold album.

More than any artist in the last 20 years
(with Etienne Daho a notable exception),
Camille has succeeded in bridging the
gulf between France's musical left field and
its mainstream, largely inhabited by syrupy
variété types who dominate light
entertainment. In musical terms she has
breathed new life into the *chanson* tradition,
opening it up to modern, even avant-garde,
approaches and contemporary reinventions.

Probably more deserving of the Björk
comparisons that Camille is frequently
lumbered with, **Emilie Simon** is an electronic
producer and singer who has also made the
leap from the alternative ghetto. Simon's
breakthrough was producing a glacially
beautiful soundtrack to the blockbuster
penguin flick *La Marche de L'Empereur*, which
was sadly replaced in the English-language
version with a mawkish Hollywood score.

Apart from this groundbreaking pair, in the
realm of more traditional singer-songwriters,
sweet-voiced **Keren Ann** has been an
emblematic figure – but **Barbara Carlotti**'s
baroque splendour, **Mansfield TYA**'s stark
intimacy, **Anais**' playful provocation and
Emily Loizeau's jazzy confections have all
brightened up the landscape. Cast the net
a little wider and you'll find garage girl groups
like **Les Plasticines** (*pictured*) and **Tu Sera
Terriblement Gentille**, the *yé-yé*-meets-Velvet
Underground sound of **Vanessa and the Os**,
and encouraging signs of female rappers –
like the militant **Keny Arkana** and sparky,
Paris-based Miami girl **Uffie** – finding a voice.

What's more, female rap/R&B figurehead
Diam's is now artistic director of Motown's
French division – the first time that the
iconic American label has opened offices
outside the US.

Actresses and models suddenly want
a piece of the singing action, a career
crossover judged more kindly by the French
than by UK or American audiences. Former
glamour girl **Carla Bruni**, arthouse darling
Jeanne Balibar and cinema star **Agnès Jaoui**
have all jumped on to the bandwagon, while
Charlotte Gainsbourg has made her first
album since she was 14 with Air and
Radiohead producer Nigel Godrich.

Speaking of comebacks, **Dani**, **Lio** and
even **Françoise Hardy**, the first lady of French
pop, have been experiencing Indian summers.
Musical emancipation has proved to be
liberating all round.

Arts & Entertainment

Olympia. *See p317.*

Mains d'Oeuvres

1 rue Charles-Garnier, 93400 St-Ouen (01.40.11. 25.25/www.mainsdoeuvres.org). M° Porte de Clignancourt or Garibaldi. **Open** *Bar* 8pm-midnight when events or concerts are on. **Admission** €8. **Credit** *Bar* MC, V.

A hub for fringe musical and performance activity in Paris, this former leisure centre for car factory workers specialises in left-field electro, rock mavericks and multimedia artists.

La Maroquinerie

23 rue Boyer, 20th (01.40.33.35.05/ www.lamaroquinerie.fr). M° Gambetta. **Open** *Box office* 2.30-6.30pm Mon-Fri. *Concerts* 8pm Mon-Fri. **Credit** MC, V. **Map** p403 P4.

Literary discussion and rock 'n' roll meet at this happening locale. It's now home to the *Inrocks'* Indie Club nights, featuring Anglo and French rock, but there are still traces of its world music roots.

Nouveau Casino

109 rue Oberkampf, 11th (01.43.57.57.40/ www.nouveaucasino.net). M° Parmentier, St-Maur or Ménilmontant. **Credit** *Bar* MC, V. **Map** p403 N5.

Bankable, loveable if rather commercial venue run by the adjacent Café Charbon, with fab acoustics, gigs and club nights featuring rock, dub and garage, and reasonable drinks prices. Get sweaty down on the floor or survey the action from the balcony.

Olympia

28 bd des Capucines, 9th (01.55.27.10.00/ www.olympiahall.com). M° Opéra. **Open** *Box office* 10am-9pm Mon-Sat; 10am-7pm Sun. **Credit** AmEx, DC, MC, V. **Map** p401 G4.

Once graced by the Beatles, Stones and the leading names in French *chanson*, this legendary venue is now mainly a nostalgia shop, although Mogwai and Gotan Project appeared recently. **Photos** *p316.*

Paris Paris

5 avenue de l'Opéra, 1st (01.42.60.64.45/www.le parisparis.com). M° Pyramides. **Open** 11pm-5am Tue-Sat. **Drinks** €10. **Credit** MC, V. **Map** p401 H5.

This sweaty *boîte* is a new addition to local nightlife, attracting youngsters and fashionistas for drunken electro and rock nights. *See also p325.*

Point Ephémère

200 quai de Valmy, 10th (01.40.34.02.48/ www.pointephemere.org). M° Jaurès or Louis Blanc. **Open** 10am-2am daily. **Credit** AmEx, DC, MC, V. **Map** p403 Q5.

Sister venue to Mains d'Oeuvres, this converted warehouse is a top spot for up-and-coming local rock acts, as well as jazz and world music.

La Scène Bastille

2bis rue des Taillandiers, 11th (01.48.06.50.70/ www.la-scene.com). M° Bastille. **Open** midnight-6am Wed-Sun. Closed Aug. **Credit** *Bar* MC, V. **Map** p407 M7.

Watch from the chill-out alcoves as the kids strut to hip hop, funk and jazz. Club nights too (*see p325*).

Le Trabendo

211 av Jean-Jaurès, 19th (01.42.01.12.12/www. trabendo.fr). M° Porte de Pantin. **Credit** MC, V. **Map** p403 inset.

This quirky, minimal-futurist spot has carved out a niche in all things alternative, from post-rock to drum 'n' bass, avant-garde hip hop to modern jazz.

Le Triptyque

142 rue Montmartre, 2nd (01.40.28.05.55/www. letriptyque.com). M° Bourse or Grands Boulevards. **Open** 9.30pm-4am Mon-Wed; 9pm-6am Thur-Sat; 8pm-2am Sun. **Credit** AmEx, MC, V. **Map** p402 J4.

One of the hippest places in town, with eclectic programming and a sweaty moshpit-cum-dancefloor. Currently a focal point for Parisian rock, with occasional high-profile guests from overseas – although Pete Doherty didn't make it through customs.

Rock in bars

The Cavern

21 rue Dauphine, 6th (01.43.54.53.82). M° Odéon. **Open** 7pm-3am Mon-Thur, Sun; 7pm-5am Fri, Sat. **Credit** MC, V. **Map** p408 H6.

This lively, atmospheric St-Germain cellar is the perfect place to check out up-and-coming bands.

Le Gambetta

104 rue de Bagnolet, 20th (01.43.70.52.01). M° Gambetta. **Open** 10am-2am daily. **Admission** free-€5. **Credit** AmEx, DC, MC, V. **Map** p407 Q6.

Slump on dilapidated sofas and check out local bands as they thump away at their guitars.

O'Sullivans by the Mill

92 bd de Clichy, 18th (01.42.52.24.94). M° Blanche. **Open** noon-5am Mon-Thur, Sun; noon-6am Fri, Sat. **Credit** MC, V. **Map** p401 G2.

The basement of this drinking emporium welcomes all sorts of bands strumming and thrashing in its back room, plus there's salsa dancing on alternate Wednesday and Sunday nights.

Le Reservoir

16 rue de la Forge-Royale, 11th (01.43.56.39.60). M° Faidherbe Chaligny or Ledru-Rollin. **Open** 8pm-2am Mon-Thur; 8pm-5am Fri, Sat; noon-2am Sun. *Concerts* 10pm Mon-Thur; 11pm Fri, Sat. **Credit** AmEx, DC, MC, V. **Map** p407 N7.

This Anglo-inspired venue hosts regular club nights, stand-up comedy and live indie acts, as well as occasional low-key performances from larger acts. Also serves up a jazz brunch on Sundays.

Chanson

Chez Adel

10 rue de la Grange-aux-Belles, 10th (01.42.08. 24.61). M° Jacques Bonsergent. **Open** noon-midnight Tue-Sun. **Credit** MC, V. **Map** p402 L3.

Patron Adel is the most renowned *chanson*-café owner in Paris, and this is reflected in the enticing repertoire of *chanson* and eastern European sounds.

The weekend starts here

Its glory days lasted no longer than six months, but **Le Bus Palladium** in Pigalle can stake a claim as one of the most chic and influential clubs of the 1960s. Revived interest in this legendary venue saw a grand reopening in September 2006, and 'Le Bus' is now back on the scene (*see p314*).

Coinciding with its relaunch, interviews with the singers, musicians, photographers and film directors who frequented it 40 years earlier attested to the venue's enduring mystique. Back in the day, Gainsbourg namechecked it in song, while the Beatles sipped rum and Cokes at its bar.

Le Bus began its brief spell in the limelight back in 1965, when dancer and part-time hairdresser James Arch became its boundlessly enthusiastic and resourceful boss. Prior to this, Arch had worked as a be-bop dancer in Club St-Germain and Caveau de la Huchette, with only limited experience of running a disco in St-Michel and organising surprise parties. He was able to negotiate the rent for a place in Pigalle for Friday and Saturday nights and Sunday lunchtimes, funding the project with a loan from his mother. Despite stiff competition, Le Bus was an overnight success, thanks to a couple of Arch's inspired innovations. The first was an open-door policy that marked it out from the snobby attitude of other venues, particularly towards *banlieuesards* – suburban kids. As a *banlieuesard* himself, from Asnières, Arch

knew all about having to dash while the party was in full swing to catch the last train or bus home. He struck a deal with tour-bus drivers to pick up and drop off suburban revellers for a nominal charge of two francs each way – hence the Bus Palladium.

Legend in leather Vince Taylor played on the second night, and pretty soon everyone who was anyone was there. Antoine and Michel Polnareff were regulars, as was Roman Polanski; trend-setting singer Stone made her mark as a dancer there, and Dalí made himself the club's unofficial ambassador. It was a place to see and be seen, launch your career or just take part in competitions for who could grow the longest hair.

Police attention, inevitable given its success, meant that the giddy good times couldn't last, and Arch was soon forced to move to other premises. Several attempts at reopening it stalled. In the mid 1990s, Le Bus gave up on live music and became a club like any other; in 2004, it closed completely.

The current refit just might work. While the new interior reflects the feel of the original, it's fitted out with what the management claims is one of the best sound systems in Europe. With stand-up comedy on Sundays, concerts on Friday and alternate Wednesday nights and the cream of homegrown DJs appearing for club events, Le Bus could have a bright future. Fittingly, there are still no dress codes or face police at the door.

Le Limonaire

*18 cité Bergère, 9th (01.45.23.33.33/http://
limonaire.free.fr). M° Grands Boulevards.* **Open**
Concerts 10pm Mon-Sat; 7pm Sun. **Credit** MC, V.
Map p402 J4.
A *bistrot à vins* where serious *chanson* takes the
limelight. Performances vary from acoustic, piano-
led *chansonniers* to cabarets.

Le Magique

*42 rue de Gergovie, 14th (01.45.43.21.32/
www.aumagique.com). M° Pernéty.* **Open** *Concerts*
9.30pm Wed, Thur; 10pm Fri, Sat. **No credit cards.**
Map p405 F10.
Artist-in-residence Marc Havet serenades punters
with politically incorrect *chanson*, plus occasional
poetry events and exhibitions.

Sentier des Halles

*50 rue d'Aboukir, 2nd (01.42.61.89.96/
www.sentierdeshalles.fr). M° Sentier.* **Open** *Concerts*
8-10pm Tue-Sat. **No credit cards. Map** p402 J4.
More a concert venue than a music bar, Le Sentier
is where celebrated and new artists entertain a discerning seated crowd.

Le Vieux Belleville

*12 rue des Envierges, 20th (01.44.62.92.66/www.
le-vieux-belleville.com). M° Pyrenées.* **Open** *Concerts*
9pm Tue-Sat. **Credit** MC, V. **Map** p403 N4.
For an authentic Belleville rendezvous, there's no
better spot than this old-style terrace café, where
accordion music and croaky-voiced *chanson* endure.

Floating venues

Batofar

*Opposite 11 quai François-Mauriac, 13th
(01.53.60.17.03/www.batofar.org). M° Bibliothèque
François Mitterrand or Quai de la Gare.* **Open** 6pm-
4am Tue-Sat. **Admission** €5-€20. **Credit** MC, V.
Map p407 N10.
Distinctively red, enduringly hip party boat, laying
on international DJs, rappers and underground
noise-merchants for an up-for-it crowd. The terrace
is open from 7pm in summer. *See also p323.*

Guinguette Pirate

*Opposite 11 quai François-Mauriac, 13th
(01.44.06.96.45/www.guinguettepirate.com).
M° Bibliothèque François Mitterrand or Quai de la
Gare.* **Open** 7pm-2am Tue-Sat. **Admission** €5-€12.
Credit MC, V. **Map** p407 N10.
Moored beside the Batofar, this rickety Chinese junk
is a good place to catch the cult/experimental end of
things, even if the speakers sometimes cut out.

World & traditional music

Cité de la Musique

*221 av Jean-Jaurès, 19th (01.44.84.44.84/www.cite-
musique.fr). M Porte de Pantin.* **Open** *Concerts* Tue-
Sat (times vary). **Admission** €17-€38. **Credit** MC,
V. **Map** p403 inset.

This Villette venue welcomes names from the four
corners of the globe, and does a fine line in contemporary classical, avant-jazz and electronica.

Institut du Monde Arabe

*1 rue des Fossés-St-Bernard, 5th (01.40.51.38.38/
www.imarabe.org). M° Jussieu.* **Open** *Concerts*
8.30pm Fri, Sat. **Admission** varies. **Credit** MC, V.
Map p409 K7.
This huge, plush auditorium attracts some of the
biggest names in Arab music.

Kibélé

*12 rue de l'Echiquier, 10th (01.48.24.57.74). M°
Bonne Nouvelle.* **Concerts** 9pm Mon-Sat. **Admission**
free-€5. **Credit** AmEx, MC, V. **Map** p402 K4.
Music from across the Mediterranean and beyond,
with a Turkish restaurant in the same building.

Satellit' Café

*44 rue de la Folie-Méricourt, 11th (01.47.00.48.87/
www.satellit-cafe.com). M° Oberkampf, Parmentier
or St-Ambroise.* **Open** *Bar* 8pm-1am Tue, Wed; 8pm-
4am Thur; 10pm-6am Fri, Sat. *Club* 11pm-6am Thur-
Sat. *Concerts* 9pm Tue-Thur. **Admission** €10.
Credit *Bar* MC, V. **Map** p403 M5.
This spacious bar lends its sound system to all
things global, but the focus is on traditional African
music. Great late-night bar too.

Théâtre de la Ville

*2 pl du Châtelet, 4th (01.42.74.22.77/www.theatre
delaville-paris.com). M° Châtelet.* **Open** *Box office*
11am-7pm Mon-Sat. *Concerts* 8.30pm Mon-Fri; 5pm,
8.30pm Sat. **Admission** €17. **Credit** MC, V.
Map p408 J6.
Music and dance of the highest order can be found
at both of its sites, with performers from Iraq, Japan,
Thailand and Brittany amid the classical recitals.
Other locations: 31 rue des Abbesses, 18th.

La Vieille Grille

*1 rue du Puits-de-l'Ermite, 5th (01.47.07.22.11/
http://vieille.grille.free.fr). M° Place Monge.* **Open**
Concerts 8.30pm Mon-Sat; 3pm, 5pm Sun. **Admission**
prices vary. **No credit cards. Map** p406 K8.
Intimate, artist-run locale, great for passionate performances of tango, French songs and klezmer, as
well as operettas, theatre and children's shows.

Jazz & blues

Baiser Salé

*58 rue des Lombards, 1st (01.42.33.37.71/
www.lebaisersale.com). M° Châtelet.* **Open** *Jazz
concerts* 10pm daily. **Admission** €12-€18. **Credit**
AmEx, DC, MC, V. **Map** p406 J6.
The 'salty kiss' divides its time between passing
chansonniers and jazzmen of every stripe.

Le Bilboquet

*13 rue St-Benoît, 6th (01.45.48.81.84/http://
jazzclub.bilboquet.free.fr). M° St-Germain des Prés.*
Open *Concerts* 9am daily. **Admission** (incl 1 drink)
€18. **Credit** AmEx, DC, MC, V. **Map** p408 H6.

The legendary Le Bilboquet – in its heyday, host to the likes of Miles Davis, Duke Ellington and Charlie Parker – has smartened itself up to reclaim its place as St-Germain's key jazz address.

Caveau de la Huchette
5 rue de la Huchette, 5th (01.43.26.65.05/ www.caveaudelahuchette.fr). M° St-Michel/RER St-Michel Notre-Dame. **Open** *Concerts* 10.15pm daily. **Admission** €11-€13; €9 students. **Credit** MC, V. **Map** p408 J7.
This medieval cellar has been a Left Bank mainstay for 60 years now. Jazz shows are followed by lively early-hours performances in a swing, rock, soul or disco vein, and attract a regular student following.

Caveau des Oubliettes
52 rue Galande, 5th (01.46.34.23.09). M° St-Michel or Maubert Mutualité/RER St-Michel Notre-Dame. **Open** *Concerts* 10pm daily. **Admission** free. **Credit** MC, V. **Map** p408 J7.
A foot-tapping frenzy thrives in this converted medieval dungeon, complete with instruments of torture and underground passages (the name translates as 'the cellar of the forgotten ones'). There are jam sessions in the week if you fancy contributing.

Au Duc des Lombards
42 rue des Lombards, 1st (01.42.33.22.88/www. ducdeslombards.com). M° Châtelet. **Open** *Concerts* 10pm Mon-Sat. **Admission** €19-€25. **Credit** MC, V. **Map** p406 J6.
This small, atmospheric den has improved its decor and seating, and started running attractive theme nights. Keep a look out for house band Le Duc des Lombards Jazz Affair.

Lionel Hampton Jazz Club
Hotel Meridien Etoile, 81 bd Gouvion-St-Cyr, 17th (01.40.68.30.42/www.jazzclub-paris.com). M° Porte Maillot. **Open** *Concerts* 10.30pm daily. **Admission** (incl 1 drink) €23-€25 Fri, Sat. **Credit** MC, V. **Map** p400 B2.
This classy hotel invites top American names and French ensembles to perform blues, jazz and vocal. Generally easy on the ear.

New Morning
7-9 rue des Petites-Ecuries, 10th (01.45.23.51.41/ www.newmorning.com). M° Château d'Eau. **Open** *Box office* 4-7.30pm Mon-Fri. *Concerts* 9pm daily. **Admission** €15-€21. **Credit** MC, V. **Map** p402 K3.
One of the best for the latest jazz exponents, with a broad policy also embracing *chanson*, blues, world and sophisticated pop.

Parc Floral de Paris
Route de la Pyramide, Bois de Vincennes, 12th (01.49.57.42.84/www.parcfloraldeparis.com). M° Château de Vincennes. **Open** *Concerts* (May-July) 4.30pm Sat, Sun. **Admission** €1.50-€3. **No credit cards.**
Every summer, well-known names serenade a chilled-out crowd at this open-air festival on the eastern outskirts of the city.

Petit Journal Montparnasse
113 rue de Commandment-René-Mouchotte, 14th (01.43.21.56.70/www.petitjournal-montparnasse. com) M° Gaîté or Montparnasse-Bienvenüe. **Open** *Concerts* 10pm Mon-Sat. **Admission** (incl 1 drink) €20. **Credit** MC, V. **Map** p405 F9.
Two-level jazz brasserie with Latin sounds, R&B and soul-gospel. Dinner (€55-€85) starts at 8pm.

Quai du Blues
17 bd Vital-Bouhot, Ile de la Jatte, 92200 Neuilly-sur-Seine (01.46.24.22.00/www.quaidublues.com). M° Pont de Levallois. **Open** *Concerts* Oct-June 10.30pm Fri, Sat. **Admission** €20. **Credit** MC, V.
If you like it black and bluesy, this is your place. Like many venues, Quai du Blues closes over the summer, reopening at the beginning of October. Dinner packages start at €27.

Le Sabot
6 rue du Sabot, 6th (01.42.22.21.56). M° St-Germain des Prés or St-Sulpice. **Open** noon-3pm, 6pm-2am Mon-Sat. *Concerts* 9pm. **Admission** free. **Credit** MC, V. **Map** p405 G7.
Another tasty jazz-while-you-eat spot, where the multitalented owner joins jazz, blues and *chanson* guests with his own piano and sax stylings.

Les 7 Lézards
10 rue des Rosiers, 4th (01.48.87.08.97/ www.7lezards.com). M° St-Paul. **Open** *Concerts* 7pm or 10pm daily. **Admission** €6-€16. **No credit cards.** **Map** p409 L6.
From fusion to bop, *chanson* to improv, and one of the finest jam sessions around (free on Sunday evenings), this cellar hosts the hottest sounds.

Le Slow Club
130 rue de Rivoli, 1st (01.42.33.84.30). M° Châtelet. **Open** *Concerts* 10pm Fri, Sat. **Admission** €9-€13. **Credit** MC, V. **Map** p406 J6.
This medieval cellar may be tiny but fills the space with boogie-woogie and dance-friendly R&B. Located opposite La Samaritaine on rue de Rivoli, it's not hard to find.

Le Sunset/Le Sunside
60 rue des Lombards, 1st (Sunset 01.40.26.46.60/ Sunside 01.40.26.21.25/www.sunset-sunside.com). M° Châtelet. **Open** *Concerts* 9pm, 10pm daily. **Admission** €8-€25. **Credit** MC, V. **Map** p406 J6.
A split-personality venue, with Sunset dealing in electric groups and Sunside catering for acoustic performances. The rep of both pulls in big names from both sides of the Atlantic, making this an essential port of call for any jazz pilgrimage to Paris.

Théâtre du Châtelet
1 pl du Châtelet (information 01.40.28.28.00/ booking 01.40.28.28.41/www.chatelet-theatre.com). M° Châtelet. **Admission** €16-€69. **Credit** AmEx, DC, MC, V. **Map** p406 J6.
This classic music hall has another life as a jazz and *chanson* venue – look out for Brad Mehldau, Juliette Greco and Bobby McFerrin in 2007.

Nightlife

From Hell to Nirvana – hitting Paris Paris on the way.

Paris no longer enjoys a reputation as a leading nightlife capital, but beneath the apparently quiet surface there's a vibrant assortment of venues throbbing to an array of sounds. Look in the right places and you'll find sweating dancefloors, dive bars stuffed with celebrity DJs, boats rocking from dusk to dawn and some of the most stylish clubs in the world. *See p327*

Paris by night: DJs pick their faves.

Since 2005, Parisian clubs have undergone a renaissance. New trendy places tend to include a range of electronic music, throwing techno, hip hop, house, disco and even rock into their eclectic mix – as epitomised by the fashion for 'selectors' rather than mix DJs. Among the new wave of clubs, the current forerunner is **Paris Paris**, an intimate basement venue that's been the talk of the town in 2006. If they're hip, they play and party here. Provided you get in, you'll be rubbing shoulders with Justice, Sebastian, Mr Oizo, Kavinsky, Busy P and other who's who members of Paris' clubbing community.

Fashion and looking cool are all-important in Parisian clubs and, in a city where outdated elitist door policies are still ubiquitous, even getting into a club can be difficult and a mark of status in itself. Often the best vibes are to be found in grubby basement dives such as the mixed-lesbian **Pulp**, where Ivan Smaghe and Chloe play Kill The DJ parties and Jennifer Cardini hosts her long running Lust night.

At Toxic, Uncle O and Agent Solo are joined by buffalo girls and all manner of strange behaviour. Their new home is itself another newcomer, **Point Ephémère** – opened by the team behind **Les Mains d'Oeuvres**, famous for occasional massive parties and regular gigs. A few years older but still a centre for big name DJs, **Triptyque** is both somewhere to be seen and to get down in.

Always top for sound, **The Rex** has just installed one of the best systems in Europe. Meanwhile **Les Bains Douches**, until recently a no-go area in stylish circles, is back on sparkling form with a new music policy and returned fashionable crowd.

Look out for one-offs by hip new labels: Ed Banger, Kitsune Midnight, Record Makers, and Freak 'n Chic and the veteran imprints Versatile, F Communications, UWE and Yellow. **Techno Parade** (*see p273*), the city's own Love Parade, is back on in September.

For super-club dancefloors, head over to **Queen**, mostly gay, and **Club Mix**, mostly mixed. And if you don't know when to stop, try **Chez Carmen**, where Parisians with a similar aversion to sleep keep the party going until lunchtime. Also worth checking for after-parties are **Batofar, Bateau Concorde Atlantique** and **Nouveau Casino**. For an overview of gay venues, *see p305* **6am eternal**.

The Bastille, the Marais, Oberkampf, the Grands Boulevards, the Pigalle and Canal St-Martin are littered with bars and small, hip venues. Good starting points for any night out, and useful places to pick up flyers, are bars such as **La Fourmi**, **Andy Whaloo** and **L'Ile Enchantee**. A number of small venues offer hip-hop and Latin nights, although these genres are less well represented in the main clubs, despite an enduring obsession with hip hop. But if dancing to salsa or world beats is your thing, there are options such as the long-serving **La Java** and **La Cabaret Sauvage**.

TIPS AND INFORMATION

Useful club listings websites include www.flyersweb.com, www.novaplanet.com, www.radiofg.com and www.lemonsound.com. Radio stations FG (98.2FM) and Nova (101.5FM) also provide listings.

The last métro leaves at around 12.45am and the first one only gets rolling at 5.45am; between those times you'll have to take night buses or taxis. Central Paris is small – it's often possible to walk to your next destination.

CLUBBING COMMANDMENTS

When clubbing in Paris, local rules apply:
1. Go out late. Parisians like hanging out at home, drinking wine and going for a good meal. This means clubbing generally happens late, so arrive at 1am or 2am.
2. Check flyers in clothes shops and DJ bars for free or reduced entry.
3. Talk loudly in English. Clubs gain kudos for being international, and like tourists because they tend to spend more.
4. Order a bottle of spirits at the door at upmarket clubs. It can get you ushered straight past the doorman, and is often cheaper than buying a round of drinks by the glass.
5. Avoid turning up with lots of pissed mates. Drunks and large gangs are almost guaranteed not to get in – unless you're all female.

Club bars

Andy Whaloo

69 rue des Gravilliers, 3rd (01.42.71.20.38) M° Arts et Métiers. **Open** 5pm-2am Tue-Sun. **Admission** free. **Drinks** €2-€10. **Credit** AmEx, MC, V. **Map** p409 K5.

Owned by the people behind Momo and Sketch in London, Andy Whaloo serves sumptuous snack food and is tastefully decorated with Moroccan artefacts. The seating is made from upturned paint cans and the DJs play everything from hip hop to techno. It can be quiet early on (*see p222*), but the atmosphere heats up as the night gets longer.

Café Chéri(e)

44 bd de la Villette, 19th (01.42.02.02.05). M° Belleville. **Open** 11am-2am daily. **Admission** free. **Drinks** €2.80-€6.50. **Credit** MC, V. **Map** p403 M3.

A popular DJ bar, especially in summer, when fashionistas flock to the terrace. Expect anything from DJ Jet Boy's electro punk to house and '80s classics. Also a chic daytime hangout (*see p228*).

La Fabrique

53 rue du Fbg-St-Antoine, 11th (01.43.07.67.07/ www.fabrique.fr). M° Bastille. **Open** 6pm-5am Tue-Sat. **Admission** free Tue-Fri; €10 Sat. **Drinks** €2.50-€11. **Credit** MC, V. **Map** p407 M7.

Local house DJs spin at this bar-club-restaurant on the busy St-Antoine stretch . It's surrounded by several other venues, so you can nip into the nearby San San or take your pick of the other bars and eateries.

La Fourmi

74 rue des Martyrs, 18th (01.42.64.70.35). M° Pigalle. **Open** 8.30am-2am Mon-Thur, Sun; 8am-4am Fri, Sat. **Admission** free. **Drinks** €2-€6. **Credit** MC, V. **Map** p402 H2.

Popular with everyone from in-the-know tourists to fashionable Parisians, Fourmi was a precursor to the industrial-design, informal, music-led bars that have sprung up around Paris – and it's still very much a style leader. Great throughout the day for coffees or a beer (*see p222*), it has a small seating area outside and an always-busy bar with DJ decks. You can stay into the early hours at weekends, but it's also a handy pre-club *rendez-vous* and flyer pick-up point.

L'Île Enchantée

65 bd de la Villette, 10th (01.42.01.67.99/ http://lileenchantee.free.fr/). M° Colonel Fabien. **Open** 8am-2am Mon-Fri; 5pm-2am Sat, Sun. **Admission** free. **Drinks** €2.50-€6.50. **Credit** MC, V. **Map** p403 M3.

Downstairs this feels like a trendy gastropub; thanks to an up-to-date music policy, it makes for a good pre-club drinking venue. Upstairs there's a bijou disco, which is where you'll find the Parisian pre-club party people taking in the tunes. *See p229.*

Lizard Lounge

18 rue du Bourg-Tibourg, 4th. (01.42.72.81.34/ www.hip-bars.com/lizard). M° Hôtel de Ville or St-Paul. **Open** 4pm-2am daily. **Admission** free. **Drinks** €5-€10. **Credit** AmEx, MC, V. **Map** p409 K6.

Café Chéri(e). *See p322.*

At this tiny basement venue, connected to an Anglo-French owned shop, regular Friday nights cater for experimental electronic live acts and DJs. Check the website for details before venturing down.

Le Troisième Lieu

62 rue Quincampoix, 4th (01.48.04.85.64/www.le troisiemelieu.com). M° Rambuteau. **Open** 6pm-2am Mon-Sat. **Admission** free. **Drinks** €2.50-€5. **Credit** MC, V. **Map** p402 K5.

Opened by Les Ginettes Armées, organisers of renowned Sunday lesbian and mixed events (*see p306*), Le Troisième Lieu tends toward electro and house. The ground floor hosts DJs mixing eclectic sounds for chatting and relaxing to, while the basement is more dancefloor.

Cool clubs

Bateau Concorde Atlantique

Porte de Solferino, 25 quai Anatole-France, 7th (01.47.05.71.03/www.concorde-atlantique.com). M° Assemblée Nationale or Musée d'Orsay. **Open** *Mid June-mid Sept* 11pm-5am Mon-Fri; 5pm-5am Sat; 6pm-5am Sun. **Admission** free-€10. **Drinks** €5-€8. **Credit** MC, V. **Map** p401 F5.

With its terrace and voluminous dancefloor, this two-level boat is a clubbing paradise in the summer. The legendary Respect crew held a popular, fondly remembered Wednesday night here and are still, alongside other cool crews like Ed Banger, involved in putting on parties at the venue. **Photo** *p324*.

Batofar

Opposite 11 quai François-Mauriac, 13th (recorded information 01.53.60.17.30/www.batofar.org). M° Quai de la Gare. **Open** 11pm-6am Mon-Sat; 6am-noon 1st Sun of mth. **Admission** €5-€12. **Drinks** €3.50-€8. **Credit** MC, V. **Map** p407 N10.

In recent years the Batofar has gone through a rapid succession of management teams, with varying levels of success. The current management focus on live programming (*see p319*) and straight club nights. In summer clubbers chill on the quayside while DJs play on deck. Inside are loads of nooks to hide in, and a robust soundsystem. **Photo** *p328*.

Chez Carmen

53 rue Vivienne, 2nd (01.42.36.45.41). M° Grands Boulevards. **Open** 6pm-noon Tue-Sun. **Admission** free. **Drinks** €5. **Credit** V. **Map** p402 H4.

The tiny but infamous gay-mixed dancefloor is where Parisian insomniacs spend their early morning hours hiding from the daylight.

Le Divan du Monde

75 rue des Martyrs, 18th (01.42.52.02.46/www. divandumonde.com). M° Pigalle or Abbesses. **Open** 7pm-2am Tue-Thur; 7pm-6am Fri, Sat. **Admission** €6-€30. **Drinks** €4-€8. **Credit** MC, V. **Map** p402 J2.

Upstairs specialises in VJ events, while downstairs holds dub, reggae, funk and world-music club nights. There are various one-off events, and it's where the Spoutnik crew holds its parties.

Spread over three levels, Lizard Lounge is a trendy Marais hangout (*see p223*). There's a boozer upstairs and a more full-on DJ bar in the booth-filled basement – often full, thanks to its modest proportions. Local jocks play a variety of contemporary styles.

Le Mandala Ray

32-34 rue Marbeuf, 8th (01.56.88.36.36/ www.manray.fr). M° Franklin D. Roosevelt. **Open** 7pm-2am Mon-Thur, Sun; 7pm-5am Fri, Sat. **Admission** free; €25 after 11pm Fri, Sat. **Drinks** €10-€15. **Credit** MC, V. **Map** p400 D4.

Created by Johnny Depp, Sean Penn, John Malkovich and Mick Hucknall, this glamorous bar-restaurant (*see p193*) attracts upmarket, well turned-out types for musically themed nights, record launches and the like.

La Mezzanine de l'Alcazar

62 rue Mazarine, 6th (01.53.10.19.99/www. alcazar.fr). M° Odéon. **Open** 7pm-2am daily. **Admission** free. **Drinks** €9-€11. **Credit** AmEx, DC, MC, V. **Map** p406 H7.

The stylish Conran-owned mezzanine bar has become a well-heeled hangout, but it still attracts top local DJs and live acts from Wednesday to Saturday nights. Thursday is set aside for live music, and the weekends feature good-time house, funk and disco.

Project 101

44 rue de La Rochefoucauld, 9th (01.49.95.95.85/ www.project-101.com). M° Pigalle. **Open** 10pm-2am Fri. **Admission** free-€5. **Drinks** €2-€4. **No credit cards. Map** p401 H2.

Arts & Entertainment

All hands on decks – **Bateau Concorde Atlantique**. *See p323.*

Elysée Montmartre

72 bd de Rochechouart, 18th (01.44.92.45.38/www. elyseemontmartre.com). M° Anvers. **Open** midnight-6am Fri, Sat. **Admission** €10-€15. **Drinks** €4-€10. **Credit** *Bar* MC, V. **Map** p402 J2.

Both a gig venue (*see p315*) and a club, Elysée hosts big nights by outside promoters, such as Open House, Panik and Nightfever for young clubbers.

La Flèche d'Or

102bis rue de Bagnolet, 20th (01.44.64.01.02/ www.flechedor.com). M° Alexandre Dumas. **Open** 8pm-2am Mon, Sun; 8pm-5am Wed-Sat. **Admission** free. **Drinks** €3-€10. **Credit** MC, V. **Map** p403 Q6.

This converted métro station recently returned under new management and has quickly won over the Parisian muso crowd with its adventurous programming, from punk to *nouvelle chanson*. *See p315.*

Folies Pigalle

11 pl Pigalle, 9th (01.48.78.55.25/www.folies-pigalle.com). M° Pigalle. **Open** midnight-dawn Mon-Thur; midnight-noon Fri, Sat; 6pm-midnight Sun. **Admission** €20 (incl 1 drink); €7 Sun evening. **Drinks** €10. **Credit** AmEx, MC, V. **Map** p402 G2.

Folies Pigalle's programme includes what claims to be Paris' only transsexual night, a *soirée* devoted to latex, plus house, R&B and electronic nights.

Le Gibus

18 rue du Fbg-du-Temple, 11th (01.47.00.78.88/ www.gibus.fr). M° République or Temple. **Open** midnight-dawn Tue-Sat; 6pm-2am Sun. *Concerts* 8-11.30pm Fri. **Admission** €5-€20. **Drinks** €5-€8. **Credit** *Bar* MC, V. **Map** p402 L4.

A famous '80s punk venue, Le Gibus has gone through plenty of different styles changes in its time. Today it takes in techno, reggae, psychedelic trance, 1980s pop and hip hop on different evenings.

Le Glaz'art

7-15 av de la Porte de-la-Villette, 19th (01.40.36. 55.65). M° Porte de la Villette. **Open** 8.30pm-2am Thur (sometimes Wed); 11pm-5am Fri, Sat. **Admission** €6. **Drinks** €3.50-€7. **Credit** AmEx, MC, V. **Map** p403 inset.

This converted Eurolines station is situated way out north-west, but its strong DJ nights and live acts pull punters in from central Paris. Breakbeat and drum 'n' bass nights have made the venue a mecca for breaks fans, and it has a nocturnal garden to chill in.

Les Mains d'Oeuvres

1 rue Charles-Garnier, 18th (01.40.11.25.25/www. mainsdoeuvres.org). M° Garibaldi. **Open** days and times vary according to event. **Admission** €8-€10. **Drinks** €3-€6. **Credit** *Bar* MC, V.

A rehearsal space and live venue (*see p317*) for new bands, occasionally the whole building is turned into a club venue with different rooms devoted to different music styles. Look for flyers or on the website.

Nouveau Casino

109 rue Oberkampf, 11th (01.43.57.57.40). M° Parmentier. **Open** midnight-5am Wed-Sat. **Admission** €5-€10. **Drinks** €5-€10. **Credit** *Bar* MC, V. **Map** p403 M5.

Handily surrounded by the numerous bars of rue Oberkampf and tucked behind the legendary Café Charbon (*see p228*), Nouveau Casino is a concert venue (*see p317*) that also hosts some of Paris' liveliest club nights from Wednesday to Saturday. Local collectives, international names and record labels, such as Versatile, regularly put nights on here.

Paris Paris
5 avenue de l'Opéra, 1st (01.42.60.64.45/ www.leparisparis.com). M° Pyramides. **Open** 11pm-5am Tue-Sat. **Admission** free. **Drinks** €10. **Credit** MC, V. **Map** p401 H5.
Currently the hottest spot in Paris, and the subject of endless column inches, Paris Paris has the Parisian club glitterati regularly passing through its doors, either to DJ or to enjoy the party – or both. Getting in isn't easy, but once inside you'll find a bustling basement where the focus is on having fun, with iPod battles between hip hop and rock crews adding to the on-the-button music policy. *See p317.*

Point Ephémère
200 quai de Valmy, 10th (01.40.34.02.48/www. pointephemere.org). M° Jaurès or Louis Blanc. **Open** 10am-2am daily. **Admission** prices vary. **Drinks** €3-€7. **Credit** AmEx, DC, MC, V. **Map** 402 L2.
Generally thought of as bit of Berlin that relocated here, Point Ephémère is one of the coolest arrivals on the Parisian scene. An uncompromising programming policy (*see p317*) delivers some of the best international electronic music to be had in town. There's also a restaurant and bar with decks and a gallery, and terrace space by the canal in summer.

Pulp
25 bd Poissonnière, 2nd (01.40.26.01.93/www.pulp-paris.com). M° Grands Boulevards. **Open** midnight-5am Thur-Sat. **Admission** free Thur; €10 Fri, Sat. **Drinks** €5-€9. **Credit** MC, V. **Map** p402 J4.
A lesbian club (*see p306*), Pulp draws a mixed crowd on Wednesdays and Thursdays for some of Paris' hottest midweek club action in this quintessential dive bar. Big nights include Kill the DJ, where Ivan Smagghe (Black Strobe) and DJ Chloe hold court, and Jenifer Cardini's Lust night.

Red Light
34 rue du Départ, 15th (01.42.79.94.53). M° Edgar Quinet or Montparnasse Bienvenüe. **Open** midnight-11am Fri, Sat. **Admission** (incl 1 drink) €20. **Drinks** from €10. **Credit** AmEx, MC, V. **Map** p405 F9.
The former Enfer ('Hell') remains a house mecca with local and global DJs spinning to a young, up-for-it, often gay, well-groomed crowd. Regular Friday and Saturday nights include Strictly House, Sound of Red Light and French Kiss.

Rex
5 bd Poissonnière, 2nd (01.42.36.10.96/www.rex club.com). M° Bonne Nouvelle. **Open** 11.30pm-dawn Wed-Sat. **Admission** free-€10. **Drinks** €5-€12. **Credit** *Bar* MC, V. **Map** p402 J4.
The Rex used its annual August holiday in 2006 to install a brand new sound system, revealed to much fanfare in September. With over 50 different sound

configurations at the DJ's fingertips, it's been designed to be a magnet for the top turntable stars. Once associated with legendary techno pioneer Laurent Garnier, the Rex has remained at the top of the Paris techno scene and occupies an unassailable position as the city's serious club music venue.

La Scène Bastille
2bis rue des Taillandiers, 11th (01.48.06.50.70/ www.la-scene.com). M° Bastille. **Open** midnight-6am Wed-Sun. Closed Aug. **Admission** €12. **Drinks** €4-€9. **Credit** *Bar* MC, V. **Map** p407 M7.
This tastefully decorated club-bar-venue-restaurant complex holds regular rock concerts (*see p317*), as well as club events from Thursday to Saturday. The agenda here changes constantly, so do check what's on. Popular gay nights too. *See p305* **6am eternal**.

Le Triptyque
142 rue Montmartre, 2nd (01.40.28.05.55/ www.letriptyque.com). M° Grands Boulevards or Bourse. **Open** 11.30pm-3am Wed; 11pm-6am Thur-Sat. **Admission** free-€12. **Drinks** €4-€10. **Credit** AmEx, MC, V. **Map** p402 J4.
Set amid the hub of club activity around Grands Boulevards, Le Triptyque stays on top of the club scene thanks to spot-on programming. *See p317.*

Wagg
62 rue Mazarine, 6th (01.55.42.22.00/www. wagg.fr). M° Odéon. **Open** 11.30pm-6am Fri, Sat; 3pm-midnight Sun. **Admission** €15 Fri, Sat; €10 Sun. **Drinks** €7-€10. **Credit** AmEx, DC, MC, V. **Map** p406 H7.
Refurbished during the makeover of La Mezzanine upstairs, Wagg went through a period attracting big name UK DJs but has settled down to be home to a well-to-do Left Bank crowd. Expect house and disco at weekends, and salsa on Sundays.

Glitzy clubs

Les Bains Douches
7 rue du Bourg-l'Abbé, 3rd (01.48.87.01.80). M° Etienne Marcel. **Open** 11pm-6am Wed-Sun. **Admission** €10-€20. **Drinks** €6-€12. **Credit** AmEx, MC, V. **Map** p402 J5.
Once a global leader, Les Bains lost its way in the 1990s, relying on its reputation to pull in tourists. This all changed recently, and now local star DJs like Busy P and international names such as Erol Alkan grace its decks. The clientele is increasingly, but not exclusively, gay. *See p305* **6am eternal**.

Le Baron
6 av Marceau, 8th (01.47.20.04.01). M° Alma Marceau. **Open** times vary. **Admission** free. **Drinks** from €10. **Credit** MC, V. **Map** p400 D5.
Owned by André and Lionel, the brains behind Paris Paris (*see left*), this small but supremely exclusive 8th-district hangout for the international jet set at one time was an upmarket brothel and has kept the decor. It only holds 150, but if you manage to get in you'll be rubbing shoulders with celebrities.

**OUR CLIMATE NEEDS
A HELPING HAND TODAY**

Be a smart traveller. Help to offset your carbon emissions
from your trip by pledging Carbon Trees with Trees for Cities.

All the Carbon Trees that you donate through Trees for Cities
are genuinely planted as additional trees in our projects.

Trees for Cities is an independent charity working with local
communities on tree planting projects.

www.treesforcities.org   Tel 020 7587 1320

Trees for Cities
Charity registration number 1032154

Le Cab

2 pl du Palais-Royal, 1st (01.58.62.56.25/www. cabaret.fr). M° Palais Royal Musée du Louvre. **Open** *bar* 11.30pm-5am Tue. *Club* 11.30pm-5am Wed-Sat. **Admission** free Tue-Thur; €20 Fri, Sat. **Drinks** €13. **Credit** AmEx, MC, V. **Map** p402 H5.

The Cabaret, now 'Le Cab', is owned by the management behind The Mix and Queen, and has had an interior facelift by Franco-Japanese designer Ora Ito. R&B and commercial house dominate the playlist.

L'Etoile

12 rue de Presbourg, 16th (01.45.00.78.70/ www.letoileparis.com). M° Charles de Gaulle Etoile. **Open** 11pm-5am Mon-Sat. **Admission** €20 (free for women Tue). **Drinks** €16-€20. **Credit** AmEx, DC, MC, V. **Map** p400 C3.

A-list celebrity hangout where guests such as Johnny Halliday, Pamela Anderson and Robbie Williams have been known to show their faces. If you're not A-list, it's seriously hard to get in.

Nirvana

3 av Matignon, 8th (01.53.89.18.91/www.le-nirvana. com). M° Franklin D. Roosevelt. **Open** 11.30pm-6am daily. **Admission** €15 (free for women before 1am). **Drinks** €10-€12. **Credit** AmEx, DC, MC, V. **Map** p401 E4.

Opened by Buddha Bar music guru Claude Challe, Nirvana is notorious for its fearsome reputation of its door staff. Inside, the hip and beautiful shimmy on the dancefloor and the club has a vaguely Eastern theme. An eclectic music selection ranges from lounge to Ibiza house.

Paris by night: DJs pick their faves

Prominent Parisian players plug their top places for a night out.

Justice, the duo behind that 'we… are… your friends' anthem and part of the on-the-button Ed Banger stable: '**Paris Paris** (*see p325*) and also Toxic parties (now at new home **Point Ephémère**, *see p325*), hosted by the best DJs in the world – Uncle O and Agent Solo… but any place a friend is playing or providing free booze.'

Dead Sexy Inc, impeccably connected electro-rock DJs and band: '**Pulp** (*see p325*) is a super-trendy hangout. Second is **La Flèche d'Or** (*see p324*). It has a great music policy, is always surprising and they have a restaurant, DJs and very cute bartenders. **Le Divan Du Monde** (*see p323*) also has great parties, like Spoutnik.'

Rapper **Uffie** and **DJ Feadz** both play house music with hip hop attitude, and are also on the Ed Banger label: '**Paris Paris** (*see p325*) is the most select place in Paris at the moment – and it's also the place where the drinks are the most expensive. But you get to meet nice people there, and the music is very good. For sound, the **Rex** (*see p325*) has been the best club in Paris for a very long time, but this summer they did a refit to make it the best soundsystem in Europe.'

DJ Chloe, female star DJ of Kill The DJ club and record label: 'The best place at the moment in Paris for me is **Point Ephémère** (*see p325*). They have a very interesting programme, and I've discovered a lot of very

good artists there. And **Les Mains d'Oeuvres** (*see p324*) is a place for experimentation, dance shows, rock concerts and special electronics nights.'

Ygal Ohayon, DJ and label manager, Versatile Records: '**Nouveau Casino** (*see p324*) is the club where Versatile organises parties. There's also live stuff there. The club where Carl Craig, Quiet Village and Rub'N'Tug have all played can only be good!'

DJ Paulette, ex-Hacienda DJ turned resident at the Mix: 'I'm biased, of course, but **Club Mix** (*see p329*) is the only real superclub in Paris. The residents play like international guests, and those include Sven Väth, MANDY, Tiga and Chloe, Lawler, Howells, Emerson and Mr C.'

Damian Harris, aka Midfield General, Anglo-Parisian DJ/producer and boss of Skint Records: '**Bateau Concorde Atlantic** (*see p323*) was the first place I went when I arrived in Paris, and I went there every night that summer. Drinks on the deck early on, down the basement once the sun goes down, then walk home as the sun comes up over the Seine. The Ed Banger party there last year was the maddest I've played in Paris.'

Jayhem, former Kojak front man and Queen resident, currently fusing electronic and Creole music as Kemit Sources: 'For jazz, there's **New Morning** (*see p320*) and for Brazilian music there's **Favela Chic** (*see p329*) – and, of course, there's **Paris Paris** (*see p325*) and **Les Bains Douches** (*see p325*).'

Arts & Entertainment

It's a hard day's night at the **Batofar**. *See p323.*

La Suite

40 av George-V, 8th (01.53.57.49.49/www.lasuite.fr).
M° George V. **Open** 12.30-4.30am Thur-Sat (often
closed for private parties). **Admission** €15-€20.
Drinks €15. **Credit** AmEx, MC, V. **Map** p400 D4.
Cathy and David Guetta are said to be behind this
venue of plush modernist leather seating, light bar
and soft colours with themed parties every night.

VIP Room

76-78 av des Champs-Elysées, 8th (01.58.36.46.00/
www.viproom.fr). M° Franklin D. Roosevelt. **Open**
midnight-5am Tue-Sun. **Admission** free. **Drinks**
€20. **Credit** AmEx, DC, MC, V. **Map** p400 D4.
The name says it all for this stylish spot – a hit with
the crowd that populates places such as Paris Paris.

Mainstream clubs

Club Med World

39 cour St-Emilion, 12th (08.10.81.04.10). M° Cour
St-Emilion. **Open** 11pm-2am Tue-Thur; 11.30pm-
6am Fri, Sat. **Admission** €15 Tue-Thur; €20 Fri,
Sat. Free for women. **Drinks** €9. **Credit** AmEx,
MC, V. **Map** p407 N10.
Part of a massive conference, restaurant and club
complex in the Bercy Village, Club Med World hosts
popular disco and '80s nights at weekends.

Club Mix

24 rue de l'Arrivée, 15th (01.56.80.37.37/www.mix
club.fr). M° Montparnasse Bienvenüe. **Open** 11pm-
6am Wed-Sat; 5pm-1am Sun. **Admission** €12-€20.
Drinks €8. **Credit** MC, V. **Map** p405 F8.
The Mix, formerly Amnesia, has one of the city's
biggest dancefloors and DJ booths, so the music is
strictly big room. Regular international visitors
include Erick Morillo's Subliminal and Renaissance
parties, while in-house events include David
Guetta's 'Fuck Me I'm Famous', 'Hipnotic' and 'One
Night With Paulette'.

La Loco

90 bd de Clichy, 18th (01.53.41.88.89/www.la
loco.com). M° Blanche. **Open** 11pm-6am daily.
Admission €5-€20. **Drinks** €6-€8. **Credit** MC,
V. **Map** p401 G2.
La Loco has a substantial and youthful following
taking advantage of its three dancefloors, which
offer different musical genres: house, dance and
chart music on weekend nights, and metal and gothic concerts during the week.

Queen

102 av des Champs-Elysées, 8th (08.92.70.73.30/
www.queen.fr). M° George V. **Open** midnight-7am
Mon-Thur, Sun; midnight-8am Fri, Sat. **Admission**
€15 Mon-Thur, Sun; €20 Fri, Sat. **Drinks** €10.
Credit *Bar* AmEx, MC, V. **Map** p400 D4.
Once Paris' most fêted gay club (*see p303*), with a
roster of star local DJs holding court, Queen's star
has faded a little. That said, it has recently introduced more theme nights and still packs 'em in
seven nights a week.

La Scala

186bis rue de Rivoli, 1st (01.42.60.45.64/www.
lascalaparis.fr). M° Palais Royal Musée du Louvre.
Open 11pm-6am Tue-Sun. **Admission** €12 Tue-
Thur, Sun; €15 Fri, Sat. Free for women Tue-Fri, Sun.
Drinks €9. **Credit** MC, V. **Map** p401 H5.
A huge central club with a commercial music poli-
cy that embraces house, techno, R&B, hip hop and
Caribbean music.

World, jazz & rock 'n' roll

Le Cabaret Sauvage

59 bd Macdonald, 19th (01.42.09.03.09/www.cabaret
sauvage.com). M° Porte de la Villette. **Open** 11pm-
dawn, days vary. **Admission** €10-€20. **Drinks**
€4-€8. **Credit** AmEx, MC, V. **Map** p403 inset.
A big top-shaped cabaret venue that's taken over by
outside promoters for occasional club nights, often
containing a world music element.

La Chapelle des Lombards

19 rue de Lappe, 11th (01.43.57.24.24/
http://chapelle.lombards.free.fr/). M° Bastille. **Open**
11pm-7am Tue-Sun. **Admission** free Tue, Wed, Sun;
€15 Thur; €19 Fri, Sat. Free for women Tue-Thur &
before 12.30pm Fri). **Drinks** €6-€12. **Credit** MC, V.
Map p407 M7.
With Afrojazz and Latino bands and DJs providing
the music, Latinos and Africans lead the dancefloor
in this popular world music venue.

Les Etoiles

61 rue du Château-d'Eau, 10th (01.47.70.60.56/
www.etoiles-salsa.com). M° Château d'Eau. **Open**
9pm-3am Thur-Sat. **Admission** €10. **Drinks** €4-€6.
Credit MC, V. **Map** p402 K3.
Rumoured to be the oldest music venue in Paris and
home to the first Parisian salsa scene in the mid
1980s, DJs and bands still electrify the dancefloor
here every weekend. These days it's more of a
French than Latin hangout, and open to beginners
– salsa lessons are available.

Favela Chic

18 rue du Fbg-du-Temple, 11th (01.40.21.38.14/
www.favelachic.com). M° République. **Open** 7.30pm-
2am Tue-Thur; 7.30pm-4am Fri, Sat. **Admission**
free Tue-Thur; €10 (incl 1 drink) Fri, Sat. **Drinks**
€6-€19. **Credit** MC, V. **Map** p402 L4.
Situated near the fashionable Canal St-Martin and
Oberkampf, the Brazilian-themed Favela Chic
attracts an international, dressy crowd for some serious samba and other full-on Latin dancing, DJs, live
acts, plus Brazilian food and drinks.

La Java

105 rue du Fbg-du-Temple, 10th (01.42.02.20.52).
M° Goncourt or Belleville. **Open** 9pm-3am Wed, Thur;
11pm-6am Fri, Sat; 2pm-2am Sun. **Admission** €5-
€10. **Drinks** €3-€6. **Credit** MC, V. **Map** p403 M4.
Tucked inside the crumbling disused Belleville market, La Java plays rock, salsa and world music, with
live bands every weekend.

Arts & Entertainment

Sport & Fitness

Cool pools and outdoor boules – while rollerskaters rule the streets.

The range of activities available to all in Paris does justice to the city's proud sporting history. The modern Olympic Games, and football's FIFA, World Cup and European trophies were all planned and developed in the boardrooms of the French capital. The **Stade de France** national stadium, to the north of the city centre, will host the prestigious Rugby World Cup in 2007 (*see p333* **Up for the cup**), just as it staged the football one so memorably in 1998.

Much is owed to the dynamic influence of an outward-looking sports press, particularly the daily newspaper *L'Equipe* and biweekly *France Football*. Their fin-de-siècle forebear, *L'Auto*, introduced the world's biggest annual cycling event into the calendar: the **Tour de France** (www.letour.fr). Beset in recent years by doping scandals, the three-week summer Tour is still a national festival. Millions flock to the avenue des Champs-Elysées in July to welcome the winner. For details of other major sports events, *see pp270-274* **Festivals & Events**.

The City Hall manages many of the facilities across the capital. For details, consult its free annual *Parisports: Guide du Sport à Paris* or view the online version at www.sport.paris.fr.

Spectator sports

The national stadium is the **Stade de France** (93210 St-Denis, 08.92.70.09.00, www.stadede france.fr), with stations on the RER B (La Plaine Stade de France) and RER D (Stade de France St-Denis) lines one stop from the Gare du Nord.

Indoor events, including judo, basketball and tennis, take place at the **Palais Omnisports de Paris-Bercy** (8 boulevard de Bercy, 12th, 08.92.39.04.90, www.popb.fr, Mᵒ Bercy). The **Stade Roland Garros** (Porte des Mousquetaires, 2 av Gordon-Bennett, 16th, 01.47.43.48.00, www.fft.fr/rolandgarros, Mᵒ Porte d'Auteuil) stages the French tennis open; the **Parc des Princes**, home of flagship football club Paris St-Germain (*see right*), also hosts rugby and other sports events.

Tickets to see many sports are sold online at www.ticketnet.fr and www.francebillet.com, and at branches of **Fnac** and **Virgin Megastore** (for both, *see p243*). For football and rugby internationals held at the Stade de France, contact the national football and rugby associations (www.fff.fr; www.ffr.fr).

Basketball

Paris Basket Racing
Stade Coubertin, 82 av Georges-Lafont, 16th (01.46.10.93.60/www.parisbasket.net). Mᵒ Porte de St-Cloud. **Tickets** from €8. **Credit** MC, V.
PBR are best known as the club where Bruges-born Tony Parker of San Antonio Spurs fame began his career – this cachet still occasionally brings stars of the NBA to play here.

Football

Paris St-Germain
Stadium *Parc des Princes, 24 rue du Commandant-Guilbaud, 16th (01.47.43.71.71/tickets & information 32.75/www.psg.fr). Mᵒ Porte de St-Cloud.* **Tickets** €18-€80. **Credit** MC, V. **Shop** *27 av des Champs-Elysées, 8th (01.56.69.22.22). Mᵒ Franklin D. Roosevelt.* **Open** 10am-8pm Mon-Thur; 10am-10pm Fri, Sat; noon-8pm Sun. **Credit** AmEx, MC, V; *Parc des Princes, 24 rue du Commandant-Guilbaud, 16th (01.47.43.72.91). Mᵒ Porte de St-Cloud.* **Open** 10am-7pm Mon-Sat & 2hrs after game on match days. **Credit** AmEx, MC, V.
If PSG didn't exist, it would have been necessary to invent them. Starved of top-class soccer in the capital, a group of donors set up PSG by amalgamating local clubs in 1970. PSG bought top stars to win silverware in the 1980s and '90s, much to the chagrin of poorer, traditional clubs – in particular their biggest rivals, Olympique Marseille. PSG's raucous *banlieue* following hardly endears them, either. Since then, PSG's star has faded, and the club are now light years away from the Champions League standard set by new football superpower, Olympique Lyon. For PSG tickets, simply book online and pick them up from any branch of Fnac (*see p243*).

Horse racing

The full racing schedule, the *Calendrier des Courses*, is published by *France Galop* (www.france-galop.com). For information on trotting, consult www.cheval-francais.com. Tickets are €1.50-€8 (free for under-18s), with free babysitting and pony rides for under-tens.

Hippodrome d'Auteuil
Route des Lacs, 16th (01.40.71.47.47). Mᵒ Porte d'Auteuil.
Steeplechasing in the Bois de Boulogne. The biggest event is the Gras Savoye Grand Steeplechase de Paris on the last Sunday in May.

Jean-Taris (*see p338*) and runs trips to the Med. **Bleu Passion** (94 bd Poniatowski, 12th, 01.43.45.26.12, www.bleu-passion.fr) runs a diving school and sells equipment.

Fencing

For a list of clubs, consult www.escrime-ffe.fr. The fencing section at the **Racing Club de France** (5 rue Eblé, 7th, 01.45.67.55.86, www.racingclubdefrance.org) is suitable for leisure or competition, with 12 fencing masters and 18 pistes. All levels and ages are welcome.

Fitness clubs

Club Med (www.clubmedgym.fr) dominates the health-club scene, with 22 branches in Paris and the western suburbs, including five Waou Clubs with spa facilities. Gyms have state-of-the-art machines and pools, and offer everything from dance classes to in-line skating outings. Single visits cost €25, annual memberships from €675.

The non-profit **La Gym Suédoise** (01.45.00.18.22, www.gymsuedoise.com) is an association that holds one-hour gym sessions in ten locations across Paris. Its method mixes stretching, cardio exercises and running to music. Membership is €75-€110 per term, or €10 per session. Unlike most gyms, there are free trials at specified locations.

There are free weekly 'Sport Nature' sessions of outdoor stretching, aerobics and running, set up by the Mairie at 13 locations around town. Check the annual *Guide du Sport* (*see p330*) or visit www.sport.paris.fr.

Club Quartier Latin

18 rue de Pontoise, 5th (01.55.42.77.88/www.clubquartierlatin.com). M° Maubert Mutualité.
Open 9am-midnight Mon-Fri; 9am-7pm Sat, Sun.
Admission *Pool* from €3.70. *Gym* from €19.
Credit MC, V. **Map** p406 K7.
Home to the Pontoise pool (*see p338*), this venerable centre off boulevard St-Germain houses no-frills fitness facilities, and has a room for step, aerobics, stretching and yoga classes. There's a sauna too.

Accessibility and simplicity are the keys to its international appeal. Men, women and children – able-bodied or wheelchair-bound – can play each other on equal terms. Whether singles (*tête-à-tête*), pairs (*doublettes*) or (most popularly) triples (*triplettes*), the game's the same. In a circle of rough ground or gravel, players must try to throw their ball nearest the jack, or *cochonet*. Turns are not taken alternately – those furthest from the jack must throw. In the team version, six balls are divided between two or three players. Whoever is closest to the jack when all the balls are used up gains a point; 13 points wins a match.

Only the top players in France earn enough from prize money and sponsorship deals to play full time. Playing in threes, according to how the game is going, each can handle all three team roles of pointer, *milieu* and shooter, throwing the initial ball, protecting their best-placed balls and skilfully shooting opponents' efforts out of the way.

To see locals in action, head to the *boulodrome* at the Jardin de Luxembourg (only members of the garden's official *pétanque* association are allowed to play), or the Arènes de Lutèce. If you fancy having a go, your neighbourhood Go Sport or Monoprix will sell a cheapish set of boules.

Espace Vit'Halles

48 rue Rambuteau, 3rd (01.42.77.21.71/www.vit halles.com). M° Rambuteau. **Open** 8am-10.30pm Mon-Fri; 9am-10pm Sat; 10am-7pm Sun. **Admission** €25/day. **Credit** AmEx, MC, V. **Map** p406 K5.
This sunken-level health club has Technogym fitness machines, a sauna and some of the best classes in the city, step and spinning especially; payment is extra for each.

Football

For information on the local amateur leagues, contact the **Ligue Ile de France de Football** (01.42.44.12.12). To join a weekend kickabout, try the Bois de Boulogne near Bagatelle, the Bois de Vincennes or the Champ de Mars.

Golf

The suburbs are full of top-rated courses suitable for all levels and budgets. Contact the **Fédération Française de Golf** (01.41.49.77.00, www.ffg.org) for more info.

Golf du Bois de Boulogne

Hippodrome d'Auteuil, 16th (01.44.30.70.00/ www.golfduboisdeboulogne.fr). M° Porte d'Auteuil. **Open** 8am-8pm daily. **Admission** €4-€5. **Credit** AmEx, MC, V.
The municipal green has one main course, putting greens and crazy golf. It's closed on horse-racing days, so check before you head out.

Golf National

2 av du Golf, 78280 Guyancourt (01.30.43.36.00/ www.golf-national.com). RER St-Quentin-en-Yvelines then taxi. **Open** 8am-7pm Mon-Fri; 8am-8pm Sat, Sun. **Admission** (annual membership €44) €37-€97. **Credit** MC, V.
The home of the French Open, this has two 18-hole courses and one nine-hole course.

Horse riding

To enjoy the lovely horse-riding trails in the Bois de Boulogne or the Bois de Vincennes, you need to join a riding club such as **La Société d'Equitation de Paris** (Centre Hippique du Bois de Boulogne, 16th, 01.45.01.20.06, www.equitation-paris.com), the **Centre Hippique du Touring** (Bois de Boulogne, 16th, 01.45.01.20.88) or the **Cercle Hippique du Bois de Vincennes** (8 rue de Fontenay, 94130 Nogent-sur-Marne, 01.48.73.01.28). Beginners can learn at the **Club Bayard Equitation** in the Bois de Vincennes (Centre Bayard, UCPA Vincennes, 12th, 01.43.65.46.87, www.clubbayard.com). Membership runs for one year (€83), or you can take a special five-day course in July or August for €275. Out near Versailles, the **Haras de Jardy** (bd de Jardy, 92430 Marnes-la-Coquette, 01.47.01.35.30, www.haras-de-jardy.com) is open every day and offers lessons by the hour for all ages, with no membership fee. The steeds on offer include Shetland ponies, ponies and horses.

Espace Vit'Halles.

Arts & Entertainment

Leisurely rides at all levels in the forests of Fontainebleau are run by **La Bleausière** (06.82.01.21.18, la.bleausiere.free.fr).

Ice skating

The most popular open-air skating rink is the free one in front of the **Hôtel de Ville**, which is open from December to February (skate rental €5). There's another rink set up at the Tour de Montparnasse. When it's frozen, people skate on **Lac Supérieur** in the Bois de Boulogne. *See also pp270-274* **Festivals & Events**.

Patinoire de Boulogne

1 rue Victor-Griffuelhes, 92100 Boulogne-Billancourt (01.46.08.09.09). M° Marcel Sembat. **Open** 4-6pm Mon; 3-6pm Wed; 3.45-5pm Fri; 10.30am-1pm, 3-6pm, 9pm-midnight Sat; 10am-1pm, 3-6pm Sun. **Admission** €5.20; €4.30 concessions. **No credit cards.**
Year-round indoor rink with free skate rental.

Patinoire Sonja Henie

Palais Omnisports de Paris-Bercy (01.40.02.60.67/ www.bercy.fr). M° Bercy. **Open** Sept-mid June 3-6pm Wed; 9.30pm-12.30am Fri; 3-6pm, 9.30pm-12.30am Sat; 10am-noon, 3-6pm Sun. **Admission** €3-€6. **No credit cards. Map** p407 N9.
Protection, helmets and skates for hire (€3).

In-line skating

Skating is a sociable affair in Paris. Every Friday night, thousands meet by the Tour Montparnasse to take to the streets en masse. They're here for **Friday Night Fever** (www.pari-roller.com), a free, fast-paced three-hour skate through the streets, open to anyone who can keep up. Cars have no choice but to grind to a halt as thousands of skaters fly by. Beginners can join the more sedate skate event run by **Roller et Coquillage** (www.rollers-coquillages.org), which sets off from boulevard Bourdon, by place de la Bastille, at 2.30pm on Sundays. The route is about 20km (12 miles) long, taking around three hours. You can hire skates from **Nomades** (37 bd Bourdin, 4th, 01.44.54.07.44, www.nomadeshop.com). For lessons for all ages, try the **Roller Squad Institute** (01.56.61.99.61, www.rsi.asso.fr). For real in-line skating and skateboard acrobatics, head for the vast **Rollerparc Avenue** (100 rue Léon-Geffroy, 01.47.18.19.19) in Vitry-sur-Seine.

Rowing & watersports

Paris residents can row, canoe and kayak for free on Saturdays at the **Base Nautique de la Villette** (41bis quai de la Loire, 19th, 01.42.40.29.90). Reserve a week in advance and bring along proof of residence and two photos.

You can go waterskiing and wakeboarding at the **Club Nautique du 19ème** (Bassin de Vitesse de St-Cloud, 92100 Boulogne-Billancourt, 01.42.03.25.24). Serious rowers can join the annual **Traversée de Paris**, part of the Randon'Aviron EDF outings open to the public. Contact the **Ligue Ile-de-France d'Aviron** (94736 Nogent-sur-Marne, 01.48.75.79.17). For a leisurely paddle, hire a boat at **Lac Daumesnil** or **Lac des Minimes** in the Bois de Vincennes, or at **Lac Supérieur** in the Bois de Boulogne.

Rugby

For a good standard of play, try the **Athletic Club de Boulogne** (Stade du Saut du Loup, av de la Butte-Mortemart, 16th, 01.46.51.11.91), which fields two teams. The **British Rugby Club of Paris** (58-60 av de la Grande-Armée, 17th, 01.40.55.15.15, www.brfcparis.com) fields two teams in the corporate league.

Skateboarding

Although the Mairie tries to clamp down, the city's skateboard scene continues to thrive. With its double-set, the riverfront courtyard at the **Palais de Tokyo** (*see p123*), known as 'Le Dôme', is popular as ever – as are the ledges and steps at **Trocadéro** (16th). **La Défense** (*see p177*) tends to be full of security guards, but is still worth exploring for smooth marble, ledges and rails; **Palais Omnisports de Paris-Bercy** (*see p330*) has vast ledges and some almighty gaps.

A more relaxed scene is found at the **place des Innocents** (by the Forum des Halles, 1st), with low ledges and smooth ground, and at the **Opéra Bastille** (11th), with small steps. Check www.paris-skate-culture.org or ask at **Street Machine** (6 rue Bailleul, 1st, 01.47.03.64.60, www.streetmachine.fr).

Cosanostra Skatepark

18 rue du Tir, 77500 Chelles (01.64.72.14.04/ www.cosanostraskatepark.net). RER Gare de Chelles. **Open** *July, Aug* 2-8pm Mon-Wed, Sat; 2-11pm Thur, Fri; 2-7pm Sun. *Sept-June* 4-11pm Tue, Thur, Fri; 2-8pm Sat; 2-7pm Sun. **Admission** €6. *Season ticket* €205; €190 under-13s. **No credit cards.**
A huge indoor street course and micro-ramp, which hosts international competitions.

Squash

No membership is necessary to play squash at the **Club Quartier Latin** (*see p335*), which charges €17-€25 per match (racket rental from €2.50). The **Standard Athletic Club** (*see p332*) rents squash courts for members or on payment of a €185 seasonal fee.

Arts & Entertainment

Squash Montmartre

14 rue Achille-Martinet, 18th (01.42.55.38.30/www.
squash-montmartre.com). M° Lamarck Caulaincourt.
Open 10am-11pm Mon-Fri; 10am-7pm Sat, Sun.
Admission from €11. **Credit** V.
Period memberships available, plus equipment hire.

Swimming

Pools are plentiful and cheap, some with fine
views or historical architecture. There's even
one that floats – the **Piscine Josephine-
Baker**. Most pools require a swimming cap
(available on site) and ban bermudas, and many
open late. Swimming to music is integral to Nuit
Blanche in October (*see pp270-274* **Festivals
& Events**). The times given below may change
during school breaks and national holidays.

Aquaboulevard

4 rue Louis-Armand, 15th (01.40.60.10.00/
www.aquaboulevard.com). M° Balard. **Open** 9am-
11pm Mon-Thur; 9am-midnight Fri; 8am-midnight
Sat; 8am-11pm Sun. **Admission** *6hrs* €25; €10
concessions. **Credit** AmEx, MC, V. **Map** p404 A10.
With year-round summer temperatures, this tropical water park under a giant atrium is great fun for
kids. An extra charge gets you a steam bath and
three saunas of varying intensity.

Piscine Butte-aux-Cailles

*5 pl Paul-Verlaine, 13th (01.45.89.60.05). M° Place
d'Italie.* **Open** 7-8am, 11.30am-1pm, 4.30-6.30pm Tue;
7am-6.30pm Wed; 7-8am, 11.30am-6pm Thur, Fri;
7-8am, 10am-6pm Sat; 8am-5.30pm Sun. **Admission**
€2.60; €1.50 concessions. **Credit** AmEx, MC, V.
This listed complex, built in the 1920s, has one main
indoor pool and two outdoor pools. The water is a
warm 28°C, thanks to the natural sulphurous spring.

Piscine Georges-Vallery

*148 av Gambetta, 20th (01.40.31.15.20). M° Porte des
Lilas.* **Open** 10am-5pm Mon, Wed, Fri; 10am-10pm
Tue, Thur; 9am-5pm Sat, Sun. **Admission** €2.60;
€1.50 concessions. **Credit** (€15 minimum) MC, V.
Built for the 1924 Olympics, this complex features a
retractable Plexiglas roof, a 50m pool and one for
kids. It reopened in 2005 after renovation.

Piscine Jean-Taris

*16 rue Thouin, 5th (01.55.42.81.90). M° Cardinal
Lemoine.* **Open** 7-8am, 11.30am-1pm Tue, Thur;
7-8am, 11.30am-5.15pm Wed; 7-8am, 11.30am-1pm,
5-7.45pm Fri; 7am-5.15pm Sat; 8am-5.15pm Sun.
Admission €2.60; €1.50 concessions. **Credit** V.
Map p406 J8.
This 25m pool has huge bay windows overlooking
a sloping garden, with the Panthéon visible just
above the trees. Mixed showers and locker area.

Piscine Josephine-Baker

Quai François-Mauriac, 13th (01.56.61.96.50/
*www.sport.paris.fr). M° Bibliothèque François
Mitterrand.* **Open** 7-8.30am, 1-3pm, 5-9pm Mon;

noon-5pm, 7pm-midnight Tue; 7-8.30pm, 1-9pm Wed;
noon-3pm, 5-9pm Thur; 7-8.30am, 1-5pm, 7pm-
midnight Fri; 10am-8pm Sat, Sun. **Admission** €2.60;
€1.50 concessions. **Credit** MC, V. **Map** p407 N10.
Moored on the Seine by the Bibliothèque
Nationale, the swish, modern Piscine Josephine-
Baker opened in 2006. It boasts a 25m main
pool, a paddling pool and café – plus a busy
schedule of exercise classes. There's a sundeck
in summer and a sliding glass roof for winter,
allowing the pool to stay open all year round.

Piscine Pontoise Quartier Latin

18 rue de Pontoise, 5th (01.55.42.77.88/www.
clubquartierlatin.com). M° Maubert Mutualité.
Open 7-8.30am, 12.15-1.30pm, 4.30-11.45pm Mon,
Tue; 7-8.30am, 12.15-11.45pm Wed; 7-8.30am, 12.15-
1.30pm, 4.30-7.15pm, 9-11.45pm Thur; 7-8.45am,
noon-1.30pm, 4.30-11.45pm Fri; 10am-7pm Sat; 8am-
7pm Sun. **Admission** €3.70; €2.20 concessions;
€9.50 for all 9-11.45pm. **No credit cards.**
Map p406 K7.
A beautiful art deco pool with two mezzanine
levels. It has private locker rooms, plus night swimming to underwater music. Small fee for lockers.

Piscine Suzanne-Berlioux

*Forum des Halles, 10 pl de la Rotonde, 1st (01.42.
36.98.44). M° Les Halles.* **Open** 11.30am-10pm Mon,
Tue; 10am-10pm Wed; 11am-10pm Thur, Fri; 9am-
7pm Sat, Sun. **Admission** €3.80; €3 under-16s.
Credit (€8 minimum) MC, V. **Map** p402 J5.
This 50m pool with its own tropical greenhouse is
good for lap swimming – but there are no lockers
(check in your belongings with the attendants).

Tennis & table tennis

The Paris Tennis system (01.71.71.70.70,
www.tennis.paris.fr) allows you to register
a password and reserve a court online, €6.50
per hour, €12.50 for indoor courts. Among the
40 municipal courts, the six at the **Jardin du
Luxembourg** (01.43.25.79.18) are convenient,
but there's a better selection at the **Centre
Sportif La Faluère** (route de la Pyramide,
12th, 01.43.74.40.93) in the Bois de Vincennes.

To find public table-tennis tables in parks
around town, consult the *Guide du Sport* (*see
p330*). Find club details at www.paristt.com.

Centre Sportif Suzanne-Lenglen

*2 rue Louis-Armand, 15th (01.44.26.26.50).
M° Balard.* **Open** 7am-10pm Mon-Fri; 7am-7pm
Sat, Sun. **Admission** from €3. **No credit cards.**
Fourteen courts, two of which are covered.

Club Forest Hill

*4 rue Louis-Armand, 15th (01.40.60.10.00/www.
aquaboulevard.com). M° Balard/RER Bd Victor.*
Open 9am-11pm daily. **Admission** prices vary.
No credit cards. Map p404 A10.
Tennis, table tennis and other racquet sports at most
of the dozen branches in and around Paris.

Theatre

Peter Brook heads an eclectic, global and often radical scene.

Théâtre des Bouffes du Nord.
See p342.

Arts & Entertainment

Paris is increasingly becoming the crossroads of European theatre. The bastion of the French Classical repertoire, the **Théâtre de l'Odéon**, is filling its newly revamped auditorium with a programme in as many languages as one finds at the Edinburgh Festival. In the suburbs, the **MC93 Bobigny** (*see p340*) continues to invite international companies to perform in their own tongues, while London-born Peter Brook still reigns as an influential director at the recently renovated **Théâtre des Bouffes du Nord**, marrying adventurous programming with global flair (*see p341* **Peter's playhouse**).

The city's theatre scene is divided into the lofty, state-run institutions headed up by the **Comédie Française** and the Odéon, and independent theatres, most of which tend to have low-brow fare and farces of little interest to an English audience. There are, of course, exceptions: the hot ticket at the end of 2006 was Isabel Adjani in Wolfgang Hildesheiner's *Maria Stuart* at the **Théâtre Marigny**.

As you would expect from the city where Ionesco's absurdist *La Cantatrice Chauve* was premiered and is still running, almost a half century later (**Théâtre de la Huchette**), experimental theatre is strong. In the Bois de Vincennes, accessible by a theatre bus, the **Cartoucherie** is a factory remade as a theatre commune that's home to five exciting and innovative resident companies. Just south of Bastille is the petite **Théâtre de l'Opprimé**, a pocket-sized venue with lofty productions, often tackling sticky political issues. (For more experimental theatres, such as the legendary **Café de la Gare**, *see pp275-277* **Cabaret, Circus & Comedy**.

BEYOND THE PERIPHERIQUE

A policy of bringing theatre to the masses has led to the funding of some exceptional theatres outside the Paris ring road. In truth, the audiences are often comprised of Parisians prepared to go the distance in their quest for culture, but the programming makes it well worth the extra few métro stops. In the northeast, the MC93 Bobigny (1 bd Lénine, 93000 Bobigny, 01.41.60.72.72, www.mc93.com) is a slick institution dedicated to promoting global cross-cultural exchange with visiting companies such as the excellent Théâtre de Complicité. The **Standard Idéal** festival of February 2007 offers the chance to see *Hamlet* in Hungarian and Vassili Grossman's *Life and Destiny*, a face-off between the forces of Stalin and Hitler, in Russian and German. The **Théâtre Gérard-Philipe** (55 boulevard Jules-Guesde, 93207 St-Denis, 01.48.13.70.00, www.theatregerardphilipe.com), housed in a century-old building and directed by Stanislas Nordey, offers quality fare for the 2007 season, ranging from Chekhov to the Et Mois Alors? festival for youngsters.

PLAYING IN ENGLISH

Productions in English, German and Spanish come to the Théâtre de l'Odéon, the Théâtre des Bouffes du Nord, the **Théâtre de la Cité Internationale**, MC93 Bobigny and the versatile stage at the Centre Georges Pompidou (place Georges-Pompidou, 4th, 01.44.78.12.33, www.cnac-gp.com).

There are three regular English-language companies. The most prominent, **Glasshouse** (http://glasshouse.monsite.orange.fr), perform contemporary English-language plays and English translations of French works. In 2007 the company will be reviving its successful rendering of Jean Genet's *The Maids* and performing a new production of *Little Women*, at the eclectic Théâtre Déchargeurs (3 rue des Déchargeurs, 1st, 01.42.36.00.02, Mº Châtelet) and the Atelier Théâtre (place Charles-Dullin, 18th, 01.42.17.05.23, Mº Pigalle, Anvers or Abbesses), as well as other venues.

Local improv troupe the **Improfessionals** (www.improfessionals.com) have been treading the boards of central Paris for the last five years offering off-the-cuff stuff.

Dear Conjunction Theatre Company (01.42.41.69.65, dearconjunction@wanadoo.fr) perform British and Irish playwrights such as Pinter and Brien Friel at the **Sudden Théâtre** (14bis rue Ste-Isaure, 18th, 01.42.62.35.00, www.suddentheatre.fr).

Shakespeare in English is performed every June at the Bois de Boulogne's Théâtre de Verdure du Jardin Shakespeare (08.20.00.75.75) by the **Tower Theatre Company** (www.towertheatre.org.uk). Look out also for regular readings of new work by Paris-based playwrights on Sunday nights at **Carr's** pub (1 rue du Mont-Thabor, 1st, 01.42.60.60.26, www.carrsparis.com).

TICKETS AND INFORMATION

For details of scheduling and programming, look in the Theatre section of the weekly *L'Officiel des Spectacles*. Further information can be found at www.parisvoice.com. Tickets can be bought at the theatres directly, at **Fnac** or the **Virgin Megastore** (for both, *see p243*) and at www.theatreonline.com. Check www.theatresprives.com for half-price tickets to performances at many of the private theatres during the first week of a new show. Two agencies that sell same-day tickets at half price are the **Kiosque de la Madeleine** (15 place de la Madeleine, 8th, closed Mon) and the **Kiosque Montparnasse** (parvis de la Gare Montparnasse, 15th, closed Mon). These agency tickets, however, tend to be for commercial shows. Queues can be long, and there's no way to contact the kiosks by phone or internet. For students, special subscriptions are available at many theatres, and most venues offer same-day rates with significant reductions.

Right Bank

Cartoucherie de Vincennes

Route du Champ de Manoeuvre, Bois de Vincennes, 12th. Mº Château de Vincennes, then shuttle bus. **Théâtre de l'Aquarium** (*01.43.74.99.61/ www.theatredelaquarium.com*). **Théâtre du Chaudron** (*01.43.28.97.04*). **Théâtre de l'Epée de Bois** (*01.48.08.39.74*). **Théâtre du Soleil** (*01.42.74.87.63/ www.theatre-du-soleil.fr*). **Théâtre de la Tempête** (*01.43.28.36.36/ www.la-tempete.fr*).
Housed in old munitions warehouses in the woods, these five independent theatres, each with its own troupe, offer first-class politically committed fare. Try and catch one of Théâtre du Soleil's spectacles featuring puppets, masks and on-stage musicians.

Comédie Française

www.comedie-francaise.fr.
Salle Richelieu *2 rue Richelieu, 1st (08.25.10.16.80/01.44.58.15.15). Mº Palais Royal Musée du Louvre.* **Box office** 11am-6.30pm daily. **Admission** €10-€35. *1hr before show* €5 for cheapest seats only; €10 under-27s. **Credit** AmEx, MC, V. **Map** p401 H5.
Studio Theatre *Galerie du Carrousel du Louvre, 99 rue de Rivoli, 1st (01.44.58.98.54/ 01.44.58.98.58). Mº Palais Royal Musée du Louvre.* **Box office** 2-5pm on day. **Admission** €10-€35. **Credit** MC, V. **Map** p401 H5.
Théâtre du Vieux Colombier *21 rue du Vieux Colombier, 6th (01.44.39.87.00/01.44.39.87.01). Mº St-Sulpice.* **Box office** 1-6pm Mon, Sun; 11am-7pm Tue-Sat. **Admission** €14-€35. *1hr before show* €10 under-27s. **Credit** MC, V. **Map** p405 G7.
The gilded mother of French theatres, the Comédie Française turns out season after season of classics, as well as lofty new productions. The red velvet and

Arts & Entertainment

Peter's playhouse

Behind an unassuming façade, in the grey shadow of the overhead métro track, facing a bustling street of Sri Lankan businesses, is one of the most innovative theatres in Europe, let alone Paris: the **Théâtre des Bouffes du Nord** (*see p342*). At its helm London-born Peter Brook, perhaps the greatest theatre director of his generation, now in his eighties.

Reopened in September 2006 after a ten-month, €2-million renovation, with a tidy café-restaurant attached to the modest box office, the Bouffes du Nord is also back under the firm managerial hand of Micheline Rozan, with whom Brook first set up in Paris 30 years ago. Performances starting at 7pm sharp, music recitals for Monday evenings, Rozan runs a tight ship. Of the 14 productions comprising the 2006-07 season, three are being directed by Brook himself, including the much lauded *Sizwe Banda is Dead*, which has already toured the world.

Set in a South African township, this challenging play keeps Brook on the same experimental quest for groundbreaking global theatre as when he left England for Paris in the early 1970s. A successful co-director of the Royal Shakespeare Company, Brook had made his name on productions such as *A Midsummer Night's Dream* using stilts and trapezes, as well as films, the most notable

being *Lord of the Flies*. Teaming up with Jean-Louis Barrault in Paris, he set up the International Centre for Theatre Research to explore the roots of drama across the globe. He took research trips outside Europe, taking experimental productions with him, using theatre spaces both basic and bizarre, from mountain tops in Iran to carpets-for-stages in the more remote parts of west Africa.

Brook had already put out feelers to set up his own theatre in Paris. With experienced cultural administrator Micheline Rozan, he searched the city for a suitable venue. They found it right behind the Gare du Nord, an obscure, abandoned 19th-century theatre with a colourful interior and a dark past. Inaugurated in 1876, the venue, located in unfashionable, dank La Chapelle, saw off a dozen directors or more. One of them, Olga Léaud, ran off with the takings. Directors came and went until Paul le Danois and Charles Malincourt took over in 1929; Malincourt committed suicide soon after; le Danois died in 1935. After sporadic music-hall shows, the theatre was closed by the authorities in 1952 when it failed to meet safety regulations.

Gaining significant state finance, Brook and Rozan had the theatre restored in six months. Intimate and egalitarian – no numbered seats, modest, uniform ticket prices – Bouffes du Nord opened with Brook's *Timon d'Athènes* in 1974. Saturday matinées were introduced, and poorer families from the suburbs encouraged to come along. There were even free shows at Christmas and Easter. Most of all, though, there have been three decades of truly challenging theatre, in English and French – condensed versions of *Hamlet*, the eleven-hour Hindu epic *Le Mahabharata* and a unique interpretation of *Carmen*, all underpinned by Brook's brave, stark settings. With Dostoevsky, Beckett and township drama already programmed, you can expect little compromise for the new season.

gold-flecked Salle Richelieu is located right by the Palais-Royal; under the same umbrella are the Studio, a black box inside the Carrousel du Louvre, and the Théâtre du Vieux Colombier. The line-up for 2007 includes Molière's *Le Malade Imaginaire* (until April) and *Le Misanthrope* (May-July).

Théâtre de l'Athénée-Louis Jouvet

7 rue Boudreau, square de l'Opéra Louis Jouvet, 9th (01.53.05.19.19/www.athenee-theatre.com). Mº Opéra. **Box office** 1-7pm Mon-Sat. **Admission** €6-€30. **Credit** MC, V. **Map** p401 G4.

This theatre is among the most beautiful in France, its Italianate decor like the interior of a jewellery box and in total contrast to its modernist fare. After a Beckett centenary festival, in 2007 there is Pirandello, Ionesco, Camus and Benjamin Britten's opera *The Rape of Lucretia*.

Théâtre de la Bastille

76 rue de la Roquette, 11th (01.43.57.42.14/www. theatre-bastille.com). Mº Voltaire. **Box office** 10am-6pm Mon-Fri; 2-6pm Sat. **Admission** €12.50-€19. **Credit** MC, V. **Map** p407 N6.

Effervescent, exotic productions are emblematic of the kind of spirit found here; the Bastille is a little smaller, a little edgier and a little funkier than many of the more grand Parisian theatres.

Théâtre des Bouffes du Nord

37bis bd de la Chapelle, 10th (01.46.07.34.50/ www.bouffesdunord.com). Mº La Chapelle. **Box office** 11am-6pm Mon-Sat. **Admission** €8-€24.50. **Credit** MC, V. **Map** p402 K2.

Landmark theatre, recently renovated and ready to go. *See p341* **Peter's playhouse**. *Photo p339.*

Théâtre Marigny

Avenue de Marigny, 8th (01.53.96.70.30/ www.theatremarigny.fr). Mº Champs Elysées Clemenceau or Franklin D. Roosevelt. **Box office** 11am-6.30pm Mon-Sat; 11am-3pm Sun. **Admission** €37-€72. **Credit** MC, V. **Map** p401 E4.

Given its location off the Champs-Elysées, deluxe interior conceived by Charles Garnier of Opéra fame, high-profile casts and illustrious pedigree stretching back to its inauguration by Offenbach 150 years ago, it's no wonder that the Théâtre Marigny is one of the most expensive nights out for theatre-goers in Paris. Still, you get the best in the business – late 2006 saw Isabel Adjani starring in *Maria Stuart*.

Théâtre National de Chaillot

1 pl du Trocadéro, 16th (01.53.65.30.00/www. theatre-chaillot.fr). Mº Trocadéro. **Box office** 11am-7pm Mon-Sat. **Admission** €9-€39. **Credit** MC, V. **Map** p400 B4.

Get here early and grab a cocktail; the lobby has a huge window with an Eiffel Tower view. Highlights for 2007 include Marivaux's *La Double Inconstance* in January and Büchner's *Léonce et Léna* (March-April), a 19th-century Romeo and Juliet. The three auditoriums range from an intimate, experimental space to a 2,800-seater.

Théâtre de l'Opprimé

78 rue du Charolais, 12th (01.43.40.44.44). Mº Dugommier. **Box office** 1hr before show. **Admission** €10-€15. **No credit cards.** **Map** p407 P9.

This small theatre with great vision borrows its name – and mission – from Brazil's Augusto Boal, who believed that theatre can change the world. The repertory is largely contemporary, the methods are inspired by Boal, and the troupe offers workshops in his technique and teachings.

Théâtre de la Ville

2 pl du Châtelet, 4th (01.42.74.22.77/www.theatre delaville-paris.com). Mº Châtelet. **Box office** 11am-7pm Mon; 11am-8pm Tue-Sat. **Admission** €11.50-€30. **Credit** MC, V. **Map** p406 J6.

The City Theatre turns out the most consistently innovative and stimulating programming in Paris. Instead of running a standard rep company, the house imports music, dance and theatre productions, ranging from the classics to the avant-garde.

Left Bank

Odéon, Théâtre de L'Europe

Pl de l'Odéon, 6th (01.44.85.40.00/bookings 01.44.85.40.40/www.theatre-odeon.fr). Mº Odéon. **Box office** *By phone* 11am-6.30pm Mon-Sat. *On site* 2hrs before show. **Admission** €13-€26. **Credit** MC, V. **Map** p408 H7.

Back in the historic Left Bank auditorium after a €30m renovation, the Odéon has a thrilling polyglot programme planned. In late 2006 Isabelle Huppert stars here in *Quartett*. This is being followed by *King Lear* in French (January-February 2007), *The Tempest* in four languages (April-June) as well as *Il Ventaglio* in Italian (May).

Théâtre de la Cité Internationale

21 bd Jourdan, 14th (01.43.13.50.50/www.theatre delacite.com). RER Cité Universitaire. **Box office** 2-7pm Mon-Fri. **Admission** €12.50-€21. **Credit** MC, V.

A polished professional theatre on the campus of the Cité Universitaire, the Théâtre de la Cité displays an international flair worthy of its setting. In addition to the main theatre and dance season, the prestigious Ecole du Théâtre National de Strasbourg occupies the stage for a short stint each summer.

Théâtre de la Huchette

23 rue de la Huchette, 5th (01.43.26.38.99). Mº St-Michel or Cluny La Sorbonne. **Box office** 5-9pm Mon-Sat. **Admission** €20; €15 concessions. **Credit** MC, V. **Map** p408 J7.

Eugene Ionesco's absurdist classic *La Cantatrice Chauve* ('The Bald Soprano') premiered in Paris in 1950; Nicolas Bataille first staged the play at this tiny theatre in 1957. The same production still runs on a double bill (€28/€20) with Ionesco's *La Leçon*. Each runs just short of an hour. A reasonable level of French should get you through the evening.

late 1700s, stop by for tea at **Aux Goûters Champêtres** (03.44.57.46.21, closed mid Nov-mid Mar) in the *hameau* at the château.

One of the few hotels in the town centre is the **Hotel du Parc Best Western** (36 av du Maréchal-Joffre, 03.44.58.20.00, www.hotel-parc-chantilly.com, doubles €100), equipped with the essentials for a good night's rest.

Getting there

By car

40km (25 miles) from Paris by N16 (direct) or A1 (Chantilly exit).

By train

SNCF Chantilly-Gouvieux from Gare du Nord (30mins), then 5min walk to town, 20mins to château. Some trains stop at Creil, then loop back to Chantilly.

Tourist information

Office de Tourisme

60 av Maréchal-Joffre, 60500 Chantilly (03.44.67. 37.37/www.chantilly-tourisme.com). **Open** 9.30am-12.30pm, 1.30-5.30pm Mon-Sat.

Office de Tourisme

Pl du parvis Notre-Dame, 60302 Senlis (03.44.53. 06.40/www.ville-senlis.fr). **Open** 10am-12.30pm, 2-6.15pm Mon-Sat; 10.30am-1pm, 2-6.15pm Sun. Closes at 5pm Nov-Feb.

Chartres

Seen from afar, the mismatched spires and brilliant silhouette of **Chartres cathedral** burst up out of the Beauce cornfields and dominate the skyline of this modest town some 90 kilometres (56 miles) south-west of Paris.

One of the finest examples of Gothic architecture, it impresses millions of tourists today – and makes you wonder: what would it have been like to have walked here as a fervent believer and seen it 800 years ago?

Chartres was a pilgrimage site long before the cathedral was built, ever since the Sacra Camisia (said to be the Virgin Mary's birthing garment) was donated in 876 by the king. The sublime stained glass of the cathedral, and its doorways bristling with sculpture, embody a complete medieval world view, in which earthly society and civic life reflect the divine order.

The town of Chartres is an attractive tangle of narrow, medieval streets on the banks of the river Eure that makes for a pleasant post-cathedral walk. Two sights merit mentioning: the **Musée des Beaux-Arts** (29 cloître Notre-Dame, 02.37.90.45.80), tucked inside the former bishop's palace, housing a collection of 18th-century French paintings by Watteau and

others; and the **Memorial to Jean Moulin**, the legendary figure of the Resistance, a war-time prefect of Chartres until dismissed by the Vichy government due to his refusal to co-operate with the Nazi authorities. He became de Gaulle's right-hand man on the ground, and died under torture in Lyon in 1943. Moulin's memorial stands a ten-minute walk west of the cathedral, at the corner of rue Collin d'Arleville and boulevard de la Résistance.

Cathédrale Notre-Dame

Place de la Cathédrale (02.37.21.59.08). **Open** *Cathedral* 8.30am-7.30pm daily. *Tower* 9.30am-noon, 2-4.30pm Mon-Sat; 2-4.30pm Sun. **Admission** *Cathedral* free. *Tower* €6.20; €4.20 students. **No credit cards**.

The west front, or 'Royal Portal', of this High Gothic cathedral modelled in part on St-Denis (*see p173*) has three sculpted doorways. Inside, there's another era of sculpture, represented in the 16th-century scenes of the life of Christ that surround the choir. Note the circular labyrinth of black and white stones in the floor – such mazes used to exist in many cathedrals, but most have been destroyed. The cathedral is, above all, famed for its stained-glass windows depicting biblical scenes, saints and medieval trades in brilliant 'Chartres blue', punctuated by rich reds. Climb the tower for a fantastic view.

English-language tours by lecturer Malcolm Miller – one of the world's most knowledgeable and entertaining experts on the cathedral – take place twice daily for most of the year (noon & 2.45pm Mon-Sat, €10, €5 students); enquire in the gift shop. In his absence, audioguides can be hired. Miller is also available for private tours (02.37.28.15.58, millerchartres@aol.com). **Photo** *p348*.

Where to eat & stay

Tourists flock to the **Café Serpent** (2 cloître Notre-Dame, 02.37.21.68.81), in the shadow of the cathedral – if it's full, there are plenty of easy options nearby. For restaurant cuisine with a riverside view, try **L'Estocade** (1 rue de la Porte Guillaume, 02.37.34.27.17, closed all day Mon & Sun evening). For fireside treats, **La Vieille Maison** (5 rue au Lait, 02.37.34. 10.67, closed Mon & Sun) serves up modern and traditional French fare in its cosy 14th-century dining room. For a local speciality, order a serving of Chartres pâté at **Le Saint-Hilaire** (11 rue Pont St-Hilaire, 02.37.30.97.57).

Two chain hotels on the ring road, not far from the town centre, are **Grand Monarque** (22 pl des Epars, 02.37.18.15.15, www.bw-grand-monarque.com, doubles from €115) and the more basic **Ibis Centre** (pl Drouaise, 02.37.36.06.36, www.ibishotel.com, doubles €73), which offers a special weekend rate of €48 until April 2007.

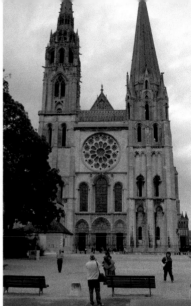

The dreaming spires of Chartres: **Cathédrale Notre-Dame**. *See p347.*

Getting there

By car
90km (56 miles) from Paris by A10, then A11.

By train
Direct from Gare Montparnasse (1hr).

Tourist information

Office de Tourisme
*Pl de la Cathédrale, 28000 Chartres (02.37.18.26.26/
www.chartres-tourisme.com).* **Open** *Apr-Sept* 9am-
7pm Mon-Sat; 9.30am-5.30pm Sun. *Oct-Mar* 10am-
6pm Mon-Sat; 10am-1pm, 2.30-4.30pm Sun.

Fontainebleau

Home to 14 French kings since François I,
Fontainebleau ('Fon-ten-blow') was once a sort
of aristocratic club where gentlemen of the day
came to hunt and learn the art of chivalry. The
town grew up around the **château** in the 19th
century, and is a pleasant place to visit, circled
by hunting forest and rock formations. The
INSEAD business school ('Euro-Harvard') on
the forest edge adds a cosmopolitan touch.

The château is bite-sized compared to the
sprawling grandeur of Versailles, but it has
been completely furnished since its restoration.
The style adopted by the Italian artists brought
in by François I is still visible, as are the
additions by later rulers – Napoleon redecorated
much of it in Empire style before leaving for
exile on Elba from the front courtyard, the
Cour des Adieux. The extensive château
gardens, park and grand canal, all free for
visitors to enter, are also worth exploring.

The 170sq km (66 square mile) **Forêt de
Fontainebleau** is part of the Gâtinas regional
nature park, which has bizarre geological
formations and diverse wildlife. Its ravines,
rocky outcrops and mix of forest and sandy
heath where François I liked to hunt is the
wildest slice of nature to be found near Paris,
and is popular with weekenders for walking,
cycling, riding and rock climbing. There are a
number of well-marked trails, such as the GR1
from Bois-le-Roi train station, but more serious
yompers would be better off with an official
map such as the TOP25 IGN series 2417-OT,
which covers the entire forest, highlighting
climbing sites, campsites and picnic areas.

Trail maps are on sale at the **Fontainebleau
tourist office**, which rents out bicycles (€20
per day) and has info on the nearby villages of
Barbizon and Moret-sur-Loing. Bikes can also
be hired from La Petite Reine (32 rue Sablons,
01.60.74.57.57, www.la-petite-reine.fr), as can
baby seats – passport or €300 deposit required.
La Bleausière riding school (06.82.01.21.18,
la.bleausiere.free.fr), in Barbizon, on the edge
of the forest, offers year-round short and long
guided tours for all ages and levels.

Château de Fontainebleau
*Pl Général-de-Gaulle (01.60.71.50.70/www.musee-
chateau-fontainebleau.fr).* **Open** *Château* June-Sept
9.30am-6pm Mon, Wed-Sun; Oct-May 9.30am-5pm
Mon, Wed-Sun. *Park & gardens* Mar, Apr, Oct

9am-6pm daily; May-Sept 9am-7pm daily; Nov-Feb 9am-5pm daily. **Admission** *Château* €6.50; €5 18-25s; free under-18s. PMP. *Park & gardens* free. **Credit** AmEx, MC, V.

This former hunting lodge is a real mix of styles – the result of centuries of additions and changes. In 1528 François I brought in Italian artists and craftsmen to help architect Gilles le Breton transform a neglected lodge into the finest Italian Mannerist palace in France. This style, noted for its grotesqueries, contorted figures and crazy fireplaces, is still visible in the Ballroom and Long Gallery. Henri IV added a tennis court, Louis XIII built a double-horseshoe entrance staircase, and Louis XIV and XV added classical trimmings. Napoleon and Louis-Philippe also spent a fortune on redecoration. The château gardens include Le Nôtre's Grand Parterre and a carp pond in the Jardin Anglais. There is also an informal château park just outside, with lawns and a canal where locals fish and visitors stop to picnic. Other activities on the site include dinghy paddling on the lake and horse-drawn carriage rides.

Where to eat & stay

Rue Grande is lined with restaurants such as the inventive, stylish **Au Délice Impérial** (No.1, 01.64.22.20.70) and **Au Bureau** (No.12, 01.60.39.00.01), which has Tex-Mex specialities in a pub setting, with DJs and bands in the evening. At No.92, picnickers can find an excellent array of local cheeses at **Fromagerie Barthélémy** (01.64.22.21.64).

For a blow-out meal, head for **Le Caveau des Ducs** (24 rue Ferrare, 01.64.22.05.05), with traditional French cuisine in a 17th-century interior of heavy oak tables and tapestries.

The charming, central **Hôtel de Londres** (1 pl Général-de-Gaulle, 01.64.22.20.21, www.hoteldelondres.com, doubles €90-€150) has free, private parking. Some of the dozen rooms have balconies overlooking the château. Set in a 19th-century post house, the elegant **Hôtel Napoleon** (9 rue Grande, 01.60.39.50.50, www.hotelnapoleon-fontainebleau.com, doubles €125-€210) overlooks an interior garden, and provides appropriately grand meals at its restaurant, **La Table des Maréchaux**.

Getting there

By car
60km (37 miles) from Paris by A6, then N7 (about 75mins). Beware of the likelihood of traffic jams when heading back to Paris on Sundays.

By train
Gare de Lyon to Fontainebleau-Avon (35mins), then bus AB (marked 'Château'). Ask for a Forfait Château de Fontainebleau (€20.80; €16 10-17s; €7.70 4-9s) at the Gare de Lyon; it includes train fare, bus connection, château entrance and audio guide.

Tourist information

Office de Tourisme
4 rue Royale, 77300 Fontainebleau (01.60.74.99.99/ www.fontainebleau-tourisme.com). **Open** *May-Oct* 10am-6pm Mon-Sat; 10am-12.30pm, 3-7pm Sun. *Nov-Apr* 10am-6pm Mon-Sat; 10am-1pm Sun.

Giverny

In 1883 Claude Monet moved his mistress and their eight children into a quaint pink-brick house in bucolic Giverny, and concentrated as much time on cultivating a beautiful garden here as painting the water lilies in it.

The leader of the Impressionist movement – his *Impression: Sunrise* gave rise to the group's name in 1874 – thrived on outdoor scenes, whether along the Seine near Argenteuil or by the Thames in London. Having once seen the tiny village of Giverny from the window of a train, he was smitten. By 1890 he had bought his dream home and soon had a pond dug, bridges built and a tableau of greenery created. As Monet's eyesight began to fail, he produced endless impressions of his man-made paradise, each trying to capture how the leaves and water refracted light. He died here in 1926.

Of the hundreds of tourists who visit here on any given day, not all are art lovers – there are no original Monets here, though you will see the

Château de Fontainebleau. *See p348.*

32 Japanese woodblock prints collected by the artist. Most visitors are simply here for the lilies, and a good photo opportunity. (Giverny is overrun with visitors snapping each other.)

The garden is a masterpiece, its famous water-lily pond, weeping willows and Japanese bridge remarkably intact; and the charming house, the **Fondation Claude Monet**, is dotted with touching mementos. But once you're back in the village, be prepared for heated arguments over finding a table at one of the scarce eating places and long queues of impatient tourists almost everywhere you turn. Get here early, or book ahead for dinner at the famous **Hôtel Baudy** museum-restaurant (81 rue Claude Monet, 02.32.21.10.03, closed Nov-Mar), where Monet's American disciples (such as Willard Metcalf and Dawson-Watson) set up their easels for several decadent years, expanding the old hotel into an art-atelier extraordinaire, complete with ballroom, rose garden and tennis courts – Cézanne stayed for a month. Today, booking accommodation for Giverny (*see below*) is essential – but you will be first to the Monet museum in the morning. Up the road, the **Musée d'Art Américain de Giverny** (99 rue Claude-Monet, 02.32.51.94.65, www.maag.org) houses works by the American Impressionist colony.

Fondation Claude Monet

84 rue Claude-Monet, 27620 Giverny (02.32.51. 28.21/www.fondation-monet.com). **Open** *Apr-Oct* 9.30am-6pm Tue-Sun. **Admission** *House & garden* €5.50; €4 students; €3 7-13s; free under-7s. **Credit** AmEx, MC, V.

Where to stay

For suggestions of hotels and B&Bs in the area, visit www.giverny.org. Pretty **Le Clos Fleuri** (5 rue de la Dîme, 02.32.21.36.51, doubles €75, closed Nov-Mar) is in Giverny, close to the Musée d'Art Américain and Monet's garden.

Getting there

By car
80km (50 miles) west of Paris by A13 to Bonnières, then D201.

By train
Gare St-Lazare to Vernon (45mins), then 5km (3 miles) taxi ride or bus from the station.

Tourist information

Comité Départemental du Tourisme de l'Eure
3 rue du Commandant-Letellier, BP 367, 27003 (02.32.62.04.27/www.cdt-eure.fr). **Open** 9am-12.30pm, 1.30-6pm Mon-Thur; 9am-1pm, 1.30-6pm Fri.

Rouen

Port, cathedral city and industrial hub, historic Rouen is more than just a medieval museum. It boasts a serious collection of fine arts, a bright city centre rebuilt after wartime destruction, a great daily market and more than enough decent restaurants for a town of its size.

Most visitors, though, do come here for the history. The **Cathédrale de Notre-Dame** is one of France's Gothic masterpieces, its façade depicted in many of Monet's canvases (the results can be seen in the **Musée d'Orsay**; *see p157*). Within lies a tomb containing the heart of Richard the Lionheart. The cathedral is also where Léon tries to seduce Emma in *Madame Bovary* – Rouen is firmly Flaubert country.

Behind it are the ruins of the Archbishop's Palace, where another key historical figure, Joan of Arc, was tried in 1431. At the time, this capital of Upper Normandy – an important centre in Roman times, attacked by the Vikings – was under English rule. Joan had commanded French forces fighting the Anglo-Burgundian alliance until her capture by the Burgundian army in 1430. Sold to the English, she was incarcerated in the castle of Philippe-Auguste. All that remains of its seven towers today is the **Tour Jeanne d'Arc**, which contains a modest collection of artefacts relating to Joan – sadly, the steep climb up its spiral staircase is not rewarded with a panorama of this interesting jumble of a city.

At the heart of Rouen, amid the colourful reproduction façades that show how the medieval centre would have looked but for World War II, is place du Vieux-Marché. As well as the site of the main market, it's another place of pilgrimage on the Joan of Arc trail – a vast cross marks the spot where she was burned at the stake. Also here are an unusual modern church built in her name, in the form of a pyre, and, in the cellar of a nearby souvenir shop, a rather disappointing museum.

Between the market and the cathedral, rue du Gros-Horloge contains the clock of the same name, a one-handed astrological remnant from the 16th century and local landmark. Just north of it, towards the main Rive Droit station that links with the swish city metro network, stands the **Musée des Beaux-Arts** (esplanade Marcel-Duchamp, 02.35.72.28.40, www.rouen-musees.com, closed Tue), one of the most prestigious fine arts museums in the provinces. In a building as grand as the collection, it contains works by some of the biggest names from the 16th to the 20th centuries, including Veronese and Rubens, as well as one of Monet's impressions of Rouen cathedral. Also on show is a series of Russian icons from the 1500s.

Rouen's **Cathédrale de Notre-Dame**.

Cathédrale de Notre-Dame

Place de la Cathédrale (www.cathedrale-rouen.net).
Open 2-6pm Mon; 8am-6pm Tue-Sun.
Admission free.
This imposing Gothic landmark, reconstructed after the war, is the third church to stand on this site. The first was built in the third century, the second was ransacked by Vikings. Most of what you see today, including the towers and spires, was put up in the 12th and 13th centuries. So too was the intricate west façade, painted 30-odd times by Monet as the light changed at different times of the day. The tombs in the cathedral's crypt contain the remains of Rollo, the Viking Duke of Normandy, and the heart of Richard the Lionheart.

Where to eat & stay

Creamy Norman cheeses, a particularly bloody local duck dish (*canard à la Rouennaise*) and desserts doused with calvados all feature on most menus in town. Restaurants cluster around place du Vieux-Marché. Among them, **La Couronne** (No.31, 02.35.71.40.90) has been serving traditional fare since the 1400s. Nearby, **Les Nymphéas** (9 rue de la Pie, 02.35.89.26.69, closed Mon, Sun and 14 Aug-5 Sept) specialises in duck, in particular duck liver with a slight cider flavouring. The best restaurant in town is **Gill** (9 quai Bourse, 02.35.71.16.14, closed Mon, Sun, 10-26 Apr and 1-26 Aug), by the Seine, where foie gras ravioli and langoustine tail salad are among the key dishes.

For comfort and location, **Du Vieux Marché** (15 rue de la Pie, 02.35.71.00.88, www.hotelduvieuxmarche.com, doubles €140) can't be beaten; a series of renovated houses grouped around an old courtyard right in the heart of town. For price and convenience, **Hôtel Le Cardinal** (1 place de la Cathédrale, 02.35.70.24.42, doubles €43-€97.50, closed 23 Dec-15 Jan) is right next to the cathedral, with terrace breakfasts served in summer.

Getting there

By car
100km (65 miles) north-west of Paris by A13.

By train
Hourly from Gare St-Lazare (1hr 15mins).

Tourist information

Office de Tourisme de Rouen
25 place de la Cathédrale, 76000 Rouen (02.32.08.32.40/www.rouen.fr). **Open** *May-Sept* 9am-7pm Mon-Sat; 9.30am-12.30pm, 2-6pm Sun. *Oct-Apr* 9am-6pm Mon-Sat; 10am-1pm Sun.

Versailles

Centuries of makeovers have made Versailles the most sumptuously clad **château** in the world – a veritable bouquet of over-the-top brilliance, and an absolute must-see. Architect Louis Le Vau first embellished the original building – a hunting lodge built in the centre of marshlands during Louis XIII's reign – after Louis XIV saw Vaux-le-Vicomte, the impressive residence of his finance minister, Nicolas Fouquet. The Sun King had the unlucky minister jailed, and stole away not only his architect but also his painter, Charles Le Brun, and his landscaper, André Le Nôtre, who turned the boggy marshland into terraces, parterres, fountains and lush groves.

After Le Vau's death in 1670, Jules Hardouin-Mansart took over as principal architect, transforming Versailles into the château we know today. He dedicated the last 30 years of his life to adding the two main wings, the Cour des Ministres and the Chapelle Royale. In 1682 Louis moved in, accompanied by his court –

thereafter, he rarely set foot in Paris. In the 1770s, Louis XV commissioned Jacques-Ange Gabriel to add the sumptuous Opéra Royal, used for concerts by the Centre de Musique Baroque (01.39.20.78.10). It still has the original spy holes Louis' bodyguards used to keep an eye on him. The expense of building and running Versailles cost France dear. With the fall of the monarchy in 1792, most of the furniture was lost – but the château was saved from demolition after 1830 by Louis-Philippe.

Versailles has hosted the official signings of many historic treaties – European recognition of the United States, the unification of Germany in 1871, the division of Europe after 1918 – and it is still used by the French government for major summits. Recently, Kirsten Dunst caroused here in the title role of Sofia Coppola's 2006 film *Marie-Antoinette*. Indeed, Hollywood golden girl Coppola and her crew were given unprecedented access to the château – including Marie-Antoinette's bedroom. In the gardens, the Grand Trianon accommodates heads of state.

The **gardens** are works of art in themselves, their ponds and statues once again embellished by a fully working fountain system. On summer weekends, the spectacular jets of water are set to music, a prelude to the occasional fireworks displays of the Fêtes de Nuit.

Beyond the gardens is the Grand Canal, where visitors can laze around in small boats, and the wooded parkland and sheep-filled pastures of the estate's park. Outside the château gates are the recently restored **Potager du Roi** (the Sun King's vegetable garden), and stables, now housing the **Académie du Spectacle Equestre**.

Versailles is currently undergoing a major overhaul, the first phase of which is due to last until 2010, so expect a little chaos and patches of scaffolding for the next few years. As well as sprucing up Marie-Antoinette's residence (*see p354*), the French state and several sponsors are funding a restoration of the **Hall of Mirrors** – a dazzling 73-metre (240-foot) gallery overlooking the garden, hung with chandeliers. Commissioned in 1678 by Louis XIV and decorated by Le Brun with scenes from the emperor's reign, it is lined with 357 mirrors. The gallery is due to reopen anew in May 2007.

Other renovation tasks mean that you may find boards obstructing the palace's grand front entrance court. Among the key works planned is the recreation of the **Grille Royale**, the vast gilded iron gateway that separated the outer Cour d'Honneur from the inner sanctum of the Cour Royale. This symbol of imperial aloofness and etiquette went missing in the revolutionary period; a newly forged gate – 80 metres (262 feet) long and weighing 15 tonnes – is due to be in place by December 2007. A weathered bronze statue of Louis XIV on horseback that usually commands the courtyard was also removed in 2006 for retouching.

In the town of Versailles, grab a *Historical Places* brochure free from the tourist office (*see p355*) and explore. The Quartier St-Louis opposite the Potager was developed by Louis XV around the Cathédrale St-Louis. Just off rue d'Anjou are the Carrés St-Louis, four market squares surrounded by 18th-century boutiques housing galleries and antiques shops. North-east of the château is the Quartier Notre-Dame, part of the 'new town' designed by the Sun King himself. Eglise Notre-Dame is where members of the royal family were baptised and married. Around the corner is the Marché Notre-Dame, a market square dating back to 1671 and restored in 1841, surrounded by restaurants and cafés. The covered market is closed on Mondays.

Bicycles can be rented from outside RER Versailles-Chantiers (pl Raymond Poincaré, 01.39.20.16.60) for €2 an hour or €12 a day.

Académie du Spectacle Equestre

Grandes Ecuries, Château de Versailles (01.39.02.07.14/www.acadequestre.fr). **Les Matinales des Ecuyers** *(to watch riding practice & visit)* **Viewings** 10.30am & 11.15am Sun. Times vary for groups and during school holidays; call for details. **Admission** €8; €4 5-18s, students. **Credit** MC, V. **Reprise Musicale** *(performance & visit)* **Performances** 8.30pm Sat; 3pm Sun. **Admission** *Daytime* €16; €8 under-18s, students. *Evening* €20; €10 under-18s, students. **Credit** MC, V.

Across from the château entrance are the Sun King's magnificent stables, restored in 2003. They house the Académie du Spectacle Equestre, which is responsible for the elaborate shows of tightly choreographed theatrics on horseback run by famous horse trainer Bartabas. Visitors can catch a show either on the weekends or at special evening performances, or attend training sessions on Sunday mornings to see how the white horses and their young riders learn their tricks.

Château de Versailles

78000 Versailles (01.30.83.76.20/advance tickets 08.92.68.46.94/www.chateauversailles.fr). **Open** *Apr-Oct* 9am-6.30pm Tue-Sun. *Nov-Mar* 9am-5.30pm Tue-Sun. **Admission** €13.50; €10 after 4pm (summer) or 3pm (winter); free under-18s. PMP, Passeport Versailles. **Credit** AmEx, DC, MC, V.

Versailles is a masterpiece – and it's almost always packed with visitors. Allow yourself a whole day to appreciate the sumptuous State Apartments, and the Hall of Mirrors, the highlights of any visit – and mainly accessible with just a day ticket (*see right* **Just the ticket**). The Grand Appartement, where Louis XIV held court, consists of six gilded salons (Venus, Mercury, Apollo and so on), all opulent examples of baroque craftsmanship. No less luxuri-

ous, the Queen's Apartment includes her bedroom, where royal births took place in full view of the court. Hardouin-Mansart's 73m long (240ft) show-piece, the Hall of Mirrors, where a united Germany was proclaimed in 1871 and the Treaty of Versailles signed in 1919, is flooded with natural light from its 17 vast windows. Designed to catch the last of the day's rays, it was here that the Sun King would hold extravagant receptions. Other private apartments can be seen only as part of a guided tour. **Photo** *p354*.

Domaine de Versailles

Gardens Open *Apr-Oct* 7am-dusk daily. *Nov-Mar* 8am-dusk daily. **Admission** *Winter* free (statues covered over). *Summer* €3; €1.50 10-17s; free under-10s. Passeport Versailles. **Grandes Eaux Musicales** (01.30.83.78.88). **Open** *Apr-Sept* Sat, Sun. **Admission** €7; €5.50 10-17s; free under-10s. Passeport Versailles. **Credit** AmEx, DC, MC, V. **Park Open** dawn-dusk daily. **Admission** free.

Sprawling across 8sq km (3sq miles), the meticulously planned gardens consist of formal parterres, ponds, elaborate statues – many commissioned by Colbert in 1674 – and a spectacular series of fountains, served by an ingenious hydraulic system only recently restored to working order. On weekend afternoons in the spring and autumn, the fountains are set in action to music for the Grandes Eaux Musicales – and also serve as a backdrop, seven times a year, for the extravagant Fêtes de Nuit, capturing the regal splendour of the Sun King's celebrations with fireworks, music and theatre.

Just the ticket

The easiest, although not the cheapest, way to see Versailles is to get a **Passeport Versailles**. It allows quick access via Porte C to the main section of the château, the audio-guided tour of the Chambre du Roi, the Grand and Petit Trianons, the gardens and their displays. You can buy the Passeport in advance from Fnac stores (*see p243*), tourist offices or any RER station (price of journey added to the ticket); or go directly to Porte C2 or D before 2pm. Those who hold a Paris Museum Pass (*see p73*) can enter via Porte B2. Those just wanting a day ticket must queue with the masses at Porte A. Any number of guided tours are available from Porte D; you must book early that morning, before meeting by Porte F.

Passeport Versailles

Admission *Apr-Oct* €20 Mon-Fri; free under-18s; €25 Sat, Sun; free under-18s. *Nov-Mar* €16 daily; free under-18s.

Trips Out of Town

Opulent **Château de Versailles**. *See p353.*

Grand Trianon/Petit Trianon/ Domaine de Marie-Antionette

01.30.83.77.43/weekend reservations 01.30.83.76.50.
Open *Apr-Oct* noon-6.30pm daily. *Nov-Mar* noon-
5.30pm daily. **Admission** *Summer* €9; €5 after 4pm;
free under-18s. PMP, Passeport Versailles. *Winter*
€5; free under-18s. PMP, Passeport Versailles.
Credit AmEx, DC, MC, V.

In 1687 Hardouin-Mansart built the pink marble
Grand Trianon in the north of the park, away from
the protocol of the court. Here Louis XIV and his
children's governess and secret second wife,
Madame de Maintenon, could admire the intimate
gardens from the colonnaded portico. It retains the
Empire decor of Napoleon, who stayed here with
his second Empress, Marie-Louise.

The Petit Trianon, built for Louis XV's mistress
Madame de Pompadour, is a wonderful example
of neo-classicism. It later became part of the
Domaine de Marie-Antoinette, an exclusive hide-
away located beyond the canal in the wooded parkland. Given to Marie-Antoinette as a wedding gift
by her husband Louis XVI in 1774, the domain also
includes the chapel adjoining the Petit Trianon,
plus a theatre, a neo-classical 'Temple d'Amour',
and Marie-Antoinette's fairy-tale farm and dairy,
known as the Hameau de la Reine. Here, the queen
escaped from the discontent of her subjects and
the revolutionary fervour of Paris by pretending
to be a humble milkmaid. The Domaine opened to

the public in summer 2006, but only its gardens
will remain fully accessible until April 2008, when
renovation work on the buildings is due for completion – call for updates. A stroll can be enlivened
by hiring hand-held digital PDA or iPod guides.

Potager du Roi

10 rue Maréchal Joffre (www.potager-du-roi.fr).
Open *Apr-Oct* 10am-6pm Mon-Fri (by guided tour
only); times vary Sat, Sun. *Nov-Mar* 10am-6pm Mon-
Fri (by guided tour only). **Admission** *Mon-Fri*
€4.50; €3 concessions; free under-6s. *Sat, Sun* €6.50;
€3 students; free under-6s. **Credit** AmEx, DC, MC, V.
The Potager du Roi, the king's vegetable garden, features 16 small squares surrounded by 5,000 fruit
trees espaliered into fabulous shapes.

Where to eat & stay

Set in a building dating back to the construction
of the château, **Le Chapeau Gris** (7 rue Hoche,
01.39.50.10.81, www.auchapeaugris.com, closed
dinner Tue, all day Wed, set menus €21-€28)
is the oldest restaurant in Versailles, and offers
French country cuisine served under wooden
beams. **Boeuf à la Mode** (4 rue au Pain,
Marché Notre-Dame, 01.39.50.31.99) is an
authentic 1930s brasserie serving steak and
seafood specialities at mid-range prices. For a
proper splurge, consider sampling the Michelin-
starred haute cuisine of **Les Trois Marches**
(Hôtel Trianon Palace, 1 bd de la Reine,
01.30.84.52.00, closed Mon & Sun, lunch €58,
dinner €160). Another long-established eaterie
is the traditional **Brasserie du Théâtre** (15
rue des Réservoirs, 01.39.50.03.21, set menu
lunch €20), which stays open until 11.30pm
for the after-show crowd from the Montansier
theatre next door. You'll also find plenty of late-
night bars around the Marché Notre-Dame.

The town centre town has several reasonably
priced hotels. One of the more historic is the
Hôtel du Cheval Rouge (18 rue André-
Chénier, 01.39.50.03.03, www.chevalrouge.fr.st,
doubles €71-€88), built in Louis XIV's former
livery overlooking the Marché Notre-Dame.
Across from the château, the **Hôtel de France**
(5 rue Colbert, 01.30.83.92.23, www.hotelfrance-
versailles.com, doubles from €141) is set in an
18th-century townhouse and has period decor.

Getting there

By car
20km (12.5 miles) from Paris by A13 or D10.

By train
For the station nearest the château, take the RER C5
(VICK or VERO trains) to Versailles-Rive Gauche; or
take a Transilien SNCF train from Gare St-Lazare to
Versailles-Rive Droit (10mins on foot to the château).

Tourist information

Office de Tourisme
2bis av de Paris, 78000 Versailles (01.39.24.88.88/ www.versailles-tourisme.com). **Open** 11am-5pm Mon, Sun; 9am-6pm Tue-Sat.

Further Afield

Champagne country

Named after the region in which it's produced, champagne – nearly all 300 million bottles a year of it – comes from the towns of **Reims** (nasally pronounced 'Rrance') and **Epernay**, some 25 kilometres (16 miles) apart. At less than two hours by train from Paris, both are ideal destinations for a day trip or a weekend break. Most champagne cellars give detailed explanations of how the drink is produced – from the grape varieties used to the strict name and quality controls – and tours finish with a sample. Don't forget your woollies, as the cellars are chilly and damp.

Epernay developed in the 19th century as expanding champagne houses moved out from Reims to acquire more space. Today, the aptly named avenue de Champagne is home to most major brands – but the best tours are at **Moët & Chandon** and **Mercier**.

In Reims, most of the major champagne houses are open by appointment only: Krug (03.26.84.44.20); Lanson (03.26.78.50.50); Louis Roederer (by appointment *and* recommendation only, 03.26.40.42.11) and Veuve Clicquot (03.26.89.53.90, www.veuve-clicquot.com). **Champagne Pommery** is set in an intriguing Elizabethan building.

Home of the coronation church of most French monarchs dating back to Clovis in 496, Reims was an important city even in Roman times. Begun in 1211, the present **Cathédrale Notre-Dame** (03.26.47.55.34, www.cathedrale-reims.com) has rich Gothic decoration that includes thousands of well-preserved figures on the portals. Look out, too, for the splendid stained-glass windows in the axial chapel, designed by Chagall. The statues damaged during heavy shelling in World War I can be seen next door in the former archbishop's palace, the Palais de Tau (2 pl du Cardinal-Luçon, 03.26.47.81.79).

L'Ancien Collège des Jésuites (1 pl Museux, 03.26.85.51.50, closed all Tue and Sat & Sun mornings) is a classic example of 17th-century baroque architecture, housing a library decorated with religious carvings and paintings by Jean Hélart. The college has also given over a considerable space to modern art.

Champagne Pommery
5 pl du Général Gouraud, 51100 Reims (03.26.61. 62.63/www.pommery.com). **Open** *mid Apr-mid Nov* 9.30am-7pm daily. *Mid Nov-mid Apr* (by appointment only) 10am-6pm daily. **Admission** (incl 1 glass) €7.50; (incl 2 glasses) €10. **Credit** MC, V.
Built in 1868, this unusual château was modelled on Elizabethan architecture so that it would stand out from the surrounding competitors. The visit takes place some 30m (98ft) underground, in 18km (11 mile) tunnels, which link 120 chalk mines from the Gallo-Roman period.

Mercier
68 av de Champagne, 51200 Epernay (03.26.51. 22.22/www.champagne-mercier.fr). **Open** *mid Mar-mid Nov* 9.30-11.30am, 2-4.30pm daily. *Mid Nov-mid Mar* 9.30-11.30am, 2-4.30pm Mon, Thur-Sun. **Admission** (incl 1 glass) €6.50; €3 12-15s; free under-12s. **Credit** MC, V.
Some 7,000 tonnes of chalk were extracted to create the 18km (11 miles) of cellars at Mercier, opened in 1858. Note the 20-tonne champagne barrel at the entrance: it took 24 bulls and 18 horses to drag it all the way from Epernay to Paris for the 1889 Universal Exposition. The 45-minute underground tour takes place on a little train and covers a stretch of tunnel that was used for mini-car races in the 1950s.

Moët & Chandon
20 av de Champagne, 51200 Epernay (03.26.51. 20.00/www.moet.com). **Open** *mid Mar-mid Nov* 9.30-11.30am, 2-4.30pm daily. *Mid Nov-mid Mar* 9.30-11.30am, 2-4.30pm Mon-Fri. **Admission** (incl 1 glass) €7.50; €4.50 12-16s; free under-12s. **Credit** AmEx, DC, MC, V.
Moët & Chandon started life in 1743 as champagne supplier to Madame de Pompadour, Napoleon and Alexander I of Russia. Since then it has kept pole position, with the largest domaine and more than 250 global outlets. In the hour-long tour, visitors are led through a section (under the grand house) of the 28km (17 miles) of chalk tunnels.

Where to eat & stay

In Reims, countless cafés and brasseries line lively **place Drouet d'Erlon**, as do many hotels. If you fancy staying at a working champagne domaine, contact **Ariston Fils Champagne** (4-8 Grande-Rue, Brouillet, 03.26.97.43.46, www.champagne-aristonfils. com, doubles €45-€48), which offers three rooms and pampers its guests. To sleep like a king, book one of the luxuriously extravagant rooms at the **Château les Crayères** (64 bd Henry Vasnier, 03.26.82.80.80, www.chateaules crayeres.com, doubles €275-€475), a grand country-house hotel set in lush grounds.

In Epernay, **La Cave à Champagne** (16 rue Gambetta, 03.26.55.50.70) does good traditional French food, as does **Théâtre** (8 pl Pierre-Mendès-France, 03.26.58.88.19, closed

dinner Tue & Sun, all Wed and 15 Feb-2 Mar,
15 July-2 Aug & 22-28 Dec). Known for its
champagnes, **Les Cépages** (16 rue Fauvette,
03.26.55.16.93, closed Wed & Sun and July &
Christmas) serves homely food.

Set in a 19th-century red-brick mansion,
Le Clos Raymi (3 rue Joseph-de-Venoge,
03.26.51.00.58, www.closraymi-hotel.com,
doubles €90-€115) is a cosy mix of traditional
and modern. Part of the international Best
Western chain, the **Hôtel de Champagne**
(30 rue Eugène-Mercier, 03.26.53.10.60,
www.bw-hotel-champagne.com, doubles
€75-€115) is comfy enough, and the **Hôtel
Kyriad** (3bis rue de Lorraine, 03.26.54.17.39,
doubles from €57) has basic, clean rooms.

Getting there

By car
150km (93 miles) from Paris by the A4. For Epernay,
exit at Château Thierry and take the N3.

By train
From Gare de l'Est, trains take about 90mins for
Reims and Epernay.

Tourist information

Office de Tourisme
*7 avenue de Champagne, 51200 Epernay (03.26.
53.33.00/www.ot-epernay.fr).* **Open** *mid Apr-
mid Oct* 9.30am-12.30pm, 1.30-7pm Mon-Sat;
11am-4pm Sun. *Mid Oct-mid Apr* 9.30am-noon,
1.30-5.30pm Mon-Sat.

Office de Tourisme
*2 rue Guillaume-de-Machault, 51100 Reims
(03.26.77.45.00/www.reims-tourisme.com).* **Open**
Jan-Easter 10am-7pm Mon-Sat; 11am-7pm Sun.
Easter-mid Oct 9am-7pm Mon-Sat; 10am-6pm Sun.
Mid Oct-Dec 10am-7pm Mon-Sat; 11am-4pm Sun.

Deauville & the Norman Riviera

In late 2006, as Oliver Stone and Brian De
Palma were hanging around **Deauville** to
promote their latest movies at September's
prestigious American Film Festival, and
moneyed Parisians enjoyed quality leisure time
at the landmark casino, the equally illustrious
racecourse, the polo field, golf courses and
marina, a local protest group was planning a
fruitless challenge to Ryanair flying here
three times a week from London Stansted.

To no avail. The hoi polloi can now rub
shoulders with the hooray Henris around
this genteel resort, the jewel in the somewhat
artificial crown that is the Norman Riviera.

Deauville boomed in the 1860s, when
Napoleon III followed in the footsteps of
his half-brother, the Duc de Morny, who built
a racecourse on an empty patch of the Côte
Fleurie, just across a narrow stretch of water
from Trouville-sur-Mer. By the early 1900s
there was a casino, a spa and grandiose hotels,
welcoming Paris jet-setters and the British
aristocracy. This early growth period has left
its mark on the town's personality: the bright
parasols and bathing huts of the famous beach-
side promenade, designed to protect ladies'
flowing dresses, are a reminder of those days.
Today spa centres and the gourmet food market
(place du Marché, Tue, Fri and Sat mornings)
attend to today's seekers of *bien-vivre*.

Compared, not unfavourably, to Cannes,
Deauville caters to old-style leisure and wealth:
there are two marinas, three golf courses,
including the only floodlit course in Europe
(02.31.14.42.00), and a yachting school
(02.31.88.38.19). The opportunities to drop
coin are endless: plush designer boutiques,
top-dollar restaurants and Paris-style cafés
(with prices to match) line the streets. Then
there's the **casino**, just behind the seafront.
This massive belle époque edifice stands like a
bastion of decadence, and cannot be missed (ID
is required and, for some rooms, formal attire).

In summer, when the population swells
from 4,500 to around 75,000, watersports and
sand-surfing keep the restless occupied. An
energetic social calendar also brings in the
crowds; there are polo and racing events all
year, and two big film festivals – the Asia Film
Festival (www.deauvilleasia.com) in March, and
then the American Film Festival in September
(www.festival-deauville.com).

The nearby 17th-century port town of
Trouville-sur-Mer shares Deauville's railway
station. Family-owned shops, narrow backstreets
and a daily fish market lend Trouville an
authenticity that its flashier sister lacks. Check
out the beach, casino (with one room decorated
as a Louisiana paddle steamer) and Napoleon's
summer residence, Villa Montebello (64 rue du
Maréchal-Leclerc, 02.31.88.16.26), which
regularly hosts art exhibitions.

A short drive or bus journey further east
is **Honfleur**, a small, very pretty fishing town
at the mouth of the Seine. Honfleur has none
of Deauville's glitz, but plenty of charm. The
old port and the narrow and winding streets
leading off it are perfect for lazy exploration on
foot; there are two sandy beaches nearby; and
the town has a long list of associations with
major artistic figures. Baudelaire spent time at
his mother's house here, and the Impressionists
were frequent visitors – the 'Honfleur School'
included Monet and Courbet. The Musée

Eugène Boudin (pl Erik-Satie, 02.31.89.54.00, closed Jan-10 Feb) contains paintings by Monet, Boudin, Jongkind and others, as well as sculptures and folk artefacts from the local area. Also worth a look is the wooden, 15th-century Eglise Ste-Cathérine (rue des Capucins, 02.31.89.11.83), with its roof built using boat-construction methods and detached belfry.

Casino Barrière de Deauville

Rue Edmond-Blanc, Deauville (02.31.14.31.14). **Open** 11am-2am Mon-Thur; 11am-3am Fri; 10am-4am Sat; 10am-3am Sun. **Admission** (over-18s only, formal dress) €14. **Credit** AmEx, MC, V.

Where to eat & stay

In Deauville, tuck into oysters at **Le Ciro's** (2 rue Edmond-Blanc, 02.31.14.31.31) on the seafront or tackle a roast lobster and rich Normandy treats at **Le Spinnaker** (52 rue Mirabeau, 02.31.88.24.40). The best of Deauville's hotel selection are the palatial **Royal Barrière** (bd Cornuché, 02.31.98.66.33, doubles €270-€390) and the half-timbered **Normandy Barrière** (38 rue Jean Mermoz, 02.31.98.66.22, doubles from €288), linked by a tunnel to the casino.

Those looking to stay on a budget should head in from the seafront – or find somewhere in Trouville-sur-Mer. A quite cheap option there is the **Flaubert** (rue Gustave-Flaubert, 02.31.88.37.23, www.flaubert.fr, doubles €90-€125).

In Honfleur you'll find **La Ferme Saint-Siméon** (rue Adolphe-Marais, 02.31.81.78.00, www.fermesaintsimeon.fr, doubles €220-€450, closed all Mon & lunch Tue), a luxury inn set in landscaped gardens, with a spa and quality restaurant. In the centre, **Les Maisons de Léa** (02.31.14.49.49, www.lesmaisonsdelea.com,

doubles €95-€220) occupies four characterful houses on place Ste-Catherine, by the church, and a cottage for four to six people (€295). Centuries-old stonework adds atmosphere to the harbour views from the hotel and restaurant **L'Absinthe** (10 quai de la Quarantaine, 02.31.89.39.00, www.absinthe.fr, doubles €105-€135, closed mid Nov-mid Dec), where the focus is on fish and seafood; the same outfit runs the nearby **La Grenouille Brasserie** (No.16, 02.31.89.04.24, closed mid Nov-mid Dec).

Getting there

By car

195km (121 miles) west from Paris by A13.

By train

From Gare St-Lazare to Deauville-Trouville (2hrs).

Tourist information

Office de Tourisme

Pl de la Bastille, 14800 Deauville (02.32.14.40.60/ www.deauville.org). **Open** 9am-noon, 2-6pm (until 7pm Apr-Oct) daily.

Office de Tourisme

Quai Lepaulmier, 14600 Honfleur (02.31.89.23.30/ www.ot-honfleur.fr). **Open** *Easter-June, Sept* 10am-12.30pm, 2-6.30pm Mon-Sat; 10am-5pm Sun. *July, Aug* 10am-7pm Mon-Sat; 10am-5pm Sun. *Oct-Easter* 10am-12.30pm, 2-6pm Mon-Sat; 10am-5pm Sun (during school hols only).

Office de Tourisme

32 quai Fernand-Moureaux, 14360 Trouville-sur-Mer (02.31.14.60.70/www.trouvillesurmer.org). **Open** *Apr-June, Sept & Oct* 9.30am-noon, 2-6.30pm Mon-Sat; 10am-1pm Sun. *July & Aug* 9.30am-7pm Mon-Sat; 10am-1pm Sun. *Nov-Mar* 9.30am-noon, 1.30-6pm Mon-Sat; 10am-1pm Sun.

Deauville.

Directory

Palais-Royal. *See p98.*

Directory

Getting Around

By air

Roissy-Charles-de-Gaulle airport

Most international flights use Roissy-Charles-de-Gaulle airport (www.paris-cdg.com), 30km (19 miles) north-east of Paris. Its two main terminals are some way apart, so check which one you need for your return flight; for information in English, call 01.48.62.22.80 or see www.aeroportsdeparis.fr. The RER B (SNCF helpline, 08.92.35.35.39) is the quickest way to central Paris (about 40mins to Gare du Nord; 45mins to RER Châtelet-Les Halles; €7.75 single). A new station gives direct access from Terminal 2; from Terminal 1 you take the free shuttle bus. RER trains run every 15mins, 5.24am-11.56pm daily. **Air France buses** (08.92.35.08.20, www.cars.airfrance.com; €12 single, €18 return) leave every 15mins, 5.45am-11pm daily, from both terminals, and stop at porte Maillot and place Charles-de-Gaulle (35-50min trip). Air France buses also run to Gare Montparnasse and Gare de Lyon (€12 single, €18 return) every 30mins (45-60min trip), 7am-9pm daily; there's a shuttle bus between Roissy and Orly (€16) every 30mins, 6am-10.30pm Mon-Fri, 7am-10.30pm Sat, Sun. The **RATP Roissybus** (08.92.68.77.14, www.ratp.fr; €8.40) runs every 15mins, 5.45am-11pm daily, between the airport and the corner of rue Scribe/rue Auber (at least 45mins); buy tickets on the bus. **Paris Airports Service** is a door-to-door minibus service between airports and hotels, 24/7. The more passengers on board, the less each one pays. Roissy prices go from €24 for one person to €12.40 each for eight people, 6am-8pm (minimum €34, 5-6am, 8-10pm); book on 01.55.98.10.80, www.paris airportservice.com. **Airport Connection** (01.43.65.55.55, www.airport-connection.com; booking 7am-7.30pm) runs a similar service, 4am-10.30pm. Prices for Roissy are €27 per person, €42 for two, then €15 per extra person. A **taxi** to central Paris can take 30-60mins depending on traffic and your point of arrival. Expect to pay €30-€50, plus €1 per item of luggage.

Orly airport

Domestic and international flights use Orly airport (English-speaking information service on 01.49.75.15.15, 6am-midnight daily, www.paris-ory.com), 18km (11 miles) south of the city. It has two terminals: Orly-Sud (mainly international) and Orly-Ouest (mainly domestic). **Air France buses** (08.92.35.08.20, www.cars-airfrance.com; €8 single, €12 return) leave both terminals every 15mins, 6am-11pm daily, and stop at Invalides and Montparnasse (30-45mins). The RATP **Orlybus** (08.92.68.77.14, www.ratp.fr; €5.80) runs between the airport and Denfert-Rochereau every 15mins, 5.35am-11.05pm daily (30min trip); buy tickets on the bus. The high-speed **Orlyval** shuttle train runs every 7mins (6am-11pm daily) to RER B station Antony (Orlyval and RER together cost €9.05); getting to central Paris takes about 35mins. You could also catch the **Orlyrail** (€5.65) to Pont de Rungis, where you can take the RER C into central Paris. Trains run every 15mins, 6am-11pm daily; 50min trip. Orly prices for the Paris Airports Service and Airport connection door-to-door facility (*see left*) are €22 for one person and €8-€14 each for extra passengers depending on the number. A **taxi** into town takes 20-40mins and costs €16-€26, plus €1 per piece of luggage.

Paris Beauvais airport

Beauvais (08.92.68.20.66, www.aeroportbeauvais.com), 70km (44 miles) from Paris, is served by budget airlines such as **Ryanair** (03.44.11.41.41, www.ryanair.com). Buses (€13) leave for porte Maillot 20mins after each arrival; buses the other way leave 3hrs 15mins before each departure. Get tickets from the arrival lounge or the shop at 1 bd Pershing, 17th (01.58.05.08.45).

Airline contacts

Aer Lingus 01.70.20.00.72, www.aerlingus.com
Air France 08.20.82.08.20, www.airfrance.fr
American Airlines 08.10.87.28.72, www.aa.com, www.americanairlines.fr
bmibaby 08.90.71.00.81, www.bmibaby.com
British Airways 08.25.82.54.00, www.britishairways.fr
British Midland 01.41.91.87.04, www.flybmi.com
Continental 01.71.23.03.35, www.continental.com
Easyjet 08.25.08.25.08, www.easyjet.com
KLM & NorthWest 08.90.71.07.10, www.klm.com
United 08.10.72.72.72, www.united.fr

By car

For car travel between France and the UK, there's the tunnel **Le Shuttle** (Folkestone-Calais 35mins) (08.10.63.03.04, www.eurotunnel.com); fast service **Hoverspeed** (Dover-Calais, Newhaven-Dieppe) (www.hoverspeed.com); or ferries run by **Brittany Ferries** (08.25.82.88.28, www.brittanyferries.com), **P&O Stena Line** (08.25.12.01.56, www.poferries.com) and **SeaFrance** (08.25.08.25.05, www.seafrance.com).

Shared journeys

Allô-Stop *1 rue Condorcet, 9th (01.53.20.42.42/08.25.80.36.66/ www.allostop.net). Mº Poissonnière.* **Open** 10am-1pm, 2-6.30pm Mon-Fri; 10am-1pm, 2-5pm Sat. **Credit** MC, V. Call several days ahead to be put in touch with drivers. There's a fee (€4.50 under 200km, 124 miles; up to €10 over 500km, 310 miles), plus €0.50 per km to the driver.

By coach

International coach services arrive at the Gare Routière Internationale Paris-Galliéni at Porte de Bagnolet, 20th. For reservations (in English), call **Eurolines** on 08.92.89.90.91 (€0.34/min), or 01.41.86.24.21, or in the UK 01582 404 511, www.eurolines.fr.

By rail

The **Eurostar** service between London and Paris takes 2hrs 25mins direct, slightly longer for trains stopping at Ashford and Lille. Check in at least 30mins before departure time. Eurostar trains from London Waterloo (01233 617 575, www.eurostar.com) arrive at Gare du Nord (08.92.35.35.39, www.sncf.fr), with easy access to public transport and taxi ranks. **Cycles** can be taken as hand luggage if they are dismantled and carried in a bike bag. You can also check them in at the Eurodispatch depot at Waterloo (Esprit Parcel Service, 08705 850 850)

or Sernam depot at Gare du Nord (01.55.31.54.54). Check-in must be done 24hrs ahead; a Eurostar ticket must be shown. The service costs £20/€45.39.

Travel agencies

Nouvelles Frontières *13 av de l'Opéra, 1st (08.25.00.07.47/www. nouvelles-frontieres.fr). Mº Pyramides.* **Open** 9am-7pm Mon-Sat. **Credit** V. Agent with 16 branches in Paris.

Thomas Cook *17 rue du Colisée, 8th (01.58.36.49.25/www.thomas cook.fr). Mº Opéra.* **Open** 10am-7pm Mon-Sat. **Credit** AmEx, DC, MC, V. General travel agent with more than 30 branches in Paris.

Maps

Free maps of the métro, bus and RER systems are available at airports and métro stations. Other brochures from métro stations are *Paris Visite – Le Guide*, with details of transport tickets and a small map, and *Plan de Paris*, a fold-out one showing *Noctambus* night bus lines. Maps sponsored by Galeries Lafayette and Printemps can be picked up at most hotels. A Paris street map (*Plan de Paris*) can be bought from newsagents or stationers (*papeteries*). The blue *Paris Pratique* is clear and compact.

Public transport

Almost all of the Paris public transport system is run by the **RATP** (Régie Autonome des Transports Parisiens; 08.92.68.77.14, in English 08.92.68.41.14, www.ratp.fr): the bus, métro (underground) and suburban tram routes, as well as lines A and B of the RER (Réseau Express Régional) suburban express railway, which connects with the métro within the city centre. National rail operator **SNCF** (08.92.35.35.39, www.sncf.com) runs RER lines C, D and E, and serves the Paris suburbs (*Banlieue*), and French regions and abroad (*Grandes Lignes*).

Fares & tickets

Paris and suburbs are divided into eight travel zones; zones 1 and 2 cover the city centre. RATP tickets and passes are valid on the métro, bus and RER. Tickets and *carnets* can be bought at métro stations, tourist offices and *tabacs* (tobacconists); single tickets can be bought on buses. Hold on to your ticket in case of spot checks; you'll also need it to exit from RER stations.
● A single ticket costs €1.40, but it's more economical to buy a *carnet* of ten for €10.90.
● A one-day *Mobilis* pass costs from €5.50 for zones 1 and 2 to €18.70 for zones 1-8 (not including airports).
● A three-day *Paris Visite* pass for zones 1-3 is €18.25; a five-day pass is €26.65, with discounts on some attractions.
● One-week or one-month *Carte Orange* passes (passport photo needed) offer unlimited travel in the relevant zones; if bought in zones 1 or 2, each is delivered as a Navigo swipe card. A *forfait mensuel* (monthly *Carte Orange* valid from the first day of the month) for zones 1 and 2 costs €51.50; a weekly *forfait hebdomadaire* (weekly *Carte Orange* valid Mon-Sun inclusive) for zones 1 and 2 costs €15.90 and is better value than *Paris Visite* passes.

Métro & RER

The Paris **métro** is the fastest and cheapest way of getting around. Trains run daily 5.30am-12.40am. Individual lines are numbered, with each direction named after the last stop. Follow the orange *Correspondance* signs to change lines. Some interchanges, such as Châtelet, Montparnasse Bienvenüe and République, involve long walks. The exit (*Sortie*) is indicated in blue. The driverless line 14 runs from Gare St-Lazare to the Bibliothèque Nationale.

Directory

Green machine

It's the pride of mayor Bertrand Delanoë and the flagship project in his vision for creating a greener, more liveable Paris. Inaugurated at the end of 2006, the slick Tramway des Maréchaux (also known as T3) covers the 8-km (five-mile) stretch just inside the Périphérique between Pont du Garigliano in the south-west and the porte d'Ivry in the south-east. Compared to the PC1 bus it replaces, the electric tram has doubled passenger capacity (with an estimated 100,000 travellers daily) and has bolstered travel speed by 38 per cent (at an average of 20kph, 12.5mph).

Most of all, though, the new line is a model of environmental karma. The tracks are covered with some 36,000 square metres (387,000 square feet) of lawns and bordered by over a thousand trees. And with car lanes slimmed down to accommodate the rails, the surrounding roads are estimated to enjoy a 25 per cent reduction in traffic, with a resulting fall in pollution and noise.

The car killed off its previous incarnation in the 1930s; there is a neat historical symmetry to the tramway's triumphant return.

Another aim of the new tram line is to consolidate links between Paris and its suburbs, and many of the 17 stations already connect with métro and RER lines. Furthermore, plans are afoot to improve these connections – notably by linking up with an existing tram in the suburbs. The commuter-friendly T2 line currently runs between the two business-heavy districts of La Défense and Issy-les-Moulineaux on the outskirts of Paris. By 2009, the southern axe will be extended to join up with the T3 station at porte de Versailles. Indeed, the tram looks set to be a big player in the city's future, with a further two lines already under construction in the *banlieue*. The Tramway des Maréchaux, meanwhile, is due to be prolonged eastwards to the Pont de Charenton by 2011, and, if all goes according to plan, it should eventually encircle the entire city.

Pickpockets and bag-snatchers are rife – pay special attention as the doors are closing.

The five **RER** lines (A, B, C, D and E) run 5.30am-1am daily through Paris and into the suburbs. Within Paris, the RER is useful for faster journeys – Châtelet Les Halles to Gare du Nord is one stop on the RER, and six on the métro. Métro tickets are valid for RER journeys within zones 1-2.

Buses

Buses run 6.30am-8.30pm, with some routes continuing until 12.30am, Mon-Sat; limited services operate on selected lines Sun and public holidays. You can use a métro ticket, a ticket bought from the driver (€1.40) or a travel pass. Tickets should be punched in the machine next to the driver; passes should be shown to the driver. When you want to get off, press the red request button, and the *arrêt demandé* (stop requested) sign lights up.

Night buses

After the métro and normal buses stop running, the only public transport – apart from taxis – are the 18 **Noctambus** lines, between place du Châtelet and the suburbs (hourly 1.30am-5.35am Mon-Thur; half-hourly 1am-5.35am Fri, Sat); look out for the owl logo on bus stops. Routes A to H, P, T and V serve the Right Bank and northern suburbs; I to M, R and S serve the Left Bank and southern suburbs. A ticket costs €2.70 with one change; travel passes are valid.

River transport

Batobus
(08.25.05.01.01/www.batobus.com).
River buses stop every 15-25mins at: Eiffel Tower, Musée d'Orsay, St-Germain-des-Prés (quai Malaquais), Notre-Dame, Jardin des Plantes, Hôtel de Ville, Louvre, Champs-Elysées (Pont Alexandre III). They run Nov-Mar 10.30am-4.30pm; Mar-May & Sept-Nov 10.30am-7pm; Jun-Aug 10am-9.30pm. A one-day pass is €11 (€5, €7 concs); two-day pass €13 (€6, €8 concs); five-day pass €16 (€7, €10

concs); one-month pass €22 (€12 concs); season-ticket €50 (€30 concs). Tickets can be bought at Batobus stops, RATP ticket offices and the **Office de Tourisme** (*see p381*).

Trams

Two modern tram lines operate in the suburbs, running from La Défense to Issy-Val de Seine and from Bobigny Pablo Picasso to St-Denis. They connect with the métro and RER; fares are the same as for buses. A third line launches at the end of 2006 (*see above* **Green Machine**).

Rail travel

Suburban attractions, such as Versailles (*see p352*) and Disneyland Paris (*see p280* **Cartoon capers**), are served by the RER. Other locations farther from the city are served by the SNCF railway; the TGV high-speed train has slashed journey times and is steadily being extended to all the main regions. There are few long-distance bus services.

Tickets can be bought at any SNCF station (not just the one from which you'll travel), SNCF shops and travel agents. If you reserve online or by phone, you can pay and pick up your tickets from the station or have them sent to your home. SNCF automatic machines (*billeterie automatique*) only work with French credit/debit cards. Regular trains have full-rate White (peak) and cheaper Blue (off-peak) periods. You can save on TGV fares by buying special cards. The *Carte 12/25* gives under-26s a 25-50 percent reduction; even without it, under-26s are entitled to 25 percent off. Buy tickets in advance to secure the cheaper fare. Before you board any train, stamp your ticket in the orange *composteur* machines located on the platforms, or you might have to pay a hefty fine.

SNCF reservations & tickets *(national reservations and information 08.92.35.35.39 (€0.34 per min)/www.sncf.com).* **Open** 7am-10pm daily. You can also dial 3635 and say *'billet'* at the prompt.

SNCF information *(Ile-de-France 08.91.36.20.20; no reservations).* **Open** 7am-10pm daily.

Paris mainline stations

Gare d'Austerlitz: Central and SW France and Spain.

Gare de l'Est: Alsace, Champagne and southern Germany.

Gare de Lyon: Burgundy, the Alps, Provence and Italy.

Gare Montparnasse: West France, Brittany, Bordeaux, the South-West.

Gare du Nord: Eurostar, Channel ports, North-East France, Belgium and Holland.

Gare St-Lazare: Normandy.

Taxis

Paris taxi drivers are not known for their flawless knowledge of the Paris street map; if you have a preferred route, say so. Taxis can also be hard to find, especially at rush hour or early in the morning. Your best bet is to find a taxi rank (*station de taxis*, marked with a blue sign) on major roads, crossroads and at stations. A white light on a taxi's roof indicates the car is free; an orange light means the cab is busy. Taxi charges are based on zone and time of day: **A** (10am-5pm Mon-Sat central Paris, €0.62 per km); **B** (5pm-10am Mon-Fri, 5pm-midnight Sat, 7am-midnight Sun central Paris; 7am-7pm Mon-Sat inner suburbs and airports, €1.06 per km); **C** (midnight-7am Sun central Paris; 7pm-7am Mon-Sat, all day Sun inner suburbs and airports; all times outer suburbs, €1.24 per km). Most journeys in central Paris cost €6-€12; there's a minimum charge of €5.10, plus €0.90 for each piece of luggage over 5kg or bulky objects, and a €0.70 surcharge from mainline stations. Most drivers will not take more than three people, although they should take a couple and two children. Don't feel obliged to tip, although rounding up to the nearest euro is polite. Taxis are not allowed to refuse rides because they deem them too short and can only refuse to take you in a certain direction during their last half-hour of service (both rules are often ignored). If you want a receipt, ask for *un reçu* or *la note*. Complaints should be made to the **Bureau de la réglementation publique**, 36 rue des Morillons, 75732 Paris Cedex 15.

Phone cabs

These firms take phone bookings 24/7; you also pay for the time it takes your taxi to reach you. If you wish to pay by credit card (minimum €15), mention this when you order.

Airportaxis *to and from Paris airports, 01.48.40.17.17/ www.airportaxis.com.*
Alpha *01.45.85.85.85/ www.alphataxis.fr.*
G7 *01.47.39.47.39/in English 01.41.27.66.99/www.taxis-g7.fr.*
Taxis Bleus *01.49.36.24.24/08.91.70.10.10/ 08.25.16.24.24/www.taxis-bleus.com.*

Driving

If you bring your car to France, you must bring its registration and insurance documents. An insurance green card, available from insurance companies and the AA and RAC in the UK, is not compulsory but is useful. As you come into Paris, you will meet the Périphérique, the giant ring road that carries traffic into, out of and around the city. Intersections, leading on to other main roads, are called *portes* (gates). Driving on the Périphérique is not as hair-raising as it might look, though it's often congested, especially at rush hour and peak holiday times. If you've come to Paris by car, it may be a good idea to park at the edge of the city and use public transport. Some hotels have parking spaces that can be paid for by the hour, day or by various types of season tickets. In peak holiday periods, the organisation Bison Futé hands out brochures at motorway *péages* (toll gates), suggesting less crowded routes. French roads are categorised as *Autoroutes* (motorways, with an 'A' in front of the number), *Routes Nationales* (national 'N' roads), *Routes Départementales* (local, 'D' roads) and rural *Routes Communales* ('C' roads). *Autoroutes* are toll roads, though some sections, including most of the area immediately around Paris, are free. *Autoroutes* have a speed limit of 130km/h (80mph); this is not adhered to with any degree of zeal by French motorists. The limit on most *Routes Nationales* is 90km/h (56mph); within urban areas the limit is 50km/h (30mph), and 30km/h (20mph) in selected residential zones.

Infotrafic *08.92.70.77.66 (€0.34 per minute)/www.infotrafic.fr*
Traffic information service for the Ile-de-France *08.26.02.20.22/www.securite routiere.gouv.fr.*

Breakdown services

The AA or RAC do not have reciprocal arrangements with an equivalent organisation in France, so it's advisable to take out additional breakdown insurance cover, for example with a company like **Europ Assistance** (0870 737 5700/ www.europassistance.co.uk). If you don't have insurance, you can still use its service (01.41.85.85.85), but it will charge you the full cost. Other 24-hour breakdown services in Paris include: **Action Auto Assistance** (01.45.58.49.58) and **Dan Dépann Auto** (01.40.06.06.53).

Driving tips

● At junctions where no signposts indicate right of way, the car coming from the right has priority. Many roundabouts now give priority to those on the roundabout. If this is not indicated (by road markings or a sign with the message *Vous n'avez pas la priorité*), priority is for those coming from the right.
● Drivers and all passengers must wear seat belts.
● Children under ten are not allowed to travel in the front of a car, except in baby seats facing backwards.
● You should not stop on an open road; you must pull off to the side.
● When drivers are flashing their lights at you, this often means they will not slow down and are warning you to move out of their path or keep out of the way. But some friendly drivers also flash their lights to warn other drivers when there might be traffic police lurking in the vicinity.
● Try to carry plenty of change, as it's quicker – and less stressful – to make for the exact-money line on *péages*. If you are caught short, some cashiers give change and most *péages* accept credit cards.

Parking

There are still a few free on-street parking areas in Paris, but they're often full. If you park illegally, you risk getting your car clamped or towed away (*see below*). It's forbidden to park in zones marked for deliveries (*livraisons*) or taxis. Parking meters have now been replaced by *horodateurs*, pay-and-display machines, which take a special card (*carte de stationnement* at €15 or €30, available from *tabacs*). Parking is often free at weekends, after 7pm and in August. There are plenty of underground car parks in the city centre. Most cost €2.50 per hour, €20 for 24 hours; some have lower rates after 6pm, and many offer various season tickets – a week at €80 or a month at €150.
Parking information for Paris
www.parkingsdeparis.com.

Clamps & car pounds

If your car is clamped, contact the nearest police station. There are eight car pounds (*préfourrières*) in Paris. You'll have to pay a €136 removal fee, plus €10 storage charge per day and a parking fine of €35 for parking in a no-parking zone. Bring your driving licence and insurance papers. Before you can pay, you need to find your vehicle – no small task. Once clamped, your car will be sent to the *préfourrière* nearest to where it was snatched, then moved on to a different pound after 72hrs. To find out where, call 01.53. 73.53.73 or 08.91.01.22.22, or try www.prefecture-police-paris.interieur.gouv.fr.

Car hire

To hire a car you must be 25 or over and have held a licence for at least a year. Some agencies accept drivers aged 21-24, but a supplement of €20-€25 per day is usual. Take your licence and passport with you. There are often good weekend offers (Fri evening to Mon morning). Week-long deals are better at the bigger companies: with Avis or Budget, for example, it's around €300 a week for a small car with insurance and 1,750km (1,090 miles) included. Costlier hire companies allow the return of a car in other French cities and abroad. Bargain companies may have an extremely high charge for damage: read the small print before signing.

Hire companies
Ada *08.25.16.91.69/www.ada.fr.*
Avis *08.20.05.05.05/www.avis.fr.*
Budget *08.25.00.35.64/ www.budget.fr.*
Calandres *01.43.06.35.50/ www.calandres.com.* Prestige cars for those who've held a licence for at least five years.
EasyRentacar *www.easycar.com.*
Europcar *08.25.82.55.13/ www.europcar.fr.*
Hertz *01.41.91.95.25/www.hertz.fr.*
Rent-a-Car *08.91.70.02.00/ www.rentacar.fr.*

Chauffeur-driven cars
Chauffeur Services Paris (06.68.56.16.88/www.csparis.com). **Open** 24hr daily. **Prices** from €80 airport transfer; €270 for 4 hours. **Credit** AmEx, DC, MC, V.

Cycling

The Mairie actively promotes cycling in the city. There are now 353km (220 miles) of bike lanes and there are even plans for a bicycle 'Périphérique' circling Paris. The Itinéraires Paris-Piétons-Vélos-Rollers – scenic strips of the city that are closed to cars on Sundays and holidays – have been consistently multiplied; the city website (www.paris.fr) can provide an up-to-date list of routes and a downloadable map of cycle lanes. A free *Paris à Vélo* map can be picked up at any Mairie or from bike shops. Cycle lanes (*pistes cyclables*) run mostly N-S and E-W. N-S routes include rue de Rennes, avenue d'Italie, bd

Fighting the fumes

How can Paris combat its perpetual traffic and pollution problems? Simply by taking cars out of the equation. This is the radical solution put forward by mayor Bertrand Delanoë in a controversial three-stage plan that aims to reduce traffic by 25 per cent in five years – and free the centre of all non-residential vehicles by 2012. After studying various alternatives, Delanoë (who drives an electric car) and his team rejected the London toll system in favour of the closed zone model used so successfully in Rome.

While the project may sound ambitious, it is essentially the logical extension of a series of traffic innovations the mayor has introduced since coming to power in 2001. Multiple bus lanes, an extra 90km (56 miles) of cycle tracks, reduced residential parking fees, and wider pavements have delivered a 13 per cent decrease in traffic, a 32 per cent increase in bicycle travel and a 19 per cent reduction in pollution on the city's main east-west thoroughfare, rue de Rivoli. With the launch of the city's new tramway at the end

of 2006 (*see p362* **Green machine**), the mayor showed his continued determination to make public transport more eco-friendly. Now, he is waging open war against the car.

During the first stage of the new plan, the speed limit will be reduced to 30kph (18.5mph) in the first four districts (the area between place de la Concorde and place de la Bastille), and current parking fines tripled. New cycle lanes will also be built along the Seine. In 2007, cars will be banned from Seine-side embankments and from the centre of Paris at weekends, while the roads around Les Halles will be pedestrianised. The final phase of the plan sees the first four districts closed to all non-residential private vehicles by the year 2012.

As a further measure against pollution, the city is covering sections of its frequently-congested ringroad, the 35km- (22-mile) long Périphérique. The first of three areas to swap noise and traffic fumes for gardens and sports fields was the north-eastern porte des Lilas at the end of 2006.

Sébastopol and av Marceau. E-W routes take in the rue de Rivoli, bd St-Germain, bd St-Jacques and av Daumesnil. You could be fined (€22) if you don't use them, which is a bit rich considering the lanes are often blocked by delivery vans and the €135 fine for obstructing a cycle lane is barely enforced. Cyclists are also entitled to use certain bus lanes (especially the new ones, which are set off by a strip of kerb stones); look out for traffic signs with a bike symbol. The Bois de Boulogne and Bois de Vincennes offer paths away from traffic, although they are still criss-crossed by roads bearing menacing motor vehicles.

Don't let the Parisians' blasé attitude to helmets and lights convince you it's not worth using them. Be confident, make your intentions clear and keep moving – and look out for scooter-mounted bag-snatchers. If the thought of

pedalling around alone in a city known for the verve of its drivers fazes you, consider joining a guided bike tour.

Cycles & scooters for hire

Note that bike insurance may not cover theft: be sure to check before you sign up.

Freescoot *63 quai de la Tournelle, 5th (01.44.07.06.72/www.freescoot. com). M° St-Michel or Maubert Mutualité.* **Open** 9am-7pm daily; closed Sun from Oct to mid-Apr. **Credit** AmEx, MC, V.
Scooters €30/day, €40/weekend, €145/week. Deposit of €1,300/€1,600 required, plus passport.
Other locations: 144 bd Voltaire, 11th (01.44.93.04.03).

Maison Roue Libre *1 passage Mondétour, 1st (08.10.44.15.34). M° Châtelet. Plus (Mar-Oct) four RATP cyclobuses at Stalingrad, pl du Châtelet, porte d'Auteuil and parc Floral in the Bois de Vincennes (01.48.15.28.88/www.rouelibre.com).* **Open** 9am-7pm daily. **Credit** MC, V (for weekend hire only).
Bike hire €4/hour, €10-€15/day, €27/weekend. Helmets come free.

Passport and a deposit of €150 both required.
Other locations: 37 bd Bourdon, 4th (01.44.54.19.29).

Paris-Vélo *2 rue du Fer-à-Moulin, 5th (01.43.37.59.22/www.paris-velo-rent-a-bike.fr). M° St Marcel or Censier Daubenton.* **Open** 10am-7pm daily. **Credit** MC, V.
Good selection of mountain bikes (VTT) and 21-speed models for hire. Five hours costs €12, a weekend €30, a month €116. Passport and €300 deposit required.

Walking

Walking is the best way to explore Paris; just remember to remain vigilant at all times. Crossing Paris streets can be perilous, as the 3,000 or so pedestrians who end up in hospital – or worse – each year can tell you. Brits must realise that traffic will be coming from the 'wrong' direction and that zebra crossings mean very little. By law, drivers are only obliged to stop at a red traffic light – and even then, many will take a calculated risk.

Resources A-Z

Addresses

Paris arrondissements are indicated by the last two digits of the postal code: 75002 denotes the 2nd, 75015 the 15th. The 16th arrondissement is divided into two sectors, 75016 and 75116. Some business addresses have a more detailed postcode, followed by a Cedex number, which indicates the arrondissement; *bis* or *ter* is the equivalent of 'b' or 'c' after a building number.

Age restrictions

For both heterosexuals and homosexuals the age of consent is 15. You must be 18 to drive, and to consume alcohol in a public place. There is no age limit for buying cigarettes.

Attitude & etiquette

Parisians take manners seriously and are generally more courteous than their reputation may lead you to believe. If someone brushes you accidentally, they will more often than not say '*pardon*'; you can do likewise, or say '*c'est pas grave*' (don't worry). In shops it is normal to greet the assistant with a '*bonjour madame*' or '*bonjour monsieur*' when you enter, and say '*au revoir*' when you leave. The business of '*tu*' and '*vous*' can be tricky for English speakers. Strangers, people significantly older than you and professional contacts should be addressed with the respectful '*vous*'; friends, relatives, children and pets as '*tu*'. Among themselves, young people often launch straight in with '*tu*'.

Business

The best first stop in Paris for initiating business is the **CCIP** (*see p367*). Banks can refer you to lawyers, accountants and tax consultants.

Conventions & conferences

The world's leading centre for trade fairs, Paris hosts over 500 exhibitions a year.
CNIT *2 pl de la Défense, BP 321, 92053 Paris La Défense (01.72.72. 17.00/www.parisexpo.fr). Mº/RER Grande Arche de La Défense.* Mainly computer fairs.

Palais des Congrès *2 pl de la Porte-Maillot, 17th (01.40.68.00.05/ www.palais-congres-paris.fr). Mº Porte-Maillot.*
Parc des Expositions de Paris-Nord Villepinte *SEPENV 60004, 95970 Roissy-Charles-de-Gaulle (01.48.63.30.30/www.expoparisnord. com). RER Parc des Expositions.* Trade fair centre near Roissy airport.
Paris-Expo *Porte de Versailles 15th (01.72.72.17.00/www.parisexpo.fr). Mº Porte de Versailles.* Paris' biggest expo centre, from fashion to pharmaceuticals.

Courier services

ATV *(01.41.72.13.63/www.atoutevitesse. com).* **Open** 24 hrs daily. **Credit** MC, V. 24-hr bike or van messengers. Higher rates after 8pm weekdays and at weekends.
Chronopost *(Customer service: 08.25.80.18.01/www.chronopost. com).* **Open** 8am-8pm Mon-Fri; 9am-3pm Sat. **Credit** MC, V. This overnight delivery offshoot of the state-run post office is the most widely used service for parcels and packages of up to 30kg.
UPS *34 bd Malesherbes, 8th (08.21.23.38.77/www.ups.com). Mº St-Augustin.* **Open** 8am-7pm Mon-Fri; 8am-1pm Sat. **Credit** AmEx, MC, V. International courier services.

Secretarial services

ADECCO International *50 rue Etienne-Marcel, 2nd (01.55.34. 78.20/www.adecco.fr). Mº Etienne Marcel.* **Open** 8.30am-12.30pm, 2-6.30pm Mon-Fri. International employment agency specialising in bilingual secretaries and office staff – permanent or temporary.

Translators & interpreters

Documents such as birth certificates, loan applications and so on, must be translated by certified legal translators, listed at the **CCIP** (*see p367*) or embassies. For business translations there are dozens of reliable independents.
Association des Anciens Elèves de l'Esit *(01.44.05.41.46).* **Open** by phone only, 8am-8pm Mon-Fri; 8am-6pm Sat.

Travel advice

For up-to-date information on travel to a specific country – including the latest news and tips on safety and security, health issues, local laws and customs – contact your home country government's department of foreign affairs. Most have websites packed with useful advice for would-be travellers.

Australia
www.smartraveller.gov.au

Canada
www.voyage.gc.ca

New Zealand
www.mft.govt.nz/travel

Republic of Ireland
foreignaffairs.gov.ie

UK
www.fco.gov.uk/travel

USA
www.state.gov/travel

Size charts

Women's clothes			Women's shoes		
British	French	US	British	French	US
4	32	2	3	36	5
6	34	4	4	37	6
8	36	6	5	38	7
10	38	8	6	39	8
12	40	10	7	40	9
14	42	12	8	41	10
16	44	14	9	42	11
18	46	16			
20	48	18			

Men's clothes			Men's shoes		
British	French	US	British	French	US
34	44	34	6	39	7
36	46	36	7.5	40	7.5
38	48	38	8	41	8
40	50	40	8	42	8.5
42	52	42	9	43	9.5
44	54	44	10	44	10.5
46	56	46	11	45	11
48	58	48	12	46	11.5

A translation and interpreting co-operative whose 1,000 members are graduates of the Ecole Supérieure d'Interprètes et de Traducteurs.
International Corporate Communication *3 rue des Batignolles, 17th (01.43.87.29.29). Mº Place de Clichy.* **Open** 9am-1pm, 2-6pm Mon-Fri. Translators of financial and corporate documents, plus simultaneous translation.

Useful organisations

American Chamber of Commerce *262 rue du Fbg-St-Honoré, 8th (01.53.89.11.00/www. faccparisfrance.com). Mº Ternes.* (Closed to the public, calls only.)
British Embassy Commercial Library *35 rue du Fbg-St-Honoré, 8th (01.44.51.34.56/www.amb-grandebretagne.fr). Mº Concorde.* **Open** by appointment. Stocks trade directories, and assists British companies that wish to develop or set up in France.
CCIP (Chambre de Commerce et d'Industrie de Paris) *27 av de Friedland, 8th (01.55.65.55.65/ www.ccip.fr). Mº Charles de Gaulle Etoile.* **Open** 9am-5pm Mon-Fri. This huge organisation provides a variety of services for people doing business in France and is very useful for small businesses. Pick up the free booklet *Discovering the Chamber of Commerce* from its head office (*above*). There's

also a legal advice line (08.92.70.51.00, 9am-4.30pm Mon-Thur, 9am-1pm Fri). **Other locations**: Bourse du Commerce, 2 rue de Viarmes, 1st (has a free library and bookshop). 2 rue Adolphe-Jullien, 1st (support for businesses wishing to export goods and services to France).
Chambre de Commerce et d'Industrie Franco-Britannique *31 rue Boissy d'Anglas, 8th (01.53.30.81.30/fax 01.53.30.81.35/ www.francobritishchambers.com). Mº Madeleine.* **Open** 2-5pm Mon-Fri; by phone 9am-6pm.
This organisation promotes contacts through conferences and social/cultural events. It publishes its own trade directory, as well as *Cross-Channel*, a trade magazine.
INSEE (Institut National de la Statistique et des Etudes Economiques) *Salle de consultation, 195 rue de Bercy, Tour Gamma A, 12th (01.41.17.50.50/ 08.25.88.94.52/www.insee.fr). Mº Bercy.* **Open** 9.30am-12.30pm, 2-5pm Mon-Thur; 9.30-12.30pm, 2-4pm Fri. Source of seemingly every statistic to do with French economy and society. Visit the reading room or search the website for free stats.
US Commercial Service *Postal address: US Embassy, 2 av Gabriel, 8th. Visit: US Commercial Service, NEO Building, 14 bd Haussmann, 9th (01.43.12.23.83/www.buyusa. gov/france or www.amb-usa.fr).*

Mº Richelieu Drouot. **Open** by appointment 9am-6pm Mon-Fri. Helps US companies looking to trade in France. Advice by fax and email.

Consumer

In the event of a serious misdemeanour, try one of the following:
Direction Départmentale de la Concurrence, de la Consommation et de la Répression des Fraudes *8 rue Froissart, 3rd (01.40.27. 16.00). Mº St-Sébastien Froissart.* 9am-noon, 2-5pm Mon-Fri. Come here to file a consumer complaint concerning Paris-based businesses.
Institut National de la Consommation *80 rue Lecourbe, 15th (08.92.70.75.92/www.conso. net). Mº Sèvres Lecourbe.* **Open** by phone 9am-12.30pm Mon-Fri; recorded information at other times. Queries on consumer, regulatory, housing and administrative matters

Customs

There are no customs on goods for personal use between EU countries, provided tax has been paid in the country of origin. Quantities accepted as being for personal use are:
● 800 cigarettes or 400 small cigars or 200 cigars or 1kg loose tobacco.
● 10 litres of spirits (over 22% alcohol), 90 litres of wine (under 22% alcohol) or 110 litres of beer.
For goods from outside the EU:
● 200 cigarettes or 100 small cigars or 50 cigars or 250g loose tobacco.
● 1 litre of spirits (more than 22% alcohol) or 2 litres of wine and beer
● 50g perfume
● 500g coffee

Tax refunds

Non-EU residents can claim a refund or *détaxe* (around 12 per cent) on VAT if they spend over €175 in any one day in one shop and if they live outside the EU for more than six months in the year. At the shop concerned ask for a *bordereau de vente à*

Directory

l'exportation, and when you leave France have it stamped by customs. Then send the stamped form back to the shop. *Détaxe* does not cover food, drink, antiques, services or works of art.

Disabled travellers

It's always wise to check up on a site's accessibility and provision for disabled access before you visit. General information (in French) is available on the Secrétaire d'Etat aux Personnes Handicapées website: www.handicap.gouv.fr.

Association des Paralysés de France *13 pl de Rungis, 13th (01.53.80.92.97/www.apf.asso.fr). M° Place d'Italie.* **Open** 9am-12.30pm, 2-6pm Mon-Fri. Publishes *Guide 98 Musées, Cinémas* (€3.81) listing accessible museums and cinemas, and a guide to restaurants and sights.

Fédération APAJH (Association pour Adultes et Jeunes Handicapés) *185 Bureaux de la Colline, 92213 St-Cloud Cedex (01.55.39.56.00/www.apajh.org). M° Marcel Sembat.* Advice for disabled people living in France.

Plateforme d'Accueil et d'Information des Personnes Handicapées de la Marie de Paris *(08.00.03.37.48).* Advice in French to disabled persons living in or visiting Paris. The Office de Tourisme website (www.paris bienvenue.com) also gives useful information for disabled visitors.

Getting around

Neither the métro nor buses is wheelchair-accessible, with the exception of métro line 14 (Méteor), bus lines 20, PC (Petite Ceinture) and some 91s. Forward seats on buses are intended for people with poor mobility. RER lines A and B and some SNCF trains are wheelchair-accessible in parts. All Paris taxis are obliged by law to take passengers in wheelchairs.

Aihrop *3 av Paul-Doumer, 92508 Rueil-Malmaison Cedex (01.41.29. 01.29/www.aihrop.com).* **Open** 9.30am-12.30pm, 1.30-5.30pm Mon-Fri. Closed Aug.

Transport for the disabled, anywhere in Paris and Ile-de-France; book 48 hours in advance.

Drugs

French police have the power to stop and search anyone. It's wise to keep prescription drugs in their original containers and, if possible, to carry copies of the original prescriptions. If you're caught in possession of illegal drugs, you can expect a prison sentence and/or a fine. *See also* **Health, Helplines**.

Electricity & gas

Electricity in France runs on 220V. Visitors with British 240V appliances can change the plug or use an adaptor (*adaptateur*). For US 110V appliances, you'll need to use a transformer (*transformateur*), available at BHV or branches of Fnac and Darty. Gas and electricity are supplied by the state-owned Electricité de France-Gaz de France. Contact EDF-GDF (08.10.34.34.75/ www.edf.fr/www.gazdefrance. com) about supply, bills, power failures and gas leaks.

Embassies & consulates

For a full list of embassies and consulates, see the Pages Jaunes (www.pagesjaunes.fr) under 'Ambassades et Consulats'. Consular services (passports, etc) are for citizens of that country only.

Australian Embassy *4 rue Jean-Rey, 15th (01.40.59.33.00/ www.france.embassy.gov.au). M° Bir-Hakeim.* **Open** *Consular services* 9.15am-noon, 2-4.30pm Mon-Fri; *Visas* 10am-noon Mon-Fri.

British Embassy *35 rue du Faubourg-Saint-Honoré, 8th (01.44.51.32.81/www.amb-grandebretagne.fr). M° Concorde. Consular services 18bis rue d'Anjou, 8th. M° Concorde.* **Open** 9.30am-12.30pm, 2.30-5pm Mon, Wed-Fri; 9.30am-4.30pm Tue. *Visas 16 rue d'Anjou, 8th (01.44.51.33.00).* **Open** 9am-noon Mon-Fri; *by phone* 2.30-5pm Mon-Fri.

British citizens wanting consular services (new passports etc) should ignore the long queue along rue d'Anjou for the visa department, and walk straight in at No.18bis.

Canadian Embassy *35 av Montaigne, 8th (01.44.43.29.00/ www.amb-canada.fr). M° Franklin D. Roosevelt. Consular services (01.44.43.29.02).* **Open** 9am-noon, 2-4.30pm Mon-Fri. *Visas 37 av Montaigne, 8th (01.44.43.29.16).* **Open** 8.30-11am Mon-Fri.

Irish Embassy *12 av Foch, 16th. Consulate 4 rue Rude, 16th (01.44.17.67.00). M° Charles de Gaulle Etoile.* **Open** *Consular/visas* 9.30am-noon Mon-Fri; *by phone* 9.30am-1pm, 2.30-5.30pm Mon-Fri.

New Zealand Embassy *7ter rue Léonard-de-Vinci, 16th (01.45.01. 43.43/www.nzembassy.com/france). M° Victor Hugo.* **Open** 9am-1pm, 2-5.30pm Mon-Fri (closes 4pm Fri). July, Aug 9am-1pm, 2-4.30pm Mon-Thur; 9am-2pm Fri. *Visas* 9am-12.30pm Mon-Fri.
Visas for travel to New Zealand can be applied for on the website www.immigration.govt.nz.

South African Embassy *59 quai d'Orsay, 7th (01.53.59.23.23/ www.afriquesud.net). M° Invalides.* **Open** *by appointment; by phone* 8.30am-5.15pm Mon-Fri. *Consulate and visas* 9am-noon Mon-Fri.

US Embassy *2 av Gabriel, 8th (01.43.12.22.22/www.amb-usa.fr). M° Concorde. Consulate and visas 2 rue St-Florentin, 1st (01.43.12. 22.22). M° Concorde.* **Open** *Consular services* 9am-12.30pm, 1-3pm Mon-Fri. *Visas* (08.92.23.84.72) or check website for non-immigration visas.

Emergencies

Most of the following services operate 24 hours a day. In a medical emergency, such as a road accident, phone the Sapeurs-Pompiers, who have trained paramedics. *See also* **Health: Accident & Emergency, Doctors; Helplines**.

Ambulance (SAMU)	**15**
Police	**17**
Fire (Sapeurs-Pompiers)	**18**
Emergency (from a mobile phone)	**112**

GDF (gas leaks)
08.10.43.32.75/www.gazdefrance.fr

EDF (electricity)
08.10.33.39 + number of arrondissement (01-20)

Centre anti-poison
01.40.05.48.48

Directory

Gay & lesbian

For information on HIV and AIDS, *see* **Health**. *See also* *pp301-306* **Gay & Lesbian**.

Health

Nationals of non-EU countries should take out insurance before leaving home. EU nationals staying in France are entitled to use of the French Social Security system, which refunds up to 70 per cent of medical expenses. UK residents travelling in Europe require a European National Health Insurance Card (EHIC). This allows them to benefit from free or reduced-cost medical care when travelling in a country belonging to the European Economic Area (EEA) or Switzerland. The EHIC replaces the E111 form and is free of charge. For further information, refer to www.dh.gov.uk/travellers or your local post office. If you're staying for longer than three months, or working in France but you are still making National Insurance contributions in Britain, you will need form E128 filled in by your employer and stamped by the NI contributions office in order to get a French medical number. Consultations and prescriptions have to be paid for in full on the spot, and are reimbursed on receipt of a completed *fiche*. If you undergo treatment, the doctor will give you a prescription and a *feuille de soins* (bill of treatment). Stick the small stickers from the medication boxes on to the *feuille de soins*. Send this, together with the prescription and details of your EHIC card, to the local **Caisse Primaire d'Assurance Maladie** for a refund. For those resident in France, more and more doctors (especially in Paris) now accept the **Carte Vitale**, which lets them produce a virtual *feuille de soins* and you to pay only

the non-reimbursable part of the bill. Information on health insurance can be found at www.ameli.fr. You can track refunds with Allosecu (08.20.90.09.00). See the Ministry of Health's website: www.sante.gouv.fr (08.20.03.33.33).

Accident & emergency

Hospitals specialise in one type of emergency or illness – refer to the Assistance Publique's website (www.aphp.fr). In a medical emergency, call the Sapeurs-Pompiers or SAMU (*see* **Emergencies**). The following (in order of district) have 24-hr accident and emergency services:

Adults
Hôpital Hôtel Dieu *1 pl du Parvis Notre-Dame, 4th (01.42.34.82.34).*
Hôpital St-Louis *1 av Claude-Vellefaux, 10th (01.42.49.49.49).*
Hôpital St-Antoine *184 rue du Faubourg-Saint-Antoine, 12th (01.49.28.20.00).*
Hôpital de la Pitié-Salpêtrière *47-83 bd de l'Hôpital, 13th (01.42.16.00.00).*
Hôpital Cochin *27 rue du Fbg-St-Jacques, 14th (01.58.41.41.41).*
Hôpital Européen Georges Pompidou *20 rue Leblanc, 15th (01.56.09.20.00).*
Hôpital Bichat-Claude Bernard *46 rue Henri-Huchard, 18th (01.40.25.80.80).*
Hôpital Tenon *4 rue de la Chine, 20th (01.56.01.70.00).*

Children
Hôpital Armand Trousseau *26 av du Dr Arnold-Netter, 12th (01.44.73.74.75).*
Hôpital St-Vincent de Paul *74-82 av Denfert-Rochereau, 14th (01.58.41.41.41).*
Hôpital Necker *149 rue de Sèvres, 15th (01.44.49.40.00).*
Hôpital Robert Debré *48 bd Sérurier, 19th (01.40.03.20.00).*

Private Hospitals
American Hospital in Paris *63 bd Victor-Hugo, 92200 Neuilly (01.46.41.25.25/www.american-hospital.org). M° Porte Maillot, then bus 82.* **Open** 24hrs daily. English-speaking hospital. French Social Security refunds only a small percentage of treatment costs.

Hertford British Hospital (Hôpital Franco-Britannique) *3 rue Barbès, 92300 Levallois-Perret (01.46.39.22.22/www.british-hospital.org). M° Anatole-France.* **Open** 24hrs daily. Most of the medical staff speak English.

Complementary medicine

Académie d'Homéopathie et des Médecines Douces *2 rue d'Isly, 8th (01.43.87.60.33). M° St-Lazare.* **Open** 11am-8pm Mon-Fri. Health services include acupuncture, aromatherapy and homeopathy.

Contraception & abortion

To get the pill (*la pilule*) or coil (*stérilet*), you need a prescription, available on appointment from the two places listed below, from a *médecin généraliste* (GP) or from a gynaecologist. The morning-after pill (*la pilule du lendemain*) can be had from pharmacies without prescription but is not reimbursed. Condoms (*préservatifs*) and spermicides are sold in pharmacies and supermarkets, and there are condom machines in most métro stations, club lavatories and on some street corners.

If you're considering an abortion (IVG – *interruption volontaire de grossesse*) but want to discuss options in detail, you may get better information and counselling from the *orthogénie* (family planning) department of a hospital than from the two organisations below (see www.aphp.fr for IVG services). While abortion rights are strongly grounded in France, there are some doctors who remain opposed. Ultrasound examinations to ascertain the exact stage of pregnancy are obligatory.

Centre de Planification et d'Education Familiales *27 rue Curnonsky, 17th (01.48.88.07.28). M° Porte de Champerret.* **Open** 9am-5pm Mon-Fri. Free consultations on family planning and abortion. Abortion counselling on demand; otherwise phone for an appointment.

Directory

High-tech travel

Responsible for running the city's public transport network, the RATP prides itself on being at the cutting edge of technology. In the last few years, city travellers have benefited from innovations such as the contactless Navigo card, an ultra-efficient electric tramway and the driverless high-speed métro line 14.

With an eye on the future, the RATP has launched plans to automate other métro lines, beginning with the main east-west thoroughfare, line 1. Buses are set for their own hi-tech makeover too. Among the proposed projects is a scheme to fulfil every urban motorist's dream by making traffic lights automatically turn green. The system relies on co-ordination between the traffic lights and the existing GPS equipment aboard the city's buses. The same GPS technology is also behind plans to offer a localised information service on plasma screens. Bus passengers will be able to watch aerial 3D views of the surrounding streets, along with expected arrival times. Most innovatively, the screens will broadcast regularly updated mini-documentaries, cultural reports, and weather and news bulletins about the different areas en route. Both these projects are currently being tested on select lines.

The mobile phone is at the heart of another series of services. Since late 2006, travellers have been able to access free, real-time information about the state of traffic via SMS or WAP. By consulting their phones, Parisians can thus be warned about any potential hold-ups. During 2007, the RATP intends to extend this service so that passengers can calculate their journey times and itineraries on their phone. Thanks to geolocalisation, the phone will even be able to point its owner to the nearest station or bus stop. In another experimental project, the mobile phone allows blind or poor-sighted travellers to be guided to an exit within a métro station. Dubbed BlueEyes, the service is made possible using Bluetooth technology and a special software. Travellers are thus pointed the right way via large arrows on the mobile phone screen or by listening to audio directions on a headset. Currently under testing, the system could eventually be adapted for use by tourists.

To make these services more widely available, the RATP is gradually equipping its stations – and entire lines – with Wi-Fi hotspots. For the moment, high-speed wireless internet access is available on bus No.38 and the RER lines A and B.

MFPF (Mouvement Français pour le Planning Familial)
10 rue Vivienne, 2nd (08.00.80. 38.03/01.42.60.93.20/www. planning-familial.org). Mº Bourse. **Open** 9.30am-5.30pm Mon, Tue, Thur, Fri; 9.30am-7.30am Wed. Phone for an appointment for prescriptions and contraception advice. For abortion advice, turn up at the centre at one of the designated time slots. The approach here, however, is brusque. **Other locations**: 94 bd Masséna, 13th (01.45.84.28.25).

Dentists

Dentists are found in the *Pages Jaunes* under *Dentistes*. For emergencies, contact:

Hôpital de la Pitié-Salpêtrière *(see p369)* also offers 24hr emergency dental care.

SOS Dentaire *87 bd Port-Royal, 13th (01.43.37.51.00). Mº Les Gobelins/RER Port-Royal.* **Open** *phone* 9am-midnight. Phone service for emergency dental care.

Urgences Dentaires de Paris *(01.42.61.12.00/01.43.37.51.00).* **Open** 8am-10pm Sun, holidays.

Doctors

You'll find a list of GPs in the *Pages Jaunes* under *Médecins: Médecine générale*. For a social security refund, choose a doctor or dentist who is *conventionné* (state registered). Consultations cost €20 or more, of which a proportion can be reimbursed. Seeing a specialist costs more still.

Centre Médical Europe *44 rue d'Amsterdam, 9th (01.42.81.93.33). Mº St-Lazare.* **Open** 8am-7pm Mon-Fri; 8am-6pm Sat. Practitioners in all fields – modest consultation fees.

House calls

SOS Infirmiers *(Nurses)* *(01.47.07.00.73).* House calls 24hrs. Costs will vary, and are higher after 8pm and at weekends.

SOS Médecins *(01.43.37.77.77 or 08.20.33.24.24).* House calls cost €35 before 7pm; from €50 after and on holidays; prices are higher if you don't have French social security.

Urgences Médicales de Paris *(01.53.94.94.94).* Doctors make house calls for €35 during the day (€60 if you don't have French social security); €50/€80 until midnight; €63.50/€90 after midnight. Some of them speak English.

Opticians

Branches of **Alain Afflelou** (www.alainafflelou.com) and **Lissac** (www.lissac.com) stock hundreds of frames and can make prescription glasses within the hour. For an eye test, you'll need to go to an *ophtalmologiste* – ask the optician for a list. Contact lenses can be bought over the counter if you have your prescription details.

Hôpital des Quinze-Vingts
*28 rue de Charenton, 12th (01.40.
02.15.20).* Specialist eye hospital
offers on-the-spot consultations
for eye problems.

SOS Optique
*(01.48.07.22.00/www.sosoptique.
com).* 24hr repair service for glasses.

Pharmacies

French *pharmacies* sport a
green neon cross. A rota of
pharmacies de garde operate
at night and on Sundays. If
closed, a pharmacy will have a
sign indicating the nearest one
open. Staff can provide basic
medical services such as
bandaging wounds (for a
small fee) and will indicate
the nearest doctor on duty.
Parapharmacies sell almost
everything pharmacies do but
cannot dispense prescription
medication. Toiletries and
sanitary products are often
cheaper in supermarkets.

Night pharmacies

**Dérhy/Pharmacie des Champs-
Elysées** *84 av des Champs-Elysées,
8th (01.45.62.02.41). M° George V.*
Open 24hrs daily.

Matignon *2 rue Jean-Mermoz, 8th
(01.43.59.86.55). M° Franklin D.
Roosevelt.* Open 8.30am-2am daily.
Pharma Presto *(01.61.04.04.04/
www.pharma-presto.com).* Open
24hrs daily. Delivery (€40 8am-6pm;
€55 6pm-8am & weekends) of
medication. Will also chauffeur your
ailing pet to the vet.

**Pharmacie Européene de la
Place de Clichy** *6 pl de Clichy, 9th
(01.48.74.65.18). M° Place de Clichy.*
Open 24hrs daily.

Pharmacie des Halles *10 bd de
Sébastopol, 4th (01.42.72.03.23).
M° Châtelet.* Open 9am-midnight
Mon-Sat; 9am-10pm Sun.

Pharmacie d'Italie *61 av d'Italie,
13th (01.44.24.19.72). M° Tolbiac.*
Open 8am-2am daily.

**Pharmacie de la Place de la
Nation** *13 pl de la Nation, 11th
(01.43.73.24.03). M° Nation.*
Open 8am-11pm daily.

STDs, HIV & AIDS

**Centre Medico-Sociale (Mairie
de Paris)** *2 rue Figuier, 4th
(01.49.96.62.70). M° Pont-Marie.*
Open 9am-5.30pm Mon, Tue, Thur;
noon-5.30pm Wed; 1.30-5.30pm Fri;
9.30-10.30am Sat.

Free, anonymous tests (*dépistages*) for
HIV, hepatitis B and C and syphilis
(wait one week for results). Good
counselling service too.

**Le Kiosque Infos Sida-
Toxicomanie** *36 rue Geoffroy-
l'Asnier, 4th (01.44.78.00.00). M°
St-Paul.* Open 10am-7pm Mon-Fri;
2-7pm Sat. Youth association that
offers information on AIDS and
sexuality, drug addiction and abuse.
Face-to-face counselling service.

SIDA Info Service
*(08.00.84.08.00/www.sida-info-
service.org).* Open 24hrs daily.
Confidential AIDS information in
French. English-speaking counsellors
available 2-7pm Mon, Wed, Fri.

Helplines

**Alcoholics Anonymous in
English** *(01.46.34.59.65/www.
aaparis.org).* 24hr recorded message
gives details of AA meetings at the
American Cathedral or American
Church (for both, *see p376*).

Allô Service Public *(39.39/
www.service-public.fr).* Open 8am-
7pm Mon-Fri; 9am-2pm Sat. A source
of information and contacts for all
aspects of tax, work and admin
matters. They even claim to be able
to help if you have problems with
neighbours. The catch: you can only
dial from inside France, and
operators speak only French.

The Counseling Center
(01.47.23.61.13). English-language
counselling service, based at the
American Cathedral.

**Drogues Alcool Tabac Info
Service** *(08.00.23.13.13/www.
drogues.gouv.fr).* Phone service, in
French, for help with drug, alcohol
and tobacco problems.

Narcotics Anonymous *(01.43.72.
12.72/www.nafrance.org).* Meetings
in English three times a week.

SOS Dépression *(01.40.47.95.95/
http://sos.depression.free.fr/).* Open
24hrs daily. People listen and/or give
advice. Can send round a counsellor
or psychiatrist in case of a crisis.

SOS Help *(01.46.21.46.46/www.
soshelpline.org).* Open 3-11pm daily.
English-language helpline.

ID

French law requires that some
form of identification be
carried at all times. Be prepared
to produce your passport or
EHIC card (*see p369*).

Insurance

See p369 Health.

Internet

ISPs

America Online *(08.26.02.60.00/
www.aol.fr).*

Club-Internet *(08.00.97.01.58/
www.club-internet.fr).*

Free *(08.92.13.51.51/www.free.fr).*

Neuf *(08.92.22.21.09/www.neuf.fr).*

Noosnet *(08.26.20.03.80/
www.noos.com).*

Orange *(32.20/www.orange.fr).*

Internet access

Many hotels offer internet
access, some from your own
room – and an increasing
number of public spaces are
setting themselves up
as Wi-Fi hotspots.

Milk *31 bd de Sébastopol, 1st (01.40.
13.06.51/www.milkinternethall.com).
M° Châtelet or Rambuteau/RER
Châtelet Les Halles.* Open 24hrs
daily.
Other locations: throughout
the city.

Language

See p383 **Essential
vocabulary**; for food terms,
see p188 **Menu lexicon**.

Left luggage

Gare du Nord

There are self-locking luggage
lockers (6.15am-11.15pm daily)
on Level -1 under the main
station concourse: small (€3.50),
medium (€7) and large (€9.50)
for 48 hours. The SNCF
luggage service (01.55.31.54.54)
can give basic details.

Roissy-Charles-de-
Gaulle airport

Bagages du Monde *(01.48.16.
84.90/www.bagagesdumonde.com).*
Terminal 1 *Niveau Arrivée, Porte
14 (01.48.16.34.90).* Open 8am-2pm
daily. **Terminal 2** *Niveau Départ,
Porte 3 (01.48.16.20.61).* Open 8am-
8pm daily. **Terminal 2F** *Niveau
Arrivée, Porte 4 (01.48.16.20.64).*
Open 7am-7pm daily. Company with
counters in CDG terminals and an
office in Paris (102 rue de Chemin-
Vert, 11th, 01.43.57.30.90, 10am-2pm
Sat only by appointment) that can
ship excess baggage anywhere in the
world, or store luggage.

Directory

Legal help

Mairies can answer some legal enquiries; ask for times of their free consultations juridiques.

Direction Départementale de la Concurrence, de la Consommation et de la Répression des Fraudes *8 rue Froissart, 3rd (01.40.27.16.00). Mº St-Sébastien Froissart.* **Open** 9am-noon, 2-5pm Mon-Fri. Part of the Ministry of Finance; deals with consumer complaints.

Palais de Justice Galerie de Harlay *Escalier S, 4 bd du Palais, 4th (01.44.32.48.48). Mº Cité.* **Open** 9am-noon Mon-Fri. Free legal consultation. Arrive early and obtain a numbered ticket for the queue.

SOS Avocats *(08.25.39.33.00/ 01.44.32.48.48).* **Open** 7-11.30pm Mon-Fri. Closed July, Aug. Free legal advice by phone.

Libraries

Every arrondissement has its free public library. To get hold of a library card, you need ID and evidence of a fixed address in Paris.

American Library *10 rue du Général-Camou, 7th (01.53.59.12.60/ www.americanlibraryinparis.org). Mº Ecole-Militaire/RER Pont de l'Alma.* **Open** 10am-7pm Tue-Sat (shorter hours in Aug). **Admission** day pass €12; annual €100; discount for students. A useful resource: this is the largest English-language lending library on the Continent. It receives 400 periodicals, as well as popular magazines and newspapers (mainly American).

Bibliothèque Historique de la Ville de Paris *Hôtel Lamoignon, 24 rue Pavée, 4th (01.44.59.29.40). Mº St-Paul.* **Open** 9.30am-6pm Mon-Sat. Closed 1st 2 wks Aug. **Admission** free (bring passport photo and ID). Books and documents on Paris history in a Marais mansion.

Bibliothèque Marguerite Durand *79 rue Nationale, 13th (01.53.82.76.77). Mº Tolbiac.* **Open** 2-6pm Tue-Sat. Closed 3wks Sept. **Admission** free. 40,000 books and 120 periodicals on women's history. The feminism collection includes letters of Colette and Louise Michel.

Bibliothèque Nationale de France François Mitterrand *quai François-Mauriac, 13th (01.53.79.59.59/www.bnf.fr). Mº Bibliothèque.* **Open** 10am-8pm Tue-Sat; noon-7pm Sun. Closed 2wks Sept & bank holidays. **Admission** day pass €3.50; annual €35.

Books, papers and periodicals, plus titles in English. An audio-visual room lets you browse photo, film and sound archives.

Bibliothèque Publique d'Information (BPI) *Centre Pompidou, 4th (01.44.78.12.33/ www.bpi.fr). Mº Hôtel de Ville/RER Châtelet Les Halles.* **Open** noon-10pm Mon, Wed-Fri; 11am-10pm Sat, Sun. Closed 1 May. **Admission** free. Now on three levels, the Centre Pompidou's vast library has a huge global press section, reference books and language-learning facilities.

BIFI (Bibliothèque du Film) *51 rue de Bercy, 12th (01.71.19.32.32/ www.bifi.fr). Mº Bercy.* **Open** 10am-7pm Mon-Fri. Closed 2wks Aug. **Admission** €3.50 day pass; €34 annual; €15 students annual. Housed in the same building as the Cinémathèque Française (*see p291*), this world-class researchers' and film buffs' library offers books, magazines film stills and posters, as well as films on video and DVD.

Documentation Française *29-31 quai Voltaire, 7th (01.40.15.72.72/ www.ladocumentationfrancaise.fr). Mº Rue du Bac.* **Open** 9am-6pm Mon-Fri. Closed Aug & 1st wk Sept. The official government archive and central reference library has information on French politics and economy since 1945.

Locksmiths

Numerous round-the-clock repair services handle locks, plumbing and, sometimes, car repairs. Most charge a minimum €18-€20 call-out (*déplacement*) and €30 per hour, plus parts. Charges are higher on Sunday and at night.

Allô Assistance Dépannage *(08.42.49.05.81/www.allocentral depannage.com).* No car repairs.

SOS Dépannage *(08.20.22.23.33/ www.okservice.fr).* Double the price of most services, but claims to be twice as reliable.

Lost property

Bureau des Objets Trouvés *36 rue des Morillons, 15th (08.21.00.25.25/www.prefecture-police-paris.interieur.gouv.fr). Mº Convention.* **Open** 8.30am-5pm Mon-Thur; 8.30am-4.30pm Fri. Visit in person to fill in a form specifying details of the loss. This may have been the first lost property office in the world, but it is far from the most efficient. Huge delays in processing claims mean that if your trip to Paris is short, you may need to nominate a

proxy to collect found objects after you leave, although small items can be posted. If your passport was among the items lost, you'll need to go to your consulate to get a single-entry temporary passport in order to leave the country.

SNCF lost property Some mainline SNCF stations have their own lost property offices.

Media

See also p385 **Websites**.

Magazines

Arts & listings

Two modest local publications compete for consumers of basic Wednesday-to-Tuesday listings details: the handbag-sized **L'Officiel des Spectacles** (€0.35) and **Pariscope** (€0.40). Look out also for **Lylo**, a free bi-monthly booklet distributed around bars and clubs, for info on gigs and DJ nights. Affiliated to Radio Nova, monthly **Nova** gives multi-ethnic information on where to drink, dance and hang out. **Technikart** tries – not entirely successfully – to mix clubbing with the arts. Highbrow TV guide **Télérama** has superb arts coverage and comes with **Sortir**, a Paris listings insert. **Les Inrockuptibles** (fondly known as *Les Inrocks; see p313*) deals with contemporary music scenes at home and abroad; it has strong coverage of film and books too.

There are specialist arts magazines for every interest. The choice of film-related titles, in particular, is wide, and includes long-established intellectual heavyweights **Les Cahiers du Cinéma**, **Positif** and **Trafic**, fluffy **Studio** and celebrity-heavy **Première**.

Business

Capital, its sister magazine **Management** and weightier **L'Expansion** are the notable monthlies. **Défis** has tips for the entrepreneur; **Initiatives** is for the self-employed.

English

The springtime **Time Out Paris Free Guide** is widely distributed in visitor venues such as hotels, and the **Time Out Paris Visitors' Guide** is on sale in newsagents across the city. **FUSAC** (France-USA Contacts) is a small-ads magazine that lists flat rentals, job ads and appliances for sale.

Gossip

The French love gossip. **Public** gives weekly celebrity updates; **Oh Là!** (sister of Spain's *Hola!* and UK's *Hello!*) showcases celebs. **Voici** is the juiciest scandal sheet; **Gala** tells the same stories without the sleaze. **Paris Match** is a French institution founded in 1948, packed with society gossip, celeb interviews and regular photo scoops. **Point de Vue** specialises in royalty (no showbiz fluff). Monthly **Entrevue** aims to titillate and tends toward features on nonconformist sex.

News

Weekly news magazines are an important sector in France, offering news and cultural sections as well as in-depth reports; they range from respected organs **L'Express**, **Le Point** and **Le Nouvel Observateur** to the sardonic, chaotically arranged **Marianne**. Weekly **Courrier International** publishes an interesting selection of articles, translated into French, from newspapers all over the world.

Women, men & fashion

Elle was a pioneer among women's mags and has editions across the globe. In France it's a weekly, and spot-on for interviews and fashion. Monthly **Marie-Claire** takes a more feminist, campaigning line. Both have design spin-offs (**Elle Décoration**, **Marie-Claire Maison**). and *Elle* has also spawned foodie **Elle à Table**. **DS** has lots to read and coverage of social

issues. **Vogue**, bought for its fashion coverage and big-name guests, is rivalled during fashion week by **L'Officiel de la Mode**. Meanwhile the underground prefers to buy more radical publications such as **Purple** (six-monthly art, literature and fashion tome), **Crash** and the new wave of fashion/lifestyle mags: **WAD** (stands for We Are Different), **Citizen K**, **Jalouse** and **Numéro**. Men's mags include the naughty-bizarre **Echo des Savanes** and French versions of lad bibles **FHM**, **Maximal** and **Men's Health**.

Newspapers

French national dailies, with relatively high prices and low print runs, are in dire straits. Only 20 per cent of France reads a national paper; regional dailies dominate outside Paris. Serious, centre-left **Le Monde** is must-read material for business types, politicians and intellectuals; despite its lofty reputation, subject matter is eclectic. The conservative upper and middle classes go for daily broadsheet **Le Figaro**, which has a devotion to politics, shopping, food and sport. Taken over in 2004 by the head of the Dassault defence and media group, it veers from controversial industrial issues. Its sales are aided by pages of property and job ads and Wednesday's **Figaroscope** Paris listings. The Saturday edition has three magazines. Founded in the aftershocks of 1968 by a group that included Sartre and de Beauvoir, **Libération**, once affectionately known as *Libé*, is shedding readers and yet to find a modern identity. In early 2005, its staff accepted a plan for financier Edouard de Rothschild to take a 39 per cent stake in the paper – only to go on a three-day strike when he later proposed 52 job cuts across the board.

It is still the preferred read of the *gauche caviar* (champagne socialists) and worth buying for wide news and arts coverage. For business and financial news, the French dailies **La Tribune**, **Les Echos** and the weekly **Investir** are the tried and trusted sources. The easy-read tabloid **Le Parisien** is strong on consumer affairs, social issues, local news, events and vox pops. Downmarket **France Soir** has gone tabloid. **La Croix** is a Catholic, right-wing daily. The Communist Party **L'Humanité** (shortened to *L'Huma*) struggles on. Sunday broadsheet **Le Journal du Dimanche** comes with **Fémina** mag and a Paris section. **L'Equipe** is the doyen of European sports dailies – Saturday's edition comes with a magazine. Its sister bi-weekly **France Football** is the bible of world soccer. Each was instrumental in setting up the game's top competitions during the golden age of French sports journalism after the war. **Paris-Turf** is for horse fans.

English-language papers

Paris-based **International Herald Tribune** is on sale throughout the city; British dailies, Sundays and **USA Today** are widely available on the day of issue at larger kiosks in the centre, though often without their supplements. The most popular (and many esoteric) English and US newspapers and magazines can be found in central bookshops (*see pp242-243*).

Satirical papers

Wednesday institution **Le Canard Enchaîné** is the Gallic *Private Eye* – in fact it was the inspiration for the *Eye*. It's a broadly left-wing satirical weekly broadsheet that's full of in-jokes and breaks political scandals.

Directory

Radio

For a complete list of all Paris radio frequencies, go to www.bric-a-brac.org/radio. Many of the following can be heard online at their respective websites. A mandatory state-defined minimum of 40 per cent French music has led to overplay of Gallic pop oldies and to the creation of dubious hybrids by local groups that mix words in French with a refrain in English. Trashy phone-in shows also proliferate. Wavelengths are given in MHz.

87.8 France Inter Highbrow, state-run; jazz, international news and discussion slots aplenty. Good cultural coverage.

90.4 Nostalgie As you'd expect.

90.9 Chante France 100 per cent French *chanson*.

91.3 Chérie FM Lots of oldies.

91.7 France Musiques State classical music channel: highbrow concerts and top jazz.

92.1 Le Mouv' New public station aimed at luring the young with pop and rock music.

93.1 Aligre From local Paris news to literary chat.

93.5/93.9 France Culture Talky state culture station.

94.8 RCJ/Radio J/Judaïque FM/Radio Shalom Shared wavelength for Jewish stations.

95.2 Ici et Maintenant/Neo New stations hoping to stir local public debate about current events.

96.0 Skyrock Pop station with loudmouth presenters. Lots of rap.

96.4 BFM Business and economics.

96.9 Voltage FM Dance music.

97.4 Rire et Chansons A non-stop diet of jokes and pop oldies.

97.8 Ado Music for teenagers.

98.2 Radio FG Beloved of clubbers for its on-the-pulse tips, this station ditched its all-gay remit in 1999.

99.0 Radio Latina Great Latin and salsa music.

100.3 NRJ 'Energy' – geddit? National leader with the under-30s.

101.1 Radio Classique Top-notch, state-run classical music station.

101.5 Radio Nova Hip hop, trip hop, world, jazz.

101.9 Fun Radio Now embracing techno alongside Anglo pop hits.

102.3 Oui FM Oui will rock you.

103.9 RFM Easy listening.

104.3 RTL The most popular French station nationwide mixes music and talk programmes.

104.7 Europe 1 News, press reviews, sports, business, entertainment. Much the best weekday breakfast news broadcast, with politicians interviewed live.

105.1 FIP Traffic and weather info, what's on in Paris and a mix of jazz, classical, world and pop. 'Fipettes', female continuity announcers employed for their come-to-bed voices, are a much-loved feature.

105.5 France Info 24hr news, weather, economic updates and sports bulletins. Reports get repeated every 15 minutes: useful if you're learning French.

106.7 Beur FM North African music and discussion.

English

You can receive the **BBC World Service** (648 KHz AM), with its English-language international news, current events, pop and drama; also on 198KHz LW, from midnight to 5.30am daily. At other times 198KHz LW carries **BBC Radio 4**, with British news, talk and *The Archers*. **RFI** (738 KHz AM; www.rfi.fr) has an English-language programme of news and music 7-8am, 2.30-3.30pm and 4.30-5pm daily. There's also the French capital's first all-English radio station, **Paris Live** (www.parislive.net).

Television

In 2005, the choice of free TV channels available in France more than doubled. Under the explosive acronym TNT (Télévision Numérique Terrestre, or terrestrial digital television), seven new channels – available via the traditional rooftop aerial with a decoder that costs about €100, or automatically to cable and satellite customers – began broadcasting. For more information, go to www.tdf.fr or pick up a copy of weekly mag *Télérama* (see p373). The channels listed below are the six 'core' stations available on an unenhanced TV set:

TF1 *(www.tf1.fr)*. The country's biggest channel, first to be privatised (in 1987). Reality shows, dubbed soaps and football are staples.

France 2 *(www.france2.fr)*. This state-owned station mixes game shows, chat, documentaries and the usual cop series and films.

France 3 *(www.france3.fr)*. This, the more heavyweight of the two state channels, offers wildlife and sports coverage, debates, *Cinéma de Minuit* – classic films in V.O. (*version originale*, or original language) – and the endearing cookery show *Bon Appétit Bien Sûr*, fronted by superchef Joël Robuchon.

Canal+ *(www.canalplus.fr)*. Subscription channel shows recent films, exclusive sport and late-night porn. A week's worth of the satirical puppets show *Les Guignols* is broadcast unscrambled on Sundays at 1.40pm.

Arte/France 5 *(www.arte-tv.com)*. The intellectual Franco-German hybrid Arte shares its wavelength with educational channel France 5 (3am-7pm).

M6 *(www.m6.fr)*. Dubbed US sci-fi series and made for TV movies, plus investigative reportage, popular science and kids' shows.

Cable TV & satellite

France offers a decent range of cable and satellite channels but content in English is still limited. CNN and BBC World offer round-the-clock news coverage. BBC Prime keeps you up to date on *EastEnders* (omnibus Sun 2pm), while Teva supplies comedy such as *Sex and the City*.

Noostv *(08.26.20.03.80/www.noos.fr)*. The first cable provider to offer an interactive video service via internet.

Money

Visitors can carry a maximum of €7,600 in currency (www.finances.gouv.fr).

The euro

Non-French debit and credit cards can be used to withdraw and pay in euros, and currency withdrawn in France can be used subsequently all over the euro zone. Daylight robbery occurs, however, if you try to deposit a euro cheque from any country other than France in a French bank: they are currently charging around €15 for this service, and the European parliament has backed down on its original decision that cross-border payments should be in line with domestic ones across the euro zone. Good news for Brits, though: if you transfer money from the UK to France in euros, you will pay the same charges as if Britain were within the euro zone (but watch the exchange rate carefully). For useful euro information online, *see p385*.

ATMs

Withdrawals in euros can be made from bank and post office automatic cash machines. The specific cards accepted are marked on each machine, and most can give instructions in English. Credit card companies charge a fee for cash advances, but their rates are often better than bank rates.

Banks

French banks usually open 9am-5pm Mon-Fri (some close at lunch); some banks also open on Sat. All are closed on public holidays, and from noon on the previous day. Note that not all banks have foreign exchange counters. The commission rates vary between banks; the state-owned Banque de France usually offers good rates. Most banks accept travellers' cheques, but may be reluctant to accept personal cheques even with the Eurocheque guarantee card, which is not widely used in France.

Bank accounts

To open an account (*ouvrir un compte*), French banks require proof of identity, address and your income (if any). You'll probably be required to show

your passport, an electricity, gas or phone bill in your name and a payslip/letter from your employer. Students need a student card and may need a letter from their parents. Of the major national banks (BNP, Crédit Lyonnais, Société Générale, Banque Populaire, Crédit Agricole), Société Générale tends to be the most foreigner-friendly. Most banks don't hand out a Carte Bleue/Visa card until several weeks after you've opened an account. A chequebook (*chéquier*) is usually issued in about a week. Payments made with a Carte Bleue are debited directly from your current account, but you can arrange for purchases to be debited at the end of every month. French banks are tough on overdrafts, so try to anticipate any cash crisis in advance and work out a deal for an authorised overdraft (*découvert autorisé*) or you risk being blacklisted as '*interdit bancaire*' – forbidden from having a current account – for anything up to ten years. Depositing foreign currency cheques can be slow, so try to use wire transfer or a bank draft in euros to receive funds from abroad.

Bureaux de change

If you happen to be arriving in Paris early in the morning or late at night, you will be able to change money at the **American Express** bureaux de change in terminals 1 (01.48.16.13.26), 2A, 2B, 2C and 2D (01.48.16.48.40) and 2E (01.48.16.63.81) at Roissy, and at Orly Sud (01.49.75.77.37); all open 6.30am-11pm daily. **Travelex** (*see right*) has bureaux de change at the following train stations – although other opening hours can vary:

Gare Montparnasse *01.42.79. 03.88.* **Open** 8am-8pm daily.
Gare du Nord *01.42.80.11.50.* **Open** 6.30am-11.25pm daily.

Credit cards

Major international credit cards are widely used in France; Visa (more commonly known in France as *Carte Bleue*) is the most readily accepted. French-issued credit cards have a security microchip (*puce*) in each card. The card is slotted into a reader, and the holder keys in a PIN to authorise the transaction. Non-French cards also work, but generate a credit slip to sign. In case of credit card loss or theft, call one of the following 24hr services which have English-speaking staff:

American Express *01.47.77.70.00.*
Diners Club *01.49.06.17.50.*
MasterCard/Visa *08.36.69.08.80.*

Foreign affairs

American Express *11 rue Scribe, 9th (01.47.77.79.28/www.american express.com). M° Opéra.* **Open** 9am-6.30pm Mon-Sat. Travel agency, bureau de change, *poste restante* (you can leave messages for other card holders), card replacement, travellers' cheque refund service, international money transfers and a cash machine for AmEx cardholders. **Other locations**: Galeries Lafayette, 40 bd Haussmann, 9th (01.45.26.78.68).

Barclays *6 rond-point des Champs-Elysées, 8th (01.44.95.13.80/ www.barclays.fr). M° Franklin D. Roosevelt.* **Open** 9.15am-4.30pm Mon-Fri. Barclays' international Expat Service handles direct debits, international transfer of funds, etc.

Citibank *125 av des Champs-Elysées, 8th (01.49.05.49.05/ www.citibank.fr). M° Charles de Gaulle Etoile.* **Open** 10am-5.30pm Mon-Fri. Clients get good rates for international money transfers, preferential exchange rates and no commission on travellers' cheques.

Travelex *52 av des Champs-Elysées, 8th (01.42.89.80.33/www.travelex.fr). M° Franklin D. Roosevelt.* **Open** 9am-10.30pm daily. Hours of other branches (over 20 in Paris) vary. Issues travellers' cheques and insurance; deals with bank transfers.

Western Union Money Transfer *(08.25.82.58.42/www.westernunion. com).* Many post offices in town (*see p376*) provide Western Union services. Transfers from abroad should arrive within 15 minutes; charges are paid by the sender.

Tax

French VAT (*taxe sur la valeur ajoutée* or TVA) is arranged in three bands: 2.1 per cent for items of medication and newspapers; 5.5 per cent for food, books, CDs and DVDs; and 19.6 per cent for all other types of goods and services.

Natural hazards

Paris has no natural hazards as such, though in recent years the town hall has produced evacuation plans to cover flooding. The deadly heatwave of 2003 led to *anti-canicule* measures for 2004, though these were widely ridiculed in the press. *See p365* **Walking**.

Opening hours

Standard opening hours for shops are 9/10am-7/8pm Mon-Sat. Some shops close on Monday. Shops and businesses often close at lunch, usually 12.30-2pm; many shops close in August. While Paris doesn't have the 24hr consumer culture beloved of some capitals, some branches of Monoprix stay open until 10pm. Also most areas have a local grocer that stays open into the night and will often open on Sundays and public holidays too.

24hr florist Elyfleur *82 av de Wagram, 17th (01.47.66.87.19). Mº Wagram*. **Credit** MC, V.

24hr garage Select Shell *6 bd Raspail, 7th (01.45.48.43.12). Mº Rue du Bac.* This round-the-clock garage has an extensive if pricy array of supermarket standards from the Casino chain. No alcohol sold 10pm-6am.

24hr newsagents include: *33 av des Champs-Elysées, 8th. Mº Franklin D. Roosevelt. 2 bd Montmartre, 9th. Mº Grands Boulevards.*

Late-night *tabacs* Le Brazza *86 bd du Montparnasse, 14th (01.43.35.42.65). Mº Montparnasse-Bienvenüe.* **Open** 6am-2am daily. **La Favorite** *3 bd St-Michel, 5th (01.43.54.08.02). Mº St-Michel.* **Open** 7am-2am daily.

Photo labs

Photo developing can often be more expensive than in the UK or USA (although developing slide films can often be cheaper). **Fnac Service** (www.fnacphoto.com), **Photo Station** (www.photostation.fr) and **Photo Service** (www.photoservice.com) have many branches around the city.

Police

The French equivalent of 999 or 911 is **17** (**112** from a mobile), but don't expect a speedy response. That said, the Préfecture de Police has no fewer than 94 outposts in the city. If you're assaulted or robbed, report the incident as soon as possible. You'll need to make a statement (*procès verbal*) at the *point d'accueil* closest to the site of the crime. To find the nearest, call the Préfecture Centrale (08.91.01.22.22) day or night, or go to www.prefecture-police.paris.interieur.gouv.fr. Stolen goods are unlikely to be recovered, but you'll need a police statement for insurance purposes.

Postal services

Post offices (*bureaux de poste*) are open 8am-7pm Mon-Fri; 8am-noon Sat, apart from the 24-hour one listed below. Details of all branches are included in the phone book: under 'Administration des PTT' in the *Pages Jaunes*; under 'Poste' in the *Pages Blanches*. Most post offices contain automatic machines (in French and English) that weigh your letter, print out a stamp and give change, thus saving you from wasting time in an enormous queue. You can also usually buy stamps and sometimes envelopes at a tobacconist (*tabac*). For more information refer to www.laposte.fr.

Main Post Office *52 rue du Louvre, 75001 Paris, 1st (01.40.28.76.00). Mº Les Halles or Louvre Rivoli.* **Open** 24hrs daily for poste restante, telephones, stamps, faxes, photocopying and a modest amount of banking operations. This is the best place to arrange to have your mail sent to you if you haven't got a fixed address in Paris. Mail should be addressed to you in block capitals, followed by Poste Restante, then the post office's address. There will be a charge of €0.50 for each letter received.

Recycling & rubbish

The city has a recently-established system of colour-coded domestic recycling bins. A yellow-lidded bin can take paper, cardboard cartons, tins and small electrical items; a white-lidded bin takes glass. All other rubbish goes in the green-lidded bins, except for used batteries (all shops that sell batteries should accept them), medication (take it back to a pharmacy), toxic products (call 08.20.00.75.75 to have them picked up) or car batteries (take them to an official tip or return to garages exhibiting the '*Relais Verts Auto*' sign). Green, hive-shaped bottle banks can be found on many street corners. More information is available at www.environnement.paris.fr.

Religion

Churches and religious centres are listed in the *Pages Jaunes* under 'Eglises' and 'Cultes'. Paris has several English-speaking churches. The *International Herald Tribune*'s Saturday edition lists Sunday church services in English.

American Cathedral *23 av George V, 8th (01.53.23.84.00/www.americancathedral.org). Mº George V.*

American Church in Paris *65 quai d'Orsay, 7th (01.40.62.05.00/www.acparis.org). Mº Invalides.*

Emmanuel Baptist Church of Paris *56 rue des Bons Raisins, Rueil-Malmaison (01.47.51.29.63). RER Reuil-Malmaison, then bus 244.*

Kehilat Gesher *10 rue de Pologne, 78100 St-Germain-en-Laye (01.39. 21.97.19/www.kehilatgesher.org). RER St-Germain-en-Laye.* The Liberal English-speaking Jewish community has rotating services in Paris and the western suburbs.

La Mosquée de Paris *2 pl du Puits de l'Ermite, 5th (01.45.35. 97.33/www.mosquee-de-paris.org). M° Place Monge.*

St George's Anglican Church *7 rue Auguste-Vacquerie, 16th (01.47. 20.22.51/www.stgeorgesparis.com). M° Charles de Gaulle Etoile.*

St Joseph's Roman Catholic Church *50 av Hoche, 8th (01.42.27. 28.56/www.stjoeparis.org). M° Charles de Gaulle Etoile.*

St Michael's Church of England *5 rue d'Aguesseau, 8th (01.47.42. 70.88/www.saintmichaelsparis.org). M° Madeleine.*

Renting a flat

Flats are generally cheapest in northern, eastern and south-eastern Paris. You can expect to pay approximately €20 per square metre per month (so, for example, €700 per month for a modest 35sq m apartment). Studios and one bedroom flats fetch the highest prices proportionally; the provision of lifts and cellars will also boost the rent.

Flat hunting

Given the scarcity of housing in Paris, it's a landlord's world; you'll need to search actively, or even frenetically, in order to find an apartment. The internet is a decent place to start: www.explorimmo.fr lists rental ads from *Le Figaro* and specialist real estate magazines; you can place a classified ad or check lettings on www.avendrealouer.fr. Thursday morning's *De Particulier à Particulier* (www.pap.fr) is a must for those who want to rent directly from the owner, but be warned – most flats go within hours. Fortnightly *Se Loger* (www.seloger.com) is also worth getting, though most of its ads are placed by agencies. Landlords keen to let to foreigners advertise in the

International Herald Tribune and English-language *FUSAC* (www.fusac.fr; for both, *see p372*); rents tend to be higher than in the French press. There are also assorted free ad brochures that can be picked up from agencies. Private landlords often set a visiting time; prepare to meet hordes of other flat-seekers and have your documents and cheque book to hand.

There's also the option of flat-sharing – one that's been growing in popularity in recent years. To look for housemates, pick up a copy of *FUSAC* or browse the 3,000-odd weekly announcements found at www.colocation.fr, which also organises monthly soirée Le Jeudi de la Colocation, an opportunity to meet potential flatmates in the flesh.

Rental laws

The minimum lease (*bail de location*) on an unfurnished flat is three years (though the tenant can give notice and leave before this period is up); furnished flats are generally let on one-year leases. During this period the landlord can only raise the rent by the official construction inflation index. At the end of the lease, the rent can be adjusted, but tenants can object before a rent board. Tenants can be evicted for non-payment, or if the landlord wishes to sell the property or use it as his own residence. It is illegal to throw people out in winter. Landlords will probably insist you present a dossier with pay slips (*fiches de paie/bulletins de salaire*) showing income equivalent to three to four times the monthly rent, and, for foreigners in particular to provide a financial guarantor (someone who will sign a document promising to pay the rent if you abscond). When taking out a lease, payments usually include the first month's rent, a deposit (*caution*) of the equivalent of two months' rent,

and an agency fee, if applicable. It's customary to have an inspection of the premises (*état des lieux*) at the start and end of the rental, the cost of which (around €150) is shared by landlord and tenant. Landlords may try to rent their flats *non-declaré* – without a written lease – and get rent in cash. This can make it hard for tenants to establish their rights – which is one reason why landlords do it.

Centre d'information et de défense des locataires *9 rue Severo, 14th (01.45.41.47.76). M° Pernety.* **Open** *by appointment* 10am-12.30pm, 2.30-3.30pm Mon-Thur. Helps sort out problems with landlords, rent hikes, etc.

Safety & security

Beware pickpockets, especially in crowded tourist hotspots. See also **Métro & RER** and **police stations**.

Shipping services

Hedley's Humpers *6 bd de la Libération, 93284 St-Denis (01.48. 13.01.02/www.hedleyshumpers.com). M° Carrefour Pleyel.* **Open** 9am-1pm, 2-6pm Mon-Fri. Closed 2wks Aug. Specialist in transport of furniture and antiques. **In UK**: 3 St Leonards Road, London NW10 6SX (020 8965 8733). **In USA**: 21-41 45th Road, Long Island City, New York NY 11101 (1-718-433-4005).

Smoking

Although smoking seems to be an essential part of French life (and death), the French state and public health groups have recently waged war against the cigarette on several fronts. Smoking is now banned in most public spaces, such as theatres, cinemas and public transport (including TGV trains), and there are increasingly strident anti-smoking campaigns. Health warnings on cigarette packets are now unignorable, and prices have soared. Restaurants are obliged to have a non-smoking area (*espace non-fumeurs*) –

Directory

though it will often be the worst corner in the house, and there's no guarantee other people seated in the section won't light up anyway. A fairly modest number of restaurateurs, encouraged by the Mairie, has opted for the *100% sans tabac* label, making their establishments entirely non-smoking.

For information about stopping smoking, contact the Tabac Info Service (08.25.30. 93.10/www.tabac-info.net). If you're a dedicated smoker, you'll soon learn that most *tabacs* close at 8pm (for a few that don't, *see p376* **Opening hours**). Some bars sell cigarettes behind the counter, generally only to customers who stay for a drink.

Study

Language

Most large multinational language schools, such as **Berlitz** (www.berlitz.com), have at least one branch in Paris. **Konversando** (01.47. 70.21.64/www.konversando.fr) specialises in international exchanges and talk.

Alliance Française *101 bd Raspail, 6th (01.42.84.90.00/ www.alliancefr.org). M° St-Placide.* Non-profit French-language school. Beginner and specialist courses start every month. Film club and lectures.

Ecole Eiffel *3 rue Crocé-Spinelli, 14th (01.43.20.37.41/www.ecole-eiffel.fr). M° Pernety.* Intensive classes, business French and phonetics.

Eurocentres *13 passage Dauphine, 6th (01.40.46.72.00/www.euro centres.com). M° Odéon.* Intensive classes with emphasis firmly on communication. It also boasts a *médiathèque*.

Institut Catholique de Paris *12 rue Cassette, 6th (01.44.39.52.68/ www.icp.fr/ilcf). M° St-Sulpice.* Courses in French culture and language. You must hold a *baccalauréat*-level qualification and be 18 or over (but don't have to be Catholic).

Institut Parisien *29 rue de Lisbonne, 8th (01.40.56.09.53). M° Monceau.* Dynamic private school offering courses in language, French civilisation and business French.

La Sorbonne – Cours de Langue et Civilisation *47 rue des Ecoles, 5th (01.40.46.22.11/www.ccfs-sorbonne.fr). M° Cluny-La Sorbonne/ RER Luxembourg.* Classes for foreigners ride on the name of this eminent institution. Teaching is grammar-based. Courses are open to anyone over 18 and fill up quickly.

University of London Institute in Paris *11 rue Constantine, 7th (01.44.11.73.83/www.ulip.lon.ac.uk). M° Invalides.* Linked to the University of London, this 4,000-student institute offers English courses for Parisians, and French courses at university level. Also offers a degree course and MAs.

Specialised

Many of the prestigious Ecoles Nationales Supérieures (including film schools La FEMIS and ENS Louis Lumière) offer summer courses in addition to their full-time degree courses – ask for *formation continue.*

Adult education courses
Information: www.paris.fr or from your local mairie. A huge range of inexpensive adult education classes is run by the City of Paris, including French as a foreign language, computer skills and applied arts.

American University of Paris *31 av Bosquet, 7th (01.40.62.06.00/ www.aup.edu). M° Ecole-Militaire/ RER Pont de l'Alma.* International college awarding four-year American liberal arts degrees (BA/BSc).

Christie's Education Paris *4 av Bertie-Albrecht, 8th (01.42.25.10.90/ www.christies.com/education). M° Ternes.* The international auction house offers a one-year diploma, ten-week intensive courses and specialisations. They organise a five-day art-history tour/class in English in September.

Cordon Bleu *8 rue Léon-Delhomme, 15th (01.53.68.22.50/ www.cordonbleu.edu). M° Vaugirard.* Courses range from three-hour sessions on classical and regional cuisine to a nine-month diploma for those starting a culinary career.

Ecole du Louvre *Palais du Louvre, porte Jaugard, place du Carrousel, 1st (01.55.35.18.00/www.ecole dulouvre.fr). M° Palais Royal Musée du Louvre.* Art history and archaeology courses. Foreign students not wanting to take a degree can attend lectures.

INSEAD *bd de Constance, 77305 Fontainebleau (01.60.72.40.00/ www.insead.edu).* Highly regarded international business school

offering a ten-month MBA course in English as well as PhDs in a range of business subjects.

Parsons School of Design *14 rue Letellier, 15th (01.45.77.39.66/ www.parsons-paris.com). M° La Motte-Picquet-Grenelle.* Subsidiary of the New York art college offering BFA programmes in fine art, photography, fashion, marketing and interior design.

Ritz-Escoffier Ecole de Gastronomie Française *38 rue Cambon, 1st (01.43.16.30.50/ www.ritzparis.com). M° Madeleine.* Everything from afternoon demonstrations in the Ritz kitchens to diplomas – but at a price. Courses are in French with English translation.

Spéos – Paris Photographic Institute *7 rue Jules-Vallès, 11th (01.40.09.18.58/www.speos.fr). M° Charonne.* Full-, part-time and summer programmes. Exchange courses with four art schools, including the Rhode Island School of Design.

Student life

Long-term visas & housing benefit

UK and other students from the European Union may stay in France for as long as their passport is valid. To also work legally during their course in Paris, they can find out more information about their rights at www.droitsdesjeunes.gouv.fr.

Foreign students from outside the EU wishing to study in Paris for longer than three months must apply for a long-term visa through the French embassy in their particular country.

Some students may be eligible to receive housing benefit, the ALS (*allocation de logement à caractère social*), which is dealt with by four CAFs (*caisses d'allocations familiales*). The 'Aide au logement étudiant' feature of their French-only website (www.caf.fr) allows you see how much you are entitled to receive; enter your postcode on the site to find which office you should contact. The section www.paris.caf.fr deals with all enquiries related to Paris.

Accommodation

The simplest budget accommodation for medium-to-long stays can be found at the **Cité Universitaire** or *foyers* (student hostels). There are 37 halls of residence set in landscaped gardens, with sports facilities and a theatre (*see p168*). Another option is a *chambre contre travail* – free board in exchange for childcare, housework or English lessons; for this, look out for ads at language schools and the American Church. For cheap hotels and youth hostels, *see chapter* **Where to Stay**. As students often cannot provide proof of income, a *porte-garant* (guarantor) who will guarantee payment of rent and bills is required.

Cité Universitaire *19 bd Jourdan, 14th (01.44.16.64.00/www.ciup.fr). RER Cité Universitaire.* **Open** *Offices* 8am-6pm Mon-Fri. Foreign students enrolled on a university course, or interns who are also studying, can apply for a place at this campus of halls of residence (but be forewarned: only about 10 per cent of the students who apply are successful). Rooms can be booked for a week, a month or for an entire academic year. Rents are approximately €300-€400 per month for a single, €200-€300 per person for a double. UK citizens must apply to the Collège Franco-Britannique, and Americans to the Fondation des Etats-Unis.

CROUS (Centre Régional des Oeuvres Universitaires et Scolaires) *39 av Georges-Bernanos, 5th (01.40.51.36.00/ 08.92.25.75.75/www.crous-paris.fr). Service du Logement: (01.40.51. 55.55). RER Port-Royal.* **Open** 9am-5pm Mon-Fri. Manages all University of Paris student residences, posts ads for rooms and has a list of hostels. Requests for rooms must be made by 1 April for the next academic year. CROUS also runs cheap canteens (listed on website) and is the clearing house for all *bourses* (grants) issued to foreign students. Call the Service des Bourses on 01.40.51.55.55.

UCRIF (Union des Centres de Rencontres Internationales de France) *27 rue de Turbigo, 2nd (01.40.26.57.64/www.ucrif.asso.fr). M° Etienne Marcel.* **Open** 9am-6pm Mon-Fri. Operates cheap, short-stay hostels from five help centres: 5th (01.43.29.34.80); 12th (01.44.75.60.06); 13th (01.43.36.00.63); 14th (01.43.13. 17.00); 20th (01.40.31.45.45).

Student & youth discounts

To claim a *tarif étudiant* (around €1.50 off cinema seats, up to 50 per cent off museums and standby theatre tickets), you must have a French student card or International Student Identity Card (ISIC), available from **CROUS** (*see left*), student travel agents and the **Cité Universitaire** (*see left*). ISIC cards are valid in France only if you are under 26. Under-26s can get up to 50 per cent off rail travel on some trains with the SNCF's Carte 12/25 and the same reduction on the RATP network with the Imagine R card.

Working

Foreign students can legally work up to 20 hours per week. Non-EU members studying in Paris must apply for an *autorisation provisoire de travail* from the DDTEFT. The job service at CROUS (01.40.51.37.52 through 57) finds part-time jobs for students. For pointers to job vacancies, consult www.crous-paris.fr/emploi.

DDTEFT (Direction Départementale du Travail, d'Emploi et de Formation Professionelle) *109 rue Montmartre, 2nd (01.44.84.41.00/ www.travail.gouv.fr). M° Bourse.*

Useful organisations

CIDJ (Centre d'Information et de Documentation Jeunesse) *101 quai Branly, 15th (01.44.49. 12.00/www.cidj.com). M° Bir-Hakeim/RER Champ de Mars.* **Open** 10am-6pm Mon-Wed, Fri; 1-6pm Thur; 9.30am-1pm Sat. The library gives students advice on courses and careers; the youth bureau of ANPE (Agence Nationale pour l'Emploi/ www.anpe.fr) can assist with job applications.

Edu France *173 bd St-Germain, 6th (01.53.63.35.00/www.edufrance. fr). M° St-Germain-des-Prés.* **Open** 9am-6pm Mon-Fri (call as hours vary). Fees €200-€500. This government-run organisation promotes the French university system abroad and assists foreign students in France. The website has further information.

Maison des Initiatives Etudiantes (MIE) *50 rue des Tournelles, 3rd (01.49.96.65.30/ www.paris.fr).* **Open** 10am-10pm Mon-Fri; 2-9pm Sat. Provides student associations with logistical assistance and Paris-based resources like meeting rooms, grants and computers. Radio Campus Paris, a radio station for students, has been broadcast since September 2004.

Socrates-Erasmus Programme Britain: *UK Socrates-Erasmus Council, Rothford, Giles Lane, Canterbury, Kent CT2 7LR (01227 762 712/www.erasmus.ac.uk).* **France**: *Agence Socrates-Leonardo Da Vinci, 25 quai des Chartrons, 33080 Bordeaux Cedex (05.56.00. 94.00/www.socrates-leonardo.fr).* The international Socrates-Erasmus scheme lets EU students with reasonable written and spoken French spend a year of their degree in the French university system. Applications must be made via the Erasmus co-ordinator at your home university. Non-EU students should find out from their university whether it has an agreement with the French university system. American students can find out more from the following:

MICEFA (*26 rue du Fbg-St-Jacques, 14th, 01.40.51.76.96/www.micefa.org*).

Relais d'accueil (Foreign students helpdesk) *Cité Universitaire, 19 bd Jourdan, 14th. RER Cité Universitaire. CROUS de Paris, 39 av Georges-Bernanos, 5th (01.43.13.66.46/www.eduparis.net). RER Port-Royal.* **Open** Sept-Nov 8.30am-4pm Mon-Fri (Cité); 9am-4.30pm Mon-Fri (CROUS). Advice on housing, getting a bank account, visa requirements, social security and university registration is available (by appointment) to foreign students at the two addresses above.

Mobile phones

A subscription (*abonnement*) will normally get you a free phone if you sign up for at least one year. Two hours' calling time a month costs about €35 per month. International calls are normally charged extra – a lot extra. The three companies that rule the cell phone market in France are:

Bouygues Télécom *(08.25.82.56.14/www.bouygues telecom.fr).*

France Télécom/Orange *(08.25.00.57.00/www.orange.fr).*

SFR *(01.71.24.00.00/www.sfr.fr).*

Dialling & codes

All French phone numbers have ten digits. Paris and Ile-de-France numbers begin with 01; the rest of France is divided into four zones (02-05). Mobile phone numbers start with 06. 08 indicates a special rate (*see below*); numbers beginning with 08 can only be reached from inside France. If you are calling France from abroad, leave off the 0 at the start of the ten-digit number. The country code is 33. To call abroad from France dial 00, then the country code, then the number. Since 1998 other phone companies have been allowed to enter the market, but France Télécom still has the monopoly on basic service. It has a useful website with information on rates, contracts and related items: www. agence.francetelecom.com.

France Télécom English-Speaking Customer Service *(08.00.36.47.75/from abroad +33 1.55.78.60.56)*. **Open** 9am-5.30pm Mon-Fri. Freephone information line in English on phone services, bills, payment, internet.

Public phones

Most public phones in Paris, almost all of which are maintained by France Télécom, use *télécartes* (phonecards). Sold at post offices, *tabacs*, airports and train and métro stations, they cost €7.50 for 50 units and €15 for 120 units. For cheap international calls, you can also buy a *télécarte à puce* (card with a microchip) or a *télécarte pré-payée*, which features a numerical code you dial before making a call; these can be used on domestic phones too. Travelex's International Telephone Card can be used in more than 80 countries (available from **Travelex** agencies, *see p375*). Cafés have coin phones, while post offices usually have card phones. In a phone box, the display screen will read 'Décrochez'. Pick up the phone.

When 'Introduisez votre carte' appears, put your card into the slot; the screen should then read 'Patientez SVP'. 'Numérotez' is your signal to dial. 'Crédit épuisé' means you have no more units left. Hang up ('Raccrochez') – and don't forget your card. Some public phones take credit cards. If you're using a credit card, insert the card, enter your PIN number and 'Patientez SVP' will appear.

Operator services

Operator assistance, French directory enquiries *(renseignements) 12.* To make a reverse-charge call within France, ask to make a call *en PCV.*

Airparif *(01.44.59.47.64).* 2-5.30pm Mon-Fri. Information about pollution levels and air quality in Paris and Ile-de-France: invaluable for asthmatics.

International directory enquiries *32.12,* then country code. €3 per call.

International news (France Inter recorded message, in French), *08.92.68.10.33* (€0.34 per min).

Telegram *all languages, international 08.00.33.44.11; within France 36.55.*

Telephone engineer *10.13.*

Time *36.99.*

Traffic news *08.26.02.20.22.*

Weather *08.99.70.12.34* (€1.39 then €0.34 per min) for enquiries on weather in France and abroad, in French or English; you can also dial 08.92.68.02.75 (€0.34 per min) for a recorded weather announcement for Paris and region.

Telephone directories

Telephone books can be found in all post offices and most cafés. The *Pages Blanches* (White Pages) list people and businesses alphabetically; the *Pages Jaunes* (Yellow Pages) list businesses and services by category order. Online versions can be found at www.pagesjaunes.fr.

Telephone charges

All local calls in Paris and Ile-de-France (to numbers beginning with 01) cost €0.11 for three minutes, standard rate and €0.04/min thereafter.

This only apply to calls towards other land phones. Calls beyond a 100km radius (*province*) are charged at €0.11 for the first 39 seconds, then €0.24 per minute.

International destinations are divided into 16 zones. Reduced-rate periods for calls within France and Europe are 7pm-8am during the week and all day on Saturdays and Sundays. Reduced-rate periods for the US and Canada are 7pm through to 1pm from Monday to Friday and all day on Saturdays and Sundays.

Cheap providers

Getting wise to the market demand, smaller telephone providers are becoming increasingly prolific and popular, as rates from giant France Télécom are not exactly bargain-basement. The following can offer alternative rates for calls – although you will still need to rent your telephone line from France Télécom:

AT&T Direct (local access) *08.00.99.00.11.*

Free *www.free.fr.* With the Freebox (Free's modem for ASDL connection), €29.99 per month gets you ten hours of free calls to land lines (additional calls: €0.01 per minute), €0.19 per minute to mobiles and €0.03 per minute for most international calls.

IC Télécom *www.ictelecom.fr.*

Neuf Télécom *08.00.95.99.59/ www.neuf.fr.*

Onetel *www.onetel.fr.*

Télé 2 *08.05.04.44.44/www.tele2.fr.*

TroisU Télécom *08.05.10.16.45/www.3utelecom.fr.*

Special-rate numbers

0800 Numéro Vert Freephone.

0810 Numéro Azur €0.11 under three minutes, then €0.04/min.

0820 Numéro Indigo I €0.118/min.

0825 Numéro Indigo II €0.15/min.

0836.64/0890.64/0890.70 €0.112/min.

0890.71 €0.15/min.

0891.67/0891.70 €0.225/min.

0836/0892 €0.337/min. This rate is for the likes of ticket agencies, cinema and transport information lines.

10.14 France Télécom information; free (except from mobile phones).

Minitel

France Télécom's Minitel, launched in the 1980s, is an enduring dinosaur: a videotext service available to any telephone subscriber. The internet has made it virtually redundant. If you come across one of these beige plastic boxes, type in 3611 for Minitel directory in English, wait for the beep, press 'Connexion', type MGS, then hit 'Envoi'. Then type 'Minitel en anglais' for the English service.

Ticket agencies

The easiest way to reserve and buy tickets for concerts, plays and matches is from a **Fnac** store. You can also reserve on www.fnac.com or by phone (08.92.68.36.22; 9am-8pm Mon-Sat) and pick them up at one of their *points de vente* (see site for full list) – or pay with your credit card and have them sent to your home. **Virgin** has teamed up with **Ticketnet** to create an online ticket office (www.virginmega.fr). Tickets can also be purchased by phone (08.25.12.91.39) and sent to your home for a €5.50 fee.

Fnac Forum *Forum des Halles, Porte Lescot, 1st (01.40.41.40.00/ www.fnac.com). M° Les Halles/RER Châtelet Les Halles.* **Open** 10am-7.30pm Mon-Sat. **Credit** AmEx, MC, V.

Virgin Megastore *52-60 av des Champs-Elysées, 8th (01.49.53. 50.00). M° Franklin D. Roosevelt.* **Open** 10am-midnight Mon-Sat; noon-midnight Sun. **Credit** AmEx, MC, V.

Time & seasons

France is one hour ahead of Greenwich Mean Time (GMT). France uses the 24hr system (for example 18h means 6pm).

Tipping

A service charge of ten to 15 per cent is legally included in your bill at all restaurants, cafés and bars. However, it is polite to either round up the final amount for drinks, or to leave a cash tip of €1-€2 or more for a meal, depending on the restaurant and, of course, the quality of the service.

Toilets

The city's automatic street toilets are not as terrifying as they look. You put your coin in the slot, and open sesame. Each loo is completely washed down and disinfected after use, so don't try to avoid paying by sneaking in as someone is leaving: you'll get covered in bleach. Once inside, you have 15 minutes. If a space-age-style lavatory experience doesn't appeal, you can always nip into the toilets of a café; although theoretically reserved for customers' use, a polite request should win sympathy with the waiter – and you may find you have to put a 20 cent coin into a slot in the door-handle mechanism, customer or not. Fast-food chain toilets often have a code on their toilet doors that is made known to paying customers only.

Tourist information

Espace du Tourisme d'Ile de France *Carrousel du Louvre, 99 rue de Rivoli, 1st (08.26.16.66.66/ www.paris-ile-de-france.com). M° Palais Royal Musée du Louvre or Pyramides.* **Open** 8.30am-7pm Mon-Fri. This is the information showcase for Paris and the Ile-de-France.

Maison de la France *20 av de l'Opéra, 1st (01.42.96.70.00/ www.franceguide.com). M° Opéra or Pyramides.* **Open** 10am-6pm Mon-Fri; 10am-5pm Sat. The state organisation for tourism in France: information galore.

Office de Tourisme et des Congrès de Paris *Carrousel du Louvre, 99 rue de Rivoli, 1st (08.92.68.30.00 recorded information in English & French/www.parisinfo.com). M° Palais Royal Musée du Louvre or Pyramides.* **Open** 9am-7pm daily. Information on Paris and the suburbs, shop, bureau de change, hotel reservations, phonecards, museum cards, travel passes and tickets. Multilingual staff.

Other locations: *Gare de Lyon* 20 bd Diderot, 12th. M° Gare de Lyon. **Open** 8am-6pm Mon-Sat. *Gare du Nord* 18 rue de Dunkerque, 10th. M° Gare du Nord. **Open** 8am-6pm daily. *Montmartre* 21 pl du Tertre, 18th. M° Abbesses. **Open** 10am-7pm daily. *Opéra* 11 rue Scribe, 9th. M° Opera. **Open** 9am-6.30pm Mon-Sat. *Pyramides* 25 rue des Pyramides, 1st, M° Pyramides. **Open** 9am-7pm daily. *Tour Eiffel* Champ de Mars, 7th. M° Bir-Hakeim. **Open** late Mar-Oct 11am-6.40pm daily.

Visas

European Union nationals do not need a visa to enter France, nor do US, Canadian, Australian, New Zealand or South African citizens for stays of up to three months. Nationals of other countries should enquire at the nearest French embassy or consulate before leaving home. If they are travelling to France from one of the countries included in the Schengen agreement (most of the EU, but not Britain or Ireland), the visa from that country should be sufficient.

EU citizens may stay in France for as long as their passport is valid. For non-EU citizens who wish to stay for longer than three months, they must apply to the French embassy or consulate in their own country for a long-term visa. For more information, contact these two offices:

CIRA (Centre Interministeriel de Renseignements Administratifs) *(0821.08.09.10 0.12€/min/www.service-public.fr).* **Open** 8am-7pm Mon-Fri; 8am-noon Sat. Advice on most French administrative procedures.

Préfecture de Police de Paris Service Etrangers *7-9 bd du Palais, 4th (01.53.71.51.68/www. prefecture-police-paris.interieur. gouv.fr). M° Cité.* **Open** 9am-4pm Mon-Fri. Information on residency and work permits for foreigners.

Weights & measures

France uses only the metric system; remember that all speed limits are in kilometres

Average monthly climate

Month	High temp (C°/F°)	Low temp (C°/F°)	Rainfall
Jan	7/45	2/36	53cm
Feb	10/50	2/36	43cm
Mar	13/55	4/39	49cm
Apr	17/63	6/43	53cm
May	20/68	9/48	65cm
June	23/73	12/54	54cm
July	25/77	15/59	62cm
Aug	26/79	16/29	42cm
Sept	23/73	12/54	54cm
Oct	20/68	8/46	60cm
Nov	14/57	4/39	51cm
Dec	7/44	3/37	59cm

per hour. One kilometre is equivalent to 0.62 mile (1 mile = 1.6km). Petrol, like other liquids, is measured in litres (one UK gallon = 4.54 litres; 1 US gallon = 3.79 litres).

What to take

Binoculars for studying high-altitude details of monuments, a pocket knife with corkscrew (for improvised picnics with food bought from the market) and – vital – comfortable shoes. If you're staying in cheap hotels, a universal plug is handy for the sink.

When to go

In July and August, when there are good deals on hotels and a good range of free summer events; the city seems empty but is more relaxed than usual. Avoid October, with its glut of fashion weeks and trade shows.

Women in Paris

Though Paris is not especially threatening for women, the precautions you would take in any major city apply: be careful at night in areas like Pigalle, the rue St-Denis, Stalingrad, La Chapelle, Château Rouge, Gare de l'Est, Gare du Nord, the Bois de Boulogne and Bois de

Vincennes. If you receive unwanted attention, a politely scathing *N'insistez pas!* (Don't push it!) makes your feelings clear. If things get too heavy, go into the nearest shop or café and ask for help.

CIDFF (Centre d'Information et des Droits des Femmes et de la Famille) *7 rue du Jura, 13th (01.42.17.12.00). M° Gobelins.* **Open** visits by appointment only.The CIDFF offers health, legal and professional advice for women.

Violence Conjugale: Femmes Info Service *(01.40.33.80.60).* **Open** 7.30am-11.30pm Mon-Sat. Telephone hotline for battered women, directing them towards medical aid or shelters.

Viols Femmes Informations *(08.00.05.95.95).* **Open** 10am-7pm Mon-Fri. Freephone service. Help and advice, in French, to rape victims.

Working in Paris

Most EU nationals can work legally in France, including UK and Irish citizens – but should apply for a French social security number. Some job ads can be found at branches of the French national employment bureau, the **Agence Nationale pour l'Emploi** (ANPE), or on its website (www.anpe.fr). Branches are also the place to go to sign up as a *demandeur d'emploi*, to be placed on file as ready for work and possibly to qualify for French unemployment

benefits. Britons can only claim French unemployment benefit if they were already signed on before leaving the UK. Non-EU nationals need a work permit and cannot use the ANPE network without having valid work papers.

Club des Quatre Vents *1 rue Gozlin, 6th (01.40.51.11.81). M° St-Germain-des-Prés.* **Open** 9am-6pm Mon-Fri. Provides three-month work permits for US citizens at university or recent graduates.

Espace Emploi International (OMI et ANPE) *48 bd de la Bastille, 12th (01.53.02.25.50/www.emploi-international.org). M° Bastille.* **Open** 9am-5pm Mon, Wed-Fri; 9am-noon Tue. Provides work permits of up to 18 months for Americans aged 18-35 and has a job placement service.

The Language Network *(01.44.64.82.23).* Helps to orient native English speakers who wish to find work teaching.

Job ads

Help-wanted ads sometimes appear in the *International Herald Tribune*, in *FUSAC* and on noticeboards at language schools and the **American Church** (*see p376*). Bilingual secretarial/PA work is available for those with good written French. If you're looking for professional work, have your CV translated, including French equivalents for any qualifications. Most job applications require a photo and a handwritten letter .

Vocabulary

In French the second person singular (you) has two forms. Phrases here are given in the more polite *vous* form. The *tu* form is used with family, friends, children and pets; you should be careful not to use it with people you do not know sufficiently well. Courtesies such as *monsieur, madame* and *mademoiselle* are used more than their English equivalents.

General expressions

good morning/afternoon, hello bonjour; **good evening** bonsoir; **goodbye** au revoir; **hi** (familiar) salut; **OK** d'accord; **yes** oui; **no** non; **how are you?** comment allez vous?/vous allez bien?; **how's it going?** comment ça va?/ça va? (familiar); **sir/Mr** monsieur (Mr); **madam/Mrs** madame (Mme); **miss** mademoiselle (Mlle); **please** s'il vous plaît; **thank you** merci; **thank you very much** merci beaucoup; **sorry** pardon; **excuse me** excusez-moi; **do you speak English?** parlez-vous anglais?; **I don't speak French** je ne parle pas français; **I don't understand** je ne comprends pas; **speak more slowly, please** parlez plus lentement, s'il vous plaît; **I am going** je vais; **I am going to pay** je vais payer; **it is** c'est; **it isn't** ce n'est pas; **good** bon/bonne; **bad** mauvais/mauvaise; **small** petit/petite; **big** grand/grande; **beautiful** beau/belle; **well** bien; **badly** mal; **a bit** un peu; **a lot** beaucoup; **very** très; **with** avec; **without** sans; **and** et; **or** ou; **because** parce que; **when?** quand?; **what?** quoi?; **which?** quel?; **where?** où?; **why?** pourquoi?; **how?** comment?; **at what time/when?** à quelle heure?; **forbidden** interdit/défendu; **out of order** hors service (HS)/ en panne; **daily** tous les jours (tlj)

On the phone

hello allô; **who's calling?** c'est de la part de qui?/qui est à l'appareil?; **this is… speaking** c'est… à l'appareil; **I'd like to speak to…** j'aurais voulu parler avec…; **hold the line** ne quittez pas; **please call back later** rappellez plus tard s'il vous plaît; **you must have the wrong number** vous avez du composer un mauvais numéro

Getting around

where is the (nearest) métro? où est le métro (le plus proche)?; **when is the next train for… ?** c'est quand le prochain train pour… ?; **ticket** un billet; **station** la gare; **platform** le quai; **entrance** entrée; **exit** sortie; **left** gauche; **right** droite; **straight on** tout droit; **far** loin; **near** pas loin/près d'ici; **street map** un plan; **road map** une carte; **bank** la banque; **is there a bank near here?** est-ce qu'il y a une banque près d'ici?

Sightseeing

museum un musée; **church** une église; **exhibition** une exposition; **ticket** (*for museum*) un billet; (*for theatre, concert*) une place; **open** ouvert; **closed** fermé; **free** gratuit; **reduced price** un tarif réduit

Accommodation

do you have a room (for this evening/for two people)? avez-vous une chambre (pour ce soir/pour deux personnes)?; **full** complet; **room** une chambre; **bed** un lit; **double bed** un grand lit; **(a room with) twin beds** (une chambre à) deux lits; **with bath(room)/shower** avec (salle de) bain/douche; **breakfast** le petit déjeuner; **included** compris

At the café or restaurant

I'd like to book a table (for three/at 8pm) je voudrais réserver une table (pour trois personnes/à vingt heures); **lunch** le déjeuner; **dinner** le dîner; **coffee** (espresso) un café; **white coffee** un café au lait/café crème; **tea** un thé; **wine** le vin; **beer** une bière; **mineral water** eau minérale; **fizzy** gazeuse; **still** plate; **tap water** eau du robinet/une carafe d'eau; **the bill, please** l'addition, s'il vous plaît

Shopping

cheap pas cher; **expensive** cher; **how much?/how many?** combien?; **have you got change?** avez-vous de la monnaie? **I would like…** je voudrais…; **may I try this on?** est-ce que je pourrais essayer cet article?; **do you have a smaller/larger size?** auriez-vous la taille en-dessous/au dessus?; **I'm a size 38** je fais du 38; **I'll take it** je prends; **could you gift wrap it for me?** pourriez-vous me faire un paquet cadeau?

Behind the wheel

no parking stationnement interdit/ gênant; **toll** péage; **speed limit 40** rappel 40; **petrol** essence; **speed** vitesse; **traffic moving freely** traffic fluide

The come-on

do you have a light? avez-vous du feu?; **what's your name?** comment vous vous appellez?; **would you like a drink?** voulez vous boire un verre?; **you have lovely eyes, you know** tu as de beaux yeux, tu sais?; **your place or mine?** chez toi ou chez moi?

The brush-off

leave me alone laissez-moi tranquille; **get lost, you cretin** casse-toi, imbécile

Staying alive

be cool restez calme; **I don't want any trouble** je ne veux pas d'ennuis; **I only do safe sex** je ne pratique que le safe sex

Numbers

0 zéro; **1** un, une; **2** deux; **3** trois; **4** quatre; **5** cinq; **6** six; **7** sept; **8** huit; **9** neuf; **10** dix; **11** onze; **12** douze; **13** treize; **14** quatorze; **15** quinze; **16** seize; **17** dix-sept; **18** dix-huit; **19** dix-neuf; **20** vingt; **21** vingt-et-un; **22** vingt-deux; **30** trente; **40** quarante; **50** cinquante; **60** soixante; **70** soixante-dix; **80** quatre-vingts; **90** quatre-vingt-dix; **100** cent; **1000** mille; **10,000** dix mille; **1,000,000** un million

Days, months & seasons

Monday lundi; **Tuesday** mardi; **Wednesday** mercredi; **Thursday** jeudi; **Friday** vendredi; **Saturday** samedi; **Sunday** dimanche; **January** janvier; **February** février; **March** mars; **April** avril; **May** mai; **June** juin; **July** juillet; **August** août; **September** septembre; **October** octobre; **November** novembre; **December** décembre; **spring** le printemps; **summer** l'été; **autumn** l'automne; **winter** l'hiver

Further Reference

Non-fiction

Petrus Abaelardus & Heloïse *Letters* The full details of Paris' first great romantic drama.

Robert Baldick *The Siege of Paris* The bloodshed, the hunger, the rats for supper: a gripping account of the Paris Commune of 1871.

Antony Beevor & Artemis Cooper *Paris after the Liberation* Rationing, freedom and Existentialism.

NT Binh *Paris au cinéma* Gorgeous coffee-table round-up of Paris sights on film.

Henri Cartier-Bresson *A propos de Paris* Classic black and white shots by a giant among snappers.

Danielle Chadych, Dominique Leborgne *Atlas de Paris* Lavishly appointed survey of Paris bricks and blocks and their movements through the centuries.

Rupert Christiansen *Tales of the New Babylon* Blood and sleaze in Napoléon III's Paris.

Vincent Cronin *Napoleon* A fine bio of the megalomaniac.

Christian Dupavillon *Paris Côté Seine* Nicely illustrated history of riverside Paris.

Julien Green *Paris* Personal account of Green's city.

Alastair Horne *The Fall of Paris* Detailed chronicle of the Siege and Commune 1870-71.

Andrew Hussey *Paris: A Secret History* Entertaining, street-level description of Paris through the ages.

J-K Huysmans *Croquis Parisiens* The world that Toulouse-Lautrec painted.

Douglas Johnson & Madeleine Johnson *Age of Illusion: Art & Politics in France 1918-1940*

French culture in a Paris at the forefront of modernity.

Marc Lemonier, Jacques Lebar *Fascinating Paris* The city in colour photographs.

Ian Littlewood *Paris: Architecture, History, Art* Paris' history and its treasures.

Colin MacCabe *Godard* A bio and accessible introduction to intellectual life in late 20th-century France.

Patrick Marnham *Crime & the Académie Française* Scandals in Mitterrand-era Paris.

François Maspero *Roissy Express: Journey Through the Paris Suburbs* Take the train: Maspero examines day-to-day life in mid-1990s Paris with photographer in tow.

Nancy Mitford *The Sun King; Madame de Pompadour* Great gossipy accounts of the courts of the *ancien régime*.

Noel Riley Fitch *Literary Cafés of Paris* Who drank what, where and when.

Virginia Rounding *Les Grandes Horizontales* Racy, entertaining lives of four 19th-century courtesans.

Renzo Salvadori *Architect's Guide to Paris* Plans, maps and a guide to Paris' growth.

Simon Schama *Citizens* Epic, wonderfully readable account of the Revolution.

William Shirer *The Collapse of the Third Republic.* Forensic account of the reasons for France's humiliating 1940 defeat.

Fiction & poetry

Louis Aragon *Le Paysan de Paris* A great Surrealist view of the city.

Honoré de Balzac *Illusions perdues; La Peau de chagrin; Le Père Goriot; Splendeurs et misères des courtisanes* Many of the best-known novels in the 'Comédie Humaine' cycle are set in Paris.

Charles Baudelaire *Le Spleen de Paris* Prose poems with Parisian settings.

Simone de Beauvoir *Les Mandarins* Paris intellectuals and idealists just after the Liberation.

Louis-Ferdinand Céline *Mort à crédit* Vivid, splenetic account of an impoverished Paris childhood.

Victor Hugo *Notre Dame de Paris* Romantic vision of medieval Paris. Quasimodo! Esmeralda! The bells!

Guy de Maupassant *Bel-Ami* Ruthless ambition in 19th-century Paris.

Patrick Modiano *Honeymoon* Evocative story of two lives that cross in Paris.

Gérard de Nerval *Les Nuits d'octobre* Late-night Les Halles and environs, mid 19th-century.

Georges Perec *La Vie, mode d'emploi* Cheek-by-jowl life in a Haussmannian apartment building.

Raymond Queneau *Zazie dans le Métro* Paris in the 1950s: bright and very *nouvelle vague.*

Nicolas Restif de la Bretonne *Les Nuits de Paris* The sexual underworld of Louis XV's Paris, by one of France's most famous defrocked priests.

Jean-Paul Sartre *Les Carnets de la drôle de guerre* Existential angst as the German army takes over Paris.

Georges Simenon The Maigret books. Many of Simenon's novels featuring his laconic detective provide vivid pictures of Paris and its underworld. See also *L'Homme qui regardait passer les trains.*

Emile Zola *L'Assommoir; Nana; Le Ventre de Paris* Vivid accounts of the underside of the Second Empire from the master Realist.

The ex-pat angle

Adam Gopnik *From Paris to the Moon* A New Yorker raises a family in this alien city.

Ernest Hemingway *A Moveable Feast* Big Ern chronicles 1920s Paris.

Henry Miller *Tropic of Cancer* Love, lust, lice and low life: bawdy, yes. Funny, too.

Anaïs Nin *Henry & June* More lust in Montparnasse with Henry Miller and his wife.

George Orwell *Down and Out in Paris and London* Work in a Paris restaurant (it's hardly changed), hunger in a Paris hovel, suffering in a Paris hospital.

Edmund White *The Flaneur: a Stroll through the Paradoxes of Paris* US ex-pat maps out some of the hidden nooks of the city's history.

Film

Olivier Assayas *Irma Vep* Jean-Pierre Léaud and Maggie Cheung endeavour to remake Feuillade's vampire classic in 1990s Paris. And fail.

Luc Besson *Subway* Christophe Lambert goes underground. Hokum, but easy on the eye.

Marcel Carné *Hôtel du Nord* Arletty's finest hour.

Jean-Luc Godard *A Bout de Souffle* Belmondo, Seberg, Godard, the Champs-Elysées, the attitude, the famous ending. Essential.

Jean-Luc Godard *Une Femme est une femme* Belmondo and Karina, and Godard's first feature in colour – the Grands Boulevards, the attitude, the music.

Edouard Molinaro *Un Témoin dans la ville* Lino Ventura on the run in 1950s nocturnal Paris. Superb *noir*.

Bertrand Tavernier *L.627* The drugs war in the 1990s, as seen from the cops' side. Gritty and polemic-making.

François Truffaut *Les 400 Coups* The first of the Antoine Doinel cycle.

Agnès Varda *Cléo de 5 à 7* The *nouvelle vague* heroine spends an anxious afternoon drifting around Paris.

Claude Zidi *Les Ripoux (Le Cop)* Cops Philippe Noiret and Thierry Lhermitte scam the whole of the Goutte d'Or.

Music

Air *Moon Safari* Relaxing, ambient beeps and sonics from that rara avis, a credible French pop group.

Serge Gainsbourg *Le Poinçonneur des Lilas* Classic early Gainsbourg: jazzy, elegant, mordant.

Thelonius Monk *The Paris Concert* A blend of the experimental and the romantically gentle.

Pink Martini *Sympathique* 'Je ne veux pas travailler' and other dinner-party starters by some French-singing Americans.

Websites

paris.webcity.fr Compendious cultural calendar, plus small ads and information on shops, hotels, restaurants, traffic conditions and more.

www.culture.fr Current and forthcoming cultural events of all kinds, in Paris and other big French cities.

www.edible-paris.com Customised gastronomic itineraries in Paris – you send your requirements before you arrive – by the editor of Time Out's *Eating & Drinking in Paris* guide.

www.eduparis.net Lots of practical advice for anyone thinking of studying in Paris.

www.euro.gouv.fr Official euro website: information, updates and online currency converter.

www.fnac.com Browse and buy the multidisciplinary Fnac's books, CDs, DVDs and electronics – and reserve tickets for all sorts of events.

www.fusac.org Online version of the free fortnightly small ads mag: jobs, removals, personals, classes and more.

www.gogoparis.com Online version of free monthly Anglo listings mag.

www.mappy.fr Maps of Paris and France.

www.meteo.fr Weather forecasts and stats from the state meteorology office.

www.pagesjaunes.fr The Paris yellow pages, with maps and multi-angle photos of every address in the city. Also has a link to the Pages Blanches phone directory.

www.paris-anglo.com An abundance of nuts-and-bolts information, in English, on living in Paris.

www.paris-art.com Contemporary art exhibitions and galleries.

www.parisdigest.com Paris listings, shopping tips and general information in English.

www.parissi.com Films, concerts and a strong calendar of clubbing events.

www.paris-tourist office.com Official site of the Office de Tourisme et des Congrès de Paris.

www.pidf.com Official site of the Paris regional tourist board: a gold mine of info on museums, events, transport, shopping et al.

www.quidonc.fr The phone book in reverse: type in a number, it tells you the owner. Can only be used in France.

www.ratp.com Everything you'll need to know about using the buses, métro, RER and trams.

www.timeout.com/paris A pick of current events and good hotels, eateries and shops.

Directory

Index

Advertisers' Index

Please refer to the relevant pages for contact details

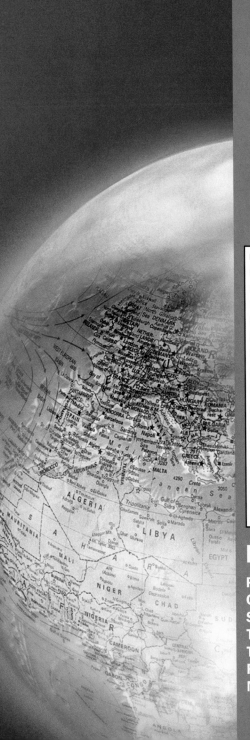

Place of interest and/or entertainment	![]
Hospital or college	![]
Railway station	![]
Parks	![]
River	![]
Autoroute	=
Main road	![]
Main road tunnel	![]
Pedestrian road	![]
Arrondissement boundary	—
Airport	✈
Church	✚
Métro station	Ⓜ
RER station	ⓇⒺⓇ
Area name	LES HALLES
Hotels	❶

Maps

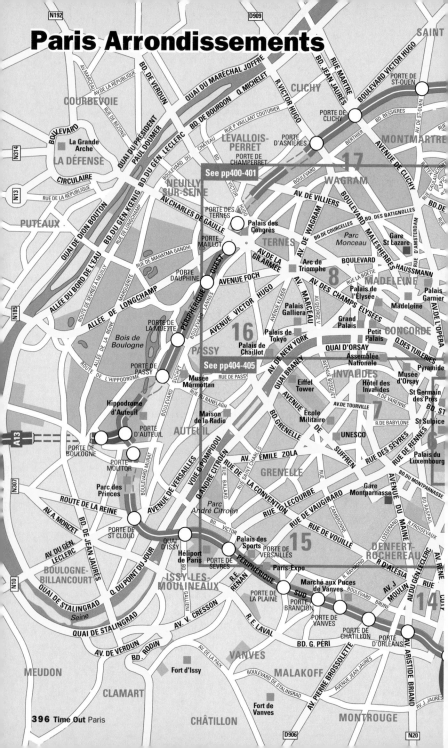

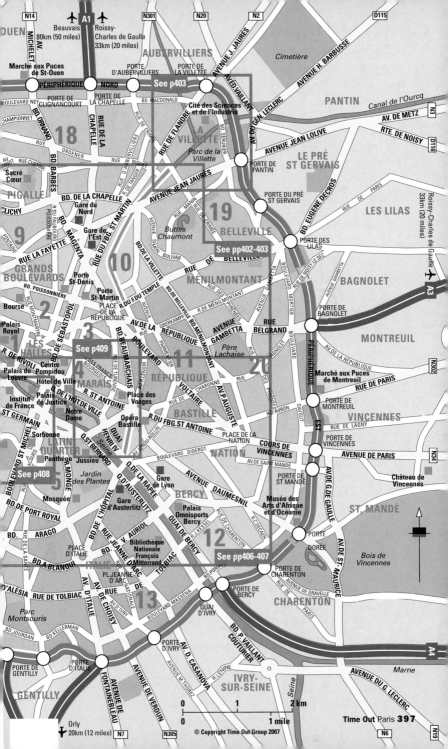

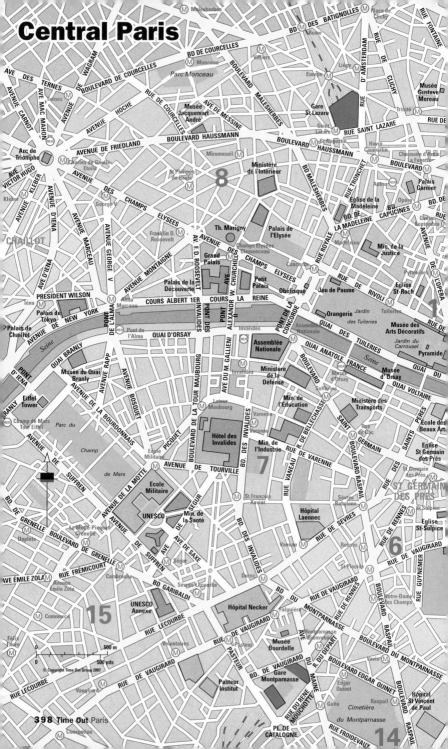

9

Pigalle
Anvers

R. NOTRE DAME DE LORETTE
St Georges
Notre-Dame
de Lorette
CHATEAUDIN

RUE LA FAYETTE
Cadet
Le Peletier

RUE LA FAYETTE

DU QUATRE SEPTEMBRE
Bibliothèque
Nationale
Richelieu

HAUSSMANN
ITALIENS
Richelieu Drouot

Banque
de France
Hôtel des
Postes
Palais
Royal
Palais Royal
Musée du Louvre
Bourse
du Commerce
Musée du
Louvre
Louvre
Rivoli

LOUVRE

Institut
de France
Hôtel des
Monnaies

BD SAINT GERMAIN
Mabillon
Odéon
St Michel

Univ
Paris VI

Palais du
Luxembourg
Jardin du
Luxembourg

5

Port
Royal
Clinique
Baudelocque
Val de Grâce
Hôpital
Cochin

Hôpital
Lariboisière
Gare
du Nord
St Vincent
de Paul

Poissonnière

BD DE MAGENTA
RUE DU FAUBOURG ST DENIS

Hôpital
Fernand
Widal
Gare
de l'Est
Gare
de l'Est

Hôpital
St Lazare

BD POISSONNIERE
BD BON NOUVELLE
Strasbourg
St Denis
Bonne
Nouvelle

Bourse
des Valeurs
RUE REAUMUR
Sentier

2

Réaumur
Sébastopol
Les
Halles
Châtelet
Les Halles
Rambuteau
Forum des
Halles
Centre
Pompidou

Pont Neuf
QUAI DE LA
MEGISSERIE
Conciergerie
QUAI DES GRANDS
Sainte
Chapelle
ILE DE LA
CITÉ
St Michel Notre
Dame
Cathédrale Notre
Dame de Paris

St Michel
Cluny
La Sorbonne
RUE DES ECOLES
SAINT
MICHEL
Sorbonne
RUE SOUFFLOT
Luxembourg
Panthéon

BOULEVARD
SAINT MICHEL
RUE GAY LUSSAC

Eglise Notre Dame
de Val de Grâce

BOULEVARD DE PORT ROYAL

BD DE MAGENTA
RUE DU FAUBOURG ST MARTIN

Château
Landon

10

Château
d'Eau

Jacques
Bonsergent
RUE DU FAUBOURG DU TEMPLE
Palais
des
Glaces
République

BD ST MARTIN
Conservatoire
National
des Arts et
Métiers
TURBIGO
Temple

Arts et Métiers
R. DU TEMPLE

BD DU TEMPLE

3

Filles du
Calvaire
Oberkampf
St Sébastien
Froissart
Musée de
la Chasse
Musée
Picasso
Archives
Nationales
MARAIS
Hôtel
de Ville

Chemin
Vert
BD BEAUMARCHAIS
RICHARD LENOIR BOULEVARD

St Paul
RUE DE RIVOLI
RUE SAINT ANTOINE
Bastille

4

Q. DE CELESTINS
BD HENRI IV
Sully
Morland
BD MORLAND
Pont Marie
Eglise
St Louis
en-l'Ile
ILE ST LOUIS
QUAI DE LA
TOURNELLE
Institut du
Monde Arabe
Cardinal
Lemoine
Jussieu
Universités Paris VI
Paris VI
Pierre et Marie Curie
RUE JUSSIEU
RUE CUVIER
Jardin des
Plantes
Gare
d'Austerlitz
Museum National
d'Histoire Naturelle
Place
Monge
Censier
Daubenton
Mosquée
de Paris
RUE CLAUDE BERNARD
Val de Grâce
RUE MONGE

BOULEVARD SAINT MARCEL
St Marcel
Gobelins

13

Louis
Blanc
Jaurès
Bolivar

BD DE LA VILLETTE
Parc des
Buttes
Chaumont

19

Colonel
Fabien

BD DE LA VILLETTE
Hôpital
St Louis
Belleville
BELLEVILLE
Goncourt
Couronnes

AVENUE DE LA REPUBLIQUE
Parmentier
St Maur

BD RD LENOIR BOULEVARD VOLTAIRE

11

St Ambroise
Richard
Lenoir
Breguet
Sabin
Voltaire

RUE DU FAUBOURG SAINT ANTOINE
Ledru
Rollin
Opéra
Bastille
AVENUE LEDRU ROLLIN
AVE LEDRU ROLLIN
AVENUE DAUMESNIL

BOULEVARD BOURDON
BOULEVARD DE LA BASTILLE
BOULEVARD DE LYON

Quai de
la Rapée
BERCY
DIDEROT
Gare de
Lyon
Gare de
Lyon
Gare de
Lyon
BOULEVARD
BERCY
Gare de
Lyon

PONT D'AUSTERLITZ
QUAI D'AUSTERLITZ
Gare
d'Austerlitz
Gare
d'Austerlitz
QUAI D'AUSTERLITZ
QUAI DE LA RAPEE

Palais Omnisports
de Paris Bercy
Hôpital
La Pitié
Salpêtrière

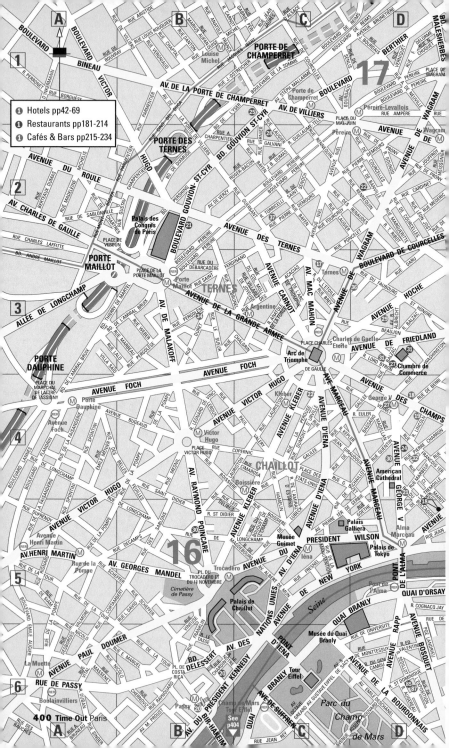

Hotels pp42-69
Restaurants pp181-214
Cafés & Bars pp215-234

400 Time Out Paris

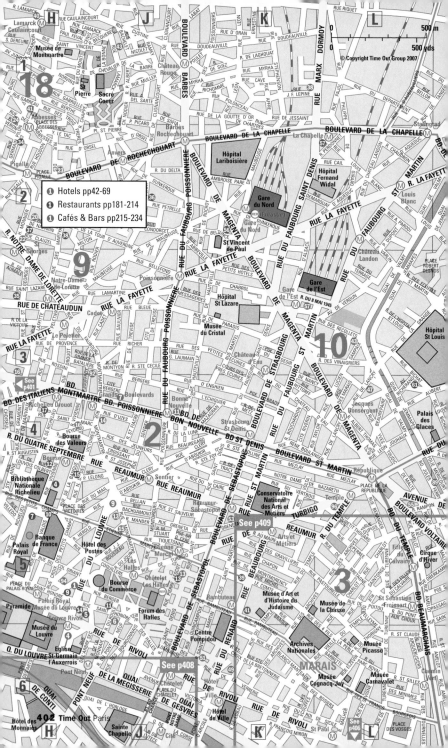

❶ Hotels pp42-69
❶ Restaurants pp181-214
❶ Cafés & Bars pp215-234

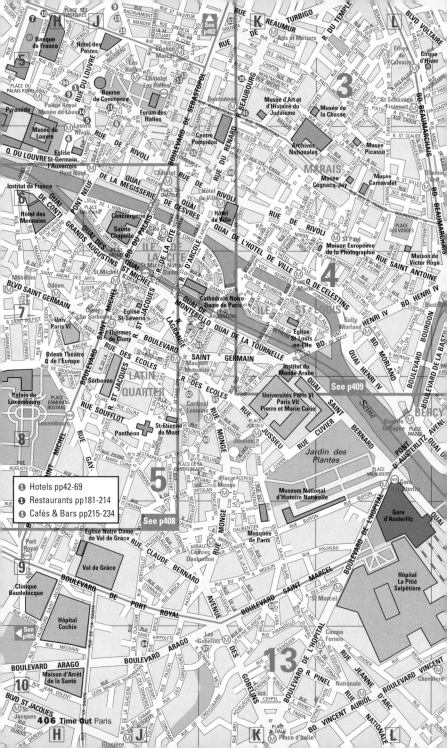

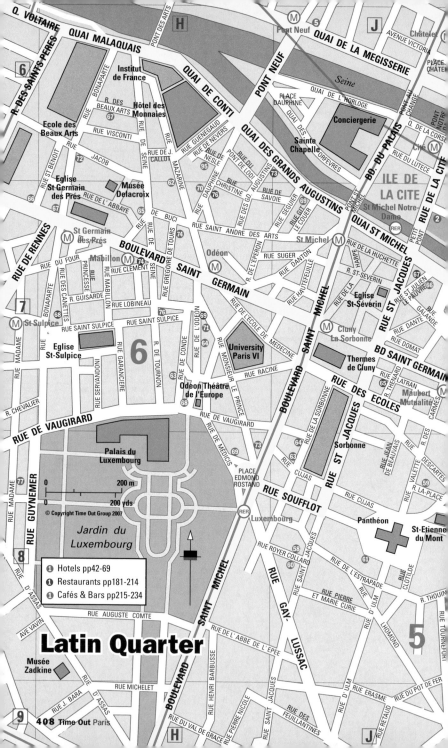

Latin Quarter

- ❶ Hotels pp42-69
- ❶ Restaurants pp181-214
- ❶ Cafés & Bars pp215-234

Musée Zadkine

© Copyright Time Out Group 2007

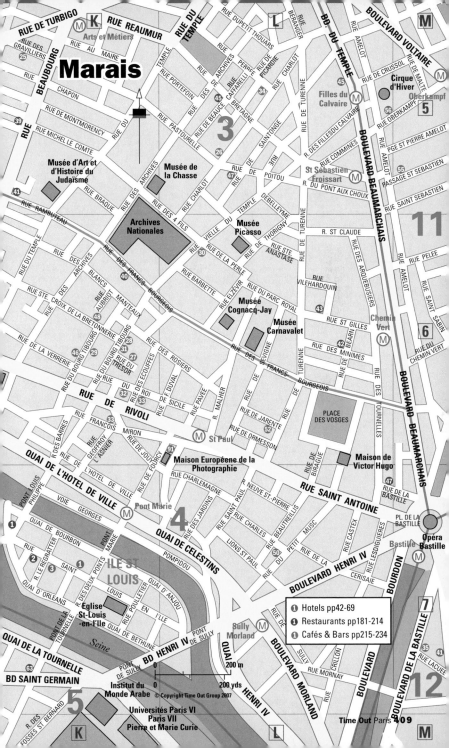

Street Index

Street Index

Paris RER

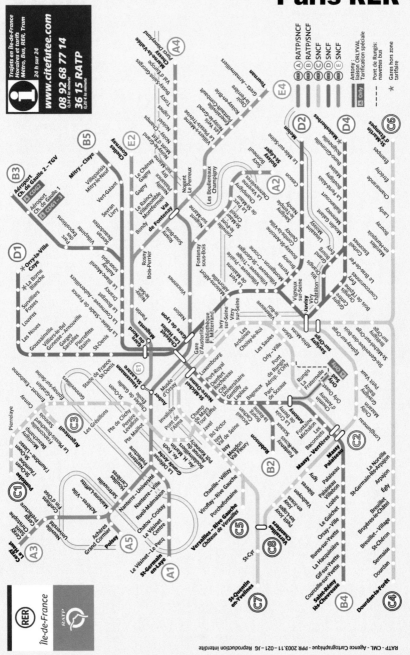

RATP - CML - Agence Cartographique - PPR 2003.11 - 021 - JG Reproduction interdite

RER
Île-de-France

RATP

Trajets en Île-de-France
Horaires et tarifs
Métro, Bus, RER, Tram
24 hr sur 24
www.citefutee.com
08 92 68 77 14
0,34 € la minute
36 15 RATP
0,20 € la minute

A RATP/SNCF
B RATP/SNCF
C SNCF
D SNCF
E SNCF

Antony -
liaison ORLYVAL
Tarification spéciale

Pont de Rungis:
navettes bus

Gares hors zone
tarifaire

Paris Métro

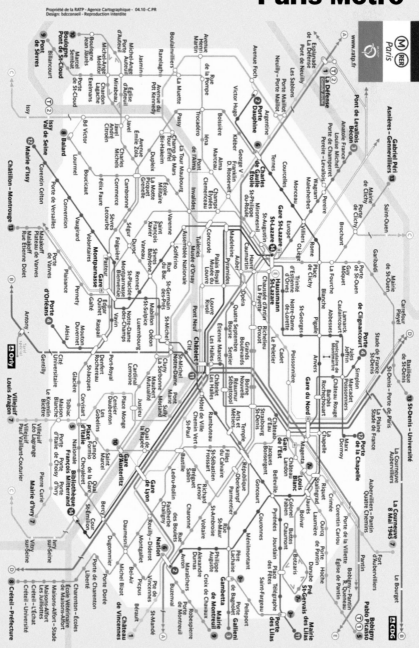